W9-BMP-538

SELF-PUBLISHING WITH AMAZON

4 BOOKS IN 1

Chris McMullen

COPYRIGHT

Self-Publishing with Amazon
4 Books in 1

Copyright © 2014, 2019 by Chris McMullen
All rights reserved. This includes the right to reproduce any portion of this book in any form.

Chris McMullen
Cover design by Melissa Stevens: theillustratedauthor.net

Updated and revised to reflect the merger between CreateSpace and KDP
Updated and revised edition published in February, 2019
First edition published in October, 2014
First printing in October, 2014

Books > Education & Reference > Publishing & Books > Authorship
Books > Education & Reference > Writing

ISBN-10: 150318420X
EAN-13: 978-1503184206

Disclaimer: Every effort was made to describe the information in this book very accurately as of the publication date. Companies make periodic changes to their websites, practices, and policies, and so this information is subject to change. The author makes no guarantees regarding the information in this book. You should check directly with each company for the most up-to-date information regarding their practices, policies, pricing, etc.

CONTENTS

A DETAILED GUIDE TO
SELF-PUBLISHING
with
AMAZON
AND OTHER ONLINE BOOKSELLERS

VOL **1**

Chris McMullen

COPYRIGHT

A Detailed Guide to Self-Publishing with Amazon and Other Online Booksellers, Vol. 1
How to Print-on-Demand with KDP Print & Make eBooks for Kindle & Other eReaders

Copyright © 2012, 2013, 2014, 2018 by Chris McMullen
All rights reserved. This includes the right to reproduce any portion of this book in any form.

Chris McMullen
Cover design by Melissa Stevens: theillustratedauthor.net

Eighth edition published in October, 2018 (CreateSpace merged with Kindle Direct Publishing)
Seventh edition published in September, 2014 (new Kindle programs, minor updates)
Sixth edition published in May, 2014 (for new cover and minor updates)
Fifth edition published in November, 2013 (to add **index** and minor updates)
Fourth edition published in May, 2013 (minor updates)
Third edition published in March, 2013 (to include references to material in Volume 2)
Second edition published in February, 2013 (regarding the discontinued 4-for-3 program)
First edition published in November, 2012
First printing in November, 2012

Books > Education & Reference > Publishing & Books > Authorship
Books > Education & Reference > Writing

ISBN-10: 1480250201
EAN-13: 978-1480250208

Disclaimer: Every effort was made to describe the information in this book very accurately as of the publication date. Companies make periodic changes to their websites, practices, and policies, and so this information is subject to change. The author makes no guarantees regarding the information in this book. You should check directly with each company for the most up-to-date information regarding their practices, policies, pricing, etc.

CONTENTS

Volume 2 Contents

INTRODUCTION

I HAVE WRITTEN AND self-published over a dozen books with Amazon. I write non-fiction books in areas that interest me. Most of my books are math workbooks, as I am very passionate about helping people improve their fluency in fundamental math skills, like algebra, fractions, and calculus. It all started after I had written a pair of volumes on the fourth dimension – another of my passions, and also the topic of several papers that I have written in the field of collider physics – when I discovered, in my search for a publisher, that Amazon had a self-publishing company.

Writing, formatting, and publishing books – the technique of trying to turn ideas into a printed work of art – has evolved into a hobby for me. I wrote this book with the aim of helping many other writers who, like myself, were not entirely satisfied with the traditional publishing industry and were considering the prospects of print-on-demand self-publishing. I have also published some puzzle books, golf books, chess books, and science books. I have learned much about the self-publishing process – many ideas that I wish I had known when I started out. While I can't pass this wisdom onto my former self, I can try to share it with other writers, such as you. This is the spirit with which I have written this book. I sincerely hope that you find much of the information helpful, and I wish you the best of luck with your books! ☺

One of my main goals in writing this book was to provide a wealth of practical information, and also to state the information concisely. I expect that you want to spend more time writing your own book, and less time listening to some other author drone on along some tangent. Thus, I have tried to stick to the point, and I have deleted several paragraphs which didn't actually provide any valuable information. I hope that you appreciate this. Also, I have tried to adopt a friendly, conversational tone, so that, hopefully, you will feel that someone (but not me – that would be creepy) is right there speaking with you, helping you publish your book with confidence.

I have tried to write this book in such a way that it reads well if you read it straight through, yet is also organized so that you can easily find the information that you're looking for if you consult the book as you need it: For example, you will probably want to have this book handy while you are applying any of the step-by-step techniques – like how to submit your book to the publisher or how to modify the content of your manuscript in order to format it as an eBook. The new 18-page index should also come in handy.

Chapter 1

Choosing a Publishing Service

Chapter Overview

1.1 Print-On-Demand Paperbacks with KDP Print
1.2 eBook Publishing Services and Online eReaders

This chapter answers questions about the following topics, and more:

- ☑ Reasons that millions of paperback books and eBooks are now self-published, and how print-on-demand services and eReaders have revolutionized the publishing industry.
- ☑ The advantages of self-publishing print-on-demand paperbacks with Kindle Direct Publishing,[1] which is an Amazon[1] company.
- ☑ A survey of some self-publishing options – such as color versus black-and-white, binding options, and book sizes.[2]
- ☑ The prospects for getting physical copies of your book to appear on bookshelves in bookstores across America.
- ☑ Popular eReaders – including Kindle, Nook, and Sony – and self-publishing services where you can make an eBook available for them.[3]

---

[1] Kindle Direct Publishing and Amazon are trademarks of Amazon.com, Inc. These trademarks and brands are the property of their respective owners.
[2] We will explore self-publishing options in much more detail in Chapter 4.
[3] Kindle is a trademark of Amazon.com, Inc. Nook and Barnes & Noble are trademarks of Barnes & Noble Inc. Sony is a registered trademark of Sony Corporation. These trademarks and brands are the property of their respective owners.

1.1 Print-On-Demand Paperbacks with KDP Print

1.1.1 A Revolutionary Self-Publishing Concept

AMAZON HAS MADE IT possible for anyone to self-publish a book and make it available for sale directly from Amazon's website either as a paperback or as an eBook. The paperback and eBook options are now both possible through Kindle Direct Publishing (KDP), which is an Amazon company.[1] (Originally, Amazon had two separate self-publishing companies: CreateSpace was for paperbacks, while KDP was for Kindle[3] eBooks. However, in October, 2018, CreateSpace and KDP merged together. Now you can publish paperbacks and eBooks using KDP, which simplifies the self-publishing process.) KDP is not only an affordable, simple, and high-paying means of selling both physical and digital copies of a book on Amazon, but KDP also offers distribution to bookstores, other online book-sellers, educators, and libraries. Paperback self-publishing is introduced in Sec. 1.1, while eBook self-publishing is introduced in Sec. 1.2.

Each chapter of this book separately addresses the issue of publishing paperback books and eBooks. For paperback publishing, we will focus almost exclusively on KDP Print, since they offer quick and easy publishing on Amazon and very high royalties, with the option of publishing your book without any fees. For the eBook option, we will often refer to Kindle, but we will also discuss publishing eBooks through other eBook publishing services – such as making your eBook available on the Barnes & Noble Nook and the Sony Reader.[3] Much of the information that is relevant for publishing paperbacks or eBooks through KDP would also relate to publishing print-on-demand paperbacks or eBooks with other publishing services.

KDP Print is a print-on-demand self-publishing service. Whereas a traditional publisher spends months producing and distributing thousands of books and then hopes to sell all of them, KDP Print manufactures and distributes books as they are sold. If a book published with KDP Print is purchased at Amazon, the book is manufactured and sent to the customer without any noticeable delay – just as if the book had been sitting on a shelf in Amazon's warehouse.

1.1.2 Advantages of Print-On-Demand and eBook Self-Publishing

The print-on-demand and eBook concepts have revolutionized the self-publishing industry. Following are some reasons that self-publishing has recently become very common:

☺ You can publish an eBook for free with Amazon, Barnes & Noble, and other popular online booksellers. You can also self-publish a paperback with KDP for free. Prior to the print-on-demand revolution, a self-published author had to pay for hundreds of books to be manufactured up front, and also pay to distribute them to bookstores. Take a moment to appreciate the benefits of this new technology.

☺ Both self-published print-on-demand paperback books and self-published eBooks can now reach a very wide audience. Since self-published books – both paperbacks and eBooks – can be made available for sale directly on Amazon's and Barnes & Noble's websites, these books are available to millions of customers throughout the world on the most popular online bookstores. KDP Print also has distribution options for physical bookstores, other online bookstores, educators, and libraries. Prior to KDP, it was very challenging for a writer to self-publish a book and persuade major book-sellers to purchase their self-published books.

☺ A print-on-demand book reaches the market almost immediately, whereas it takes six months to a year, on average, for a traditionally published book to reach the market; eBooks reach the market in a matter of hours. Print-on-demand paperbacks and eBooks are the quickest ways to publish time-sensitive material, such as a book that relates to current events or ways to deal with the present state of the economy.

☺ It is difficult and time-consuming to get a book published with traditional publishers, but it is very easy to publish a book with KDP or to publish an eBook with a variety of eReaders. Traditional publishing requires purchasing the current copy of *Writer's Market*, writing query letters, sending self-addressed stamped envelopes to several publishers and/or agents, and waiting months to hear a response, which often includes many rejection letters even if the book does get published. More and more authors are choosing to save the hassle, headache, rejection, and lengthy waiting period of the traditional publishing process by instead self-publishing with a print-on-demand publisher and/or publishing an eBook.

☺ You can earn a larger royalty for your book using KDP for paperbacks, and publishing eBooks with Amazon, Barnes & Noble, etc. (see Sec.'s 4.1.4-5 and 4.2.5).

☺ It's possible to self-publish your book using a company that you trust: KDP is an Amazon company, Kindle and Nook are Amazon and Barnes & Noble eReaders.

☺ You can promote your book as little or as much as you would like. You don't have to commit to a great deal of book promotion in order to persuade an editor to publish your book.

☺ Print-on-demand books are available indefinitely. Millions of traditionally published books are available for a couple of years and then become unavailable. This is because thousands of books were manufactured up front, and once those copies were sold, the publisher determined that there was not demand to publish thousands more. A print-on-demand book can be available for sale for decades, earning royalties for a lifetime.

☺ You can self-publish your book just the way you like it. No editor will modify your book. No publisher will require you to make conceptual or physical changes to your book, simply because the publisher feels that those changes would earn the publisher more profit (or worse, if it is just to cater to the whims of an editor). You are in full control of the content and appearance of a self-published book.

☺ It's easy to make revisions, even after your book is published. If you want to make a change to your book, you don't have to create a new edition. Your revisions reach the market very quickly, since your book is printed on demand.

☺ You can skip the struggle of breaking through the publishing industry as a first-time author. If your self-published book is successful, it could help you to publish a second book through a traditional publisher.

☺ If you change your mind, your self-published book can be retired. You are still free to pursue traditional publishing.[4]

☺ Some publishers are actually using KDP Print and similar print-on-demand services, and are also publishing eBooks. That's right: Publishers are realizing the many benefits of print-on-demand and eBook technology, and are using it themselves. Some publishers actually publish print-on-demand paperbacks and eBooks the same way that you can do it yourself! You can skip the middleman, publish print-on-demand paperbacks and eBooks directly yourself, and thereby earn a larger royalty.

1.1.3 Disadvantages of Print-On-Demand and eBook Self-Publishing

To be fair, there are some disadvantages of self-publishing to consider:

☹ Self-published authors do not receive an advance on their royalties. It's possible to earn thousands of dollars up front if you can get a book published with a traditional publisher. Celebrities and well-known writers can earn huge advances, like a hundred thousand dollars, but that's not typical. A modest advance of five to ten thousand dollars is more likely, yet still challenging to come by for a first-time author. The publisher must really believe in your book to be willing to invest in a large advance.

  ☺ Although you are likely to earn much more money in the near future if your book is traditionally published, print-on-demand and eBook self-publishing can accrue a significant amount of money over the long term. If you could receive a $10,000 advance, but then after one year your book is retired and that's the only money you ever receive, or if you could receive $2,000 a year on average over the course of three decades – which would you prefer? When you self-publish a book, you can potentially continue earning royalties on it for the rest of your life.

☹ Your book is much more likely to appear on the bookshelves at Barnes & Noble and other bookstores if your book is traditionally published. Top bookstores are much

---

[4] If you used a free ISBN from KDP Print, a traditional publisher won't be able to use this same ISBN. Other details relating to the ISBN are discussed in Sec. 4.1.6.

more likely to order physical copies of books from established publishers, where books have passed a review process.

- ☺ You can make your book available to bookstores through KDP Print's Expanded Distribution channel. Your book may appear on Barnes & Noble's website this way,[5] but it's much more unlikely that physical copies of your book will appear on their bookshelves if you self-publish your book.

- ☹ If you're a celebrity or if you have expertise in the area in which you are writing, this increases your chances of getting published traditionally, along with a healthy advance.
  - ☺ On the other hand, this would also help your self-published book have success. Celebrities already have an audience; and expertise is an asset in nonfiction.

- ☹ Having an editor review your book and accept it for publication may provide a sense of satisfaction or may serve as a status symbol. Anybody can self-publish a book, but only a select group of books are accepted for publication.

- ☹ If you get published traditionally, it may open many wonderful opportunities. If your book is successful, it may make it much easier to get a second book published.
  - ☺ If your self-published book is successful, you will also establish a fan-base, many of whom will be looking for more books. On the other side, if you traditionally publish a book, many fans may buy your second book even if it's self-published. If Stephen King self-published a novel, don't you think it would still be a bestseller?

- ☹ Some features of a physical book are not currently available through KDP Print. For example, KDP Print specializes in softcover books. A variety of other options, such as spiral bound books, are readily available through various traditional publishing houses.

- ☹ You need to create your own PDF files for the interior and cover of your book if you self-publish. You can't just send a hard copy to the publisher.
  - ☺ Fortunately, once your book is typed, it's very easy to convert the interior to a PDF file, and it's not so painful to make a nice cover – as explained in Chapters 2-3. Also, if you absolutely don't want to do this yourself, it's possible to hire out freelance help.

- ☹ You have to promote your own work when you self-publish.
  - ☺ However, most publishers also expect authors to promote their own books. You pretty much have to promote your own work no matter what. One difference is that when you self-publish, you don't have to make promises to the editor in an effort to get your book published.

---

[5] If you search for my name at Barnes & Noble's website, you will see that books that were self-published with KDP Print have, in fact, become available for sale there. But you probably won't find my books in their stores.

1.1.4 Choosing a Print-On-Demand Self-Publishing Service

If you decide to self-publish your book, you must choose your publishing service(s). There are actually many self-publishing options. Self-publishing services usually specialize either in paperback books or eBooks. There are also a few that provide other options, such as hardcover books.

I recommend self-publishing your book both in print and as an eBook. This way, you reach the largest possible audience (and you'll be eligible for **Kindle MatchBook** – see Sec. 4.2.7). There are millions of people who buy physical books, and there are also millions of people who buy eBooks. If you only publish one way or the other, you are missing out on a potentially large market. You will probably earn a much larger royalty on eBooks, percentage-wise, which allows you to price your book lower to, hopefully, sell more copies. Again, we will discuss paperback self-publishing services throughout Sec. 1.1, and return to eBook self-publishing services in Sec. 1.2.

KDP Print is a very popular self-publishing service for softcover books. I have used KDP Print (and also CreateSpace, before it merged with KDP) for all of my self-published paperbacks (over a dozen titles), and continue to trust them and consider them to be the best self-publishing service. Therefore, in this book I will focus on KDP Print for softcover self-publishing. In a moment, I will discuss how to find a few alternatives, but first I will list many reasons that I prefer KDP Print over other services:

✓ A book can be self-published with KDP Print for <u>free</u>. It's reasonable to invest about $15 to self-publish your book with KDP Print. This is a very low-cost service. (This low cost lets you hire out a few services, like editing or cover design, in case you feel that you really need help with some aspect of the publishing process.)

✓ Once your book is self-published with KDP Print, you can make it available for sale at Amazon for free. In this way, your book reaches a huge market very easily.

✓ Since KDP Print is a print-on-demand publisher, your book is always in stock. Your book shows as 'In Stock' on Amazon's website. Your book is manufactured and shipped whenever it sells. It will still be available for purchase several years from now.

✓ KDP Print is an Amazon company. I first signed up with KDP Print because I love Amazon, and have been a long-time loyal customer. My trust of Amazon was extended to KDP Print, and it turned out to be a good decision for me.

✓ The royalties are very good. Percentage-wise, it is much higher than traditional publishers pay even well-known, established authors (unless you choose to price your self-published paperback very low).

✓ It is very easy to self-publish a book with KDP Print. You will be guided through the process in Chapters 2-4.

✓ Expanded distribution options are available, allowing your book to potentially reach physical bookshelves, sell on other websites, and even sell to libraries.[6]

✓ KDP Print specializes in quality trade paperback books, with high-quality 60# paper and laminated full-color covers.[7]

✓ Authors can buy copies of their own books for very cheap – as little as about $2 per book (see Sec. 4.1.4) for a black-and-white interior, depending on the number of pages.

✓ You set the list price of your book. In this way, you actually control the sales price[8] of your book and control your own royalty. We will explore this more in Sec.'s 4.1.4-5.

✓ You can choose between white or cream pages and black-and-white or full-color interior. There are numerous trim sizes to choose from. They offer multiple ISBN options.

✓ As an author, you get detailed sales reports. Sales post on your KDP sales dashboard in as little as a few hours after books are purchased on Amazon. You can see which book sold when, and exactly what your current total of royalties is for the month. There are numerous ways to filter and search through your sales reports, too.

✓ Help is available when you self-publish with KDP. There are many useful help pages, you can ask questions in the KDP community – where other self-published authors can share their experience – and you can even talk directly with a sales representative by email or telephone. It's also possible to hire freelance help, if you are willing to pay for it, such as designing a cover, editing a manuscript, or illustrating your book.

Even though I'm a big fan of KDP,[9] I still encourage you to explore your publishing options to see which option is the best fit for you. If you want to explore the traditional publishing route, you need to find a copy of the current *Writer's Market*,[10] read a few books on writing

---

[6] Royalties are somewhat lower for expanded distribution options, as we will see in Sec.'s 4.1.4-5.

[7] If you're looking for a hardcover option, you'll need to find another printer for that, such as Ingram Spark or Barnes & Noble's Nook Press (but note that Nook Press's hardcover option won't be available on-demand: it's just for ordering author copies).

[8] The actual selling price of your book may vary. Amazon or another bookseller may choose to offer a discount, and some other booksellers may actually charge more than the list price that you set. Amazon will show the price that you set as the list price, and if they choose to sell it for less it will show that your book is on sale.

[9] Yes, I do love KDP. It worked out very well for me. I'm not sure if I would have published any books, let alone dozens of paperback titles, if not for them. Remember, I was not paid or even encouraged by Amazon or KDP in any way to write this book. When I wrote this book, these companies had no idea that I was writing such statements. This is not a sales pitch nor an advertisement – just a simple recommendation from a satisfied customer. I encourage you to explore all of your publishing options.

[10] *Writer's Market* comes out with a new edition every year, and also has different books for different genres (like poetry). You can save a bundle of money if your local library has a copy to borrow. You might also explore free information about query letters, book proposals, and finding publishers and literary agents – using your favorite search engine. Many publishers' websites have information about their manuscript submission policies – many big publishers don't accept unsolicited materials and require you to have an agent, but there are some that welcome proposals straight from the author and have detailed advice about how to prepare the proposal.

book proposals and query letters, and consider finding a literary agent. However, if you wish to self-publish, you can skip all of that and focus more time on writing your own books.

KDP Print's major competition is Ingram Spark, which launched in the middle of 2013. Ingram is a major distributor to bookstores. When a self-publisher uses KDP's Expanded Distribution option, one result is that the book is listed in Ingram's catalog. Ingram Spark is the self-publishing version of Lightning Source, which is a major print-on-demand service used by many small publishing companies. You can learn more about Ingram Spark from their website, www.ingramspark.com. One possible advantage is a discount for bookstores, although getting your print-on-demand book in any bookstore is a challenge, and works best when you show up and deliver your books in person (for which this discount option doesn't matter); having a bookstore find your book in the Ingram catalog and stock it is very unlikely. Personally, I remain loyal to Amazon and use KDP Print because I love the opportunities that Amazon has created for authors. I also like the easy access to Amazon offered by KDP, with a book that's always in stock through print-on-demand. However, Ingram Spark looks like an excellent company comparable to KDP Print. You should check them both out and decide for yourself. (A third option is Lulu.)

Beware of publishing services (like vanity presses) that require you to invest hundreds, or even thousands, of dollars to publish your book. Some of these are scams intended just to get your money. Others are legitimate – i.e. they will actually publish your book – but probably will not sell enough copies for you to break even. A traditional publisher won't charge you any fee to publish your book, and will sell many, many more copies of your book than those publishing services that demand a large payment. I strongly recommend using either a self-publishing or traditional publishing option that is FREE.

There are self-publishing services that charge you only for the cost of printing your books, and allow you to buy as few books as you would like to have printed. (In the previous paragraph, I was talking about publishing services that require you to pay a few hundred to thousands of dollars, and publish your book for you – i.e. you are paying for the privilege of having your book published. Since it's so easy to do this for free, it's not a privilege that you should have to pay for.) In this case, if the service is legitimate, you will at least have hundreds or thousands of copies of your book to sell to show for your self-publishing investment. However, you then have to distribute and sell your own books. This is the way self-publishing was a couple of decades ago. These days, you can use a print-on-demand self-publishing service and skip the hassle of having to distribute or sell your own books. I highly recommend using a free print-on-demand self-publishing service, and not paying money to have hundreds of copies of your book shipped to your home.

Another option is through R.R. Bowker. This is a major company that sells ISBN numbers and compiles lists of published books. If you want to be your own publisher or if you want to self-publish, you could purchase an ISBN directly through R.R. Bowker. (KDP Print offers a free ISBN option, yet still allows you to purchase your own ISBN.) R.R. Bowker also allows you to pay a fee to make your manuscript visible to publishers. I don't recommend paying a fee to get your book published, and publishers are so overwhelmed with manuscript proposals that I can't imagine too many editors finding a gem this way and then contacting the author about publishing his/her book. If anything, it seems that a small or unheard-of publisher is more likely to contact you through this method. If you want a publisher to notice you, you need to do the hunting (or get an agent to do it) – the big publishers are not hunting for you unless you happen to be a celebrity or a popular, established author.

If you explore other self-publishing options, I recommend the following:

⊗ Don't pay a fee – since you can get the same (or better) quality and service for free.

⊗ Only send your manuscript to a reputable, established company.

⊗ Independently (i.e. don't trust their own testimonials) verify that many other authors have achieved some measure of success with that publishing service.

For the remainder of this book, I will focus specifically on KDP Print features when I describe how to self-publish a softcover book. I will also describe a variety of eBook publishing services, such as how to publish on Amazon's Kindle and Barnes & Noble's Nook, when I describe how to self-publish an eBook.

1.1.5 Self-Publishing Options

Let us now discuss some self-publishing options, since knowing what options are available may impact your choice of publishing service. Each of these options will be considered again in more detail in a subsequent chapter. Here is a sample of which options are available with KDP Print:

✓ KDP Print specializes in softcover books with glossy or matte covers (the matte finish is a new feature). They also offer free software to convert your softcover book into Kindle format (but, as this book will explain, it's fairly simple to do this on your own). There are no hardcover or binding options – e.g. you can't have your book spiral bound through KDP Print. If you are specifically looking for hardcover books, board books, or spiral-bound books, for example, you should explore other publishing services.

✓ The cover will be printed in full color, but you must choose between a black-and-white interior and a full-color interior. Black-and-white costs much less than full-color, which means you make a much greater royalty for the same list price (or you can sell a black-and-white book for less than a full-color book and make the same royalty). Unfortunately, if your book has 300 pages, and only 1 page needs to be in color, you still have to choose the full-color interior option as if your entire book were in color – i.e. you don't save anything by printing fewer pages in color.

✓ There are 15 trim sizes to choose from, 12 of which are industry-standard trim sizes. The smallest is about the size of a mass market paperback – 5" by 8" – and the largest is the size of a standard sheet of paper – 8.5" by 11".

✓ Black-and-white books can be printed on white or cream paper.

✓ The covers are not only full-color, but are laminated – this makes the book more durable. The books are high-quality, and the printing and binding are professional. The interior is printed on 60# paper, which is thick and sturdy. Many other publishers print paperback books on cheaper paper, which is more likely to tear – this is especially true of puzzle books, workbooks, mass market paperbacks, and international editions. The cheaper paper helps other publishers sell books at very low prices, while the high-quality paper that KDP Print uses will help your book stand out in quality.

✓ Your book must have a minimum of 24 pages. The maximum varies, depending upon whether you choose black-and-white or full-color, the trim size, and whether the paper is white or cream. A black-and-white book can have as many as 828 pages, and a full-color book can have as many as 500 pages – depending on the trim size.

✓ If your book has at least 100 pages, you can include spine text – which makes your book's title visible on a bookshelf. If your book has less than 130 pages, but more than 100 pages, the spine text has to be very narrow – the publisher requires you to leave room on both sides to allow for printing variations, so that the spine text doesn't wrap around to the front or the back of the cover.

✓ Unfortunately, you can't print on the inside of the front or back cover. You can't put a design there or put useful reference information there, for example. The inside of the front and back cover will just be white. One or more pages will be added to the end of your book: The last page will have a bar code at the bottom (which has an important number if you want to report a manufacturing defect to KDP) and state when and where the book was manufactured; the rest of this page will also be plain white.

✓ You are in complete control of your own manuscript when you self-publish with KDP Print. No editor will suggest any content changes and nobody will check your spelling or grammar (unless you want to pay for these optional services). They just check that you followed the manuscript submission guidelines. So you are solely responsible for any typos, mistakes, formatting issues, etc.

✓ When you self-publish with KDP Print, you just need to publish your book in order to have your book made available for sale at Amazon (it's free!). You can also have your book made available for purchase through other Expanded Distribution channels (now free – it used to be $25), which allows other booksellers, libraries, and schools to purchase your book directly through the publisher.

✓ You need to make a PDF file for the interior and cover of your book (described in detail in Chapters 2-4). It's very easy to do, but for those who absolutely want to avoid doing this, it's possible to hire freelance help.

✓ You can find a variety of helpful information on the KDP help pages (on everything from formatting to marketing), and a community forum where you can ask experienced authors for help or advice.

1.1.6 Prospects for Getting Your Book in Bookstores

Before we get into eBooks in Sec. 1.2, let's address one more issue that may be on your mind: What are the prospects for getting physical copies of your book to appear on bookshelves in bookstores across America?

KDP Print is an Amazon company, and makes it very easy to make your book available for sale on Amazon's website, but Amazon doesn't have bookstores across the United States like Barnes & Noble or Books-A-Million. However, KDP Print does offer an Expanded Distribution option (it's now free – it used to be $25). The Expanded Distribution channel allows online booksellers, libraries, schools, and even traditional in-store booksellers to purchase your book directly from the publisher (you also make less royalty through the Expanded Distribution channel than if your book sells directly through Amazon). If you select the Expanded Distribution channel, your title will be included with the catalog that KDP Print provides to bookstores, libraries, and schools. So it is possible for your book to magically appear on a bookshelf in a bookstore, but it is very unlikely that it will just show up there all by itself.

If you select the Expanded Distribution channel, here is what will likely occur. First, some online booksellers will sell copies of your book on your Amazon listing where customers can purchase New or Used books from other sellers. On the one hand, you make a higher royalty when customers buy your book directly from Amazon than through one of these other sellers. However, customers tend to prefer purchasing directly through Amazon – for one, they are eligible for Super Saver shipping (and any special offers, if there are any) when they buy your book directly from Amazon. Also, when potential buyers see that your book is not only sold by Amazon, but also by other booksellers selling books on Amazon, it makes your book seem more widely distributed – it gives your self-published book more credibility.

Secondly, you may be able to find your book for sale on other websites. For example, there is a very good chance that your book will become available at Barnes & Noble's and Books-A-Million's websites (through Expanded Distribution). You can find most of my titles on these and other websites, and all of my titles have been self-published through Amazon. If nothing else, the Expanded Distribution channel will greatly enhance your online reach.

If you would like to see physical copies of your books on bookshelves somewhere, you probably need to take the initiative and visit your local bookstores. Start out with small local bookstores, as they often like to support local authors – their friends, family, and acquaintances are likely to give them a little extra business. Show the owner or manager a copy of your book – or if you have multiple titles, spend some time preparing an appealing catalog of your books on your computer, and print it out – and inquire about the prospects of having your hard work show up on their bookshelves. Booksellers can go to Ingram's website (they have a special catalog for bookstores) and purchase your book directly from the publisher. You can also purchase books at a special author price from KDP Print and try to sell them directly. It is reasonable to get your books to appear on some bookshelves with one of these methods. If you want your books to be distributed to larger bookstores, go to their websites and read the guidelines for publisher submissions. Barnes & Noble, for example, has a detailed set of guidelines for what you need to do in order to have them consider selling your book in their bookstores (online is much easier, in-store is much more challenging). It's probably very unlikely for your self-published book to show up in Barnes & Noble bookstores, but it is reasonable to get your book in smaller bookstores. See Sec. 4.1.7 and Chapter 8 for more information about this. If you really want to see your book sitting in Barnes & Noble, maybe you should give traditional publishing a shot (or become a publisher yourself).

1.2 eBook Publishing Services and Online eReaders

1.2.1 A Brief Introduction to the eBook Concept

THERE ARE MANY different kinds of eReaders. Amazon has the Kindle, Barnes & Noble has Nook, Sony has the Reader, and so on.[11] Each brand of eReader also comes in a variety of models, varying in the size of the screen and whether or not the images are in black-and-white or color. For example, the Kindle Fire is Amazon's color eReader.[12] Even cell phones, tablets, and laptops can serve as eReaders.

There are a few incentives for publishing exclusively on the Kindle, but there is a wider market available if you publish your eBook on a variety of eReaders.[12] Authors and publishers who make their books available for Amazon's Kindle may choose to include their titles with Kindle Select. Inclusion with Kindle Select requires publishing exclusively with Amazon, so if you choose this feature, you can't also publish the same (or similar) eBook with any other eBook services. Two benefits of Kindle Select are: (1) Kindle Unlimited and Prime members may borrow your eBook for free, and if they borrow your Kindle Select title for free, Amazon pays you a royalty for this; and (2) you may make your eBook available at a discount with a Countdown Deal or for free (this time, without earning royalties) to all buyers for as many as seven days in a three-month period, which can be a useful tool for promoting your book. The

---

[11] Kindle, Kindle Fire, and Amazon are trademarks of Amazon.com, Inc. Nook and Barnes & Noble are trademarks of Barnes & Noble, Inc. Sony is a registered trademark of Sony Corporation. These trademarks and brands are the property of their respective owners.

[12] We will address the choice of where to publish your eBook in Sec. 4.2.1.

main disadvantage of going with Kindle Select is that your book will be available to a wider audience if you publish your eBook on a variety of eReaders. We will return to Kindle Select features, including the pros and cons, in Sec. 4.2.7.

Like print-on-demand self-publishing, the eReaders are revolutionizing the publishing industry. Amazon, Barnes & Noble, Kobo, Sony, and other eBook publishing companies have successfully marketed their eReaders such that millions of customers now own eReaders, and therefore millions of people are purchasing eBooks for their eReaders. In addition, it is fairly easy for anyone to publish an eBook – you don't have to be a publisher or even a traditionally published author. As a result, millions of eBooks are now being published, including numerous self-published eBooks by first-time authors.

The technology of the eReaders has brought many new possibilities for buying and reading books. If you suddenly want a book now, and you have an eReader, you can literally start reading the book in a few moments. You no longer have to wait until the bookstore opens, and you don't have to wait weeks for a book that was out of stock. Once you get hooked with an eReader, you won't ever buy another bookmark: eReaders automatically mark your place. You can also highlight the eBook, and quickly check the definition of a word without getting up from your chair to get a dictionary. The eReaders have many other features of convenience. Unlike paper, the technology of eReaders encourages books to be written in color: Whereas the cost of printing in color is often prohibitive of publishing a book in color, this is not the case with eBooks (however, pictures add to memory, which is an issue). Another interesting feature of eBooks is that they can also be interactive – like games.

Since no money is spent on paper or print cartridges, eBooks can be potentially be published with a lower list price than a paperback or hardcover book, and the royalties paid to authors are often much higher. Authors who publish their own eBooks can make royalties of up to 70%, whereas the standard royalty for traditionally-published books is about 15%. If you publish a paperback book for $7.99, the same book could be easily sold as an eBook for $2.99, yet the author might easily draw a larger royalty from the lower-priced eBook. Just imagine selling more copies because the cost of the book is less, while also making more money for each book that you sell. This is why millions of eBooks are being published. Similarly, since many eBooks have a list price between 99 cents and $2.99, millions of eBooks are being purchased: For $20, you can buy 7 eBooks or 3 paperbacks – which is the better deal?

Unfortunately, not all eBooks have a low list price. Some traditional publishers have made bestselling books into eBooks, but have held out at the higher price. Some books that have sold millions of copies for $9.99 in the bookstore are also selling for $9.99 as eBooks. These publishers are drawing a royalty of up to 70% for their eBooks – while they make much less profit if they sell the paperback book for the same price – and choosing not to share one penny with the reader of the eBook edition by reducing its cost. I've been disappointed with the eBooks by a few of my favorite authors – that the publisher didn't choose to discount the eBook compared to the price of the paperback (and, usually, the big-name publisher's eBook has many formatting errors, which the paperback lacks). When the publisher doesn't discount the eBook, I buy the paperback book instead.

However, there are thousands of good, low-priced eBooks. Most authors and publishers do pass the savings onto the readers, and they probably sell many more eBooks by doing so. Those few publishers who don't discount their eBooks hopefully don't sell as many eBooks (they certainly don't deserve it – I suggest not supporting this practice).

In general, traditionally published books that are offered as eBooks don't sell for $3.99 or less; they are usually $5.99 and up. Even if the eBook list price is less than the paperback list price, traditional publishers usually don't publish their eBooks too cheap. Many self-published eBooks, on the other hand, sell for 99 cents or $2.99. Many buyers are willing to take a chance on a self-published eBook that interests them simply because the eBook is so affordable. The higher prices of the traditional publishers' eBooks are good for self-published authors. (These are the main trends, presently. There are a few exceptions, both ways – i.e. self-published books with a high list price, and inexpensive eBooks by bestselling authors.)

There is one more important advantage that an eBook offers over a paperback book: Once you sell enough paperback books, some of them will be resold as used books. Authors don't receive royalties for books that are resold. However, when an eBook sells, it won't be resold, cutting into the author's royalties.

1.2.2 A Note on eBook Formatting

The main issue with publishing an eBook is formatting the eBook. If your manuscript consists only of plain text, the formatting will be very, very easy. If you have a lot of rich text formatting – like fancy fonts , headers, footnotes, bullets (•), tabs, WordArt, text effects, textboxes, etc. – in your manuscript, you will have to do some editing in order to make your book format nicely as an eBook. If you have numerous pictures or equations, these will also add to the work that you must do to format your eBook.

Some formatting features that are possible with paperback books are not possible with eBooks. The reason behind this is to give the reader control of things like font style, font color, and font size. The editor of a paperback book decides how large the font will be and which font will be used, whereas the reader of an eBook is given control over these things. Another difference is that there is no such thing as a 'page' in an eBook. Therefore, an eBook does not have a table of contents with page numbers. Instead, a table of contents in an eBook consists of a set of links to click on that take the reader directly to the beginning of each chapter (this is called an active table of contents).

Since the reader may change the font size, the publisher has virtually no control over how much text will appear on the screen at any time. If you're publishing a novel, this isn't as important, but if you're publishing a children's picture book, a puzzle book, or a math workbook, for example, the formatting of the eBook becomes somewhat more complicated. We will discuss how to format your manuscript into a quality eBook in Sec. 2.2.

Another issue with the formatting has to do with the variety of eReaders available. Some customers will have color eReaders, many will have black-and-white eReaders. Some eReaders have a large screen, many have a small screen. You must consider these different options if you want your eBook to appear well for all of your buyers. Additionally, there are a few subtle differences in the way that an eBook will appear on eReaders sold by different companies. Your eBook may look a little different on Kindle than on Nook, for example. If you're publishing flash cards, with the question on one picture and the answer on the next picture, your eBook won't work very well if customers see both pictures on the screen at the same time, for example. Thus, it's important for you to learn what your eBook looks like in every form in which it is available. We will consider these differences in Chapters 2 and 4.

Chapter 2

Formatting Your Book Interior

Chapter Overview

2.1 Using Microsoft Word to Make a Paperback Interior
2.2 Revising Your Manuscript to Create an eBook

This chapter answers questions about the following topics, and more:

- ☑ If you are planning to sell your book as an eBook as well as a paperback book, there are several points that you will want to consider when you format your manuscript.
- ☑ The advantages of using Microsoft Word to format your book interior.
- ☑ Important differences in recent versions of Microsoft Word.
- ☑ Formatting tips, such as page size, font selection, linespacing, headers, page borders, page numbering, margins, footnotes, citations, columns, tables, pictures, equations, and more.
- ☑ Front and back matter, including the title page, copyright page, contents, acknowledgments, introduction, foreword, references, index, biography, and more.
- ☑ How to convert your Microsoft Word document into a PDF file.
- ☑ Why the file for your eBook will be considerably different from the file for your paperback book interior.
- ☑ How to revise the file for your paperback book interior to create an eBook.
- ☑ Formatting pictures and equations for your eBook.
- ☑ How to create an active table of contents using hyperlink bookmarks.

2.1 Using Microsoft Word to Make a Paperback Interior

2.1.1 Advantages of Using Microsoft Word

IF YOU HAVEN'T ALREADY typed most of your book, I highly recommend using Microsoft Word to prepare your manuscript for convenience and ease of use (Adobe InDesign and Serif Page Plus are professional alternatives). Even if you have already typed much of your manuscript with a different word processor, you can still save it with a .doc extension and then open it with Microsoft Word (or copy and paste the contents into a blank Word document). Advantages of using Microsoft Word to format your book interior include:

✓ The more recent editions of Microsoft Word (starting in 2007) have a built-in feature (or a link that will take you to Microsoft Word's website to add the feature for free) to convert your finished manuscript from a Word document to a PDF file. This will be very convenient, since you must first convert your manuscript files – one for the interior and one for the cover – into PDF files in order to self-publish with KDP.

✓ Microsoft Word is also highly compatible for making eBooks. Many companies who sell eReaders, such as Amazon, provide many useful tips for publishing your eBook specifically with Microsoft Word. You can also easily convert your Microsoft Word document into HTML or other formats, which may be better-suited for your eBook.

✓ This and the next chapter will specifically describe how to use a variety of features of Microsoft Word to format the interior and cover of your book and eBook.

✓ Other software that you may use, such as clipart or a more professional PDF conversion program, is very likely to be compatible with Microsoft Word.

✓ Microsoft Word has numerous features to help you make a very professional looking book, as will be described in this and the next chapter.

2.1.2 Differences in Recent Versions of Microsoft Word

You will want to note that there are some important differences in the recent versions of Microsoft Word, some of which are described below. I will describe the specifics for how to use Microsoft Word 2010 in this book. Many features are implemented much differently in Microsoft Word 2003, while most features are the same or similar in Microsoft Word 2007.

❖ Microsoft Office introduced new file extensions in 2007. The default format for Word documents now includes a .docx extension, which does not work in editions of Microsoft Office from 2003 and earlier. The newer editions of Word (2007 and 2010) can read both types of documents, but the older editions (2003 and earlier) can't open a file with a .docx extension. This is important if you intend to use more than one computer as you type your book, or if you collaborate with a coauthor. If you start writing your book in Word 2007 or 2010 and then try to open your file in Word 2003 on another computer, you won't be able to do it unless you first save it with a .doc extension (by changing the "Save As Type" option to a Word 1997-2003 Document). If your manuscript includes many formatting features that are only available in the 2007 and 2010 editions, it may look considerably different when saved in the old format.

❖ Word 2007 and 2010 include an option to save your file as a PDF file. The first time that you choose this option, Windows may open your internet browser (it will probably ask for your permission first) and take you to Microsoft's website in order to download this free feature. This is very convenient because most self-publishing services, including KDP Print, require you to submit your manuscript files in PDF format. Earlier editions of Microsoft Word did not have this file conversion option.

❖ Numerous features available with Microsoft Word changed location between 2003 and 2007. There are now several tabs that appear at the top of the program – including File, Home, Insert, Page Layout, Mailings, Review, View, and others (like Format) that are not always present. If you are accustomed to using Word 2003 and suddenly change to Word 2007 or 2010, you will notice this abrupt change, and will need to relearn how to use various features. It's also an issue if someone is helping you use a feature on Microsoft Word (or if you are searching for help online): Make sure that you are getting advice for your version of Word; otherwise, the instructions may not be helpful. **Little has changed from 2010 to 2013 to 2016.**

❖ There have been numerous changes in the options for drawing and formatting pictures between Word 2003, 2007, and 2010. For example, in Word 2003 you had freedom in the size of the gridlines and could place an object virtually anywhere on the page; in 2007, the grid was simply on or off and just one size; but in 2010, some of the flexibility has been revived. For the most part, the picture formatting options improved a little from 2007 to 2010. However, one noticeable change is the selection pane. In previous versions of Word, you could draw a rectangle with the cursor to select multiple drawing objects, but in Word 2010 you have to instead go into the selection pane and choose them one by one within the pane. The selection pane makes it easier to grab objects that are hiding behind other objects, but also makes it more difficult to grab several objects at once (I wish the old method would work, too).

❖ The equation editor received a major overhaul in 2007. This is important if you plan to type equations or formulas in your book. If so, and you plan to publish your book as an eBook, you should read Sec.'s 2.2.6-7 about formatting equations for an eBook before you spend much time typing them. If you go back and forth between Word 2003 and the newer versions, your equations will get converted going between .doc and .docx formats. In Word 2007, the equations sometimes didn't format properly when converting to PDF, but I haven't observed this problem with Word 2010.

2.1.3 Briefly Explore the Features of Your Version of Microsoft Word

Check out the features of your Word edition. At a minimum, I recommend that you check your file saving options as follows. Open a blank document in Microsoft Word and find where to Save As. If you have 2007 or 2010, you will click on a File tab at the top left of the screen, then select Save As. After selecting Save As, see if Word Document, Word 97-2007 Document, and PDF are three of the many options in the window that pops up. In 2007 and 2010, click the bar next to Save As Type in order to find these options.

It is worth browsing the tabs that appear at the top of the screen in Word 2007 or 2010. This will help you see where most of the formatting options are found, and you might see something of interest when you do this. When you have a Word document open, at the top of the screen you should see a variety of tabs: From left to right, if you have Word 2007 or 2010, you should see File, Home, Insert, Page Layout, References, Mailings, Review, and View (it could be a little different, as some tabs depend upon what features you may have already installed and others only appear when you've selected a relevant item in your document, such as a picture, table, or equation). Click on each tab and take a few moments to browse through the variety of formatting options at your disposal. We will explore many of these features of Word as we describe them in this book. As we describe a feature, I recommend that you open Microsoft Word and try it out.

2.1.4 Choosing the Trim Size

We will focus on how to use Word to format a paperback book throughout Sec. 2.1, then turn our attention to the eBook format in Sec. 2.2. Even if you only plan to make an eBook edition, you will still want to read this section (i.e. Sec. 2.1) first, as many of the features of Word will be described in Sec. 2.1 (and not be repeated in Sec. 2.2). If you do plan to publish an eBook edition, you may find it useful to read both Sec.'s 2.1 and 2.2 before you finish writing your book. In Sec. 2.2, when we consider how to convert the paperback manuscript into an eBook, we will see that a few features of Word – like bullets and page headers – will not be in your eBook edition, and a few features – like equations, textboxes, and pictures – complicate the conversion process. You may wish to be aware of these eBook-conversion issues (again, discussed in Sec. 2.2) before you type your manuscript.

We will now discuss how to format your manuscript in Microsoft Word 2010 with a paperback version of your book in mind. The first thing that you should do is select the page size. I recommend browsing Amazon for other books similar to the one that you are writing to see what size paperbacks are common for that type of book. Mass market paperbacks common with popular fiction, for example, have a small size (like 5.5" x 8.5"). Keep in mind that most self-published authors will not compete well with titles that have been mass produced. So if you are writing fiction, you might prefer trade paperback size, which is a little larger. A workbook or textbook tends to be fairly large (like 8.5" x 11"). One nice thing about a smaller book is that it is more portable. If you don't mind doing extra formatting work, you could potentially offer two editions of your book in different sizes. For comparison, the paperback edition of this book is 8" x 10".

There is also a financial factor to consider in choosing your book size. If you publish with KDP Print, the factor is indirect, since KDP Print pays the same royalties regardless of the page size. Your book's royalty does depend on the page count, however. If you have a smaller book, you will probably have more pages. The first 108 pages of a black-and-white paperback and the first 40 pages of a color paperback are free. If your book is longer than this, each extra page costs you 1.2 cents for black-and-white and 7 cents for color. So if you have a black-and-white paperback that would be 200 pages with a 7" x 10" size, but 250 pages with a 5" x 8" size, for example, you would draw 60 cents more royalty per book with the 7" x 10" size than the 5" x 8" size.[13] Remember, the page count only matters if you have more than 108 pages for black-and-white and 40 pages for color. There are also benefits of having more pages, even though each page costs you a little in royalties. Your spine label can be larger, and therefore be easier to read, if you have a higher page count, for example. Also, some customers may look at the page count when considering whether or not your book is a good value. (These figures are for US sales. They are different for sales in other countries.)

There are several page sizes to choose from if you publish with KDP Print. The following trim sizes accommodate 24-828 white pages (black-and-white print), 24-740 cream pages (black-and-white), and 24-480 white pages (color): 5" x 8", 5.06" x 7.81", 5.25" x 8", 5.5" x 8.5", 6" x 9", 6.14" x 9.21", 6.69" x 9.61", 7" x 10", 7.44" x 9.69", and 7.5" x 9.25". An 8" x 10" option only accommodates 24-440 white pages (black-and-white), 24-400 cream pages (black-and-white), and 24-480 white pages (color), and 8.5" x 11" accommodates 24-630 white pages (black-and-white), 24-570 cream pages (black-and-white), and 24-480 white pages (color). Finally, there are a few non-standard trim sizes: 8.25" x 6" and 8.25" x 8.25" each accommodate 24-220 white pages (black-and-white), 24-200 cream pages (black-and-white), and 24-212 white pages (color), and 8.5" x 8.5" accommodates 24-630 white pages (black-and-white), 24-570 cream pages (black-and-white), and 24-480 white pages (color). Be sure not to exceed the maximum page count for the trim size that you select (also noting whether your book will be in black-and-white or in color, and, if in black-and-white, whether or not it will be on white or cream paper).

Some of these trim sizes are industry-standard, others are custom trim sizes. If you hope to sell your book through bookstores or online retailers, you definitely need to choose an industry-standard trim size. If you print in black-and-white on white paper, the following trim sizes are industry-standard: 5" x 8", 5.06" x 7.81", 5.25" x 8", 5.5" x 8.5", 6" x 9", 6.14" x 9.21",

---

[13] It might not be a 50-page difference for your book. It depends on your margins, font size, etc. When your book is completed, you can try changing the page size and see how this impacts your page count.

6.69" x 9.61", 7" x 10", 7.44" x 9.69", 7.5" x 9.25", 8" x 10", and 8.5" x 11". (So 8.25" x 6", 8.25" x 8.25", and 8.5" x 8.5" are custom trim sizes.) If you print in black-and-white on cream paper, you only have four industry-standard choices: 5" x 8", 5.25" x 8", 5.5" x 8.5", and 6" x 9". If you print in color (white paper is then the only option), the following are industry-standard trim sizes: 5.5" x 8.5", 6" x 9", 6.14" x 9.21", 7" x 10", 8" x 10", 8.5" x 8.5", and 8.5" x 11".[14] It is possible to enter your own dimensions for the trim size – up to 8.5" x 11.69" – but with limited distribution options (see Sec.'s 4.1.7 and 4.1.9).

2.1.5 Setting the Page Size

To adjust the page size and margins of your Word 2010 document, follow these steps:

1. Click the Page Layout tab (all of the tabs appear at the top of the screen), and then (instead of clicking Size) click the tiny arrow (that looks like 🔲) in the bottom right corner of the Page Setup group (the group appears toward the top of the screen when you are in the Page Layout tab).

2. A popup window with the Page Setup options will open when you do this. First, find where it says Apply To (near the bottom of the window) and change This Section to Whole Document – since you want to change the page size and adjust the margins for the entire document, and not just a few of the pages (that's why it's better to open the Page Setup window than to choose the Margins or Size options directly).

3. You should see three tabs in this popup window: Margins, Paper, and Layout. In Layout, you can check a box if you would like different options for the first page, and another box will allow the odd-numbered pages to be different from the even-numbered pages. The odd pages appear on the right and the even pages appear on the left (open a book and look at the page numbers on the right and left sides). You might want different headers on odd and even pages, or you might want to place page numbers on the outside of each page (which will be the right side of odd pages and the left side of even pages), for example. I recommend checking both boxes.

---

[14] This information was current, according to KDP's website, as of the publication of this book. You can visit kdp.amazon.com to view the current options: Click the Help link at the top of the screen, click Paperback Manuscript Guide under Prepare Your Book, scroll down to Step 1, and look for the word Options. Click the Options link to view the table of trim sizes. Although this table shows several industry-standard cream trim sizes, beware that many of these may not apply to cream paper: Before the merger between CreateSpace and KDP, CreateSpace's website included a footnote stating that only four of these were industry-standard for cream paper. If you plan to use cream pages and enable Expanded Distribution, you should contact support to check the latest status on industry-standard trim sizes specifically for cream paper. (It's possible that KDP's website or options will have changed since this note was written.) It's strange that both cream paper with black-and-white and white paper with color both have limited options, yet the options are different. If you really want to check on the latest options, you can email or call a representative at KDP (first login to your account, then click Help at the top of the page, and then click the Contact Us button at the left).

4. If you would like any page to be centered vertically (top is better for most), change the Vertical Alignment from Top to Center in the Layout tab (and change Apply To).
5. Now go into the Paper tab (still in the Page Setup popup window) and select your page size. Unfortunately, some industry-standard trim sizes are not default page sizes in Microsoft Word.[15] However, you can still type in the width and height of the page manually.
6. Close the Page Setup popup window and reopen it to see if the width and height are the same: In some editions of Word and various PDF converters, like Adobe, I have had issues with the program changing the page size to different values if the values that I entered were close to one of the default page sizes. If it does change slightly, the main thing to know is that each page of your file will be centered on the printed pages. If you need to, you can go with a page size that's a little larger than what you want, and increase the margins to compensate for the difference.

Note that you will need to increase the page size a little bit if your book will have images near the edge that need to bleed. When an image is designed to extend to the very edge of the page, we say that the image bleeds to the edge. An artistic page border or a page background, for example, might be intended to bleed to the edge of the page. If you have any images that need to bleed, you must add .125" to the outside margins – including the top and bottom. Therefore, you must also add .125" to the width and .25" to the height of your book. When your book is printed, each page will be cut – cutting .125" off of each outer edge of your file's page size in order to meet the specified trim size. Any images that bleed must extend this extra .125" beyond the pages final (i.e. after it is cut) trim size. This provides a little tolerance in the cutting so that you don't get a narrow white strip between the image and the page edge. For example, if you have an 8" x 10" book, and you have at least one image that needs to bleed, you should make the page size 8.125" x 10.25" and also adjust the margins to account for the extra .125" in width (add 0.125" to the left and right margins, but subtract .125" from the gutter) and 0.25" in height (add 0.125" to both the top and bottom margins). You must also ensure that any images that need to bleed extend to the edge of the page (completely across the margin) on the screen after doing this.

Images that do not bleed are considered to be live elements, and must be at least 0.25" from the final (after it is cut) page edges – so if your file allows for bleed, any live element must be 0.375" from the page edge on your screen. When you click the View tab in Word, you can check the Ruler box in order to help measure distances; the numbers are in inches, and the dots between them are in 1/8" (0.125") increments. All text, including textboxes, must also be a minimum of 0.25" from the (final) page edges.

In the Page Setup tab, set the Orientation as Portrait – not Landscape. If, for example, you select 6" x 9" as your trim size, you can't make a 9" x 6" book simply by choosing Landscape. If you would like the width to be longer than the height, your only option is the custom trim size

---

[15] Maybe this would change in the future if enough people politely asked Microsoft to add them as defaults…

of 8.25" x 6", and still you must use Portrait – not Landscape. The spine will always be on the left side, which is always the longer dimension (except for 8.25" x 6"). (Note: You could take a screenshot of each page in Landscape, paste the image into a document in Portrait, and rotate the image. But when you look at the final product it will seem like the spine is in the wrong place, and Amazon's Search Inside feature will probably be rotated, too. Therefore, I don't recommend trying this.)

Note that KDP offers Word template files (see Chapter 5 for common formatting issues).

2.1.6 Setting the Page Margins, Including the Gutter

Follow these steps to set the page margins, including the gutter:
1. Click the Page Layout tab and then click the tiny arrow in the bottom right corner of the Page Setup group.
2. With the Page Setup popup window still open, click the Margins tab.
3. Be sure to set the margins for the Gutter, too, and place the gutter on the Left; also, check the box for different odd and even pages (see Sec. 2.1.5, Step 3). With Gutter set to Left, the gutter appears on the left of odd pages and the right of even pages.

The gutter is in addition to the side margin. For example, if your gutter is 0.5" and your left/right margins are 0.75", your overall inside margin will be 1.25" (at the left of odd pages and the right of even pages), while your outside margin will be 0.75" (at the right of odd pages and the left of even pages). Your inside margin needs to be at least 0.375" for 24-150 pages, 0.75" for 151-400 pages, 0.875" for 401-600 pages, and 1" for more than 600 pages. The minimum required outside margin (including top and bottom margins) is 0.25", but at least 0.5" is recommended.

I recommend the following margins for most books, unless you add page borders: 0.5" top, 0.5" bottom, 0.5" left, 0.5" right, and 0.5" gutter. This will make your inside margin 1" and your outside margin 0.5". If you have page borders, you might want to add a little more room for them: 0.6" top, 0.6" bottom, 0.6" left, 0.6" right, and 0.4" gutter. These were the margins for the book that you're holding (unless you're reading the eBook), so you can see for yourself whether you would prefer larger or smaller margins. If you add headers and page numbers, Word will not place them in the margins – instead, the number of text lines that you have on each page will decrease a little bit in order to make room for the header and page number. Therefore, you want to add the header and page number (we will describe how shortly) before you start making sure that each page looks perfect – since adding these features to a book that was typed without them will suddenly reposition lines throughout your file. You might want larger margins, for example, if you anticipate that your reader would like plenty of room for annotation. If you write a puzzle book or a study guide, for example, the reader may wish to make several notes on the side of the page.

2.1.7 Choose Color or Black-and-White, and Why You Need to Decide Now

Decide whether your book's interior will be in black-and-white or in full-color. Even if you just want one picture on one page to be in color, in order to do this you have to choose the full-color option. Unfortunately, you must pay the full price for color even if your book only uses color sparingly. Color is more expensive than black-and-white, especially if your book is much longer than a typical children's book. We will explore pricing and royalties in detail in Sec.'s 4.1.4-5, but for now let's talk about the difference between black-and-white and color pricing, since you should have this in mind as you format your book (as we will soon explain).

A black-and-white book (but the cover will be in color) costs $2.15 plus 1.2 center per page over 108 pages, whereas a color book costs $3.65 plus 7 cents per page over 40 pages. For a book that sells directly from Amazon's website, your royalty will be 60% minus the cost of your book. If your book is 40 pages or less, you will lose $1.50 from your royalty by choosing color instead of black-and-white. If your book is longer than 40 pages, you will also lose about 6 to 7 cents per page beyond 40 pages, in addition to the $1.50. These values are for US sales.

Here are a couple of examples. Suppose you have a 130-page book. Your book would cost $2.41 in black-and-white ($2.15 + 22 x $0.012) and $9.95 in color ($3.65 + 90 x $0.07).[16] If you priced the book at $9.99, you would receive a royalty of $3.58 (0.6 x $9.99 − $2.41) for a black-and-white book; if the book is in color, you can't even price it at $9.99 (since the book's cost would exceed 60% of the list price). If you priced the book at $19.99, you would receive a royalty of $9.58 (0.6 x $19.99 − $2.41) for black-and-white, but merely $2.04 (0.6 x $19.99 − $9.95) for color. A color book with many pages is very expensive, and requires a high list price; a black-and-white book has a relatively low cost even with a high page count, and can be priced reasonably and still draw a good royalty. Your book must have much visual appeal, or instructive use of color, for example, in order to warrant a large difference in royalty that comes from publishing a book with a high page count (compared to 40 pages) in color.

Let's look at another example that's not so extreme. Suppose you wish to publish a 40-page children's book. The book would cost $2.15 for black-and-white and $3.65 for color. If you priced the book at $9.99, your royalty would be $3.84 (0.6 x $9.99 − $2.15) for black-and-white and $2.34 (0.6 x $9.99 − $3.65) for color. A children's book with many pictures will look much more appealing in color, so if the page count is not too high, it is probably much better to publish the book in color.

Why is the decision between color and black-and-white important when you are formatting your book? The answer is that it will affect how your book looks in print. If you have text or figures that are in color, but choose to print your book in black-and-white, there may be a significant change in appearance between the colorful image (or text) that you see

---

[16] KDP has a handy royalty calculator so that you can play with possible scenarios when deciding how to publish and price your book: From kdp.amazon.com, click the Help link at the top of the screen, click Royalty Overview under Royalties & Payments, click Paperback Royalty, and select the first item.

on your screen and the grayscale image that you see on paper. You can get a preview of this change by converting your file to PDF (described in Sec.'s 2.1.16 and 4.1.8) and printing it out in grayscale – though it could still be somewhat different than the printed page of your actual book. Text that is in bold red has an eye-catching appearance, but in grayscale it comes out as a soft gray that has much the opposite effect, for example. In such cases, your black-and-white book may look better if you change all of your text to black. Similarly, you might want to consider drawing images in Word in black, white, and gray instead of color if you will be publishing your book in black-and-white (but also make a set in color for an eBook edition).

If you are publishing your book in color, you will want to note that the colors that you see on the screen are not exactly the same as the colors that you will see on the printed page. Thus, if you plan to publish your book in color, you might like to be aware of this while you are writing or formatting your book, rather than find out for the first time when your proof arrives in the mail. We will discuss this issue in Sec. 3.1.4, as it will also affect the colors of your book's cover regardless of whether your interior is black-and-white or color.

If your book will have figures, note that we will describe some color-shifting and formatting issues regarding figures in Sec. 3.1.4. We will also discuss the formatting of pictures and how to draw images in the following chapter. So if you would like to learn how to draw pictures or insert photos into your manuscript, just wait until we get to Chapter 3.

2.1.8 Page Borders and Shading, Columns, and Page Layout Options

Microsoft Word also has some features to help decorate your pages. For example, you can find watermarks, change the page color, and insert page borders in the Page Layout tab. If you use these features, you might want to test it out and see if it will show up in a PDF (as described in Sec. 4.1.8). Some of the fill effects (like patterns and gradients) available in Page Color look much different in print than on the screen – the scale may change between your file and the actual book. Also, these page layout features will not show up in an eBook edition. Your interior can really stand out if you include these fancy page borders, but the design could also be a distraction for readers. The paperback edition of this book has a page border to help you judge the effect. Here is how you can browse through the available page borders, and – if you find one that you want to use – how to add it to your book:

1. Go the Page Layout tab, click on Page Borders, and choose the Page Border tab in the popup window.
2. Browse through Art to find several decorative borders. Once you select one border, you can simply use the up (↑) and down (↓) arrows on your keyboard to scroll through the entire list (and see a preview of each in the upper right corner of the popup window). The first several are in color, while the rest are in black-and-white.

Note: Visit http://chrismcmullen.wordpress.com/2014/07/04/page-numbers-in-microsoft-word-2010 for a free article (with screenshots) showing how to properly format page numbers and headers in Word.

3. If you use a page border, be sure to go into Options in the popup window and change Measure From to Text (otherwise there will be a glaring gap between the page gutter and the text margin near the gutter).

4. The Options window also allows you to change the distance between the border and the text. For this book, I used the following distances between the text and page border: 10 pts top, 0 pts bottom, 10 pts left, and 10 pts right. The discrepancy between the top and bottom reflects that the header is thicker than the footer (there is just a page number in the footer).

5. I also went into the Page Layout tab, clicked the little arrow in the bottom right corner of the Page Setup group, selected the Layout tab in the popup window, switched to Whole Document in Apply To, and set Header to 0.6" and Footer to 0.5". This was needed to create even space between the border and page edge as well as between the text and border. Depending upon the thickness of your page border and how the size of your header compares to your footer, you might need to use different values from these. Play with the options and see how it look (go to the View tab and select One Page).

6. In the Preview area of the popup window, you can remove any of the four sides of the page border, in case you want your page border just to be on the top or left of the page, for example, instead of all the way around.

You can manually force a page break by going into the Insert tab and clicking Page Break. I recommend not forcing page breaks until your book is complete. Otherwise, any revisions that you make to your book can easily change the place where you want to insert your page break. For example, if you add or delete a sentence to a paragraph, this changes the number of lines on a page. When you proofread your manuscript, pay careful attention to the page breaks, as this is a common place to find extreme formatting problems. If you use the Page Break button (instead of using the Enter key) to force a page break, this will help you if you want to convert your manuscript to an eBook file later. **Tip**: Click Page Layout, choose Breaks, then Next Page (under Section Breaks) instead of Page Break (see Chapter 5).

Most books are written in a single column. Newspapers and magazines often appear in double columns. Answer keys may appear in multiple columns. If you want to make columns, go to the Page Layout tab and select Columns. If you choose More Columns (at the bottom), you will find several column options, like changing the spacing between columns or adding lines between them.

Sometimes, you may want to insert a column break instead of a page break, in order to force text to the top of the next column. Do this by going to the Page Layout tab and finding Breaks and then choosing Column from the list.

Or visit my blog, http://chrismcmullen.wordpress.com, click the button near the top called Microsoft Word Tutorials, and click the link for the page numbering tutorial. You'll be glad you did.

2.1.9 Headers, Footers, and Page Numbers

Most books have a page header. A page header includes text (sometimes with some artistic design, too) that appears at the top of every page. You can have an odd-page header, an even-page header, and a first-page header that are all different (but only if you select the corresponding options in Step 3 in Sec. 2.1.5). Many traditional books have the title on the odd page header and the author's name on the even page header, for example. A famous author has some name recognition; it might not have the same effect for a self-published author to include his or her name on half of the pages through a header. You could place the title on the odd page header and subtitle, if you have one, on the even-page header, for example, or you could be creative and use the headers decoratively. You could do without a header if you want to, but your book may look more professionally formatted if you use headers. The paperback edition of this book has the title on odd-numbered pages and the chapter name on even-numbered pages (if instead you have the eBook edition, if there is any header it is probably the title and/or author and was placed there by your eReader, not by the author or publisher); **Sec. 5.1.4 shows how to make different headers for each chapter.**

To add a header, a footer, and/or page numbers, follow these steps:

1. Click on the Insert tab and look for the Header & Footer group, which includes Header, Footer, and Page Number. **See Sec. 5.1.4 regarding Roman and Arabic numerals.**
2. There are several default options to choose from (find more by using the scroll bar).
3. After you add a header or footer, you can edit the header/footer area by going to the same place and selecting Edit Header or Footer down at the bottom of the list – or you can simply double click with your cursor in the header's (or footer's) location.
4. Type the text of your header in this area, and add any decorations that you might want. In this book, I added a long line beneath the header by choosing the border options in the Paragraph group of the Home tab (while I was in the header area). If you choose Borders and Shading at the bottom of the border options, a popup window will allow you to change Apply To from Text to Paragraph.
5. Exit the header or footer area by double-clicking with your cursor somewhere in the body of your manuscript. **See Sec. 5.1.4 about different headers for each chapter.**

In the Insert tab, in the Header & Footer group there are also several page number options. You can change the style of your page numbers and the number of the first page by selecting the Format Page Numbers option. You can edit the design by double-clicking a page number – add characters around your page number, or decorate your footer, for example, the same way that you edit the header (double-click anywhere in the body of your text to exit the footer). If you place the page number on the right side of odd pages, you will probably want to place the page number on the left side of even pages (in order for this distinction to be possible, you must have checked the box for different odd and even pages in the Page Layout tab after clicking the icon at the bottom right of the Page Setup group).

2.1.10 Tabs, Justified Text, Bullets, and Paragraph Styles

You can indent a paragraph simply by pressing the tab key. With the Ruler checked in the View tab, you will see little gray triangular markers on the ruler showing you where the tab is. You can move these markers to increase or decrease a tab. The top triangle usually appears at the half-inch mark, and the bottom triangle usually appears at the left edge of the line. The bottom marker controls the indent of the subsequent lines of the paragraph, while the top marker controls the indent for the first line of the paragraph. If you will be making an eBook, tabs present a formatting issue, which we will discuss in Sec. 2.2.4 – in that case, I highly recommend using the method of Sec 2.2.4 instead. You can find more paragraph options by clicking the little icon in the bottom right corner of the Paragraph group in the Home tab.

Another important feature is the justification of your text. You can find the icons for left, center, right, and full justification in the Paragraph group of the Home tab (these icons are composed of little horizontal lines). The body text of almost all books is justified full, not left. This book is justified full: See how the text is even on the right side and the left side?

See the examples of left, right, centered, and fully justified text blow. The first paragraph has a jagged right edge, while both edges of the last paragraph are even. Microsoft Word automatically adds blank space between each word when you click the full justify icon in order to make every line exactly the same length. Your book will look much more professional in appearance if you justify full instead of justifying left.

> This paragraph is justified left. This paragraph is justified left. This paragraph is justified left. This paragraph is justified left. This paragraph is justified left. This paragraph is justified left. This paragraph is justified left. This paragraph is justified left. This paragraph is justified left.
>
> This paragraph is justified right. This paragraph is justified right. This paragraph is justified right. This paragraph is justified right. This paragraph is justified right. This paragraph is justified right. This paragraph is justified right. This paragraph is justified right. This paragraph is justified right.
>
> This paragraph is centered. This paragraph is centered. This paragraph is centered. This paragraph is centered. This paragraph is centered. This paragraph is centered. This paragraph is centered.
>
> This paragraph is justified full. This paragraph is justified full. This paragraph is justified full. This paragraph is justified full. This paragraph is justified full. This paragraph is justified full. This paragraph is justified full. This paragraph is justified full. This paragraph is justified full.

When you open a new document in Word, you will need to change the defaults. By default, new documents are justified left; you will need to change this to full for most of your manuscript, and many headings will need to be centered. Also, Word's default is to add space after every line. This paragraph has Word's default line spacing. See how it looks different than every other paragraph in this book. Click the little icon in the bottom right corner of the Paragraph group in the Home tab. Change the Spacing After from 10 pt to 0 pt and change the Line Spacing from 1.15 to 1 to correct the defaults. If you had already typed some or all of your manuscript, you will need to select all of it before readjusting the defaults (find the Select tool on the far right of the Home tab to Select All).

In the home tab, you can find paragraph borders and shading. This allows you to shade an entire paragraph or to add a border around a paragraph. At the bottom of the list of the Borders and Shading icon (click the arrow just to the right of the icon to find this list), select Borders and Shading to find all of the possibilities. If you select some text, you can also choose to place a border just around the text instead of the whole paragraph (but you will find that some options that apply to paragraphs don't apply to selected text). Some samples of what you can do with borders and shading are shown here in this paragraph. Beware that a few of the fancy Styles may not print quite the same in your paperback book as they look on the screen.

If you are typing a list, you might want to use bullets; but keep in mind that bullets won't appear in an eBook (but see Sec. 2.2.3 for a way to achieve the bullet effect in an eBook). In the Home tab, you can find three different bullet icons in the Paragraph group:

- The left bullet icon allows you to use symbols for your bullets.
- ☺ You can change the symbol to a checkmark or a smiley face.
- ☺ All of the bullets in the list will be the same if you use symbols. I made different bullets here, however, by starting brand new bullets. These two smiley face bullets are part of the same bullet list, while the others are separate bullet lists. At the beginning of the line, press Backspace (maybe twice) as one way to remove the bullet.
- You can even use a picture as the symbol for a bullet. Choose define new bullet (first click the arrow next to the bullet icon), then Picture, and then Import to browse for your picture.

1) Here we have numbered bullets.
2) They automatically increase when you press the Enter key.
3) This numbered list has three bullets.
1. The rightmost bullet icon is outline format – for creating a multi-level list.
   a. This "a." appeared when I pressed the Tab key.
   b. The "b." appeared when I pressed Enter.
      i. I hit Tab again to create a new sublevel.

2.1.11 Drop Caps, Font Sizes and Styles, Headings, Symbols, and Text Formatting

Most traditionally published books use a drop cap for the first letter of each chapter. As an example, one was used to begin this paragraph. You can easily do this in your own book using Microsoft Word, following these steps:

1. First, go to the Insert tab and choose Drop Cap.

2. Select your drop cap, return to the Insert tab, click Drop Cap again, and explore the Drop Cap Options.

3. If you place your cursor in the drop cap, you can change the font size and other font options as usual (using the Font group in the Home tab).

4. Place your cursor in the drop cap, then select the dashed blue rectangle that appears, and you will see 8 little blue rectangles at the corners and midpoint of each side: You can resize your drop cap by grabbing one of these 8 little blue rectangles and moving your cursor.

5. If you want the letter of the drop cap to be flush against the left side, place your cursor to the left of the letter in the drop cap, and hit the backspace key.

You can find most of the text options in the Home tab. This is where you can select a font and change the font size. You'll want to ensure that the font is easy for the reader to see and understand; some fonts are harder on the eyes. This book was written with Calibri size 12 font. (If you wish to make a large print edition of your book it needs to have a font size of 16 or larger.) A smaller font size can allow you to have fewer pages, which increases your royalty if you have over 108 pages black-and-white or over 40 pages color; but you don't want readers to complain that the book was difficult to read because the font was too small. If you have a library of fonts to choose from, beware that many specialized fonts do not allow free commercial use. Since your book will be available for sale, you are using the font for commercial use. Check with the company that distributed the font to see whether or not they permit commercial use of the font. Some companies allow commercial use with your purchase, some require a fee or purchase of a more expensive edition of the software, and others prohibit commercial use all together. Much clipart and many pictures have similar copyright restrictions, so you should inquire about commercial use restrictions before using any fonts, clipart, or other images. Even Office comes in personal and professional versions.

If you want to explore fonts quickly, type one sentence in a document, highlight the sentence, and browse through the fonts. You will see the sentence change into each font as your cursor is placed over the font. Alternatively, after highlighting the sentence, click the little icon in the bottom right corner of the Font group in the Home tab, and click on a font.

Note: Published books use **one** space after a period, not two. There is a compelling article on this that you can find on this by searching for "Space Invaders" by Farhad Manjoo.

Boldface and italics (these and other font options are available in the Home tab) are common ways to make print words stand out. **Boldface** is common in headings. *Italics* are used to give stress to a word or for book titles. There is a school of thought that you should avoid the use of underlining when typing. When you would underline the title of a book when writing by hand, you instead italicize the title when typing. I guess it just looks funny to some people to see a phrase or sentence underlined. There, you can judge for yourself. Underlining a single word could be effective: Personally, I like to use it with the word 'not,' as in, "Use italics, not underlining." If you want that 'not' to stand out, it seems to do the job. Well, it would stand out better if there weren't any other underlining on this page; the less underlining you have, the more effective it will be. The ab (but not abc – look carefully) icon in the Font group of the Home tab can be used for highlighting (gray would be the logical choice if your book is black-and-white). If you choose black highlighting, you need a light font (use white if your book is black-and-white), and white may read better if you make it boldface: Compare normal to **bold**. A couple of fancy options in body text (as opposed to WordArt, which we will discuss in Sec. 3.1.6) include the A icon, which might be useful in a heading, as in HEADING, and the abc icon, which is for strikethrough. After using the outline option (highlight your text and then click the A icon), there are four options at the bottom – Outline, Shadow, Reflection, and Glow – that can help you perfect it. You can find a few more font options by clicking the little icon in the bottom right corner of the Font group in the Home tab, including the Advanced tab that you will see in the popup window and the Text Effects option at the bottom. CAPS are common in HEADINGS. It's considered rude to type sentences in CAPS – people think of this as yelling. However, if you're writing fiction, you may use CAPS for a quote from a character who is, in fact, yelling.

You may want to do something special with headings (not to be confused with a header). Headings include the titles and subtitles of a chapter, the titles of front and back matter (like a table of contents or an appendix), and any other groups of word that you would see above the body of your text. It is common to write headings with a larger font, as in Chapter 2. Headings usually stand on their own line, with one or two linespaces below them. Some headings are centered, others are justified left.

Bold Heading

The heading above is centered, boldface, large, and has two linespaces (blank lines) below it (hit the Enter key twice or add space after paragraph). Main headings may even include some symbols or artistic design to help them stand out and add decoration to your book. The following examples were made using the A icon (for Text Effects in the Home tab):

EXAMPLE EXAMPLE EXAMPLE EXAMPLE EXAMPLE.
EXAMPLE

You can also make a heading using *WordArt*, as we will learn how to do in Sec. 3.1.6. In this case, I highly recommend going into the Format tab (which appears only after you select the WordArt), and change Wrap Text to In Line With Text.

The default Styles that you see in more than half of the Home tab allow you to quickly format text. These can be really handy to make an eBook format from your paperback format, or vice-versa. If you want to use them, first modify the Styles (see Sec. 2.2.4).

If you use the subscript and superscript icons in the Font group in the Home tab, this might be lost if you convert your book to an eBook – but feel free to use them for your paperback. You can make the same effect by inserting an equation (to be described in Sec. 2.1.13), but this will also cause some formatting issues in the eBook edition. We will explore this in Sec. 2.2.

If you are looking for special symbols, you can find most of them by going to the Insert tab, clicking Symbol, and selecting More Symbols. Many standard symbols are in "(normal text)" besides Font in the window that pops up, but you can find some more by changing "(normal text)" to one of the other fonts. (The organization of those symbols could probably be improved…) MS Gothic, for example, has many symbols to choose from (it even includes Chinese and Hindi language symbols, for example). Way at the bottom of the list, you can find some common icons in Webdings and Wingdings 1-3. If you are looking for mathematical symbols, also explore inserting an equation (we will discuss equations in Sec. 2.1.13). Following is a brief sample of symbols that you might find to be useful:

$$© ® é Ω ⅝ ™ ❶ ÷ æ ∞ ☺ ✋ ✂ ✎ → ↑ ✗ ♦ ☂ 🖥 蜷$$

2.1.12 Footnotes, Citations, Cross-References, and Plagiarism

If you want to add a note without interrupting the flow of the text, you might do it with a footnote, like the one you see at the bottom of this page.[17] In the References tab, choose Insert Footnote. You can find the footnote options by clicking the little icon in the bottom right corner of the Footnotes group. For example, you can number your footnotes with Roman numerals (I, II, III, IV, etc.) or symbols (*, †, #, etc.). You can also link to longer notes placed at the end of your book using endnotes instead of footnotes. Endnotes are appropriate for a bibliography – a list of citations or references. Use Cross-reference to refer to figures, chapters, sections, tables, and pages. For example, instead of typing "as described on page 42," you could use a cross-reference so that you only have to type the text, "as described on

---

[17] This is the 17th footnote of this book.

page," and the number 42 will appear automatically (and will automatically change if the referenced text happens to change page – which may happen if you add, remove, or modify any part of the document that precedes the referenced text). Add the cross-reference to the text or item on that page (page 42 in this example) that you are referring to. That way, after some editing if the item happens to move to page 43, the page number will automatically update. However, this won't apply to the eBook edition of your book (see Sec. 2.2.3), so if you use cross-references, you'll have to change them for the eBook.

Be sure to avoid plagiarism, which is defined in the following note. If you copy one or more sentences – or even just a phrase – from any other source, enclose the sentence(s) in quotation marks and cite the source (using a style of citation appropriate for your genre). For example, suppose that I included the quote, "I do things like get in a taxi and say, 'The library, and step on it,'" [24], the [24] would refer to the 24th reference of my bibliography, where I would cite my source. The 24th reference of my bibliography would then list the author of the quote, David Foster Wallace, and the title of the novel where the quote was taken from, *Infinite Jest*. Styles for how to cite the reference differ. Instead of numbering the references in a bibliography, the references may be alphabetized. In that case, instead of writing [24] to indicate which reference the quote is attributed to, you might include the last name and year, as in [Wallace, 1996]. Find the style appropriate to your genre – and just choose one if there doesn't seem to be a standard in your genre. You can learn about a variety of citation styles by searching for "citing references" with your favorite internet search engine, for example (and sorting through the search results to determine which sources are most reliable).

> **Plagiarism**: Copying the work of another – even as little as a single phrase – and passing it off as your own is called plagiarism. Failure to cite your source – even if you paraphrase instead of quote – is an instance of plagiarism.

Don't overdo the length of the quote or the frequency of quotations from the same source. Provided that you properly cite (i.e. acknowledge) the source of your quote, you can quote with "fair use." If you feel the need to quote excessively, you must first obtain written permission from the author. Consult an attorney if you would like legal advice.

You still need to cite your reference if you paraphrase instead of quote. If you find written information and rewrite it in your own words, even though you didn't copy the exact same words, you must still acknowledge the source of your information. For example, Mark Twain once said, "'Classic' – a book which people praise and don't read." If I want to write the following, I still need to cite my source: A classic is a book which people praise without ever having read [Twain]. You don't use quotes when you paraphrase, but you must still cite the reference with brackets [] or a footnote. Place the brackets (with either the reference number or name, according to the citation style that you follow) or footnote at the end of the paraphrase, and write the complete source of the information (which usually consists of author and title) in the corresponding bibliography (or, in the case of a footnote, it will appear at the bottom of the page).

Failure to use quotation marks for direct quotes or to indicate the source of your quote or paraphrase is a serious problem that can come with serious legal repercussions.

Even quotes may carry legal repercussions. You're not allowed to quote lyrics from a song or poem (unless it's in the public domain). For other material, quotes may be used only in "fair use." Research **fair use** online or contact an attorney to learn more about this.

2.1.13 Using Microsoft Word's Equation Editor

The best way to format a formula is to insert an equation. If you save your document as a Word Document, you will be able to use the new equation editor; if you save your document as a Word 97-2003 Document, only the old equation editor will work. In the latter case (or if you have an old edition of Word), go to the Insert tab, select Object, and choose Microsoft Equation 3.0. If you convert your Word Document to a Word 97-2003 Document (which may be useful for making an eBook, as we will discuss in Sec.'s 2.2.6-7), any equations that you have will be converted to the old format. Since I have been describing how to use Word 2010 (which also applies to Word 2007 in most cases), I'm going to describe how to use the new equation editor (the old one is also pretty intuitive).

Go to the Insert tab and select Equation. Click on the top half of the Equation icon to type your own equation (as the list of default equations is very limited). Much of the equation can simply be typed, as in $y = mx + b$. Notice that letters are automatically italicized. The convention is to italicize symbols, but not units. For example, in $t = 3$ s, the t is the symbol for time, while the s is the unit seconds. You can un-italicize a letter by highlighting it and then selecting Normal Text in the Design tab, or you can go to the Home tab and hit the italics icon. Note that the Design tab only appears when you are in the equation.

If you want to make a fraction, you can type a / and then a space when you finish (of course, you must first insert the equation and then type this in the equation), as in $\frac{x}{y}$, or you can go to the Design tab (after first inserting an equation and then placing your cursor in that equation), select a Fraction, and then type the numerator and denominator into it. Exponents can be made by typing a caret (^) between the base and exponent and then hitting space, as in a^b, or by choosing Script in the Design tab. The Radical option in the Design tab is used to make squareroots like $\sqrt{7}$. You can find many other equation features, like integrals, sums, trig functions, and brackets on the right side of the Design tab. For example, the following was made by selecting Matrix:

$$\begin{pmatrix} 2 & 3 \\ 5 & -1 \end{pmatrix}$$

If you type formulas, you will want to go to the Design tab (you must place your cursor in the equation first) and click the little icon in the bottom right corner where you see the table of symbols (it looks like a triangle with a short line above it). Next, click the triangle next to Basic Math. This is where you can find many mathematical symbols, including Greek letters and arrows. If you can't find the symbol here, you can also try inserting a symbol from the Insert tab (rather than the Design tab). If you need a rare symbol that you just can't find anywhere, you could always draw your own picture, resize it, and insert it wherever you like (see Sec.'s 3.1.8-9 to learn how to draw a picture). Following is a brief sample of common math symbols: $\pm \infty \times \approx \in \theta \hbar \geq \Leftrightarrow \perp$. If you would like to add an accent to a symbol in an equation, choose Accents from the Design tab. That's how I made $\vec{A}$ and $\overline{12}$, for example.

Equations may look different if they are in line with the text versus being completely alone on their own line. Compare the equation $\sin \theta = \frac{\sigma}{\hbar}$ with the same equation that appears by itself below. One equation is a copy and paste of the other — it automatically changed when it appeared on its own line (if you add anything else next to it, it will change format — looking smaller, like the one above, to fit on the line of text).

$$\sin \theta = \frac{\sigma}{\hbar}$$

2.1.14 Inserting and Formatting Tables and Adding Captions to Figures/Tables

You can make a table by selecting Table from the Insert tab. If you select Insert Table, you can choose exactly the number of rows and columns that you want. If you place the cursor in the table or highlight cells in the table, you will see Design and Layout tabs appear. Click these tabs to find the table formatting options. In the Layout tab, use Properties to position the table in the center, and to find some options for cells, rows, and columns. In the Properties window that pops up, click Options to change the cell margins or to wrap or fit the text in the cell. You can add or remove rows or columns and split or merge cells in the Layout tab. You can easily change row or column widths and heights by changing the measurements that you see in the Layout tab (first highlight the row or column that you wish to modify). There are 9 icons in the Layout tab that let you position the text in any part of the cell (choose the central one if you want to center your text both horizontally and vertically). The Distribute Rows and Columns icons let you even the widths of rows and heights of columns. If you don't want your text to read left to right, try using the Cell Direction icon.

	Column 1	Column 2	Column 3
Row 1	16	32	64
Row 2	8	4	2

Use the Design tab (which appears when you have the cursor in the table) in order to change the colors, shading, and borders. There are some default shading/border schemes to choose from. To make manual adjustments (or to make changes after selecting one of the default schemes), click Borders and Shading. I made the diagonal split above using an option in Borders. Grab the line to choose a different line style (like a dashed line). Grab the ½ pt pen size to change the line thickness to some other value. After applying a line style, click somewhere above or below the table in order to get the cursor to function normally again.

Type numbered captions below all figures and tables. Start with, "Fig. 3" or "Table 2," for example. This makes it easy to refer to figures and tables throughout the text – e.g. you might write in the body of your text, "as you can see in Fig. 4." After numbering the figure or table, write a complete sentence with proper punctuation that describes the figure or table. You might want to use a narrower margin for figures and captions in order to make it clearly separate from the main text. You can do this by clicking the icon in the bottom-right corner of the Paragraph group in the Home tab and typing 0.5" (or another value) for both Left and Right. See the example of a caption below.

Fig. 7. This is an example of what a caption looks like. This would be the 7th figure of the book. The margins of the caption are narrower than the body text so that it is not confused with the main text.

A Note for Novices: Many of the "how-to" instructions will probably seem abstract if you simply read through them. If you really want to learn how to use Microsoft Word, turn on your computer, open Microsoft Word, sit down at your computer, and try the instructions out as you read this book. The instructions will make much more sense if you try to find the things that the book is describing.

If you are new to Microsoft Word and have trouble understanding something, first try pressing the F1 key or clicking the circled question mark (?) in the upper right corner of the screen, which will take you to Microsoft Word Help. If that doesn't help, try asking a friend for help; there are also numerous help forums online where you can swiftly seek help with common computer issues. Once you get a few things clarified, you might find that other instructions begin to make more sense. As you understand the organization of Word a little better and how it works, and as you gain confidence that you can figure it out, you will probably find that things are much simpler than they may have first seemed.

As a teacher, I find that the greatest obstacle is often <u>confidence</u>. When you have doubts, you give up before you solve the problem. When you have enough confidence that you can figure it out yourself if you only just persist, you are usually able to solve the problem.

2.1.15 Copy/Paste, Undo/Redo, and Zoom Options

On the left side of the Home tab, you can find Cut, Copy, and Paste options. It may be more efficient to hold down the Ctrl button on the keyboard and press X for cut, Ctrl + C for copy, and Ctrl + V for paste. It is sometimes helpful to click the little arrow under Paste instead of just pasting. For example, if you copy/paste your ISBN from KDP into your book, you can save a little time by choosing the Keep Text Only icon (otherwise, it tries to do a complicated paste of formatting styles, which takes longer). After you paste something into your Word document, you will see an icon near the end of it, which allows you to adjust the formatting (to match the source or destination, for example, or just to keep the text only). When you proofread your book, the Find and Replace options at the far right of the Home tab should be useful. For example, if you find that sometimes you write Chapter 3 and other times Ch. 3 when referring to a chapter, you can use Replace to make all of them the same.

Note the undo and redo buttons at the very top of the screen (near the save icon). You can also undo by pressing Ctrl + Z and redo with Ctrl + Y. If you make a mistake, correct it by hitting the undo button or pressing Ctrl + Z. If you want to undo the last several things you've done, hit the undo button repeatedly. If you change your mind, hit the redo button or Ctrl + Y. These buttons are precious! But beware: If you press undo several times and then make a change to your document, the redo won't work.

In the View tab, you can zoom in just as much as you want. I like to use the Page Width option when I'm typing and One Page or Two Pages to check the formatting of each page of the document. Use the Zoom button for more options. I also like to check the Ruler box, which serves as a useful measuring tool.

2.1.16 Saving Your File, Backups, and PDF Conversion

I have some advice regarding saving your file that could potentially save you a lot of headaches and frustration. First, save different versions of your file. For example, suppose you named the file for your manuscript as MyBook. After you type a chapter or so, go to the File tab and choose Save As (not Save). Now call your file MyBook2. A chapter or so later, call it MyBook3. Every once in a while, a file becomes corrupt – it won't open no matter what you do. If you save different versions every chapter or so and your file does become corrupt, a previous version will probably still work. This way, you might lose just one chapter instead of the entire manuscript. Save your file frequently – every few minutes (but only change the version every chapter or section). If you sit down and type five pages, you will be frustrated if the power goes out, or if your computer simply decides to freeze on you, just before you click Save. You can't save your file too often, but you might (and probably will) become very frustrated if you don't save it frequently enough.

The default save option is Microsoft Word format with a .docx extension. I recommend saving your Word documents this way (except where I have noted otherwise in this book in the context of publishing eBooks). If you are working on multiple computers, where one computer has Word 2003 (or earlier), you will need to choose Save As (in the File tab) and change Save As Type from Word Document to Word 97-2003 Document. This will save your file with the older extension – i.e. it will be .doc instead of .docx.

Don't save your file in only one place. You can save it to your hard drive, save another copy to a jump drive, email a copy to yourself, etc. Computers have frequent problems. If you write several books, you will almost certainly have problems with some of the files. If you save different versions and store multiple copies of your book in multiple places, you protect yourself from losing a great deal of work. Remember which one is the most recent version!

You can convert your document to PDF using the Save As option from the File tab. The first time that you do this, you may be taken to the internet to Microsoft Office to download this free feature. We will discuss the conversion to PDF further in Sec. 4.1.8.

2.1.17 Preventing and Dealing With Memory Problems

A richly formatted book can cause memory problems when using Microsoft Word – even if you have a new, top-of-the line computer with ample hard drive memory and RAM. The following items make your file increasingly complex:

- ☹ Pictures, clipart, line drawings, tables, textboxes, WordArt, and equations.
- ☹ Illustrations that you make in Word where you do not group the items together (we will discuss grouping in Sec. 3.1.8) and are positioned In Front Of or Behind Text add to the complexity more than grouped items that are positioned In Line With Text.
- ☹ Page borders, page colors, headers, footers, and page numbers.
- ☹ Footnotes, endnotes, and cross-references.
- ☹ Frequent rich formatting of text.
- ☹ Comments added using features in Microsoft Word's Review tab.
- ☹ Built-in table of contents or index inserted from the References tab.

Memory problems can cause the file to become corrupt and create problems trying to open, modify, and save the file. There are a couple of ways to help prevent this. One thing you can do is focus on writing plain text until your manuscript is complete, and add the above features after the text is finished. This way, you can save a simple file with all of your text. Then, in the worst-case scenario at least you won't have to retype any text.

Another thing that you can do is follow the advice in Sec. 2.1.16. By frequently saving files with different names (just add a version number when you save it), you have a previous version to fall back on if one file has issues; and by saving your file in multiple places, if you do have computer issues (like a problem with your hard drive or a virus), this increases your chances of finding some version of your file to work with.

You can also separate your book file into pieces. For example, if you have a 400-page book with several pictures, tables, and rich formatting, you could divide it up into four 100-page files. You can also make tables and line drawings in a blank file and save them by themselves, and only copying and pasting them into your main document at the end of your project.

2.1.18 Spelling, Grammar, Word Count, and Review Options

In the Review tab, you can find the spelling and grammar checkers. Spellcheck is very useful. If this is on, every word that Word's dictionary doesn't recognize will be underlined in red. When you finish typing your book, carefully browse through the file to find all of these red underlines – these are potentially misspelled words. Your book will make a poor impression if there is frequent misspelling. The spellcheck is not foolproof, but it does help you catch many potential mistakes. If you accidentally type 'the' instead of 'then,' it won't be a misspelling since 'the' is still a word. So you do need to proofread your book carefully, too.

Also use the grammar check, which also checks capitalization. You can find grammatical suggestions underlined in green. The grammar check is not perfect because the English language is highly complex, but it will help you catch sentences where you forgot to capitalize the first word, repeated words, verb tense issues, and fragments, for example.

Don't like Word's autocorrections? Click the File tab, click Help down at the bottom of the list, choose Options, and click Proofing. There are several boxes that you can check or uncheck, depending upon your preferences, and you can find more by clicking AutoCorrect Options.

If you are collaborating with another author, you can add comments in the Review tab. A comment allows you to highlight selected text and have a line connecting the selection to a note placed in the margin. This is a convenient way to add annotations without modifying the content of the document.

Near the bottom left of the screen, you can find the page count and the word count, which can be very handy. Click on the word count and it will even break it down to characters with and without spaces. This will be useful when you type your book's description, since there is a limit to how many characters you can use.

2.1.19 Figures, Pictures, Clipart, WordArt, and Textboxes

We will learn a few more things about Microsoft Word in Chapter 3, including how to draw pictures, how to import and format pictures and clipart, and how to use and format textboxes and WordArt (we will also discuss the issue of formatting pictures specifically for the eBook in Sec. 2.2.5). Remember, most clipart comes with a copyright restriction that prohibits commercial use, but some versions of clipart software do allow commercial use; you should always find out about commercial use before using clipart in your book. Just to be clear: What I'm saying is, if you want to learn how to draw figures, format pictures, insert clipart and format WordArt and textboxes, read Chapter 3.

If you insert a figure on its own line (as opposed to being positioned beside a paragraph), center the figure and add a caption beneath it as described in Sec. 2.1.14. (We will discuss how to position figures in Sec. 3.1.8 – first find the third group of numbered steps, then find Step 10.) If you have a large figure that you would like to be on its own page, use the Page Break feature in Insert. I suggest not doing this until your file is virtually complete, otherwise any revisions to the text that previously came just before the figure might need to move to the page just after the figure. If you need to break a line up mid-sentence, so that the first part of the sentence precedes the page break and the second part of the sentence comes after the figure, press Shift + Enter at the point where you want to chop the sentence, and cut and paste (Ctrl + X then Ctrl + V) the second part of the sentence to move it. Make sure that the second part doesn't begin with a space ( ); if so, just delete the space.

2.1.20 Title Page, Copyright Page, Table of Contents, and Other Front Matter

Before we move onto the eBook, let's discuss front and back matter. These are sections that appear at the beginning and end of your book, such as a table of contents and glossary. You should have some front and back matter, but you might not want to go overboard with this. You will find several ideas here to choose from.

Your book should begin with a title page; you can find one on the first page of this book. I suggest looking at a variety of books' title pages before making your own. The title page should have the book's title and the name(s) of the author(s). If your book has a subtitle, you might want to include that, too. Textbooks often include the names of the universities where the authors teach. Traditionally published books would also include the name of the publisher; if you choose an ISBN option where you use your own imprint (see Sec. 4.1.6), you could include that on your cover. Consider using WordArt and adding pictures or artistic decorations to your title page (described in Chapter 3).

The copyright page is usually a plain text page that lists your book's title, the name(s) of the author(s), the name of the publisher, the ISBN number (you will have both ISBN-10 and EAN-13 numbers), the copyright date, edition number, and copyright notice. Some books also include the subject of the book (like nonfiction \ writing \ publishing \ self-publishing). If your main target is Amazon, you can browse the categories there and use that to designate the subject. Traditionally published books also include a series of numbers that shows which printing was used. You can get a lot of ideas by reading a variety of copyright pages. In your copyright notice, you want to make it clear that the right to reproduce any portion of the book in any form is reserved (by the author or publisher). I have a very simple copyright notice in this book; some authors have a lengthy paragraph here, getting into the specifics; and some copyright notices strive to persuade readers not to make copies of the work and distribute them (as if the people who would do that would bother to read the copyright notice, and as if the copyright notice may actually affect their actions). If you write a fictional work, include a statement that explains that all of the characters are fictional, and that any resemblance to actual people is purely coincidental. The main thing you want from your copyright notice is legal protection. If you would like legal advice, then, of course, I'm obliged to recommend that you seek legal counsel from an attorney for all of your legal questions.

Readers will find it useful if you have a table of contents (a must for nonfiction). Keep in mind that your front and back matter will be included in Amazon's Search Inside feature. The title page, copyright page, table of contents, and introduction are the first sections that a customer will see when using the Search Inside feature. Therefore, you want these sections to look professional in order to make a good impression; and if your book is lacking any of these sections, it may stand out as a glaring omission. The heading (not header) for your table of contents should be Contents or Table of Contents. One way to make the table of contents is to insert an actual table. In Sec. 2.1.14, we described how to make a table in Microsoft Word. Alternatively, you could make two columns (as described in Sec. 2.1.8). Either way, you want your first column to be very wide and the second column to be very short. The table of contents usually doesn't show gridlines, so if you insert a table, highlight all of the cells (but be careful not to highlight any area before or after the table, or you might not get the option you need), go into the Design tab, click on Borders, and remove all of the borders.

Most books have an introduction or foreword at the beginning of the book. The introduction is usually written in the third person. If you write your own introduction, this means not to use the pronouns I, me, and my, but instead to write as if you know the author and wish to describe his or her book. (However, if you read my introduction for this book, you can see that I wrote it in the first person. I opted for a personal touch with this book, so I thought that this was appropriate.) A foreword usually is written by someone else. Traditional publishers include a foreword written by a famous author in the same genre, and advertise on the front cover that the book includes a foreword by so and so. If you know anybody who has name recognition that may add to the value of your book in this way, if you can get him/her to agree to write a foreword for your book, it serves as a marketing tool.

If you would like to acknowledge anyone – such as the support of your family, appreciation for your fans, a colleague who offered valuable discussions, the advice of a friend, or grammatical corrections offered by a reader – you can include an acknowledgments section with your front matter. You can also include a dedications page if you wish to dedicate your book to someone in particular (or even to a pet!).

2.1.21 About the Author, Bibliography, Index, Glossary, Catalog, and Other Back Matter

Back matter often includes one or more of the following sections. A glossary is useful if your book includes a lot of jargon – terms that the reader probably was not familiar with before reading your book. An index is useful with nonfiction books where a reader is likely to be searching for a specific topic. Almost every textbook has an index for this reason. An index is not useful in a book that will be read once through, but is very handy when there are specific topics that a reader is likely to search for, but not otherwise find easily. Some books include an afterword. In this internet age, many younger readers will appreciate a page of useful links to related websites – but if you do this, note that your links may quickly become outdated, and you will need to frequently update your book if you want to keep the links current. Nonfiction books often have an appendix, which contains useful information that some readers may want to explore, but which didn't quite fit into the contents.

You can provide some insight into the person who wrote the book (that's you!) with an About the Author section. You should probably write the About the Author section in the third person, as if it were written by someone else who is describing you (or you can ask someone to write this section about you). Some authors include a picture here, too. Come on, don't be camera shy. Your readers want to know about you. I'm a family man, so my photo includes a picture of my daughter. Your photo can also show your passion for your hobbies or pet or the subject in which you write, if your picture is taken while you do whatever it is that you love.

You should include a References or Bibliography section if you have any works to cite. Whether to call it References or Bibliography depends on the field in which you are writing, as does which convention to follow to cite your references properly. In physics, we cite references by placing a number in brackets, like [3], following the place in the text where we paraphrased or quoted the source or where we otherwise wish to credit a prior work, and then we have a References section at the end in a numbered list with all of the works that were cited. Other conventions use letters from the last name, for example. You can find entire books devoted to the subject of properly citing references, so instead of making a long diversion on the subject of citations, I'm going to ask you to do some research and find the method of citations that applies to your work and read up on it there (also, since there are multiple conventions, this way you can seek the convention that is appropriate for your work).

Front and back matter provides an opportunity for marketing, too. Traditional publishers take full advantage of this. If you buy a fictional work by a famous author who has written dozens of books, you will find numerous quotes about how awesome the book is from several popular book reviews, you will find a sample chapter of the next book in the series, and you will find a catalog of the author's or publisher's other books. I've seen mixed feelings about whether self-published authors should do this and to what extent. I do think that a catalog of your other books is appropriate, especially since customers who like your book will probably be interested in your other works. You might want to avoid too much marketing in the front and back matter of your book, though; most people don't like advertising and sales pitches. I included a full catalog of my books at the end of this book as a sample of what a catalog might look like, not so much because I thought you would be interested in my other books (especially, since my other books are not on the subject of self-publishing like the one you are reading, but much different subjects like math, golf, chess, and science). In the catalog, you could just list your titles in bullet format, or you could copy and paste the pictures of the front covers of your other titles into your book.

Keep in mind that each page of front matter and back matter costs you money – 1.2 cents black-and-white and 7 cents color (even if the page itself is black-and-white – every page counts as color if you choose a color interior) – unless your book is 108 pages or less black-and-white or 40 pages or less color. (These are current values for books sold in the US.)

2.1.22 Professional Formatting and Editing Services

It is possible to hire freelance help to format and edit your book for you. I recommend doing it yourself. It is pretty easy to use Word to format your book professionally. Try all of the features that I just described and you should, I hope, feel confident that you can do it. You <u>can</u> do it. Be positive!

If your English is poor, you might consider hiring a basic copyediting service to correct spelling and grammatical mistakes. Otherwise, I suggest not spending money on professional formatting and editing services. Until you publish your book, you don't know how much you might earn from your royalties. Unfortunately, not all self-published books are highly successful. If you publish your book for free, rather than investing money up front, you won't be starting out in the hole.

2.2 Revising Your Manuscript to Create an eBook

2.2.1 Reformatting Your Paperback Book File into an eBook

YOUR FILE FOR THE eBook version of your book may be significantly different from the file for the paperback version of your book. One reason is that a paperback book reads differently than an eBook. A page is well-defined on a paperback book: Numbering the pages provides a handy reference, we know exactly how each page will look when we publish the book, and we can add headers and page borders to each page.

In contrast, eReaders do not at all respect the concept of a 'page.' They are designed to let the reader control such things as the font size and font style. Since the reader will set the font size to his/her liking, there is no way to control how much information appears on the screen at any given time. Additionally, eReader screens come in many different sizes. Some buyers will read the eBook on a cell phone, others on a large computer monitor.

Page numbers, page headers and footers, and page borders will <u>not</u> be part of the eBook, since pages have no meaning. Similarly, any page margins or font size that you set may not apply to your eBook. However, the font size that you select may affect the starting point for the font size that is displayed, and the reader can then increase or decrease the font size from this point – so starting with a typical font size, like 12, may be a good idea. There are a variety of eReaders out there, and then some people use their cell phones and personal computers to read eBooks, too. You want your eBook to look good on any device.

There is one page feature that <u>will</u> work with Amazon's Kindle (but not necessarily all eReaders): The page break feature can force the eBook to begin a new page at a given point on the Kindle. You can use page breaks to ensure that a new chapter always starts on a fresh screen. If you make a puzzle or flash card book, you can make sure that the answers start on a new screen – it would be silly to have the question and answer on the same screen.

There are some other common manuscript features which eReaders will also <u>not</u> accommodate: eBooks do not respect tab spacing, most special characters (symbols), fonts that are not very common, textboxes, and fancy text effects (like glow). Most eReaders also do not respect tables, bullets, and footnotes, but the latest version of Kindle supports basic tables, simple bullets, and endnotes (test out whether or not your table will work – go through the initial publishing steps and check the preview). You <u>may</u> use **boldface** and *italics* for a heading (not header), phrase, or a sentence; but don't use it for an entire paragraph or more. <u>Underline</u>, ~~strikethrough~~, super^{scripts}, and sub$_{scripts}$ work on most eReaders.

You see the problem: If you've already typed your book without all of this in mind, now you have to completely reformat your book to convert it to an acceptable eBook format. Be sure to save the new file with a different name so that you will still have the old pre-eBook format in addition to the new file specifically formatted for an eReader. You would hate to make all these changes and then discover that you'd lost your original. Again, save your files in two or more different places – like your hard drive, a jump drive, and by email in case something happens to one of the files (unfortunately, it is too common to have file problems).

2.2.2 Freelance eBook Conversion Services

Amazon currently doesn't offer paid eBook conversion services, but there are several freelance individuals and businesses who do. Amazon maintains a list of eBook conversion services on the KDP help pages. Login to Amazon KDP, click the help link at the top of the page, select See

All Formatting Resources under Prepare Your Book, and click on the link on the right column under Professional Services.

Following are some suggestions when hiring freelance help with eBook conversion:

- Ask if you can get a short sample (like the beginning and first chapter) formatted for a reasonable fee (or even free) before committing to full eBook conversion.
- Explore eBooks that the person or business has formatted for other authors. Check the quality of those eBooks.
- Seek independent recommendations and referrals from multiple sources (who don't all know one another).
- Keep in mind that you have no idea how well your book might sell. While you want to publish a quality eBook, you also want to keep your expenses to a minimum when you don't have any idea if your book will sell at all.
- If you hire professional help for eBook conversion, make sure that they will attend to all of the important details that are described here. You'll be quite frustrated if you pay money and wind up with a poorly formatted eBook.
- What file format will they give you when they are finished? Many professionals will give you a MOBI file or EPUB file, but if you don't have the right tools, you won't be able to edit this file if you need to make changes. How much will you need to pay if you discover mistakes and need to update your book later? (And what if that person retires or goes out of business?) **Note**: For an eBook, you **don't** want a PDF file.
- Most authors don't publish just one book. While it might seem reasonable to pay for eBook conversion for one book, if you wind up publishing several books, this expense will really add up over time.

2.2.3 Removing Headers, Footers, Page Numbers, Borders, Bullets, and Page References

The first you thing you should do is remove all headers, footers, and page numbers from your file:

1. Select all of the text (using Select at the far right of the Home tab) in your document.
2. With all of the text selected, go to the Insert tab, and find the Remove option at the bottom of Header.
3. Do the same for Footer and Page Number.

If you used page borders or shading, go to the Page Layout tab, open Page Borders, choose the Page Border tab, select Whole Document in Apply To, and change Setting to None. You must also remove any borders or shading that you may have applied to paragraphs or text.

You will also need to revise your table of contents and remove your index, since they refer to page numbers which are nonexistent in an eBook. You could change the page numbers to section numbers, but you can also include links that take the reader directly to the page. We will describe how to add such links to your contents and index in Sec. 2.2.8.

Remove extra line breaks. You get a line break each time that you press Enter. You should not have two or more consecutive line breaks in your eBook (if you had several consecutive line breaks, you probably need a page break instead). You can view all of the formatting marks in your Word document by pressing the ¶ button in the Paragraph group of the Home tab. If you press this button once, it will show all of the formatting marks. Press it again if you want to hide them.

Remove any bullets (although Kindle may support very simple ones). You can click the bullet icon in the Home tab to remove it, or place your cursor at the beginning of each bullet and use the Backspace key (you might need to do it twice to get to the left margin). If you really want some mark like a bullet, you can achieve this manually. You can just type a number, like (1), manually and place it before the line. I don't recommend trying to recreate the tab (and, remember, the usual tab spacing doesn't work): Since most eReaders have a small screen, any tabs cut into the already limited text that is displayed on the screen. Many symbols are not recognized by eReaders, in case you are thinking of inserting symbols (like ☺) in place of the usual bullet. You can enter a *small* picture (you don't want a *large* picture at the beginning of the line), in principle, but that also presents a formatting issue (see the issue with formatting equations in Sec.'s 2.2.6-7). Some simple text that the eReader recognizes is best. You will be able to view a sample of the eBook before it is published, so you will know if a symbol is not recognized (we'll get to this point shortly, too).

Look for any page references. It will be very frustrating for a reader to find a reference like "see page 24" in your eBook since there aren't any page numbers in an eBook. Use Word's Find feature at the far right of the Home tab to quickly find every instance where you used the word 'page.' If you may have used any abbreviations for page – like p., pp., or pg. – you need to find those, too. (If you search for 'p,' you will pull up every word that has a 'p' in it – so search for 'p.' instead in order to limit your results.) Instead of referring to the page, refer to the chapter or section number – like "see Sec. 3.5" instead of "see page 24."

If you used Word's Cross-reference tool, you need to manually replace these with numbers. For example, if you used the Cross-reference tool in the References tab to number all of your figures, delete those and manually type the number of each figure in. The same goes for references to chapters, sections, and any other cross-references that you may have used.

2.2.4 Reformatting Text and Paragraphs, Including Textboxes and Special Symbols

If you did not use a common font, you need to change it to a font that is very likely to be recognized, such as Times New Roman, Arial, or Calibri. Remember, the font can be changed by the customer on his/her eReader. If you used multiple fonts in your original file, make sure that all of them get changed. The simplest thing is to Select All from the Home tab (on the far right) and then choose a common font.

Did you use any textboxes? Cut (select the text and hold Ctrl and press X while still holding Ctrl) and paste (using Ctrl + V) the text from the textbox into the body of the document, and then delete the empty box that remains behind (select it, then select it again at one of its edges, and press delete). However, you may be able to treat a single word or short phrase of WordArt as a picture (but perhaps not for all eReaders), but even so it will format much better as plain text than as a picture (since it may be too small to read on some eReaders, especially cell phones that have a small screen). If it doesn't format as a picture when you preview your eBook (see Sec.'s 4.2.8-11), you can copy/paste it into Paint to make it a picture – but, again, it will format best as plain text (copy/paste it into the text and delete the WordArt box), since then customers can resize the font to their liking. If you want to leave short WordArt as a picture – or at least test it out – select the WordArt, go into the Format tab, choose Wrap Text, and select In Line With Text (afterward, you may need to use copy/paste to position it exactly where you want within the body of your text).

Similarly, remove any Drop Caps that you may have used (at the beginning of a chapter, for example). If you want to achieve a similar effect, highlight the first letter and increase its font size, or, perhaps better, use SMALL CAPS for the first few words.

Most eReaders recognize curly quotes (', ', ", and ") and dashes (– and —) provided that they are made using the Alt key (e.g. hold down Alt while typing 0150 to make –). Don't make dashes using Word's AutoFormat feature because a few Kindle devices may not recognize them when made this way. **See Sec. 5.2.1 regarding the use of special symbols with Kindle.** For a device that doesn't support curly quotes, replace these with straight quotes.

Tables are not supported by most eReaders. Kindle's new software is supposed to support tables, but I would test this out first (Sec.'s 4.2.8-11 will describe how to preview your eBook). You can take a picture of a table (with a Snipping Tool, or print it and scan it), but if the text is small it may be difficult to read on a small eReader like a cell phone. Instead, it may be better to state the same information in plain sentence form instead of a table.

Remove any use of multiple columns, since eReaders do not support them.

Most eReaders also do not support footnotes or endnotes. In this case, you will have to remove them – you can cut/paste the text within the body of the text instead, or you can insert a number in brackets, like [4], after the text, and move the footnotes to the end of the chapter or section (a simple numbered list, in plain text in the body of your text – not footnotes, not endnotes, and not bullets). However, Kindle will automatically convert your footnotes into hyperlink bookmarks (you should test this out to be sure and see how well it works). You can also create your own hyperlink bookmarks (see Sec. 2.2.8).

Use of the tab key is <u>not</u> recognized by eReaders. Also, do <u>not</u> use the spacebar to make tabs. If you used the tab key or spacebar to indent the first line of each paragraph (or anywhere else), you need to replace all of these indentations with a method of indenting that is supported by eReaders. (Kindle may automatically indent the first line of each paragraph, but, if so, it may not do so consistently and might indent shorter or longer than you would like. Many eReaders do <u>not</u> automatically indent.)

First, you must delete all instances where you pressed the tab key or pressed the spacebar successively to create tabs. Save your Word document, then resave it with a different name (so if something goes haywire, you will still have the original as back-up). Press the ¶ button in the Paragraph group of the Home tab in Microsoft Word to show codes. Next, press the Replace button (at the far right of the Home tab), then click the More button, then click the Special button, and select Tab Character (if instead you used successive spaces to create tabs, use the same number of spaces in the Find What field – instead of the Tab Character). Leave the Replace with field empty. Click the Replace All button. This will remove all of the tabs.

Now you need to indent the first line of each paragraph (and add indentations anywhere else where you once had them and would like to keep them). You can do this for the entire document (but then you'll want to undo it for paragraphs where you don't want the first line to be indented, like the title, author, copyright page, contents, headings, etc.), or you can highlight as many paragraphs as you want and do it for all of the highlighted paragraphs at once (and then repeat the process as many times as needed). In the former case, use the Select All tool to the far right of the Home tab – you can do this at the same that you implement the Normal Style (to be described a few paragraphs from now). After highlighting the paragraphs that you to automatically indent, in Word 2010, click the little arrow in the bottom right corner of the Paragraph group on the Home tab, change Special to First Line, and enter a value in inches (like 0.25"). Note that long indentations may not format well on an eReader with a small screen. Instead of using the standard 0.5" indentation, it might be better to use a value between 0.2" to 0.3". (Chances are that some of your paragraphs already had a First Line set instead of the tab, since Word automatically does this as you type – but even if that's the case, some of your paragraphs were not, especially the first paragraph of a section. You want to ensure that there are no tabs anywhere, so it's important to do this step even if you found that some paragraphs had the First Line option already set. Also, First Line was probably set to 0.5" instead of a smaller value, so it needs to be reset anyway.) Remove any blank linespaces between paragraphs (or they may not indent properly) – created by hitting the Enter key twice at the end of a paragraph (like the one after this paragraph).

All non-centered stand-alone lines (with linespace above and below), including left-aligned headings, must have First Line indent set to 0.01"; otherwise, they will automatically be indented. To not indent any other line, like the first line of a chapter, use 0.01". Don't set First Line indent to (none); otherwise it will be automatically indented. For example, if you have blank lines in your table of contents or copyright page, be sure to adjust First Line indent to 0.01" or there will be automatic indentations of these lines. If you use a Drop Cap (not recommended in the eBook as it creates formatting problems on some devices), that paragraph should also have a 0.01" indent. Do you have any other paragraphs or lines where you don't want automatic indents? (Don't use automatic indents where you do want indents, either; it's better to set First Line to 0.3", or whichever value you are using, or it might not be consistent. Also, some eReaders may not automatically indent.)

Set First Line indent to 0.01" for any line like this that you don't want indented.

When formatting your eBook, Word's AutoCorrect feature can automatically do things that affect your eBook's formatting, but which you don't see (when you read an eBook where the paragraph style – such as font style or size, or justification – changes abruptly, this is probably the cause of the problem) – even though you don't see it in Word, your readers will definitely notice it in the eBook file (so it's important to examine your eBook carefully when using the preview tool – described in Sec.'s 4.2.8-11). Turn the AutoCorrect feature off before you make any further revisions to your eBook. In Word 2010, select the Review tab, click the Spelling & Grammar icon, click the Options button, in Proofing click the AutoCorrect Options button, select the AutoFormat As You Type tab, and uncheck all of these boxes.

Make sure that your linespacing is set to single or 1.5 and that the At field is left blank. Do this using the little arrow in the bottom-right corner of the Paragraph group of the Home tab. You should Select All and change the entire document to single or 1.5 with nothing set in the At field just to be safe.

If you want to avoid abrupt changes in paragraph style – like the font size or style suddenly changing from one paragraph to the next – you need to make your entire document 'normal.' Your eBook looks like the style is the same throughout when you view it in Word, but there are probably style changes that you don't see in Word – however, if there are hidden style changes, your customer will definitely see this with the eReader. You need to eliminate these style changes that are hidden in Word, but which will be very visible on the eReader. Before you do this, save your file the way it is and resave it with a new version (as a back-up, just in case something goes wrong). The simple way to do this is to Select All and click the Normal option at the left of the Style group in the Home tab – but not yet because first you need to modify the Normal option.

Right-click the Normal option at the left of the Style group in the Home tab and choose Modify to define what you want the Normal style to be: Choose a simple font and a size around 12, but no larger than 14, then click the Format button and select Paragraph. In this Paragraph popup window, set Left and Right to 0", change Special to First Line, set By to a value between 0.2" to 0.3", change Before and After to 0 pt (not the default 10 pt), adjust Line Spacing to Single or 1.5 (but not the default 1.15), ensure that the At field is blank (no value), and adjust Alignment to Left (Kindle, for example, will automatically justify Full).

Unfortunately, implementing the Normal style change will also make some changes that you don't want: You'll just have to unchange them individually. For example, if you want your section and chapter headings to have a larger font and to be **boldfaced**, you'll have to manually redo all of this. Right click Heading 1, for example, in the Style group in the Home tab, to make a style similar to Normal, but larger and with the boldface button pressed (for example), to make a convenient heading style to apply individually to each heading. You can create multiple heading styles for different types of headings.

Any other formatting that disappears when you implement the Normal style change will have to be reformatted, too (be sure that the AutoCorrect options are completely turned off). Look for **boldface**, <u>underline</u>, centering, and changes in font size – compare your original file to the new one. Manually add these features back into your file. If you would have a ton of reformatting to do, you could try previewing what your eBook file looks like now (see Sec.'s 4.2.8-11) – if you don't see abrupt changes in style, you might be able to get away without normalizing your text (but if your end product has those changes – this method will help to remove them). **Note: Chapter 5 (in Volume 2) discusses Styles in much further detail.**

If you created any page breaks by pressing the Enter key several times, remove those blank linespaces (with the Backspace key) and use Page Layout > Breaks > Next Page instead. Don't separate sections with multiple linespaces – instead, make a line of symbols, like * * * to indicate section breaks (like the example that follows). Alternatively, you can insert a small picture or icon that relates to the theme of your eBook to separate sections.

* * *

Try to remember whether or not you inserted any special symbols in your document. Unfortunately, most special symbols are not recognized by eReaders. The way to know for sure is to view a sample of your eBook when you go to publish it (this is described in Sec.'s 4.2.8-11): Usually, you will see a ⍰ everywhere you used a symbol that the eReader does not recognize. Be sure to change all of the ⍰'s to a recognized symbol: Any ⍰ visible in your published eBook will stand out like a sore thumb. Sometimes, if you use unsupported characters, you instead find a jumble of crazy symbols like áäæéê; you definitely want to find and change those, too. <u>**Beware that Fire supports symbols that the old Kindle doesn't.**</u>

So exactly which characters <u>are</u> supported? Obviously, the list includes uppercase and lowercase unaccented letters of the English alphabet (A-Z and a-z), single Arabic digits (0-9), and most of the punctuation marks that you find on a standard keyboard. Letters with common accents (like é, á, and æ) are supported, but many accents are not. The copyright symbol (©) and registered trademark symbol (®) are supported, but the vast majority of special symbols that you find in Symbol in the Insert tab are <u>not</u> supported. You can find a picture of symbols that Kindle supports, for example, by going to Kindle's homepage, which is https://kdp.amazon.com/self-publishing/help, then clicking Formatting FAQ down near the bottom left under Frequently Asked Questions, and then clicking the second Here under the question, "What characters are supported in KDP?"

You need to find all of the unsupported special characters and change them to something else in order to prevent ⍰'s (or jumbles of characters like áäæéê) from showing up in your published eBook. In some cases, you might be satisfied with a standard symbol that looks similar. If you really want the original symbol, you could produce the same symbol as a picture (I don't mean that you have to draw it yourself – just copy and paste it into Paint and save the file as a JPEG image). Be sure that the format of the picture is In Line With Text (click the picture, go to the Format tab, and choose Wrap Text). However, this is not a perfect solution, so you don't want to do it frequently. For one, the resolution of the image may be lower than the original symbol (generally, you get a higher-resolution image by making the image larger in the original program before you copy and paste it into Paint – which suggests making the symbol with a very large font size before you copy and paste it). Another problem is that the size of the picture will be fixed: The reader may increase or decrease the font size of text to his or her liking, but your picture will not change size. So the picture of your symbol could be very small or very large compared to the text – and it might be smaller than the text for one customer, but larger than the text for another customer. You want your picture to be about the average size of text (around 12 points), yet still have high resolution. (So if you used a very large font size to make the picture of your symbol, now you want to make sure the picture's size on the eReader is comparable to the text instead of being very large there, too. Note that the size of the picture as you see it in your Word document may not be the same as a customer sees on the eReader. When you view the sample of your eBook as you are about to publish it – Sec.'s 4.2.8-11 – you will then have some idea of how the size of your picture will compare to the text around it.) Yes, we will discuss pictures – we're getting there.

Also, look for fancy text effects (like glow) and any special text formatting that may not be supported (you can leave equations for now, which we will discuss shortly), as you also need to change these.

2.2.5 Formatting Pictures for an eBook

We will discuss how to format pictures in Sec. 2.2.5, and then discuss how to format equations in Sec.'s 2.2.6-7. (We will discuss how to draw and edit pictures in Chapter 3; Sec. 2.2 is on formatting for the Kindle. Also, we discussed how to make equations in Sec. 2.1.13.) If you have pictures or equations, you want them to look nice on the customer's eReader. You want to keep in mind that eReaders come in a variety of screen sizes: A cell phone screen is smaller than a typical eReader, and a PC monitor is much larger than any eReader; people read eBooks on eReaders, cell phones, and personal computers. You want your eBook to look nice on any screen. Also, keep in mind that some customers will have color eReaders, but others will have grayscale eReaders. Suppose that one of your pictures is a graph and you refer to the 'red' line: Any customer with a black-and-white screen will not know which line is red.

The first thing is to convert images to JPEG file formats (line-art and text in images work better as GIF). This includes any pictures that you drew yourself using Word's drawing tools. You may be able to leave equations that you made with Microsoft Word provided that you save your document with a .doc extension instead of a .docx extension (go to the File tab, choose Save As, and select Word 97-2003 Document instead of Word Document). WordArt that is In Line With Text (click on it, go to the Format tab, and choose Wrap Text) may be okay, too (you will see for yourself when you view the sample of your eBook as you are about to publish it – see Sec.'s 4.2.8-11).

Following is a simple way to convert your picture to a JPEG file. (An even simpler way would be to use a Snipping Tool, if you have one.) Of course, it would be more professional to create images with PhotoShop or Gimp than to paste images from Word to Paint.

1. Select the image in Word, copy it (hold down Ctrl and press C while holding Ctrl down), and open Paint (you can find it in Accessories in your Start Menu if you have Windows). But don't paste the image into Paint yet.

2. When you first open Paint, you see a white rectangle (the 'canvas'). Place your cursor over the smaller white rectangle in the bottom right corner of the canvas. When you do position your cursor correctly there, it will turn into a double arrow, then you can drag the cursor (by holding down the left button of your mouse and moving the cursor). Do this to make the canvas <u>much</u> smaller.

3. Now paste your image into Paint (press Ctrl + V). If the image is smaller than the canvas, undo the paste (Ctrl + Z), make the canvas smaller, and try again until it isn't. You want the image to be larger than the canvas was before you pasted the image. When the image is larger than the canvas was, the canvas will automatically enlarge to accommodate it (that's what you want). This is important: Otherwise you get extra white space in your picture that you don't want.

4. After pasting your image into Paint, go to the View tab and Zoom In or Out as needed to get a good view of the image. Don't zoom in too far: Make sure that you can see the entire canvas (white rectangle) on the screen. Zoom in (or out) just far enough that the canvas is as large as you can make it without only seeing part of it.

5. Now return to the Home tab in Paint. If you need to crop your image, grab the Select tool, place your cursor at the upper left point where you want the cropped image to begin and drag the cursor (by holding the left button down while you move it) down to the right. As you do this, you will see a dashed black rectangle. If the black rectangle isn't positioned exactly where you want it, click somewhere outside the canvas and then try again. Once you are happy with the black rectangle's size and position, press the Crop button in the Home tab.

6. Now press the Resize button to change the size of your image. Make sure that the Maintain Aspect Ratio box is checked if you want the picture to look the same way when it is resized. In a moment, we will discuss how to choose the picture size.

7. When you are ready to save your picture, click the File icon in the top left corner of Paint, choose Save As, and select JPEG picture (or PNG if there is text or line art).

8. After you have saved the JPEG file, return to Microsoft Word.

9. Remove the old picture from your Word document (just select it and press the Delete key).
10. Insert its replacement as a JPEG file by going to the Insert tab, pressing Picture, browsing for the location of your file (where you just saved it when you were in Paint), and inserting your file into Word.

You can have an image as large as 2500 pixels on the longest size, but this is overkill: The actual eReader screen won't have more than about 1000 pixels (we will discuss the pixel size of eReaders in the next paragraph). Larger images also make your file size larger. (We will discuss file size in a few paragraphs; you probably want to consider this point before you begin resizing your images. **Also, see Sec.'s 4.2.2 and 4.2.4.**) If you have a large picture designed to fill the screen, you need a high pixel count. If you want your picture to be smaller, a lower pixel count is appropriate (but note that pixel count is <u>not</u> the same as picture size). If you are using your picture for a symbol and want it to be about the size of your text, it will be a very small picture. See how large the picture is when you first paste the JPEG file into word – this may give you a rough idea. You'll see how it will actually look on the eReader when you view the sample as you go to publish the eBook (see Sec.'s 4.2.8-11). Unfortunately, the way you best learn how to perfect the picture formatting is through a little trial and error.

Do you want to make a full-page picture that will completely fill the screen? You won't be able to do this perfectly (and keep your aspect ratio fixed), since eReader screens come in different aspect ratios. Many authors who don't realize that Kindle Fire has a different aspect ratio than the Kindle eInk, for example, become frustrated when they find that their pictures fit perfectly on one screen, but not on the other. It's not possible, though, because these screens have different aspect ratios. What you can do is design your pictures to completely fill the screen (minus minimum, automatic margins) of a particular eReader screen. For example, if you are targeting the Kindle Fire, strive to match its aspect ratio. The Kindle Fire and Nook Color have displays that are 600 pixels by 1024 pixels, while the Kindle eInk 6" and the black-and-white Nook have displays that are 600 pixels by 800 pixels. The Kindle Fire HD 7" is 800 pixels by 1280 pixels. **I recommend skipping ahead to read Sec. 4.2.2, which discusses in more precise terms how to perfect large images for a variety of eReaders.**
    Insert picture, right-click the image, click Size and Position, and set Scale to 100%.
Pixel count affects the resolution of the image. Another important consideration is the size of the original image. If the image was low-resolution to begin with and you increase the pixel count, it will appear blurry. The way around this is to begin with a larger image. If you drew the picture in Microsoft Word, you can redraw it as a larger image. (You can simply lock the aspect ratio – click on the image, go to the Format tab, click the little icon in the bottom right corner of the Size group, select the Size tab, and choose Lock Aspect Ratio – and then resize the object in Word – manually enter the size in the same place where you locked the aspect ratio, or grab the bottom right rectangle of the object and drag the cursor. However,

some images will look significantly different when you do this: Lines may not meet at precisely the same place and relative thicknesses may change. So it may be better to draw a new image.) You can make the page as large as 20" by 20" in Word, so you can make a very large image if you want. If you made the original picture with a different program, you can explore that program's options to find out whether or not it is possible to make a larger image (or higher resolution image) to begin with – **but see Sec. 4.2.2 for a note about Nook**.

Cropping and resizing the image in Paint will permanently change the image. The eReaders do not respect cropping and resizing that you do in Word. So if you want to make the picture larger or smaller, you have to go back to Paint and do it there. If you simply resize the picture in Word, that won't affect how large the picture looks on the eReader.

There is a trade-off between how large and sharp a picture looks and how large the file is. So let's consider file size for a moment. Several large, high-resolution images have a significant impact on file size. If you have numerous equations or little pictures, this will really increase the size of your file, too. First of all, every eReader has a maximum file size, so if your file exceeds this threshold you won't even be able to publish your eBook with that eReader. (We will discuss ways to effectively shrink your file size in Sec. 4.2.4.) Secondly, a larger file size may cut into your royalties (as explained in Sec. 4.2.5).

For example, if you opt for the 70% royalty rate with Amazon's Kindle, a delivery fee of 15 cents per megabyte (Mb) is subtracted from from your list price before taking 70%. For example, suppose that you set your list price at $2.99 and the file size is 10 Mb. The delivery fee would be $1.50 (15 cents/Mb x 10 Mb), so you would earn 70% of $1.49, which is $1.04 (0.70 x $1.49) per sale. If you could shrink the file size down to 5 Mb, you would instead earn $1.57 per sale: The delivery fee is reduced to 75 cents ($15 cents/Mb x 5 Mb), and 0.70 x $2.24 = $1.57. The extra 5 Mb costs you 53 center per sale ($1.57 – $1.04) in this example.[18]

If your eBook contains several pictures, and you make all of your pictures 20" x 20" in Word and then save them as 2500 pixels x 2500 pixels JPEG images in Paint, you will have a very, very large file. You want to find the happy medium where you have large pictures with a good resolution, while at the same time keeping the file size down. **See Sec.'s 4.2.2 and 4.2.4.**

There are a couple of things that you can do to decrease the file size. We will explore this more fully in Sec. 4.2.4, but for now you should carry out the steps that follow. This will decrease your file size significantly if the pictures take up much of your total file size.

1. Select one of your pictures, go to the Format tab, choose Compress Pictures (near the left side of the panel, in the top right corner of the Adjust group), uncheck the box that says to Apply Only To This Picture (by unchecking this box, it will apply to every picture), check the box that says to Delete Cropped Areas of Pictures, and change the

---

[18] If you don't like math, don't sweat it. You will find a handy royalty calculator when you go to publish your eBook and/or paperback book, so you won't need to do any arithmetic to know exactly what your royalty will be. The eReader will measure your file size when you download it, and the computer will do the calculation for you. You can play around with the list price and see how it affects your royalty.

Target Outpt to Email Resolution (96 ppi). (Simply resizing a picture by dragging in a corner will <u>not</u> reduce the memory.) Older Word versions: try right-clicking the image.

2. Click on a second picture to ensure that the same settings apply to it – just to ensure that every picture did change as intended (once in a while, strangely, you have to do this to a couple of pictures in order to make it fully take effect).

Make sure that all of your figures are In Line With Text. When you insert a JPEG file using the Picture button in the Insert tab, the default is In Line With Text. If you want to check the positioning, select the picture, go to the Format tab, and press the Text Wrap button. You want In Line With Text in order to position your picture exactly where you want it. You definitely do <u>not</u> want your picture to float using In Front Of Text or Behind Text (those options position the picture at a precise point on a 'page,' but there are no 'pages' in eBooks).

Kindle users can zoom in on pictures, but the way to do this is not obvious. Since it's not easy to find the zoom option, many Kindle users aren't aware that it's possible to make the pictures larger. If you have a Kindle Fire, for example, you double-click a picture with your finger in order to zoom in on the image. Also, a picture sometimes looks larger in portrait mode than landscape mode, or vice-versa. Users toggle between modes by simply rotating their eReaders 90°, just like using most cell phones. If you have a very detailed picture, and observe when you check the sample as you are ready to publish your eBook that zoom could be of value when reading your eBook, you might consider including a note. Find the first picture of your eBook where you feel that this is important. After the figure, include a note similar to the following note. You might want to shorten such a note. Also, for many figures the landscape/portrait option doesn't actually make a difference – if that's the case with your pictures, you might just mention the zoom option.

[**Photo viewing tip**: Many eReaders have a zoom option. For example, on the Kindle Fire, double-tap your finger on a picture to zoom in on it. Also, try rotating your eReader 90 degrees between landscape and portrait.]

For picture books, check out the new Kindle Kids' Book Creator. This new Amazon tool is easy to use (and it's free). I have a free tutorial on how to use it on my blog:

http://chrismcmullen.wordpress.com/2014/09/04/how-to-use-the-new-kindle-kids-book-creator-tutorial

2.2.6 Formatting Stand-Alone and Mid-Sentence Equations for an eBook

If you typed any equations by going to the Insert tab and selecting Equation, your equation will have serious formatting problems unless you save your file with a .doc extension (instead of a .docx extension). In order to do this, go to the File tab, choose Save As, and change Word

Document to Word 97-2003 Document – but don't do this yet: First, turn all of your stand-alone equations into JPEG files (as described below), and then change the file format. After saving the file as a Word 97-2003 Document, you may be able to reduce your file size somewhat by saving the file back as a Word Document while also checking the box that says to Maintain Compatibility With Previous Versions Of Word (this option only comes up when resaving a .doc file with a .docx extension). I suggest waiting until the rest of your eBook is complete before resaving your file in different formats. (When you go to open a file, you can tell the difference between a .doc file and .docx file if you look carefully. If you view icons, you will notice a slight difference in the 'W.' If you place your cursor over the file and wait a moment, it will tell you if it is a Word Document or a Word 97-2003 Document.)

If you have equations that are in the body of the text (as opposed to being on their own line), you will want to format them so that they look approximately the size of the text when the customer reads the eBook on his/her eReader. When the customer adjusts the font size, all of the text will becomes larger or smaller, but equations and pictures will not. This makes the text look larger than the equations or vice-versa, and also makes the equations look like they are above or below the line (and also affects the line spacing on the screen) – because the bottom of the equation is lined up with text, but the equation has some white space underneath. The best you can do is have the equations be about the same size as the text when the customer first opens the eReader. What you see on the sample when you are about to publish it (once again, we will discuss that in Sec.'s 4.2.8-11) is where you want the text and equation size to roughly match.

Equations placed on their own line can (and probably should) be made larger than equations that are parts of sentences. You can copy and paste (with Ctrl + C and Ctrl + V) your equation into a new Word document temporarily, increase the font size to a much larger value, and copy and paste the equation into Paint (see Sec. 2.2.5) in order to make a JPEG picture out of it. Then you can insert the JPEG file for your equation into your Word document the same way that you do for all other pictures. A large, high-resolution image will enhance the appearance of your equation. If you have some equations that are mid-sentence and others that are on their own line, having the ones on their own line as a JPEG file will prevent those equations from getting resized if you follow my suggestion for how to resize the mid-sentence equations. You might consider moving mid-sentence equations to be on their own line (so you will need to adjust your original sentence, too, if you do this), since you can make a larger equation this way. Mid-sentence equations may not look as good as a large equation on its own line can (since you can make it a large picture on its own line).

It's not easy to format a book with a large number of equations. Long equations are especially difficult to format so that they are easy to read (especially, small details like exponents and subscripts) on eReaders with small screens. If you wrote a textbook or otherwise have numerous equations in your book, I suggest going through the process of trying to format just a few pages (pick those with the most challenging formatting issues) and see how it looks when you view the sample as you are about to publish it (see Sec.'s 4.2.8-11). (I'm not saying to publish a few pages of your book – I'm saying to go through the process so that you can view a sample of a few pages of your eBook, then go ahead and delete it instead of finishing the publishing process. If you have pictures, tables, or rich formatting of any kind, it would be wise to make such a sample and see how it looks before you go through a great deal of trouble to reformat your book. First, see if the trouble will be worthwhile.)

2.2.7 Resizing Mid-Sentence Equations

Note that this section applies to mid-sentence equations only. Make sure that any stand-alone equations have already be converted into JPEG images (not only that, but you must have deleted the original equation and inserted the JPEG file in its place) before you follow these instructions. **Save a new version of your file in case you don't like the result.**

Beware: Equations in Word tend to be problematic for Kindle, and completely unreadable on one or more specific devices. Your best bet is to use JPEG images, and these tend to work best when placed on their own line between paragraphs.

If you made your equations with Word 2007 or 2010 using the Equation button in the Insert tab, there is a trick (for Kindle – not necessarily all eReaders) that you can apply to increase or decrease the size of mid-sentence equations relative to the text. Intuitively, you might expect that if the equations are typed with a size 12 font and that the font size of the text is also 12 pt, they should match. Unfortunately, it doesn't always turn out this way. When you view the sample of your eBook as you are almost ready to publish it, if you need to adjust the size of mid-sentence equations relative to the text, here is what you can do:

1. Go back to the Word Document with the .docx extension (don't use a Word 97-2003 Document with a .doc extension, and don't use a Word Document that was saved in such a way as to be compatible with Word 97-2003 documents).
2. Find one of your equations and make sure that you can place your cursor within the equation and format it as usual (if instead it opens in a new window with the old 2003 equation editor, you don't have your Word Document in the correct format).
3. Select all of your text (using the Select button at the far right of the Home tab), increase or decrease the font size of the document (don't worry, you will change it back in a moment) so that the font is larger if you want your equations to look larger relative to the text and the font is smaller if you want your equations to look smaller relative to the text.
4. Save your file as a Word 97-2003 Document with a .doc extension (again, using Save As).
5. Select all of your text again, and now return the font size to its original size.

This changes the size of your equations relative to the text. View a new sample where you go to publish your eBook (Sec.'s 4.2.8-11) and see if this is good enough. Unfortunately, you may need to do this a couple of times using a little trial and error if you want to perfect it. When you are satisfied with the result, you will want to go back and increase the font size of headings and any other text that had been larger than the body text (since all of the text became the same size when you used Select All).

2.2.8 Reformatting Your Table of Contents and Index, and Adding Hyperlinks

You need to revise your table of contents and index (if you have one). Don't format your table of contents (or your index) as an actual table. Start out by just compiling a list without page numbers, placing each row of what was your table on its own line (use the Enter key to go onto the next line) in the body of your text. Be sure to keep your heading (Table of Contents) and the page break that came before the table of contents (and remove your index). Instead of including page numbers, you can include section numbers (like 'Sec. 3.5' instead of 'Page 53') – but you really don't even need section numbers if you use hyperlinks.

When your (single-column) list is complete, you are ready to add links to it. It's not complicated at all, and Word 2010 has a built-in tool for it. By adding links, customers will be able to click the link to Chapter 4 or your Glossary, for example, and go directly there on their eReader. This is called an Active Table of Contents, and it provides Easy Navigation for the customer (that's the jargon for it).

There are two ways to make an Active Table of Contents. One method is to use Word's built-in Table of Contents tools, which works as a cross-reference. Unfortunately, the built-in Table of Contents tool is not supported by all eReaders (such as Smashwords – Sec. 4.2.10). The second method is to use Word's bookmark tool. I recommend the bookmark method, especially if you plan to publish your eBook with a variety of eReaders.

Following are the instructions for making an Active Table of Contents using Word's built-in Table of Contents tool. Remember, this method is <u>not</u> supported by all eReaders.

1. Place your cursor on an empty line (just hit Enter to make one), go to the References tab, press Table of Contents (on the left side), and select Insert Table of Contents (near the bottom of the list).
2. In the window that pops up, uncheck the box that says to Show Page Numbers (since you don't want to have page numbers in your table of contents) and check the box that says to Use Hyperlinks Instead Of Page Numbers.
3. You will see the following message in the body of your text: "No table of contents entries found." That's okay because we will now add the entries.
4. Highlight a heading that you want to link to the table of contents, like "Introduction" or "Chapter 4" (wherever you find that heading – a separate word or phrase that precedes the text of a section of your book).

5. Go to the Home tab and select a heading style that you like (there are several headings to choose from in the Styles group on the right half) – be sure to choose a 'heading,' not something else, and make sure that the heading stands alone by itself (as opposed to being part of a paragraph). Right-click a heading style if you want to modify it.

6. Now go to the References tab and press Update Table in the Table of Contents group (at the left).

7. If it worked, this heading will appear in your table of contents.

8. Place your cursor over the heading in the table of contents and then, while holding Ctrl, click the heading with the mouse (first press Ctrl, then click it while still holding Ctrl). This will take you directly to the page where that section begins.

9. Add other entries to your table of contents the same way.

The second method of creating an Active Table of Contents is to use bookmarks. This is the method that I recommend. Following are the instructions for making an Active Table of Contents using bookmark hyperlinks (starting with your single-column list):

1. Don't use any bookmarks that Word may have automatically generated. Instead, be sure to make your own bookmarks as described below.

2. Go to the first item that will appear in your Table of Contents – it may be Chapter 1 or the Introduction, for example. Find the actual heading in your eBook (not the words from your single-column list). Highlight the words in your section heading (Chapter 1, or Introduction, for example).

3. With the section heading highlighted, go to the Insert tab and click Bookmark.

4. Type the name of the section without spaces (e.g. Chapter1) and click Add.

5. Repeat these steps for every section heading that will be included in your Active Table of Contents.

6. Now highlight the text in the first item in the single-column list that will become your Active Table of Contents (e.g. Chapter 1 or Introduction).

7. With the text still highlighted, go to the Insert tab and click Hyperlink. Select Place In This Document, choose the corresponding bookmark, and press OK.

8. Repeat these steps for every item listed in your Table of Contents (but don't link the Table of Contents heading to itself).

When you go to publish your eBook, be sure to test out the links in your Active Table of Contents in the preview (see Sec.'s 4.2.8-11) to ensure that it works correctly and that the formatting is satisfactory.

After you have made your Active Table of Contents, be sure to delete the list you had compiled in preparation for it. If you are reading the eBook edition of this book, you can see how this works: Go to the Active Table of Contents near the beginning of the book and click on the various links there.

You can add hyperlinks within the body of your text, too: You can create a bookmark hyperlink, which works like your Active Table of Contents, to take readers to another point in your eBook (e.g. if in your paperback book you said, "See Sec. 4.3," in your eBook you can turn this into a hyperlink so that if a reader clicks it, the eReader will take the reader directly to Sec. 4.3); or you can create a hyperlink for a web page, which takes readers outside of your eBook to the internet (e.g. if you want to provide the web page for NASA, you can do this as a hyperlink so that a customer who clicks on the web address in their eReader will go directly to that webpage, as in http://www.nasa.gov).

If you want to add an internal hyperlink (i.e. to direct a reader to a specific section of your eBook), do this by using Word's bookmark tool. We discussed this a few paragraphs ago – i.e. the second method of creating an Active Table of Contents. The function works the same way for all internal hyperlinks. For example, you can create a bookmark for Sec. 4.2, then add a bookmark hyperlink anywhere you would like to refer to Sec. 4.2.

You can add an external hyperlink (i.e. to a webpage) by highlighting the text, clicking Hyperlink on the Insert tab, and typing the full web address (including the http:// part) in the Address field (the Text To Display field may be different from the web address). Be sure to include the http:// in the Address field or the hyperlink will <u>not</u> work in the converted eReader file. After inserting the hyperlink, press and hold down the Ctrl button while left-clicking on the hyperlink to test it out – if it doesn't take you to the webpage, check that you typed it correctly (better to copy/paste the rest of it into the field, then add the http:// to the beginning manually if it isn't already there – instead of 'typing' it).

To create a hyperlink to an email address, type just the email address in your text – such as nobody@nowhere.com – but add mailto: to the beginning of the email address in the Address field of the hyperlink popup window (or the hyperlink will <u>not</u> work in the converted eReader file).

When you preview your eBook file (see Sec. 4.2), remember to test out all of the hyperlinks in your Active Table of Contents and any other internal or external hyperlinks that you created. It would also be a good idea to test them out now in Word.

Do <u>not</u> include hyperlinks to marketing pages for your affiliates. Some eReaders (if not all) do not allow this, and so this may cause your eBook not to get published (or to become unpublished later). You <u>may</u> include a hyperlink for your author webpage (at the end of the eBook, for example) or to a webpage that lists your other eBooks, for example; the problem is linking to advertisements and affiliates' marketing pages.

Don't include too many hyperlinks. Many eReaders have a touchscreen where the reader uses his/her finger to advance the page: If there are several hyperlinks on a page, the reader may inadvertently click a hyperlink while trying to turn the page, which can be quite frustrating for the reader. Also, bear in mind that a reader who was happily enjoying your eBook and clicks on an external hyperlink in your eBook might not return to continue reading your eBook – so avoid providing distractions for the reader in the body of the text. The best place for external hyperlinks is a separate page toward the end of the eBook.

End your eBook with a brief thank you note, a list of any other books that you've written, a hyperlink to your author page, hyperlinks to your FaceBook page or blog posts, and perhaps an email address and a brief About the Author section, which could include an appropriate author photo. The last page of your eBook is a good place for brief, tasteful marketing (not advertising or links to affiliated marketing pages, but to your other works): If the reader made it to the end of your eBook, they may have enjoyed your eBook enough to be interested in more of your writing. The end of your eBook is a golden opportunity.

2.2.9 Formatting Adjustments and Community Help Forums

Although I have mostly referred to Kindle, you can use the same file for other eReaders, with few exceptions. For example, the latest version of Kindle is supposed to support tables, but most eReaders may not support them yet. You may need to make a few adjustments for rare differences between eReaders (we will discuss some of these differences in Sec. 4.2). When you view your sample for a particular eReader, you will see first-hand if you need to make any formatting adjustments. We will discuss how to publish your eBook with a variety of eReaders – not just Kindle – in Sec.'s 4.2.8-11.

If you run into specific problems and can't find the solution in this book, remember that you can discuss your publishing experiences with other self-published authors like yourself. If you encounter a problem with picture formatting with your eBook – or any other publishing problem – chances are that other authors have had the same problem and figured out a solution, and someone will likely to be happy to help you. For example, you can ask questions to be answered by other self-published authors of Kindle eBooks at the following community forum (for Nook and other eReaders, see Sec. 4.2.12):

http://forums.kindledirectpublishing.com/kdpforums/forumindex.jspa

If you type your issue into the search field of your favorite internet search engine, there is a good chance that you will find the answer there, too.

Now would be a good time to explore the links in the Resources section at the back of this book. You can find some useful publishing resources there.

Note: My latest self-publishing guide, *Kindle Formatting Magic*, provides comprehensive, in-depth instructions for how to format a Kindle eBook. Although the book you're reading now covers all of the basics, my other book is an encyclopedic reference. (Another guide, *Paperback Formatting Magic*, will be coming in 2019.)

Chapter 3

Creating a Book Cover

Chapter Overview

3.1 Using Microsoft Word to Make a Paperback Cover
3.2 Converting Your Cover Into an eBook Thumbnail Image

This chapter answers questions about the following topics, and more:

- ☑ How to create a single-page document that includes the front cover, back cover, spine, and allows room for slight printing variations.
- ☑ How to make spine text and center it perfectly, how to center text and images on the front and back covers, and how to know where the bar code and ISBN will appear.
- ☑ The importance of having a cover that looks nice both as a thumbnail image and as a paperback book cover, and how to preview what the thumbnail image will look like.
- ☑ How to make a cover that looks nice both as a thumbnail image and in paperback.
- ☑ What information you want to be clearly visible on your thumbnail image.
- ☑ Formatting options for textboxes and WordArt, how to draw color pictures using Word's built-in drawing tools, and how to insert pictures.
- ☑ A variety of tips for making a cover in Microsoft Word, such as how to save memory if you have several images, allowing for slight printing shifts, and preventing color variations.

3.1 Using Microsoft Word to Make a Paperback Cover

3.1.1 Finding Sample Covers

BROWSE THROUGH A VARIETY of sample covers. First look at the covers of your own books at home. Then take a trip to the library or bookstore. Next, view a variety of covers by browsing through Amazon's, Barnes & Noble's, and other booksellers' websites. Look at the covers of both paperback books and eBooks. It is important to view both paperback covers and thumbnail images.

Find a book that you can hold in your hand and view online at the same time. Do this with a few books for which you really like the cover. Compare how the cover looks in person to how the thumbnail image looks. Ultimately, you want your book cover to look good both as a paperback book and as a thumbnail image.

Note some covers that you particularly liked, and also find some covers that really didn't appeal to you. Make some notes of what stood out both ways – good and bad. You definitely want to keep this in mind as you design your cover.

Looking through covers, you're not just contemplating what looks great and what looks awful. You're also getting ideas for what is possible, which colors go well together, how large the font needs to be to make key words stand out, and various ways in which a cover might grab attention, for example. Note the different items that you find on covers, like the title, subtitle, author, what goes on the spine, descriptions and quotes on the back cover, etc.

I have included samples of a variety of my books. It's not because I thought that my own covers were the best. Rather, it's that it was very easy to obtain permission to use them, and I could use my own covers for free. I did, however, make most of my covers myself, and most of the images are pictures that I made from scratch using Microsoft Word's drawing tools. (However, I have hired a cover designer for a few books, including this one.) You can also make your own cover and draw your own images with Microsoft Word – or you can take photos and use those pictures – as I describe how to do in this chapter. You will learn how to draw pictures in Microsoft Word in Sec.'s 3.1.8-9, and how to format pictures in Sec. 3.1.12.

If you are reading the paperback version of my book, you can see what the front covers of some of my books look like in color as they appear on the front and back cover. If you are reading the eBook, all of the cover images in the eBook edition are in color. I selected the samples on the cover, and in the following figures, to try to show some variety – I didn't choose which covers to place there based on how popular the books are.

In addition to the front covers, you can find samples of some of my full cover spreads on the following pages. These show you what my Word files looked like for the full cover, including the front cover, back cover, and spine. Your cover will have a similar layout to these full cover spreads. I included my full cover spreads mainly to help you understand this layout.

This detailed guide will take you step-by-step through the self-publishing process, including both print and eBook editions. Learn how to format the interior of your book using Microsoft Word, reformat your interior file for the eBook edition, use Word's drawing tools to make illustrations, and publish your book to be available on Amazon and other major online retailers. Find detailed discussions of important issues like how to set the price of your book, differences in color for images viewed on a screen compared to images printed on paper, and the benefits and disadvantages of enrolling in KDP Select.

The author, Chris McMullen, has self-published over a dozen different types of books on Amazon.com. He is experienced with the techniques and details, and is sharing his knowledge with you through this guide. This handy reference shows you how to format your book, design a cover, self-publish your paperback with Create Space, and self-publish your eBook with Kindle, Nook, Kobo, and Smashwords.

$9.00 USA

MCMULLEN   A DETAILED GUIDE TO SELF-PUBLISHING WITH AMAZON AND OTHER ONLINE BOOKSELLERS   VOL. 1

Chris McMullen

A DETAILED GUIDE TO
SELF-PUBLISHING
with
AMAZON
AND OTHER ONLINE BOOKSELLERS

VOL 1

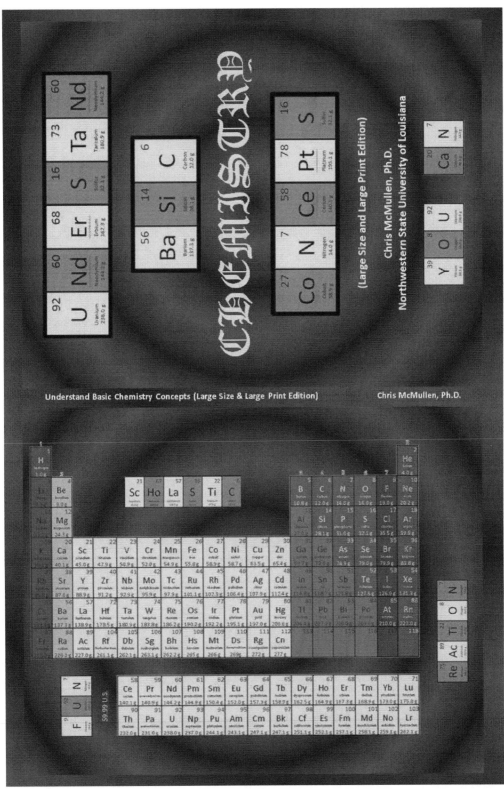

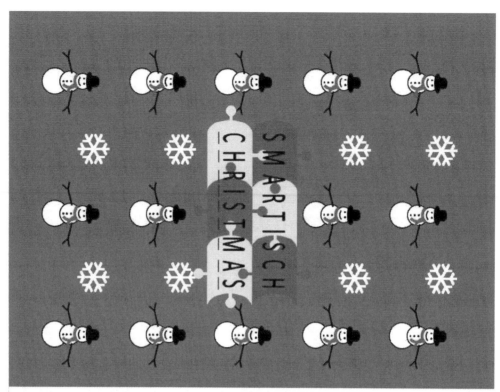

MASTER
LONG
DIVISION
PRACTICE WORKBOOK

Includes Answers!

$$52 \text{ R } 1$$
$$7\overline{)365}$$
$$350$$
$$15$$
$$14$$
$$1$$

$$28 \text{ R } 8$$
$$28\overline{)792}$$
$$560$$
$$232$$
$$224$$
$$8$$

Improve Your Math Fluency Series

Chris McMullen, Ph.D.

This *Master Long Division Practice Workbook* is designed to help students develop proficiency with their long division skills by offering ample practice. This book is conveniently divided up into six parts:

- Part 1 reviews the fundamental division facts with one-digit divisor and quotient since swift knowledge of these is critical toward long division mastery.
- Part 2 focuses on basic long division problems with single-digit divisors. Part 2 does not include remainders. This way students are not challenged with too much too soon.
- Part 3 includes two-digit divisors.
- Part 4 introduces remainders with simple problems that have one-digit divisors and dividends with no more than two digits.
- Part 5 expands on Part 4 to include dividends with more digits.
- Part 6 involves two-digit divisors, multi-digit dividends, and remainders.

A multiplication table is provided for students who are not yet fluent with their division facts.

$$31 \text{ R } 9$$
$$17\overline{)536}$$
$$510$$
$$26$$
$$17$$
$$9$$

$$1{,}709 \text{ R } 20$$
$$25\overline{)42{,}745}$$
$$25$$
$$177$$
$$175$$
$$24$$
$$0$$
$$245$$
$$225$$
$$20$$

$9.99 U.S.

Master Long Division Practice Workbook   Chris McMullen, Ph.D.

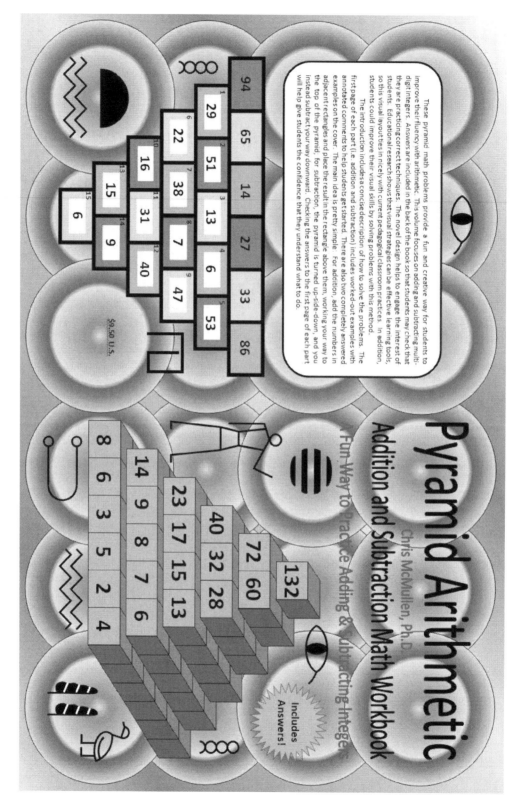

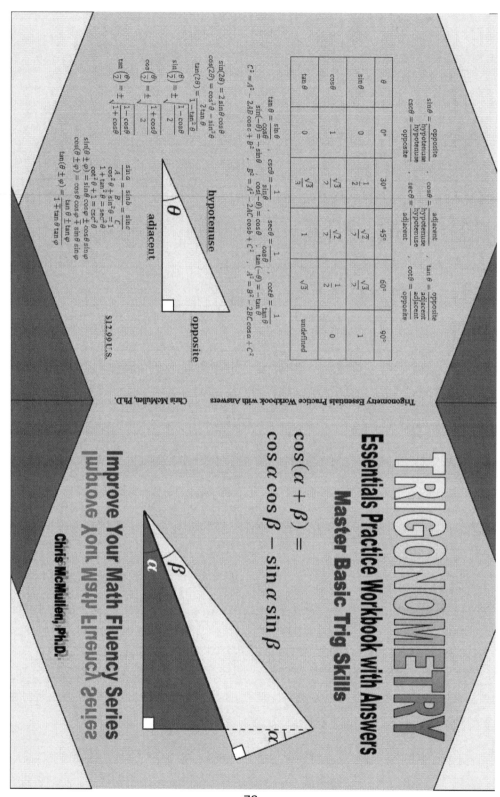

GOLF WORD SCRAMBLES   Chris McMullen and Carolyn Kivett

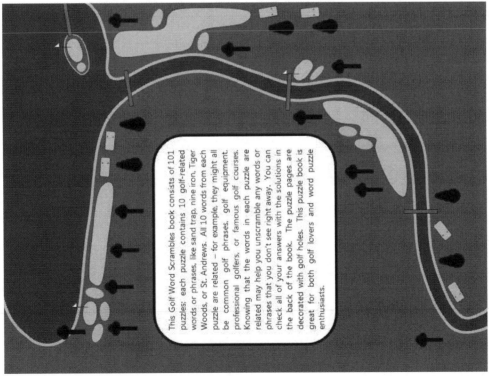

This Golf Word Scrambles book consists of 101 puzzles; each puzzle contains 10 golf-related words or phrases, like sand trap, nine iron, Tiger Woods, or St. Andrews. All 10 words from each puzzle are related – for example, they might all be common golf phrases, golf equipment, professional golfers, or famous golf courses. Knowing that the words in each puzzle are related may help you unscramble any words or phrases that you don't see right away. You can check all of your answers with the solutions in the back of the book. The puzzle pages are decorated with golf holes. This puzzle book is great for both golf lovers and word puzzle enthusiasts.

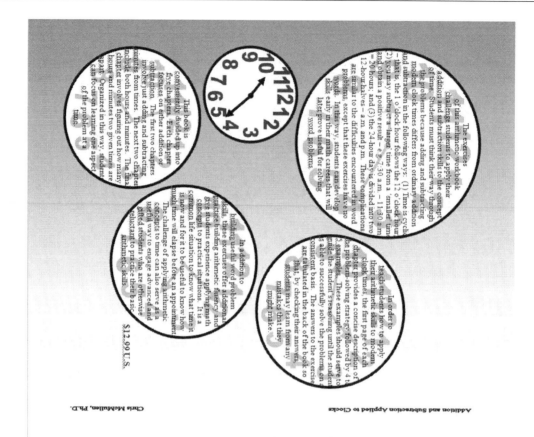

Addition and Subtraction Applied to Clocks

Chris McMullen, Ph.D.

$12.99 U.S.

ADDITION AND SUBTRACTION

APPLIED TO CLOCKS

Includes Answers!

Chris McMullen, Ph.D.

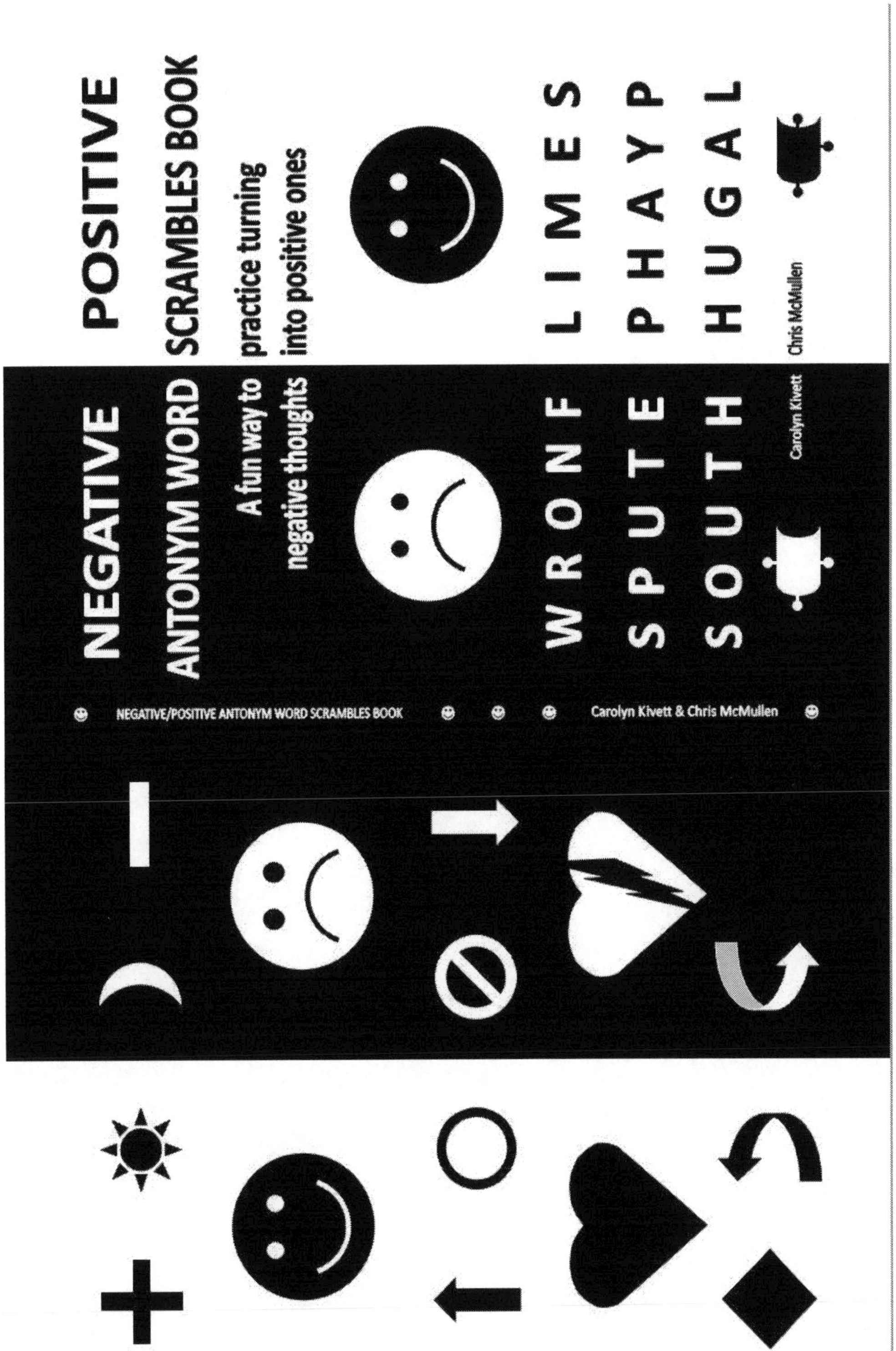

POSITIVE SCRAMBLES BOOK

practice turning into positive ones

L I M E S

P H A Y P

H U G A L

Chris McMullen

NEGATIVE ANTONYM WORD

A fun way to negative thoughts

W R O N F

S P U T E

S O U T H

Carolyn Kivett

NEGATIVE/POSITIVE ANTONYM WORD SCRAMBLES BOOK

Carolyn Kivett & Chris McMullen

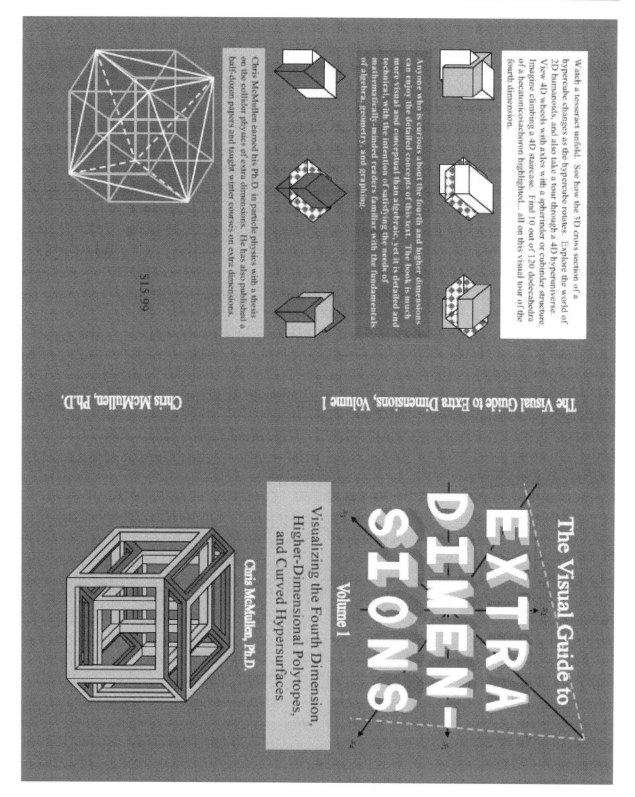

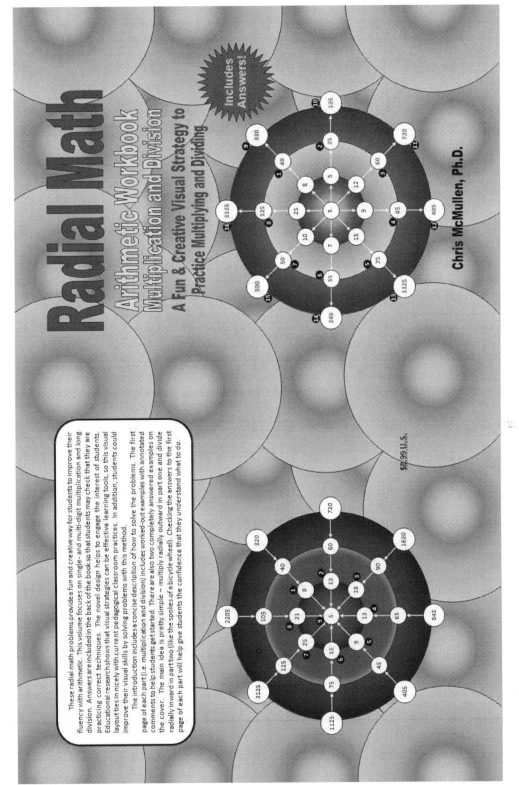

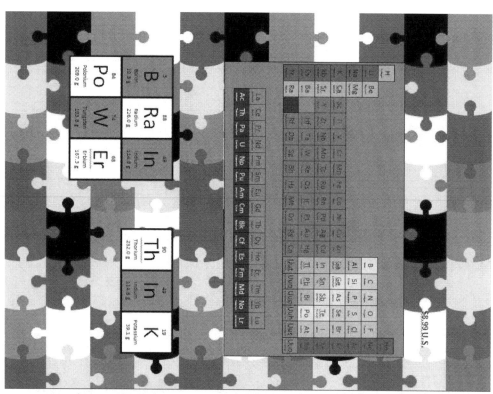

3.1.2 What Should You Include on Your Cover?

Your front cover must include the full title and the names of all of the authors. The full title on your front cover file, the title on the title page, the title on the copyright page, and the title that you enter when you go to publish your paperback book must all match exactly. However, you don't need to include the subtitle on your cover; this is optional. Spell the names of all of the authors exactly the same way on the cover, title page, copyright page, and as you enter them when you go to publish your book. You might have an illustrator or editor, for example, to acknowledge in addition to the authors.

All of the text of the title does not need to be the same size, does not need to lie on the same line, can have a symbol replace a letter (like a planet replacing an 'O'), and can even be separated or spread out considerably (as long as it is reasonably obvious how to correctly read the words of the title in order). You probably want a few key words to be larger and to stand out effectively. The key words should be easily visible in the thumbnail image.

Most front covers feature some art. However, many very appealing and effective covers don't have anything that you might normally regard as art – many just have simple patterns of solid colors, stripes, or simple shapes. You don't necessarily need good drawing or art skills in order to design a great cover. You probably observed some simple covers that were very nice when you were browsing through covers. When it comes to the thumbnail image – and this is where most Amazon buyers will first see your book – simple is often much more effective than complex. The main ingredients are key words that stand out and are easy to read combined with an appealing color scheme (note which combinations of colors seemed appealing to you when you were browsing covers – and if you're not confident with your own judgment or those of your friends, you can search for opinions about good color schemes on your favorite internet search engine).

If your book has 130 pages or more, include a label on the spine, too. In fact, it is worth having this many pages (in case you were planning to submit a slightly shorter book) so that you can add spine text to your cover. A book looks more professional when you see the title and a combination of the author, publisher, and a logo on the spine. Also, it makes the book much easier to find when it is sitting on a bookshelf: So if you have any aspirations of getting a local bookstore to buy and sell copies of your book, you really need to include spine text. If your book has over 100 pages, you can still include spine text, but due to printing tolerances, there is a chance of the edge of the spine text wrapping onto the front or back cover; also, the spine text is required to be quite small on a thinner book. A book of 100 pages or less can't have spine text on the cover. (We will describe how to add spine text in Sec. 3.1.7.)

Keep in mind that buyers will see the back cover of your book when they use the Search Inside feature on Amazon. The back cover can be decorative, or it can be functional, or both. One way to make the back cover functional is to include a description of your book. If your book has been professionally reviewed, you can include a quote from the review on your cover. The back cover can also include a brief biography of the author, or highlight the author's qualifications. The back cover provides an opportunity to help market and sell your book. You can even put a table or picture on the back cover that may be helpful to the reader – like a map, if you are writing a fantasy book, or a multiplication table, if you are writing a math workbook. I included pictures of a variety of my book covers on the back cover of this book because I thought that these color pictures of covers might be helpful to some of my fellow, soon-to-be self-published authors when they go to design their covers.

Your back cover will automatically include a bar code and ISBN number. You can predict precisely where this will be placed, as described in Sec. 3.1.5. (If you really would like it placed elsewhere, try contacting the company with whom you self-publish your paperback – such as KDP. After logging into your account, click Help at the top and then scroll down and click Contact Us at the left.) Consider including the list price on the cover, too. Big chain bookstores, like Barnes & Noble, require the list price of the book (which is the list price that shows on Amazon's listing) to be on the cover in order to be eligible to have your book stocked in their stores. However, this does not affect eligibility for online sales, and it is not easy to get big chain bookstores to stock your book on their shelves (see Sec. 4.1.7 and Chapter 8).

3.1.3 Design With Both the Paperback and Thumbnail Image in Mind

It's very important for the front cover of your book to look nice as a thumbnail image because this is the first thing that prospective buyers will see on Amazon and any other websites where you paperback book is sold. The thumbnail image helps customers to visualize holding your paperback book in their hands. The actual cover of your paperback book – including the front cover, spine, and back cover, is also important because customers who buy your book will see it firsthand (their friends and family members will likely see it, too).

Many people are significantly influenced by the cover of a book. Do you know anybody who has a coffee table book decorating their living room, who mostly appreciates that the cover looks nice? You're not trying to sell a coffee table book, and you want people to read your book and value it for the content, but my example does show one common way that a cover is important to buyers. Similarly, some customers like holding a book that looks nice and sounds interesting when they read it in a bus or on a plane, for example. You may find that you have friends or family who have some books that they bought because they looked or sounded interesting, but never got around to reading. Again, you don't want your book to go unread, but you can see in this case that the appearance of the book may factor into the purchase decision.

The content is important, but many readers will not judge your book solely by the content. The thumbnail image helps to draw interest in the book, and the actual cover helps to continually recall interest in the book – and to interest other potential readers. If a customer buys your book online, it may be a week or more before the book arrives in the mail. When the customer opens the box, you want the cover to revive his or her interest in your book. When the customer sees your book lying around, you want the cover to remind the customer to read your book (of course, captivating content can achieve this, too – but the customer has to start reading your book before he or she can be captivated by the content; the cover can help to capture the reader's interest before the book is ever opened).

The cover should do more than just catch attention or create interest. It should look professional in appearance in order to make a good impression. The cover can also provide information about the book and/or the author, and can help to sell or market your book.

Several factors affect how professional your cover looks. Any misspellings or grammatical mistakes on the cover give a poor impression right off the bat, so it's definitely worth very carefully proofreading all of the text on your cover. Also, check the images over carefully when you review your proof to ensure that there aren't any formatting errors – such as intersecting lines that should meet at their edges, but are a little misaligned. The cover text should be easy to read in person, and the key words should be easy to read on the thumbnail image. The color combinations that you see on the cover should look appealing both on the screen and in print. (Even if you publish your book with a black-and-white interior, the cover will be color.) Overall, the cover should have a good aesthetic feel to it. Including spine text and centering it properly on the spine and including the list price on the cover can also help to create a professional look. A professional cover is also tasteful and inoffensive.

It doesn't take a Picasso for a cover to draw interest from readers. A simple cover is often more effective than a complex cover. You also don't want the cover to seem too busy.[19] Books with the best-looking covers don't always sell well. Although the appearance of the cover is important, it's not the only factor that affects sales – content, reviews, qualifications of the author, recognition of the publisher, and so on, are important, too.

Here is one way that a cover can be quite simple, yet still be effective. The cover could have a few large, key words that are easy to read on the thumbnail image, and the background could include a few large rectangles (one above the other) – all with an appealing color scheme. Without even a picture, such a cover can be effective. It is easy to vary this approach – change the large rectangles to some other pattern, or add an image. I'm not saying that you should avoid anything more complex: Rather, I'm saying that if your goal is to keep the cover design as simple as possible, your cover could still be effective. I have a few sample thumbnail images below that exemplify this simple scheme. These thumbnail images aren't for real books – I just made them up to illustrate a few ways that the design scheme of a cover can be simple.

---

[19] A couple of my own covers are a little too busy, such as the astronomy book shown on the front cover. For the most part, I have tried to keep my covers from looking too busy, and I recommend this as a general rule.

 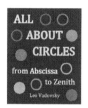 

You don't make both a cover file and a thumbnail image for your paperback book. If you publish your book with KDP, they will create the thumbnail image for your Amazon and other online bookstores' listings from your cover file. So you want to anticipate how the thumbnail page will look, based on your file for the entire cover that includes the front cover, back cover, and spine. After you make the cover for your book, you can preview how the cover will look as a thumbnail image as follows:

1. Add (so remember to remove them afterward) a few large rectangles (click Shapes in the Insert tab) that block out the back cover, spine, and any background that extends beyond the edges of the cover (you will be able to do this easily the same way that you draw the temporary edges of the cover, spine, and bar code in Sec. 3.1.5).
2. Change the zoom (the Zoom button is in the View tab) to a small number, like 10% to 20% (it depends on how large your monitor is, for one).
3. Open Amazon and adjust the zoom until your cover looks about the same size on the screen as the thumbnails that you see there.

This will give you an indication of what your book's cover will look like as a thumbnail image. You will also get to preview the thumbnail image of your book when you proceed to publish your book (as described in Sec. 4.1.9). If you're not satisfied with the preview, it's worth making some adjustments.

3.1.4 Color Shifts and Other Printing Issues

Beware that the colors that you see when you view your cover on the screen in Microsoft Word (or your PDF file) may not look exactly the same as when you receive a copy of your paperback book. This is not the publisher's fault; instead, it has to do with the difference between how colors are made on a computer monitor versus how they are printed on paper.

Here is the technical reason for the variation. Many computer monitors use a RGB (red, blue, green) color scheme. This is a color addition scheme where the combination of two or more colors can be used to make any other color. The monitor shines light from two or more colors at the same point on the screen to create the desired color there. Printers generally use a CMYK (cyan, magenta, yellow, black) color subtraction scheme. In this case, you view reflected light from the page. Here, the colors mix according to the rules for pigmentation, which is different than for mixing light.

The CMYK process used by printers is, from a conceptual standpoint, more limited than the RGB process. As a result, it is difficult to achieve the exact same color with a printer as that color appears on a screen. There may also be a difference in brightness, contrast, and other qualities between the image that you see on the screen and the actual cover.

The printing process used by KDP Print is excellent, but – as with printing in general – does not perfectly reproduce the colors that you see on the screen. You may notice slight variations in color. For example, a blue may appear a little darker on the printed page and a little brighter and lighter on the screen. You can print your cover if you have a color printer (scaled down to a smaller size, unless your printer accepts large sheet sizes – like 11" x 17"): Although it won't be the same printer that is used by the publisher, it might be better than only looking at the screen.

On a related note, you can draw with hundreds of colors on your computer monitor, but the publisher's printer won't print in this many different hues and shades. So if your cover has three different shades of green, for example, you might only see two different shades of green on your actual cover. If you use a few different shades or hues of the same color, try to ensure that no two of the colors look too similar.

	Color	Red	Green	Blue
	Aqua	0	255	255
	Black	0	0	0
	Blue	0	0	255
	Fuchsia	255	0	255
	Gray	128	128	128
	Green	0	128	0
	Lime	0	255	0
	Maroon	128	0	0
	Navy	0	0	128
	Olive	128	128	0
	Purple	128	0	128
	Red	255	0	0
	Silver	192	192	192
	Teal	0	128	128
	White	255	255	255
	Yellow	255	255	0

There is one thing you can do if want to try to control the colors to some degree: When you choose a color, select More Colors, choose the Custom tab, and enter precise values for Red, Green, and Blue. The table on the previous page lists the RGB values for the 16 standard basic web colors. If you want to look up the RGB values for additional colors (such as orange or brown), try searching for "red green blue values colors," for example, with your favorite internet search engine. The previous table appears in color if you are reading the eBook version of this book with an eReader that supports color. Unfortunately, most of these 'standard' web colors are not the same color as Microsoft Word 2010's default colors. For example, when you select 'green' in the list of what they call Standard Colors, it turns out to be different than the 'green' that you get when you manually type in the standard RGB values for 'green' from the previous table.

Another issue that you might have with your images is termed 'flattening.' The publisher flattens images when they convert the PDF file that you submit to the final PDF file that will be used to print your book. Usually, if anything, the color may shift a little bit due to flattening. You can flatten the image yourself if you purchase Word-to-PDF conversion software that has an option to flatten the images. However, this is probably an unnecessary expense. Alternatively, you can convert the images to JPEG files following the instructions of Sec. 2.2.5 – although the quality of the image in the paperback book or its cover may be better by not converting the image to a JPEG file. At least, see if you are content with your images after first trying the free PDF conversion that is available with Microsoft Word 2010. If not, keep in mind that it might not be flattening that is the problem: As we just mentioned, color-shifting may also be attributed to inherent differences between printing and producing an image on a screen.

Not every effect that you can create on the screen will show up in your physical paperback book, and in some cases the effect may look somewhat different. This may be an issue if you use some of the fancier options – like setting transparency, or choosing a default texture or pattern. The pattern may be scaled differently in the printed image than it appears on the screen, for example. The printing process is excellent overall – I'm very pleased with the results, and continue to use KDP Print for my paperback self-publishing needs – but I have observed occasional discrepancies. If you are a perfectionist and notice subtle details, you must realize that the printing process is not a perfect reproduction of what you see on the screen.

There are also sometimes slight variations in positioning, alignment, and the cut of the book cover. You have to allow for slight printing tolerances. I've ordered hundreds of books, and very rarely had more than just a slight issue. I have had a couple of noticeable problems, which were promptly resolved, and these haven't occurred for a couple of years. If you see a significant printing problem – like something being off by ¼", you should contact KDP to report it along with the number printed on the very last page of your book (which will help them track the problem to its source). After logging into your account, click Help at the top, then click Contact Us at the left (you may need to scroll down first). Be courteous in your communication and keep an open mind – a mistake could turn out to be your own.

3.1.5 First Draw Temporary Edges of the Cover, Spine, and Bar Code

The first step in creating a cover is choosing a sufficient page size and then marking on the page where the boundaries of the cover, spine, and ISBN bar code will be. This is pretty straightforward to do as you will be able to follow step-by-step instructions.

When you open a new Word document to serve as your cover file, you will need to adjust the page size in order to accommodate the front cover, back cover, spine, and room for images to bleed at the edges. There is a simple formula that you can use to calculate precisely what the minimum page size will be. I will provide the formula with KDP Print in mind; if you use a different publisher, the calculation may be a little different.

The first step is to compute how wide the spine will be. Since the thickness of your book depends upon how many pages there are in the book, you will need to know the page count for your book. When you open the file for your book's interior, Microsoft Word shows the page count in the bottom left corner. If the page count is an odd number, add 1 to the page count since you must have an even number of pages (this is because each piece of paper has 2 pages – one page on each side). As examples, if your book has 133 pages, count this as 134 pages instead; but if your book has 152 pages, just leave it as 152. (If you have an odd number of pages, you might consider adding 1 more page to it – otherwise, the last page will just be blank. Actually, there will be another two or four pages after that: The very last page will have a bar code and date of manufacture on it. However, any pages that KDP Print adds at the back do not affect your royalty calculation.)

You also need to decide whether you will print your book on white or cream paper because the thickness is slightly different. (However, if your interior will be in color, then white paper is your only option.) In order to determine the spine width, multiply your page count by 0.002252" (0.002347" for color) for white paper and by 0.0025" for cream paper:

For white paper: spine width = number of pages x 0.002252 inches (0.002347" for color).
For cream paper: spine width = number of pages x 0.0025 inches.

For example, a 150-page black-and-white book on white paper has a spine width of 0.3378" (that's 150 x 0.002252), while a 150-page book on cream paper has a spine width of 0.375" (that's 150 x 0.0025).

Next, what is the trim size of your book? You had to select this before you set the page size for the interior of your book. Note that the trim size is not the same size as the page size if you allowed room for images to bleed. The actual dimensions of your book will match the trim size (within reasonable tolerance). You might want to recall the available trim sizes listed in Sec. 2.1.4.

The first dimension of the trim size is the book's width, while the second dimension is the book's height. For example, an 8" x 10" book has a width of 8 inches (across from left to right, when the book is closed) and a height of 10 inches (top to bottom).

Now we can calculate the trim size of your cover. The width of your cover will be two times the width of your book's trim size plus the spine width. The height of your cover will equal the height of your book's trim size.

> Width of cover trim size = (width of trim size x 2) + spine width.
> Height of cover trim size = height of trim size.

For example, suppose that we have an 8" x 10" book with a spine width of 0.42". The cover trim size will have a width of 16.42" (that's 8" x 2 + 0.42") and a cover height of 10".

If you want to have images (such as a color background) extend all of the way to the edge of the cover (as opposed to live elements – like text – which must be 0.125" from the cover edges), you must submit a cover file image that measures 0.25" wider and 0.25" taller than your cover trim size in order to allow for images near the edge of the cover to bleed. (The extra 0.25" allows for 0.125" bleed on each side – left and right or top and bottom.)

So if the cover trim size is 16.42" x 10" (as it was in the previous example), then the image in your cover file must be at least 16.67" x 10.25" (where 0.25" was added to both the width and height).

KDP permits you to submit a larger cover image than needed, provided that you center everything on the page (there is a simple way to do this with Word, which we will learn shortly). However, I do **not** recommend this because it often results in unexpected changes to your cover file during file review. Change the page size by clicking the Size button on the Page Setup group of the Page Layout tab, then More Paper Sizes at the bottom of the list. Enter the values of the width and height, including bleed. In my previous example, the width would be 16.67" and the height would be 10.25". Be sure that everything is centered properly on the front cover, spine, and back cover of the PDF cover file that you submit. You're much less likely to have resizing or repositioning issues if you size the cover perfectly.

Let me describe conceptually what we are going to do, and then I will provide step-by-step instructions, followed by a couple of illustrations. We're going to set the page size and then add 5 rectangles. The 5 rectangles will serve as guides to show you the boundaries of the front cover, back cover, spine width, and ISBN bar code (yep, that's only 4 – the 5th will serve to help place the ISBN bar code rectangle correctly). When your cover is completely finished, you will delete these 5 rectangles. They are temporary, but very useful as they serve to help you place your cover text and pictures exactly where you want them.

Following are the instructions for adding the 5 guide rectangles:

1. First, set the page size to a size that is equal to your cover trim size plus bleed, or to a size that is larger than this. In my example with an 8" x 10" book with a spine width of 0.42", we determined that the cover trim size plus bleed was 16.67" x 10.25". In that example, the page size needs to be 16.67" x 10.25". (Don't make your cover any larger than necessary, or it improves the chances of your cover being adjusted during the file review process.) Go through the calculation of the spine width and the cover trim size plus bleed for your book, following my examples.

2. Go to the Page Layout tab, click Size, choose More Page Sizes at the bottom of the list, and enter the width and height for your cover file.

3. Also in the Page Layout tab, click Margins and set all of the margins to 0". You will receive an error message in a popup window: Click Ignore.

4. In the View tab, click One Page so that you can see your entire cover on the screen.

5. Go to the Insert tab. Choose Shapes. Select the rectangle that has square corners (not the one with rounded corners). Since there are two rectangles that look similar, be sure to choose the right one.

6. Your cursor will now look like a plus (+) sign (like the crosshairs of a scope). Place the cursor somewhere on the page and press the left button on your mouse. A rectangle will appear on the screen.

7. With the rectangle selected (it was already selected unless you have since clicked somewhere else – if so, click on the rectangle to reselect it), go to the Format tab. (This Format tab only appears when a drawing object is selected.) Click on Shape Fill (but not the left part of the button). Choose No Fill (beneath the Standard Colors) so that you can see through the rectangle.

8. With the rectangle still selected, return to the Format tab. Click on Shape Outline (but not the left part of the button). First choose Black (near the top). Then go back into Shape Outline, click Weight, and choose 1 pt or less (in order to decrease the thickness of the outline).

9. With the rectangle still selected, again return to the Format tab, and on the far right change the width and height to match the trim size of your book. For example, for an 8" x 10" trim size, set Width to 8" and Height to 10".

10. With the rectangle still selected, click Copy in the Home tab (or hold down the Ctrl button while pressing C on your keyboard). Then click Paste (or Ctrl + V) twice. Now you will see 3 rectangles. One rectangle is for your front cover, one is for the back cover, and the third is for the spine width. Grab one rectangle (but the edge – you can't grab the middle when the color has been set to No Fill) and change its width to match the spine width of your book. Recall the results of your spine width calculation. This third rectangle should be very narrow (probably less than one inch unless you have a very long book).

11. Grab one of the large rectangles and move it to the far left of the screen. To do this, click the edge of the rectangle with the left button of your mouse and hold the left button down as you drag it across the screen. Release the button when you finish.

12. Grab the narrow spine width rectangle and place its left edge against the right edge of the far left large rectangle. After you get it close, with the spine rectangle selected click the left (←) or right (→) arrow keys to line the edges up as well as you can.

13. Now grab the second large rectangle and place its left edge against the right edge of the spine width rectangle. Line up the edges as well as you can.

14. Select all three rectangles. There are a couple of ways to do this. One way is to click on one rectangle, press the Ctrl button on your keyboard, and while you are holding down the Ctrl button, click the other two rectangles. This way is frustrating if you mis-click anything before you finish. The other way is to click one rectangle, go to the Format tab, and click Selection Pane. A selection pane will appear at the right of the screen. Click on the word Rectangle 1 (or any other number) in the selection pane, hold down the Ctrl button on your keyboard, and then click on the names of the other two rectangles.

15. With all 3 rectangles still selected, in the Format tab, click the Align button and choose Align Top (this will line all 3 rectangles by their tops).

16. With all 3 rectangles still selected, in the Format tab, click Group and then select Group from the list.

17. Click elsewhere on the screen to deselect the rectangles, then select the group of rectangles (be sure to click the group only once). Go to the Format tab, select Position, choose More Layout Options (at the bottom of the list), choose the Position tab in the window that pops up, and in both Horizontal and Vertical, click Alignment and choose Centered. This will center the group of 3 rectangles on the screen.

18. Insert a fourth rectangle following Steps 5-8 again. Set the size of the rectangle to 2" x 1.2" following the instructions in Step 9.

19. Insert a fifth rectangle (you can use copy/paste instead of making a new one – this way you don't have to set the fill and outline again) and change its size to 0.25" x 0.25".

20. Position the small square (0.25" x 0.25") in the bottom right corner of the large (like 8" x 10") rectangle on the left. Then position the ISBN bar code rectangle (2" x 1.2") so that its bottom right corner touches the upper left corner of the small square.

21. Group all 5 rectangles together like we did in Steps 14-16.

If you followed all of the steps correctly, your cover guide will look like the illustration on the next page. I suggest saving just the guide by itself (before completing your cover) in case you publish more books in the future. The second illustration that follows shows the cover spread for this book (shrunk down to fit on the page of this book) with the guide rectangles on it. This will help you see the purpose of the guide rectangles that you made.

Top left corner of page

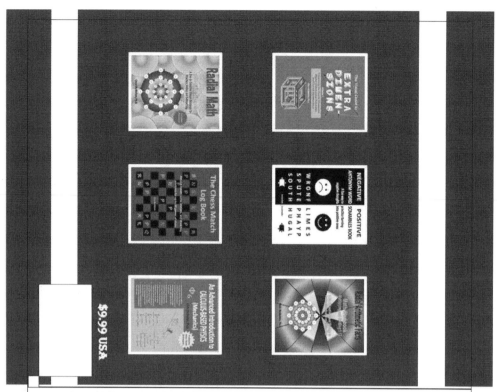

The gray border in the first illustration just serves to show where the page boundary is. View each of the previous two pages with the book turned sideways with the spine at the top – i.e. the 'bottom' of each page is at the outer page edge, while the 'top' of each page is at the spine. Doing so, you can see that the 'left' rectangle represents the back cover and the 'right' rectangle represents the front cover.

In Sec. 3.1.6, we will learn how draw and format textboxes and WordArt, and, then in Sec. 3.1.7, we will apply this to add text for the title, author, spine, description, price, etc. In Sec.'s 3.1.8 and onward, we will learn how to draw, format, and insert pictures. You will want to make one large picture for your background (which you will learn how to do in Sec. 3.1.10) – which could simply be a very large solid rectangle.

Remember to allow room for images to bleed 0.125" (or slightly more, but not less) beyond the cover guide that we made. For a simple background, add a rectangle the size of the page of your cover trim size + bleed (width = trim width x 2 + spine width + 0.25", height = trim height + 0.25"), center it on the page, change Wrap Text to Behind Text, and set Shape Fill to a color of your choice. Remember to keep all text within 0.25" of your cover guide boundaries. Don't put anything where the ISBN bar code will go (otherwise the bar code will cover it up). Any images that extend near the edge should either stop 0.25" before reaching the edge of the cover guide or should extend 0.125" beyond the edge to allow for bleed.

3.1.6 Formatting WordArt and Textboxes

WordArt and textboxes allow you to create text that can grouped together with images to form pictures, to create floating text that can be placed anywhere in the document, or to create text that can be rotated. The text in text boxes and WordArt can be formatted just like ordinary body text using the features in the Font group in the Home tab, and also fancier text effects that can be found in the Format tab. In older versions of Microsoft Word, there were significant differences between textboxes and WordArt,[20] but now you can achieve the same effects with either textboxes or WordArt. The main distinction now is that WordArt starts out looking a little fancier than a textbox when you first type your text. I prefer WordArt for short phrases or single words, and textboxes for sentences or paragraphs.

WordArt

This is a textbox. You can remove the 'box' from the textbox if you want to. You can also format it to look like WordArt, if you want.

---

[20] There used to be fancier text effects for WordArt, but only more basic formatting options for textboxes. In Microsoft Word 2010, you can find the same features for textboxes and WordArt in the Format tab.

Is this a textbox or WordArt? Actually, it could be made either way.

To create WordArt, go to the Insert tab, click WordArt, and choose any of the A's as a starting point. A rectangle will appear on the screen with a message that says, "Your text here." Place your cursor in the message, delete the message, and type your text into the WordArt.

Grab the WordArt by placing the cursor over the dashed rectangle that surrounds the WordArt and clicking the left button of your mouse once; this causes the rectangle to become solid instead of dashed. Go to the Format tab (which only appears when the WordArt is selected) in order to change the style of the WordArt. Since the same formatting options are available for both WordArt and textboxes, let's discuss how to insert textboxes before we describe the various formatting options.

To insert a textbox, go to the Insert tab and click Text Box. I prefer to pick the basic textbox in the top left corner, and then format it to my liking. Set your cursor on the screen and click the left mouse button to insert the textbox. Place your cursor inside the textbox in order to type text into it. Grab the textbox the same way that you grab WordArt. However, unlike WordArt, the rectangle always looks solid.

A variety of things that you can do with a textbox or WordArt includes:

➤ Select the textbox or WordArt by clicking the edge of the rectangle.

➤ Edit the text by placing your cursor within the text.

➤ Note the distinction between selecting the box versus editing the text. Select the box by grabbing the edge of the rectangle, and edit the text by putting the cursor where the text is. In both cases, you click on the textbox or WordArt, but in different ways. WordArt will have a dashed rectangle when you are editing the text and solid rectangle when you select it, but a textbox will look solid either way. For either one, you will see 8 tiny white circles (at the corners and midpoints of the sides) when it selected, and your cursor will be flashing when you are editing text. Sometimes, when you try to select the box, the first time that you click the box it is ready to type instead; in that case, click the rectangle a second time to properly select it.

➤ Move a textbox or WordArt by selecting it and dragging the mouse (move the mouse while holding down the left button). Once it is very close to where you want to place it, use the arrow keys (→, ←, ↑, and ↓) on the keyboard to move it a small distance in order to position it precisely where you want it.

➤ Resize the textbox or WordArt by first selecting it. When it is selected, you should see 8 tiny white circles – one at each corner and the midpoint of each side. When you place your cursor over one of these circles, you will notice (without clicking) that it turns into a double arrow (↔). Place your cursor over one of the circles and drag the mouse (hold down the left button while moving the cursor) to change the size of the box.

➢ You can rotate a textbox or WordArt. One way to rotate the entire box is to go to the Format tab and click Rotate. You can quickly rotate the box 90° clockwise (Rotate Right) or counterclockwise (Rotate Left). For other angles, click More Rotation Options and enter the angle directly into the Rotation field in the Size tab. If you Flip the entire box, the text will still read forward, not backward. Another way to rotate the entire box is to select the box and place your cursor over the green circle above it. Then drag the cursor to rotate the box (click the left button of your mouse and hold it down while moving the mouse).

➢ You can also rotate the text within the box as opposed to rotating the entire box. To do this, go to the Format tab and select Text Direction.

➢ Change the style and size of the font in the Home tab the same way that you format ordinary text. This, along with other standard text formatting options available in the Home tab, such as boldface and highlighting, were described in Sec. 2.1.11. You can also include standard paragraph formatting from the Home

Some standard formatting options:
❖ Bullets.
❖ **Boldface**, *italics*, underline.
❖ Highlighting, ~~strikethrough~~.
❖ Superscript, subscript.

tab in textboxes and WordArt, such as bullets and linespacing (as described in Sec. 2.1.10). For the fancier formatting options available in the Format tab, see the remaining bullets on this list.

➢ Insert an equation into a textbox or WordArt by clicking Equation from the Insert tab (see Sec. 2.1.13).

$$y = \sum_{i=1}^{N} x_i^2$$

➢ Note that, in the Format tab, there are a Shape Fill and Shape Outline in addition to a Text Fill and Text Outline. This is because you can fill the box itself with color and also outline the box, and you can also fill and outline each letter of the text. Compare the WordArt examples below to see the distinction between filling and outlining the shape versus the text.

➢ Both Shape Fill and Text Fill allow for gradients and patterns in addition to solid colors. You can find more options within Gradients by selecting More Gradients, such as choosing a preset gradient pattern or changing the direction of the gradient.

GRADIENT

➢ Shape Outline and Text Outline each allow for a variety of solid and dashed outlines (choose Dashes) – including double or trip lines (choose More Lines and then select Compound Type) – as well as the option to vary thickness (select Weight).

➢ Change the shape of the box by clicking Edit Shape in the Format tab. Alternatively, you can insert a shape from the Insert tab, click to insert the shape, right-click the shape, and select Add Text. Note the Callouts available in the selection of shapes, which are designed to have text pointing to a picture (of a person, for example). When you select a callout (by clicking at its edge), look for the tiny yellow diamond (near the point), and drag it (by left-clicking it and moving the cursor while holding the button down) to move the pointer of the callout.

➢ You can find fancy text options in Text Effects in the Format tab, including Shadow, Reflection, Glow, Bevel, 3-D Rotation, and Transform. For example, in Transform you can make the text follow a path or you can warp the text. Find more options at the bottom of each list (such as 3-D Options or Shadow Options).

WARPED   *This infinite sentence reads as follows:*

➢ You can also apply Shadow, Reflection, Glow, Soft Edges, Bevel, and 3-D Rotation to the shape of the box – as opposed to the text – by choosing Shape Effects in the Format tab. Note the distinction between Shape Effects and Text Effects.

➢ Note that there are several preset styles to choose from in the Shape Styles group of the Format tab.

This was a default Style.

➢ You can also change the way that a textbox is wrapped in your document by selecting Wrap Text in the Format tab. In your book cover, choose In Front of Text so that you can position the textbox wherever you want. In the interior file for your book, choose In Line With Text or Square instead of In Front of Text, as this reduces the complexity of your file. When you choose In Line With Text, you can also center it or align it with either margin using the icons in the Paragraph group of the Home tab. When adding a textbox to a drawing that you make in Word, select In Front of Text (for every item in the group – drawing or textbox), group the textbox(es) and other drawing elements together (choose Group in the Format tab), and then change Wrap Text to In Line With Text (you must select the entire group, without also selecting a specific item in the group, in order to do this). For a wrapped textbox or WordArt, modify the distance between the box and body text choosing Wrap Text in the Format tab, then More Layout Options, and finally the Text Wrapping tab.

➢ If you are using a textbox or WordArt as a label in a diagram, remove the outline of the textbox and the fill by selecting No Fill in Shape Fill and No Outline in Shape Outline.

> ➤ Change text alignment by selecting Align Text in the Format tab. Click the little arrow in the bottom right corner of the WordArt styles group in the Format tab and select TextBox in order to adjust the internal margins.

Once you have made one textbox or WordArt, if you wish to make another one similar to the first it may be more convenient to copy/paste the original (using Ctrl + C and then Ctrl + V) instead of making a new textbox. However, if you do this, be sure not to accidentally paste a textbox into a textbox (this happens if you have a textbox selected when you paste).

3.1.7 Title, Author, Spine Text, Cover Price, and Other Text

In this section, we will discuss how to use textboxes and WordArt to make all of the text for your book's cover. Then, in subsequent sections, we will describe how to draw images and how to add drawings, photos, clipart, and other images to your cover. I suggest not adding a background for your cover until later, as this will make it easier to select objects on your cover without accidentally grabbing the background. We will also discuss how to make a background in the following sections.

It will probably be useful to switch back and forth between zoom options as you make your cover. When you want to see the entire cover on your screen, select One Page in the View tab. When you prefer a close-up so that you can read small text easily and place images or text precisely, try Page Width, 100%, or click Zoom to choose another value, such as 200%, in the View tab.

You should presently have a file started with a large page size and 5 rectangles positioned to serve as the guides for the front cover, back cover, spine width, and ISBN bar code, as described in Sec. 3.1.5. It should presently look like the image below:

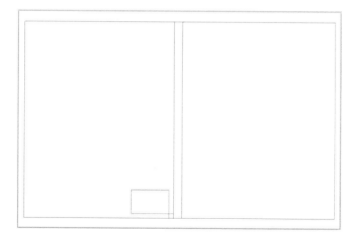

Start out by typing the full title of your book in one or more textboxes. Your front cover must contain the full title exactly as you enter it when you publish it if you choose to publish with KDP Print (but the subtitle – if you have one – is not required to appear on your cover; that's optional). Your title can be split over multiple lines, and words on one line do not need to read perfectly straight across, so long as the order of the words is clear and each word can be clearly made out. If you want any words to appear larger or in a different font, for example, create different textboxes or WordArt for them. You can even use a picture for a letter, such as a basketball for an 'O' in the title of a sports book. You can even make the individual letters of a word separately – for example, you can make every letter of a word outlined with a circle and then stagger the letters (the sample below was made by grouping each letter together with a circle and then using the Bring Forward option in the Format tab; use Wrap Text to position the WordArt in front of the shape). There is ample opportunity to be creative, should you wish to exercise it, in the design of your cover. You may wish to read Sec. 4.1.3 before finalizing your title.

If your title extends onto two or more lines, consider entering each line in a different textbox or WordArt instead of using the Enter key to go onto the next line. This will allow you to place the text closer together, vertically, for example. If you do use two or more textboxes or WordArt for your title and you want the font to be the same throughout, double-check that the font has the same size in each box (it's also a good idea to visually check that the letters of each textbox or WordArt appear exactly the same if you're trying to match them – in addition to checking the font size number).

If you would like a textbox or WordArt to be centered on the front or back cover, one way to do it is to make the textbox or WordArt the same width as the front cover and center the text within it. Be sure to check that the text does not extend all of the way to the edge of the cover, though: The text must be at least 0.25" from the cover edge. Remember, the cover guide that you made includes a rectangle to show you the front and back cover edges. Copy and paste the 0.25" x 0.25" square, then move this square (drag it with the cursor) to any cover edge if you want to check that there is at least 0.25" between the text and cover edge. Alternatively, you can make a narrower textbox or WordArt, center the text within it, and align the box with the cover rectangle – by selecting both the textbox/WordArt and the front or back cover rectangle (it must be ungrouped from your cover guide before doing this – click

Ungroup in Group in the Format tab), clicking Align in the Format tab, and then Align Center. (Select multiple objects by clicking one, holding Ctrl, then clicking the second – or select one on the Selection Pane available from the Format tab, hold Ctrl, then click the second.)

You may want a few words of your title to be readily visible in your thumbnail image. If so, you need a very large font size for these words. If you would like the font to be larger than 72 pt – the maximum default font size that you get when you click the arrow next to the font size in the Font group of the Home tab – click on the font number (which will highlight the number in blue) and type the number that you would like to try (such as 96 or 144). You may wish to refer to the end of Sec. 3.1.3, where we discussed how to preview what the thumbnail image will look like as you design your cover in Microsoft Word.

Remember that you want your cover to look good both as a thumbnail image and as a softcover book. While a large font size helps to make text more readable on the thumbnail image, it might not look as good to have a very large font when holding the book itself. With this in mind, you might just want a few key words to be very large, and many of the words to be much smaller. Consider both how the actual cover and thumbnail image will look as you design your cover.

We discussed a variety of text effects in Sec. 3.1.6, which you can apply to your textboxes and WordArt. Bear in mind that you want the text – especially, key words – to be easily read. Some font styles and text options are easier to read than others. You also want to apply an appealing color scheme. See what the text looks like with and without **boldface** – some fonts look better on the cover one way or the other. Similarly, explore the difference between having a Text Outline color as well as setting the Outline color to No Color; also, try making the Text Outline the same color as Text Fill, compared to making the two colors contrast. Trying out various options is the best way to help you make decisions.

You must also include the full name(s) of all of the authors on the front cover, and spell each name the same way that you enter it when you publish your book. Other names of contributors, like an illustrator or editor, may not need to be on your cover, but should be mentioned somewhere – like the title page and copyright page. See Sec. 4.1.9 regarding contributors that you might acknowledge, and also about author names and pen names.

You may wish to use a smaller font for the author's name than for the title, unless you have name recognition – as is the case with celebrities and already popular authors, but is also the case for authors who write a nonfiction book in a field of their recognized expertise, for example. On the other hand, if you're really proud to have your name on the book and want it to stand out, go ahead and make it large – remember that it is your book, so you should be happy with the design of your cover. If an author has special qualifications that relate to a nonfiction book – such as professional experience or a relevant degree – you may want to include this information with the author's name.

If you want to center the author's name on the cover page, or align it with other text, for example, select the items (click on one, hold Ctrl, and click the others – you can also select the items in the Selection Pane from the Format tab), go to the Format tab, and choose the Align button.

You can include the subtitle of your book on the front cover, if you have one, but you may also choose not to do so. A subtitle may provide additional information that may be useful to a potential buyer who is looking at your book in person. This may not be important unless you have plans where many potential customers will be checking your books out in person compared to the number of sales that may come from browsing for your book online. You may find it difficult to fit a subtitle on the cover in addition to the title, author(s), and whatever artwork or pictures you may have in mind, yet still have the cover look nice as a thumbnail. If so, it may be best to leave the subtitle out.

Think about the positioning of any images that you plan to use when you place your title and author text on the front cover. You could have the title at the top, name at the bottom, and a large image in between, for example – but if you view dozens of book covers, you will see that there are many other ways that you can choose to place the title, author(s), and images. If your cover will feature one main image, you probably want to design the title and author text around it. If you plan to use multiple images of about the same size, think about how you want to place them – e.g. you might scatter the images around, or you could group them together or place them symmetrically. In these cases, you should also plan the position of the images first, then place the title and author text around them. If, on the other hand, your cover design will feature a pattern that is uniform throughout, your cover text will not be dictated by the position of your images.

You might want to highlight a brief, important note on your front cover in a way that stands out. For example, if you write a workbook, you might want to emphasize that it includes the answers; or if you are writing a book in a mystery series, you might want to highlight the series name. One way to do this is with a starburst or a callout. In order to do this, follow these instructions:

1. Go to the Insert tab and select a shape of your liking, such as one of the stars.
2. Click on the arrow in the bottom right corner of the Size group on the far right of the Format tab and check Lock Aspect Ratio in the Size tab.
3. Adjust the size of the shape by selecting it, placing your cursor over one of the small white circles at the corner (but <u>not</u> a side) of the rectangle, and dragging your cursor.
4. Select a Shape Fill, Shape Outline, and other formatting of your liking.
5. Insert a textbox or WordArt and add text. Adjust the font style, size, and formatting.
6. Select the shape and the textbox (or WordArt) by clicking on one, holding down Ctrl, and clicking on the other.
7. Choose Align in the Format tab, then Align Center and Align Middle. If you're not happy with the centering, you can always use the arrow keys on the keyboard to adjust it.

8. While the shape and textbox (or WordArt) are both selected, group the objects together (available in the Format tab).
9. Position the combined shape where you would like it by selecting the shape and dragging your mouse.

It is also possible to add text directly to a shape (by selecting the shape, right-clicking it, and choosing Add Text), instead of making them separately and grouping them together. However, by making them individually, it is generally easier to center the text precisely and you can also position text with much narrower margins between the text and the shape.

Does your book have enough pages to include spine text? A book of 100 pages or less is not thick enough to include spine text (if you include it with a cover file that you submit to KDP Print, and if your book doesn't have more than 100 pages this will be flagged during file review). If your book has fewer than 130 pages, the spine text will have to be very narrow in order to allow for printing tolerances so that the spine text does not wrap around to the front or back cover. Thus, it may be better to omit spine text if your book is under 130 pages. If your book has 130 pages or more, you should take full advantage of the opportunity to add spine text to your cover. In fact, if your book is presently a little short of 130 pages, this is a good incentive to add a few more pages.

In order to add spine text to your book, first insert a textbox. Type the text for your title and author(s) into this textbox on a single line. Actually, it would be better to copy and paste (using Ctrl + C and Ctrl + V) the text for your title and author from the copyright page of your interior file into the textbox for the spine text in your cover file (since it's easier to check for spelling mistakes and other typos on the copyright page than it is in the spine text). You can enter the text in separate textboxes, but you know that they will be perfectly aligned if they are in the same textbox. Add several spaces between the title and author(s) to create some separation between them.

Select the textbox, go to the Format tab, choose Rotate, and click Rotate Right 90°. Be sure to choose right, not left, in order to achieve the proper orientation: This is an industry standard so that all books have their writing in the same direction on the spine. Your library would look funny if a few books had the spine text rotated the other way. Find some of your own books and study the orientation of the spine text and check that yours is rotated correctly. When you receive a proof of your book, remember to compare the orientation of your spine text to that of traditionally published books.

Be sure to center the spine text within the textbox. After you choose a font style and other formatting of your liking, adjust the font size and the number of spaces between the title and author(s) until your spine text has suitable length, thickness, and positioning. You can place the spine text exactly on the center of your cover file by clicking Position in the Format tab, going to More Layout Options, and changing Alignment to Centered in both Horizontal and Vertical. If you happen to change the height of thickness of your spine text (which could simply result from changing the font style, for example), you will want to re-center the spine textbox on the page.

Ensure that you leave at least 0.0625" on either side of your spine text between the two cover folds. If your book is short (around 130 pages), this may require using a smaller font size than you would prefer. If you submit your cover file to KDP Print, they will let you know if you did not leave enough room on either side of your spine text, and you will be asked to shrink the spine text down in order to allow for reasonable printing tolerances. (Once you pass the file review, you will be able to order a printed proof – which I highly recommend – in order to inspect the cover and interior carefully.)

Remember to account for the ISBN bar code placement when designing your back cover. You don't want an important image or text to get covered up by it. Recall that the cover guide that you made in Sec. 3.1.5 accounts for the precise placement of the ISBN bar code.

Most books have some text on the back cover, although occasionally a book will only have a picture and the ISBN bar code. A back cover description can provide a sample of your writing, and also provides the opportunity to do one or more of the following:

☺ Describe your book and draw interest in your work.

☺ Explain how your book is distinguished from similar titles.

☺ Include a biography of the author(s).

☺ Highlight your experience and qualifications.

☺ Help to market your book. For example, if any magazines have reviewed your book, you can include quotes from them.

If you write a book with a black-and-white interior, the cover is the only place that you can include color pictures. If you are writing a chemistry book, you can include a periodic table on the back cover, and if you are writing a fantasy book, you can include a map on the back cover. Should you have valuable content that you would like to appear in color, but you have a black-and-white interior, consider adding it to your back cover. The back cover of this book (if you are reading the paperback edition) includes both descriptive text and thumbnails of some of my book covers. I included these color pictures of front covers as a sample of book covers to supplement the large black-and-white covers from Sec. 3.1.5.

Your book will look more professional if you add a cover price. There is no standard location for the cover price. However, you should find some position where it looks natural, and there shouldn't be any alignment concerns that may stand out in the reader's mind (like feeling that it isn't quite centered within its area). If you will be making your book available on Amazon UK and Amazon Europe (meaning continental Europe) through KDP Print (this option is free, so why not take advantage of it – unless you happen to have content that isn't supposed to be sold in one or more of those countries), your book might look a little more impressive if you state your price in USA dollars, UK pounds, and EUR euro. For example, your cover price might be $8.99 USA, £5.59 UK, €6.98 EUR. To add these symbols, go to the Insert tab, click Symbol, choose More symbols, go to the Symbols tab, change From to ASCII (decimal), and enter the character code. The character code is 0163 for the pound symbol (£) and 0128 for the euro symbol (€).[21] In Sec.'s 4.1.4-5, you will learn how to set your price in pounds and euro in addition to dollars.[22]

The picture below shows an example of what your cover might look like when your text is complete, prior to adding any images and before removing the guides. The layout of your cover may be somewhat different, but you should presently have a title, author(s), spine text (if your book has at least 100 pages), a cover price, and other text (such as a description). The main point is to see how your text appears before adding other images.

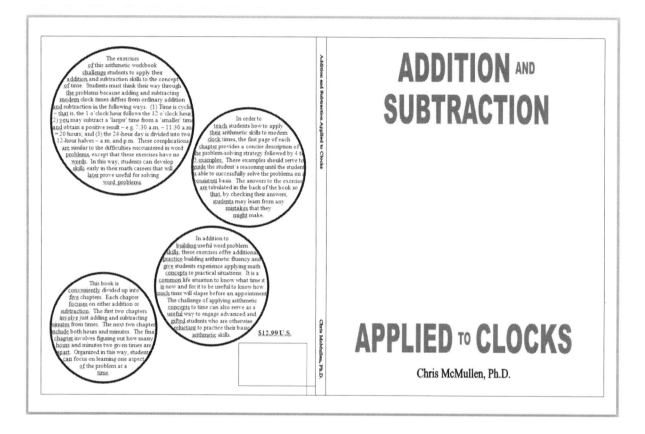

Be sure to remove the guides when your cover is in its final form. However, it would be wise to save a version of your cover (with a different file name, of course) that includes the guides, just in case you need to modify your cover later (e.g. if your page count increases with revisions).

---

[21] If you're having trouble finding a specific symbol that you're looking for, try typing "shortcut key for ___" in your favorite internet search engine. You can very often discover the character code this way.
[22] Did you know that euro should not be capitalized and that the plural does not have an 's'?

3.1.8 How to Make Illustrations Using Microsoft Word's Drawing Tools

If you wish to make your own pictures, I highly recommend using Microsoft Word. It is very easy to use – especially, if you read this section and try making each image as you read the instructions. You can make very professional images simply by drawing in Microsoft Word.

I do not recommend using Paint. I have had many students express a preference for Paint when I teach them how to use Word, but the only reason for their preference was that they were already used to Paint. Many pictures that I have seen drawn in Paint look very unprofessional. For example, diagonal lines often look noticeably jagged in Paint, but straight in Word. There are many more features in Word to help you align images and enter values for width and height, for example, which help you draw with precision. Use Word instead of Paint, and make your book look much more professional. (Better yet would be Adobe PhotoShop.) It is easy, and you can do it. If you really want to learn how to draw pictures in Microsoft Word, sit down at your computer as you read this section, open Microsoft Word, and try to make each image yourself. Again, I'm preparing instructions with Microsoft Word 2010 in mind; Microsoft Word 2007 is similar.

Before we get started, let me remind you of the color issues that we discussed in Sec. 3.1.4. Strangely, the preset colors in Microsoft Word 2010 do not include many of the 16 standard web colors, and a few colors that seem like standard colors are not quite the same as the 16 standard web colors. Even what Microsoft Word calls 'Standard Colors' when you click on Shape Fill or Shape Outline are not all the same as the standard web colors. As a result, if you go with the defaults instead of entering RGB values, you might find (as we discussed in Sec. 3.1.4) that the colors that you see on the cover are slightly different from what you see on the screen. I recommend using the RGB values in the table in Sec. 3.1.4 for the 16 standard web colors. You will also want to look up the RGB values of other useful colors which are not in the table – like orange and brown. You can easily find a more comprehensive table by searching for "RGB values" with your favorite internet search engine.

Here is how to enter the RGB values for a color: When you are choosing Shape Color or Outline Color, go into More Shape Colors or More Outline Colors and enter the RGB values in the Custom tab. Once you have used a color once, you will be able to quickly find it in Recent Colors the next time that you click on Shape Fill or Shape Color (until you close Microsoft Word – then the next time you open the program, you need to do it again).

Avoid drawing a picture from scratch inside your book interior file. Instead, first draw the picture in a new blank document (with your book file closed – and any other programs that take a significant chunk of your computer's memory closed). Save your picture file (so you have a backup copy, just in case). Group the images of your picture together and, for an interior image, also change Text Wrap to In Line With Text. Then you can open your book interior file or cover file, and copy and paste the completed picture.

This will minimize the risk of running into memory problems – like having to restart your computer or having a file become corrupt. Drawing the image in your book file sometimes causes problems, but pasting the completed picture already grouped together and in line with text usually doesn't cause a problem. We will learn how to group objects together and change the text wrap later in this section.

So let's get started. Go to the Insert tab and click on Shapes. This is the place to start anytime you want to draw a picture. Note the New Drawing Canvas at the bottom of the list that appears when you click on Shapes. You don't have to use a drawing canvas, but you might find it convenient to draw your picture on a canvas. You can try drawing the pictures with and without a canvas, and see which you prefer.

Select a shape and adjust its formatting as follows. It would be good practice to see if you can make each of these images.

1. Go to the Insert tab, click Shapes, and choose one of the shapes.
2. When you select one of the shapes, your cursor will change into a plus (+) sign. Place your cursor on the screen and click the left button of your mouse to insert the shape.
3. Select the shape with your mouse. When a shape is selected, a Format tab will appear at the top of the screen. Go into the Format tab.
4. Set the Shape Fill and Shape Outline. Choose More Shape Colors or More Outline Colors to set the RGB values (see Sec. 3.1.4). Note the distinction between White and No Fill: If you place one shape over another, No Fill will let you see through it. If you use No Fill, you will have to grab the edge of the shape in order to select it. Similarly, remove the outline from a shape by choosing No Outline.
5. If you want to blend multiple colors together in the fill, select Gradient (in Shape Fill), then More Gradients, and then Gradient Fill. Note the preset color schemes available for gradients.

6. In Shape Outline, you can change the thickness of the line in Weight and the pattern in Dashes. At the bottom of each list, More Lines offers more options, like a double line.
7. If you change your mind about which shape you want, you don't actually need to delete it and start over. Instead, you can simply select Edit Shape in the Format tab, and then choose a new one.
8. Explore the variety of Shape Styles available in the Format tab. You can certainly create many more effects than just what you see in Shape Styles, but it's nice to be familiar with preset styles, since they are easy to make.

9. When you click on a shape, you will see 8 little white circles – one at each corner and the midpoint of each side. For many shapes, if you look closely you may also find one or two little yellow diamonds. If you grab and drag (hold the left button of your mouse while moving the cursor) the little yellow diamond, it will adjust the shape's shape. For example, the four different pictures below were all made from the 5-point star shape – the only difference is that the little yellow diamond was used to adjust the shape.

10. Resize a shape as follows. Select the shape. Place your cursor over one of the 8 little white circles and your cursor will transform into a double arrow (↔). Drag the cursor to resize the shape. The corners allows you to change the width and height together, while the sides allow you to change just the height or just the width. Another way to resize the shape is to click on the shape, go to the Format tab, and enter the Width and Height directly. This is especially useful if you want to create different types of shapes and make them all the same height or width.

11. Sometimes you want to lock the aspect ratio so that the shape looks the same when you resize it. To do this, select the shape, go to the Format tab, click on the little arrow in the bottom right corner of the Size group (on the far right), choose the Size tab in the popup window, and check the box to Lock Aspect Ratio. For example, if you want to make a circle and change its size without having it turn into an ellipse, you must lock the aspect ratio before you resize it.

12. There are two different ways to rotate a shape. One way is to select the shape, place your cursor over the green circle, and drag the mouse. Alternatively, you can set the rotation angle precisely by going to the Format tab, selecting the little arrow in the bottom right corner of the Size group, choosing the Size tab, and typing an angle in the Rotation field. If you click Rotate in the Format tab, you can quickly rotate the shape 90° or flip the object horizontally or vertically.

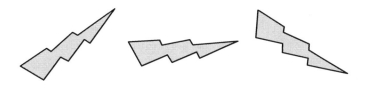

13. In the Format tab, if you click Shape Effects, you can choose from Shadow, Reflection, Glow, Soft Edges, Bevel, and 3-D Rotation. You can find Options at the bottom of each list. For example, in 3-D Rotation Options, click 3-D Format in the popup window and enter a value in order to increase the Depth (otherwise, the shape won't look 3-D). Note that 3-D Rotation Options allows you to rotate a shape in ways that aren't possible with the other two methods of rotating a shape (described in Bullet 12). All six images below are the same basic plain rectangle with different Shape Effects.

14. You can really alter a shape by clicking Edit Shape and then Edit Points from the Format tab. For example, insert a circle and choose Edit Points. You will see 4 small black rectangles appear; these are the 'points' that define the shape. Place your cursor over one of these small black rectangles and drag your cursor. The shape won't look much like a circle when you do this. As you drag your cursor, note the blue line that appears. Try rotating this blue line to learn how it affects the shape. Also, try stretching the blue line. Next, right-click a point and choose Delete Point. Now right-click somewhere on the boundary of the shape and select Add Point. Right-click a point and switch from Smooth, Straight, and Corner. As you can see, you can make all sorts of custom shapes using the Edit Points feature. Each image below was made simply by editing the points of a basic circle.

15. If you want to move a shape, just grab it and drag your mouse – unless you want to move it just a little bit, then use the arrow keys (↑, ↓, ←, and →) on your keyboard to place it at a precise position on the screen.

16. Don't forget the value of the undo and redo buttons at the top of the screen (or use Ctrl + Z and Ctrl + Y).

Next, explore the assortment of lines, arrows, and curves that you can make:

1. In the Insert tab, click Shapes, and first select the basic Line tool. Position your cursor somewhere on the screen and click the left mouse button to insert a line.

2. When you select the line, you will see a tiny white circle at each end. Place the cursor over one of these little white circles and drag it to reposition one end of the line.

3. Grab and drag the little white circle at one end of the line to change the length of the line and its orientation. See if you can make a horizontal line and a vertical line by doing this. If you look closely, you can see a subtle difference between a line that is perfectly horizontal and one that is close but not quite – the one that is not quite horizontal will appear just slightly jagged. When making horizontal and vertical lines, be sure to get the orientation just right.

4. If the line is horizontal or vertical and you want to resize it, just type the new Width or Height at the right of the Format tab. If the line is tilted and you want to resize it without changing the tilt, first lock the aspect ratio (see Bullet 11 in the previous list) and then enter a new Width or Height.

5. Format the line by clicking Shape Outline in the Format tab. Here, you can change the color, width, and pattern. Explore the options in Width and Dash in Shape Outline, and look for More Lines while you are there to find more effects.

6. You can also insert a single (→) or double (↔) arrow by clicking Shapes. The formatting options for arrows are just like lines, except that you can also change the style and size of the arrowhead. In the Format tab, choose Shape Outline, click Arrows, select More Arrows, then pick Line Style in the popup window in order to change the size and style of the arrowhead. You can turn a line into an arrow following these same steps.

7. The Arc tool in Shapes in the Insert tab allows you to draw a circular arc. You can format it just like lines; you can even add an arrowhead to it. If you add a Fill Color to the arc, it will look like a pie slice. If you want to draw one-half of a circle, one way to do it is to use the arc tool, draw a semicircle, and add a Fill Color. Lock the aspect ratio of the arc before you resize it (see Bullet 11 of the previous list) – otherwise, it will stretch into an ellipse, instead of being circular.

8. There is another tool that allows you to draw a curve that doesn't look circular. Find the shape called Curve and select it. (When you click Shapes in the Insert tab, just place the cursor over a shape without clicking and wait a minute – the name of the shape will pop up in a moment.) As usual, the cursor will turn into a plus sign (+) when the Curve tool is selected. What's different is how you insert the curve: Place the cursor somewhere on the screen and click the left mouse button once to begin using the Curve tool, then move the cursor to another point and click again, move the cursor to a third point and click again, and continue doing this until your curve is complete – and then press the Enter key on the keyboard. You can format a curve the same way that you can format a line, and in addition you can Edit Points on a curve (as described in Bullet 14 in the previous list).

9. If your third (or more) click when using the Curve tool is on the initial point, a closed curve will result. Note that all of the shape formatting options apply to a curve (whether it is open or closed), including Shape Fill and Shape Effects.

10. The Freeform tool (also in Shapes in the Format tab) works the same way as the Curve tool, except that it connects straight line segments together instead of fitting a curve through the points. The Freeform tool is useful for drawing irregular polygons, for example. If you are trying to draw something rectangular using the Freeform tool, try turning on the Gridlines (see Bullet 4 of the next list).

11. The Scribble tool allows you to "draw" by holding down the left button of your mouse and dragging it, but you might find it challenging to draw smoothly with this tool. If you happen to have a touchscreen monitor, you can probably draw freehand much better with that than you can with the Scribble tool. If you do have a touchscreen monitor, there will be a special tab for the touchscreen drawing tools.

12. If you just want to draw a tiny point, there are a couple of ways that you could do it. One way is to insert a circle from Shapes (in Insert), lock the aspect ratio (see Bullet 11 in the previous list), and make the circle much smaller (see Bullet 10 in the previous list to recall how to resize a shape). You can also reduce the circle's size by setting Shape Outline to No Color – or making it the same color as the background and increasing the Width of the outline. Another way to draw a tiny point is to type a period (.) into a textbox or WordArt – or enter a dot from the symbols menu (click Symbols from the Insert tab) if a period is too small.

● ● ·

Shapes, lines, arrows, arcs and other curves, and textboxes and WordArt form the building blocks with which you can draw just about anything on Microsoft Word that you could create on paper by hand. Following are some tools that are useful for combining shapes together to form composite images:

1. Select multiple objects by first clicking on one, and then holding down the Ctrl button on the keyboard while selecting the others. If you open the Selection Pane in the Format tab, it will help you select objects that are not easy to grab.

2. Use the Align button in the Format tab to align two or more objects – after selecting them – according to Left, Right, Center, Top, Bottom, or Middle. Note that Center means horizontally, while Middle means vertically. There are also new buttons in Microsoft Word 2010 to align a picture to a page or a margin.

3. Another new feature in Microsoft Word 2010 is the Distribute option available when you click Align in the Format tab. Create even spacing between multiple objects by using Distribute Horizontally or Distribute Vertically.

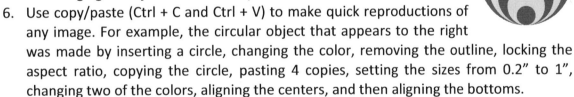

4. You can place objects at precise points on the screen and draw right angles with the Freeform tool (described in Bullet 10 of the previous list), for example, with the aid of the gridlines. In Microsoft Word 2007, you could simply turn the Gridlines on or off in the View tab. In Microsoft Word 2010, they have revived some of the Microsoft Word 2003 flexibility of gridlines and placed these features with the Align button in the Format tab. When you click Align, you can toggle between viewing and not viewing gridlines, and you can also adjust the Grid Settings. Turn the gridlines on when you want place objects on the grid and check the box to Snap Objects To Other Objects when you want objects to meet together – but remove these options when you want the freedom to place an object anywhere. You can also change the grid size.

5. The Bring Forward and Bring Backward buttons in the Format tab help to layer objects – i.e. to control which object is placed before another. If you click the bottom part of these buttons, you find more options – like bringing an object all of the way to the front or back.

6. Use copy/paste (Ctrl + C and Ctrl + V) to make quick reproductions of any image. For example, the circular object that appears to the right was made by inserting a circle, changing the color, removing the outline, locking the aspect ratio, copying the circle, pasting 4 copies, setting the sizes from 0.2" to 1", changing two of the colors, aligning the centers, and then aligning the bottoms.

7. When multiple objects are selected, you can group them together using the Group button in the Format tab. You can also Ungroup them the same way.

8. If you select multiple objects and rotate (see Bullet 12 in the first list of this section) them, they will rotate individually unless you first group them together – in that case, the group will instead rotate as a whole.

9. A group of images may not look as nice if it is resized. Even if you lock the aspect ratio, there may be some noticeable and undesirable changes. One problem is that the thicknesses of the lines do not change automatically if you resize an image. Similarly, text does not change size when you resize a group. Alignment imperfections can also be magnified when a group is enlarged. There is a definite advantage to drawing the picture the right size the first time.

10. Drawing elements have a default Text Wrap that is In Front of Text. When your image is finished, if you insert it into your interior book file, you can change the Text Wrap to In Line With Text or Square in the Format tab. Grouping multiple objects together and wrapping them In Line With Text will help to minimize the risk of complex file issues; keep the number of free-floating (In Front Of Text) pictures to a minimum (only do that when there is no other way to position the picture exactly where you want it). In your cover file, on the other hand, you should use In Front Of text: This file just has one page, and you need the flexibility of placing images anywhere on the screen. If you change Text Wrap to In Line With Text or Square, for example, you won't be able to use some drawing features unless you change it back to In Front Of Text. So if you need to revise a text-wrapped figure, first change Text Wrap to In Front Of Text temporarily.

If you have figures and/or tables that you will be describing in the body of your text, your book will look more professional if you include numbered captions below each figure. For example, many books have a numbered caption of the form, "Fig. 3. The total United States budget is plotted over the course of 100 years." This helps readers quickly find the figure that you are referring to, and the description below the figure helps readers understand what the figure represents. I didn't include figure captions with this book, however, since most of the figures are simple shapes and it didn't seem necessary to include a sentence between the pictures of the book covers to tell you that they are book covers. Well, I did include one caption in the figure below so that you could see an example of a caption.

Add textboxes and WordArt to label your figures. If you do, change both the Shape Outline and Shape Fill to No Color and No Fill, respectively – it doesn't look nice when all of the text labels are surrounded by black rectangles, for example.

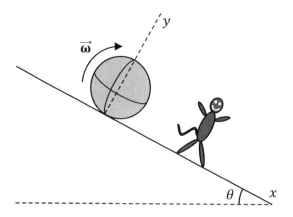

Fig. 1. A ball rolls without slipping down an incline, chasing a frightened monkey.

3.1.9 Sample Drawings and How to Make Them

Here is a brief sample of the variety of pictures that you can draw with Microsoft Word 2010 by applying what you learned in Sec. 3.1.8. It would be good practice to see if you can reproduce some of these pictures.

Let's begin with a few basic three-dimensional geometric objects. There are few different ways that you can draw a cube. The simplest way to make a cube comes with the least flexibility in customizing it: Go to Insert, select Shapes, and choose Cube (by clicking on its picture). If you look closely, you'll notice that the sides are shaded differently. One option that you do have with this preset cube can be found by clicking the tiny yellow diamond (◊) near its top left corner (visible only after you select the cube). If you click the tiny yellow diamond and drag it, it will reshape the cube.

If you want more flexibility with your cube, there are two other ways that you can draw it. One way is to insert a square and two parallelograms from Shapes, and join them together to form a cube. One parallelogram will need to be rotated. You will also have to drag the little yellow diamond to change the shape of each parallelogram, and also adjust the height and width of each. It will take some trial and error to make the three pieces fit together precisely in the shape of a cube.

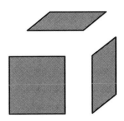

A third way to draw a cube is to first make a hexagon and then add three edges to it. Turn on the Gridlines and use the Freeform tool to make a hexagon (or insert a hexagon and select Edit Points to reshape it). You can draw dotted edges to show the hidden back side of the cube by copying and pasting the solid front edges.

Yet another option is to draw a rectangle and add thickness to it in the 3-D Rotation Options (you must switch to 3-D Format in the popup window). If there is a specific way you want the object to look, you might find it challenging to make a cube this way.

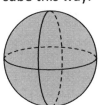 A sphere can be drawn by first inserting a circle and then using the Arc tool (in Shapes) to help illustrate the three-dimensional roundness. Once you make one arc, you can copy and paste it to quickly make the others. Including both solid and dashed arcs can help to distinguish between the front of the sphere and its back.

If you are clever with gradients and shadows, you can also use these tools to draw a sphere. In the sphere at the right, the Gradient is a preset color choice (Fire) with Radial Type and the rightmost Direction selected. The Rotation Angle was set to 330° to make the gradient's direction  match that of the shadow. Play with the Shadow Options to try to get the shadow to match the sense of light created by the gradient's effect.

You can find a basic cylinder in Shapes (called Can), where the end will be lighter than the body. A cylinder can also be made by increasing the Depth (you can also change the Depth Color) in 3-D Format within the 3-D Rotation Options. However, you gain the most flexibility in creating a cylinder from two Ovals with Shape Outline, one Rectangle with Shape Outline set to No Color, and two straight lines, as illustrated below. The rolling hollow cylinder illustrated below was drawn from three Circles, one Rectangle, some Lines, an Arc with an Arrow end, a Brace, and some equations that were inserted into textboxes.

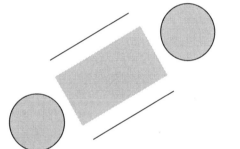
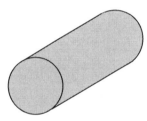
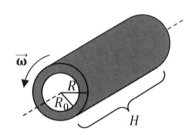

Most objects can be drawn by putting common geometric shapes together, as we will see in the following examples. For example, a flower can be drawn by using Circles for petals, a Curve for the stem, and combining Arcs together to form leaves. Similarly, a football can be drawn using arcs and lines. The bunch of grapes illustrated below was made by stacking numerous copies (use Ctrl + C and Ctrl + V) of an Oval atop one another.

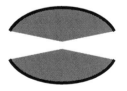

You can draw a present by adding some ribbon and a bow to a cube. In the present that follows, two rectangles were used for the ribbon, while the bow was made out of a Circle and six Ovals. Rectangles can also be used to make a piano or organ keyboard.

A cube can be copied and pasted several times, and these cubes can be stacked together to form a pyramid. To make the pyramid shown to the right, first make one cube. Then copy the cube and paste two copies of it. Place the two copies side by side and Align them by their bottoms. Group the two side-by-side cubes together, then copy and paste the group. Place one group in front of the other. Next, make three cubes in a row, then make two copies of that row. Make the bottom layer the same way. Finally, group each layer together, and then stack the layers.

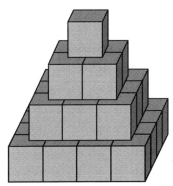

The concave lens in the ray diagram below was actually made from two Moon shapes and two Triangles. Another way to make it would be two add two arcs with white Shape Fill in front of a Rectangle.

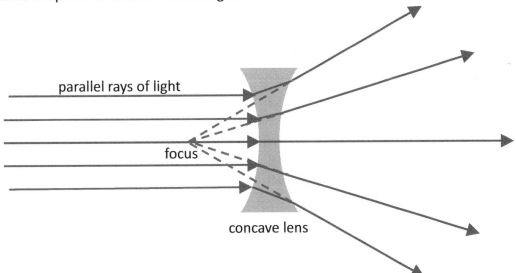

The easiest way to construct a complex image is to break it down into a combination of simpler shapes. For example, if you want to draw a person, the simplest way to do it is to make a stick figure. The following illustration shows how a snowman was created from Circles, Lines, Rectangles, Arcs, and Ovals. If you want to draw a monkey, for example, you could make a stick figure person and add a tale; an improvement upon this would be to use ovals and circles instead of lines.

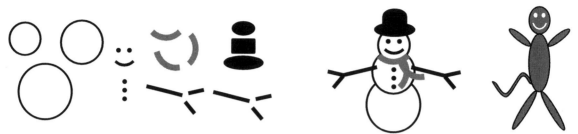

The simplest curves to make are Arcs (remember to lock the aspect ratio before resizing an Arc if you want it to remain circular instead of becoming elliptical). Other curves can also be made quite nicely using the Curve tool, but you have to practice with this tool and exercise some patience to perfect your curves. Now would be a good time to review how to use the Curve tool (see Bullets 8-9 in the second list of Sec. 3.1.8) and how to Edit Points (see Bullet 14 in the first list of Sec. 3.1.8).

The green and fairway of the following golf hole were drawn using the Curve tool. When you first attempt the Curve, just try to get something close – you aren't going to make the perfect curve on your first try. Don't delete the curve and start over until you get it right; instead, once you get one in the ballpark, use the Edit Points feature. The fairway below has 11 points – see if you can find the 11 'corners.' (The fairway's 11 points are fairly easy to find, whereas some of the green's 7 points are more subtle). You can reproduce the fairway by making a closed Curve with 11 points that are in roughly the same positions as the 'corners' of this fairway. Remember that you can right-click a point and adjust the blue line to reshape the curve at that point. As I said, it takes some practice and patience to perfect use of the Curve tool, but you can create more complex images if you master this tool. The bunkers are Ovals and the trees were made from Circles. The tee boxes are Rounded Rectangles.

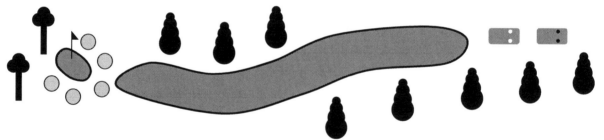

The right-handed coordinate system below was drawn with Curves, Arcs, Lines, and Arrows.

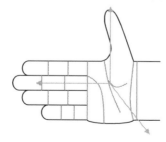

3.1.10 Making a Background for Your Cover

One way to make a background image for your book cover is to simply add a large rectangle. The rectangle could have a single color, or it could be a gradient or a pattern, for example. See the first list of bullets in Sec. 3.1.8 regarding how to insert a shape, change its color, and add a gradient or pattern to a shape. If you would prefer to use an imported picture as your background, see Sec. 3.1.12 regarding how to insert and format a picture.

After you insert a background rectangle, select the background rectangle and change Wrap Text (in the Format tab) to Behind Text. Now you will see all of the text and pictures of your cover in front of the background rectangle.

Change the size of the background rectangle to match the cover trim size + bleed (width = trim width x 2 + spine width + 0.25", height = trim height + 0.25"). For example, for an 8" x 10" book with a spine width of 0.42", the cover trim size plus bleed is 16.67" x 10.25". Type the dimensions directly at the far right of the Format tab. After centering the background rectangle (see the next paragraph), be sure that your background rectangle extends at least 0.125" beyond the cover edges marked by your guide (so that the colors will 'bleed' all of the way to the edges); it's okay if the rectangle extends more than this amount.

Now center your background rectangle: Click Position in the Format tab, go to More Layout Options, choose the Position tab, and change both Horizontal and Vertical to Center.

You can make more than one background rectangle. For example, you may want to have a different background for the front cover, spine width, and back cover. You can even add a border to your front and back covers. The cover guide that we made in Sec. 3.1.5 will help you piece your background together. Make rectangles for the front cover, spine width, back cover, and border, then position these rectangles where you would like them, and group them together. They should line up precisely where they meet and fill the entire page. Change the position of the background rectangle group to Behind Text.

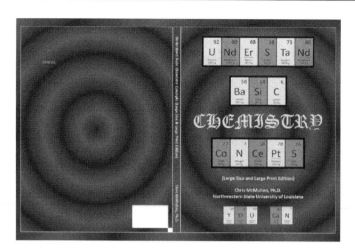

Consider saving your background rectangle for last – otherwise, when you select text and images on your cover, you might find that you accidentally grab the background instead.

3.1.11 Copyright Restrictions on Photos, Clipart, and Other Images

If you will be publishing a book that will be available for sale, you need to be aware that most clipart and photos have a copyright restriction that does not allow them to be used for commercial use. Including a picture in a book or on its cover is considered to be commercial use if the book will be available for sale. If you violate the copyright policy of the copyright holder, you put yourself in a situation where you may be sued by the copyright holder.

Unfortunately, if you click on Clip Art in the Insert tab, the clipart available from Microsoft Office's website is <u>not</u> available for commercial use (which you will see if you read the fine print, which is not always easy to find). Much of the clipart and the vast majority of photos that you may find on the web are also <u>not</u> available for commercial use. Even if you purchase a cd with thousands of photos or clipart images, these are <u>not</u> available for commercial use unless you find a statement on the box that clearly states that you may use it for commercial use.

Some clipart collections do allow commercial use of the clipart and photos, but many do not. Those that do write this statement clearly on the box – they want you to notice this statement on the box, as it may increase your chances of buying their product. Those that do not allow commercial use sometimes do not mention this anywhere on the box – you have to hunt through all the legal fine print later to discover that you can't use the images for commercial use. Sometimes you have to buy a more expensive edition to get the license for commercial use, but beware that some products still are <u>not</u> available for commercial use even if you buy the most expensive version. Make sure that you find the statement in writing before purchasing a collection.

A few companies may allow you to purchase a commercial use license if you write to them. They may ask you for specific details in writing – like how you intend to use the image and how many books you expect to sell. They might also ask you to include a specific statement in the book, declaring the origin of the image. It is also common that they won't allow you to use the image as it is, but will request that you either use it as part of an image or make some change to the image – this way, everyone that uses the image will have a different variation of it. (However, it's <u>not</u> acceptable to make a variation of an image or use an image as part of another picture when commercial use is not permitted.)

There are even special fonts that do not permit commercial use. Microsoft Office itself even comes in student, personal, and professional editions (and even that license doesn't extend to everything, like clipart).

On the other hand, you can sometimes find clipart, photo collections, and fonts that are available for free and allow commercial use, so it pays to do some research. Many of the photos available from NASA (www.nasa.gov) are available for free download and do allow for commercial use, provided that you make it clear that NASA did not participate in the writing or publication of your book.[23] Even then, you must be careful, because some of their photos do have copyrights held by individuals (you have to read the photo credits of each photo to find out).

If there is a specific photo that you want to use, try contacting the copyright owner. You may use the image for commercial use if you obtain written permission. Make sure that you obtain permission in writing – and check with an attorney to make sure that the writing is satisfactory – from the copyright owner (check on this, too) and that the writing clearly allows commercial use of the specified image. If you have written permission to use an image, acknowledge the copyright holder in the caption below your figure.

Similarly, when you are browsing covers to get ideas for your cover, don't copy covers that you see. Focus on understanding your design options – like how to layout the cover, which color schemes work well, and what features you could include (like starbursts or book reviews from magazines) – but don't copy specifics (like sentences from the cover or diagrams that you've seen). Copying or paraphrasing text is also a copyright violation called plagiarism. You're also not allowed to reproduce a picture (unless you've been granted commercial use). Note that drawing from scratch a copy of a picture that you've seen is a copyright violation, too. There are even some places or images that you aren't allowed to photograph – such as taking a photo of the Eiffel Tower at night – and use commercially.

---

[23] If you want to use these images, first read their "Image Use Guidelines."

3.1.12 Inserting and Formatting Pictures and Clipart

As mentioned Sec. 3.1.11, don't use the Clip Art button in the Insert tab to find clipart and other images because you're not permitted to use any pictures that have a copyright restriction against commercial use.

Instead, you will need to either draw your own figures, take your own photos, or find a library of clipart and pictures which clearly states that commercial use is allowed.

First, turn off picture compression. Go to the File tab, look for Options, which is hiding below Help and Save & Send. Click Options, pick Advanced, scroll down to Image Size and Quality, and check the box for Do Not Compress Images in File. Choose the maximum PPI.

To insert a photo, clipart, or any other picture that you don't draw in Word, go to the Insert tab, click Picture, browse for your picture, click on the picture's filename, and click the Insert button on the popup window. If you select the picture (by clicking on it), a Format tab will appear at the top of the screen (only when the picture is selected). In the Format tab, there are several tools that you can use to format the picture in Microsoft Word.[24]

1. You can remove a background by clicking Remove Background. When you select this, a square will appear in the picture, which you can resize (by placing your cursor over one of the little circles or squares that appear at the corners and midpoints of the sides, and holding down the left button while moving the mouse to drag the cursor). When you finish resizing the square, click anywhere else on the screen outside of the picture. The black space in the background of Venus[25] was removed from the photo below following this procedure.

2. If you want to remove a color from the picture and Remove Background doesn't do the job, you can make one color in your picture transparent. To do this, click Color, choose Transparent Color, and click somewhere on the picture that has the color that you want to make transparent. Beware, though, if you make red transparent – for example – it will make every red in the picture transparent. Also, you will be able to see anything that may be behind the transparent color (such as the background).

---

[24] If you have some fancy photo-editing software, you may find a greater variety of options by editing your pictures in that program instead of Word. Also, when you publish an eBook, adjustments that you make in Word may not show up (i.e. you might see the original image instead) unless you copy and paste the modified image into Paint (see Sec. 2.2.5) and save it as a new image.

[25] This photo is from NASA's image gallery (www.nasa.gov). NASA did not participate in the writing or publication of this book.

3. It is often useful to crop a photo – i.e. to remove part of the background or to select just a particular image from a picture. Click on the bottom half of the Crop button (on the right side of the Format tab) to find the cropping options, which include Crop To Shape, Aspect Ratio, Fill, and Fit.

4. Crop To Shape can serve a similar purpose compared to removing a background, but it can also be used in other ways. If you want to take a close-up, or frame a picture with a different shape, for example, Crop To Shape will be useful. In the photo below, Uranus' moon Titania[25] was cropped to the shape of a circle. Note that removing the background or setting black to transparent would also have removed the dark surface of the moon in addition to the black space. The Apollo 17 photo[25] below was cropped to the shape of a trapezoid. When cropping to a shape, after you select the shape, deselect the object (by clicking elsewhere on the screen), reselect the object, and then click the top half of the crop button to adjust the boundary of the shape. (If instead you try adjusting the boundary without first deselecting the object, the aspect ratio of the object will change as you adjust it.)

5. If you make a mistake or change your mind after formatting a picture, click Reset Picture to revert back to the original. This button (on the left of the Format tab) can be very handy (so can the Undo and Redo buttons at the top of the screen – or use Ctrl + Z and Ctrl + Y).

6. You can adjust the color and tone of your picture by clicking Color (at the left of the Format tab). Also, explore the variety of Artistic Effects (this button is next to the Color button). The photo of the sun[25] below was recolored in Pencil Grayscale.

 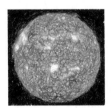

7. You can add an outline to a picture by choosing Picture Border. In addition to choosing a color for your border, you can adjust the Width and select from a variety of solid and dashed outlines in Dash (which includes double lines – choose More Lines at the bottom to adjust settings like Compound Type and Dash Type). The 1969 moon landing photo[25] featuring Buzz Aldrin (taken by Neil Armstrong) below has a gray picture border.

8. Compare the two photos of earth[25] below. If you click Remove Background or set a Transparent Color and then add a Picture Border, the border will have a rectangular outline, as in the photo on the left. If instead you Crop to Shape and add a Picture Border, the border will have the outline of the cropped shape, as in the right photo.

9. There is a good selection of preset Picture Styles available in the center of the Format tab. You can customize your own style by clicking Picture Effects, which has the following options: Shadow, Reflection, Glow, Soft Edges, Bevel, and 3-D Rotation. You can find more options at the bottom of each list – when you click 3-D Rotation Options, for example, in the popup window you can also explore 3-D Format options. The Sombrero galaxy[25] below is shown in a few different styles.

10. Resize or rotate pictures the same way as you resize or rotate any drawing object in Microsoft Word. See numbers 10-12 in the first list of bullets in Sec. 3.1.8 to review how to resize and rotate drawing objects.

11. There are also several standard formatting features that are often useful. In Wrap Text, choose In Front of Text when you want to make a composite picture from multiple pictures. Use Group to group them together when the picture is complete, and change Wrap Text to In Line With Text when inserting a picture into your book's interior. Set Wrap Text to In Front of Text when adding a picture to your cover so that you can place it anywhere on the screen. The Align button is helpful for aligning two or more pictures by their tops, left sides, or centers, for example.

12. You can also edit a picture by using Microsoft Word's drawing tools (described in Sec. 3.1.8), and you can insert a textbox or WordArt (see Sec. 3.1.6) to add labels.

If you edit a picture in Microsoft Word, note that the picture will generally revert back to its original form in an eBook. Word does not change the file for your picture – it just displays the edited picture when you open Word. However, when you submit your Word document for your eBook, the original picture is loaded when the file is converted into your eBook. Fortunately, there are ways around this. For example, if you crop a photo in Word, you can delete the cropped portions of the photo by clicking on the Compress Pictures button in the Format tab and checking the corresponding box. To save other changes, you can copy and paste the edited photo into Paint (see Sec. 2.2.5), save the new photo as a JPEG file, and insert this modified photo back into Word. Don't do this with the paperback version of your book – just the eBook version.

If you crop and otherwise edit pictures in their native program (such as photo-editing software), you may find more editing options than Word has. Also, make sure that any changes to the pictures are permanently saved before inserting them into the Word file for your eBook.

A tool that can be particularly handy is a Snipping Tool. Many new computer models have a Snipping Tool on the Start Menu. If not, you may be able to find this tool online. When you open the Snipping Tool, it allows you to make a rectangle, capture an image on the screen, and save it as a JPEG file. (Again, you must be careful that anything you copy is not protected by copyright, trademark, or commercial use restrictions.) For example, suppose that you want to enlarge an image from your paperback book for use in an eBook: You could zoom in on the image in Word, use the Snipping Tool to capture the enlarged image, and save it as a JPEG file for your eBook. Also, note that the latest version of Microsoft Word has a Screenshot tool. To use it, first open the image in a separate window (it can't be in the same file that you are using), and adjust the window exactly as you want the Screenshot to appear. Click the top half of the Screenshot button (in the Insert tab) to select an available Screenshot.

Another way to make a picture is to scan it. If you draw a colorful children's book, for example, you can scan the images with a scanner (or even photograph them), save them as JPEG files, and insert them into your Word document. Test this out before scanning on a large scale to check the resolution of your scans. Insert a sample scan into a Word document, click Save As and choose PDF, then print out the page from your PDF file. It may not be the same quality as your final book, but it will help to give you some indication of how the PDF file's resolution compares to what you see on the original paper.

It's important to have high-quality images, both in print and in eBook format – especially, if you have several pictures in your book. It is not uncommon when publishing an eBook for the author to begin with high-quality images, but discover that the pictures aren't nearly as good when reading the eBook on one or more devices. It would be wise to make a file with a few representative pictures, go to Amazon's Kindle and begin the publishing process (don't fill out everything – just the bare minimum for it to let you upload the file), upload the file that just has the few sample pictures, and view converted eBook file on the Kindle previewer to see what the pictures will look like (view them both in the black-and-white version and in the Kindle Fire version). If you're not happy with them, strive to find ways to improve them (you can find suggestions in Sec. 4.2). Also, look at the file size, calculate the number of pictures that you plan to make, and estimate the total file size. We will discuss how to publish an eBook on Kindle (and other platforms), along with the issue of file size, in Sec.'s 4.2.2, 4.2.4, and 4.2.8-11.

Some documents do <u>not</u> scan well. For example, if you have a pile of lecture notes and just want to scan them in, you might find that the resulting book does not have sufficient quality – especially for an eBook, if the images are highly detailed. However, some images <u>do</u> scan well with a high-resolution scanner or camera. You may be able to make the background pictures for a full-color picture book this way – but if the pictures include writing, that may be too detailed (instead, add the writing with textboxes after inserting the pictures into Word). If you will be making an eBook version of your manuscript, it is smart to preview how the images will look before you begin converting your book into an eBook.

Finally, let's briefly discuss two other types of pictures that you may wish to make: graphs and flowcharts. You can find all of the ingredients for making these by clicking Chart (for graphs) or SmartArt (for flowcharts) in the Insert tab. If you have two columns of data and want to make a graph, you probably want to make an X Y (Scatter) plot instead of a Line (even if the data set is linear, you probably don't want what Word calls a Line graph). There are also a variety of Bar and Pie charts to choose from. In SmartArt, there are several different types of flowcharts that you can make; once you choose a basic design, you can modify it to suit your needs.

When inserting a figure into the interior file for your book, consider adding a caption to describe the figure (as described in Sec. 2.1.14). This is common in traditionally published books, and will help your book appear professionally edited.

3.1.13 Adding Photos, Clipart, and Other Images to Your Cover

Most of the images that you include on your cover should in some way relate to your book. For example, if you publish a puzzle book, you could include a close-up of the puzzle on the front cover, or if you publish a fiction book that features hockey players, you could include a photo that relates to hockey. Pictures on your front cover can help show customers what your book is about.

Insert pictures, clipart, and other images into your cover – and format them – as described in Sec. 3.1.12. In your cover file, change Wrap Text (in the Format tab) to In Front of Text for all of your images except for the background (which should be Behind Text). If you want to draw your own figures, see Sec.'s 3.1.8-9. Select multiple objects and use the Align button in the Format tab to center or otherwise align images (e.g. you might want to center an image with the front cover rectangle of your cover guide by selecting both and aligning them – but be sure to ungroup your front cover rectangle first).

Group multiple images together (by selecting them – hold down Ctrl while selecting the images, or use the Selection Pane in the Format tab to select them while holding down Ctrl – and clicking on Group in the Format tab) to help minimize the risk for PDF conversion issues, objects wandering around as you move other objects, and to help reduce problems that may arise from the file becoming highly complex. In Word 2007, for example, it wasn't uncommon for the cover file to look quite different in the PDF than it did in Word unless you grouped multiple images together.

Some authors include a picture of themselves either on the cover (the back cover is probably more common) or on an author page near the end of the book. Many readers are curious about the person behind the words. If you are not too shy, consider doing this. If you are attractive and photogenic, maybe it is even worth including on the front cover. But remember, customers are buying your book, not your photo. Also, consider whether you have a face that suits the type of book that you are writing – survey some people (not just close friends and family, who may offer a biased opinion) to see what they think.

If you draw an image in Microsoft Word and need to resize it, group all parts of the images together, lock the aspect ratio (click on the little arrow at the bottom right corner of the Size group in the Format tab), and then resize the picture (either by dragging a corner or by manually entering the width or height on the Format tab – sometimes, you have to open the Size popup window to make this work). Unfortunately, an enlarged or reduced image doesn't always look the same, so sometimes you have to ungroup the parts of the picture, resize text, adjust thicknesses, and improve alignment by moving objects around.

If you would like to use a photo as a background, see Sec. 3.1.12 regarding how to insert, resize, and format the photo. Also, recall that we discussed how to insert a background, in general, in Sec. 3.1.10. Change the Text Wrap of the background to Behind Text. I suggest saving the background for last – otherwise, you may find yourself accidentally grabbing the background when you are trying to select and edit other objects.

When your cover is complete, place a sheet of paper over the back cover to study how the front cover looks (and similarly analyze the back cover and spine). Then zoom out considerably (look in the View tab), place a sheet of paper over the back cover, and study how the thumbnail image looks. Solicit opinions from friends, family, and acquaintances.

Remember to remove the cover guides that we drew in Sec. 3.1.5 when your cover is finalized. However, you should save a next-to-final version of your cover file (with a different file name, of course) with the guides included, just in case you need to revise your cover.

3.1.14 Cover Help, Including Free and Paid Cover and Illustration Services

In case you may be interested in receiving help – free or paid – creating artwork or designing your cover, we will discuss some alternatives to doing it all by yourself in this section.

First, KDP has a free Cover Creator (KDP has this both for paperbacks and eBooks.) This program is easy to use – it launches directly from the page where you publish your book. It includes free artwork and fonts to choose from, and makes the cover design simple. Designing your own cover following the instructions in this chapter provides the most flexibility – and is also pretty straightforward to do – but if you want some free artwork to choose from and a way to make design even simpler, you should check out Cover Creator. Since Cover Creator is free, you should at least give it a try before investing in any paid services. We will describe how to launch Cover Creator in Sec. 4.1.9.

KDP also offers another free service that can help you with your cover design: KDP Print can build you a cover template in a PNG or PDF format. (If you want a template in Word, I recommend following the step-by-step instructions in Sec. 3.1.5.) You can get a PNG or PDF template for your cover by following these steps:
1. Visit KDP's website: kdp.amazon.com.
2. Click the Help link at the top of the page.
3. Click See All Formatting Resources under Prepare Your Book.
4. Click the Cover link in the first bullet point under Paperbacks.
5. At the left, select your trim size from the dropdown menu.
6. Enter the page count for your interior file.
7. Choose the paper color. For a color interior, choose color (even though the paper will technically be white). For a black and white interior, choose white or cream.
8. Now you can download a PNG or PDF template of your book cover.

Before we discuss paid services, let's talk about one more thing that you can get for free: help and advice. If you have questions about the publishing process, you can contact KDP by clicking the Help link at the top of the page after you login to your KDP account. You can also get help from fellow authors by asking questions in a community forum. For example, at KDP the community forum is easily accessed via a link at the top of the page (after you login to your KDP account).

https://www.kdpcommunity.com/s/?language=en

Whether you have a specific question or even a general topic in mind, if you type your issue into the search field of your favorite internet search engine, there is a good chance that you will find the answer there, too.

There are freelance illustrators who offer professional (paid) services to help you with your cover design. This can include purchasing artwork, hiring an illustrator, or even paying to have the entire cover designed for you. Awesome artwork could make your book very eye-catching and help you fall in love with your own book, but it's probably the content that should be more meaningful than your cover. Like any investment, paying for artwork is a risk. Think about how many books you will have to sell just to break even if you invest money in the production and publication of your book. If instead you publish your book for free, you won't be starting out in the hole. For this reason, I recommend doing it yourself – or at least give it a shot and see how it turns out. Back to the comment I made about loving your cover – when you put your own creativity, time, and effort into the book cover project, that can also help you enjoy your own book cover.

Note that KDP doesn't currently offer paid services. Prior to the merger between Create-Space and KDP, CreateSpace discontinued their paid services. However, KDP does maintain a list of professional design services. Click the help link at the top of the page, click See All Formatting Resources under Prepare Your Book, and click the link at the right under Professional Services. You can find a list of designers under Book Cover Creation. This is just a small list. There are hundreds of designers and illustrators available for hire which aren't on that list.

If you want to explore paid services from other companies and individuals, try searching for them with an internet search engine, asking questions in community help forums for authors, talking to other authors that you know, and looking for friends or family members who have artistic talents. Do some research and be wary of paying for services from entities or people that you don't know: It would be wise to find a sample of the service first and also find fellow authors who can vouch for the service.

3.2 Converting Your Cover into an eBook Thumbnail Image

3.2.1 Why You Need a Different Thumbnail Image for Your eBook

PAPERBACK BOOKS AND eBooks have different types of covers. There are obvious structural differences: The cover file for your paperback book includes a front cover, spine, back cover, and extra room around the edges for colors to bleed, whereas your eBook cover just needs a front side. Also, the front cover of your paperback must be designed to match the trim size of your book, which probably won't be the ideal aspect ratio for the cover of your eBook. Furthermore, when you submit your paperback book cover, it will be in the form of a PDF file. When you submit your eBook cover, it will be in the form of a JPEG file.

Another difference is that your paperback book cover needs to look good both as a thumbnail image and in person, but your eBook's cover will primarily be viewed as a thumbnail image. Sometimes, it is wise to refrain from making the font too extremely large for a paperback cover, thinking of how it will look in person; instead, easy-to-read is very important for the eBook cover. In this case, you might make some of your text larger. Since your eBook cover will primarily function as a thumbnail image, it's not necessary to include finer details that will be difficult to make out in the thumbnail.

Even the rules for making the paperback and eBook covers differ: The front cover of your paperback must contain every word of your book's title in order, but this is not required for eBook covers with some eReader companies. If you do include every word of your title on the cover and try to make every word easy-to-read on the thumbnail image, if you have a lengthy title there will scarcely be room for images. Consider highlighting key words and increasing their font size, while still leaving ample room for images on your eBook cover.

You also have the opportunity to make a higher-resolution image for your eBook cover. I recommend making the highest-resolution image that will be accepted. We will return to this point – including how to do it – in the next section; for now, it is one more reason to design a new cover for your eBook.

For these reasons, I recommend modifying your paperback cover file to create your eBook cover file (instead of copying the thumbnail image from KDP, for example). It's easy to do, as explained in Sec. 3.2.2: You already have the ingredients for your cover, we're just going to modify them – so it will be much easier than starting from scratch.

If you do modify your paperback book's cover, which I'm suggesting is worthwhile, to make your eBook cover, also consider having the two covers look similar, though not exactly the same. If the covers look considerably different, readers may be confused into thinking that they are really two different books instead of two editions of the same book. A reader who unknowingly buys the same book twice may not be too happy about it. (You also have the opportunity to make this clear in your book's description.) If the books look similar, but a little different, that will be consistent with having two different editions – one paperback, one eBook – of the same book.

Let's discuss how you can use the exact same image for your eBook cover and paperback book front cover. Although I don't recommend this, I will still tell you how to do it. If you publish your paperback book on Amazon, you can get a copy of the front cover of your book directly from Amazon's website: You could open your book's detail page, right-click on the front cover image, select Save As, and save the file to your computer. However, if you do this, the image will probably be lacking in resolution. If you simply open the picture with image software and increase the image size (while preserving the aspect ratio), the quality of the image will probably be lacking.

If you have a Snipping Tool on your computer, Microsoft Word 2010, or any other program that offers a Screenshot, you can take a Screenshot of your cover. Adjust the View until you can see (at least) the whole front cover. With a Snipping Tool, make a rectangle that just outlines the front cover and capture this image. With Microsoft Word 2010, open a new document (leaving the front cover open), go to the Insert tab in the new document, click the top half of the Screenshot button, and select an available Screenshot. Copy and paste the

Screenshot into Paint (see Sec. 2.2.5), crop the image as desired, resize the image (see Sec. 4.2.2), and save your eBook cover as a JPEG file.

3.2.2 Designing Your eBook Cover

Before you design your eBook cover, browse a variety of eBook thumbnail images. For some of the books, compare the eBook thumbnail image to the paperback or hardcover thumbnail image – this will help you gauge how similar or dissimilar a typical eBook cover looks compared to its paperback or hardcover counterpart. Following are a couple of sample thumbnail images for some of my own eBook covers for which there is a corresponding paperback cover. The eBook thumbnail appears at the left side of each pair, while the paperback thumbnail appears at the right side of each pair. In each case, observe that the paperback cover is more detailed, the text in the eBook thumbnail is easier to read, and the eBook thumbnail is wider. (Yes, I broke my own rule by not making them very similar...)

Following are a few of my eBook covers for which I don't have a corresponding paperback book.

 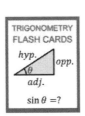 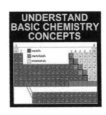

You will need to submit a cover file as a JPEG file. (Amazon's Kindle also accepts TIFF images, and other eReader requirements will differ. We will discuss eBook publishing requirements for a variety of companies in Sec.'s 4.2.1, 4.2.4, and 4.2.8-11.) I suggest making your eBook cover in Word, using many of the same elements from your paperback cover – but perhaps modifying their sizes.

You can easily make a JPEG file from an eBook cover that you create in Word. When your eBook cover is ready, select the entire image (change View to One Page and click in the gray area to the left of the page to do this quickly) and follow the instructions in Sec. 2.2.5 to convert your cover into a JPEG file.

Set the page size in Word using the Page Layout tab. You can make either dimension – height or width – as large as 20". I recommend making the height 20" in order to maximize the resolution of the cover that you make in Word. You can have a square cover, which would then be 20" x 20"; this will give you a square thumbnail image. When a website – such as Amazon – displays their eBooks side-by-side with equal cover heights, some books appear wider than others because they don't all have the same aspect ratio. A square book with maximum resolution will appear widest. It may not be the case that wider is better. However, if you want wider, go with 20" x 20".

When you decide on your aspect ratio, keep in mind that your cover JPEG file may be added to the beginning of the eBook (in addition to your title page) – depending on the eReader company. In this case, you may want the aspect ratio of your cover to match the aspect ratio of the eReader. For example, if you want to match the Kindle Fire and Nook Color aspect ratios, choose 11.7" x 20"; for the Kindle eInk 6" and black-and-white Nook, choose 15" x 20"; and for the Kindle Fire HD 7", choose 12.5" x 20". Another consideration is that your thumbnail may look more uniform if it matches the aspect ratio of most of the other eBooks of its genre.

To make your eBook cover, you can simply copy (Ctrl + C) and paste (Ctrl + V) textboxes, WordArt, drawings, photos, and other pictures from your paperback book cover into your eBook cover. You will probably need to resize most, if not all, of the textboxes and images. Remember that if you click on the little arrow in the bottom right corner of the Size group at the far right of the Format tab, you can choose to lock the Aspect Ratio before resizing. Also, a group of images may not look as nice when it is first resized – you may need to change the font size, line thicknesses, and adjust alignment to recreate the quality of the original image. You can Zoom out in the View tab to preview what the eBook will look like as a thumbnail image, and you will also get a preview of the thumbnail when begin the publishing process (although the actual thumbnail usually looks sharper than the preview).

Amazon recommends an eBook cover with an aspect ratio of 5:8 and a longest dimension with 4500 pixels. The width will then be approximately 2813 pixels. A page size of 12.5" by 20" creates this aspect ratio. While 5:8 matches Kindle Fire devices, it's more important how the thumbnail looks before buying the book. With that in mind, 5:8 may be too narrow; many designers prefer 6:9. **Note that KDP has a Cover Creator tool.**

If you do this, you will need a different cover for a Nook eBook since a Nook cover can't have more than 2000 pixels on the longest side (unless Nook has updated their requirements). You can simply open your JPEG file in Paint and resize the longest dimension to 2000 pixels. If you use the 5:8 aspect ratio, your width will have about 1250 pixels.

Chapter 4

Self-Publishing Your Book

Chapter Overview

4.1 Publishing Your Paperback Book with KDP Print
4.2 Publishing Your eBook Online

This chapter answers questions about the following topics, and more:

- ☑ Detailed instructions for how to publish a paperback book with KDP.
- ☑ Pricing your book, selecting categories, adding a second Browse category at Amazon, choosing keywords, adding a subtitle, and a discussion of KDP options.
- ☑ Making your paperback book available in bookstores and libraries.
- ☑ Detailed instructions for how to publish – with information about pricing – an eBook on Amazon's Kindle, Barnes & Noble's Nook, the Sony Reader, and more.[26]
- ☑ The problem of using the brand of the eReader in the description of your eBook, why it's not really a problem, and what to do instead.
- ☑ Differences between the paperback and eBook versions of your book's description, keywords, and categories.
- ☑ Your paperback Amazon listing and Kindle Amazon listing will be linked together, such that either page shows both versions of your book.
- ☑ An introduction to Smashwords[27] – a free publishing service that makes your eBook available on a variety of eReaders.

---

[26] Kindle and Amazon are trademarks of Amazon.com, Inc. Nook and Barnes & Noble are trademarks of Barnes & Noble, Inc. Sony is a registered trademark of Sony Corporation. Smashwords is a registered trademark of Smashwords. These trademarks and brands are the property of their respective owners.

4.1 Publishing Your Paperback Book with KDP Print

4.1.1 About KDP and Amazon[27]

I RECOMMEND PUBLISHING THE paperback edition of your book with Kindle Direct Publishing (KDP), for reasons that I described in Chapter 1. KDP is an Amazon company. I love and trust Amazon as both a consumer and as an author. I gave KDP (and prior to that, CreateSpace, which has since merged together with KDP) a shot because of Amazon's reputation, and have come to love and trust KDP, too. These bookselling and publishing giants have created many opportunities for small business owners and self-published authors. Amazon frequently features success stories of small, family-owned businesses that sell their products on Amazon as well as success stories of self-published authors. I'm happy to support a huge business that gives the small guy a fighting chance.[28]

We all know that Amazon is an online bookstore giant (which also sells many other products besides books). As a potential self-published author and Amazon customer, you may want to take a moment and consider how Amazon's history impacts you. When Amazon emerged as a giant online bookseller, they made a very bold move: They allowed customers to resell their used books (regardless of where they were purchased), and listed the used book sales on the same detail page as for the new books. Traditional publishers and bestselling authors were not happy about this, as they did not (and still don't) draw royalties[29] on the resold copies: Customers who visited Amazon online to order a bestselling book could choose – as an alternative to paying the cover price for a new book – to purchase a used book for as little as one penny (and bestselling mass market paperbacks often were selling for just one penny). Traditional publishers were a major supplier to Amazon, yet Amazon went against the traditional publishers' wishes, benefiting the small guy: Consumers could buy books for less, consumers could resell their books (many used books sold very quickly and brought a much better price than a yard sale ever would), and many small businesses found a great avenue for selling new and used books.

---

[27] KDP and Amazon are trademarks of Amazon.com, Inc. These trademarks and brands are the property of their respective owners.

[28] I was not endorsed to write this book by Amazon, KDP, or CreateSpace. I was <u>not</u> paid nor encouraged in any way to show my support for these companies in my book. Neither company was aware that I was writing or self-publishing this book until the work had already been completed (and these companies are probably too huge to ever take notice of this book, let alone read it and see that I have recommended them). These are my honest opinions; you are encouraged to do some research and form your own opinions.

[29] Don't freak out about this. In Sec. 4.1.7, I will explain how the sale of third-party used and new books probably helps the self-publisher much more than it hurts.

Amazon's next major moves, which significantly impacted the publishing industry, were to introduce the Kindle and to advertise CreateSpace. Both Kindle and CreateSpace provided incredible self-publishing opportunities for authors. (CreateSpace has since merged with KDP.) I first learned about CreateSpace when I was shopping at Amazon. I found a link at the bottom of Amazon's webpage that read, "Independently Publish with Us." This link briefly described Kindle and CreateSpace, and invited me to visit their websites. There are now millions of paperback books and eBooks being published this way. The editors of big publishing houses have long decided which books we should be able to read (and write), but now Amazon (and other companies, like Barnes & Noble and Kobo, with their eReaders) are providing millions of new books to choose from. I recognize and appreciate what Amazon has done for both self-published authors and consumers, and so I continue to support Amazon both ways.

KDP is an Amazon company that has been helping authors make their work available on Amazon and other distribution channels (such as other booksellers and libraries). KDP's paperback option is a print-on-demand service, meaning that they print and bind your book when it sells. This way, there is no inventory to manage, and your book is always in stock and never goes out of print (unless, for some reason, you decide to discontinue production of your book). Your book will show as 'in stock' on Amazon's website, and is ready to ship if a customer purchases it. The print-on-demand technology is what makes self-publishing possible – you can self-publish for free (there are no setup fees). You don't have to purchase any of your own books (unlike old-fashioned self-publishing, where you would buy hundreds or thousands of copies up front and try to sell them directly to bookstores). Since KDP is an Amazon company, your self-published book will be listed with Amazon,[30] available for purchase by millions of potential customers around the globe. You can even make your book available for sale in Europe (if so, they will print your book on demand in Europe and ship it from Europe to save shipping costs). There is also an Expanded Distribution option, which allows other booksellers and libraries to buy copies of your book and sell them. KDP also provides tools, resources, customer service, and a community forum, all of which provide help for you to self-publish your work. The royalties are excellent, too (see Sec.'s 4.1.4-5). I don't imagine that you will find another self-publishing service that makes your book more visible, offers better royalties, and also comes for FREE. It's an amazing combination!

KDP's primary competitor is Ingram Spark, which charges with a setup fee. Since Ingram Spark offers a hardcover option and since illustrated children's books sometimes sell best in hardcover format, it's not uncommon for authors of illustrated children's books to use KDP for paperback and Kindle editions and also create a hardcover edition through Ingram Spark. Note that Nook Press offers a hardcover option if you just want to order author copies, but Nook Press doesn't currently offer print-on-demand sales and distribution of paperback or hardcover books (but this may change in the future as Nook Press continues to evolve).

---

[30] This is provided that your book doesn't have unacceptable content, such as pornography, offensive material, and public domain content.

Most of the material from Sec.'s 4.1.2-8 – such as preparing your book description and choosing keywords – will apply regardless of where you publish your paperback book, even though I will generally speak with KDP in mind. In Sec. 4.1.9, I will specifically outline how to publish your paperback book using KDP.

If you would like more information about KDP, you can visit their website directly (kdp.amazon.com); or you can visit Amazon's website (www.amazon.com), scroll down to the bottom of the page, and click Independently Publish With Us. You can login with your Amazon account, or if you wish you can sign up for a new account for KDP. Then, when you login, it is very easy to contact them if you have any questions that you would like to ask. Click the Help link at the top of the screen, then look for the Contact US button on the left side. I've used this option myself, and have always communicated with a courteous, knowledgeable support specialist. Other ways to get questions answered include the KDP help pages and the Community Help forum, where you can speak with other self-published authors.

4.1.2 Preparing a Description and Biography

You will need to prepare a description of your book for online booksellers. Amazon will use your description on your book's detail page. Most other online booksellers, like Barnes & Noble, which are available through the Expanded Distribution, are not presently using this description – it's up to them. Therefore, you should focus on your Amazon audience when you prepare your description, and then revise your description if you also publish an eBook version of your book.

Customers browsing through Amazon who come across your book will be able to read your book's description. Therefore, the purpose of your description is to inform potential readers what your book is about in order to help them make their purchase decision. Your main goal is to provide a clear indication of what the customer is buying. If your customer expects your book to be one thing, but it turns out to be something else, the result could be a negative review. Thus, you don't want to 'oversell' or 'under-describe' your book: If your book sounds like the best thing since sliced bread, but doesn't live up to the description, or if there isn't enough information for the customer to understand exactly what he/she is getting, the customer may leave a negative review – which will affect potential sales in the future.

Your book will have a Search Inside feature on Amazon (though it may take a few weeks before this feature is added to your book), which allows the customer to preview the contents, introduction, other front and back matter, the back cover, and sample pages. Because of this, some authors make the mistake of not describing the book well, thinking that the customer will be able to sample the book firsthand. The problem with this is that many customers purchase books without using the Search Inside feature. You just have to accept this fact and make your description clear. The consequence for an unclear description could be a negative review; it doesn't help to be able to say, "You could have looked inside!"

In addition to providing a clear picture of what your book is about, your description provides a writing sample. Customers won't assume that the author of the book also wrote the book's description (unless you want to advertise this point in the description – it might be more professional to write in the third person, as if someone else is describing your book), unless perhaps the customer is another self-published author (which is not at all unlikely, as many self-published authors like to support the self-publishing concept). Rather, the description is the first form of writing that the customer associates with your book: If there are obvious spelling or grammatical mistakes in the one-paragraph description, in the customer's mind, that won't bode well for the quality of the book itself.

There is a limit to how long your description can be: When you self-publish with KDP, your description must be 4,000 characters or less (estimated at about 760 words).

I recommend typing your book's description in Microsoft Word. There are a few advantages of doing this and later using copy/paste to transfer your description to the publisher:

- You can easily check the character count. Click the word count in the bottom left corner of the screen, and a window will pop up to show you the character count. You want "Characters (with spaces)."
- Use Word's spelling and grammar checker to help reduce the chance for such mistakes. These checkers are not foolproof, though, so you still need to read the description carefully (and have friends/family check it, too). These checkers will help to catch a few obvious mistakes, though.
- It will be easy to find your description if you need to modify it for your eBook.

The nature of your description depends on what type of book you are publishing. For fiction, you want to inspire interest in your story without giving away the plot (definitely, don't spoil the ending). Since characters can attract interest in a book, describe key characters involved in the story. The setting of the story may also draw interest: A reader might want to enjoy the feeling of living someplace exotic, or might appreciate being able to relate to a story from their home city, for example.

In nonfiction, you want to make the range and depth of the content very clear. While you should mostly describe your book, you want to show how it is distinguished from similar titles (not by mentioning other books directly or putting other authors down, but by describing what is unique about your book). Describe any special features that your book includes, such as an answer key, a glossary, or over a hundred figures. Readers will want to know such things as whether your book is comprehensive or focused on a narrow topic, whether it is an introduction for beginners or presented at a high level for experts, and whether it is written with clear language that anyone can understand or written at a technical level. You want to make the contents clear (since not everyone will Search Inside to see the table of contents). If the author has any special qualifications that relate to the book (such as a degree in the subject area, or several years of experience in the field), highlight this.

I suggest reading descriptions of other books for inspiration (but don't plagiarize the content). Browse descriptions on Amazon and also read back covers and dust jackets of books that you have (or visit a library or bookstore).

You are not permitted to include contact information in your description, such as an email address or even a website URL. Also, you may not include any reviews, quotes, or testimonials in your description. If you have a professional Editorial Review, Amazon will post that review separate from your description. You can't use your description to ask customers to review your work. You're not allowed to advertise or promote in your description. Also, you can't use DHTML, Java Scripts, or any executables in your description.[31]

While you want to provide sufficient detail so that the potential reader has a clear description of what your book is about, having a description that is too lengthy might also deter some readers. A concise description is often effective, provided that it doesn't omit important details. A shorter description may be better for fiction; leaving an air of mystery might even stir a little interest. On the other hand, I've come across many short descriptions that didn't tell me what I really wanted to know: If you take a chance on such a book, you're not going to be happy if it doesn't turn out to be what you were looking for. There is a balance somewhere in between, where you provide all of the pertinent information in a concise description. I suggest erring on the side of too much, rather than too little, information in the case of a nonfiction book.

If you have a long description, you may want to find a way to organize it into parts to help readers find what they are looking for. Unfortunately, if you use the tab key to make indentations, the paragraph breaks will not show up in the description for your book on Amazon (although they will show up for a Kindle book). There are some alternatives. You could use one-word section headings in CAPS (but don't use CAPS extensively – it's unacceptable), as illustrated in the following sample description. You can also number the sections of your description – like (1), (2), etc. – or use symbols – like the asterisk (*), but many nonstandard symbols won't show up – in order to help show the divisions. **Once published, you can format your description better at Author Central (see Sec. 6.1.4).**

Following, I have a couple of my sample descriptions to help get you started. These descriptions are for nonfiction books. The first description is fairly long, and features occasional use of the CAPS key to create divisional breaks. The second description is fairly concise. Again, I selected my own descriptions because it was easy to get permission to use them, not because I thought you'd be interested in a book about chemistry or the fourth dimension. I recommend that you check out a variety of other book descriptions.

---

[31] This covers most of what you need to avoid including in your description for Amazon. Visit Amazon and other booksellers' websites to learn all of the exclusions that apply.

Understand Basic Chemistry Concepts

OVERVIEW: This book focuses on fundamental chemistry concepts, such as understanding the periodic table of the elements and how chemical bonds are formed. No prior knowledge of chemistry is assumed. The mathematical component involves only basic arithmetic. The content is much more conceptual than mathematical. AUDIENCE: It is geared toward helping anyone – student or not – to understand the main ideas of chemistry. Both students and non-students may find it helpful to be able to focus on understanding the main concepts without the constant emphasis on computations that is generally found in chemistry lectures and textbooks. CONTENTS: (1) Understanding the organization of the periodic table, including trends and patterns. (2) Understanding ionic and covalent bonds and how they are formed, including the structure of valence electrons. (3) A set of rules to follow to speak the language of chemistry fluently: How to name compounds when different types of compounds follow different naming schemes. (4) Understanding chemical reactions, including how to balance them and a survey of important reactions. (5) Understanding the three phases of matter: properties of matter, amorphous and crystalline solids, ideal gases, liquids, solutions, and acids/bases. (6) Understanding atomic and nuclear structure and how it relates to chemistry. (7) VErBAl ReAcTiONS: A brief fun diversion from science for the verbal side of the brain, using symbols from chemistry's periodic table to make word puzzles. ANSWERS: Every chapter includes self-check exercises to offer practice and help the reader check his or her understanding. 100% of the exercises have answers at the back of the book. COPYRIGHT: Teachers who purchase one copy of this book or borrow one copy of this book from a library may reproduce selected pages for the purpose of teaching chemistry concepts to their own students.

The Visual Guide to Extra Dimensions, Volume 1

Watch a tesseract unfold. See how the 3D cross section of a hypercube changes as the hypercube rotates. View 4D wheels with axles with a spherinder or cubinder structure. Imagine climbing a 4D staircase. Find 10 out of 120 dodecahedra of a hecatonicosachoron highlighted... all on this visual tour of the fourth dimension. The book is much more visual and conceptual than algebraic, yet it is detailed and technical, with the intention of satisfying the needs of mathematically-minded readers familiar with the fundamentals of algebra, geometry, and graphing.

You can also add an author biography to your book's Amazon detail page. Since many books do not include an author biography below the description, including one can add a professional appearance to your book's Amazon page. Of course, a biography will also help readers learn more about the author behind the book, and any relevant experience and qualifications.

Before CreateSpace merged with KDP, CreateSpace offered the option to include an About the Author section which would show up on your book's Amazon page. Since CreateSpace has merged with KDP, the best way to add a biography (or About the Author section) is through Author Central. Chapter 6 will show you how to manage author pages via Author Central. For now, we'll focus on how to prepare a biography or about the author section. Once it is ready, visit Author Central (described in Chapter 6, in Volume 2 of this book) to add your biography.

As with your description, I recommend first typing your biography in Word to check for spelling and grammar mistakes, and to check the character count. The same provisions out-lining what you can or can't include with your description also apply to your biography.

What do you want your readers to know about you? They might be curious about your background, relevant qualifications, or previous publications. Some will wonder what your hobbies and interests are. Readers will probably appreciate being able to see some of your personality as they read your biography. As it is another writing sample (though again, it will seem more professional if it is written in the third person so that it appears that another person wrote about you – rather than speaking in the first person as if you wrote it yourself, even if that was the case), it's very important to make a good impression by avoiding spelling or grammatical mistakes. If you struggle with spelling and grammar, it will be worthwhile to receive proofreading assistance with your description and biography.

(In addition to a biography associated with your author profile which will show on each of your books' Amazon pages, Author Central allows you to post an optional About the Author section that is separate from your biography. In most cases, the About the Author section is unnecessary, since the biography already describes the author. I recommend preparing a biography, but leaving the optional About the Author section blank.)

Following is a sample biography that I included with my books on the fourth dimension. It is a bit long because I felt the need to establish my qualifications in this field. In general, I would suggest a shorter biography on your book's detail page, but include a longer biography on your Author Page.

Chris McMullen is a physics instructor at Northwestern State University of Louisiana. He earned his Ph.D. in phenomenological high-energy physics (particle physics) from Oklahoma State University in 2002. Originally from California, he earned his Master's degree from California State University, Northridge, where his thesis was in the field of electron spin resonance. He has published several papers on the prospects for discovering large superstring-inspired extra dimensions at the Large Hadron Collider, which is his area of specialization. Dr. McMullen published The Visual Guide to Extra Dimensions, Volumes 1 and 2, to share his passion for the geometry and physics of the fourth dimension. He also wrote these books, Full-Color Illustrations of the Fourth Dimension, Volumes 1 and 2, to help illustrate the geometry of a fourth dimension of space. Dr. McMullen was fascinated with a fourth dimension of space when he first read Rudy Rucker's introduction to the subject during high school. He happened to be working on his Ph.D. in particle physics when Arkani-Hamed, Dimopoulos, and Dvali wrote a famous technical paper motivating large superstring-inspired extra dimensions, which transformed the subject of the fourth dimension from philosophy to a plausibly experimental science. Dr. McMullen has published these general-audience books on the fourth dimension to share his passion for the math and physics of extra dimensions. One of his favorite sayings is: May your contemplation of a fourth dimension of space enhance the dimensionality of your thoughts.

The following sample About the Author section is for a Christmas word scrambles book that I coauthored. It is somewhat more concise than the previous biography, and also shows an example of when an About the Author section might be useful.

Chris McMullen and Carolyn Kivett are a son-and-mother combination who teamed up to write a variety of word puzzle books and, recently, some children's books, such as math flash cards for the Kindle. CHRIS MCMULLEN holds a Ph.D. in theoretical high-energy physics (aka particle physics) from Oklahoma State University. He teaches physics at Northwestern State University of Louisiana. In addition to solving verbal and math puzzles, he enjoys playing chess and golf and writing books in his spare time. His mother, CAROLYN KIVETT, loves solving verbal puzzles, such as anagrams and crossword puzzles. She runs a small business in southern California where she manufactures covers for outdoor entertainment centers and golf cart enclosures from scratch. She enjoys the challenge of sewing materials into new geometric shapes, which is a three-dimensional visual puzzle. She loves to collect teddy bears and sunflowers, and also enjoys playing golf.

4.1.3 Selecting a Browse Category, Keywords, and Title/Subtitle

You will need to select a browse category for your book's detail page on Amazon. If you also publish an eBook, you will need to select two browse categories.

Visit Amazon's website and browse through the books. Click Books on the left of their home page, then choose Books from the list. On the left-hand side, you will find a list called "Books Categories." Explore these categories and their subcategories to discover what options are available.

Next, type in key words that relate to your title in the Search field at the top of the screen. Make sure that 'Books' is selected (as opposed to 'All' or a specific category) because you want books from various book categories to show up in your search. Find books that are similar to your book, open their detail pages, and see what browse categories they are listed in. This will help you decide which categories are a best fit for your book.

KDP lets you choose two browse categories. When you finish selecting your categories, examine them carefully to make sure that two categories were indeed selected. It's very easy to select only one category when you believe that you selected two, so after you close the window, examine the categories closely. (Before CreateSpace merged with KDP, you could only select one category. A nice benefit of the merger is that now you can select two.)

In addition to selecting a category, you will need to add keywords to associate with your book. Keywords help potential buyers find your book when they use the search field at Amazon.[32] Your book will already be searchable at Amazon using any combination of words from your title and subtitle. In addition, your book will be searchable using up to 7 set of keywords that you enter when you publish your book. You may enter multiple words in each of the 7 keyword fields. It's incorrect to think that you can only enter one word in each field. Try to keep each keyword field below 50 characters (spaces included). (Prior to the merger between CreateSpace and KDP, you could only enter 5 keywords and there had been a strict limit of 25 characters. This is another benefit from the merger.) Note that you may change the keywords later if you think of something better or if you want to see whether changing the keywords might affect your sales (but beware that you will lose any keyword relevance that you may have built up over time when you remove or modify any existing keywords).

I recommend typing possible keywords into the search field at Amazon to test out the popularity of the keyword. Plus, as you do this, you may discover keywords that you hadn't thought of. After you type a few letters, you will see a list of popular searches come up. Keep in mind that a keyword is not necessarily a single word, but may be a group of words or a phrase. Make a list of all of the relevant keywords, and make notes about which ones seem more popular. This list will help you choose the best 7 sets of keywords. Don't use quotation marks (") or underscores (_) with your keywords.

---

[32] Other online booksellers, like Barnes & Noble, which may sell your book through the Expanded Distribution channel, will probably not use these keywords. If not, you can always consider contacting them and inquiring about the prospects of having relevant keywords added to your book. First, give them plenty of time (a month or more) to get your book properly listed, then see if your book comes up in the keyword search at their website (I mean to check if it comes up at all – it probably won't be on the first page if it comes up).

The most important factor in choosing your keywords is that they be very relevant to your book. It's not just popularity that you're looking for. It doesn't do you any good to use a very popular keyword that doesn't relate to your book, like using Tiger Woods as a keyword for a book that doesn't even mention Tiger Woods (that will just upset customers). Ensure that the keywords closely relate to your book's content. The keyword could relate to your content (like "medical thriller"), the setting (like "San Diego"), or the type of book (like "workbook"), for example. The keyword may even be another term for a word used in your title. For example, a book that is entitled, *Scary Word Search Puzzles*, should have "word find" as one of the keywords because some people will be typing "word find" instead of "word search," and the book should show up either way.

Another factor is the popularity of the keyword. If you want your book to be discovered in searches at Amazon, you want to use a keyword which potential buyers will be searching for frequently. If your keywords are only searched for once every few months, almost nobody will discover your book through your keywords. When you start typing a keyword in a search at Amazon, if the keyword does not show up at all, you know that it will be a very rare search. You definitely want to use keywords that have been typed frequently enough to show up on the list of keywords. Very popular keywords will show up after just typing a couple of letters, less popular keywords require typing more letters.

However, using the most popular keywords might not be the best idea (as long as the keywords that you do use are searched for with a reasonable frequency). Here's why: If the keyword is exceedingly popular, the keyword search will pull up thousands of matches, and your book may be way down at the end of the search (where it is unlikely to be found). If instead your keyword is moderately popular and pulls up, say, 50 matches, there is a much better chance of your book being visible in the search results. (Even if your book is way down at the end of the search results, it may still be discovered – as explained in Chapter 7.)

The points below relate to keywords. **Learn how to get into special categories at** https://kdp.amazon.com/self-publishing/help?topicId=A200PDGPEIQX41.

- Popularity changes with time. If you check the popularity of keywords today, you might find that the order of their popularity is different next month. A keyword that you choose today could even become obsolete in the future. The current popularity is based on the frequency with which that keyword has been used recently.
- Plurals may make a difference. For example, if you search for "fraction book," the order of the search results changes if instead you search for "fractions book." However, you probably don't need to make separate keywords for both singular and plural – as long as you have one, your book will probably show up the other way, too. For example, if you use "fraction book" for one keyword, you probably don't need to waste a second keyword for "fractions book." You can always test this out after your book is published (and waiting a reasonable time period for all of the keywords to be added to your book's Amazon detail page).

- The word "book" may be implied. For example, if you have the word "pirates" in your title, your book will probably show up in a search for "pirates book" without having to waste one of your keywords to make "pirates book." You can always test this out after your book is published (and keep in mind that your book could be way down at the end of the search results).
- The order of your keywords may make a difference. For example, "writing practice" is different from "practice writing." If the keyword is popular both ways (i.e. compared to reversing the word order), you could choose one of the keywords and see if your book is searchable both ways. If not, and you want it to be, you will have to change one of your other keywords to accommodate this (since you can only have 5).
- The popularity of the keywords (and the order of the search results) changes when you search in 'All' compared to searching in 'Books' or even searching in a specific category (and it's also different when searching for your eBook in Kindle). Explore all of these options when choosing your keywords.

Keywords help to make your book searchable, but not necessarily visible: Your book might not be in the first several pages (though it could be on the first page – you won't know until you try it out), and it could be down at the end of the pack (if so, that could change in time). In Chapter 7, we will discuss how customers will be able to find your book if it is way down at the end of the pack, and how your book might become more visible as time passes.

One way to decide which 7 sets of keywords to use is to conduct a survey among family, friends, and acquaintances. Ask them what they would type into a search if looking for a book like yours and see what the common responses are.

You should have keywords in mind when you develop the title and subtitle for your book, since your book will also be searchable through combinations of words in your title and subtitle. Note that words in your title are more important than words in your subtitle because your book may not be searchable by words in your subtitle in Amazon's European (and other) websites or with other online booksellers (if you use these distribution channels).

A title or subtitle that simply consists of keywords probably won't be the best title. A catchy or interesting title can be very effective, and often such titles only include a few keywords, if any. Most fiction titles are catchy, but have no keywords of their own. Nonfiction titles tend to include a few keywords that help to indicate what the book is about.

A subtitle is optional. When your book shows up in search results at Amazon, the subtitle will appear after the title, separated by a colon. So if you have a long title and subtitle, the overall title will look very long. Sometimes, concise can be more effective. If you don't have any keywords in your title, you may want to include a subtitle in order to add a couple of keywords which briefly help readers to see what your book is about.

It's very important to spell the title and subtitle correctly: Since this is the first thing that a potential buyer will read, you don't want these to make a poor impression. The title and subtitle also need to sound good – which may be more important than keywords.

If you are publishing a series of books with volume numbers, you may want to consider adding the volume number to the title or subtitle. There is also a separate place to enter the volume number when you publish your book.

4.1.4 Calculating the Cost of Your Book and Your Royalty

In this section, I'll show you how to calculate your royalty for paperback books published with KDP. In Sec. 4.2.5, we'll discuss eBook royalty calculations. In order to calculate your royalty, first you need to figure out the author's cost of the book. The author's cost is how much it costs the author to buy the book directly from the publisher. Unless you have a lengthy book and choose a color interior, the author's cost is actually quite affordable (these are US rates):

$ A black-and-white book costs $2.15 plus 1.2 cents per page over 108 pages.
$ A color book costs $3.65 plus 7 cents per page over 40 pages.

Note that if you have an odd number of pages, you have to add 1 page to your page count (since there are two sides to every sheet of paper).

Here is an example: Suppose that you have a 200-page black-and-white book. The author's cost is $3.25. The breakdown is as follows. Subtract 108 from 200 to find that it is 92 pages over. Multiply 92 by $0.012 (that's 1.2 cents expressed in terms of dollars) to get $1.10. Add this to $2.15 to get the author's cost of $3.25.

If you want to skip the math, don't worry – you can. KDP has a calculator on their website that will figure the author's cost for you. After logging in to KDP, click Help, click Royalties Overview under Royalties & Payments, choose Paperback Royalty, select How We Calculate Paperback Royalties, and find the Royalty Calculator button at the right. The 'per book' cost is the author's cost.[33]

Let us first discuss the royalty calculation for books sold directly by Amazon.[34] When a customer buys your book directly from Amazon, KDP pays you 60% of the list price minus the

[33] You don't get a discount by buying in bulk. Rather, since the cost is quite cheap, they don't charge us more when we buy a small quantity. However, you do save on shipping if you purchase multiple books.

[34] If a used or new book sells from a third-party seller at Amazon, you earn no royalty. However, if you use the Expanded Distribution, there will be some sellers offering copies of your book (usually new, but sometimes they call it used) who purchase their wholesale copies from KDP. If this happens, you will earn royalties from the Expanded Distribution channel when they purchase your book wholesale. For reasons that I will explain in Sec. 4.1.7, there are some incentives for customers to buy your book directly from Amazon – instead of buying new or used copies (whether they are from customers reselling their copies or Expanded Distribution sellers).

author's cost of your book. For example, if the author's cost of the book is $3.25 and the list price is $9.99, the royalty will be $2.74 per book. To figure this out, multiply the list price by 60% as follows: $9.99 x 60% = $5.99. Then subtract the author's cost: $5.99 – $3.25 = $2.74.

You can download a royalty calculator from KDP's website. After logging in to KDP, click Help, click Royalties Overview under Royalties & Payments, choose Paperback Royalty, select How We Calculate Paperback Royalties, and find the Royalty Calculator button at the right. You will also be able to play with the list price and royalty calculation when you enter the list price for your book during the publishing process (see Sec. 4.1.9).

You make a different royalty if you sell books through distribution channels other than Amazon. In addition to selling books on Amazon, you can sell books directly through Amazon Europe (and Japan and other countries) and through the Expanded Distribution channel (if you check this box when you publish). You can use KDP's royalty calculator to see what royalty you will draw in each of these distribution channels; you will also have the opportunity to play with the numbers (i.e. type in different list prices and see what the royalties will be) when you go through the process of publishing your book.

The royalty rates for Amazon.com sales and Expanded Distribution sales are summarized in the table below. (Prior to the merger between CreateSpace and KDP, CreateSpace had an eStore, which is no longer available. Few authors sold copies through the CreateSpace eStore.)

Distribution Channel	Royalty
Amazon's Website	60% minus author cost
Expanded Distribution	40% minus author cost

For example, if you set your list price at $7.99 and the author's cost of your book is $2.51, your royalty would be $2.28 for sales at Amazon ($7.99 x 0.6 – $2.51) and 69 cents for Expanded Distribution sales ($7.99 x 0.4 – $2.51). Note that the Expanded Distribution channel is optional: When you publish, there is an optional checkbox that you can mark to include this channel. All of the sales channels are free, including the Expanded Distribution channel (see Sec. 4.1.7). (Expanded Distribution used to cost $25, but now it's free.)

The royalty is also 60% minus the author cost for sales through Amazon UK and Amazon Europe. The difference is that sales through Amazon's UK and other European websites (including France, Germany, Spain, and Italy) have a different author cost and may also have a different list price.

When you select distribution options for Amazon UK and continental Europe, books purchased through Amazon UK and Amazon's other European website are manufactured in Great Britain or continental Europe. This way, European customers can purchase your book without having to pay an outrageous shipping charge to send the book from the US to Europe.

The list price for books sold through Amazon UK is set in pounds (£); this is called Great Britain pricing (GBP). The author's cost and royalty are also figured in pounds. The author's cost for GBP is £0.70 plus £0.01 per page for black-and-white books and £0.70 plus £0.045 per page for color (unless the book has fewer than 110 pages for black-and-white or 42 pages for color, in which case the fixed cost is £1.70 or £2.05.) For example, a black-and-white book with 150 pages has an author's cost of £2.20 in GBP (£0.70 + £0.01 x 150).

The list price for books sold through Amazon's continental Europe (EUR) websites is set in euro (€). The author's cost and royalty are also figured in euro. The author's cost for EUR pricing is €0.60 plus €0.012 per page for black-and-white books over 108 pages and €0.60 plus €0.06 per page for color books over 40 pages (otherwise, it's €1.90 or €2.40). For example, a black-and-white book with 150 pages has an author's cost of €2.40 in EUR pricing (€0.60 + €0.012 x 150).

To figure your royalty for GBP and EUR sales, multiply your list price by 60% and subtract the author's cost of your book. For example, if your book has list prices of £5.50 and €6.82 and author's costs of £2.20 and €2.40, respectively, your GBP and EUR royalties will be £1.10 (0.6 x £5.50 − £2.20) and €1.69 (0.6 x €6.82 − €2.40). Of course, you may choose to have these royalties deposited into a US bank account in US dollars (but if you prefer to be paid in pounds or euro and have it deposited in Europe, that's possible, too).

4.1.5 Setting the List Price and Royalty for Your Book

When you self-publish a book, you control the list price. Since your royalty depends on the list price, you control how much royalty you make for each book that you sell. It's not the royalty that you make per book that matters, though: If you're trying to maximize your income, it's how much royalty you draw overall that counts. For example, if you could sell many more books by dropping your price a little, you might make more royalty overall. However, book sales do not always increase when the price is dropped. You want to choose a lower list price if it means more royalty overall, but you don't want to lower your price when it won't improve sales enough to increase your overall revenues. It's a challenge to set the perfect price. In this section, we will describe a few different methods for setting the list price of your paperback book, and explore a variety of factors that you may want to consider when you set the list price for your book.

The standard royalty for a traditionally published book is 15%. For comparison, you should see what list price would give you the standard 15%. I'm not saying that you should use 15% to determine your royalty. Rather, a self-published book should probably draw a greater royalty than 15%. For one, there is no guarantee that you will sell a large number of copies, so you want to ensure a fair royalty on those that you do sell. A second reason is that you're doing your own editing and publishing services: You're not just being paid as the author, but as the editor and publisher, too. Hence, you should make more than just the author's standard share. Nonetheless, it's a useful starting point to see what list price would give you a 15% royalty, and then you can go from there.

The formula for making your KDP royalty for Amazon sales equal to 15% is:

$$\text{list price} = \text{author's cost} \times 20 \div 9$$

For example, if the author's cost of your book is $2.38, a list price of $5.29 would give you a 15% royalty for sales at Amazon (since $2.38 x 20 ÷ 9 = $5.29). Your royalty would be 79 cents per book – that's 15% (since $5.29 x 0.15 = $0.79). You should calculate what the 15% royalty list price is for your book, just for your reference. (First, you will need to calculate the author's cost of your book, as described in Sec. 4.1.4. Remember, you may use KDP's royalty calculator. To check that the royalty is indeed 15% – multiply the list price times 0.15 to check.) In general, I recommend earning a royalty that is much **higher** than 15%. This was just a starting point.

One problem with a royalty of 15% through Amazon sales is that you probably won't make any royalty (or significant royalty) through Expanded Distribution sales (this sales channel is now free). While the royalty for Amazon sales is 60% of the list price minus the author's cost, the Expanded Distribution royalty is 40% of the list price minus the author's cost. In the previous example, with a list price of $5.29, if you calculate 40% of the list price, you get $2.11 (that's 0.40 x $5.29) – there's nothing left when you subtract the author's cost of $2.38. Therefore, the list price would need to be higher in order to offer books through the Expanded Distribution channel.

As I already mentioned, it is reasonable to draw a royalty of greater than 15% for a self-published book, since you're doing more than just writing the book – you're editing it, formatting it, publishing it, designing your own cover, etc.[35] Therefore, it may be more reasonable to make your Expanded Distribution royalty (instead of your Amazon royalty) equal to 15% of your list price. Let's see what this comes out to. The formula for setting the list price so that the Expanded Distribution royalty will be 15% is:

$$\text{list price} = \text{author's cost} \times 4$$

For example, if the author's cost of your book is $2.38, a list price of $9.52 would give you a 15% royalty for Expanded Distribution sales (since $2.38 x 4 = $9.52). Your royalty would be $1.43 cents per book sold through the Expanded Distribution channel – that's 15% (since $9.52 x 0.15 = $1.43). In this case, your Amazon royalty would be $3.33 (that's $9.52 x 0.6 – $2.38), which is 35% for Amazon sales. You should apply the above formula to your book for your reference, and also figure out what the royalty would be for both Amazon sales and Expanded Distribution sales.

Setting your royalty to make 15% on Expanded Distribution sales is not necessarily the best list price for your book. We will now consider a variety of factors that may influence what list price you set:

---

[35] If you invest money in any of these services, you also want to recoup some of your start-up funds.

$ Check out the competition. Search for other books that are similar to yours to see what the going rate is. Potential buyers will be comparing book prices when they shop. If your book is way overpriced, they may prefer a more economically priced title. On the other hand, if your book significantly cheaper, they might assume (perhaps incorrectly) that your book is shorter, less detailed, or lesser quality – i.e. they might believe that "you get what you pay for." If you just blindly price your book for a 15% or 35% royalty, for example, you may lose sales if it turns out that your book is not competitively priced.

$ Pay attention to details when you price the competition. For example, paperback books generally cost less than hardcover books. Your book will be softcover[36] if you publish with KDP, so you should base your price on paperback editions. Look at how much material you get for your money: A book might be cheap if it has little content, and it might be more expensive if it is very long. Other details that you should consider include whether the book is in color or black-and-white, whether it has several quality illustrations, and special qualifications of the author. A book with unique features might earn a higher price. Is there anything special about your book that would drive buyers to spend a little more?

$ Keep in mind that your book is self-published. If buyers will be comparing your title to traditionally published books – especially, if the other titles include bestselling authors or major publishing houses – consider how the price of your title might influence a potential customer's purchasing decision when your book appears alongside these other titles in their Amazon search results. You can take this two ways, though, so it's not entirely clear cut: You might think that your list price should be a little less to entice readers your way, or you might think that you need to draw a higher royalty if your expectation is that you're not going to sell as many books.

$ Who is your primary audience? If you're hoping for most of your business to come from new customers who happen to find your book in Amazon search results, you may want your book to sell for a little less than traditionally published titles that are similar to yours. However, if you're planning to drive many of your sales through marketing (or sell books in person, after a seminar, or from your own website, for example), then your price can be somewhat higher (and help you recover any marketing expenses, too).

$ There are occasionally special offers. For example, years ago books priced $9.99 or less were eligible for Amazon's 4-for-3 program (where customers could by 4 books for the price of 3). The 4-for-3 program was apparently discontinued in February of 2013. Browse books to see if there may be any special offers going on at Amazon.[37]

---

[36] If you're interested in a hardcover option, see Sec. 4.1.9.

[37] It's possible that the 4-for-3 program will return someday. It wouldn't hurt to check.

$ Another very important number to have in mind is $35. When a purchase (of eligible items) totals $35 or more, Amazon buyers can choose free shipping (called FREE Super Saver Shipping). If you were planning to set a list price in the mid-twenties, you may want to set the list price high enough for Amazon customers to receive free shipping.[38] Similarly, if you are planning to have a two-volume set, if the list price of each volume is high enough for the pair to total $35 or more, customers will be able to purchase the pair with free shipping.[39] If there are any Special Offers available, customers can take advantage of those and also receive free shipping if the total comes to at least $35.[40] If you have a series of books that you were planning to price at $7.99 each, if instead you price them at $8.99 each customers will be able to buy 4 and qualify for free shipping (without having to hunt for a cheap fifth book). But $35 is *irrelevant* for *Prime* shoppers.

$ You should consider FREE Super Save Shipping even if you only plan to publish a single book and your price will be well below the $35 threshold: Explore which books customers are likely to buy in addition to yours. You want typical combinations to come out just over $35 rather than just under $35. Books do tend to sell in combinations at Amazon: After a few customers buy the same combination of books, when a future customer buys one book, Amazon has many marketing tools that help to promote the sale of other books in the combination (such as notes that other customers who bought this book also bought these other books). Again, $35 is *irrelevant* for *Prime* shoppers.

$ The list price is not the same as the selling price. Amazon (and other booksellers, if you opt for Expanded Distribution) may choose to sell your book at a discount from the list price. If so, you still receive royalties based on the list price, not the actual selling price. A book with a higher list price is more likely to be on sale compared to the list price than a book with a lower list price. If you were thinking of selling your book for $15 to $18, for example, it's possible that if you go with $18, it will wind up being on sale. There is no guarantee that a book of any list price will be discounted, and is totally at the discretion of Amazon (or other bookseller); you have no say in this.

$ Contrary to common economic intuition, a lower list price does <u>not</u> always produce more sales. Why not? Some customers believe "you get what you pay for." Some have bought cheap books and found them to be shorter than they were expecting, lesser quality than they were hoping, or were otherwise dissatisfied. There may also be a critical price where the book is already such a good value that dropping the price won't make any difference. Thus, a lower price won't guarantee improved sales.

---

[38] However, you must also consider the possibility that Amazon may offer customers a discount, placing your book on sale for a price less than your list price.

[39] Again, if you price each volume at $18.50 and Amazon places either volume on sale, the customers won't qualify for free shipping – so you might allow a little room for a possible discount.

[40] When the 4-for-3 program was available, customers could qualify for free shipping if all four books added up to $25 (this is now $35), even if the total was less than $25 after removing the cost of the free book.

$ On the other hand, sometimes a lower price will drive many more sales. This is especially true when many customers perceive a book to be noticeably overpriced. If a book is significantly more expensive than similar titles, a few customers may buy it with the "you get what you pay for" mentality, but many customers may also feel more comfortable going with the lesser risk of the average price range. If a lower price affects FREE Super Saver Shipping, that may also play a significant role in how frequently the book sells.

$ Who is your audience? If many of the potential customers looking for books similar to yours tend to like good deals, then a lower price is more likely to drive more sales. If you're writing a nonfiction book about saving money or finding great bargains, for example, then your book *should* be economically priced. At the other extreme, customers tend to spend more money on technical textbooks and luxury books.

$ The effect of price is not easy to predict. A lower price provides a better deal. In some cases, the deal attracts more customers and pays off; in other cases, the lower price may actually hurt sales. A higher price sometimes suggests that a book is more serious, more detailed, or otherwise better; other times, a higher price deters sales.

$ You do have the option of changing your price if you want to experiment and see how price impacts sales. If you do this, it may be better to err on the high side to begin with and try lowering your price; if instead you raise your price, it may deter any customers who have observed the price hike.

$ Don't focus solely on how price will affect whether a potential customer will purchase your book: You must also consider how the customer will <u>feel</u> about the book's value <u>after</u> buying and reading your book. If a customer purchases your book, but later feels that it wasn't a good value, this increases your chance of receiving a negative review. When a customer opts for a more expensive book – thinking that "you get what you pay for" – the customer also has increased expectations. If you do price your book higher, you definitely want your readers to be satisfied with the value of their purchase.

$ Maybe royalty isn't your main concern. If you're more interested in selling as many books as possible (even if it means drawing less royalty income overall), or if a very affordable price is more important to you than your book revenues, then you might set your list price somewhat differently than an author who is mainly trying to maximize his or her overall royalties. This might be the case, for example, if you have written a book that attempts to spread awareness of a disease and how to prevent it.

$ You can't offer a list price that would make your royalty negative, so the absolute minimum list price is the list price for which your royalty would be zero. If you want to offer books for sale through the Expanded Distribution channel, your list price must also be high enough that the Expanded Distribution royalty is above zero. (You will be able to check these royalties when you go through the actual publishing process.)

$ You will probably have third-party sellers offering new and/or used copies of your book for sale at Amazon and other online booksellers. Some of these will be sellers who purchase your books through the Expanded Distribution channel, if you select it. Others will be customers who are reselling their used copies. If you choose a high list price (say, $15 or more), it's more likely for new or used books to sell for a healthy discount compared to Amazon's selling price, which will increase the temptation for potential customers to buy from a third-party. If you choose a low list price (say, under $10), third-party books will probably not seem as tempting – especially, if customers may buy enough books to qualify for FREE Super Saver Shipping.

$ Most list prices end with .99 or .95. Retailers have been doing this for ages: When buyers see a price of $7.99, they sometimes focus on the 7 – not seeing it as $8. For example, if you were planning to sell your book for $13, consider selling it for $12.99 instead. The reason is not to 'trick' your readers. Rather, the .99 and .95 ending is so common that your book might seem more professionally-priced if you have the common ending. If you strongly dislike this common pricing scheme, though, feel free to make a statement and end your list price with .50, for example. In rare circumstances, you might even be able to make the price relate to the theme of your book: For example, imagine a list price of $13.13 for a book about superstitions or a list price of $7.77 for book about Las Vegas.

$ Basic economics[41] tells you that – assuming your main goal is to maximize your royalty income – the best price is a compromise between supply and demand. Basic economics also assumes that more people would buy your book at a lower price and fewer people would buy your book at a higher price – i.e. that the price will affect the demand. The latter is certainly true if you overprice your book: Try setting your list price at $500 and see how many copies you sell! There is also a psychological element involved: If the price is too cheap and customers don't recognize the value that they are getting (they recognize the great price, but wonder if it's because the product is cheap, too), they might choose to go with the middle price range instead. Since your book will be published on demand, you have virtually an infinite supply of books. So if you want to approach this from the perspective of economics, what you're really trying to gauge is the demand (and how it will be split between your book and similar titles). If you can create a higher demand through marketing, you can price your book higher; if there is little demand, it may take a lower price to attract customers.

---

[41] The entire subject of economics is based on maximizing your profits. Are people are more important than profits? Perhaps we should reinvent the subject of economics to maximize other things, like making the world (not just one individual's world) a better place. Just because you might make more money by charging a higher price doesn't mean that you *should* charge a higher price. However, I'm not trying to persuade you to make less royalty income than you can. I'm just trying to present a variety of perspectives to help you make an informed decision. The other side of this argument is that your hard work *deserves* every penny that you can earn.

$ Retailers often start out high and work their way down. There may be a high demand when a product is released to the market. Customers willing to spend more money buy products in this stage. As the price is gradually lowered, it becomes affordable to more customers. This strategy removes some of the guesswork from pricing the product. However, it can also create disgruntled customers (who might leave a negative review for a book) when they see it sell for less than they paid for it.

How did I set the price for this book? First, I searched for "self-publishing" and similar keywords on Amazon in Books. I ignored the eBooks when pricing the paperback. The first page of search results had paperback list prices ranging from $14.95 to $24.99. All of these list prices were discounted except for the $14.95 book. As I continued further into the search results, the first few cheaper self-publishing books that I came across (under $10) appeared to be shorter, less detailed works (or were much more focused – like how to publish an article rather than a book).

I observed that a list price between $15.99 and $19.99 would be competitive. Potential buyers might not take my book seriously if I made my list price well below $15.99, and I would probably lose many sales with a price of $20 or more. Also, a list price in the $15.99 to $19.99 range would increase the chances of having my book placed on sale at a discount. I feel that this book is highly detailed and quite comprehensive, focused on the information that many self-published authors would be looking for, and full of helpful ideas (these were my goals – you may judge the final product for yourself) – i.e. I didn't see a reason to set the list price below $15.99 based on content. Thus, I believed that this book would be a good value within the $15.99 to $19.99 price range.

Also, I felt that my book had a significant advantage over some of the competition. This book was clearly self-published (Amazon lists the publisher as CreateSpace Independent Publishing Platform) following its own instructions. What I was really amazed to see in my search results for self-published books was how many books about self-publishing were actually published by traditional publishers! If they know so much about self-publishing, why didn't they self-publish <u>their</u> own books about how to self-publish?[42] It seems reasonable to me that if you want to buy a book that will teach you how to self-publish, you ought to buy one from a self-published author who is successful enough at it to self-publish his/her own book. I knew that any potential buyer who checked out my book and clicked on my author profile would see that I have actually self-published dozens of books. I felt that this qualification – which helps set my book apart – could either merit a higher list price, or could make a list price of $15.99 or so seem like a better value.

---

[42] Mine is not the only self-published book about self-publishing that you can find in paperback. My point is that too many of the books on the subject of how to self-publish – and especially the top search results at the time – were not actually themselves self-published.

Secondly, my book on self-publishing describes both paperback publishing and eBook publishing, whereas most self-publishing books either do one of two things: (1) Focus on just one publishing platform, like paperback or Kindle (but not both in detail); or (2) describe self-publishing in general terms (but not go into great detail for many of them). I want you to have an excellent paperback book and a well-formatted eBook, too, and so I have attempted to provide in-depth coverage for both formats. While I do mostly have KDP in mind, much of the content is also relevant for Nook, the Sony Reader, and other publishers; and later in this chapter I will lay down the details of how to self-publish an eBook with a variety of eReaders. This also helps my book on self-publishing stand out.

I therefore had a couple of compelling (or so I believed) reasons to put my list price at the higher end of the $15.99 to $19.99 bracket. I was planning to sell the paperback edition of this self-publishing book with a list price of $15.99, but as you can plainly see, I instead chose to set the list price of this paperback book at $9.99. I hope you appreciate the savings. ☺

Why did I set the list price at $9.99 instead of $15.99? Here are the reasons for my decision:

$ When I first published this book, Amazon's 4-for-3 program was still in effect. When the program was available, it was a great incentive for authors and publishers to price their books $9.99 or less. Although the 4-for-3 program was apparently discontinued in February of 2013, I opted to keep the original price. Personally, I'm very reluctant to raise prices (I'm sure you don't mind that I didn't). ☺

$ My audience mainly consists of aspiring self-published authors. Throughout this book, I've been advising you to keep your publishing investment to a minimum: Setting the list price at $9.99 instead of $15.99 helps you do this. $9.99 is my rock-bottom price – I only make about 50 cents when it sells through the Expanded Distribution, since this book has over 200 pages.

$ Almost all of my books are priced between $6.99 and $9.99. This price range has worked well for many of my other books. Once you find something that seems to work for you, it's hard to make yourself try something different. The only books that I have with a list price over $9.99 are technical physics books that have so many pages (like 500 pages) that I couldn't set the list price under $10 and still be eligible for the Expanded Distribution. If this book had another dozen pages or so, I wouldn't have been able to set the list price at $9.99.

I took a risk pricing this book at $9.99. Customers who see that my book is $5 below the typical price range of similar books might not see this as great savings – unfortunately, they might wonder what this book is lacking. I hope that you find that it's not lacking content or quality compared to similar titles – and even if the quality isn't lacking, potential customers won't know this (unless I'm so lucky to be blessed with reviews that say so).

I highly recommend that you conduct a survey among family members, friends, and acquaintances. They will help to give you some idea of what the book is worth. Your closest friends and family members may overprice your book: Your book and effort is likely to be worth much more to them than to a complete stranger. After they price your book, if you wind up selling it for less than they suggest, be sure to hit them up for a purchase: Tell them, "Look, I priced it less than you thought it was worth – so you have to buy one now." ☺ Be sure to say it with a smile!

Thinking about lowering your price? Consider this: For every $1.00 that you lower your price, you lose 60 cents from your royalty. In order for the price drop to increase your overall royalty income, you must not only sell more books, but the additional sales must be enough to compensate for the 60 cents per book that you are losing from your royalty.

Here is an example: Suppose that your book is priced at $9.99, your royalty is $3.00, and you presently sell an average of 30 copies per month. You're making an average of $90 per month presently. If you reduce your list price to $8.99, your new royalty will be $2.40. In order to still make $90 per month now, you must sell at least 38 books per month. In this example, you would have to sell at least 8 more books every month just to show a slight improvement in your monthly royalty income. The question that you have to ask yourself is this: Do you have reason to believe that 38 people were on the verge of buying your book last month, but 8 of them decided not to buy it because the price was $9.99 instead of $8.99? This is probably unlikely, in this example, unless there is a compelling reason – such as similar titles selling for $9.50, so now your book is 50 cents less instead of 50 cents more.

What if you dropped the price down to $7.99? Now your royalty would be $1.80 and you would need to sell 50 books per month just to make the same royalty – that's an extra 20 books per month. If you drop the price down to $6.99, your royalty would be $1.20 and you would need to sell 75 books per month. How about $5.99 – that's a bargain compared to $9.99, right? Well, you would make 60 cents per book, so you would have to sell 150 books at $5.99 just to make the same monthly royalty as you would with a $9.99 list price.

The point of my example is this: If sales aren't what you expect, dropping the price is not necessarily the answer. For one, you might not even increase your sales with a lower price (it happens). Even if you do sell more books by dropping your price, you have to sell many more books for the lower price to improve your monthly royalties.

However, lowering the price is sometimes the answer. It's important to price-match similar titles. If customers can find a book equivalent to yours for a lower price, then price may be more of a factor. However, if you are regularly selling copies every month, then price is probably not deterring customers from buying your book. On the other hand, if your sales are really slow and there are other equally visible similar titles selling for less, which also have frequent sales (as judged by watching the sales rank) – it could be that price is the hurdle (but there are other factors, too, including reviews, quality of the writing, quantity of content, publishing brand, appeal of the cover and description, better marketing strategy, etc.).

If price makes a significant difference for any Special Offers or eligibility for FREE Super Saver Shipping, then price may be more important. For example, when the 4-for-3 program was available, if your book was priced at $10.99, reducing the price to $9.99 *could* (but there are never any guarantees with sales) have made a significant difference. If there are currently any Special Offers like the 4-for-3 program, consider whether or not a small price change might significantly impact sales.

In general, unless the list price is quite low or quite high compared to the typical price range of similar titles – and unless the list price is on the verge of affecting eligibility for Special Offers – if you're not satisfied with your sales, it's probably not because of your book's list price. The best thing that you can do to impact sales is not changing the price, but developing effective marketing strategies and actively marketing your book (see Chapter 8).

I'm not trying to advise against giving customers a low price. I'm in favor good deals and savings, and most of my titles reflect this in the price. Rather, I'm trying to make two main points about low prices: (1) A lower price might not bring in more royalties, and (2) if you're not happy with your sales, lowering the price might not solve your problem. A lower price has its own advantages, even in the case where a lower price doesn't bring in as much monthly royalty. For one, the reader who purchases your book and recognizes that it's a great value will be happy to have found a good bargain. If it gets advertised that your book is a great value (that's a big 'if' – just because you feel that the list price is low doesn't mean that most customers will feel that your book is a good value) – as advertised by word-of-mouth or book reviews – this could have a significant impact on sales.

If you elect to sell your book at Amazon's European websites, you will also need to establish a good list price for your book in pounds (£) and euro (€). The same principles apply, but there are a few notable differences. For one, your author's cost in pounds and euro might be different from your author's cost in US dollars after conversions. You can calculate the cost of your book in each currency as described in Sec. 4.1.4, then look online for currency conversions to see if your book effectively costs you more or less in Great Britain and continental Europe. If so, you may want to take this into account when you set your list price. Another difference is that you may have a much greater demand in the US than you will have in Europe. This also may affect your choice of list price.

It would be wise to explore the list prices of similar titles in the UK. To do this, go to Amazon's homepage, scroll down to the bottom, and click on United Kingdom under the Amazon logo. Search Amazon's UK website the same way that you would search their US website – just type your keywords into the search field. You can similarly visit Amazon's websites in France, Spain, Italy, and German, but you'll encounter a significant difference: These websites are not in English. If you speak French, Spanish, Italian, or German, then it will be easier for you explore similar titles on one or more of those websites. If not, maybe you have a friend who speaks one of those languages. You can even find translation services on the web (including some that are free) to help you do searches on the European websites.

There is also a very easy way to set the list price for your book in GBP and EUR pricing: When you publish your book with KDP, it will automatically suggest a GBP or EUR price based on the US price. This suggested price is based on the average exchange rates over the past week. Although the exchange rate will fluctuate over the course of time, your list price will not change unless you manually go into your account and update the list price. Also, note that the suggested list price does not give you the equivalent US royalty.

4.1.6 Deciding on Your ISBN Option

If you self-publish with KDP, you have two different ISBN options. Even if you publish your book elsewhere, you can still choose the second option, which we will discuss last.

The first option is free: You can choose to have an ISBN assigned by KDP. When you choose the free ISBN option, on your book's Amazon detail page the words "Independently Published" will appear where Amazon ordinarily lists the name of the publisher. (It used to say "CreateSpace Independent Publishing Platform[43]" before CreateSpace merged with KDP.) It will probably also show "Independently Published" for other online retailers (like BN.com) if you enable the Expanded Distribution channel.

There are advantages and disadvantages of the free ISBN option. Obviously, you save money because it's free. A second advantage is that your book will also be eligible to be distributed directly to libraries and academic institutions if you select the Expanded Distribution option.[44] This is only an advantage if you choose the Expanded Distribution channel and if you expect to sell a significant number of books to libraries and schools through this channel. If you choose a different ISBN option, you may still be able to distribute your book to libraries – just not through the same channel. See Sec. 4.1.7 regarding this possibility.

Note that the free ISBN assigned by KDP can only be used with KDP (you can't use the same ISBN with another POD service like Ingram Spark) and only applies to the paperback edition (the ISBN for the paperback edition doesn't apply to eBooks or hardcover editions).

The main advantage of spending money on the ISBN option is that you can choose your own imprint. This way, an imprint of your own choosing will show up for the publisher's name instead of "Independently Published." If you don't want it to be obvious that your book was self-published, for example, you could invest a little money with the second ISBN option and choose your own imprint. If you plan to publish a series of books, it may have a more professional appearance if you add your own imprint (and design your own logo for your book cover and copyright page). Do some research before choosing an imprint name to be sure that you're not copying an imprint name that might be already used or even trade-marked: If your

---

[43] Some of the online retailers through the Expanded Distribution channel listed the publisher as CreateSpace instead of CreateSpace Independent Publishing Platform.

[44] As we will see in Sec. 4.1.7, the Expanded Distribution option is now free (it used to cost $25).

imprint is similar to an imprint already used by a major publishing house, for example, you could get sued over it.

Personally, I'm proud to be a self-published author. I'm grateful for the self-publishing opportunities that Amazon has provided, and I'm pleased with my experience with KDP. I have chosen the free ISBN option for many of my books. I happily wear the badge that identifies my book as having been self-published through KDP (and previously CreateSpace). The more quality books that are easily identified as self-published books, the better will be the image of the self-published author, which will help to promote sales of self-published books. Also, there are hundreds of thousands of self-published authors, and many self-published authors support other self-published authors when they make their purchases. The self-published tag can work both ways: While it may deter some readers, it might attract others who support the concept. The genre of your work and the audience for your book may be significant factors, too, since self-publishing is viewed in a different light by different people. You have to decide for yourself which is better for your book. Choose carefully: Once you select your ISBN option, you're stuck with it for that title.

The second option is available no matter how you publish your book: You can purchase your own ISBN directly from Bowker at www.myidentifiers.com. It costs $125 (presently) to purchase an ISBN for a single book, and they entice you into buying ISBN's in bulk by offering multi-ISBN discounts. For example, you could spend $250 for 10 ISBN's instead of $125 for one. If you would like to use an ISBN for the eBook version of your book (optional), you will need a different ISBN for the eBook edition. Similarly, if you revise your book to make a second edition, offer a hardbound edition, or make a large print or any other edition of the same book, you will also need a new ISBN for each edition. If you decide to buy your ISBN's directly from Bowker, you should purchase at least 10 ISBN's unless you're 100% positive that you will only have one edition of your book (not even both paperback and eBook). Note that the information in this paragraph is specifically for residents of the United States.

(In the early days of CreateSpace, there used to be four ISBN options. They used to have an option to invest $10 for a custom ISBN. It would let you choose your own imprint name without having to go to Bowker. However, this option was discontinued a couple of years prior to the merger with KDP. CreateSpace also used to offer a $99 custom universal ISBN. The idea behind the custom universal ISBN is that it was portable: If you changed your mind, you could unpublish your book with CreateSpace and republish it elsewhere using the same ISBN. Note that the free option isn't portable: When you use KDP's free ISBN, you're not allowed to use the same ISBN with any other publishing services.)

If you plan to publish several titles of your own, or if you plan to start your own publishing company, purchasing ISBN's directly from Bowker may be the way to go. Note that if you have a previously published book and now want to republish it and you have the necessary rights to do this and use your old ISBN, then your title, author, and binding type (paperback) must match exactly this information as it is already listed with Bokwer.

Regardless of whether you choose KDP's free ISBN or you buy your ISBN directly through Bowker, your title will be registered with the Books in Print database, which lists the title and author information for all books that have ISBN's.

If you purchase an ISBN from Bowker, note that you do <u>not</u> need to purchase a barcode if you are publishing with KDP: KDP will automatically place an ISBN bar code on your back cover (as described in Sec. 3.1.5). On the other hand, if you have your own barcode, you're not required to use KDP's barcode. Also note that you can't change the title, author name, or type of binding after you purchase your ISBN from Bowker and list this information with them.

4.1.7 Online Booksellers, Libraries, European Sales, and Expanded Distribution Options

In this section, we will first discuss how your book can potentially be distributed to online booksellers, libraries, schools, and even physical bookstores with KDP's Expanded Distribution option. We will then describe Great Britain and continental Europe distribution channels through KDP. The remainder of this section applies even if you don't choose to publish with KDP: We will explore possible direct distribution of your books to libraries and physical bookstores – this second time, we will discuss how you might accomplish this without using the Expanded Distribution option.

If you decide to select the Expanded Distribution channel for a book that you publish with KDP, you may do so for free (it used to cost $25). The Expanded Distribution opens up several avenues for selling your book other than direct sales at Amazon, including many other book-sellers, libraries, and schools. However, you draw a greater royalty from Amazon sales and a lesser royalty from Expanded Distribution sales:

$$\text{Expanded Distribution royalty} = \text{Amazon royalty} - 20\% \text{ of your list price}$$

For example, if your list price is $8.99 and your Amazon royalty is $3.03, your Expanded Distribution royalty will be $1.23 (that's $3.03 − 0.2 x $8.99). See Sec.'s 4.1.4-5 for more details about the royalty calculation.

Note that there are some eligibility requirements for the expanded distribution:
- ✓ Your book will <u>only</u> be eligible for distribution to libraries and academic institutions through the Expanded Distribution if you use a free ISBN assigned by KDP (see Sec. 4.1.6). If you purchase your own ISBN through Bowker, for example, you <u>won't</u> be able to select this Expanded Distribution channel (but they can still order through Ingram).
- ✓ Your book will <u>only</u> be eligible for distribution to bookstores and online retailers if you use an industry-standard trim size (see Sec. 2.1.4). If you use a custom trim size, you <u>won't</u> be able to select this Expanded Distribution channel.

Since you make a greater royalty from Amazon sales than from Expanded Distribution sales, you may be wondering if it is actually worth the opportunity to make less royalty through other channels. If your book is only available for sale directly through Amazon, for example, then customers won't be able to buy your book through some channel that pays you less money. However, the Expanded Distribution does have some benefits that may make the investment worthwhile:

➤ Your book will be included in major catalogs – including Ingram and NACSCORP – available to bookstores and online retailers. Most bookstores and online booksellers – including Barnes & Noble – purchase their books from the catalogs of these major distributors. If a potential buyer who has heard of your book walks into Barnes & Noble, for example, he/she won't be able to order your book from them unless they find it in such a catalog listing.

➤ A variety of online booksellers – such as Barnes & Noble – will probably (there is no guarantee) create a listing for your book on their website. If you search for my name at Barnes & Noble's and Books-A-Million's websites, for example, you will find my books there – available directly from these booksellers, and listed as 'in stock.' I know that some of my books sell this way because many of my books have a sales rank at Barnes & Noble's website.

➤ Third-party sellers will probably list new and/or 'like new' copies of your book for sale at Amazon (in addition to any customers who may choose to resell or trade-in their used copies). They 'purchase' their books wholesale through the Expanded Distribution channel, and offer them for sale on Amazon. Actually, they probably will not buy your book in advance: Since your book is a print-on-demand title, they may only purchase your title if it sells – at which point it will be printed (not necessarily at KDP – it could be a third-party printing service) and shipped. These third-party sellers lend credibility to your book: It looks like a popular, professional book when there are several retailers offering it for sale at Amazon. These third-party sellers probably help sales overall rather than cut into your royalties, as we will discuss soon.

➤ The more ways that your book is available for sale, the greater the chances of customers discovering your book. Greater visibility helps sales across all channels. Every customer who buys and reads your book has the potential to share your book with family and friends – or even post a note about your book on FaceBook or Twitter.

➤ (Before the merger between CreateSpace and KDP, CreateSpace had a wholesale site called CreateSpace Direct. Certified wholesalers could purchase Expanded Distribution books directly from this site. There is no mention of a similar site for wholesalers in the KDP help pages. However, local booksellers, libraries, and retailers can still purchase your book through Ingram, and if you choose KDP's free ISBN libraries can also use Baker & Taylor. We really aren't losing anything by not having CreateSpace Direct, since most bookstores and libraries are far more likely to use Ingram anyway.)

➤ If your book has a free KDP-assigned ISBN (see Sec. 4.1.6), your book will be listed with Baker & Taylor. In this way, your book will be available to libraries and academic institutions. (If not, they can still order from the Ingram catalog.)

Updating your book is free. (There was originally supposed to be a $25 update fee with the Expanded Distribution channel before KDP merged with CreateSpace, but in practice this fee was never charged.) If you need to revise the interior or cover files for your book, this is free with KDP. (Note that some other print-on-demand publishers do charge an update fee.) Your updated files should take effect at Amazon immediately, though the Look Inside feature may take several days to update. (Tip: Include a brief alteration to your copyright page, like a version number and date, so that you can tell which version of your book shows in the Look Inside.) It may take 6 weeks or so for your changes to reach all of the Expanded Distribution partners. Note that third party sellers and prior customers may sell older versions of your book.

Let's return to a comment that I made about third-party sellers offering your book for sale on Amazon. First, Amazon is probably not the only place where third-party sellers may offer your book for sale – they may sell it from their own website, many other online booksellers (like Barnes & Noble or AbeBooks), European and other websites, or even their own physical bookstore (or other store that also sells books). If they purchase your book through the Expanded Distribution, you will earn royalties regardless of where or how they sell your book. So while you might draw less royalty when an Amazon customer buys your book from a third-party seller on Amazon than if the customer bought your book directly from Amazon, that same third-party seller (and several other booksellers that don't list titles on Amazon) may sell copies of your book a variety of other ways, too. Even if you don't select the Expanded Distribution option, there may still be third-party sellers offering your book for sale on Amazon – once a customer has finished reading your book, it may very well get resold on Amazon (by the customer, or buy a bookseller that received your customer's book by purchasing it a discount or through trade-in); in this case, you don't earn any royalty for the third-party sale. So no matter what, your book will probably be available for sale by other sellers.

Nevertheless, many customers will prefer to buy your book directly from Amazon instead of from third-party sellers. There are many incentives for customers to buy your book directly from Amazon, even if third-party sellers are selling new or like new copies of your book at a discounted price:

☺ Most customers trust Amazon more than the third-party sellers. Amazon does offer an A-to-Z guarantee, and allows sellers to choose Fulfillment by Amazon – both of which make buying used and new books from third-party sellers seem safer. Even so, most customers still prefer to buy their books directly from Amazon unless the savings is significant.

☺ Customers only earn FREE Super Save Shipping (or Prime shipping) when they purchase new books or books where the seller chooses Fulfillment by Amazon. Many customers spend $35 or more when they purchase books (or have Amazon Prime membership) in order to qualify for free shipping. If a customer buys a third-party book that is not fulfilled by Amazon, the shipping charge is $3.99. A cheaper third-party book doesn't look as attractive when you add a $3.99 shipping charge to the total.

☺ Third-party books often do not qualify for Special Offers. If there are any Special Offers available (such as credits for MP3 downloads or the 4-for-3 program), this may be a great incentive to buy directly from Amazon.

I have added Expanded Distribution to virtually all of my books, and in every case I am quite pleased with my decision. This maximizes the visibility of my books, and even makes my Amazon listings appear more serious through the presence of the third-party sellers. Expanded Distribution is the reason that my books are available on Barnes & Noble's website, and some of my books are purchased there – you can tell from the sales rank.

The direct effect of the Expanded Distribution may not be as much as you might hope. For example, for my top two selling titles in 2012, Expanded Distribution accounts for about 5-10% of the quantity of books sold and about 2-5% of the royalties. For one of my top five selling titles, Expanded Distribution accounts for 25% of the number of books sold and 12% of the royalties. Every title is different. I have some titles that rarely sell through the Expanded Distribution, and I also have one title where 35% of the number and 20% of the royalty comes through the Expanded Distribution. Titles that sell regularly on Amazon (i.e. at least once every few days) also tend to sell occasionally (though not as frequently) through the Expanded Distribution channel. If your book sells at least once every few days (hopefully better) on Amazon, it would probably draw some sales through the Expanded Distribution, too. Since Expanded Distribution is relatively new, it is still growing and will likely improve. In the past 10 years, there have been a few rare occasions with bulk orders (hundreds of copies of one title) through the Expanded Distribution. Although this is rare, it can happen.

As authors, we give up a substantial royalty (see Sec. 4.1.4) in order to sell our books through the Expanded Distribution channel (if we select this option) compared to direct sales on Amazon. We do this for the opportunity to sell some of our books through bookstores, libraries, schools, etc. We could sell a large number of books this way – hundreds, or even thousands – or we could sell 5% to 10% of our books this way. Like any investment, the best we can do is make an informed decision, but the outcome is not guaranteed. If you want bookstores and libraries to purchase your title – through the Expanded Distribution or via a more direct approach – you can improve the chances for this by targeting them in your marketing campaign. We will discuss how you might approach libraries and bookstores later in this section (while marketing strategies are described in Chapter 8).

Like KDP, Kindle, Nook, and the notion of print-on-demand publishing, the Expanded Distribution channel is still growing. There are more self-published authors every day, there are more eBooks available on Kindle, Nook, and other eReaders every day, the way that booksellers and libraries purchase their books is still evolving, there are more small publishers each year, and even traditional publishers are adapting to modern technology. So keep in mind that sales through the Expanded Distribution may improve.

Let me make one more point about the Expanded Distribution channel: Whereas Amazon royalties are reported when KDP manufactures your book, it may take a couple of months for a book sold through the Expanded Distribution to be included on your royalty report. So if you add the Expanded Distribution to your title, don't expect to see sales through this channel for a few months. Even then, the sales you are seeing through this channel have a lag of one to two months. If a bookseller does purchase several of your books, you may not even learn about it for a month or two. Thus, if you select the Expanded Distribution channel, you should prepare yourself to be patient as you monitor the progress of your Expanded Distribution sales.

Another way to improve the visibility of your book is to sell your book in Europe. You can do this by choosing the Amazon UK and Europe distribution channels. I highly recommend it, since this channel is <u>free</u>. When you select Amazon UK and Europe, your book will become available on Amazon's websites for the United Kingdom (amazon.uk), Spain (amazon.es), France (amazon.fr), Germany (amazon.de), and Italy (amazon.it). Not only that, but when your book is sold through these European websites, KDP will print your book in the UK or continental Europe. This allows European customers to purchase your book with free or discounted shipping, for example. This gives you an advantage over any books that are not in stock in Europe – customers won't have to pay international shipping and handling charges in order to purchase your book.[45]

There are very good prospects for selling your book in the United Kingdom (at amazon.co.uk), as English is the national language in England, Ireland, and Scotland – and since there are many common interests among the United States and the United Kingdom. For example, in the first few months since the Amazon Europe channel has been launched through KDP, Amazon UK accounts for 5% to 10% of my paperback sales for my top selling titles. I have a couple of titles where 20% of the sales come from Amazon UK, but also titles that sell much more rarely in the UK than in the US. The main factor is how relevant your book is in Europe. Also, if you can find ways to market your book to a European audience, that will help boost sales through Amazon Europe (Chapter 8 discusses marketing).

Another consideration is language. British English is similar to American English, but there is a different vocabulary and the grammar is not quite the same. For example, whereas we refer to the 'trunk' of a car, this is called a 'boot' in the UK. Spelling is a little different, too: For example, many words that end in -or in American English instead end in -our in British English, as in 'colour.'

---

[45] European customers will pay a value added tax (VAT), which varies from country to country. The VAT is 0% for books purchased in Great Britain, for example, and 7% in France and Germany. The VAT for Denmark is 25%. You can find a VAT chart at http://www.amazon.co.uk/gp/help/customer/display.html?nodeId=502578.

English is not the national language in continental Europe, which will make it tougher to sell books in Spain, France, Germany, and Italy. However, there is an audience for English books in continental Europe. For one, there are many Americans living in or visiting continental Europe. For another, many Europeans learn English as a foreign language (just as Spanish and French are foreign languages taught in the US). All of my books are written in English, but I do sell a few books to customers in continental Europe.

Amazon Europe was launched only a few months prior to the (original) publication of this book. It is still growing, and has much potential for significant sales – especially, in the United Kingdom. It also takes time for your book to develop associations with other titles in the UK.

Amazon also has websites in other countries, including Canada (amazon.ca) and Japan (amazon.co.jp). There is now distribution to Canada, Japan, and other countries. Distribution to other channels is currently growing (with Australia and Mexico on the near horizon). Some countries (like Canada) may pay the same royalty as for Amazon.com sales, but others may be part of the Expanded Distribution channel.

Before CreateSpace merged with KDP, there had been a CreateSpace eStore. The eStore is no longer available. However, in many ways this is an improvement:

- Very few authors succeeded in selling books through the CreateSpace eStore. Most self-published authors sell almost all of their paperbacks through Amazon.com.
- The CreateSpace eStore wasn't very customer friendly. It was very difficult for customers to search for books on the eStore, they had to setup a new account with CreateSpace, and they couldn't apply Prime shipping.
- Sales through Amazon.com help with sales rank and customers also bought lists.

The reality is that 99% of authors would sell more books by referring customers to Amazon than they would by directing customers to an eStore. It's still possible to sell books directly:[46] You don't need an eStore for that. You can create your own website or sell in person.[47]

We will now return our attention to libraries and bookstores – in particular, what more you can do besides simply purchase the Expanded Distribution option in KDP and hope for libraries and bookstores to find your title in a very extensive catalog.

Libraries search for books through the Library of Congress Database. The Library of Congress homepage can be found at http://www.loc.gov/index.html. All books listed in the Library of Congress database have a Library of Congress Control Number (LCCN). Thus, you must have an LCCN if you want your book to be included in this database. How do you get a LCCN for your self-published paperback. That's a good question.

Before CreateSpace merged with KDP, you could contact CreateSpace and ask them to apply for an LCCN on your behalf for $49. Note that the application fee did <u>not</u> guarantee that your book would be included in the database. Now that CreateSpace and KDP have merged,

---

[46] There are advantages to having customers purchase your book directly through Amazon instead of selling your book directly to the customers (like helping to populate customers also bought lists), as we will see in Chapter 6.
[47] To do this successfully requires marketing (the topic of Chapter 8).

will KDP apply for an LCCN on your behalf for $49? To find out, contact KDP support: Click the Help link at the top of the page, then scroll down and look on the left for a Contact Us button. If not, you may need to apply directly with the Library of Congress.

Unfortunately, the Library of Congress doesn't send out notices of rejection or acceptance. After applying for an LCCN, if you want to see if your book has been added to the database, you need to check the catalog (http://catalog.loc.gov/). Not all books may be eligible: For one, think about whether your title would be a good fit for a library (a workbook or puzzle book where the reader would ideally write in the book is not good for a library, for example). Remember, you can contact KDP support if you have questions that you would like to ask a KDP representative – such as inquiring for more details about the LCCN Assignment.

It's important to note that you **can't** add an LCCN **after** a book has been published. After you click the Publish button, your book is published and it's too late to add an LCCN. If you're republishing material that was previously published, it's also too late to add an LCCN.

Traditionally published books that have an LCCN list this number along with the bibliographic information on the copyright page (in addition to the title, author, publisher, copyright notice, publication date, ISBN,[48] etc.). If you obtain an LCCN, your book will probably look more professional if you also do this; you can find a variety of traditionally published books to help you get ideas for how to add this to your copyright page.

The LCCN comes in two different forms – Cataloging in Publication (CIP) and Preassigned Control Number (PCN). Basically, all print-on-demand (POD) books – that includes any book published with KDP – that are made available for libraries to purchase are assigned a PCN, whereas traditionally published books that are likely to be acquired by libraries are assigned a CIP. Unfortunately, this puts your print-on-demand paperback at a disadvantage when it comes to library purchases: The PCN (instead of a CIP) is a clear signal to the librarian that your book is printed on demand, and not traditionally published. Nonetheless, books with a CIP or PCN are included in the Library of Congress database and may be purchased by libraries. You can find more information about the CIP, PCN, and LCCN at http://booksandtales.com/pod/aloc.php or by using a search engine.

Whether you have a CIP or PCN, your book is just one fish in a vast ocean. So the fact that your POD book will have a PCN is not the real obstacle: Rather, if your goal is to get your book into libraries, you need to help librarians learn about your book. Librarians are familiar with specific titles and types of books that readers ask for when they speak with the librarians. When a book becomes popular through marketing (described in Chapter 8), sometimes several people go to the library to search for it. If you are highly effective at marketing, this is a possibility. Alternatively, you can visit libraries and show the librarian your book. Your local library may have an interest in having your book – especially, as many local people may know

---

[48] Don't confuse the ISBN with the LCCN. The ISBN is a book identifier that every book has; the LCCN is a different number used for library catalogs.

you and want to read your book. So the libraries in your city are the best places to start. Generally, librarians are friendly and very interested in getting people to read and helping them find what they want to read.

Libraries are more apt to purchase books that are likely to be read and of interest to local readers. It may help if you can make the case that your book fits this criteria. Useful data may help – such as a good sales rank, favorable reviews, or official book reviews.

Authors who draw a significant royalty from sales to libraries often get a corporation to purchase a large quantity of their books and donate them to libraries across the country. Every business has a portion of their budget allocated toward donations because there is a tax incentive for doing this. Many businesses already have their annual donations lined up, but some are flexible. You can search for business who may be willing to make donations online, but anyone else who found their information online will also be approaching them – and for many other causes besides donating books to libraries. You may have a better chance with local businesses. When you contact the business, ask for the opportunity to make a presentation. You want to outline the benefits of donating your books to libraries, keeping in mind the many other charitable causes that the business could otherwise support. If your book spreads awareness of a disease or if the intended audience largely includes very low income families, for example, this will help make your cause stronger. Think about whether or not there may be great value to the community in making it possible for thousands of people to read your book for free at libraries. Will your book improve literacy, help train people for a job, or spread cultural awareness, for example? Businesses understand selling points and value, so this is what they will be looking for. Also, remember that you can offer your book for a substantially discounted price: You can purchase your book at the author's cost directly from KDP and pass a portion of this savings onto the potential business investor (if so, highlight the savings that you are passing on in your presentation).

If you are successful in getting any libraries to buy a copy of your book – especially, your local library – encourage people to visit the library to read or check out your book. If your book just collects dust on a shelf and you write a second book, the library probably will not be interested in purchasing another dust collector; but if your book is frequently read, asked for, and checked out, the library is more likely to be interested in subsequent books that you write.

Finally, let's consider how you might get copies of your book in physical bookstores. If the only thing you do is opt for Expanded Distribution, your book will just be one of millions of books listed in a very extensive database. Bookstores will be happy to order your book for any customer who specifically asks for it, but isn't likely to spot your book in the database and order it to stock on their shelves. It's up to you to spread awareness of your book, market your book, and approach bookstores.

First approach small local bookstores and other small businesses that sell books (antique stores, for example). They like to support local talent, like to stock books that major book-stores (i.e. their competition) don't have on their shelves, and they know that local authors have relatives, friends, and acquaintances who live nearby and may very well come inside to purchase their books.

Next approach major bookstores in your city. You *might* have a positive experience with your effort, so it's worth trying – you won't know until you try. They might be happy to support a local author – again, they realize that a local author is likely to have a local following, and hence many potential customers. They might even offer you a chance to sit down for a couple of hours and sign copies of your book that customers purchase (if so, you really need to spread the word and get relatives, friends, and acquaintances to show up for your appearance). On the other side, the worst they can do is say, "No thank you," and it won't be the end of the world. They are more likely to direct you to a bureaucratic process for how to get our book considered for possible purchase than to tell you 'No.' If so, they might give you some useful advice – and it doesn't hurt to ask questions or ask for advice.

If you feel strongly that your book would be a great fit for a major bookstore chain to stock, you should browse their website. For example, you can find Barnes & Noble at www.barnesandnoble.com. Once there, find a link to Publisher & Author Guidelines at the bottom of the page. You'll see that Barnes & Noble orders books from publishing companies. If you use your own imprint (see Sec. 4.1.6), you are essentially your own publishing company, but you may also need to do more to be your own publishing business – like having a corresponding tax ID number (you can learn about starting a business and getting such a number in your state by searching online). In addition, the publishing company has to submit a catalog of books; you can see that a catalog with few entries or that features mainly or a few authors won't seem as serious as the extensive catalogs that traditional publishers will submit. There are also other requirements, like having the title and author printed on the spine and a cover price listed on the book that is the same as the published list price (and the published list price has to be the same for Barnes & Noble, Amazon, and everyone else). Also, as with libraries, the bookstore database may make a distinction between traditionally published books and print-on-demand books.

Barnes & Noble is likely to include your paperback book on their website if you simply opt for the Expanded Distribution with KDP, is likely to order your paperback book for any customer who walks into their store and asks for it (provided that they can find it in their catalog, which means that you need to select the Expanded Distribution), and allows authors to self-publish eBooks for Nook. However, getting your paperback book stocked in their bookstores will not be an easy prospect. There is no harm in trying, though. You might get some helpful advice by talking to employees or management at your nearest store. Remember, businesses do want to stock products that will sell well. If you're able to meet with a person with the authority to make or influence purchase decisions and, after showing that person your book, the person predicts that your book will be a hot seller – chances are, they will want to stock your book and find a way to get it done. If you're getting the runaround or not getting interest – and your book idea has been considered – it may be because they don't predict much success from stocking your book. If you get the opportunity to pitch your book, you need to demonstrate your own belief in your book; and it will help to have any supporting data and information – like your marketing plan, sales rank, and book reviews.

Barnes & Noble is not the only major bookstore. Not all bookstores have the same policies. Search for other bookstores and research their policies (start by visiting their websites). If you are determined to get your book onto some bookshelves, your motivation and perseverance are likely to make the difference.

If a bookstore does show interest in ordering your book, be prepared to help them find your title. You can tell them that your book is listed with Ingram and NACSCORP if you selected the Expanded Distribution or if you purchased your ISBN directly from Bowker. Most authors who succeed at getting local stores to stock their books approach the stores in person with a PR kit (after researching this) and sell author copies that they purchased directly from KDP (rather than referring stores to Ingram's catalog). The benefit of selling author copies is that the reduced cost of the author copy lets you offer a 40% discount (off the list price) to the store as an incentive for stocking your book.

If you are successful in getting any bookstores to stock your book, encourage customers to shop in those bookstores. If you write subsequent books, whether or not bookstores are willing to purchase your latest book to stock on their shelves will very much depend on how well or poorly your first book sold in their store.

4.1.8 How to Convert Your Interior and Cover Files to PDF

You will probably need to convert your interior and cover files to PDF format in order to publish your book. Why 'probably'? KDP now allows you to submit a Word document (with .doc or .docx extension) or rich text file (with .rtf extension) instead of a PDF for the interior file, if you prefer. Also, if you use KDP's free Cover Creator tool (Sec. 4.1.9), you won't need to submit a PDF file for your cover. So it's actually possible to avoid having to convert your files to PDF.

<u>However, formatting may change significantly if you upload a Word document.</u> Also, I recommend designing and making your own cover, as described in Chapter 3, instead of using the Cover Creator tool. This gives you the greatest flexibility in your cover design. If you make your own cover, you will need to convert the file to PDF format before you submit it.

The simplest way to convert a Word document to PDF format is to open the file in Microsoft Word, go to the File tab, choose Save As, change Save As Type to PDF, and select Standard (instead of Minimum). If the PDF for your cover doesn't look the same as your Word file, try selecting pictures and grouping them together (to learn how to select and group objects, in Sec. 3.1.8 find the third group of numbered steps and then find Step 7).

For most purposes, Word's built-in[49] PDF converter is satisfactory for converting Word documents to PDF format. However, if you have images, Word will reduce the DPI with the Save As feature, so a free converter is better. If you have a very richly formatted file that you had to split up into separate Word documents, you can combine all of the files together into a single PDF file using a more sophisticated PDF converter. If you have an advanced need for a PDF converter with more options – like being able to flatten figures (you may receive a note about this, which KDP may do for you, when you submit your PDF files) – there are a variety of PDF converters to choose from. You can find many free PDF converters online. Adobe has a wide range of PDF software programs, many of which are quite expensive; there are several less expensive alternatives, such as Nuance PDF Converter Professional.

If your PDF converter has the option to embed the fonts, select this option. (In Word, when you Save As, click Tools, then Save Options, and check the box to Embed Fonts In The File.) Also, if not using Word's built-in PDF converter, check to see if there is an option to flatten the figures – that way, they won't be manually flattened by the publisher.

I recommend that you perform your own PDF conversion (with Microsoft Word's Save As feature, at least) rather than submitting a Word document and having KDP convert the file to PDF for you. If instead you upload a Word document (or rich text file), beware that KDP's conversion to PDF may make changes to the layout of your document. For example, if you have floating pictures (i.e. not in line with the text), the pictures may move if you submit a Word document instead of submitting a PDF file.

4.1.9 How to Publish Your Paperback Book with KDP

If you're still undecided about whether or not to use KDP as your publishing service, consider contacting a representative. Before I self-published my first book, I contacted CreateSpace (this was years before CreateSpace merged with KDP). They answered my questions, were courteous and professional, and did <u>not</u> pressure me to get started. KDP has similarly been courteous and professional in my communications with them. If you already have an Amazon account, you don't actually need to sign up for a new account with KDP: Your Amazon account will work. However, if you prefer, you may sign up for a new account for KDP. (Signing up for a free account does not commit you to anything.) After you login, click the Help link at the top, then scroll down and look for a Contact Us button on the left.

Following are step-by-step directions for how to publish your paperback book with KDP once you have completed your interior and cover book files (for help with that, see the previous chapters):

---

[49] You may be directed to Microsoft Office's website for a free download of the PDF converter. It's quick and easy – just follow the on-screen instructions. **For optimal pictures, use a different PDF converter instead.**

1. Sign up for a free account (or, if you already have an Amazon account, you may use that instead). It's free, with no strings attached. Visit KDP at kdp.amazon.com.
2. Once you login, click the Bookshelf link at the top of the page. Click the option to add a new paperback book.
3. Hover over any of the blue hyperlinks to learn more about that feature. As an example, hover over the link called, "How to provide accurate series information." In a few cases hovering doesn't work: In those cases you must click on the hyperlink. As an example of this, click link called, "Learn more about entering your title information."
4. At any point, you may click the Save as Draft button at the bottom of the page to save your progress. When you complete a page, click Save and Continue to advance to the next page of the publishing process. There are three pages all together: The first page includes book details and metadata (like keywords and categories), the second page is where you upload your interior and cover files, and the third page lets you set your list price and displays your royalties by country.
5. Select the language for the book. It's not asking about which language you speak or the language of your country. It's asking in which language did you write the book. The languages displayed on the dropdown menu are currently supported. Note that some languages aren't currently supported for publishing a book at KDP.
6. Enter the title of your book. It's best to do this by copy/paste instead of typing the title directly into this field. Open your interior book file (in the native program – like Microsoft Word – not the PDF file). Go to the copyright page. Check your title carefully to make sure that everything is spelled correctly. Highlight the title on your copyright page and copy the title (hold Ctrl and press C if your interior file is in Microsoft Word). Return to your internet browser. Paste (press Ctrl + V) the title into the field.
7. Proofread your book title: You would hate to have a typo in the book's title, so it's worth an extra proofread. If you have a lengthy title, you may want to place your cursor inside the title field and press End on your keyboard to see if the entire title is present. If you want to shorten your title, keep in mind that there is also a subtitle option. The title that you enter in the title field must be exactly the same as the title on your book cover file and the title on the first page of your interior book file. So if you revise your title, be sure to change it in the cover and interior files for your book, too. The subtitle does not need to appear on the cover or the title page of your book.[50] (We discussed titles and subtitles in Sec. 4.1.3.)
8. If you have a subtitle, enter it in the Subtitle field. Your title and subtitle will appear together, separated by a colon (:), in Amazon search results. Think about how this will look when a potential customers sees your book in the search results. A longer subtitle

---

[50] Words in the title will show up in searches on Amazon US, Amazon websites for other countries, and other booksellers' websites (if you select the Expanded Distribution). Words in the subtitle will show up in searches on Amazon US, but may not show up on other websites (they may on some, but not others).

provides more information up front and may add more keywords, but a very long title/subtitle can also deter customers. Try doing some searches on Amazon and see how you feel (and you can poll friends and family) about search results that are short or long. A short title/subtitle is less informative and uses fewer keywords, but sometimes effectively intrigues potential customers.

9. Check that the length of the title and subtitle combined doesn't exceed 200 characters (including spaces). Copy/paste the title and subtitle into a blank document in Word, and click on the word count shown in the bottom left corner in order to check the value of Characters (with spaces). Although the maximum length is 200 characters, as a general rule customers browsing search results are more likely to stop and read titles that are fewer than 60 characters long (especially in fiction).

10. If your book is (or will be) part of a series and you want your volumes to be numbered, enter the series title and the volume number. If you add this, the volume number will appear in parentheses in the form (Your Series Title Book 2) at the end of your title and subtitle in Amazon search results.

11. I would leave the Edition number blank when you first publish your book. In the future, if you republish with significant updates, you can add an edition number. You should also include a brief change to your copyright page (like v2 for version 2 followed by a date). This way, when you see your book you will instantly know which edition it is.

12. Enter the name of the primary author in the author field. The author must have a last name or a surname, but you're not required to include the first name or middle name. You may add a prefix (e.g. a medical doctor might include the prefix Dr.) or a suffix (like III, as in John Henry III, or like Ph.D. if you have an advanced degree for a nonfiction book that relates to your area of expertise). Think about how you want your name to appear. The author's name(s) entered here must exactly match the name(s) from the cover and title page. Do not write the author's name in CAPS. If the author's name uses consecutive initials, like C.D. McMullen, enter the initials separately in the First Name and Middle Name fields (do not enter them together in the same field).

13. Consider whether or not you want to publish your book in your own name or in a pen name. There are many advantages of using your own name. Especially, friends, family, and acquaintances – anyone who recognizes your name – is a potential customer. People enjoy the rare occasion where they can read a book and know personally who the author is. If you use a pen name, you lose your name recognition. If you have expertise in your field or popularity (even having thousands of friends on FaceBook gives you some popularity), name recognition is an even greater advantage. Traditional authors often use a pen name when they write in two or more genres – e.g. using their real name for literary works and a pen name for juvenile fiction. There may be some legal issues involved in use of a pen name; if you would like legal advice, consult an attorney.

14. Did anyone else help with your book, such as a coauthor or illustrator? You can add other authors and contributors by selecting the type of contributor from the drop-down menu under Contributors and then click the Add button. There are many options here, such as "Editor" or "Foreword." Be sure to credit everybody who contributed toward your book; there may be legal ramifications if anyone is left out. You may need to hire an attorney to make legal contracts regarding how royalties are to be distributed, or to inquire about "works for hire." Note that an illustrator is generally someone who created pictures for the interior of a book, and that this field generally isn't for a cover designer. A cover designer is generally credited elsewhere (such as the copyright page along with the designer's website), but you should work out these details with your cover designer if you have one.

15. Add the description of your book in the Description field (see Sec. 4.1.2). I recommend copying and pasting your description from a Word file instead of typing it directly into the Description field. For one, you can use Word's spellcheck feature to help catch some typos. Secondly, in Word, if you click the word count box at the bottom left of the screen it will tell you how many characters (with spaces) you have used in the description. There is a limit of 4,000 characters, including spaces. You can find Amazon's policy for the description in the KDP help pages (click Help at the top, click Enter Book Details under Publish Your Book, click Description, and click Our Metadata Guidelines). Note that limited, simple HTML is permitted: However, since KDP doesn't provide a preview for this, I highly recommend that you prepare your original book description as plain text and then use Author Central to format your book description after your book is published (as described in Chapter 6).

16. Select your publishing rights. If you wrote the book yourself from scratch without using material from others, and if you haven't signed a contract giving your rights to anyone else (such as a publisher), you should generally own the rights to your book. (If you're publishing public domain content, be sure to read all of Amazon's information about public domain works to ensure that you satisfy Amazon's policies on this.)

17. I highly recommend adding 7 sets of keywords in the Your Keywords fields (see Sec. 4.1.3). **Don't** use quotation marks, underscores, commas, etc. Avoid duplicating combinations of words from your title or subtitle – since those combinations already function as keywords. For example, if your subtitle is A Spy Novel Set in World War II, it's unnecessary to use "spy novel" as keywords – since your book will already be searchable with those keywords. Each keyword field may include multiple keywords. For more advice on choosing keywords, review Sec. 4.1.3. Keep the character count below 50 characters (including spaces) for each field. If you type your keywords in Word, you can check the character count there – and also use the spellcheck feature to help avoid typos. (A nice thing about the merger between CreateSpace and KDP is that CreateSpace only let you enter 5 keyword fields, and each was limited to 25 characters. It's much better now.)

18. Click the Choose Categories button to select up to two categories appropriate for your book (see Sec. 4.1.3). There are often multiple categories that seem to fit, but you can only select two from the drop-down menu. You might browse through categories on Amazon to help determine which categories are best: Find other books that are similar to yours, see which browse categories they are listed in (open their Amazon page and scroll down near the bottom to find this), and also compare sales rank (the lower the number, the more frequent the sales, in general – but see Chapter 7). Note, however, that the categories that you can choose from are not quite the same as Amazon categories. In other cases, the category that you're looking for is actually there, but not where you expect to find it; sometimes it pays to be persistent and explore a variety of options. Also see the next bullet point regarding special categories. (A nice thing about the merger between CreateSpace and KDP is that CreateSpace only let you choose one category. It's no longer necessary to contact support to request a second category. You can't add a third category manually or by request, but if a third category falls into one of the special categories described in the next bullet point, it may be possible for your book to get listed in three or more categories. Beware that occasionally your keyword list may get your book into a category that you don't want it to be in: Read the next bullet point to learn more.)

19. Amazon has special categories that your book can only get listed under if you use the right combination of keywords. For example, if you have a fantasy book appropriate for the Sword & Sorcery category, you must enter the following keywords in one of the keyword fields: sword sorcery magic dragon quest. (You can type them all in a single keyword field: You don't need to put each keyword in a different field. This way, you would still have 6 remaining keyword fields for other keywords.) You can find a table on the KDP help pages listing the keyword requirements for special categories. Click the Help link at the top, click Enter Book Details under Publish Your Book, choose Categories, click Browse Categories, and click Categories with Keyword Requirements. Note that there are different tables for US and UK categories.

20. Be sure to click the Save button to add your categories. After you close the category selection window, your categories should appear above the Choose Categories button. Check these carefully.

21. If your book is written in large print (or if you make a special large print edition of your book), you may check the Large Print box. Generally, the font size must be 16 points or higher for most font styles in order to qualify as large print.

22. Answer the question regarding Adult Content.

23. When you are satisfied with page 1 of the publishing process, click the yellow Save and Continue button at the bottom of the page in order to advance onto page 2. You will need to have your interior and cover files ready for page 2.

24. Select your ISBN option. Recall that we discussed this choice in Sec. 4.1.6. Once you choose your ISBN option, it can't be changed. (Well, if the book isn't published yet, you could delete the project and start a new one.) Also, ensure that you are happy with your title and author fields before selecting your ISBN option.

25. If KDP provided you with an ISBN, you will now see your ISBN-13 on the screen. If you want this to appear on your copyright page, now is the time to copy and paste it into the interior file for your book (before converting the file to PDF). When you go to paste these numbers in Word, click the arrow on the bottom of the Paste button in the Home tab (instead of using Ctrl + V) and choose the Keep Text Only option (otherwise, you may have to wait for a long delay).

26. I recommend that you don't do anything where it says Publication Date. Why? If you don't mess with the Publication Date, Amazon will automatically set the publication date on the day that you click the magic Publish button. This will maximize your book's exposure with the Last 30 Days and Last 90 Days filters, which proves to be valuable for many new books. (If instead you set today's date as the publication date, then order a printed proof, read the proof carefully, and make corrections, by the time that you actually publish your book, you might not get any exposure from the Last 30 Days filter. It's best to leave the default setting so that your 'Live on Amazon' date is used.)

27. Choose your Interior settings: Click Black & White on Cream Paper, Black & White on White Paper, or Color on White Paper.

28. Select the Trim Size for your book. The default size is 6" x 9". To choose a different trim size, click the Choose a Different Size button. The industry-standard trim sizes (which includes the popular trim sizes shown at the top) offer the widest distribution options. Note that custom trim sizes (which you can enter at the bottom) aren't eligible for some distribution channels within the Expanded Distribution option. Note that the maximum size is 8.5" x 11.69". If you click the Compare All Sizes link (in the trim size selection window), you can compare the various options available.

29. Select bleed or no bleed. As discussed in Sec. 2.1.5, bleed is appropriate when you have pictures that need to extend to the very edge of the page.

30. Choose matte or glossy for your cover finish. You can browse books similar to yours in a bookstore to see which is common for books like yours.

31. Before you upload your interior file, proofread it carefully, it's very important to remove any typographical, spelling, grammatical, and formatting mistakes from your book. If spelling and grammar happen to be your weakness, I do recommend exploring the possibility of seeking help with this (such as a basic copyediting service). You should also order a printed proof and proofread that carefully. I always find typos in print that I missed when proofreading on the screen.

32. KDP now allows you to submit a .pdf, .doc, .docx, or .rtf file, but PDF is recommended (others often cause formatting problems). Look it over before submitting the file to

KDP.[51] In Microsoft Word 2010, open your Word document, go to the File tab, choose Save As, change Save As Type to PDF, check the box for Standard, explore the Options, and click Save (if you have images, use a free PDF converter instead). Once you are happy with the PDF for your interior book file, click the Upload Paperback Manuscript button at KDP, click the Browse button, find your book on your computer (or jump drive, perhaps), and click Open.

33. It may take a few minutes for KDP to process your file.

34. If you have trouble uploading files, make sure that your internet browser is up-to-date and change the browser settings to (temporarily) allow popups. Also try switching web browsers, like Mozilla Firefox or Internet Explorer, as this often resolves the problem. If you still have trouble, try asking for help on the Community forum.

35. Either Launch Cover Creator and follow the instructions for how to make a cover, or choose the second option to upload a print-ready PDF cover (Chapter 3 discussed how to make a cover). Uploading a print-ready PDF cover gives you the greatest flexibility in customizing your own cover exactly the way you want it. Once you have made your own book cover file in Word, open your Word document, go to the File tab, choose Save As, change Save As Type to PDF, check the box for Standard, explore the Options, and click Save. Check your PDF carefully. Once you are happy with the PDF for your cover book file, click Upload Your Book File, click the Browse button, find your book on your computer (or jump drive, perhaps), click Open, and then click Save. Be sure to remove the guides before saving your final PDF if you added the cover guides described in Sec. 3.1.5.

36. Click the yellow button called Launch Previewer. This lets you check the formatting of your book online. You can often catch a few formatting mistakes this way before you order a printed proof.

37. Note that KDP will <u>not</u> edit or revise your files; KDP will <u>not</u> proofread your book; KDP will <u>not</u> check for most formatting or other mistakes. Your book will print straight from the files that you submit. You are responsible for correct editing and formatting.

38. When you are satisfied with page 2 of the publishing process, click the yellow Save and Continue button at the bottom of the page in order to advance onto page 3.[52]

39. In most cases, you may select all territories. If you only hold the rights to your book in selected territories, then you should select individual territories. This list lets you pick the territories in which you hold the distribution rights. (This isn't a list of where your book will be distributed. It's just a list of where you hold the rights to publish.)

---

[51] They may need to make slight revisions to the PDF file that you submit – e.g. to manually 'flatten' images.

[52] Before CreateSpace merged with KDP, CreateSpace had an Interior Reviewer used before submitting your files for approval and a separate Digital Proofer used after the files were reviewed. With KDP, the online previewer accessed through the Launch Previewer button is similar to the Interior Reviewer and Digital proofer. There is just one previewer now. I actually like KDP's previewer better, and find that it is friendlier with more web browsers.

40. Your book will automatically be distributed to Amazon US and Europe. (Well, if you don't hold the distribution rights for Europe and indicate this correctly in the previous step, then your book shouldn't be distributed to Europe.)

41. Do you wish to include Expanded Distribution? Note that the Expanded Distribution royalty is lower than the Amazon.com royalty, which may force you to set a higher list price than you originally had in mind in order to earn a significant royalty for Expanded Distribution sales. We discussed Expanded Distribution royalties in Sec. 4.1.7. I include Expanded Distribution with almost all of my books: The only time I don't is when I wish to set a lower list price than the Expanded Distribution would allow. (It used to cost $25 to enable Expanded Distribution, but this channel is now free.) You can experiment with your list price and see how it impacts your Amazon.com and Expanded Distribution royalties (see the next bullet point).[53] If you wish to include the Expanded Distribution channel, check this box. Then move your cursor to the side and make sure that this box remains checked. (If you don't want Expanded Distribution, make sure that this box remains unchecked.)

42. The Pricing & Royalty section lets you enter a list price. I recommend setting a list price that is **significantly higher** than the minimum list price: Beware that the minimum list price will earn you **zero** royalty through at least one channel. Assuming that you wish to earn a royalty for your hard work, you should make your list price sufficiently higher than the minimum. The Pricing & Royalty section shows you the printing cost of your book and the royalty for each channel. Click the dropdown arrow to see the printing cost and royalty in other countries, such as the UK, France, and Japan. (Note that some countries, such as Canada, are automatically set by your US list price. Unless this has changed recently, paperback sales in Canada pay the same royalty as US sales.)

43. In some other countries, Amazon includes a value added tax (VAT) with the displayed list price. The price with the VAT included is shown to the right. If you like for your list price to end with .99 (a common pricing strategy) and if you wish for the price with the VAT included to end with .99, you'll have to play around with the list price a few times in order to get the price with the VAT "just right."

44. I highly recommend that you click Save As Draft, order a printed proof, wait for the printed proof to arrive, read through your printed proof carefully for proofreading and formatting mistakes, make the corrections, and upload a revised interior file on page 2 of the process before you publish your book. You only get one chance to make a good first impression, so take the time to perfect your book first.

45. Click the link labeled "Click here to request a proof copy." You can choose to have your proof printed from the Amazon marketplace of your choice. The email usually comes in a matter of minutes, but it could be hours. When the email comes, it will include a link that takes you to Amazon to place your proof order.

---

[53] See Sec. 4.1.5 to see how royalties are calculated.

46. When your printed proof arrives, first check the cover carefully. Then browse through it page by page for formatting issues. Finally, take your time to proofread your book carefully, resting your eyes and refreshing your mindset often.
47. When you finish proofreading your book, revise your Word file and make a new PDF file. Upload this PDF file on page 2 just as before. Save and Continue to page 3.
48. Read Amazon's terms and conditions before you publish your book.
49. When you are ready to publish your book, press the yellow Publish Your Paperback Book button. It usually takes 12 to 24 hours to find out if your files are approved. If so, you should receive an email stating that your book is now live. (It should be available in the US at this point, but may take up to a few days for other countries.) If there are any blocking issues, you should receive an explanation of what the problem is. In this case, you'll need to correct the problem and upload new files. A common example is when your spine text is slightly too large.

Following are a variety of other useful notes, such as what you need to do before you can be paid for royalties:

❖ Your detail page will be updated several times over the course of time – several times during the first month, and occasionally thereafter – so don't be surprised if it initially seems rather incomplete. You have to wait patiently and see how it progresses. It can take weeks or months to develop a customers also bought list.

❖ Explore your book's detail page at Amazon. Check the title, subtitle, series info, author name, and cover. Read through the description carefully. Check out the Look Inside. Read through the beginning of your book carefully. The best way to revise your book's description is through Author Central (Chapter 6), but if you do this, copy and paste the HTML for your description from Author Central into the description field on your KDP Bookshelf and click Save As Draft (otherwise, if you republish your book, or simply change the price or keywords, KDP will overwrite the existing description).

❖ Once your book sells, scroll down your book's detail page at Amazon to check which categories it is listed under. If the category that you would like to add doesn't appear on its own, contact KDP support and politely ask if it would be possible to change your book's browse categories. You can choose up to two browse categories. Include your suggested browse categories in the form Books > Business & Investing > Small Business & Entrepreneurship > Entrepreneurship (first search on Amazon to find your desired categories).

❖ Ensure that your title, subtitle, and author name (especially, a pen name) do not infringe upon any copyrights or trademarks. For example, you can't write a *Chicken Soup* book or a book *for Dummies* – so be sure not to include these words (and other phrases that are part of popular series) in the title or subtitle of your book. Once again, If you have copyright, trademark, or other legal questions, consult with an attorney.

❖ With the Amazon UK or continental Europe[54] distribution channels, any books that you sell directly through these Amazon websites will be manufactured in the UK or continental Europe and shipped from there, which greatly reduces shipping time and allows customers to potentially buy your book with free shipping incentives. Keep in mind that there are language differences: Even in the United Kingdom, British English has some important differences from American English; and in other countries, English is not the native language. Of course, there are people in continental Europe who speak English, who will serve as your customer base for sales for Amazon Europe. However, if you are fluent in another language or can find an inexpensive, but good, translation service, you may be able to attract Spanish- or French-speaking customers, for example (not just in Europe, but even in Mexico, South America, or Canada, for example). Foreign language books can be sold from Amazon US as well as from Amazon Europe. Although books sold through Amazon UK and Amazon Europe have the list price and royalty figured in pounds or euro, you may choose to have your royalties deposited in US dollars in a US bank account.

❖ Royalties for a given month are paid 60 days after the month ends. There may be a minimum royalty accumulation needed before your royalties can be paid (but this may depend on whether or not you select direct deposit and where you reside).

❖ You must enter some information in your account before you can receive royalty payments. This includes a social security number for income tax reporting. After you login, click Your Name's Account at the top of the page in order to enter or update your account information.

❖ You can delete your book anytime up until the moment when you click the publish button. Make sure that you are happy with your book – and have reviewed your proof carefully – before clicking the publish button. We will discuss what to look for when proofing your book and how to make revisions in Chapter 5. Once you publish your paperback, it can't be completely removed from Amazon: If you unpublish the book, it will remain on Amazon in case customers wish to resell used copies.

❖ We will discuss how to order a proof, how to edit your proof, what to look for when you review your proof, how to revise your proof, and how to solve common problems in Chapter 5.

❖ Your title and author information will be locked once you select your ISBN option. If you want to change your title, author, or your ISBN option, you must delete your book and start over.

❖ Once you publish your book, customers can buy it. It may take a day or a few days before your book appears on Amazon. It may take weeks before some features are

---

[54] Yes, the United Kingdom (UK) is part of Europe: The distinction here is whether your book will be manufactured in and shipped within the UK or whether it will be manufactured in and shipped to continental Europe. Amazon has multiple European websites, including the UK, France, Germany, Spain, and Italy.

activated, such as the Search Inside feature. It will take time for your book to become more visible in searches on Amazon. It will take many sales before your book is linked with other books – e.g. for Amazon to list your book on other books' detail pages where it says, "Customers Who Bought This Item Also Bought." Sales may start out slow; if so, they may gradually build up. The best thing you can do to improve sales is develop an effective marketing plan. We will discuss marketing ideas in Chapter 8. Most books do <u>not</u> sell well all on their own. A new book is buried down in search results. Sales help to build sales, and to spread awareness of your book. Most books that succeed do so because of a good marketing strategy: Marketing helps to make customers aware of your book and to drive sales. There are millions of books for sale. Authors who succeed in getting their books to be in the top 200,000 (or better) out of millions of books almost always achieve this through some form of marketing. As we will see in Chapter 8, there are a variety of free or cheap marketing strategies that authors can use to help improve their sales.

❖ If you opt for Expanded Distribution, some books sold through this channel may be printed with some other print-on-demand service (i.e. other than KDP). Therefore, you may notice slight printing variations for books sold through the Expanded Distribution channel. Colors may vary slightly. A third-party may use different paper, so the paper thickness may also vary slightly.

❖ Unfortunately, you can't create discount codes nor can you put your book on sale.[55] It is possible that Amazon will discount your book periodically (without any notice). Note that Amazon will pay your full royalty based on the list price, so if Amazon discounts your book, it doesn't impact your royalties. There is no guarantee that Amazon will ever discount your book, but over the years it has happened with several KDP (and CreateSpace) books. If you create a Kindle eBook version of your book, it is possible to put the Kindle eBook on sale (via a Countdown Deal) if your book is enrolled in KDP Select. For the print edition, one way to sell copies at a discount is to order author copies and sell them directly (a few authors are fairly successful at this).

❖ Once you approve your proof and your book begins to sell at Amazon, you can track the progress of sales by viewing reports. (We will discuss how to order your proof, what to look for when you order your proof, and common issues in Chapter 5.) Click the Reports link at the top of the page.[56]

---

[55] When CreateSpace had an eStore, it was possible to create a discount code that worked for the eStore (but the discount code didn't work at Amazon). However, few customers were willing to buy books through the CreateSpace eStore (because they had to create a new account, weren't eligible for free shipping, etc.). In general, it is much easier for authors to get customers to buy books at full price on Amazon than it was to get customers to buy books at a discount through the CreateSpace eStore. (A major reason is that if a customer qualified for free shipping at Amazon, through Prime or Super Saver Shipping, the total cost would actually be less at Amazon even without the discount.)

[56] It's worth spending a few minutes to explore the variety of reports available.

❖ The default view is the Sales Dashboard. This shows eBooks, paperbacks, free eBook promotions (if applicable), and Expanded Distribution sales (if applicable). The second graph, for KENP read, applies to Kindle eBooks that are enrolled in KDP Select. Scroll down below the graphs to find a handy royalty table, which shows royalties earned in each country. Back at the top, you can change the date range (such as Month-to-Date) or filter the results (for example, by country).

❖ Note that the graph on the Sales Dashboard shows orders, whereas the table at the bottom shows royalties earned. Especially for eBooks there can be noticeable delays and discrepancies between the order report and royalty report on this page (since orders and royalties aren't synchronized). Note also that there can be a delay of a couple of days between when a book is purchased and when the royalty shows on the reports, while other times it will show immediately. (In rare cases when Amazon uses a third party to fill an order, there can be a delay of several weeks in reporting royalties.)

❖ There are a few rare situations in which you won't see a royalty show up for a paper-back sale. One example is when customer A buys a book and returns it, and the same book is sold to customer B. In this example, suppose you know customer B, but had no idea about customer A. You would never see customer B's royalty show up on your report because you had already been paid the royalty when customer A bought the book. Another example is when Amazon decides to stock up on a book (for example, during the holidays): You might see a large order one day, and then no sales at all for several weeks (until every copy of that large order finally sells).

❖ You can find more sales and royalty data by clicking the View Reports link at the left-hand side of your Member Dashboard. Royalty Details will show you all of your sales in the order in which they were sold (unless you click the heading at the top of one of the columns). Royalty by Title shows you how many of each book you sold and also the royalty that you made in the US, GB, and Europe for each book. In any of the tabs, click Run New Report to modify the reports – e.g. you can show a report for the entire year by changing the dates.

❖ There are a variety of reporting options, such as Historical and Prior Months' Royalties. Ad Campaigns helps you manage any advertising that you may choose to do. (You can now advertise both paperbacks and eBooks; it used to be eBooks only. Advertising can help you get some exposure, but isn't cost-effective for every book.)

❖ When a book sells on Amazon, the royalty is typically reported when the book is manufactured – which could be a matter of hours, but may also be a few days.

❖ When a book sells through the Expanded Distribution, it can be several weeks before the royalty is reported. Most Expanded Distribution royalties are currently reported at the end of the month – and these royalties may be for books that sold in a previous month. So it might be a few months before you can tell if your books are selling through the Expanded Distribution. Remember, sales may be a growing process – it takes time for all of the features to work on Amazon, for your book to get noticed, etc. If sales are slow starting out, there is the potential for growth. The best way to help grow sales is through marketing (see Chapter 8).

❖ If you have both paperback and Kindle editions of the same book, the Kindle edition will show up in Kindle searches and the paperback edition will show up in book searches even if the two editions are linked together. If someone opens your paperback edition, it will be very clear that you also have a Kindle edition, and vice-versa (unless, of course, they open your eBook from an eReader). You should also be aware that if your paperback and Kindle editions get linked together, reviews from both editions are collected together. So, for example, if someone leaves a negative review to complain about the formatting of your eBook, this review will be included with the reviews for your paperback book. You might not like it, but that's the way it is. Therefore, if you have an eBook edition of your paperback book, it's very important to have good formatting – since a negative review will affect the sale of both editions of your book. On the other hand, if a customer leaves a positive review for either edition, that will help the sale of both books. At least, it works both ways.

If you need help, have questions, or come across specific problems, read the paragraph at the end of Sec. 4.1.1, which describes how you can ask questions to KDP representatives and how you can get help from fellow authors.

Be sure to follow the content guidelines:

https://kdp.amazon.com/en_US/help/topic/G200672390

You can find a comprehensive list of what is not allowed at the above link. The list below is not comprehensive, but may include a few things that you might want to be aware of:

⊗ Obviously, pornographic, obscene, or offensive material is <u>not</u> allowed.

⊗ <u>Don't</u> give out any personal information in your book description, the title of your book, a review, or your biography. This includes phone numbers, addresses, email addresses, and webpages. You can include contact information inside your book (such as the copyright page or About the Author section).

⊗ <u>Don't</u> mention the price in the description.

⊗ <u>Don't</u> spoil the plot in your description.

⊗ <u>Don't</u> include reviews, quotes, or testimonials in your description or biography.

⊗ <u>Don't</u> ask customers to review your book in your description or biography.

⊗ Advertisement and promotion is <u>not</u> allowed in your description or biography.

4.2 Publishing Your eBook Online

4.2.1 Where to Publish Your eBook

Y OU CAN PUBLISH YOUR eBook with a variety of eReaders – including Amazon's Kindle, Barnes & Noble's Nook, Sony's eReader,[57] and more – all for <u>free</u>. Some authors publish their eBooks with all of the major eReaders, while some publish their eBooks exclusively with Amazon's Kindle. The reason that some authors choose to publish their eBooks only with Kindle is because Amazon's KDP Select program provides an incentive to authors for doing so. I suggest that you read Sec. 4.2.7, which discusses both the pros and cons of the KDP Select program, before you commit to where you will publish your eBooks. If you decide not to enroll your eBook in the KDP Select program, then I highly recommend publishing your eBook with all of the major eReaders (at a minimum).

There is a third alternative: A commitment to the KDP Select program is not permanent, but comes in 90-day intervals. Some authors initially enroll their eBooks in the KDP Select program, and then opt out after the 90-day period ends. In this way, they enjoy the benefits of the program for a few months, and then publish their eBooks will all of the major eReaders after this period. This 90-days period gives you a chance to test the program out and see if you like the benefits enough to keep your eBook enrolled in it. This also gives you time to revise your eBook's formatting specifically for other eReaders.

Regardless of where you choose to publish your eBook, I highly recommend publishing your eBook directly with each eReader company that you choose. For example, publish a Kindle eBook directly from Amazon's website (as described in Sec. 4.2.8) and publish a Nook eBook directly from Nook Press, which is Barnes & Noble's eBook publishing website (as described in Sec. 4.2.9). Since there are formatting differences between Kindle, Nook, and other eReaders – there are even formatting differences between the different types of Kindles, like eInk and Fire, for example – you will be able to preview exactly how your eBook will look on each eReader by publishing your eBook directly with each company. Amazon's preview tool for Kindle will even show you how your book will look on an iPhone and an iPad when customers with those devices purchase your Kindle eBook from Amazon.

Some authors choose to publish their eBook with a company like Smashwords, which publishes your eBook on most of the major eReaders for you (note that you still have the option to select whichever eReaders you want to publish with). The formatting may be better if you adapt your eBook to best fit the different types of eReaders, since formatting features

---

[57] Kindle and Amazon are trademarks of Amazon.com, Inc. Nook and Barnes & Noble are trademarks of Barnes & Noble, Inc. Sony is a registered trademark of Sony Corporation. These trademarks and brands are the property of their respective owners.

may vary from one eReader to another. This is especially true if you have large pictures or rich formatting, equations, or tables. When you publish directly with the eReader company, you can use the eReader's preview tool to see exactly how your eBook will appear on that company's eReaders. If you don't elect to publish your eBook with Kindle Select, then I <u>do</u> recommend publishing your eBook on Smashwords (as described in Sec. 4.2.10); Smashwords does provide some free benefits, like a free ISBN and the option of publishing with Apple. However, you should also consider publishing directly with Nook and other eReaders, when possible, instead of having Smashwords publish your eBook with them for you. At the very least, I suggest beginning the publishing process with Nook in order to use their preview tool – this way, you can see if the same eBook file will format well on Nook.

There are other eBook aggregators that are similar to Smashwords. An interesting option that may be worth researching is BookBaby (which, by the way, also has a paperback option). Another alternative to Smashwords is Draft2Digital.

If you do publish your eBook with multiple eReaders, you should be aware that some eReader companies, like Barnes & Noble, require the list price to be <u>no higher</u> than the list price anywhere else (and also no higher than the paperback edition of the same book). Other companies may choose to pricematch a competitor's price for your eBook (and, depending on their terms and conditions, they may pay you a royalty based on the matched price instead of the list price that you set with them). This is important to keep in mind if you make your eBook temporarily free with one eReader service – since a competing eReader may, if you published with them, too, also offer your eBook for free during the same period.

Note that eReaders impose different memory limits on your content file size. The content file size limits of the three major eReaders are summarized in the following table; the file for the interior of your eBook file must be below these limits. If you want to find out what the file size is for your eBook, find your file in the Documents or Computer folder on your computer, right-click in the white space where the files are shown in the folder and change View to Details, and then look for the file size in kilobytes (KB) – or right-click on the filename, click Properties, and look for the file size in the General tab. See Sec. 4.2.4 to learn ways that you might decrease the memory size of your file; even if the file size doesn't exceed the maximum limit, decreasing the file size might also increase your royalty (see Sec. 4.2.5).

eReader	Maximum Content File Size
Amazon's Kindle	650 MB (650,000 KB)
Barnes & Noble's Nook	20 MB (20,000 KB)
Sony Reader	5 MB (5,000 KB)[58]

---

[58] This is the file size limit if you use Smashwords to publish your eBook with the Sony Reader (see Sec. 4.2.10).

Amazon's Kindle, Barnes & Noble's Nook, Sony's Reader, and the Kobo[59] eReader are the major eReaders. Customers can also purchase eBooks for tablets (like the Apple iPad, Microsoft Surface, Google Nexus, and Samsung Galaxy Tab), laptops, PC's, and even their cell phones. One way to read an eBook on a laptop or PC is to download Kindle's or Nook's software for the PC – which allows customers to purchase Kindle or Nook eBooks and read the eBook on their laptop or PC. We will discuss how to publish directly with Kindle in Sec. 4.2.8, and directly with Nook in Sec. 4.2.9. You can't publish directly with Sony's Reader, but you can make your eBook available for Sony's Reader using Kobo or Smashwords, as we will describe in Sec. 4.2.10. If you publish an eBook with Smashwords, you can also make it available for other eReaders, as we will see in Sec. 4.2.10.

4.2.2 Perfecting Large Pictures for a Variety of eReaders

Different eReaders – even those offered by a single company – come in a variety of aspect ratios. This makes it <u>impossible</u> to create full-page pictures that completely fill the screen on every eReader (and still preserve the original aspect ratio of your pictures). The best that you can do is target a couple of specific eReaders – like the Kindle Fire and Nook Color – and design full-screen pictures around those devices.

Let me illustrate the underlying problem with an example. Suppose, for example, that you plan to take advantage of KDP Select and publish exclusively with Kindle: In this case, if you are designing a full-color picture book, you might choose to target the Kindle Fire. The problem is that many customers may buy the eBook for their cell phones, other brand tablets, laptops, and PC's. An eBook that is published exclusively with Kindle may still be read on a variety of devices. The Kindle Fire is long and skinny. If you make long, skinny pictures that completely fill the screen of the Kindle Fire, there will be noticeable gaps at the sides of the picture when the same eBook is read on other devices – and these gaps will be more pronounced when the eBook is read on a device that has a screen that is much more square. In the other extreme, if your pictures are nearly square, when a customer reads your eBook on the Kindle Fire, there will be a large gap underneath the picture. Obviously, it will be easiest to make out the details of a picture that completely fills the screen; when the picture's

---

[59] Kindle and Amazon are trademarks of Amazon.com, Inc. Nook and Barnes & Noble are trademarks of Barnes & Noble, Inc. Sony is a registered trademark of Sony Corporation. Kobo is a registered trademark of Kobo, Inc. These trademarks and brands are the property of their respective owners.

aspect ratio doesn't match the device's aspect ratio, there will be a gap below or gaps beside the picture. Apps that automatically adjust the aspect ratio don't solve the problem: This fills the screen on each device, but may greatly distort the picture to accomplish this.

To make matters worse, customers have a choice of holding the device in portrait mode or landscape mode. If you design pictures for the Kindle Fire, for example, which is long and skinny, if the customer holds the Kindle Fire in portrait mode and your picture fills the screen, the picture will be very small with very large gaps when another customer holds the Kindle Fire in landscape mode. Some customers have such a strong tendency to hold the device in a particular orientation that they may not try the other. (You can always include a note suggesting which orientation is best for viewing your book, but a few customers will still do as they please. Remember the age-old adage, "The customer is always right.") A square picture will have a very significant gap regardless of how the customer holds a device with a long, skinny screen, but will look about the same regardless of whether the customer holds the device in portrait or landscape mode.

Since an eReader can be held in portrait or landscape mode (controlled by turning the eReader 90°, so that the device can sense, via gravity, the distinction between 'top' and 'bottom'), it's important to design the orientation of your pictures with your intended mode in mind. The 'bottom' of your picture (as you see it on your screen when you submit your eBook file) will always match the 'bottom' of the eReader. Thus, when the customer switches between portrait and landscape mode, the picture rotates with the device. If you submit a picture that looks sideways to you when you view your eBook at home, it will <u>always</u> look sideways to the customer no matter which mode the customer chooses. When you proofread your eBook, make sure that no pictures look sideways in the preview (or it will be a disaster).

To make matters worse, every eReader has built-in margins (these are in addition to any margins that you may add using the Paragraph tab in Microsoft Word). The margins apply whether the eReader is showing text or images. You <u>can't</u> make a full-screen picture because of these automatic margins. Furthermore, the aspect ratio of the usable screen space is different from the aspect ratio of the actual screen size. As a result, if you make a picture with the same aspect ratio as the screen size, it won't quite fill the usable screen space. If you want a picture to fill the usable screen space of a specific device, you must figure out the new aspect ratio that is created by the automatic margins.

Amazon eReaders	Screen Aspect Ratio
Kindle Fire HD 8.9"	1200 x 1920 (5:8)
Kindle Fire HD 7"	800 x 1280 (5:8)
Kindle Fire	600 x 1024 (≈3:5)
Kindle Paperwhite	758 x 1024 (≈3:4)
Kindle Keyboard	600 x 800 (3:4)
Kindle DX	824 x 1200 (≈2:3)
Kindle Touch	600 x 800 (3:4)
Kindle 6"	600 x 800 (3:4)

Barnes & Noble eReaders	Screen Aspect Ratio
Nook HD+	1280 x 1920 (2:3)
Nook HD	900 x 1440 (5:8)
Nook Tablet	600 x 1024 (≈3:5)
Nook Color	600 x 1024 (≈3:5)
Nook Simple Touch	600 x 800 (3:4)
Nook Classic	600 x 800 (3:4)

Sony Readers	Screen Aspect Ratio
Sony Reader	600 x 800 (3:4)
Sony Pocket	600 x 800 (3:4)
Sony Touch	600 x 800 (3:4)
Sony Daily	600 x 1024 (≈3:5)
Sony PRS	600 x 800 (3:4)

Other eReader Devices	Screen Aspect Ratio
Kobo Inc.	600 x 800 (3:4)
Kobo Touch	600 x 1024 (≈3:5)
Samsung Papyrus	600 x 800 (3:4)
Microsoft Surface	768 x 1366 (≈4:7)
Apple iPad 3rd Gen.	1536 x 2048 (3:4)
Apple iPad	768 x 1024 (3:4)
Apple iPhone 5	640 x 1136 (≈4:7)
Apple iPhone 4	640 x 960 (2:3)

Most other brands of basic eReaders are presently 600 x 800 (3:4), but trends are changing. The ≈ symbol means that the aspect ratio is approximate (rather than exact).

The aspect ratios of the vast majority of eReaders range from 4:7 (where the width is just 57% of the height) to 3:4 (where the width is 75% of the height) in portrait mode. In landscape mode, the range is from 4:3 (where the width equals 133% of the height) to 7:4 (where the width equals 175% of the height). Keep in mind that a few screens, like the monitor of a PC, can only be viewed in portrait mode. The 3:4 aspect ratio is very common among classic-style eReaders. Although this aspect ratio is the most common aspect ratio on the table shown on the previous page, the latest round of eReaders are the tablet size – like the Kindle Fire HD and Nook HD – which have aspect ratios of 3:5 and 5:8. This is the aspect ratio that customers with the latest technology will have. It's tempting to gear full-color, full-page eBooks toward this tablet size – but then the iPad is 3:4 and many cell phones, like the iPhone 5, are 2:3.

Many authors size their pictures with a 3:4 aspect ratio, using 600 pixels x 800 pixels, which matches the display size of most eReaders. This aspect ratio will look reasonably good on a variety of devices. The 3:4 aspect ratio looks okay on long, skinny devices like the original Kindle Fire. The 3:4 aspect ratio also looks okay even if customers use landscape mode for a picture that was designed with portrait mode in mind, for example. On the other hand, if you make a long, skinny picture specifically with the traditional Kindle Fire, which is 3:5, or the new Microsoft Surface, which is 4:7, in mind, for example, these may not look as good on an eReader that is 3:4 – especially, on a small device like a cell phone. Thus, if you want to accommodate the greatest variety of eReaders, 3:4 may be a good fit.

Note that pictures with 600 pixels by 800 pixels will not perfectly match 3:4 devices because of the internal margins that every device has. For example, suppose that the display screen has a size of 3.6 inches by 4.8 inches (the diagonal is then 6 inches, corresponding to a 6" display size, which is common among 3:4 eReaders). If the internal left and right margins are each 0.1875 inches (that's 3/16") and the top and bottom margins are each 0.375 inches (that's 3/8")[60], then the usable screen size is 3.225 inches by 4.05 inches. In this case, a picture size of 637 pixels by 800 pixels will match the aspect ratio of the usable screen size, and best fill the screen. On some devices, the customer can actually choose from a few different margin settings – which makes it impossible to precisely plan for the actual margin size. One disadvantage of 640 pixels by 800 pixels (which is equivalent to 600 pixels by 750 pixels, except that 640 x 800 is slightly higher resolution) is that 600 x 800 may look somewhat better than 640 x 800 on skinnier devices like the Kindle Fire.

Similarly, if you make your pictures 600 x 1024 with the Kindle Fire in mind, if you account for the internal margins, 610 x 1024 may fit the usable area of the display better – depending upon the customer's choice of the internal margin size.

Perhaps the common 600 x 800 is the best fit for a variety of devices.

---

[60] The top margin may be slightly thicker than the bottom margin due to the presence of the heading (i.e. the title of the eBook that appears on a small line at the top of the screen).

Some programmers have actually developed applications to help adapt the picture size for various eReaders. Some applications allow you to set one dimension to 100% and the other dimension to Auto. This way, the picture fills the screen; but the disadvantage is that the aspect ratio is not fixed – so the image may be stretched horizontally or vertically, as needed to fill the screen. Some images will look funny if stretched; in that case, automatically stretching the image to fill the screen may not be a good idea. There are other applications that include two different sets of images for two different types of devices. If you're interested in checking out the latest applications that may be available to help adapt your images to a given device, try searching for them on your favorite search engine (there are always new applications coming out) or try asking fellow authors about this on community help forums (see Sec. 4.2.12). For example, check out Kindlegen (you can find a link for it at http://www.amazon.com/gp/feature.html?docId=1000729511), which is an Amazon tool, and Mobipocket Creator – when you upload an eBook for publishing with Kindle, Amazon auto-matically converts it to Mobipocket format (with a .mobi file extension), so Mobipocket is actually a tool that is used by Amazon (but also beware that these tools may have become obsolete or outdated, or may no longer be fully supported at Amazon).

There are two other properties of your images that you need to consider besides the aspect ratio: One is the pixel count, which affects both the resolution of your images and the memory size of your file; the other is picture size – i.e. how large the picture looks.

Your picture won't show in higher resolution than the display size. For example, if you make pictures that are 900 pixels by 1200 pixels, they will only show with a resolution of 600 x 800 on an eReader with a 600 x 800 display. On the other hand, if an eReader has a higher resolution display than the images that you submit, your full-screen pictures (we'll learn how to do that in Volume 2) will not appear as sharp as the full-screen pictures of eBooks that use the optimal resolution. For example, a third-generation iPad has a 1536 x 2048 display: A picture that is 1536 x 2048 will appear 2.5 times sharper than a 600 x 800 image viewed with this device. Higher resolution images appear sharper, but they also increase the memory of the content file size. We will discuss the problem of memory in Sec. 4.2.4, and we will see how this may affect the possible list price and your royalty in Sec. 4.2.5.

You lose resolution when you decrease the pixel size of your image, but you don't increase the sharpness when you increase the pixel size. For example, if you begin with a 150 x 200 image and resize it to 600 x 800, the image will not appear sharper. If you want sharp, high-resolution pictures, the original picture must already have high resolution. If you started with a 1500 x 2000 image, resized it to 300 x 400, and then change your mind about it – go back to the original 1500 x 2000 image and then resize it as needed (don't increase the size of the 300 x 400 image). Similarly, if you draw a small image in Word, copy/paste the image into Paint, and then increase the pixel size, your image won't look nearly as sharp as if you first create a very large image in Word (the page size can be as large as 20" x 20", so you can make a 20" x 20" image) and then decrease the pixel size to the desired amount (see Sec. 2.2.5).

The size of the image affects how large it appears on the eReader screen. If you don't want a picture to fill the screen, make it smaller. The physical dimensions of the picture correspond to the picture's size, and the pixel count corresponds to the picture's resolution. If you make full-page pictures 600 x 800, then a picture with half the width and half the height should have a resolution of 300 x 400, for example (don't waste memory by making smaller images have more resolution than needed).

If you want to get the size of your pictures and the resolution right, what you should do is make a small sample of a variety of pictures – I mean a variety of sizes and resolutions – and then go through the minimal steps of the publishing process (see Sec.'s 4.2.8-4.2.11) needed to upload a content file (not the entire book – just a few pages with sample images). Then view the images with the publisher's previewer. If you are dissatisfied with the images, make some changes to the images and resubmit them. Perfect your technique before you make the pictures for your entire eBook. Authors who draw dozens of pictures first and then proceed to publish their eBooks often become very frustrated; the less frustrating way to proceed is to draw only a few sample pictures, learn how to draw them so that they format to your satisfaction, and then draw the remaining pictures.

Amazon's Kindle won't display an image larger than the screen size. Therefore, if you submit a picture that is larger than the display size, it will automatically reduce the size of the image so that it fits on the screen. However, not all eReaders may do this. For example, with Barnes & Noble's Nook, if your picture has a higher pixel count than the eReader can display, your picture may overfill the display and be cut off. If your pictures are 600 x 800, you should not experience this problem. For pictures with higher resolution, you may want to resize them for any eReaders where this may be a problem. Remember, you can easily preview the pictures for your eBook on any eReader by going to the publisher's website, uploading your content file, and using the publisher's preview too (see Sec.'s 4.2.8-4.2.11).

Note that this section has been devoted solely to pictures that appear in your eBook's content file. The cover picture is a different matter – you should make it as high resolution as the publisher allows (see Sec.'s 4.2.8-4.2.11).

Want or need help or advice? See Sec. 4.2.12 and Sec.'s 4.2.8 thru 4.2.11.

4.2.3 Revising Your Paperback Book Description for Your eBook

Since your eBook may be somewhat different from your paperback book – due to differences in formatting features, pictures, equations, etc. – if you have already written a description for your paperback (as described in Sec. 4.1.2), you may want to revise it for your eBook.

One important difference between an eBook and a physical book is that eBooks don't have definite page sizes. Instead, the eBook's size is based on memory (in kilobytes). The memory itself doesn't really tell a customer how long the eBook is though – since pictures, tables, equations, and rich formatting (that which the eBook's publisher allows) take up memory. For example, an eBook can have a huge file size, yet be very short because it mostly consists of full-screen, high-resolution images.

The description of your eBook should make the length of your eBook very clear. This way, a customer will be less likely to complain that the eBook is shorter than expected. For example, for fiction, is your book a collection of short stories (each less than about 10,000 words), a novelette (about 10,000 to 20,000 words), a novella (about 20,000 to 50,000 words), or a novel (about 50,000 to 100,000 words)? A customer who purchases an eBook expecting a typical 'book' will be disappointed if it turns out to be a novella, for example.

It may be helpful to include the word count in your description. In Microsoft Word, when you open your eBook file you can find the word count in the bottom left corner. You can also use this to check the word count of your eBook description if you type it in Word: There is a 4000 word limit for Kindle descriptions, for example.

If your book includes color pictures, state this in your description. Customers who have color eReaders like to take advantage of this. Does your eBook have any special features, such as an active table of contents (see Sec. 2.2.8)? If your eBook has features that many eBooks lack, this may be a selling point for potential customers.

As with your paperback book, eBook customers primarily want to know what your book is about. So don't get carried away with word count, pictures, and other eBook features to the point that it's difficult for customers to determine if your content suits them.

Since Amazon, Kindle, Barnes & Noble, Nook, Sony, etc. are trademarks of their respective owners, the eBook publisher may choose not to allow you to use these brands and names in the description of your eBook. The main problem that most eBook authors run into is wanting to specifically declare that the eBook is a Kindle edition or a Nook edition, for example, in the title or description. The eBook publisher may not want to give any implication that your eBook may be 'endorsed' by the publisher, and so the publisher probably will not allow you to make such declaration. If you're writing an eBook that helps customers make the most of their Kindle Fire or helps customers publish games on the Kindle Fire, for example, then you may be able to include 'Kindle Fire' in your title; if so, be sure to provide a declaration of the actual company that owns the brand name and trademark (and speak to an attorney to see if this will suffice). Consult an attorney for legal advice on this matter; I'm only suggesting that the publisher or brand might not allow you to do this – only an attorney will be qualified to advise you on what you should or should not do.

It's not really necessary to declare that your eBook is a Kindle edition, for example. Amazon will include the words 'Kindle Edition' after your title on your Amazon detail page, so it will be clear that this edition of your book is a Kindle eBook, even if this is not in the title.

You might consider including a brief biography at the end of your description. You should sign up for a free Amazon author profile via Author Central (Chapter 6) and post your full biography at Author Central. When customers shop on their computers at Amazon, your Author

Central biography will show up on your book's Amazon detail page. However, many customers shop for Kindle eBooks on their Kindle devices (or tablets or smart phones), and the experience often doesn't show as many features as when shopping on a PC, Mac, or laptop. It might be worth adding your most pertinent qualifications to the end of the eBook description (but the description won't show in full at first; customers will need to click a Read More link).

Some eBook publishers allow linespaces in the description in order to help divide the description into paragraphs; but they will probably not respect tab spacing for indentations.

Following is a sample description for my eBook, *An Introduction to Basic Astronomy Concepts (with Space Photos)*:

> This eBook provides a highly visual and colorful introduction to a variety of basic astronomy concepts: (1) Overview of the Solar System (2) Understanding the Lunar Phases (3) Understanding Solar and Lunar Eclipses (4) Understanding the Seasons (5) Evidence that the Earth is Round (6) Models of Our Solar System (7) Laws of Motion in Astronomy (8) Beyond Our Solar System. This eBook features numerous NASA space photos. (NASA did not participate in the writing or publication of this eBook.) Many diagrams, like the heliocentric and geocentric models or explaining the phases of the moon, were constructed by combining together NASA space photos instead of simply drawing circles. Educators may use this material for the purpose of teaching astronomy concepts to their students. The content is suitable for a general interest audience, as well as those who may be learning astronomy and are looking for some supplemental instruction that is highly visual and focused on a variety of fundamental concepts.
>
> There are about 17,000 words in this eBook and over 100 color images. (The paperback edition of this eBook has 186 pages.)

4.2.4 Managing the Cover and Content File Sizes

There are three important reasons for managing the size of your content file:

1. First, if your file size exceeds the limits tabulated in Sec. 4.2.1, you won't be able to publish your eBook with each eReader unless you are able to reduce the content file's memory below that eReader's file size limit.
2. Secondly, the size of your file may impact your royalties, as described in Sec. 4.2.5.
3. Also, the file size impacts the customer. A larger file uses up more of the customer's available memory, and on an older device can take a long time to download.

Remember, you can find out what the size of your content file is by finding it in the Documents or Computer folder on your computer, right-clicking on the filename, clicking Properties, and looking for the file size in the General tab.

Pictures, equations, and tables hog most of the file's memory. You may be able to reduce the size of your file by compressing the pictures. In Microsoft Word, select a picture (just click on it) in your file, go to the Format tab that appears after you select it, click Compress Pictures, uncheck the Apply Only To This Picture box, and select a Target Output. E-mail resolution (96 ppi – pixels per inch) will give you the minimum possible file size. Before you try this, save the original version of your file, then save a new version of your file (with a different filename) with the revised Target Output. This way, you will still have the original.

If you need to shrink your file size further, there are other changes that you can make to achieve this, such as:

❖ Try changing the file format between .doc, .docx, .html, and .pdf, for example (also, check which file formats each publisher accepts – see Sec.'s 4.2.8-11). In Word, click the File tab and choose Save As to resave the file with a different format. After you change the file format, first check to see if the file size decreased – if so, then view the file carefully (some features may not look the same after the change). Also, a file that looked fine on the publisher's preview in one file format may look different after the change, so be sure to check the preview. The file format with the least memory might have several formatting problems – so check this carefully in the preview.

❖ Did you use an application, like Kindlegen or Mobipocket Creator? Some applications that provide helpful picture formatting options significantly increase the file size. If you used an application such as these, compare your eBook file to the original file (i.e. before you used the application) to see if it increased the file size. If so, weigh the benefits of the improved picture formatting with the effect that it has on your royalty.

❖ Decreasing the resolution of your pictures may reduce your file size. You want to find the best compromise between sharp images and a reasonable file size.

❖ If you have a lot of content, consider splitting your eBook into multiple volumes. In order to do this successfully, there must be enough content in each volume that the customers will feel that the content that they receive in each volume is worth the price of the volume. Customers won't be happy if you have a short eBook that they feel is worth $3.99 and split it up into two $2.99 eBooks, for example; but if you have a long novel, for example, that customers would value at $9.99, they should not mind spending $4.99 for each of two separate volumes.

❖ If you really need to cut your file size and you've already implemented the other suggestions that apply, consider whether or not there is any memory-hogging content (like a picture or table) that you are willing to part with or that you are willing to recast in a plain form (e.g. putting the same information in plain text).

❖ If you have equations, see the suggestion in Sec. 2.2.7.

Go through the minimum publishing steps required (see Sec.'s 4.2.8-4.2.11) to upload your content file and view a preview of your eBook to see how the pictures look after resizing them. You want to find the right compromise for your eBook between the royalty that you earn (which may depend on the file size, as explained in Sec. 4.2.5) and the quality of your pictures.

Some eReader publishers have maximum file size limits on the cover, too. Nook Press, for example, the publisher for Barnes & Noble's Nook, places a limit of 2 MB (2000 KB) on the size of the cover file. Since the cover is a JPEG file, if your picture exceeds this limit, one way to reduce the cover file's memory is to open the file in Paint (or better yet, professional image editing software) and resize it with a lower pixel count.

4.2.5 List Price and Royalties for Your eBook

Your royalty will depend on the publisher of your eBook. Amazon has two options for royalties of Kindle eBooks: One option is a flat 35% of the list price; the other option is 70% of the adjusted price (after subtracting the delivery cost from the list price) for eligible eBooks sold in qualifying countries (and a flat 35% otherwise). The main eligibility criteria is that your eBook does not contain public domain content. In the US, the delivery cost is 15 cents per megabyte (MB) of the content file size after Amazon automatically converts your book to Mobipocket (.mobi) format. In the UK, the delivery cost is £0.10 per MB and in Europe it is €0.12 per MB. If you have a large file size, the flat 35% royalty rate could actually be higher than the 70% royalty option, so it's worth checking both options. After you upload your book for publishing with Amazon Kindle, you will be able to use Amazon's royalty calculator to check the royalty for your eBook with each method. If your book is available for less – e.g. if the paperback edition is selling for less than your eBook through some channel or if your eBook is available for a free promotion through some other channel, then Amazon will price-match your eBook and pay your royalty based on the lower price.

You set the list price for your eBook. The maximum list price for a Kindle eBook is $200 for the 35% royalty rate and $9.99 for the 70% royalty option. The minimum list price depends on your converted content file size. For the 35% royalty option, if your converted content file size is not greater than 3 MB, you may price your Kindle eBook as low as 99 cents; if it is greater than 3 MB, but not greater than 10 MB, you may price your Kindle eBook as low as $1.99; and if it is greater than 10 MB, the minimum price is $2.99. Visit https://kdp.amazon.com/self-publishing/help?topicId=A301WJ6XCJ8KW0 to find the pricing limits for other countries. For the 70% royalty option, the minimum list price is $2.99. Customers who purchase your eBook in other countries may also pay a value-added tax (VAT) – see Sec. 4.1.7.

The 70% royalty option provides an incentive for publishers and authors to price their Kindle eBooks between $2.99 and $9.99 – Kindle eBooks priced below $2.99 or above $9.99 are only eligible for the 35% royalty rate. It also provides an incentive to keep your content file size down – since every MB of memory subtracts 15 cents per sale from your royalties. If it qualifies for the 70% royalty, don't price your eBook between $10.00 and $20.00 – since you would actually make more money by pricing your eBook $9.99 and choosing the 70% royalty.

If you want to price your book under $2.99 – and are therefore willing to accept the 35% royalty rate – there is an incentive to keep your content file size under 3 MB (since you are then eligible for a 99 cents list price) or under 10 MB (which qualifies you for a $1.99 list price). If the file size exceeds 10 MB, then the minimum list price is $2.99.

We will now consider a few examples to see how the royalty rates are calculated for Kindle – but remember, Amazon will also have a royalty calculator available when you go to publish your eBook. Suppose, for example, that your eBook has a file size of 5 MB. If you price your eBook at $1.99 (the lowest possible in this example), your royalty will be 70 cents (since only the 35% option applies) – since $1.99 x 0.35 = $0.70 (your actual royalty could be a penny less than this). If you price your eBook at $2.99, your royalty will be $1.05 with the 35% option – since $2.99 x 0.35 = $1.05 – and $1.57 with the 70% option – since ($2.99 – 5 x $0.15) x 0.7 = ($2.99 – $0.75) x 0.7 = ($2.24) x 0.7 = $1.57. In this example, you would have to sell more than twice as many eBooks at $1.99 than you would at $2.99 with the 70% option in order for the $1.00 discount in the list price to increase your overall royalties.

Let's look at another example where the file size is 2 MB. In this case, your eBook is eligible for a list price of 99 cents. If you price your eBook at 99 cents, your royalty will be 34 cents – since $0.99 x 35 = $0.34. If instead you price your eBook at $2.99, your royalty will be $1.88 with the 70% option – since ($2.99 – 2 x $0.15) x 0.7 = $1.88. You have to sell 6 times as many eBooks at 99 cents as you would at $2.99 in order for the 99 cents list price to increase your overall royalties. For example, if you sell 20 eBooks in the month at $2.99, your royalty would be $37.60, whereas you would need to sell 111 eBooks at $2.99 just to make the same royalty. Some eBooks do sell well at 99 cents or $1.99, but some eBooks don't.

The list price should reflect the quantity and quality of the content. If your eBook has only a little content – like a novella or a short picture book – you might not sell *any* books for $2.99; in that case, a lower price of 99 cents could make a huge difference.

I highly recommend searching for eBooks that are similar to yours and noting their list prices. Also, look for important differences between each eBook and yours – such as the use of a traditional publisher, well-known author, approximate page count, and substantial differences in content. Check the sales ranks, too, to see how well similar eBooks are selling, and note the visibility of each eBook in the search results. Pricing similar titles will help you establish what price range is appropriate for your eBook.

If your eBook is also available in paperback, the list price of your eBook should probably offer customers a discount compared to your paperback selling price (which could be less than its list price, especially if it is on sale). If it does, Amazon will highlight the savings of the Kindle edition compared to the paperback edition so that potential customers see this as a clear discount – that's a nice incentive for doing this. As with paperback books, an eBook with a lower list price does not always (although it sometimes does) increase sales (see Sec. 4.1.5 for a discussion of pricing and royalties).

If you have the rights to sell your eBook in other countries, you also need to set the list price of your eBook for those countries. You can have Amazon automatically calculate a list price for your eBook in those countries based on your US list price. If you prefer to set your list prices manually, you should first visit the websites for Amazon in other countries (such as Amazon UK) in order to establish the price range of similar titles in those countries. If you set a different list price for each European country, Amazon may occasionally need to match the price (e.g. when a customer in one country has a choice of buying your eBook from two different countries, that customer is entitled to the lower price).

I priced this eBook at $4.99 for US sales, which offers a 50% discount compared to the paperback edition. I felt that the paperback price was already a great value (as I explained in Sec. 4.1.5, I found similar paperback titles selling for $14.99 to $24.99; and I also believe[61] that you get a great deal of detailed and helpful information for both paperback and eBook publishing in my book, and it has the advantage of being self-published – compared to a traditionally published author trying to teach you how to self-publish). Even so, I feel rather strongly that eBooks should provide a healthy discount compared to paperback books – after all, look at all the printing, paper, and shipping/handling that is not involved in the purchase of an eBook – which is why I priced the eBook edition 50% less than the paperback edition of this book.

If you choose to enroll your Kindle eBook in the KDP Select program, you also earn royalties when your eBook is borrowed by customers. We will discuss the KDP Select Program, including how the royalty is determined for borrows, in Sec. 4.2.7.

I recommend using the same list price for your eBook regardless of where you publish it. Some publishers, like Barnes & Noble's Nook, require your list price to be no higher than any other sales channel.

Nook Press – the publisher for Barnes & Noble's Nook – pays 65% if your list price is between $2.99 and $9.99 and 40% if your list price is between 99 cents and $2.98 or between $10.00 and $199.99. It would be foolish to price your Nook eBook between $10.00 and $16.23 – since you would actually make a higher royalty with a list price of $9.99! The royalty for Nook eSales is often better than the royalty for Kindle eSales since Nook Press does <u>not</u> charge a delivery fee (instead, Nook Press simply imposes a maximum file size of 10 Mb) – such that 65% with no delivery fee may be better than 70% after a delivery fee; and, of course, for other price ranges, 40% is better than 35%.

---

[61] But please form your own opinion (if you haven't already).

If you publish your eBook with Smashwords, you can make it available for Kobo, Sony, and other eReaders. Sony used to have a store specifically for Sony Reader books, but is now using Kobo books. Make your eBook available with Kobo to reach Sony customers.

Kobo pays a 70% royalty for a wider range of list prices than Kindle or Nook – a list price in the range of $1.99 thru $12.99 qualifies for the 70% royalty at Kobo. For list prices outside of this range, Kobo's royalty rate is 45%, which also beats both Kindle and Nook. However, Kobo does require the list price of your eBook to be at least 20% less than the price of your paperback edition (if you have a paperback edition of your eBook).

4.2.6 ISBN, Keywords, and Categories for Your eBook

Unfortunately, if you have a paperback book, you are **not** allowed to use the same ISBN for your eBook. If you would like to have an ISBN for your eBook, you must either purchase one from Bowker (as described in Sec. 4.1.6) or get one from an eBook publishing company like Smashwords (Sec. 4.2.10) that has a free ISBN option. You can publish an eBook for most eReaders without having an ISBN for it. The main exception is the Sony Reader, which requires the eBook to have an ISBN (remember, you can get a free ISBN from Smashwords).

Even if you don't purchase an ISBN for your eBook, you must still use exactly the same title and author information for both your eBook and your paperback one (if you have one). You are not supposed to add any extra words to the title of your eBook (Amazon, for example, states this very clearly next to the area where you enter the title for your eBook). There is generally not a separate place for the subtitle (but there are places to enter the name of a series and the volume number). If you have a subtitle, you might be allowed include it with the title, separated by a colon – provided that the combination of title and subtitle does not exceed any maximum character length. Note: KDP recently added a subtitle option.

You will have the opportunity to specify keywords associated with your eBook when you publish it. Most of what we discussed regarding how to select keywords in Sec. 4.1.3 also applies to eBooks; I suggest reviewing that section for some important advice. However, there are a few important differences:

- Kindle Direct Publishing with Amazon allows 7 sets of keywords (with up to 50 characters per set). Beware that if you include several words in a single keyword (like "how to self-publish a book," your title will only show up in search results when a customer enters all of those words. So you can't make more than 7 keywords by grouping words together. When you publish an eBook for Nook, on the other hand, there is no limit on the number of keywords, but there is a limit of 100 characters overall.
- The common keyword searches on Amazon are different from common keyword searches on Kindle, for example. You just have to use a Kindle to see what's popular.

- If you publish both an eBook and a paperback book, you can choose to have the keywords of one edition supplement the keywords of the other – instead of doubling up and using the same keywords for both. This may increase your book's visibility.
- A customer who is browsing for Kindle eBooks from a PC might include a keyword like "digital" or "ebook" along with other keywords. However, keep in mind that customers who are shopping from a Kindle device probably won't include words like 'ebook' when they search for eBooks – since only Kindle eBooks will show up in search results when the customer is holding a Kindle in his/her hands. Unfortunately, it's **against the rules** to include the word "Kindle" with your keyword lists.

You will also need to specify browse categories for your eBook. Review Sec. 4.1.3, which discusses how to select browse categories for your paperback book. Kindle Direct Publishing allows you to enter up to two browse categories for your eBook. If you find more than two categories, using different categories for your paperback book and your eBook is one way to have your books show up in more searches.

4.2.7 Amazon's KDP Select, Kindle Unlimited, and MatchBook

Amazon has a few Kindle programs that you should be aware of: KDP Select, Amazon Prime, the Kindle Owners' Lending Library (KOLL), and Kindle Unlimited. Amazon Prime and Kindle Unlimited allow customers to borrow Kindle eBooks instead of purchasing them. Authors who elect to participate in KDP Select are paid for each Amazon Prime borrow and for each Kindle Unlimited download, but the payment isn't the same as a usual royalty: Instead, authors are paid based on the number of pages read.

Kindle Unlimited is a subscription service that costs readers $9.99 per month for unlimited reading of hundreds of thousands of books, which includes all KDP Select books (plus 100,000 other books, but notably absent, presently, are most books by major publishing houses). Customers can store up to 10 borrowed books at a time. After that, they must return a book before downloading a new one through Kindle Unlimited. Note that Kindle Unlimited is now available in several countries (in the beginning, it was just the United States).

Amazon Prime is different. Amazon Prime charges customers an annual fee of $99. The benefits of Prime include free two-day shipping of millions of eligible items (with no minimum purchase), the opportunity to borrow one KDP Select book per month, and access to Prime Instant Videos. Unlike Kindle Unlimited, Prime customers can only borrow one book per month. (Prime, like Kindle Unlimited, is available in Europe.)

I'm a member of Kindle Unlimited and Prime myself, and so are many other customers (and self-published authors).

You must enroll your eBook in the KDP Select program in order for your eBook to be included in the KOLL program (if you publish multiple eBooks, you have this option for each individual eBook – i.e. you *don't* have to enroll *all* of your eBooks in the program). There are some good incentives for publishers and authors to enroll their eBooks in the KDP Select program – listed below – but you must also make a commitment if you do this: Any eBook enrolled in the KDP Select program must be available exclusively on Kindle during the enrollment period (which comes in 90-day intervals). You may have paperback editions of your book available with other publishers, but if you enroll your eBook in the KDP Select program, you may <u>not</u> publish that eBook with Nook, Sony, or any other channel besides Kindle (they do have software that automatically checks on this). Your list price must also be between $0.99 and $9.99 in order to be eligible for the KDP Select program. Also, keep in mind that customers are more likely to purchase a $0.99 eBook rather than borrow it.

Publishers and authors have the following incentives to enroll their eBooks in the KDP Select program:

$ Authors are paid royalties for eBooks that are borrowed for free in the KOLL program. This includes all Amazon Prime borrows as well as Kindle Unlimited downloads. The royalty for a borrowed eBook depends on the number of normalized pages read.

$ The KDP Select fund is often $20,000,000 or more – e.g. it was $23,400,000 for September, 2018. Every time a customer borrows your eBook through the KOLL program, you receive a share of the KDP Select fund based on the number of "normalized pages" that the customer reads.

$ Your royalty for sales is still the same as described in Sec. 4.2.5. Your royalty for eBooks borrowed through the KOLL Program depends on how many pages of eligible eBooks are read through Kindle Unlimited (and to a much lesser extent, Amazon Prime) during the month. Amazon doesn't tell us how much they will pay for each "page" read until the 15th day of the following month. Then you must open your Prior Months' report (look on the second page of the report) and do a little math to figure this out (or visit my blog at www.chrismcmullen.com, as I post the amount each month). For example, for September, 2018, on October 15th we found out that Amazon paid $0.00488 per "page" read for the month of September. It is usually between $0.004 and $0.005 per "page," but has occasionally been above half a penny per page read.

$ You can make your eBook free for up to 5 days in every 90-day enrollment period. You do <u>not</u> earn royalties when customers 'buy' your eBook for free. However, you can greatly increase your audience around the world using this free promotion opportunity. Customers who 'purchase' your eBook during the free promotion who like your eBook may tell friends and family about your eBook. Free promotion 'sales' may help to associate your eBook with other eBooks (so that your eBook will appear in the list of "Customers who bought this item also bought" eBooks) and improve your chances of getting book reviews (but there are no guarantees).

$ If you have multiple eBooks available on Kindle and at least one is enrolled in the KDP Select program, when you make one eBook free, some customers who enjoyed your eBook might purchase one or more of your other eBooks in the future. If you have a series, periodically making the first volume free could be a helpful marketing strategy.

$ A new alternative to the free promo is the Kindle **Countdown Deal**. You can't do both free promos and Countdown Deals in the same 90-day period. The Countdown Deal allows you to set a temporary price reduction that shows as a discount to customers and also shows when your sale will end.

$ An eBook enrolled in the KDP Select program earns 70% royalties for sales in Japan, India, Brazil, and Mexico; otherwise, the royalty is 35% in these countries.

$ At the end of the 90-day enrollment period, you may opt out of the KDP Select program. Enrolling for at least one 90-day period allows you to take advantage of the free promotion opportunity. This is a good incentive to at least test the program out.

Some authors like the KDP Select program; others don't. If you want to hear fellow authors discuss what they did and didn't like about the program, and how successful it was or wasn't for them, try asking about it on Kindle's community help forum (see Sec. 4.2.12). I have enrolled almost all of my eBooks in the KDP Select Program. Presently, the eBooks that I have published with other eReader brands were either prior to Amazon's KOLL program or were eBooks that I have published (mostly with Nook) on behalf of fellow authors.

Authors who feel that their eBooks are successful with the KDP Select program tend to love it. Those who don't receive many borrows or don't get as much out of the promotional tools tend to opt out of the KDP Select program and explore publishing with Nook, Sony, Kobo, Smashwords, and other eReaders in addition to Kindle. Your eBook will have greater availability if you publish it in more places, and some of the competition is removed from other eBook publishing platforms – i.e. any eBook enrolled in the KDP Select program won't be selling on Nook, Sony, Kobo, Smashwords, etc.

Don't confuse the KOLL program with Kindle Book Lending. Borrowing and lending have different meanings in these two programs. A customer may lend your eBook to friends and family through the Kindle Book Lending program. In the case of Kindle Book Lending (unlike the KOLL program), no royalty is paid. Customers can lend your eBook through Kindle Book Lending even if your book is not eligible for the KOLL program (but you may choose to opt out of Kindle Book Lending if your eBook is on the 35% royalty option). An eBook that is loaned through the Kindle Book Lending program is only available for 14 days (and during this period, it is not available to the lender).

Another new program is Kindle **MatchBook**. (This does not require enrollment in KDP Select.) MatchBook provides an incentive to customers to purchase your Kindle eBook together with your paperback edition. To participate in the MatchBook program, you must select the option to discount your eBook for any customer who purchases your paperback.

4.2.8 How to Publish Your eBook with Amazon's Kindle

This section will provide step-by-step instructions for how to publish an eBook with Kindle Direct Publishing (KDP), which is Amazon's Kindle publishing service.[62] It's very important to get the formatting right. If your eBook provides a "poor customer experience," your eBook may be unpublished. Also, if you have a paperback edition of your eBook, the two editions may get linked together – so that a negative review of your eBook due to poor formatting may adversely affect the sales of your paperback edition, too. See Sec. 2.2 regarding how to format your eBook; note that many standard features available in common word processors such as Microsoft Word do <u>not</u> work in eBooks (as explained in Sec. 2.2). For help making figures, see Chapter 3; for help formatting pictures specifically for an eBook, see Sec.'s 2.2.5 and 4.2.2. We discussed how to design a cover for your eBook in Chapter 3. If you are having trouble with the file size, see Sec. 4.2.4. Once your eBook content and cover files are ready for publishing, here are the directions for how to publish your eBook with KDP:

1. Most of the steps for publishing a Kindle eBook with KDP are very similar to publishing a paperback with KDP, which were outlined on pages 168-175. I will outline all of the steps here, but I won't repeat the same information in nearly as much detail this time. Sign up for a free account (or, if you already have an Amazon account, you may use that instead). It's free, with no strings attached. Visit KDP at kdp.amazon.com.
2. Once you login, click the Bookshelf link at the top of the page.
3. From your KDP Bookshelf, click the option to add a new Kindle eBook.
4. Select the language in which the book was written. Note that some languages aren't currently supported for publishing a book at KDP.
5. Enter the title of your book. If you have a subtitle, enter it in the Subtitle field. Check that the length of the title and subtitle combined doesn't exceed 200 characters.
6. If your book is (or will be) part of a series and you want your volumes to be numbered, enter the series title and the volume number.
7. An edition number is optional. (I recommend using this when making revisions.)
8. Enter the name of the primary author (or a pen name) in the author field.
9. If you have a paperback edition of the same book, both the title and subtitle need to match exactly (along with the author name, spelled and punctuated – e.g. if there are initials – exactly the same way) in order to get the two editions linked together automatically on Amazon. (If the two editions don't automatically link within 72 hours of both editions going live, contact support to request to have them linked manually.)
10. Add any other contributors, such as an editor or illustrator.
11. Add the description of your book in the Description field (see Sec. 4.1.2)

---

[62] Kindle and Amazon are trademarks of Amazon.com, Inc. These trademarks and brands are the property of their respective owners.

12. Select your publishing rights. We discussed this on page 170.

13. I highly recommend adding 7 sets of keywords. We discussed this on page 170.

14. Click the Choose Categories button to select up to two categories appropriate for your book (see Sec. 4.1.3). We discussed this on page 171.

15. For children's books, you may optionally add age or grade information. This may help parents who are shopping for a specific age or grade range, for example.

16. There is a new pre-order option. This is helpful if you can generate pre-order sales from your fan base. However, lack of pre-order traffic will hurt your pre-release sales rank. My recommendation is to use the pre-order only if you have strong fan support.

17. Click your preference for Digital Rights Management (DRM). Hover over the link labeled, "How is my Kindle eBook affected by DRM?" to learn more about DRM. One of the Author Earnings Reports shows that books without DRM tend to outsell books with DRM, especially in the $3.99 to $5.99 price point. However, this could be a reflection of what bestselling authors tend to do rather than what eBook customers tend to look for: Most eBook customers probably don't know or care much about DRM.

18. Click the Upload eBook Manuscript button. Find and select your eBook's content file, then click Open. The following file formats are supported: .docx, .doc, .zip, .htm, .html, .epub, .mobi, .pdf, .rtf, or .txt. However, PDF is not recommended. I recommend .docx, .doc, .zip (especially for a picture book, where the zipped folder combines a filtered webpage and the corresponding image files folder: see Step 19), or .epub (if you've researched the steps to produce a Kindle-friendly eBook in .epub format and if you've validated your .epub file). Note the link that outlines the KDP content guidelines.

19. Does your eBook have pictures? If so, for the Kindle edition, I recommend that you open your Word file, click Save As, select Webpage (Filtered), and click okay when the pop-up window comes. Close the Word file. Find your newly created HTML file on your computer. Right-click it and click Send To Compressed (Zipped) Folder. Find the Image Files folder (of the same name) and drag it into the Compressed (Zipped) Folder. Try uploading this zipped folder to KDP in Step 18 (and preview your eBook carefully).

20. Once your uploaded file is fully processed, it will display a list of words that may be misspelled. Review these carefully. If there are mistakes, correct them and repeat Step 18. Once you're satisfied, you may choose to ignore any remaining spelling flags.

21. Either Launch Cover Creator and follow the instructions for how to make a cover, or choose the second option to upload your own cover (Sec. 3.2 discussed how to make an eBook cover). Uploading your own cover gives you the greatest flexibility in customizing your own cover (in JPEG or TIFF format) exactly the way you want it.

22. Click the yellow button called Launch Previewer. This lets you check the formatting of your book online. In addition, I recommend that you click the link called, "Preview on your computer." First download and install Kindle Previewer, and then download your .MOBI file. Open the .MOBI file with Kindle Previewer. Note that Kindle Previewer is

considered more reliable than the convenient online previewer. I recommend using both previewers and the variety of options available. You can almost always catch a variety of formatting mistakes before you publish by using these previewers.

23. Use the Device drop-down menu to preview your eBook on Kindle, Kindle Fire, Kindle Fire HD, iPhone, and iPad – you want to ensure that your eBook formats well on each of these devices. You can also view the orientation in both portrait and landscape. It should look great one way, and at least satisfactory with the other orientation – since a few customers may use their preferred orientation instead of whichever appears better. The buttons on the bottom allow you to advance the page.

24. The formatting of your eBook may have a very significant impact on sales frequency and customer reviews, so it is well worth investing the time to preview your eBook thoroughly – and it is also well worth investing any time needed to make necessary revisions. <u>I strongly recommend that you proof your eBook files carefully</u> (Sec. 5.2).

25. Note that KDP will <u>not</u> edit or revise your files; KDP will <u>not</u> proofread your book; KDP will <u>not</u> check for most formatting or other mistakes. Your book will display directly from the files that you submit. You are responsible for correct editing and formatting.

26. The publisher and ISBN information are optional. You can act as your own publisher and make your own imprint (but **don't** enter KDP, Kindle, Kindle Direct Publishing, Amazon, or CreateSpace), but, if so, do research to search for the name that you choose to avoid using the same imprint as another publisher and, especially, to avoid using any name that may be trademarked. You may **not** use the same ISBN from your paperback book for your eBook. If you would like an ISBN for your eBook, you can purchase a separate ISBN for your eBook through Bowker (as described in Sec. 4.1.6). You can get a free ISBN with Smashwords, but that's intended for use when you publish directly through them (Sec. 4.2.10). Most Kindle eBooks don't use an ISBN for the simple reason that it's *completely unnecessary*: Amazon assigns each Kindle eBook a unique ASIN, which serves the same purpose.

27. If you want to enroll your eBook in the KDP Select program (described in Sec. 4.2.7), check the box at the top of the page. Be sure to read the terms and conditions before you sign up.

28. Select the territories where you have the right to sell your eBook.

29. Choose a royalty option. These are described in Sec. 4.2.5.

30. Enter your list price for Amazon US. See Sec. 4.2.5. Beneath the pricing area you will find the size of your content file after conversion; if this seems rather large, see Sec. 4.2.4. Click Other Marketplaces to set your list price in other countries. Note that it's different from paperback pricing: This time the prices that you enter include VAT.

31. If you also have a print edition, you may enroll in MatchBook (Sec. 4.2.7).

32. The Kindle Book Lending box will automatically be checked. You can only uncheck this box if you opt for the 35% royalty option.

33. Read the terms and conditions (there is a link for them).
34. Click the Save and Publish button when you are ready. Amazon will send you an email when your eBook becomes available on Amazon US – usually about 12 hours.
35. I strongly recommend that you find a Kindle that you can use to purchase your eBook as soon as it becomes available. This way, you can see firsthand exactly how your Kindle eBook looks. If you find any problems, you may submit a revision (though your original may sell before the revised version becomes available).

4.2.9 How to Publish Your eBook with Barnes & Noble's Nook

Nook Press is the eBook publishing service for Barnes & Noble's Nook.[63] Note that there are important differences between Kindle formatting and Nook formatting – e.g. Kindle provides some table support, and large, high-resolution images may overfill Nook's display screen (see the end of Sec. 4.2.2). Therefore, you will probably need to adapt your content eBook file for publishing with Nook. You will have the opportunity to preview how your content eBook file looks on different Nook devices, so if there are any problems, you can revise your files and resubmit them. Also, read the note about Nook figures near the end of Sec. 4.2.2.

Remember, you can't publish your eBook with Nook or any other channel if your eBook is enrolled in the KDP Select program (and if you start that program and later cancel it, you still can't publish your eBook elsewhere until the 90-day period expires).

If you publish with Smashwords (see Sec. 4.2.10), they can publish your eBook with a variety of eReaders for you, including Nook. However, there may be differences in formatting from one eReader to another. If you want to use Smashwords to publish with Nook, I recommend that you at least go through the initial steps of publishing your eBook with Nook Press so that you can use the free preview tool, which will show you exactly how your eBook will appear on Nook and Nook Color. This way, you can see if the same eBook file is suitable for Nook before you have Smashwords publish your eBook for Nook. You should also compare Smashwords' royalty for Nook sales (60%) to the Nook Press royalty (65%).

When you are ready to publish your eBook with Nook, follow the instructions below. Some of the notes that I included in Sec. 4.2.8 for KDP publishing also apply for Nook publishing (such as being sure to enter the exact title of your eBook and not to add extra words, like "Nook Edition") – in those cases, the information might not be repeated again here. Also, I'm not going to include all of the reminders again (like mentioning, "See Sec. 4.2.5 regarding how to set your list price"). **Note: PubIt! is now Nook Press.**

1. Visit www.nookpress.com, the website for Nook Press. Sign up for an account.
2. Login to your Nook Press account. Click the Create New Project button.

---

[63] Nook, PubIt!, and Barnes & Noble are trademarks of Barnes & Noble, Inc. These trademarks and brands are the property of their respective owners.

3. Enter the title of your eBook.
4. Browse for and upload the content file (.doc, .docx, .html, .rtf, or.txt) for your eBook. Remember, the maximum file size for the Nook content file is 20 MB. Click any of the links to see Nook's formatting guidelines (e.g. see the issue with **subscripts**).
5. Enter the list price (it can't be higher than the list price of your eBook through any other channel), the publication date, the publisher (this could be your own Imprint or your name, but it can't be KDP or CreateSpace), and up to 5 contributors.
6. Preview your eBook with Nook and Nook Color. If you encounter problems, see Sec. 4.2.12 (but if your images exceed the page size, see the note near the end of Sec. 4.2.2). I strongly recommend that you proof your eBook files carefully (Sec. 5.2). Note that page breaks may not show on the preview – a problem for some picture eBooks (see the page break tip in Sec. 2.1.8).
7. Browse for and upload the JPEG cover file for your Nook eBook. Note that the maximum dimension is 2000 pixels for a Nook cover, whereas it is 2500 pixels for Kindle. Nook has a maximum cover (not content) file size of 2 MB.
8. Enter the ISBN number if you purchased a separate ISBN from Bowker specifically for the eBook edition of your book (you can't use the paperback ISBN). Also, note that Smashwords has a free ISBN option if you publish an eBook with them (Sec. 4.2.10).
9. Check 'yes' and enter the series name and number if your eBook is part of a series.
10. Indicate if your eBook is also available in print and, if applicable, the page count.
11. Indicate whether or not your eBook includes public domain content.
12. Use the drop-down menu to select the appropriate age group for your audience.
13. If your eBook is not in English, change the language in the drop-down menu.
14. Select the territories where you have the rights to publish your eBook.
15. Select a digital rights management option.
16. Nook allows you to enter up to five categories, which is pretty cool (Amazon currently only allows up to two). ☺
17. Enter up to 100 characters worth of keywords (a counter will show you how many characters remain as you type) separated by commas. You should try searching on Nook – or at least on Barnes & Noble's website for Nook eBooks – to see which popular keyword searches may be relevant for your eBook. You can enter more keywords by choosing shorter keywords, whereas the number of search results is likely to be smaller for a longer keyword (but customers may also be more likely to search for shorter keywords than longer ones).
18. Your eBook description may have up to 5000 characters.
19. You may add an About the Author section of up to 2500 characters.
20. If you have a legitimate editorial book review, you may enter it. If you have a review, but don't know if it qualifies – ask first (click the Support tab at the top right).

21. Read the statement carefully, check the box, and click the Put On Sale button when you are ready to publish your eBook. At any time, you can click the Save button and come back to your eBook later.
22. You can track sales with the My Sales tab at the top of your dashboard.
23. If you have problems, issues, questions, concerns, or just want to meet fellow Nook authors, see Sec. 4.2.12.

4.2.10 How to Publish Your eBook on Sony's Reader and More with Smashwords

A self-published author can't publish an eBook directly with Sony,[64] but an eBook that is published with Smashwords can be made available for the Sony Reader (through Kobo) in addition to a variety of other eReaders, including Barnes & Noble's Nook and even libraries through Baker & Taylor. As mentioned previously, I recommend publishing your eBook with each eReader individually, when possible – or at least going through the initial steps of the publishing process with each eReader, like Nook, in order to see how your eBook looks on the publisher's previewer. Your royalty may be different if you publish your eBook with other eReaders using Smashwords compared to direct publishing (in some instances, though, it could actually be higher with Smashwords, so it's worth comparing). You can use Smashwords to publish your eBook with the following eReader companies:

✓ The Sony Reader Store (Reader), now through Kobo, Inc.
✓ The Apple iBookstore (iPhone and iPad)
✓ Barnes & Noble (Nook)
✓ Kobo, Inc. (Kobo)
✓ Baker & Taylor (public libraries)
✓ Smashwords' website
✓ Diesel, Aldiko, and more

Remember, Sony's Reader will not accept eBooks that do not have an ISBN specifically for the eBook edition. If you would like an ISBN for your eBook, Smashwords offers a free ISBN option; alternatively, you can purchase a separate ISBN for your eBook from Bowker (see Sec. 4.1.6). If you use Smashwords to publish your eBook with Kobo, you will also need an ISBN for that (you can also publish with Kobo directly, as described briefly in Sec. 4.2.11). Note that Sony no longer has a separate store: Publish with Kobo to reach Sony customers.

Publishing with Smashwords comes with some benefits, such as a free ISBN option for your eBook, distribution to libraries, and free marketing and selling tools (for example, Smashwords has a Coupon Manager).

---

[64] Sony is a registered trademark of Sony Corporation. Smashwords is a registered trademark of Smashwords. These trademarks and brands are the property of their respective owners.

Smashwords also provides some helpful literature for free. To find this, from the Smashwords homepage (www.smashwords.com), click the How To Publish On Smashwords link. I highly recommend that you read the <u>free</u> *Smashwords Style Guide* by Mark Coker (find it under, "Getting Started is Easy as 1-2-3"), which is also available for <u>free</u> on Amazon (you can read it with your Kindle or download the free Kindle for PC). If you scroll down to the bottom of the page (the same page you pulled up from the Smashwords homepage after clicking the How To Publish On Smashwords link), you can find more useful literature. This includes, the *Smashwords Book Marketing Guide* by Mark Coker (also free at Amazon), the *Secrets to Ebook Publishing Success* by Mark Coker (also free at Amazon), and a blog post, *How to Self-Publish an Ebook with Smashwords* with contributions from 31 veteran Smashwords authors. It is definitely worth investing the time to read these and follow the advice if you would like for your eBook to successful.

Follow the instructions below in order to publish your eBook with Smashwords. Some of the notes that I included in Sec. 4.2.8 for KDP publishing also apply to publishing with Smashwords – in those cases, the information might not be repeated again here. Also, I'm not going to include all of the reminders again (like mentioning, "See Sec. 4.2.5 regarding how to set your list price").

1. Visit the Smashwords homepage at www.smashwords.com.
2. Sign up for a new account and login to it.
3. Click the Dashboard link near the top of the page.
4. Click the Comments/Questions/Customer Support link at the top of the page. Explore the links above, which will answer several questions that you may have. I recommend clicking the Distribution FAQ link and the Earnings & Payment Schedules Link. From the latter, scroll down to "How are earnings calculated?" to learn how Smashwords royalties are computed for sales through a variety of eReaders.
5. When you're finished exploring the options in Step 4, scroll up to the top of the page and return to your dashboard (by clicking the Dashboard link).
6. Read the free *Smashwords Style Guide* and revise the formatting of your eBook, if necessary. This guide is actually short, although when you first open the file it might seem rather long. The guide also tells you how to avoid AutoVetter errors, which is very important because your eBook won't be included in the Smashwords catalog until all AutoVetter errors have been resolved. <u>Don't</u> stop reading when the guide you reach the Frequently Asked Questions – there are many useful notes beyond that section, such as formatting tips and requirements for the title and copyright pages.
7. The formatting of an eBook is a little different for SmashWords than other eBook publishing services. Here are a few examples:
    a. There is a 5 MB limit on the size of your content file (compare to 20 MB with Nook and 650 MB with Kindle).
    b. Save your content file as a Word document with a .doc (not .docx) extension.

   c. Your cover file should be in JPEG format.

   d. Your cover image must be at least 1400 pixels wide; 1600 x 2400 is the recommended cover image size. The exact title and author must appear on your cover image. The price may not appear on your cover image. You can't have a hyperlink or web address on your cover, or advertisements.

   e. You must have a special note in the copyright page of your eBook. Either include "Smashwords Edition" or "Published by ___ at Smashwords" where you fill in the blank (___) with your name (don't underline your name, of course). Place this on its own line in the copyright page (without the quotes, of course).

   f. You must use the bookmark method for creating an Active Table of Contents, and not Word's built-in table of contents tool (see Sec. 2.2.8). Also, you need to bookmark the Table of Contents heading (but <u>don't</u> add a hyperlink to it) and name this bookmark ref_TOC.

   g. If you have any bookmarks that are not part of your Table of Contents, rename them with a ref_ at the beginning of the names of those bookmarks.

   h. Smashwords does <u>not</u> support Word's cross-referencing tool. If you used any field codes, you must remove them (consult the *Smashwords Style Guide*).

   i. Read the note near the end of Sec. 4.2.2 regarding pixel count (600 x 800) and full-screen images potentially appearing larger than the eReader screen.

   j. Prices at Apple must end in .99 (like $2.99 or $3.99). If you want to have the same list price everywhere (some eReaders require their list price to be no higher than anywhere else), you should price your eBook with this in mind.

8. When you are prepared to publish your eBook with Smashwords, click the Publish link at the top of your dashboard.

9. Enter the information for your eBook. Upload the cover and content files.

10. Preview the Smashwords edition of your eBook very carefully in Word before you upload your files. When you press the Publish button, your eBook will show up on the Smashwords website. You want your eBook to be as nicely formatted as possible when you first publish it, since your eBook may be highly visible for 15 minutes or so on their homepage after you click the Publish button.

11. When you finish entering the information and uploading your files, read the publishing agreement carefully, and if you accept the agreement click the Publish button.

12. Read Step 27 of the *Smashwords Style Guide* to learn how to preview the various formats of your eBook file. Check these files carefully and revise any content issues.

13. You will receive an AutoVetter report regarding the formatting of your eBook (not as observed by a person, but based on criteria that a computer program is looking for). Read your AutoVetter report and correct any issues that are flagged. These issues can significantly affect the distribution of your eBook, or the lack thereof. Check the *Smashwords Style Guide* for common AutoVetter errors.

14. Track sales of your eBooks in the Dashboard section of your Smashwords account.
15. If you have problems, issues, questions, concerns, or just want to meet fellow Smashwords authors, see Sec. 4.2.12.

4.2.11 Publishing with Other eReader Companies

If you opted not to participate in the KDP Select program (described in Sec. 4.2.7), I recommend maximizing the visibility of your eBook by publishing your eBook with several eReaders. Once you've published your eBook with a couple of different eReaders, you should find that the process becomes easier and that the steps are very similar.

Not every eBook publishing service has a strong reputation among authors or readers. The big three – i.e. Kindle, Nook, and Sony – have built strong reputations both among many authors and readers. Before you publish with other eBook companies, I recommend talking with other authors and/or readers about their experiences with those companies. While many of these companies do have good reputations, there are some common complaints with a few eBook publishing services – so it would be wise to learn what these are from your fellow authors before you publish your eBook with them.

There are more eBook publishing services than the couple that I'm listing below. I just selected a couple to help you get started; you can find many other brands at Smashwords. If you would like to find more eBook publishing services, try using your favorite internet search engine.

➢ You can publish with Kobo, Inc. by visiting www.kobobooks.com, scrolling down to the bottom of the page, clicking the Authors & Publishers link, and then clicking Kobo Writing Life.

➢ Check out www.apple.com/itunes/sellcontent, which has information related to publishing iBooks for the iPad or iPhone. Click the Online Application link under Sell Your Books. Click the Learn More link to see important details. Note that Smashwords (Sec. 4.2.10) is an Apple-approved aggregator. Return to the previous webpage (if you clicked the Learn More link) and explore the iAuthor tool, which includes a lot of cool features exclusively for designing a book for the iPad.

➢ Alternative eBook distributors (to Smashwords) include BookBaby and Ingram Spark.

4.2.12 Get Additional Help, Meet Fellow Authors, or Find Support for Your eBook

If you come across problems and can't find the solution in this book (such as needing more help with picture formatting), remember that you can discuss your publishing experiences with other self-published authors at the following community help forums. There is a good chance that other authors have had the same problem and figured out a solution, and someone will likely to be happy to help you. These forums are also a good place to go if you have questions, concerns, or would like to meet fellow self-published authors. In addition to community help forums, eBook publishing services also have support pages with instructions for how to publishing your eBook, frequently asked questions, and a method of contacting a representative with help. There is also a good chance that you will find the answer to your problem/question/concern/issue if you type your issue into the search field of your favorite internet search engine. The important thing to remember is that you are not alone. There are thousands of other self-published authors who are encountering similar problems when they self-publish their eBooks. Many authors have valuable advice that they could share – often, wisdom that they have gained from their mistakes – if only someone would ask for help.

The community help forum for Kindle eBooks can be found at:

https://kdp.amazon.com/community/index.jspa

Also try searching Kindle's self-publishing help pages:

https://kdp.amazon.com/self-publishing/help

If you need to submit revisions, look for the heading "Updating Your Published Book" on the left-hand side of the webpage – if there are significant changes, click on the Notifying Customers of Book Updates link. Two other useful links are Conversion Resources and the Frequently Asked Questions. Also explore the "Featured Guides" for more help. It is possible to delete a title from your dashboard, which will make it impossible for a customer to purchase your eBook, but it may not completely remove all trace of your eBook from the internet.

The Nook Press community help forum for Nook eBooks is available at:

http://bookclubs.barnesandnoble.com/t5/NOOK-Press-Help-Board/bd-p/NOOKpress

To access Nook Press's help and support pages, simply click the Support tab at the top of your Nook Press dashboard.

Smashwords provides a wealth of help directly on their website – such as self-publishing style and marketing guides (see Sec. 4.2.10), support pages (click the Comments/questions/ customer support link at the top of the page), and a FAQ link and a How to Publish on Smashwords link at the top of their homepage (you can see both of these when you're *not* logged in to your account). On their homepage, scroll down and look on the left to find useful links under "Publish on Smashwords." Just below that, you can find "Socialbuzz," with links to FaceBook and Twitter if you're interested in meeting other authors who have self-published eBooks with Smashwords.

Remember, you can also contact the eBook publisher directly – try looking for "contact us" options in their support and help pages.

A DETAILED GUIDE TO
SELF-PUBLISHING
with
AMAZON
AND OTHER ONLINE BOOKSELLERS

VOL **2**

Chris McMullen

COPYRIGHT

A Detailed Guide to Self-Publishing with Amazon and Other Online Booksellers, Vol. 2
Proofreading, Author Pages, Marketing, and More

Copyright © 2013, 2014 by Chris McMullen
All rights reserved. This includes the right to reproduce any portion of this book in any form.

Chris McMullen
Cover design by Melissa Stevens: theillustratedauthor.net

Fifth edition published in February, 2019 (KDP merged with CreateSpace)
Fourth edition published in October, 2014 (new Kindle programs and minor updates)
Third edition published in May, 2014 (for new cover and minor updates)
Second edition published in January, 2014 (to add **index** and minor updates)
First edition published in April, 2013

Books > Education & Reference > Publishing & Books > Authorship
Books > Business & Investing > Marketing & Sales > Marketing

ISBN-10: 1484037243
EAN-13: 978-1484037249

Disclaimer: Every effort was made to describe the information in this book very accurately as of the publication date. Companies make periodic changes to their websites, practices, and policies, and so this information is subject to change. The author makes no guarantees regarding the information in this book. You should check directly with each company for the most up-to-date information regarding their practices, policies, pricing, etc.

CONTENTS

Volume 1 Contents

INTRODUCTION

THE FACT THAT YOU'RE reading the introduction to the second volume of this book shows that you're not only interested in putting an excellent book together, but are also motivated to perfect and promote your book. This makes a huge difference, and therefore we will reconsider a few suggestions from the first volume. For example, in Volume 1, I recommended making a free cover for two reasons (which I didn't reveal at the time; rather, I only emphasized saving money and how long it may take to recover the investment). First, you will see firsthand how well you can design your own cover, which will serve as the basis for comparison. If you shop for cover help, you will be able to measure how much the artist is improving over your own ability. Secondly, whether or not you should invest in a fantastic cover depends on several factors, such as how much time and effort you will put into revisions and marketing. You're showing some interest in this because you have this book open presently, so we'll reconsider this point in Volume 2.

Self-publishing success involves several factors. Just having a great book concept is the tip of the iceberg. There are tens of thousands of incredible books and hundreds of thousands that had the potential to be incredible books (but the execution wasn't perfect). The first step is to have an attractive cover. Nobody will discover how good your book is until they first discover your book. The second step is to have an interesting blurb, which shows how much harder it can be to write just a few words than very many. Next, customers look inside your book. It takes professional editing and formatting to get customers who discover your work to read it. Once they begin to read, the book must be well-written and engaging. Finally, a great story (for fiction) or excellent content (for nonfiction) will help to establish the book as a good book. If also the book evokes powerful emotions and has memorable characters (for fiction) or is extremely useful or entertaining (for nonfiction), it may be a great book.

Marketing is only useful if the packaging (cover, blurb, and formatting) is professional. There isn't much point in drawing interest into a product that many people won't buy. If the cover, blurb, or sample doesn't look professional, the customer will wonder if the content is similarly lacking in effort. There are hundreds of thousands of books that are professional all the way through. So why read a book that appears less than professional?

A great cover and blurb will only be effective if the book is first perfected. Reviews and the very important prospect of word-of-mouth sales depend on this. Edit and revise your book to perfection. If you're willing to do this, then a fantastic cover and an effective marketing plan can significantly impact the potential success of your book. In this book, you will learn how to perfect your book from cover to cover and how to market your book successfully.

Chapter 5

Editing Your Proof

Chapter Overview

5.1 Proofing Your Paperback
5.2 Proofing Your eBook

This chapter answers questions about the following topics, and more:

- ☑ How the cover, title, and other elements of your book can help market it.
- ☑ Getting feedback before your publish and how this can help create "buzz."
- ☑ How to make even-page headers show the name of each chapter.
- ☑ Using Roman numerals for front matter and Arabic numerals for the main text.
- ☑ Perfecting your cover design and the importance of having an excellent cover.
- ☑ What to look for when you receive your paperback proof.
- ☑ Why you should receive at least one proof as a hard copy.
- ☑ When it's okay to proof your paperback book electronically.
- ☑ Possible variations and differences between your proof and customers' paperbacks.
- ☑ What to do if the proof is significantly different from your interior or cover file.
- ☑ Submitting revisions to your interior or cover files.
- ☑ Other things you need to proof besides your book, like your description and biography.
- ☑ Improving the description for your book.
- ☑ Using Word's Styles and perfecting the formatting of your eBook.
- ☑ What to look for when you proof your eBook.
- ☑ Warnings that some eBook publishing services may make you wait one or more days before submitting changes once you publish your eBook.
- ☑ Submitting revisions to your eBook interior file or thumbnail image.

5.1 Proofing Your Paperback

5.1.1 Before Submitting Files for Review

MANY INDIE AUTHORS submit their files for review prematurely, and also approve their proofs too early. You want your book to appear as professional as possible, which will help it to stand out in a good way, and you want to give your book the best possible chance of success. Take your time, consider everything carefully, invest a little more time and effort where it may help, and strive to avoid amateur mistakes (like rushing the book to market too soon).

This mistake is very natural. It takes a great deal of time, effort, writing, revising, and commitment just to write the book in the first place. The process consumes some authors to the extent that they are often up in the middle of the night working. After months of writing, you feel a strong desire for the project to be complete and to get some recognition and appreciation for your hard work.

That's when you discover how much more effort is needed for editing, formatting, cover design, preparing a blurb, and marketing. Writing the book is actually the easy part, especially since you enjoy writing. Most authors don't enjoy editing, formatting, and marketing, but they are just as important for the potential success of your book. It's easy to shirk on these aspects and rush the book to market for that feeling of satisfaction and the prospects for reaping some rewards from the time that you've invested (and any money that you may have put into it, too). However, you'll be far more satisfied and have much better prospects for some measure of success if you strive to perfect the full package.

I'd rather read a book that tells a great story, but has a poor cover, some editing and formatting mistakes, and wasn't marketed well than to read a book that tells a mediocre story, but has a fantastic cover, professional editing and formatting, and was marketed effectively. But that's not a choice that customers face. Most people won't find a book that's not visibly marketed, several won't read a book if the reviews complain of editing or formatting problems, and many won't notice a book among other thumbnails if the cover doesn't appeal to them. As a result, a mediocre writer with highly effective marketing skills will often be much more successful than a great writer who struggles with marketing. I'm not saying that it's necessarily fair, but it is what it is. Strive to perfect the full package and your book will have the best chance for success.

In a few paragraphs, we will consider a few important details that you can still change before you approve your proof. I believe that you'll be happy that you didn't skip ahead to the next section. Have a little patience, as there are a few other important points that I feel compelled to make first. For example, if you think it may be too late to make changes, you might be wrong. Also, I would like to stress the importance of trying to perfect your work now.

If you used a free ISBN from Amazon, you can still delete your title and start over if you haven't already approved your proof. If you invested in an ISBN or other services and would still like to make changes, contact Amazon KDP to discuss your options. Depending on the situation, you may still have the opportunity to start fresh without a sunk cost. Once you choose your ISBN information, you can't change your title, author, and other information that relates to your ISBN, but you can delete your book all together and add a new title if you haven't already approved your proof. If you have approved your proof and haven't enabled any sales channels, then you can also just start a new title. Even if you have enabled sales channels, you can disable sales channels (but in this case, your original title will probably still show on Amazon for potential used sales, even though it won't be available for sale new). Where there is a will to start fresh, there probably is a way. The main issue is that if you've already invested in money in the title, you want to contact Amazon KDP and ask if there is any way to transfer that investment into a new title (or if they can revise your current title).

Most self-published authors have very little money to invest toward cover design, professional editing, marketing, etc. But authors do have time; they may not always exercise the patience to take as much time as they could, yet this is much easier than finding money to invest. Time is money. So if you lack money, invest time. There are many resources available to help you design a better cover. You can proofread and revise repeatedly and find other pairs of eyes to help. You can collaborate with other authors and help one another edit. There are many free marketing tools available. Lack of money is not a valid excuse for not perfecting your cover, writing, promotion, etc. Invest the time to do it right.

Don't get caught in the common lazy trap. If you just want to get your work out there to find out if it's good before you invest time in it, don't publish your work. Instead, join a writing group (online or in person) for such feedback. Once you publish your work, you're beginning to develop your image and reputation. Do this with your best work from the onset. Don't think, "If my book sells and people like it, then I'll invest in a cover," or, "If anyone complains about the editing, then I'll fix it." These things can actually affect, quite significantly, if your book sells and how much, and whether or not people will like it. Also, if anyone leaves a one-star review complaining about editing, it's permanent. Make every effort to put your best work out there in the beginning. There are thousands of indie authors wishing they had.

So which features of your book should you consider possibly changing before submitting your files for review? Let's reconsider your cover, title, blurb, price, and your image as an author. It's also very important to develop a marketing plan before you publish. The vast majority of indie authors first publish, then later on consider marketing as an afterthought. A marketing plan – which can be relatively simple – can give your book a significant edge.

Test your book out before you publish. You can show your book to family, friends, and acquaintances, but it's far more important to gauge how complete strangers will react. Don't ignore family and friends – try both. Make a revised version of your front cover where you change the text to something like, "This is not the real title of this book," and print it out (in color). Show this to dozens of strangers and ask them two questions: (1) What do you think this book is about? (2) What do you think about the cover? If 70% of your sample thinks that your book is a romance, when it's really a thriller, you have a problem. Even if your book is a romance, but they think it's erotica, you still have a problem. It's much better to receive invaluable feedback like this before you publish than afterward.

With your second question, you may receive helpful suggestions, like whether or not the font is legible, if the cover seems too busy, and whether or not the colors work well together. You might come to learn that while only a few people are talented artists, almost everybody is an art critic. Be prepared to show a "thick skin." You want to solicit honest advice. Don't defend your work and you'll receive more honest opinions. Don't try to satisfy every comment that you hear. You have to try to filter out the good from the bad, and you also have your own tastes and style to consider. If you did the art yourself and tend to get defensive easily when others criticize your work, find a friend to do this for you (in your complete absence). Start building a positive image as an author. If you get in an argument with a stranger about your cover and they post this story on the internet, your book might be sunk before the ship ever sails. Be professional at all times to build the best possible author image.

You can get such feedback just about anywhere. Keep the cover with you for one day and show it to everyone you interact with. If you absolutely can't make yourself feel comfortable doing this for one day (or persuade a friend to do it on your behalf), then use the internet. Even if you do feel comfortable asking in person, you can also supplement this with the internet. Post online and get feedback, but not just from people who know and like you (as would be the case with social media – their feedback may be helpful, too, but you really need to gauge the opinions of strangers).

Next, print out a page that has just the title as it appears on your front cover (remove the picture, author, and everything else – however, if your font color is light, change the background to a dark color instead of white). Show this to a different group of strangers (i.e. people who haven't seen your cover). Ask them what they think your book is about. You want your cover, title, and blurb to present a unifying picture and to reinforce one another. Ideally, anyone who looks at your cover, reads your title, or reads your blurb (any one of the three all by itself) should be able to identify your book's genre and have some idea of what to expect.

Therefore, you should separately print out your blurb (your book's description) and show it to several people who haven't seen your cover or read your title. By doing this three times (once for the cover, title, and blurb), you actually get more exposure for your book prior to its release. Don't think of it as more work. Think of it as a combination of valuable input and free marketing. Remember, you're also trying to establish your image as a professional author.

When you solicit opinions on your cover and title, here's something else you would like to gauge. First, watch closely to see how they react. If the cover has a striking image, you should see some pop in their reactions; if your cover is just so-so (or worse), you may be able to judge this from their reactions. Next, you want to judge whether your cover or title are memorable. At some point during your interaction, put these papers away, then just as they're about to walk away, ask them to please describe the cover or repeat the title (whichever it was). Did you have a striking image that they will retain well or a short, catchy title that is easy to remember? You want them to remember your title easily and for a long period of time because this significantly improves your chances of getting word-of-mouth sales, which are the most valuable sales you can get (the book also has to be good – both content and aesthetics – to get these). If the picture is memorable, it will help them recognize your cover. Some customers don't make immediate purchase decisions, but those who don't often wind up buying products that they remember. How many times do you choose one brand over another in the store simple because you've heard of it? Recognition – both by sight and by name – is important.

Now you may see the value of having a short title. If you browse the bestseller lists, you may learn that most of these books have just three words or less in their titles! We'll return to this issue in Sec. 5.1.5.

Remember, these polls give you exposure. This way, you're beginning a small marketing campaign before your book is even published. If your cover looks nice or your title sounds interesting, a few people whom you interact with may ask when your book will be available. Be prepared for this marketing opportunity. You want people to look for your book later (even if they don't ask you directly, you can still make this effort). When will it be available? How will they find it? Think about the answers to these questions. Even better, prepare a press release package (see Sec. 8.1.14). We'll return to the necessity of developing a marketing plan in the next section, along with other valuable pre-release marketing suggestions, like preorders.

Strive to perfect your cover, title, and blurb before you seek opinions. You're more likely to generate interest in your work this way, and you'll also receive more effective feedback. We will discuss how to this in Sec.'s 5.1.3-5. If you revise your cover, title, and/or blurb significantly after receiving feedback, consider showing them again after the revisions. You'll receive new feedback and, if the feedback is better, develop a helpful measure of confidence. (Confidence is an important skill in marketing success, but so is humility. You need both. Beware of overconfidence and bragging, and also avoid the other extreme of lacking confidence.) You will also increase your pre-sale exposure. (This exposure is a minor thing in itself. If you interact with a hundred people who show interest, it might be just a few – but you never know; people do like to read books by authors they have met, and they might appreciate that you sought their advice – who actually buy your book, and it might not be for quite some time. Do it for the feedback, not for the promotion. At the same time, all of the little things that you can do in the way of marketing do add up.)

I recommend reading this chapter *before* submitting your files for review. In addition to considering possible changes before it may be too late to make them, you might also avoid some common mistakes (such as those described in Sec. 5.1.6). It's much better to prevent mistakes than to correct them later.

Copyright registration is another thing that you might want to do before you publish. Your work is already under copyright protection once you have typed or written it. I recommend that you keep your files (especially, a sequence of versions showing the development of your book over the course of time), just in case. If you are the copyright owner of the work (i.e. you wrote it yourself and were not a work for hire, and have not granted the copyright to anyone else, such as a publisher), then you provide your copyright notice in the copyright page of your book. Copyright registration is optional protection that you can obtain by filling out a form and submitting a copy of your manuscript to www.copyright.gov with a fee ($35 online and $65 via mail, presently).

Amazon has contacted a few authors to request verification of copyright ownership. Presently, it has only happened to a small percentage of authors, but it has happened. For example, if Amazon realizes that two different authors have published essentially the same material or if someone complains to Amazon that copyright may have been violated, Amazon will ask the author(s) to verify copyright ownership. In such instances, the simplest, most effective way to respond is to submit proof of copyright registration. If you don't have copyright registration, your work is still copyrighted, and there are still ways to demonstrate copyright ownership – it's just not quite as easy. I'm not an attorney. If you would like legal advice, contact an attorney. You can also find some helpful resources and learn more about copyright law at www.copyright.gov.

5.1.2 The Importance of Having a Plan

Most authors click Approve Proof to publish their first book without any sort of plan for how they will help stimulate sales. As we will learn in this section, you can start out with a simple, yet effective, marketing plan, which can make a significant impact on the success of your book. The problem is that most writers excel at writing or storytelling, but don't have any marketing skills – or associate marketing with social media, advertising, and salesmanship (but it's not!). We'll explore free and low-cost marketing ideas in detail in Chapter 8. For now, we'll focus on simple, yet effective ways to help stimulate sales when you release your book.

As of February 2013, there are 20,000,000 paperback books, nearly 8,000,000 hardcover books, and almost 2,000,000 Kindle eBooks for sale on Amazon. Just in the last 30 days, 80,000 paperbacks, 30,000 hardcovers, and 60,000 Kindle eBooks have been published. More than 5,000 books are released every day just on Amazon.[1] What do these numbers mean to you? How will anyone ever discover your book? Customers must discover your book before there is any chance that they will read or buy it.

---

[1] These numbers were found by browsing Books and Kindle eBooks, respectively. Some of these books are different editions of the same book or re-releases of previous books, and so the actual number of *new* books may be somewhat smaller than these figures suggest.

Publishing is a highly competitive business. There are millions of books on the market, including a hundred thousand new releases. Out of these millions of books, only the top 5,000 sell several copies per day on average; the top 50,000 sell a couple of copies per day on average; and millions of books just sell a few copies per month or less.

You're not just competing with other self-published authors. Many of the top selling books are published by the big traditional publishers or were written by established popular authors. It may be instructive to browse the bestsellers in your genre. You may see that you don't have to be a big name or have a big publisher to achieve success, and you can learn a few of the secrets to success by studying (and even reading) books that are proven to sell well. The bestsellers tend to have excellent covers, short and clear descriptions, and a visually attractive sample in the Look Inside. Their product pages tend to look professional. Look for other features, like editorial reviews, quotes from readers, an author picture and link to an author page, and which categories the book is listed in. This should help give you some ideas.

A marketing plan can help jumpstart sales, which may help make your book discoverable by other potential customers and which helps improve your prospects for reviews (since customers need to read your book before they can review it). If instead you just throw your book out there and very few people discover your book, your book will have a history of poor sales rank, which itself can affect sales. You don't need to invest in the marketing. There are simple, free ideas available. I will reveal what these are in a few paragraphs. Patience, please.

Let me first discuss something else that's equally important – something that you must do in order to prevent the marketing plan from backfiring. First, you must perfect your book from cover to cover and your product page. It won't do any good to drive sales to your book if any feature of your book or product page seems unprofessional – that will put many prospective customers off, and may result in negative customer reviews.

Your cover will show up next to other covers in search results. Customers are more likely to notice a cover that attracts interest. If your cover and title attract interest (and signify the correct genre), customers will check out the product page and read the description. If the product page appears professional and the description engages their interest, customers will Look Inside. If the sample looks professional, customers will read the first chapter. If the first chapter holds their interest and customers don't encounter mistakes or anything that spoils their mood, customers will buy your book. If the book is professionally edited and formatted, the story is good, and the characters are memorable, customers will leave good reviews; but if there are mistakes or issues that you could have corrected, these are likely to show up in bad reviews. So many factors affect the prospects for sales and reviews.

Some authors think along these lines: "You shouldn't judge a book by its cover," "Great storytelling is more important than technically correct writing," and, "If the story is great, customers will spread the word." You're absolutely right, philosophically, but that's not the way book buying works in practice. The reality is that the cover strongly impacts buying decisions, the quality of the writing does affect reviews, and you need people to read your book (and not be distracted by editing or formatting issues) before they can spread the word. The other side is this: Why should customers spend money on a book that wasn't perfected?

Here's the thing. There are tens of thousands of books that have fantastic covers, enticing descriptions, professional product pages, a professional Look Inside, are professionally edited and formatted, tell great stories, and feature memorable characters. If your book only has a few things on this list, why should customers buy your book when there are tens of thousands of books available that have everything on this list? Remember, you don't necessarily need money to perfect these things – you can invest some time instead. We'll discuss how to perfect your cover, interior, and blurb in Sec.'s 5.1.3-5.

You need to have your book and product page perfected when you release your book if you want your marketing plan to be effective. If instead you release your book and save these things for later, your book is more likely to start out with a mediocre sales rank and – if there are writing or story issues in the content – receive some negative reviews. It's much more difficult to overcome a history of a mediocre sales rank and negative reviews than it is to do everything right in the first place. So don't procrastinate. You can favorably impact the potential success of your own book by doing everything right in the first place.

What simple, free ideas are available for a marketing plan that can help stimulate initial sales (and through those sales, hopefully, some reviews, too)? Note that a complete list can be found in Sec. 8.1.2. First off, you can begin to develop a following before your first book is ever released. Start with people you know – friends, family, acquaintances, and coworkers who may appreciate your work. Most of the books that people read were written by authors they know very little about. When the rare opportunity presents itself, people like to be able to say, "I know that author," and especially, "I knew her before she became famous."

Start with friends, family, acquaintances, and coworkers. Keep them informed about the progress of your book – but don't overdo it. Show them how much time and effort you're putting into it; emphasize the various challenges that you've come across and how you've handled them. If you've asked them for any input – whether it's on part of the content or just the cover – they may feel a little more attached to and interested in your work.

Next, tap into your social networks (again, don't overdo it or you get tuned out). You may have many more acquaintances there. Have you posted your cover, title, and description there and asked for feedback? You want to increase the "buzz" about your upcoming book. It's unrealistic to expect everyone you know to buy your book or to buy it on the day it comes out. However, the more people who know about your book, the better. Someone who isn't interested in your book, but knows about it, might tell a friend who does read your genre.

Strive to increase the anticipation for your new release. "Did you hear that Jane wrote a mystery and it's coming out next month?" Such word-of-mouth advertising can be very helpful, but you can improve on this. You want them to know a little more. What striking characteristic does your book have? Compare the previous quote to the following quotes. These can be more effective. "Jane's cover is incredible. You have to see it." "One of Jane's characters is just as memorable as Gollum from *The Hobbit*." "Jane spent years just doing the research for her book." "I heard that Jane's book could be the next *Harry Potter*." "I read an excerpt from Jane's book, and the writing conveys some powerful emotions."

You want to identify ways that your book stands out and promote this. Share this. Don't try to tell people to advertise for you – or worse, tell them what to say. Rather, share a part of your book that's likely to generate "buzz" about your book. If your cover is awesome, the more you show it and request feedback, the more buzz you might get about your cover. If you've put a great deal of time into writing and revisions, working with an editor, doing research, and so on, mention this in conversations, occasionally post this on your social networks, etc. Don't heavily plug your upcoming book or the information may be tuned out; less than 10% of your posts might mention your book or your work on it, for example.

Friends, family, acquaintances, and coworkers are just the beginning. If you took my suggestion from the previous section to solicit feedback from strangers, this helps to build your following. Next, look for local press coverage. Local newspapers often like to feature local authors, for example. We'll discuss this and other marketing ideas (such as writing articles, which can be highly effective) further in Chapter 8. I hope that you see the importance of learning more about marketing and developing your marketing strategy <u>before</u> you release your book. It would be a great idea to skip ahead and read Sec. 8.1.2 now.

The following that you build and the "buzz" that develops in anticipation of your book's release can help to stimulate early sales.[2] Strive to visualize this – in a positive way, with the confidence that you can pull it off. Read Chapter 8 before you publish. There you can learn about other important pre-release marketing strategies, like how to get your book listed as Coming Soon on Amazon with the option of preorders (sales that you can get before your book is ever released) – that's what the big publishers do – but note that preorders themselves are described in Sec. 7.1.8. You also want to learn how to develop a long-term marketing plan; what we've discussed so far is just to get you started.

Your author image is very important. Every person you interact with, anything you post online, any email or text message that you send, and every other form of communication that you have with anyone helps to portray your image as an author. You want these posts, comments, blogs, conversations, and such to show you in a positive light as a professional author, knowledgeable about writing in his/her genre, of good character, etc. Strive to build a positive image and establish a "brand" as an author. Above all, accept criticism (and offer thanks for it – except in written reviews on your book's product page), don't act rashly or emotionally, and don't respond to any criticism defensively, snobbishly, or accusingly. A single outburst of unprofessional conduct can bring an avalanche against your book far greater than any marketing that you can do. We will discuss this further in Chapters 7-8.

---

[2] Beware that anyone who may have a financial interest in your book, such as immediate family, is not permitted to review your book on Amazon.com. If they do, their reviews are very likely to be removed at some point. We'll discuss marketing and the prospects for receiving reviews further in Chapters 7-8.

If you will be releasing both paperback and eBook editions, you will want to time their availability. In order for them to become available simultaneously, you should have them all ready and set to go (meaning that you've already inspected your printed proof and previewed your eBook on all devices, and are happy with both), so that all that remains to be done is to click the buttons to publish. It will take about 12 hours for your eBook to go live and although your paperback might show up in one to three days (but not always), it will take longer for your product page to grow (see Chapter 7). You can also establish your paperback early with preorders, or launch a hardcover edition first (learn more in Sec. 7.1.8 and Chapter 8).

You may want your eBook edition to be released prior to your paperback edition, or vice-versa. This way, provided that you successfully market the release of your book, you may be able to stimulate early sales twice – once with each release – since some people prefer eBooks, while others prefer paperback (or hardcover). Many traditional publishers apply the multi-release strategy with different editions. They often release the more expensive hard-cover first; but in your case, you might actually draw a greater royalty on a cheaper edition.

Will you be publishing one book, several books, or a series? The answer to this question affects your marketing strategy. If you have a series, or if you will have a few related books, you want to maximize your exposure for the first book. In this case, your goal isn't to make the greatest profit from the first book, but to maximize the number of sales. The idea is that the more people who read your first book, the more people will get drawn into the series. The catch is that your first book better be very good in order to make customers come for more. Many authors actually give their first book away for free or offer giveaway promotions with their first books with long-term success in mind (we'll return to this point in Chapter 8).

5.1.3 Perfecting Your Paperback Cover

Your cover is a very important marketing tool. A great cover helps to get your book discovered in search results. The cover should attract attention and signify the genre. Customers browsing through search results on Amazon are usually looking for a specific type of book, and they tend to click on appealing covers that look like the types of books that they normally read. Therefore, it's very important to study the covers in your genre to see what customers are accustomed to seeing.

A great cover can make a huge difference for a book that has a good description, professional product page, great story, memorable characters, and a professional Look Inside. A mediocre cover on a great book can significantly deter sales. A great cover on a mediocre book can inspire original sales, but then the reviews may eventually reflect that the book is mediocre. You won't be guaranteed success by having a great cover, but not having a great cover may greatly limit your book's potential. Give your book the best chance of success with the best cover you can make given your resources (which may be greater than you think).

Almost all top-selling authors believe that a highly successful book needs to have a fantastic cover. The content is more important to the reader, but the cover significantly helps in determining to what extent your book will be noticed in search results. The content is irrelevant when customers don't notice and explore the book. Just imagine your book lying atop a customer's desk or table when company comes over. If the guests notice your book and think, "Wow, that looks interesting," your book suddenly becomes a conversation piece. It's not just Amazon search results that may be affected by your cover: Your cover may be seen on buses, subways, airport terminals, and anywhere else that a customer might read your book in public. Word-of-mouth sales can make for highly effective, yet free marketing.

The cover has more importance than just attracting attention, signifying the genre, and emphasizing a few words that suggest what the book is about. It also represents an image of your professionalism and attention to detail. In practice, people *do* judge a book by its cover. When the cover is poor or mediocre, a potential buyer naturally wonders if the content is similarly lacking in effort. If the content isn't lacking, make a cover that isn't lacking either.

Does *every* book need a super cover? The cover is very important for most books, but there may be a few exceptions where a good cover may suffice. A cover is extremely important for most genres in fiction and for many nonfiction books that are more likely to sell by being wanted than by being needed. Nonfiction books that inform readers how to do something, provide technical help, include valuable knowledge, and so on may be able to get away with just a good cover. In this case, a simple cover can be quite effective, so long as it is visually appealing, the right words are emphasized and clear in the thumbnail, and the cover doesn't violate any of the rules for making a good cover (to be described soon). But here's the thing: If there are two similar nonfiction books providing helpful information – all other things being roughly equal, as far as the customer can tell – the one with the better cover will win.

I've heard some amazing success stories from authors who significantly improved their original covers – in many cases, going from one sale per day or less to several copies per day. Their blurbs, stories, editing, formatting, and characters were good, too; the new and improved covers helped call attention to their books. If the book is good, it's worth the cover.

What makes a cover good or great? It's not just about the art. There are some lousy covers that are highly detailed artistically or have well-crafted images, and there are some exceptional covers that are virtually lacking in art. However, for fiction, you definitely need some sort of imagery to signify the genre and show what the book is about. It doesn't have to be art (except perhaps for a few genres, like fantasy, where art is common); it could be a quality photo.

Covers involve many factors. If any aspect is poor, it can single-handedly ruin the effect. There is text for the title and author (at least), there may be art or photos, there can be decoration, and covers have a background. The quality of the images must be high – not just in terms of DPI, but also by being "clean," not having red-eye, looking sharp, etc. The text must be clear. Colors must coordinate well. Even the layout is important.

Shortly, we will consider a variety of ingredients that go into designing a cover and how to perfect them. In Volume 1, I described how to make a cover, while I have saved the secrets for perfecting the cover until Volume 2. Why? Partly, I didn't want to limit your creativity; if you've already attempted a cover, then you have a draft to serve as a useful starting point. Secondly, since you're reading the half of the book that concerns perfecting your proof and marketing, it suggests that you have the motivation to produce a good enough book for which an excellent cover may make the difference.

For this very reason, we should also reassess whether or not it may be worthwhile to invest in a nice cover. In Volume 1, I suggested saving money. If you will be following the advice of Volume 2 on how to perfect the content and if you're also motivated to market your book (e.g. by trying to create "buzz" for its release), then investing in a nice cover is more likely to reap dividends for you. You may have witnessed your own cover design potential firsthand if you've already attempted a draft of your cover. If so, this may help you decide how much a professional cover may improve over your own ability. Many successful authors have invested in cover design. For people with highly effective marketing skills, it's a no-brainer – they already have a plan for how to recover the investment through sales. Ask yourself how confident you are in your own book. Do you believe that it's good enough to succeed? Bear in mind that if you do hire a professional designer, your book may be featured on their website, which offers you a little exposure in return. If you're wondering about costs, hold onto your question for a moment.

There is an exception. There are a few indie authors who expect to sell most of their books in person. This is common for salesmen or speakers who travel around the country to give presentations. They sell most of their books in person when the presentation is over. If that's you, and you don't expect your book to be discovered through search results, then just having a satisfactory cover may be in order. Otherwise, strive for a great cover.

Now let's get into the cover secrets! The first step is to avoid common mistakes, which can turn a potentially great cover into a lousy cover:

☺ **Text that is hard to read** because of a poor or fancy font. Clear and legible is much better than fancy. Some fonts often create a negative reaction. Research your font selections online to find out for which context they're more often used and how appealing they seem to be (Wikipedia lists research statistics on this for many fonts).

Old English textis notthateasy to read

Comic Sans has a tendency to produce a negative reaction from readers.

☺ Problems with image quality. Pictures that appear **blurry, jagged, or pixelated** – in print or online – create a poor impression (we'll discuss how to correct these issues in Sec. 5.1.6). Inspect the quality of the images in the printed proof carefully.

☺ Poor photographs. Photos should be **well-lit**, properly **touched up** (like removing red-eye), precisely **cropped** (if needed), and professional in appearance.

☺ Using low-resolution images. Google images and other stock images often have 96 DPI. (These images may also be easily recognized from having been used on many occasions.) Ideally, all images should be **300 DPI** in the native program and if you insert them into Word you must take steps to avoid automatic compression (see Sec. 5.1.6).

☺ Text or pictures are not clean. It's very common for letters or pictures to have little **stray marks** around them. Either find a graphics program that can help you clean these up or don't use those pictures. Stray marks or dots around letters or pictures offer a poor first impression of your book.

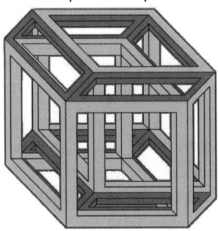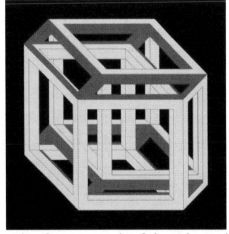

☺ Wrong choice of words emphasized in the title. If some words of the title are larger (or otherwise emphasized) over others, choose just the most relevant words. It's a common mistake to make the long words smaller and the short words larger just because the larger words wouldn't fit otherwise. Keep the author(s), other contributors, and subtitles smaller than the title. Names shouldn't be prominent unless they are famous.

☺ Poor contrast, **colors clash**, or poor color coordination. Research (online) which colors work well together – two colors that create good contrast often work well next to one another – and which colors tend to clash with one another. There should be good contrast between the text and background so that the text is easy to read. Red text on an orange background, for example, will be very difficult to make out. It's so important to seek feedback (as described in Sec. 5.1.1) on your cover because what seems fine to you might turn out to be fairly unpopular.

☺ The cover is **too busy**. The purpose of the cover is two-fold: First, grab attention (in a positive way), then lure readers from the intended audience. For the second part, the cover must make it clear which genre it falls in (by having a cover that fits into the styles common in its genre) and indicate what the book is about (from a primary image and a few emphasized words that stand out on the cover). Extra images and details make it this more difficult to determine. Many artists want to show off their talent by including artistic detail and indies feel a natural inclination to fill up every blank space on the cover, but it's a mistake. Some very popular traditionally published children's books with artists who have a knack for artistic detail have simple covers with one main image. The reason for this is that they want the main image and a few empha-sized words to stand out and they want the main image to be memorable. (I have made this mistake myself, as you can see in the pictures below.)

☺ Text arranged in a way that is **difficult to read**. Words that appear vertically, diago-nally, or have the letters staggered take longer to read. Occasionally, it may be pos-sible to achieve a good effect by using a special effect for one or two words, but it's a risk. The title should be clear and easy for the reader to figure out. Definitely, don't write an entire title with a font that's not quick and easy to read, and don't apply any fancy fonts or text effects to nonstandard words (like names or foreign words). Layout all words horizontally because they're much easier to read this way.

☺ Hand drawings that aren't expertly done. There are many magnificent covers in this age of graphic arts. Unless you're selling a coloring book, crayons are a really bad idea; so are colored pencils. Drawings or paintings must be professionally done. If a potential customer can find any fault in it, this will be used as an excuse not to buy the book. It's a challenge for hand-drawn cover art to compete with covers that take advantage of the possibilities of graphic arts. Even photos must appear **professional and clean** in order to compete.

☺ Something on the cover looks **unnatural or out of place**. Check all of the objects in the background to make sure that none of them are in an awkward position compared to the foreground images. If there are any semi-transparent images in the foreground, check if any background objects are inside them. I saw a book once with a semi-transparent man in the foreground and ski slopes in the background, and when I looked closely, there was a skier inside of his head! Such a mistake is a sales killer.

☺ Picture looks **distorted**. This common mistake occurs when the author uses a picture for the front cover that doesn't have the same aspect ratio as the cover size. Changing the aspect ratio to match the shape of the cover will distort the images. This especially makes people appear very unnatural.

☺ Text embedded in a jpeg picture appears **blurry or pixelated**. Use a textbox instead. Go to the Insert tab and choose WordArt or a textbox. While this is selected, go to the Format tab and set both Shape Fill and Shape Outline to no color (these are different from Text Fill and Text Outline, which you may wish to adjust). Text prints much better when it's not part of a jpeg picture.

TEXT   TEXT

☺ Including the word "**by**" before or above the author name. Some people view this as amateurish. The author clearly wrote the book – there isn't really any reason to include this word. Don't give anyone an excuse not to take your work seriously.

by
Chris McMullen

There is more to making a great cover than simply avoiding mistakes. Following are some of the 'secrets' to designing a successful cover. I selected some examples from covers that you can find on Amazon. It will be highly instructive to take the time to check out these covers.

☺ **Striking cover designs** grab attention; the cover just pops out at you. It's not necessarily a picture that has to be striking; some other effects can also elicit a *Wow!* Stark contrast – bright against dark – can catch attention, even without images (but for most fiction, you really need a relevant image). An interesting picture can also stand out, but you want to make sure than anything that stands out does so in a good way (and signifies the genre and relates to the content).
- *Shatter Me* by Tahereh Mafi literally is an eye-opener.
- *CIN: "Lynn, Lynn, the city of sin. You never come out the way you went in"* by Christina Leigh Pritchard stands out among other thumbnails.
- *Grace Lost* by M. Lauryl Lewis features a striking zombie picture.
- *Random Rationality* by Fourat Janabi is unique and simple, yet detailed.
- *The Guardian of Threshold* by A. A. Volts is bright, yet soft.

☺ It's not just the quality of art or a photograph. It doesn't take a Picasso to sell books. Strive to make the cover appealing. Good use of color, nice **contrast**, **bright** imagery, pleasing to look at, a main image that catches attention – such things help to build cover appeal. Nothing out of place or **distracting**, not **too busy**, easy to understand images and text, one main image (and no more than three images) – these things help to avoid an unappealing cover. **Shadows must be consistent with the light source.**
- *Merry Christmas* by Susan Rohrer effectively uses a touch of color.
- *Instant Feng Shui* by Trish McCabe, Caleen Mulock, and Ken McCabe features just a simple picture, yet looks warm and appealing.

☺ Having a **memorable cover** helps with marketing. When people recognize your cover upon seeing it again, it helps establish the book's brand (people generally purchase products they have heard of before – i.e. they recognize it). You want buyers to think, "I remember seeing this before." One main image is easier to remember than multiple images. A **short title** is easier to remember than a long title. You're more likely to get invaluable word-of-mouth sales if you have a short, memorable title (no hard words to spell, relates to the content). Research actually shows that people best recall covers that send a **unifying message** (single font used, title and images signify the genre and relate to the book). Having something zany on your cover – like a rhinoceros doing cartwheels – may catch attention, but doesn't provide the same recognition that we strive for as a cover that sends a unifying message relevant to the content and genre.

- *Illusions* by Chantilly Chanel Austin is memorable for its unique concept.
- *Reapers Inc.* by Dave Hunter has a simple, yet highly effective style.
- *Money Saving Emergency Plan* by Dave Ramson is a little zany, yet this works because the signal clearly relates to the content and genre.

☺ **Simplicity** is key. Don't get carried away with artistic detail. Artists and indie cover designers naturally feel inclined to try to fill every void. Supplemental images cause the primary image and title to be less memorable. An artistic border design may be okay, but shouldn't detract from the main image and text. Adding a little detail that makes the book appear more professional is good provided that it doesn't interfere with sending a clear message and recognition (many traditionally published books have a starburst, for example, that does this – sample traditionally published books in your genre to see what features they add to help distinguish their covers without detracting from the simplicity of design).

- *My Vampire Prom Date* and other stories by Shawn Pfister is striking, yet simple and not too detailed.
- *Through These Eyes* by Tom Bradford and Michael Risley creates an eye-catching effect with a simple design.

☺ Limit the number of images on the front cover to **three or less**. One is often best – it stands out better and it's easier to recall that way. If there are multiple images, they must all be **related**. What do a witch, a lion, and a knight all have in common? Nothing, so they shouldn't be on the same cover! They might all be in the story, but you're trying to sell books to people who haven't read the story yet. Don't include multiple images that aren't inherently related. While one image is usually best, there are occasions where two images can work together well – such as separation between protagonist and antagonist, or a romance (although a couple can also appear together with the effect of one image). Images may also appear in the foreground with another image in the background. If so, ensure that the background is not too busy.

- *Abandoned Treasure* by Ken Acha features a single, yet striking, image.

☺ Create good **contrast** – especially between text and the background. For example, white and black provide excellent contrast, yellow contrasts well with blue or purple, and red stands out well on black. Yet there are different hues and tones, so what's true in general doesn't always hold. Try playing with the colors (there are many color programs on the web that you can experiment with – i.e. programs that designers use to place colors beside one another and see how they look together) to see what produces nice contrast to your eye, and also seek external opinions because not all perceptions are identical and you want the cover to appeal to a majority of buyers.

- *The Black Dragon* by W. D. Newman features a dragon silhouette.
- *Fated* by Kazine Phoenix has contrasting butterfly wings.
- *Fine to Fab* by Lisa Lieberman-Wang has white text contrasting with purple.
- *Miso for Life* by Mai Xuan Bui, Wendy Toliver, Jenny Baranick, and Quyen Ngo has a busy foreground that contrasts well with the empty background.

Primary	Colors it often stands out with
red	yellow, black, white, gray
green	blue, black, gray, purple, pink, yellow
blue	yellow, white, pink, green
yellow	blue, black, red, orange, gray, brown, purple, pink
orange	black, white, yellow, brown, purple
brown	white, yellow, orange, pink
purple	yellow, white, black, pink, green, orange
pink	black, blue, brown, purple, green, yellow, white
black	white, yellow, pink, red, orange, green, purple, gray
white	black, brown, purple, blue, red, orange, gray, pink
gray	white, yellow, green, red, black

☺ At least part of the cover should be **nice and bright**. Even if most of the cover is dark, there at least needs to be some part that is quite bright to create contrast. In general, bright covers tend to attract more attention than dark covers; they also tend to put the buyer in a better mood. Dark covers may be more common specifically in horror, but even then the text or part of the imagery must still be bright to offset this and create the needed contrast. When you look at the top sellers in your genre, see how many of them look bright (also check if they agree with the advice in this book).

- *The Psychology of the Soul* by Angel Cusick is glowing.
- *The Haunted* by J. A. Templeton looks bright among other thumbnails.
- *I Don't Think So!* by Debbie Happy Cohen broke some of these rules (that's okay given its title), but uses color effectively in a different way.

☺ Try to restrict your cover design to **three colors**. This goes hand in hand with simplicity, recognition, easy to understand, unity of presentation, and having colors that work well together. Three is the magic number that traditional publishers use. Most of the imagery should feature just three main colors. Photographs and artwork sometimes have many colors. In this case, which colors stand out? The entire cover – text, artwork, photos, designs, etc. – should revolve around just three main colors. There should be one dominant color, so instead of having three equal colors, an old rule of thumb is to use 60% for the primary color, 30% for the secondary color (the primary and secondary should stand out well from one another), and 10% for the accent color (which should complement the primary or secondary). If you need more than three colors, try using different tints and shades of the three main colors.

- *Kindle Marketing Ninja Guide* by R. L. Adams is black, purple, and white.
- *Cinder* by Marissa Meyer makes use of black, white, and red.
- *The Girl Who Fell Beneath Fairyland and Led the Revels There* by Catherynne M. Valente and Ana Juan features purple, orange, and red.
- *Thoroughly Modern Monsters* by Jennifer Rainey uses green, white, and black.

☺ Another way that three is a magic number for cover design has to do with the **rule of thirds**. This rule suggests that the primary image might be better placed one-third the width and height from the edge than it would if it were centered. The problem of centering the main image is that it divides the cover into equal halves. Rather than cause the viewer to see the cover as equal halves, the rule of thirds helps the main image stand out. One main image is more memorable than two equal halves, so this helps with recall and associating the main image with what the book is about. There are a few exceptions, such as a mirror image contrasting design (e.g. portraying the protagonist and antagonist) or a cover that is symbolic of a battle (which may be appropriate for a war book).

- *Your World is Exploding* by Christopher Dessi applies both the rule of thirds and the three-color rule effectively.
- *Debugging with Fiddler* by Eric Lawrence has the center of the fiddle's body positioned approximately one-third from the right and bottom edges.
- *Happiness in Your Life – Book One* by Doe Zantamata features a butterfly that is one-third down from the top.

☺ Use colors that work well together. First, choose two colors that **stand out well** from one another for the primary and secondary. The third color – the accent – should **complement** one of the first two colors. If you have a main image, the colors need to **coordinate** with this. Since text needs to be clear, black text often appears against a light background and white text is usually used on a dark background. However, red text can stand out well on black, and red also catches attention. Yellow text can also stand out well on black, purple, and navy blue, although white tends to be more clear.

It's a challenge to coordinate all of the colors of the cover – text, images, and background. That's why it's so important to check out the colors that work well together in the top sellers and also to seek external opinions on your cover design.

- *The Last Man* by Vince Flynn blends white, red, and black effectively, and the title text – in orange – complements the red.
- *Book Writing Made Simple* by Kalinda Rose Stevenson has an appealing blue that contrasts well with yellow pencils and white letters.
- *Ever After* by Kim Harrison blends red, black, and yellow with a fiery effect.

☺ Use colors that send **relevant messages** for your genre and content. Different colors convey different emotions – e.g. red may evoke a sense of passion, while yellow may evoke cheerfulness. Observe that a single color is often associated with multiple emotions – e.g. green may be associated with money (especially dark green), but it also represents safety. Soft pastels are used for a feminine book, strong bold colors indicate a masculine book, and bright vibrant covers are geared toward children. Certain colors are common within a genre – e.g. romance covers often feature red for passion, while financial books tend to have dark green for money or blue for trust.

- *Touched* by Corinne Jackson features a red rose, which symbolizes the romance and power featured in the novel.
- *Freakonomics* by Steven D. Levitt utilizes green to signify money and safety.
- *Etiquette & Espionage* by Gail Carriger attracts females with a pink background.
- *The Power of Habit* by Charles Duhigg seems to promise happiness with its bright yellow background.
- *The Money Class* by Suze Orman combines white for safety, black for power, and gold for wealth – symbolizing a powerful, safe means to establish wealth.

Color	Emotions that it may evoke
red	passion, strength, power, danger
green	safety, healing, money
blue	stability, trust, health
yellow	happiness, intellect
orange	joy, enthusiasm, encouragement
brown	confidence, casualness
gold	wealth, prestige, wisdom
purple	power, luxury, ambition
pink	feminism, romance
black	power, elegance, mystery, death
white	purity, perfection, safety
gray	tradition, dullness

☺ Some colors also have **specific effects** in cover design. Red text and images tend to stand out and catch attention; it is sometimes used as an accent to help stimulate a sense of urgency (it's common on "click here" buttons on the internet). Green provides a sense of relaxation. Yellow and orange can be used effectively to call attention as highlighters. However, yellow needs to appear with dark colors to create contrast, and shouldn't be used when trying to convey masculinity, prestige, or stability. High quality is symbolized by gold. White suggests simplicity, while blue represents knowledge and expertise. Blue also helps to convey trust. Navy blue is cheaper, whereas purple is luxurious and gold is prestigious. Black adds a sense of depth. A black background helps light colors stand out, yet text is harder to read on a black background. Black and white together look formal.

- *Think and Grow Rich* by Napoleon Hill symbolizes knowledge and expertise with blue, high quality with gold, and has an orange accent in the background.

☺ **Consistency and unity** are very important factors for getting a potential buyer who notices your cover to click on your book. The images need to be unified – i.e. they must clearly go together. For example, a spaceship goes with a picture of the stars; but a cheerleader does not go with a robot (even if the story has both a robot and a cheerleader – remember, the buyer doesn't know the story yet). Use just a couple of different fonts on the cover to have consistent text. All of the fonts should be easy to read, but most of the text should be in the clearest font. The font styles should go together, too. The images, color scheme, and font styles of the cover must all send the same unified message, and this message must be consistent with the title, description, and content of the book. This is critical because inconsistent, non-unified messages among these elements deter book sales. If the title sounds like a romance, while the images look more like erotica, for example, this mismatch will create buyer confusion, and confused buyers tend to prefer a book that sends a clear message. It's a very common mistake for one of the elements – title, images, colors, font, blurb, and content – not to fit in. Check all of this carefully and seek external feedback to check that your message is 100% unified. Your cover helps to market your book.

- *Dangling Without a Rope* by Barbara Belmont sends a unified message.
- *Bible Cryptograms* by Marie Matthews focuses on the theme of the book.

☺ Design a cover that clearly **signifies your book's precise genre**. Readers are accustomed to reading books in that genre. When they see a cover that looks like the kind of cover they are used to seeing, it mentally registers that this book might be something they would read, and they click on it. If your book doesn't signify the genre, your intended audience won't be clicking on your book in search results. Check out the top sellers in your genre – and separate traditional publishers from others; both may be useful, but it may be helpful to know the difference – to see what imagery, color schemes, and font styles are characteristic of the genre. Also explore similar genres (e.g. in romance, compare adult, young adult, and erotica) to see how those books are distinguished from your genre. Don't make the mistake of using a cover that belongs in a slightly different genre. If the wrong audience clicks on your book, they won't buy it.

- *Die for Me* by Amy Plum screams teen romance.
- *Wait for You* by J. Lynn is a contemporary romance; it is distinguishable from both teen romance and erotica.

☺ The cover needs to relate to your book's content. Can people guess what your book is about just by looking at the cover? Obtain external (i.e. not from friends and family) input on your cover as described in Sec. 5.1.1 to learn what people think your book is about just by looking at the cover. This will help you see if your cover relates to the content. If you want to have just a few words in your title, which is common among the top sellers (especially, in fiction), you can add a little further clarification with a subtitle or an informative line on your front cover. However, a subtitle will appear together with your title – separated by a colon – in search results on Amazon, which may give the appearance of a longer title in the search results. If you don't want a subtitle, you can still add an informative line on the front cover (much like a subtitle). However, keep in mind that people will only read this line if they see the cover in person or take the time to enlarge the front cover view on Amazon; you can't expect this line to make up for anything that the title, images, or color scheme may be lacking.

- *Space! A Kids Book about Space* by Brian G. Johnson appears child-oriented.
- *Who Dat Cookin'* by Todd-Michael St. Pierre, Jeff Walsh, and Lori Walsh sends a clear message this this is a Louisiana cookbook.

☺ The entire cover needs to look professional, including the back cover and spine. The spine text (if your book has at least 102 pages) should be well-positioned and easy to read from a distance. Write the spine text in CAPS to make more effective use of a very narrow spine. While the front cover needs to be appealing both as a thumbnail and in person, your back cover should primarily be designed around its look in print. Back cover text needs to be clear and arranged in a very appealing way. After you order your first printed proof, show it to people for opinions – be sure to ask about the back cover, too – as described in Sec. 5.1.1. Visit different locations and don't stand in one place like a solicitor. You don't have to make special trips – just carry your cover, title, blurb, or proof with you and seek advice from people you naturally interact with (you don't need to approach complete strangers – it can be people you were going to briefly speak to anyway; but if you do intend to approach strangers, bring a friend for company and safety). Sometimes, you might even be able to approach people who may have an interest in your book. For example, if you're writing a book that relates to golf, bring this material with you every time you visit a golf course.

- *Men Are from Mars, Women Are from Venus* by John Gray, the hardcover edition, has the same style throughout the front, spine, and back.

☺ Minor professional touches can make a big difference. Develop a little logo that you can put on your books – both on the cover and on the copyright page. This will help you establish a visual brand – readers will come to associate this logo with your work. Traditional publishers often use little design marks, add fine print, include a starburst, and apply subtle touches that help give the cover an overall professional feel. Study the front, back, and spine of several professionally designed covers in your genre to learn these secrets.

- *Boundaries* by Henry Cloud and John Townsend includes the website, logo, and category on the back cover in addition to quotes (see the customer image).

Of course, there are exceptions to every rule. Just remember, there are millions of covers that break one or more of these rules that aren't selling well, but only a few covers breaking the rules that do sell very well. At the very least, don't break any of these rules unless you can think of a compelling reason to do so.

Should you pay for professional cover help? That depends on your situation. If you plan to sell most of the books in person (e.g. following a presentation), then a basic cover may suffice. For technical nonfiction or how-to books, a simple cover can be effective and the information that people need will help drive sales. Fiction, especially, along with nonfiction that people may want, but don't necessarily need (a chemistry workbook or a book that describes how to paint a house fall under need, whereas a guide to wine tasting or a biography of Napoleon fall under want) are more likely to sell when seen in online searches if they have great covers. Even word-of-mouth sales strongly depend on the quality of the cover.

Unless your book happens to fall under an exception (like selling mostly in person or a nonfiction book that people need – and even then, if there is much competition, a great cover can give you an edge), you need a wonderful cover in order to be highly successful. The next thing to consider is how well you can do by yourself (which you can gauge best if you first attempt this), and how much better a professional cover may be. Try the free and low-cost options first (to be discussed toward the end of this section) and try to get honest input from strangers. If it turns out that you have a gift for the graphic arts, you might wind up with a great self-made cover. At the very least, you will see how little or how much a professional cover might be able to improve upon what you can do by yourself.

Next, you must consider how good the book is and how much marketing you are willing to do. If there may be any issues with the storyline, editing, formatting, blurb, characterization, etc. – or if the book concept just might not be of much general interest – then a great cover may not pay off. It would be a waste to have an incredible cover attract a great deal of attention, only for most of the potential buyers to wind up not purchasing the book because (a) the blurb didn't catch their interest, (b) they found typos, grammatical errors, or formatting mistakes in the Look Inside, (c) there were several bad reviews that mention editing or storyline problems, or (d) the free sample wasn't what they were expecting from the cover.

Do some research to see how well similar books are selling. This will help you judge the potential of your concept. You don't want to invest heavily in a concept that has little interest.

How strongly do you believe in your book? How much time and effort are you willing to invest in your book? Are you seeking help with editing? If you feel strongly that your story is great, that your editing and formatting will be excellent, and that there will be popular interest in your book, then you should be willing to invest in your belief. This investment will give your book the best chance of success.

Also, consider how much time and effort you are willing to invest toward marketing (even if it's just free and low-cost marketing), and how effective your marketing campaign may be. We will discuss several free and low-cost marketing strategies in Chapter 8; the question right now is how motivated and diligent you may be in pursuing this. Any author who has any natural aptitude for marketing – e.g. if you are in the advertising business, that must be the case – should easily be able to make an investment in an amazing cover pay off. If you have a unique situation that may be of interest to the press – like writing a book that draws on your experience as a triplet or overcoming dyslexia to produce a well-written book – this is a marketing edge that you may be able to apply to help recover the cost of professional cover help. However, even if you don't have any marketing advantages, provided that you're willing to learn about how to market your book effectively and are also willing to make a long-term commitment to diligently marketing, an investment in a great cover can pay off in the long run (especially, if the content of your book is as good as the cover, both in terms of ideas and the editing and formatting). If you're highly motivated to try to create "buzz" for your book and to seek external opinions as I've already recommended, then you're already on the right track.

Professional cover design comes in a variety of price ranges. Some graphic artists sell premade covers from $10 to $100. This requires browsing to find one that's a good fit for your book. When using this option, find out whether or not other authors may be able to use the same cover – otherwise, there may be several similarly looking books. Many illustrators work with writers to provide custom cover designs for $100 to $1000. It's not necessary to spend $1000 to get a great cover; many wonderful cover designs are produced at the lower end of this price range.

Amazon KDP doesn't offer professional design services. (Prior to the merger between KDP and CreateSpace, it had once been possible to pay for professional design services. However, this service included a few drawbacks, such as not being able to interact with the artist with the more affordable options and difficulty with later revisions. CreateSpace also advertised an option to create a cover through crowdSPRING.) However, Amazon KDP does maintain a list of professional services on the KDP help pages. The cheapest option is free, since you can use the Cover Creator tool or upload your own PDF. If you wind up publishing several books in the future, the savings will really add up.

There are a few advantages of searching for your own custom cover designer online: there are less expensive options ($10 to $100 for premade covers and custom covers starting at around $100), you can learn more about the artist's ability and experience before signing up, and you may be able to interact with the artist extensively throughout the project (inquire about this before you commit). I had always designed my own covers until I wrote a 100-page fictional work called *Romancing the Novel* – an extended analogy about a man who has a very passionate relationship with a book. This cover stumped me, so I searched online for help. I discovered a talented artist, Melissa Stevens, at http://www.theillustratedauthor.net, and was very pleased both with the result and the process. I spent $300 on my cover. There are many great artists out there, and you can find very good custom designs starting at around $100.

When shopping for an illustrator, first check out the artist's portfolio. Look for samples that suit your genre and content, where the artwork pops out at you and looks professional. See if the sample covers follow the rules that I have listed previously. Browse for the books on Amazon to make sure that they are real books and see if the illustrator is listed on the cover or copyright page. See if anyone you know has ever hired a professional illustrator that he/she can recommend.

Next, contact the artist and try to interact with him/her for a while through the exchange of some emails. Such interaction will help you judge the artist's character, interest in your project, knowledge, etc. Here is a sample of what to inquire about:

- ✓ What is the artist's background, experience, etc.?
- ✓ What technique(s) does the artist use?
- ✓ Does the artist create the images or use stock images?
- ✓ How does the artist know that the images are not under copyright?
- ✓ How will you know that copyrighted images from others have not been used?
- ✓ To what extent will you be involved in the process?
- ✓ Can the artist describe briefly his/her vision for your cover?
- ✓ Can you see a brief mock-up before you sign the contract?
- ✓ Who owns the cover (probably the artist) and under what circumstances will you be able to use it (probably just for the cover of one book for as long as it's available)?
- ✓ Will the cover be displayed on the artist's website (if so, it increases your book's visibility, but bear in mind that most people who will see it are themselves writing books, and so it might not affect sales)?
- ✓ Can you display the cover on your own website, too?
- ✓ If you have legal questions about the contract, you should consult an attorney.

Whether you invest $10 or $1200 on cover design, it's worth calculating what it will take just to recover the investment. Divide your (potential) investment by the book's royalty (see Sec.'s 4.1.5 and 4.2.5) to determine how many books must be sold just to break even. For example, if you invest $300 on cover design and your royalty will be $3.27, you will have to sell 92 copies just to break even. A top-selling book can recover this quickly, whereas it can take several months to recover this investment if the book only sells a few copies per week.

Finally, we'll explore free and low-cost solutions. Designing your own cover is free, but can be a challenge to do professionally. Chapter 3 provides a tutorial on how to draw with Microsoft Word, but some objects are much easier to draw well than others. A digital camera with sufficient resolution can be used to take a high-quality photo. You want to make sure that your images have 300 DPI. Divide the pixel count of the width and height by the actual width and height that the image will have on the printed page (click on the image after you insert it in Word and go to the Format tab to see its dimensions) to determine the DPI. Also see the notes in Sec. 5.1.6 about how to prevent Word from compressing the images.

Although drawing skills aren't involved in photography, there are some photography skills needed to produce good results – e.g. the person or object should be well-lit, the objects must be in focus, the background needs to be suitable, etc. If you photograph a person, get written permission to use the photo (unless, perhaps, they are minor people in the background in a public place). Some objects, like the Eiffel Tower at night, are trademarked. I'm not an attorney. If you have legal questions, contact an attorney.

There are many free and low-cost stock photos and artwork collections online or on CD's. As described in Sec. 3.1.11, be sure that the owner of the image clearly allows commercial use of the image (some collections do not allow commercial use even for paid images). Check that the images will be 300 DPI. Many free images that allow commercial use are just 96 DPI, which may look blurry or pixelated in print. Many of the images available on the internet are copyrighted, do not allow free commercial use, and are only 96 DPI. If the image is over 80 years old, it is now in the public domain. If it is less than 80 years old, you need express written permission to use the image. The best thing is if the image or collection clearly states that commercial use is allowed. Otherwise, you must contact the copyright holder, who will probably charge a fee for use of the image. If somebody gives you a picture, make sure that they hold the copyright and get their express written permission to use it for your cover.

There are still many free and low-cost image collections that do have 300 DPI and allow for commercial use. Take the time to explore these options and you might be able to make a fantastic cover economically. Find authors whose covers you like and ask where they got their images, or inquire about stock images on a community forum for writers or self-publishers (such as Amazon KDP).

You can also get free help. There are many experienced small publishers on the Amazon KDP community forum, for example, who often provide helpful answers to questions asked by aspiring authors. If you have any friends or acquaintances with experience using Photoshop or other graphic arts programs, they may be willing to help you get started. If you have Photoshop or other photo-editing software, you should spend a few days playing with it. Once you learn the basics, you might find that you can make a nice cover yourself this way.

This section of the book has been quite long, but it is fitting because cover design is that important. Just a few details remain, and we will finally move on. It would be wise to read the other sections of this chapter before you finalize your cover. For example, you should allow for printing variations and tolerances and other issues described in Sec. 5.1.7, and learn how to prevent Word from compressing your images in Sec. 5.1.6.

Remember, your cover is also a reflection of you and your image as an author. However you make a cover, you should be happy with it. I enjoy making my own cover. Not every one of my self-made covers is perfect, but I enjoyed the satisfaction of creating them myself. (I hired a designer for this book.) I even have the experience of making a few of the mistakes that I have outlined in this book (such as making a few covers that are too busy). May you benefit from my experience and research on cover design by avoiding those mistakes. ☺

5.1.4 Perfecting the Interior for Your Paperback

Many little details, like avoiding widows, orphans, and rivers, or adding design marks to the copyright page, can help make the formatting look much more professional and less amateurish. Compare with a variety of traditionally published books – including some in your genre – to help discover what details can help your book stand out in a good way.

One thing you'll notice is that the title page, copyright page, contents, dedications, acknowledgements, and preface usually don't have any page numbers, the introduction and foreword generally have lowercase Roman numeral page numbers (iv, v, vi, etc.), and starting with Chapter 1 the page numbers are Arabic (7, 8, 9, etc.). When page numbering does begin, it's not with page 1, but the actual position in the book. For example, if the introduction begins on the fifth page in the book, page numbering will start on page v, and if the first chapter begins on the seventh page in the book, its page number will be 7.

There is a trick to using a different style of page numbers for different sections of the book in Microsoft Word. The first step is to use section breaks instead of regular page breaks. Remove page breaks and instead go to the Page Layout tab, click on Breaks, and select Next Page (both going to Insert and clicking Page Break and going to Page Layout and choosing Breaks and then Page prohibit professional page numbering and headers) anywhere that you wish to tell Word that you want to start using a new style of page headers or numbers. Using Next Page (instead of an ordinary page break) tells Word when a new section is beginning. If you want to have different page numbering styles (including none at all for the first few pages), you must first tell Word (by using Next Page) when the new sections begin.

If you haven't already done so, insert page numbers as described in Sec. 2.1.9. Note that you can add symbols before and after the page number – e.g. your page numbers can look like -31- instead of just 31. Highlight the page number to change the font size or style. To remove page numbers, click the bottom portion of the Page Number button.

Place your cursor in the page number area to pull up the Design tab for headers and footers. Check the box for different odd and even pages. If you would like the first page of the section to have different formatting, check that box, too.

I like to start at the beginning of the book and work forward. I adjust the page numbering and headers section by section through the book, each time checking the previous sections to make sure that any changes made to the new sections don't mess up the prior sections (it will probably happen a few times, so you want to inspect it frequently). It's also wise to back up your file at this point two different ways – like email and jump drive – and to make a new version number for your file (like Book2.docx instead of Book1.docx). If you experience file corruption issues while working on headers and footers, you'll be glad you have a back-up.

The 'magic' button is called Link to Previous. The Same as Previous flag disappears when the Link to Previous button is clicked. This allows you to change the footer style from none to Roman numerals or from Roman numerals to Arabic numbers, or to change the starting page number of that section. Double-check that all of the odd-numbered pages are actually on odd pages in your document.

Headers can be changed between sections the same way. Many traditionally published books have the title on odd-numbered pages and chapter names on even-numbered pages (in cases where the chapters have names). To change the header name between sections, use Next Page under breaks in Page Layout to define new sections in Word, place the cursor in the header area, and use Link to Previous to remove the Same as Previous flag.

Word sometimes gets a little fussy when several page numbering and header changes are made. Occasionally, you just have to remove the page break, reinsert the Next Page section break, and try it again. You may even have to delete the current break between chapters, reinsert it and the Next Page section break, and change the header again. If you have a PDF converter that allows you to combine PDF files together, a simple fix when Word gets fussy is simply to split the file into two or more separate files – then after converting to PDF, you can join the files back together.

Note that Word's two-page view does <u>not</u> correctly show what the book will look like: This view shows the odd pages on the left and the even pages on the right, whereas when you open the actual book, the odd pages will appear on the right with the even pages on the left. You can temporarily adjust this by inserting a blank page at the beginning, but that might mess up your page numbering and headers. You will be able to see the two-page spreads correctly in Amazon KDP's Interior Reviewer when you upload your book (if you choose the Guided Setup option) and Digital Proofer after file review (and you can still make revisions after using these tools).

All of the odd-numbered pages must be on the right in the open book, which means that the odd-numbered pages must appear on the left in Word's two-page view. Word's two-page view is simply backwards: Just understand and realize this, but don't try to 'fix' it. The first chapter should begin on an odd-numbered page. There are books where every chapter begins on an odd-numbered page, even if it means inserting a blank page to do this; but there are more books where the chapter (except for Chapter 1) begins wherever it happens to be – odd or even. Check what is most common in your book's genre and go with that.

Times New Roman and Calibri are default fonts on different editions of Microsoft Word, such that many self-published books use these font styles. Some people feel that these fonts give an amateurish look. However, there are many fonts similar to these, and it's hard to pick a font out from another that is very similar. I used Calibri for this book because I felt that it looks clean and clear for this how-to guide. Garamond, Palatino Linotype, and Georgia are popular for fiction in size 12 fonts among many indie authors looking for something different than Word's defaults. Minion and Dante are popular fonts for traditionally published fiction, but these aren't preinstalled on Word. It is worth researching fonts online to see what may be common in your genre. Wikipedia even provides statistics for how readers react to a variety of fonts – Comic Sans, for example, often creates a more negative impact.

Many well-educated people believe that there should be two spaces after a period and before the first letter of the following sentence. I believed this myself until I read an interesting article called "Space Invaders" by Farhad Manjoo in *Slate Magazine*. This is what our teachers were taught, and so this is what they passed onto us. However, if you examine traditionally published books carefully, you will see that they only use one space after the period. This can make a marked difference on full justification, for example. So if you want a professional appearance, use a single space after a period; this will become even more important in eBooks, as we will learn in Sec. 5.2.1. I actually used 2 spaces in Volume 1, but 1 space in Volume 2. This way, you can compare the two volumes and see the difference. **Tip:** If you have a habit of two-spacing, use the Replace tool on the Home tab to see if you had any double spaces.

Word's default indent is 0.5", which is larger than what most traditionally published books use – 0.2" to 0.3" is common. I used 0.3" for this book, which has wide pages. Compare Volume 2 to Volume 1, which had a wider indent. Which fits your eye better? Measure the indentations for a variety of books in your genre to see what is common. Traditional publishers actually measure their indents in terms of an 'em,' where 1 em is the width of the uppercase M. In this way, the size of the indent depends on the font style and size.

The indentation of this book is set to just over 2 ems. In full justification, the spacing of the first line tends to look better if the indent is smaller. Thus, an indent of 1 to 1.5 ems is common with smaller pages or wider margins. However, the indent needs to be clear, and an indent of 1 em isn't as easy to recognize on a large printed page.

Traditional publishers almost always use full justification[3] – not left alignment. Self-published authors sometimes align the body text left because this is the default alignment in Word; other times, they do it because they don't like the gaps that they see in fully justified

---

[3] Like many words in English, 'justified' has multiple meanings. Sometimes, 'justified' is used to imply that both sides are even, in which case 'fully justified' would seem redundant. However, 'justified' has a broader usage to mean that the text is even or properly positioned, in which case left-aligned text or right-aligned text are partially justified. Hence, some people refer to 'left-justified' and 'right-justified.' Since these terms are not uncommon, the use of 'fully justified' here may help to avoid possible confusion.

text. However, if you think about it, there are really large gaps at the end of the line when text is aligned left – this is called "ragged right" because the ends of the lines look ragged. Use full justification for a professional appearance.

There is a way to reduce the size of the gaps in fully justified text: hyphenation. You can manually hyphenate words by looking up the natural breaks in a dictionary. Don't bother with this until your manuscript is complete; otherwise, any revisions may cause hyphenated words to move and no longer appear at the end of a line. An alternative to hyphenation is kerning.

Word actually has a built-in Hyphenation tool in the Page Layout tab. Turn it on by setting Hyphenation to Automatic. If you use this tool, go into Hyphenation Options and increase the Hyphenation Zone to about 0.4" to avoid excessive hyphenation. You can also limit the number of consecutive hyphens. Check the final manuscript carefully because it may hyphenate words that you don't want hyphenated (e.g. a long heading that spans two lines might look funny if hyphenated). To manually correct an automatic hyphen, place the cursor before the first letter of the word, then hold down Shift and press Enter (then also delete the space that precedes this word at the end of the previous line). Again, don't bother with any manual hyphenation until your book is perfected. **Tip**: Go to the File tab, scroll down below Help to find Options, click Options, find Advanced, click on Layout Options at the very bottom (you can click this, even though it doesn't look like something to click on), and check the box that says to hyphenate the way that WordPerfect does.

There are two types of dashes, which are longer than hyphens and are used differently. The short en dash (–) and the long em dash (—) are used as separators; they are different from hyphens (-). A hyphen (-) appears in some compound words and is also used to join two words together to make compound adjectives, as in, "This is a well-known way to make a compound adjective." A dash is used to create separation between parenthetic elements. Either use the shorter en dash (–) with spaces around it or the longer em dash (—) without spaces, but not both – it's generally better to be consistent—don't be inconsistent like this sentence. Note the space around the en dash (–), but not the em dash (—), in the previous sentence. Word's AutoFormat feature can turn two consecutive hyphens into an en dash, but you can make the en and em dashes more properly by holding down Alt and typing 0150 and 0151, respectively. The Alt method is better if you may be making an eBook edition, too. Not everyone agrees on which dash is better to use; see what traditional publishers use in your genre. The em (—) dash is also used following the end of a quotation in lieu of quotation marks to indicate the author (but this time, with space), as in the example below.

> Better to write for yourself and have no public, than to write for the public and have no self. — Cyril Connolly in *The New Statesman*

Traditional publishers use approximately single line spacing. Setting the line spacing to double or even just 1.5 is not only unconventional, it makes the text much more difficult to read (however, those settings are good for proofreading as they allow room for editing marks). The best line spacing might not be *exactly* single spacing, though. Traditional publishers refer to 'leading,' which is the distance between the baselines of two consecutive lines of text. For example, for 12-pt font, the leading may be set to 14 pts, which is 17% leading (comparing the 2-pt difference to the 12-pt font size). Setting the leading to around 20% to 25% is typical. To do this, go to the Paragraph dialog box (click the funny icon in the bottom-right corner of the Paragraph group in the Home tab), choose Exactly under the Line Spacing option, and set the size of the leading in pts (e.g. 14 pts). Check to see how closely this compares to single spacing in Word. Print out a page and compare it to traditionally published books in your genre that have a similar font height (measure the font height of similar letters to check this), and adjust your leading if you would like to reproduce those models.

You can make your book look much more professional by eliminating widows, orphans, and rivers from your book. Don't bother adjusting these until your book is virtually complete, otherwise you may need to adjust them again after making revisions. A widow is a single line of a paragraph that winds up being on a different page from the rest; an orphan is a single word or a few short words on the last line of a paragraph; and a river is formed when the gaps between words happen to line up to create a long gap running down a paragraph. A widow (left), orphan (center), and river (right) are shown in the figure below. (In the middle diagram, you can also see gaps in the bottom line that could be corrected through hyphenation.)

Traditionally published books usually do not have widows or rivers, but orphans are not uncommon. Widows, rivers, and orphans can be removed by editing the text, in principle, but in practice, writers first perfect the text and then design the formatting around the text – authors generally don't design the text around the formatting. Other ways to remove these features include adjusting individual lines (by adjusting hyphenation or forcing a short word onto the next line – by placing the cursor before the word and pressing Shift + Enter), kerning (highlight the text that you want to kern – i.e. adjust the space between characters – then right-click, choose Font, and select the Advanced tab), or making slight adjustments to the spacing before or after paragraphs (in the Paragraph dialog box) or to the line spacing. You'll need to remove these features from the eBook edition (if you make one).

Word does have automatic Widow/Orphan Control (open the Paragraph dialog box and select the Line and Page Breaks tab). However, using this automatic control will result in gaps at the bottom of the pages. Therefore, it's best to remove widows and orphans manually. The Amazon KDP templates often have one or more of the boxes checked in the Line and Page Breaks tab in the Paragraph dialog box: Uncheck these boxes for optimal results.

Professional publishers also take the time to vertically justify the text – i.e. to make all of the pages of full text line up at the top and bottom. Viewing multiple pages at once, you can go page by page through the book and adjust vertical spacing, as needed, to achieve this. If you have mostly text, like a novel, you should also have the same number of lines on almost every page. You can adjust the spacing before or after paragraphs (in the Paragraph dialog box) for stand-alone lines – like headings, figures, and equations, adjust the kerning, or make slight adjustments to line spacing, for example, to vertically justify text. The two volumes of this book are littered with pictures and bullets, so you might not have noticed it (unless you have an eye for such formatting details – which will help you greatly with the layout of your own book). Compare them: Volume 2 shows a subtle improvement. In comparison, a novel or other book that consists mostly of text will stand out visually if it is not vertically justified.

A few pages should be centered vertically, while most of the pages should be aligned at the top and vertically justified to also line up at the bottom. However, the initial and final pages of a chapter may not line up at the top and bottom. The title page, copyright page, and a few other pages (consult traditionally published books in your genre to see which) are often centered vertically. You can center these pages vertically by going to the Page Setup dialog box, choosing the Layout tab, setting Apply To on This Section, and changing Vertical Alignment to Center. Make sure that you used Page Layout > Breaks > Next Page to create the page breaks (if not, remove the page break and use Next Page instead), otherwise you might find a blank page inserted or other pages affected vertically when you make this change.

The first page of a chapter usually doesn't start at the top of the page, but is generally dropped down a few lines (alternatively, increase the space before the chapter heading in the Paragraph dialog box). Chapter headings are often boldfaced and centered, but not underlined. Look at some traditionally published books in your genre for ideas regarding what the beginning of each chapter can look like. You should also use a drop cap (see Sec. 2.1.11) unless you have any chapters where the first paragraph doesn't have enough lines to exceed the height of the drop cap. (In that case, don't use any drop caps; consistency is important.) The first few words of the chapter often also appear in UPPERCASE (again, use traditionally published books in your genre as models).

Self-published authors often neglect the formatting and details of the first few pages of the book – i.e. the title page, copyright page, contents, etc. These are the first pages that a prospective buyer sees when he/she clicks to Look Inside. Make these as professional as possible to make a striking impression. Inspect these pages closely in a variety of traditionally published books to see what information, details, formatting, and fancy design marks they add to these pages. The printing codes on the copyright page won't be relevant since your book is printed on demand, and you won't have library information (unless you purchased an LCCN – see Sec. 4.1.7). You also won't have a publisher name unless you use an ISBN option with your own imprint (see Sec. 4.1.6); you <u>can't</u> write "published by Amazon" (or Kindle or KDP). However, there are many ways to make these pages look highly professional, so taking the time to research your options and perfect these pages can give you an edge.

Traditional publishers have an appealing logo. If you use your own imprint, you should also develop your own logo (if so, you should explore any legalities involved). The logo may appear on the spine, back cover, title page, and/or copyright page (see where traditional publishers place their logos).

Avoid writing The End when you reach the very end of the content. Just like writing "by" on the cover or title page, some people perceive this as amateurish. Why risk losing any sales?

Remember that there are marketing opportunities in your front and back matter. Keep in mind that if your email address is in the front matter, it may get spammed – and possibly just from the Look Inside. Some authors create a special email address just for their books, but then they must remember to check them periodically. Readers can also connect with authors through Facebook, Twitter, a discussion forum at the author's website, and so on.

You might not want to go overboard on contact information and marketing. Readers who enjoy your book will be interested in learning more about you and seeing what else you've written, but at the same time people tend to have an aversion to advertising and salesmanship. I usually don't include a catalog of my books. I only included it with this book to show what a catalog might look like. In my recent books, however, I have included a couple of pages that have pictures and descriptions for a few related books; you can see a sample of this on the page following the catalog at the back of this book (but those don't relate to this book...).

Many authors include an About the Author section at the back of the book with a photograph, biography, and contact information – such as the link to their blog or author website, email address, and Facebook and Twitter author accounts (you probably want to create a separate account for your author profile, which will be in addition to a personal profile that you may already have). Thinking ahead to marketing, consider adding a book club or fan club. If so, you want to set this up before releasing your book so that you can provide information about it at the end of your book. We'll talk more about this in Sec. 6.2.6.

Another thing you can do is include a sample chapter at the end or your book. If you write a series of books, include the first chapter (but no more than what the Look Inside will show for free) of the next book in the series. Remember that customers like to receive a good value for their money. This means that the front matter, back matter, sample chapter, etc. shouldn't make a large percentage of the overall content (otherwise, customers may complain about this in reviews).

Some of the comments that I made about formatting the cover in the previous section also apply to formatting your interior, especially if you have images, tables, or textboxes. For example, text embedded in jpegs doesn't format well – it's better to leave the text out of images and instead add WordArt or textboxes.

We've mostly examined how to format your interior file professionally in this section. The art of proofreading and editing will be discussed in Sec. 5.1.8. I've made a few of these formatting 'mistakes' myself in previous books (such as avoiding hyphenation); or, rather, my own style has changed with time and experience. Vertical justification, for example, didn't seem as important as maintaining precise consistency in vertical spacing, for example, when I first began writing and publishing, but I've since come to see the light.

Before we move on, I want to say a few words about content. Mainly, since this book also covers the important subject of marketing, I want to point out and emphasize that content and marketing do share a relationship. As the writer and publisher, you have the flexibility to be as creative as you wish with your content (and even with the formatting). However, you should beware that the choices you make regarding your content do impact how successful your marketing efforts may be.

Ask yourself how much artistic freedom you wish to embrace as a writer versus how successful you want sales to be. You can write to explore this freedom or you can write toward successful sales – and very often writing mainly with the freedom and independence in mind doesn't provide optimal sales. So another thing to ask yourself is whether you're willing to compromise on the freedom to some extent.

Let me address the issue of how to write with successful sales in mind, with the under-standing that the more you deviate from this path, the more it may affect the sales of your book. If your goal is to have a bestseller, the answer is right there before your eyes: First read bestsellers in your genre to learn what readers in that genre are accustomed to, what attracts those readers, what content has proven success, what rules you absolutely aren't allowed to break (go ahead and break them – but some rules, like not having a happy ending for a romance novel, may greatly deter sales if broken), which writing styles work, etc. Read the top sellers in that genre, including the top self-published sellers – since you also want to see how those other indie authors broke through. Hopefully, you've already read some books in your genre; you want to truly understand what your intended audience loves and expects.

Research takes time, but it can pay off. In addition to reading bestsellers to master the genre, there is also the issue of mastering the craft of writing in the genre. In order to gain a professional edge, many authors join writing groups, book clubs, and critique groups in an effort to improve their grammatical writing and their writing style. You learn some basic rules of writing – like writing actively instead of passively, and which types of writing to avoid – and some more subtle tips that can help your writing stand out. Developing bestselling content takes much time and effort, but in the long run it can make a huge difference.

If you want to exercise your creativity and independence, consider this: If instead you write your first two books traditionally, geared toward excellent sales, once you attain some measure of success and have a following, you can then afford to exercise creative freedom in your third book and it will actually reach a large audience. If instead you exercise your creative freedom in your first book, you might not have much of an audience for it. Look, creativity can mean many different things. By all means, feel creative and artistic as a writer. When I speak of exercising creative freedom in regards to sales, I mean that if you exercise the freedom to break the rules and expectations for your genre, it will probably hurt sales. Readers appreciate certain kinds of creativity, but most readers don't like it when authors break the unspoken rules for what is or isn't accepted in each specific genre.

5.1.5 Perfecting the Blurb and Other Features

The description for your book – called the blurb – is a sales pitch. It shouldn't sound like a sales pitch, but it should be designed to help sell the book. After seeing your cover and title, the blurb is the next thing that customers see – and it's the one major hurdle that you have to jump to make customers Look Inside instead of walking away. Only a percentage of the potential customers who read your blurb will click to Look Inside. You want to maximize this percentage as much as possible by writing a highly effective blurb.

I like to joke that it's very easy to write 50,000 words, but quite a challenge to write 50 words or even just 5. Many self-published authors can relate to this when they try to condense their 50,000 word (maybe more, maybe less) book down to the size of a modest blurb. But therein lies the problem: Your description is not a summary of your book. It's a sales pitch that should sound like it's telling the reader what your book is about, while not sounding like a sales pitch. But don't forget that the blurb is your salesman, and the only salesman standing there at the doorway to your book online!

I didn't mention this in Sec. 4.1.2 when I described how to prepare the description. Then, I wanted you to prepare a first draft of your description, and I also didn't want to hamper your creativity by providing too much direction. But now it's time to talk about how to improve your blurb to be more effective.

Most likely, your present blurb is too long, especially if your book is fiction. Shorter blurbs tend to be more effective. I happen to write technical books – like how-to guides, science books, and math workbooks – so my own descriptions are fairly long. Unless you're writing similar books, your description should be quite short. Some blurb writers will tell you that your blurb should even be short if you write technical books. However, in the case of technical nonfiction and textbooks, expertise is an important factor, and so a longer description that makes that expertise clear can also be effective. For fiction and less technical or entertaining nonfiction, shorter is better.

Why? Because people tend to be impatient. Just visit any metropolitan area and experience the traffic for a few hours and you will see firsthand that most people are impatient. It doesn't just apply to traffic; it applies to book buying, too.

One reason that bestselling books tend to have short titles – three words or less – is because buyers are impatient. The general rule of thumb is that you have 3 seconds for the customer to get interested in your title and thumbnail image – so both have to be very clear and send a unified message to attract the right reader in just 3 seconds. (But all of the details of the cover are important because some customers will stare at the large image of your cover for a while once they open your book's product page.) Then, when the customers click on your book, there is a 5-second rule for the blurb. The beginning of the blurb should attract the reader's interest – and reinforce the message conveyed by the title and cover – within 5 seconds. If they like what they read, you have another 5 seconds to hold their interest.

Some customers see a long blurb and instantly return to the main page; that's the danger of overwhelming the customer who sees more than he/she wants to read to learn about your book. Consider separating your blurb into two or three block paragraphs with spaces in between. (The description that you enter at KDP will have plain formatting, unless you use basic HTML as described in Chapter 6. What you need to do to format your blurb is go to AuthorCentral; you can revise your description there with some basic formatting tools. We'll learn how to do this in Chapter 6.)

The blurb is a challenge for authors to write because the description has much to accomplish with a minimum of words and judicious word choice. Here is what the blurb needs to accomplish:

- ✓ Grab the reader's attention right off the bat.
- ✓ Relate to the content and reinforce the title and cover; and clearly signify the genre.
- ✓ Build interest in your book and hold the reader's attention throughout.
- ✓ Express ideas very clearly and with a vocabulary appropriate for the audience.
- ✓ Use perfect spelling and grammar, with an appealing writing style.
- ✓ Include the same keywords that you entered through Amazon KDP (for your paperback or your eBook), but only if the blurb sounds good as you do this. Keywords must be less than 15% of your blurb, at the most (and a list of keywords at the end will look funny). This may affect your book's visibility in search results to some extent (probably not by introducing new keywords, but by reinforcing those you enter when you publish).
- ✓ Provide an idea of what the work is about; but not with a detailed summary.
- ✓ Arouse the reader's curiosity.
- ✓ Let the work speak for itself; bragging deters sales (however, accurately describing the author's related qualifications or what distinguishes this from other books is relevant).
- ✓ Accurately describe the content; making it seem better than it is will backfire.
- ✓ Be concise and written in the third person.
- ✓ Ultimately, persuade the reader to Look Inside. Many blurbs end with a question.

Writing a highly effective blurb is a formidable task, but can really pay off. Many authors revise and revise and revise their blurbs in an effort to perfect them. Some authors do extensive research on effective blurb writing (there are even books that describe this art, but you may be able to find free examples and ideas online). The problem with doing all of that research is that your description will still be unique and geared toward your book. These guides and books will teach you some terminology and discuss a few key concepts, but when it comes down to it, it will still be a challenge to come up with a great blurb geared toward your own book.

You need a starting point: If you have a short summary, begin with this. Look at your summary and decide what main ideas may interest readers. Not the plot itself, but some ideas from the content may be relevant. For fiction, if the first chapter sells the book, start by summarizing *only* that. Do you have any characters that you can make the reader fall in love with in a very short description? You'll need to introduce the protagonist briefly, at a minimum (for fiction). What features would interest readers most? If you've shared drafts of your work with others, their feedback can help you answer some of these questions.

Then you try to write the description. It's a draft – just a place to start. Then read my checklist for what your blurb should accomplish, and rate how your blurb accomplishes each step on a scale of 1 to 5 (1 very little, 5 very well). Getting opinions from others on this would be wise – since a variety of other people will be reading your description when they find your book. (If anyone rewrites your blurb, be sure to get their written permission to use it.) This checklist will then help you see which elements of your blurb need improving.

Revise the description, get more feedback, and so on. Initially, spelling and grammar are the least of your worries. Think structurally, conceptually. How effective are the ideas, which ideas are best and worst, what can you remove to shorten it? But after several revisions, you also want to perfect your spelling and grammar. **A single mistake in the blurb may cost you many sales.** If you make any spelling, grammar, or style mistakes in a short description – which is very prominently placed and vital to the success of your book – it doesn't bode well for the book itself being well-written. Your final blurb should <u>not</u> be a summary of the book.

In Sec. 6.1.4, we'll learn how you can use AuthorCentral to format your blurb with boldface, linebreaks, and so forth. You can do this prior to publishing with HTML, but once your book is available on Amazon, you can also reformat your blurb through AuthorCentral.

Note that there are two common uses of the word 'blurb' in publishing. Sometimes, it refers to the text that appears on the back cover, and other times it refers to the description on the product page; the latter is often different, and may be shorter. The blurb I have been discussing in this section is the description for your book on its product page, although some of the same ideas may apply to the back cover text. Back cover text may also include quotes from customers or reviews (but not Amazon's), or information about the author, for example.

Next, you need to make a strapline for your book. The strapline is a single, short sentence designed to attract interest in your book. Now you must condense your blurb down to a single sentence. Well, the strapline doesn't have to accomplish as many things. It functions a little more like an advertising slogan (but not quite). Here is what an effective strapline should do:

✓ Include a hook that gets people interested in your book.
✓ Signify the genre and relate to the content.
✓ Be short, concise, and easy to remember (maybe even catchy).

The strapline can serve many purposes. You can include it on a stand-alone line at the beginning of your blurb, with a blank line between (note that blank lines may be added through AuthorCentral after publishing, but can also be added at KDP). Use it at presentations or anytime that you have a chance to speak to a group of people about your book. Even if you also provide a longer description of your book or read a sample chapter, still use your strapline before and/or after. People are much more likely to remember the strapline, and it has your hook – some idea that will help to get people interested in reading your book. They are more likely to buy your book – and even tell others about it – if they can remember something about it, so you want your strapline to be memorable. Your strapline may even come in handy on a website, on your blog, and in your marketing efforts.

As long as we're considering condensed descriptions of your book, let's reconsider your title one more time. Remember, most top sellers have titles with just three words or less because they convey information quickly and are easy to remember. This also comes in handy when marketing – you can write, "Your Name, Author of __, __, and __," concisely if you use short titles. A great title has impact, hidden subtlety, signifies the genre, and relates to the content (such that a potential reader can guess how without already having read your book).

A descriptive title that uses keywords may work in nonfiction – especially, for more technical books. Shorter titles tend to be more effective in fiction and less technical or more entertaining nonfiction; but even for technical nonfiction, longer can be a deterrent.

There is one more place where the 5-second rule comes in play: the Look Inside. Once the customer looks inside, the front matter and first pages need to seal the deal. Format and design these pages as professionally as possible. Perfect the beginning of your book. Again, grammatical, spelling, or formatting mistakes in the Look Inside are sales killers as they don't bode well for the remainder of the book. The more professional the appearance of the Look Inside, the greater the chances that the customer will buy the book. The first chapter needs to grab and hold attention – and send a unified message along with the title, cover, and blurb. If your book has a slow start (you're more likely to close the deal if you come out with your best stuff), consider adding an excerpt of a better part to your front matter. Choose the front matter wisely because you don't want to bore the reader with a great deal of dull front matter before getting into the action. The style and quality of the writing will also impact the reader's decision. You want the words to flow well, for the reader to enjoy the read, and to be fascinated by the content and characters (which need to fit the genre – it needs to match up with the type of audience your cover, title, and blurb attract).

While you must strive to perfect the blurb and Look Inside, you don't want to create a huge disparity between these and the rest of your book. If your title, cover, blurb, and Look

Inside are effective at getting sales, this will backfire if the rest of your book doesn't live up to the expectations that these create – through negative customer reviews. Once you succeed in getting sales, to have continued sales – or to benefit from word-of-mouth sales – the content itself must be very good in terms of ideas, writing style, grammar, spelling, and formatting.

How about your name? Is it easy to spell, and easy to remember? Does it sound good, and fit your genre? If not, that might be one reason to consider using a nickname or pen name. On the other hand, your own name may be easier to market than a pen name. Everyone you meet is a potential reader – and if you tell everyone you meet what your pen name is, it kind of defeats the purpose of having one. If your first name is tough to spell or remember, but your last name isn't, you might use your first initial (or first and middle initials) along with your last name – or use a nickname if you have one (you can always start now).

One more piece of writing to perfect is your biography. As mentioned in Sec. 4.1.2, there are two similar fields available through AuthorCentral. The main field is called a biography, and the related field is called About the Author. In most cases, there is no reason to use the About the Author section: The biography is sufficient. Note that both sections will show up on your book's product page at Amazon if you fill out both sections. (Before CreateSpace merged with KDP, it had been possible to enter the About the Author section when you published the book. Now the only way to complete either the biography or the About the Author sections that show on a book's product page at Amazon is to do this through AuthorCentral.) I highly recommend visiting AuthorCentral (where you can login with the same account that you use at KDP, if you wish) because you can also spruce up your book description at AuthorCentral.

You want your biography to read well and be interesting, provide curious readers some information about you, and build credibility as the author for the kinds of books that you write. If you have relevant experience, include that. Write your biography in the third person, so that it sounds like someone else wrote it (you can even ask someone else to write it – provided that they write biographies very well – but get their written permission to use it). Biographies are often boring, so if yours reads well (yet appears professional – a little fun and personality can be effective, but don't cross the proverbial line), this bodes well for the book. On the other hand, any mistakes in the writing may deter sales.

Other writing that you may want to perfect before you publish is marketing material. Consider reading Chapter 8 before you publish your book. For optimal results, marketing is something that begins months before your book goes live and continues for years afterward.

Lastly, let's reconsider price one last time. Price was discussed in great detail in Sec.'s 4.1.4-5, so I will restrict myself to two new points that relate to marketing. First, writing is an art, and as with all art, value is based on perception. Perceived value is something that you can create through marketing. Also, customers often perceive a low price as being of little value, and a higher price as having greater value. On the other hand, if you price your book higher, your book better deliver the perception of high value – otherwise, customer reviews may reflect the disparity. Also, if the price is too high, many customers will have to pass on it.

It's a common mistake for self-published authors to undervalue their work. Intuitively, authors feel that if they drop the price, sales will increase. Usually, dropping the price doesn't increase sales unless the book was originally priced higher than similar, popular titles. Even if dropping the price does increase sales, it still might not increase the overall royalties because your per-book royalty is less with a lower list price. What often happens is that customers see a price that's too low compared to similar, popular books and perceive it to be a cheap book in terms of content. If you price your book fairly compared to similar, popular titles and your book is good, the best thing you can do for sales is marketing. Part of marketing is about creating a good, accurate perception of your book and spreading awareness of this. This way, marketing and price can work together to suggest that the book has high value.

The second point I wish to make regarding price is relevant if you have a series or if you will write more books that are similar enough that customers who read one and enjoy it may be interested in the other(s). In this case, the primary goal with the first book isn't to maximize royalties – rather, it's to maximize exposure. The idea is that the more people who read your first book, the more people will purchase your other books. Some authors even go to the extreme of giving the first book of a series away for free (economically feasible for eBooks – see Sec. 8.1.18). Alternatives include discounting the price of the first book, creating interest with giveaways and other promotions, and putting the first book on "sale" periodically. We'll discuss this further in Chapter 8.

Your first book has to be very good for this to work. It doesn't do any good to attract more readers of the first volume unless it hooks them to want to read subsequent volumes. Also, while all positive exposure is generally good, you really want to increase your exposure with the right audience. So you should direct any promoting that you do with the first book specifically toward your target audience.

The point is that if you have a series, you want the first book to give you the greatest number of readers, not necessarily the maximum royalty. Provided that the first book is good enough to hook readers into the series, this may give you greater royalties in the long run.

5.1.6 Common Paperback File Review Issues

In this section, we will focus on some issues that commonly arise when uploading and submitting files for review at Amazon KDP. We will discuss how to order a proof, what to look for when checking your proof, and how to submit corrections in subsequent sections.

The first place where you are likely to encounter these problems is when you use the Interior Reviewer tool at Amazon KDP. This tool is available if you use Guided Setup. Note that the Interior Reviewer is not always 100% accurate in the issues that it identifies. Also, some of the issues are just recommendations, while other issues must be fixed; but Interior Reviewer doesn't tell you which are which.

For these reasons, some experts like to skip Interior Reviewer. However, Interior Reviewer can be helpful, especially as it visually shows you the out-of-live zone and can show you specifically where the issues are. When you submit your files to Amazon KDP, they provide a similar (but often somewhat different) list of issues. Amazon KDP may not identify exactly where the problem is, whereas Interior Reviewer will flag the problem visually right in your book. This is the advantage of using Interior Reviewer. This tool saved me a great deal of frustration once: It flagged a stray character in the out-of-live zone. I have no idea how that character got there, and never would have believed it was there without this tool pointing right to it; I may never have found it by just browsing page by page through my file. Therefore, I recommend using Interior Reviewer, provided that you remember that some issues that it identifies may be not be accurate and some issues don't necessarily need to be fixed.

If you have trouble with the functionality of Interior Reviewer, try switching browsers (or even computers) – e.g. from Internet Explorer to FireFox (and possibly adjusting browser settings). It may take several minutes (if you have a really large file – approaching the limits of what can be uploaded, it may take much, much longer) for Interior Reviewer to open your book. Once it does, you see your book in a two-page spread, with the odd-numbered pages on the right and the even-numbered pages on the left, just as if you're reading your book (there is even an artificial lighting effect to help create this illusion).

The out-of-live zone is clearly marked, and you can see how your margins compare to these limits. If anything is flagged as being in the out-of-live zone, you will be able to see exactly which objects are in this area. You can also see how your pages look in print layout, aesthetically. If you're not happy with this, now is a good time to modify it.

Interior Reviewer will give you numbered comments (if there are any) in the top right corner. Click on any of these numbers to find the problems in the file – it will jump to that page so you can see it visually. Two common issues that Interior Reviewer finds are problems with margins (such as text in the out-of-live zone) and images with fewer than 200 DPI.

Amazon KDP will reject the file if there is text in the out-of-live zone, so if you get this message, you should find the flag(s) to see what Interior Reviewer found. You can't have text (or glyphs or other text-like symbols) closer than 0.25" from the page edges. If you have images that bleed (i.e. images that extend to the page edges), then text needs to be at least 0.38" from the oversized page edges (if you have bleed, your page size in Word must also be 0.25" taller and 0.13" wider than the trim size). Also, if you have any images that extend into the out-of-live zone, then they must extend all of the way to the oversized page edges (and you must choose the option with bleed in order to do this).

If you have any text (or glyphs or other text-like symbols) in the out-of-live zone, your file will be rejected. One way for this to happen is if your outside margins are less than 0.25" (or less than 0.38" if your file has bleed); using the exact minimum may also trigger an error (so 0.26" or 0.39" may be safer than 0.25" or 0.38"). Another way to have text in the out-of-live zone is to have a textbox with Text Wrap set to In Front Of Text or Behind Text, which is placed too close to the edge of the page. If there is any text embedded in the pictures, ensure that such text isn't in the out-of-live zone.

Any images that extend partway into the out-of-live zone will also cause the file to get rejected. Either push the images all of the way to the oversized page edges (if your book will have bleed) or pull them back inside of the out-of-live zone. If you have images that you want to be full-page, (first the book must have bleeds) right-click on them, go to the Format tab, select Wrap Text, and choose In Front of Text (unless *every* page in the book is full-page, then you should use 0" margins and In Line With Text). Full-page images must match your oversized book size (i.e. greater than the trim size) and completely fill the page; if there are any gaps along the edges, these can cause the file to be rejected. (Ideally, a full-page picture should be correctly sized to match the oversized page – i.e. after accounting for bleed – of the book when the picture is made. Otherwise, if you adjust the aspect ratio of the picture to fill the page, the picture will appear distorted.)

Remember, Interior Reviewer isn't 100% accurate. If you checked all of the flags and believe that Interior Reviewer may be wrong, the best way to find out is to submit your files for review. After file review, Amazon KDP will tell you if there is, in fact, any problem in the out-of-live zone that must be corrected.

A related issue that you could have is an insufficient interior margin. The interior margin must be at least 0.38" for a book with 150 pages or less, 0.75" for 151-400 pages, 0.875" for 401-600 pages, and 1" for 601 pages or more. The interior margin equals the value that you set for Gutter plus the value that you set for Left/Right in Word. (What Word calls a gutter, most publishing manuals refer to as a half-gutter. The gutter is extra space near the binding that can't be used.) We discussed margins in Sec. 2.1.6.

Interior Reviewer will also flag images that it believes to have a resolution of fewer than 200 dots per inch (DPI). Amazon KDP recommends 300 DPI for optimal printing; images with fewer than 200 DPI may appear blurry or pixelated in print. The DPI issue will not cause your file to be rejected – it's recommended that you correct the problem, but not required.

It's also possible to get an image with more than 200 DPI flagged as having less than 200 DPI. Remember, Interior Reviewer isn't 100% accurate. That said, more often than not, the image actually has less than 200 DPI and the self-publisher doesn't realize (or believe) it. The problem is that Word has a tendency to automatically compress images – even if you check the box that tells Word not to do this! Therefore, many times the images have actually been compressed down to as little as 96 DPI, but the author doesn't realize it.

Here is how to avoid having images less than 200 DPI:

1. First, use pictures that are already 300 DPI to begin with. Depending on how you made the picture, you must check the device (e.g. camera or scanner) or software program to see what the original DPI is. Also, if you resize the picture, this may change. Divide the pixel height by the actual height in word to get the DPI for the height, and similarly calculate the DPI for the width. You can increase the pixel count (in Paint may be

better than nothing, but other options are better than Paint), but adding these invented pixels isn't an ideal substitute from having higher-resolution images.

2. Turn off picture compression. Click File, scroll down below Help to find Options, choose Advanced, scroll down to Image Size and Quality, and check the box that says, "Do not compress images in file."[4] You must do this before inserting pictures. Otherwise, remove the pictures and reinsert them after doing this.[5]

3. Don't use copy/paste to insert images into the file. Instead, go to the Insert tab and click on the Picture button.

4. Avoid resizing your images in Word; pre-size them in the native program before inserting them into Word. Also, it's best to format images in the native program, rather than reformatting them in Word.

5. Don't upload a .doc, .docx, or .rtf file to Amazon KDP. Instead, convert your Word document to PDF yourself and submit the PDF file.

6. To convert your file to PDF, don't go to File, Save As, and choose PDF. The best option is to use a different PDF converter and print to PDF (instead of using Save As). Make sure that the PDF converter saves the images at 300 DPI and embeds the fonts (depending on what program you use, you may have to adjust the settings). It would also be desirable to have a PDF converter that can flatten transparency. There are many free Word-to-PDF converters available on the internet (but you must beware of viruses, spyware, and malware – so have a good anti-virus program on your computer, and see if you can get a recommendation from a trustworthy source).

Some images look good even if they have less than 200 DPI, while others look blurry or pixelated. The best test is to order a printed proof and see what it looks like.

Don't upload a .rtf, .doc, or .docx file to Amazon KDP, regardless of whether or not your file has images. Amazon KDP's conversion to PDF often causes unexpected formatting changes. Therefore, it is much better to convert your Word document to PDF and upload a PDF file. If you don't have any images, you can use Word's convenient Save As PDF feature.

Once you have investigated any issues that Interior Reviewer has flagged and are ready to proceed (remember, Interior Reviewer isn't 100% accurate, so sometimes it helps to submit files for review even if there are outstanding issues in Interior Reviewer), submit your files for review. When Amazon KDP replies (often in 12 to 24 hours), they will identify any issues that need to be fixed if your files are rejected, and may notify you of any other issues (such as images with less than 200 DPI). Interior Reviewer isn't always consistent with Amazon KDP's file review, and Amazon KDP's file review isn't always consistent – a number of people have reported resubmitting the exact same file with different results from the previous file review.

---

[4] As with Volume 1 of this book, the instructions are specifically for Word 2010. In Word 2007, go to Format, then Adjust Group to find this option. In Word 2003, right-click on a picture, then choose Format Picture > Picture.
[5] This was also mentioned in Volume 1 on page 120, at the beginning of Sec. 3.1.12.

We'll now discuss a few common issues that are reported after file review (aside from margins and DPI, which we have already discussed). One such issue may be that you need to embed the fonts in your PDF. For this, you need to use a Word-to-PDF converter that allows you to embed fonts and figure out how to do this. However, there are some fonts that don't allow embedding; in that case, the font designer is not permitting commercial use of the font. You may be able to learn more about this by trying to research the font online or inquiring about this in Amazon KDP's community help forum.

Another issue that may arise is if your spine text is too large for the spine width. Your spine text must be narrow enough and precisely positioned such that there is at least 0.0625" between the spine text and each spine edge. If not, Amazon KDP may shrink your spine text. They will notify you if they do this. If so, you should at least look at the printed proof and see if the resizing meets your satisfaction. The better option is to resize it yourself and submit a new cover file. If your book has 101 pages or less, spine text isn't allowed. In this case, Amazon KDP may remove the spine text from your cover.

Most images are created with transparency. Amazon KDP will usually tell you if your submitted interior and/or cover files contain images with transparency. If so, Amazon KDP may manually flatten these images. The images may look somewhat different if they are manually flattened. You can avoid this problem by using a PDF converter that allows you to flatten the images before you submit the file to Amazon KDP. At the very least, inspect the printed proof carefully to see if the images meet your approval (and if not, you'll have to find a PDF converter that can flatten them for you – or you can turn your images into JPEG images as described in Sec. 2.2.5, but then you must do so in a way that retains quality and DPI).

See Sec. 5.1.11 if you encounter problems that you need help with. If you feel that your file may have been rejected in error, try resubmitting the same files and see if you get the same error messages the second time (once in a while, this actually works). If needed, try posting your issue on the Amazon KDP community forum. Very often, someone else will have experienced the same problem and will know how to solve it.

Beware that Amazon KDP will not revise or edit your files for you. They won't correct any formatting, editing, or other mistakes that you make; they don't read your book. The files print just the way you submit them. It is the author's responsibility to find and correct any and all mistakes in the files. Amazon KDP only looks for specific file review issues – like checking for problems with margins, resolution of images, images with transparency, using the exact same title on the cover and title page, using the same author name on the cover and title page, writing "published by Amazon KDP," and other things of this sort (and you can't rely on them to catch all of these things, either). Inspect your files and printed proof very carefully.

Occasionally, Amazon KDP does make small changes to the cover file. I already mentioned how they may adjust the spine text. They may also shrink or reposition images on the cover (and may not notify you of this). It's also possible for the thumbnail image to be off. We'll discuss these two issues in Sec. 5.1.8.

5.1.7 How to order a Proof

Once Amazon KDP approves your files, you can order a proof. There are two options – viewing a digital proof and ordering a printed proof. View the digital proof first and then, if you're happy with that, order a printed proof next. You should at least order one printed proof, otherwise there may be significant problems that your customers will see before you do. For one, images look differently in print than they do on the screen. Also, almost everybody (including grammar experts) catches mistakes in print that they didn't see on the screen.

It would be wise to check the PDF carefully before you submit it to Amazon KDP. It's very common to find mistakes in the PDF, and you can save valuable time by catching them before you upload them to Amazon KDP.

There are two ways to view a digital proof – Digital Proofer and a PDF proof (which may differ slightly from the PDF that you upload – e.g. if transparency was flattened, the images may look different). Digital Proofer shows you your book in two-page spreads by default so that it looks like an open book, and also allows you to view your cover spread and a 3D cover.

I recommend first using the Digital Proofer. If you have trouble getting this to open, try switching browsers – e.g. from Internet Explorer to FireFox – or updating your browser, or even adjusting the internet options in your browser.

Once you get Digital Proofer to open your book, first study your cover carefully. The spine edges are clearly marked, which helps you check that the spine text is properly centered. Check the text on the cover, including the spine (it's easy not to notice mistakes here) – any typos on your cover will stand out to potential customers like a sore thumb. Check the positioning of images. See if the bar code appeared exactly where you expected it to be.

Look for the row of icons at the top right in Digital Proofer: The left icon shows you a 3D view of your cover. You can even spin the cover in 3D mode. This is a great way to check for centering on the front cover, spine, and back cover. Click the Stop button when the cover reaches the view you want. Close the 3D view when you're ready to check the interior.

Like Interior Reviewer, you can find a list of file issues on the right side of Digital Proofer; it flags issues like images with less than 200 DPI or images where transparency was flattened. You should inspect these flags. Check the title page carefully – the last thing you want to have is a glaring typo on the first page. Scroll through the book in the two-page spread to check for formatting problems. When you finish, change the view to show many pages at once. Sometimes your eye will catch a formatting issue the many-page view. Check that the text lines up at the bottom in both the many-page and two-page views.

In the two-page view, check for improper page breaks, and look for consistent styles and formatting throughout the book. Catching these errors now may minimize the total number of printed proofs that you need to order in the long run.

You may also want to view the PDF proof. Some people find it better to look for formatting mistakes in the Digital Proofer and editing mistakes in the PDF proof. If you find any mistakes in the digital proofs, I recommend correcting them and resubmitting your file – and repeating the process as needed until you don't see mistakes in your digital proofs. Then order a printed proof.

As I already mentioned, you really need to have at least one printed proof to see exactly what your customers will be receiving. Don't let your customers see the printed proof before you do; otherwise, they might point out something in a review that you should have caught and corrected yourself before publishing. You should also carefully check what should be the very final proof of your book in print. Almost everyone catches mistakes in the printed proof that weren't seen digitally – except for those authors who don't check the printed proof (their books tend to have more mistakes that they don't know about).

Sometimes, you check a printed proof and find one little typo to correct. If you're just changing one little thing (or a few little things), you may opt to just view a digital proof and skip the printed proof. BUT BEWARE: One little correction can create a chain reaction, causing many major formatting problems. There are true stories of self-published authors who made one little change and wound up with hundreds of defective books because they didn't realize that one tiny change could mess up the whole book. Even the smallest change can affect things like page breaks – and an improperly positioned page break can be a disaster.

If you're just making one little correction, look at your printed proof (which had the mistake) and the digital proof (which has the correction – meaning after the revised file was reviewed) and compare them carefully. Start at the position where the mistake was made. First read that sentence and make sure that the revised sentence is, in fact, correct. Then check the formatting from that point forward slowly, page by page, until the original printed proof (with the mistake) and the revised digital proof match up. Let me recommend ordering another printed proof anyway. Every once in a while, something that wasn't changed comes out a little different the second time. There is no better option than holding the completely final, perfect printed proof in your hands and seeing for yourself that it is indeed perfect.

5.1.8 What to Look for When Checking Your Proof

Begin by inspecting your cover carefully. Since the cover is the first thing that prospective customers will see, it's worthwhile to invest the time to check it very thoroughly; it's also easy to do, since there is just a front, back, and spine.

Read the title slowly. Then speak the title slowly as you read it (you might hear something that you didn't see). Repeat for the author(s) and other contributors, subtitle, spine text, back cover text, and any other text on your cover. The cover is just about the worst place to have a typo. It's easy to have a typo on the spine, especially since it looks small and sideways on the computer monitor. Hence, you should check the spine text very carefully. Also check the orientation of the spine text in the printed proof: Make sure that it's not backwards compared to traditionally published books. It should be obvious if your spine text is upside down if you insert your book between traditionally published books on a shelf.

Does the font look reasonable? Old versions of Word used to squeeze and stretch text if the textboxes and WordArt were resized, so if you used an older edition of Word to make your cover (or if you used another software program that may do this to text), then you should copy/paste the text into a blank document, make it the same size and style, print it out, and compare the text to your cover.

Find a second pair of eyes to check over your cover. You can't expect anyone else to do as thorough a job as you yourself should do, but other people may find mistakes that you are missing and might offer a valuable suggestion.

Check the centering of text and images (that you intended to be centered) on the front cover, back cover, and spine. Another thing you might examine is even spacing near the edges and between different elements (text and images) on your cover.

Images often appear different in print than they do on the screen. We discussed reasons for this in Sec. 3.1.4. Printed images may appear darker than they look on a monitor, and there may be color shifts. Two slightly different hues of the same color may look identical in print. Study the colors of your text, images, and background and compare them with the original cover as viewed on the monitor. If you're not pleased with what you see in print, you need to make adjustments (and it may take a little trial and error to get it just right). Colors don't always print exactly the same every time – if you order 100 copies of your book, the colors won't look the same on all of them. There can be slight printing variations. If Amazon KDP flattened transparency, you may be able to reduce some slight printing shifts by instead uploading a PDF for the cover that already has transparency flattened (you just need to find a PDF converter – possibly free, online – that provides this option).

See if any images or text look blurry, jagged, or pixelated. If so, this is likely caused by having images under 300 DPI. Sec. 5.1.6 discussed how to keep Word from compressing images. If you used a different program to make your cover, find the settings that control the DPI. Also check the DPI of the original image – if that's too low, you found your problem.

Look at large plain colors and see if they printed smoothly. Large plain black areas often have issues, especially if there were textboxes lying in front of them; sometimes, the "black" color inside of the textbox is noticeably lighter than the "black" color in the background. Try flattening the cover in the PDF program (find one with this option) and see if that helps. If not, you can try combining the black background object and textbox together into a single jpeg image, although a jpeg image may not have lines and text that are as smooth as the original. Another option is revising the color scheme for your cover – but before going to that extreme, try posting your issue on the Amazon KDP community forum to see if anyone can suggest a better solution.

Are there are any straight lines or straight edges of objects near the cover edges? If so, these can accentuate any slight trimming imperfections. For example, if a book is trimmed at a slight angle, it can make a line that should be parallel to the edge look like it's slanted. Also, if you made a border for your cover, due to slight trimming variations, the border may not look perfectly even on every copy of your book that is printed. Use a piece of paper to cover 1/8" of one edge of the cover at a time and see how that appeals to your eye. If you're content with that degree of printing variation, then it's probably not an issue to worry about.

Similarly, the spine may be off by 1/8" on either edge due to slight printing variations. Therefore, spine text won't always be centered, either side (i.e. front or back) may wrap 1/8" onto the spine, and the spine may wrap 1/8" onto either side. This is most noticeable if there is a sudden change in color between the spine and either side. It's just 1/8", and very often the spine may be dead-on. You have to weigh the pros and the cons.

Look closely for possible resizing and repositioning issues. Amazon KDP occasionally re-sizes and repositions elements on the cover; and, if so, they may not inform you about it. If you observe this and prefer to avoid it, try cropping the size of your cover file to just the cover with bleeds. A couple of years ago, we used to be able to submit a cover with extra back-ground (i.e. a larger file than just the cover with bleeds), and as long as it was centered, it would print just fine. Recently, however, I and other authors have noticed occasional resizing and repositioning when the submitted cover is larger than it needs to be. You do have to add 0.25" to both the width and height to allow for bleeds, and you do have to figure in the spine width, but don't make the width and height of the cover file any larger than the minimum requirements and this will help prevent possible resizing and repositioning.

I sometimes notice slight centering issues with the Amazon KDP thumbnail image, even when the submitted cover file is exactly the minimum size. However, the Amazon thumbnail is often centered properly even when the Amazon KDP thumbnail isn't.

Now it's time to open the book and look inside. You need to do two separate things: read the text itself and check the formatting. Trying to do both at once will probably result in many mistakes not getting caught – e.g. formatting mistakes distract from the text, and when you get focused on the text, formatting issues might not be noticed. Therefore, you should browse through once to check formatting and separately read the text for proofreading.

Here are formatting issues to look for:
- ✓ Is the style and size of headers and footers consistent throughout the book? Proofread the header text carefully. If you used the chapter headings for the even-page headers, double-check that these match the actual chapter names.
- ✓ Check that all of the pages are numbered correctly and that the style is consistent throughout the book (except for switching from Roman numerals to Arabic numbers).
- ✓ Spend a few moments looking at each page for possible problems with the page layout. Look for strange page breaks, linebreaks, changes in justification (like a sudden change from full to left or centered), changes in font style or size, inconsistent line spacing, inconsistent indents, and variations in the space between headings and para-graph text.

- ✓ Inspect the table of contents and index. Check each page reference to make sure that it refers to the right page. Do the chapter names from the table of contents match the actual chapter headings? Read these carefully. Make sure that your chapter headings have consistent style both in the table of contents and throughout the book.
- ✓ Search for references to pages (e.g. "see page 42"), figures (e.g. "see Fig. 3"), tables, equations, chapters, etc. and check to see if the numbers are correct.
- ✓ Check for consistency in bullets – e.g. using the same size indents, being consistent with whether or not the indents hang, etc.
- ✓ Inspect page borders, figures, equations, tables, captions, and textboxes.
- ✓ If you intended to line up the bottom of every page, thumb through the book quickly to check the vertical justification.
- ✓ After enough rounds of editing, when you finally believe that the text is perfected, you will need to attend to any manual formatting issues that you may have saved for last – such as manually dealing with hyphens, widows, orphans, and rivers (as described in Sec. 5.1.4). Note that changing one of these issues may affect others, so you'll have to keep a lookout for this. Look for hyphenation issues, wide gaps between words (that could be the result of automatic hyphenation not realizing that a "word" like Create-Space can be split in two), widows, orphans, and rivers in your "final" proof. You will also need to recheck most of the items from this list.

Keep in mind that any changes that you make to the text may cause changes to the formatting. Even a single small change may create a domino effect – e.g. it can create an unnatural page break which can carry over for many pages. Any time you make revisions to your text, you must carefully proof the book for formatting issues afterward.

Following are things that you should look for as you carefully read the text:

- ✓ Examine the title page carefully. Take a moment to make sure that the title and author(s) are exactly the same on the front cover, spine, title page, copyright, and on your bookshelf at Amazon KDP. As a customer, I have occasionally spotted a typo in the title of a book in search results on Amazon. You definitely want to make sure that your title is perfect.
- ✓ Don't ignore the copyright page and other front matter. These are the first pages that a prospective customer will see when using the Look Inside feature at Amazon. Invest some time to see if they are as professional as you can get them.
- ✓ Similarly, you want to nail the first few chapters, which may show in the Look Inside. Any mistakes here can cause potential sales to be lost. Make sure that your eyes are fresh and check the beginning of your book a few times. Are these pages captivating?
- ✓ Also rest your eyes and rejuvenate yourself frequently as you read the remainder of the book. If a reader judges that there are too many typos, this may be reflected in reviews, which can potentially impact sales.

✓ Look for spelling and grammatical mistakes. If you haven't already done so, click on the Spelling & Grammar button in the Review tab in Word and carefully check every instance that Word shows as a possible mistake. However, there are many mistakes that Word doesn't catch – e.g. "their playing by the shore" (instead of "they're"), "be there at ate o'clock" (instead of "eight"), and "the boxes punched him in the face" (instead of "boxer"). Use Word's spelling and grammar checker to catch some mistakes, but don't rely on it. You must proofread your book carefully to find many typos and mistakes that Word won't catch for you.

✓ It's very common to mean one word, but use another similar word – such as a homophone or a word that has similar spelling. Some examples include "its" and "it's," "their," "there," and "they're," and "week" and "weak." Such mistakes are easy to make without knowing it, but can really annoy readers if you don't catch them. Hence, it's very important to proofread thoroughly, carefully, and repeatedly.

✓ Also look for repeated words. For example, "the" is often repeated, especially when one "the" comes at the end of one line and the next "the" begins the next line. You can find these in Word by entering "the the" (without the quotes, of course) in the Find tool on the Home tab.

✓ Check the punctuation. Make sure that questions actually end with question marks, and not periods. Consult a style guide to see if you used colons, semicolons, commas, quotation marks, and parentheses appropriately. Even if you already know the rules, you must still check each colon, semicolon, comma, etc. for possible typing mistakes.

✓ Verify the storyline, plot, character development, chronology, etc. Any mistakes in the plot or storytelling can be huge sales killers. The problem you have is that you already know the story, so it's hard to read and think through the story the same way that a reader will. You really need a second (and third, and so on) pair of eyes to read the story and give you feedback – especially, someone you can count on to tell it like it is.

✓ "Make sure that quotes face the right direction," as in this quote, 'and this one.'

✓ Check that the short hyphen (-) is used to hy-phen-ate words – while the longer en (–) or even longer em (—) dash is used as a separator. Also check for consistency – i.e. use either the en dash or the em dash, but not both, for a separator. However, the longer em dash (—) is correct as an interrupter at the end of a line or to attribute the author of a quotation, even if you are using the en dash (–) as a separator.

✓ Look for changes of tense – e.g. suddenly switching from past tense (e.g. "she sang wonderfully") to present tense (e.g. "she sings wonderfully"). (Of course, there are exceptions, such as: "She sang wonderfully back then and still sings wonderfully today.") Also check for incorrect changes in person – e.g. narrating in the first person singular (I, me, my) and suddenly switching to narrate in the third person (he, him). There are occasions where the person should change; you want to eliminate the cases where it shouldn't change, but does. (However, a how-to guide may be less formal.)

✓ In general, active writing is favored over passive writing. That is, good writing tends to "show" more than "tell." For example, compare "it is very cold today" with "although he wore a thick jacket, a scarf, a ski hat, and mittens, he was still shivering." Don't change every instance where you "tell" to "show." Rather, try to gauge whether or not you tell too often and show too little – in which case, you want to try to show more and tell less – and when you do tell, consider whether or not showing would have been more appropriate (there are many minor points that aren't worth detracting from the story to show, so sometimes telling is better).

✓ Did you overuse adverbs that end with –ly? Adverbs also tend to be passive rather than active. For example, "she returned to her bedroom sadly" tells that she was sad, whereas "she wiped the tears from her eyes on her way to the bedroom" shows that she was sad. Some technical nonfiction books, however, do use –ly adverbs more.

✓ Various forms of the verb "to be" (is, are, was, were, been, etc.) also tend to tell rather than show, and are sometimes even useless words. For instance, "to be" is superfluous in "seems to be obvious." However, this style is sometimes used in technical works.

✓ Check for other useless words and redundancies like "wastefully useless."

✓ Some words and phrases are essentially filler – that is, the same information can often be conveyed without using them. (It's true! See!) Some common filler words include "although," "that," "whereas," "in fact," "in general," and "as opposed to." It's okay to use these words sometimes, but you should check if you overuse them. It also depends on the context; these words tend to be used more frequently in technical nonfiction and textbooks.

✓ Are there any words that you personally tend to overuse? If so, search for them in Word and consider finding alternatives to them. Here, it helps to know your own bad habits, which you could learn by receiving unbiased feedback from others.

Be sure to make revisions to both your paperback and eBook files (except for those changes, such as page header adjustments, that only apply to one or the other). You'd hate to have a mistake in your eBook, for example, that you corrected in your paperback, but forgot to also fix in the eBook.

It's nearly impossible to catch all of our own mistakes. For one, we often "see" what we meant to write instead of what we actually wrote. Many top-notch writers who have thoroughly mastered grammar and the elements of writing and style seek editors and other unbiased readers to check through their work to suggest possible mistakes and provide feedback. Even professional editors themselves hire others to edit their own writing. Having another pair of eyes look over your work is invaluable, and quite necessary.

Hiring a professional editor can make a huge difference. Many professional editors charge $300 and up. There are less expensive editing services, too. The challenge is finding someone who will do an excellent job at an affordable price, and who you can trust to protect the confidence of your work. Find writing that you can verify they have edited (easiest, when they are listed as the editor); if spelling and grammar aren't your strong suits, find someone with fluency in this to judge writing that they have edited. Request a free (or at least, low-cost) sample of a small number of pages – such as your first chapter – and see if they edit that to your satisfaction. That way, you have an expectation of what you may be getting before investing too much time and money. The prospective editor or editing service should present you with a contract. A clause in the contract about you retaining ownership of the work and the editor protecting your confidence should help ease any concerns of this sort that you may have. (I'm not an attorney; you should consult an attorney for all of your legal questions, and to check over the contract.) It's mutually beneficial if the editor will accept 50% of the payment upfront and the remainder upon receipt of the edited manuscript. (Before Create-Space merged with KDP, CreateSpace offered basic copyediting services. Amazon no longer offers paid editing services to self-published authors. However, Amazon does maintain a list of paid service providers on the KDP help pages. Another way to find editors is to ask authors or search for discussions on community forums for authors.)

Note that there are different types of editors. Basic editing consists of just checking for mistakes in spelling and grammar. You can also get editing help with writing style, storyline suggestions, formatting, etc. If you seek editing help, you want to know exactly what you're getting (and you should first determine which type of help you want).

See Sec. 5.1.11 if you have questions about editing or formatting. There are also some editors and small publishers on the KDP community forum who provide professional services. I haven't used them, and so I can't recommend any of them one way or the other; I just know that there are some regulars there who show expertise in many questions that they answer.

In Volume 1, I recommended publishing your book for free, whereas in Volume 2, I'm suggesting that hiring cover and editing help could make a significant difference. Why? By reading Volume 2, you're showing interest in perfecting your book and learning about market-ing. The author who takes the time to perfect the content of the book, attend to all of the details, and is willing to learn how to effectively market (and also is willing to do the work) is much more likely to reap the benefits of a great cover and good editing. Volume 1 was focused on getting the book written and published. The author who rushes through that, but doesn't take time to perfect the book and market, shouldn't invest in cover design and editing. Also, if you tried all of this yourself first, now you have seen firsthand and can assess more properly to what extent your cover, formatting, and editing might be improved through professional help.

There are a few other things that you need to proof besides the book itself. Login to Amazon KDP and proofread your description carefully. Also, carefully double-check the tittle, subtitle, and author(s) and other contributors. A second pair of eyes can also be helpful for proofing your description (and again when you prepare your biography). These are among the first things that prospective buyers will see, so they are well worth perfecting.

After you publish your book, you should also check the Amazon page for your book. Make sure that the title on Amazon correctly matches the title as you entered it at Amazon KDP, for example. It's worth checking your book's product page periodically – if there happens to be any glitch in the system that could affect sales, you want to know about it so you can report it to Amazon (there is a form for this on the page, or ask KDP to report this for you).

5.1.9 Before You Approve Your Proof

Rush, rush, rush! People are usually in a rush, and naturally impatient. This affects cover design and blurb writing through the 5-second rule. But customers aren't the only ones who tend to show impatience – authors do it, too. Most self-published authors rush their work out to the wolves. Slow down, take it easy, resist the temptation to get your work out there as quickly as possible, and avoid this much-too-common mistake.

Authors spend months – sometimes years – writing. This is the result of a great deal of effort, and reflects much diligence and motivation. The completion of the manuscript is a major accomplishment just in itself.

So now what will the author *do* with this book? Publish it, of course. That's when the writer suddenly realizes that writing the book was the easy part! It may have been a great deal of work, but it's something that the author felt that he/she knew how to do, and writing is a hobby that the author enjoys. After the book is written, the author is faced with a great deal of work that is unfamiliar. Publishing the book involves the fickle art of writing a query letter and book proposal, searching for publishers and literary agents, selling your book to strangers who are often more interested in your resume and marketing skills than the writing itself, and dealing with an overwhelming rejection ratio. The alternative, self-publishing, involves a variety of unfamiliar skills – formatting, editing, publishing, cover design, marketing, and even public relations – including skills which the writer may not enjoy or excel at (such as the illustrations involved in making a cover or the social prowess and public relations skills entailed in marketing).

After all of the work done to write the book and the additional work needed to publish the book, the writer naturally feels a very strong compulsion to be finished with it once and for all, to get the book to the market and be done with it, and hopefully get some pats on the back through feedback for the amazing feat of finishing the book. Realize this: Your task is not complete when you publish the book by clicking the Approve Proof button. Successful authors invest much time in marketing, and the most successful authors begin their marketing campaign before the book is launched. The book even has marketing in itself, so taking the time to perfect the cover, blurb, and content can itself have a significant impact on sales.

Most self-publishers rush their book out to the market only to regret this later. They don't regret writing the book. What they regret is not taking more time to perfect the book, getting feedback and help, learning more about marketing, and developing a plan. I see these kinds of comments on the community help forums (especially, at KDP) quite frequently:[6]

- "I got a bad review saying there were typos. Can anyone suggest a cheap editor?"
- "Sales are really slow. Please give me feedback on my cover."
- "My blurb doesn't seem to be working. Advice would be appreciated."
- "A review says there are formatting problems, but it looked great in the preview."
- "Does anyone have some good marketing suggestions?"
- "Is it possible to unpublish a book and republish it later?"

I sometimes provide my two cents in an effort to help them. I appreciate that they have realized that they need help and are trying to improve their books. However, it would have been wiser to seek this help before publishing their books. Don't wait for a bad review or slow sales to motivate you to improve your book. You can revise the book, but you can't remove the bad review and the history of slow sales will affect your sales rank after the revisions. The wiser course is to seek feedback and help – and properly invest the time to perfect the book – prior to publishing.

With your first book, you're establishing yourself as an author. Start out with the best product you can and create a positive, professional image for yourself as an author. Your image is part of your marketing.

Look at what traditional publishers do by example. They often have a whole team of people – who specialize in editing, formatting, illustration, marketing, etc. – work on a book for 6 months after it's written. They spend 6 months perfecting the book, and also use this 6-month period to build "buzz" for the book and develop promotional plans (the author is generally expected to do much of the promotion himself/herself, but the publisher may send out advanced review copies, press release materials, and a host of other things that we will consider in Chapter 8).

The indie author spends an average of one month doing these things all by his or her lonesome self, whereas publishers have a team of experts doing these same things for 6 months. Yet the self-published book is available online in the same search results as traditionally published books. If you want your book to be competitive, exercise the patience to spend more time perfecting your book, seeking and receiving valuable help and feedback, creating "buzz" for your book, and learning how to develop an effective marketing plan.

Sales usually don't come to you; you have to help drive sales through marketing efforts. Many of us enjoy the "art" of writing, but the reality is that selling books is a "business." Learn how to translate the passion that you have for your book into a passion for sharing your book with others – and you can use this to motivate yourself to learn how to become successful at marketing your book.

---

[6] These are not actual quotes from any particular users, but instead represent a variety of common questions.

Read Chapter 8 before you publish your book. Strive to create buzz for your book. Develop a marketing plan and motivate yourself to carry it out. Don't expect instant results. Train yourself to relax and exercise patience. Have you thought about the concept of pre-orders? You can learn about preorders in Sec. 7.1.8. You know that you were successful in creating buzz when you sell several copies of your book through preorders. This can give your book a good jumpstart. Instead of starting out with slow sales and struggling to make up for it, strive to start out with several early sales and meet the challenge of maintaining the sales.

One other thing you may want to do before you approve your proof is obtain copyright registration. This was described toward the end of Sec. 5.1.1.

5.1.10 Making Revisions to the Paperback

You can revise your cover and interior file as many times as you want prior to publishing your book; there is no limit. Simply click on your book on your Member Dashboard and click Interior or Cover in the Setup column. From there, you can upload a new file and submit your files for review again. You can't make changes to your file while they are in review; you have to wait for Amazon KDP to complete their file review, and then you will be able to submit revisions to your files.

You can make other changes, too – such as modifying your description, about the author, keywords, sales channels, and browse categories. However, there are a few things that can't be changed without deleting your title and starting over: Your title, subtitle, author(s) and other contributors, and ISBN are locked after you make your ISBN selection. If you used the free ISBN option, you can delete your title and start over at any time prior to clicking Approve Proof (well, if your files are in review, you may have to wait for that). If you invested in an ISBN or other services, you probably don't want to delete and start over – and lose that investment. In that case, you should call support, explain your situation, and ask if they can make the change you need or if they can transfer the service(s) that you paid for onto another book so that you can start over. It shouldn't hurt to ask.

Think carefully before you click Approve Proof. Once you do that, you can no longer delete your book. However, if you want to unpublish your book, you can disable all sales channels. Although that will prevent Amazon from selling new copies of your book, your book's detail page may remain on Amazon permanently – allowing any customers who may have a copy to sell their copies used. You can also retire your book after disabling all sales channels, but again that won't prevent Amazon from still retaining your product page. Once you enable the Amazon sales channel and approve your proof, you can expect your Amazon product page to remain there forever, even if you unpublish your book. Also, once you claim a book on AuthorCentral, it will remain on the list of books on your Author Page at Amazon indefinitely.

What if you want to make changes after you publish? Not a problem![7] The quickest way to update your book description or About the Author sections at Amazon are through Author-Central (see Sec. 6.1) – though you'll still need to revise your description through Amazon KDP for Expanded Distribution outlets. You can also revise your files, browse categories,[8] keywords, sales channels, etc. – just not your ISBN or title information.

Your book will be unavailable for purchase from Amazon during the time it takes to upload the new file(s) and approve the new proof. It can take as little as 12 to 24 hours for this, if you proof your book digitally. Check the digital proof (see Sec.'s 5.1.7-8) very carefully. Remember, a single small change can wreak havoc if that small change causes big adjustments to your page layout – e.g. through unappealing page breaks. Look carefully for formatting problems. If instead you order a printed proof, your book may be unavailable for a week or more, which can have a major impact on your sales rank.

Should you make a new edition? It's optional. You can update your book without making a new edition. If you made a change based on information posted in a review and wish to make it clear that your book has been revised, you can choose to include a note to this effect in the description (but don't make any reference to the review whatsoever; also, see Chapter 7 to learn more about customer reviews). Another thing you might do is make some change to the copyright page. It can be a subtle change that only you would notice (if you don't want it to be obvious that there is a new version), or you can write something like 2nd edition, Version 4, updated 3/14/13, etc. At the very least, this will be helpful for you. Why? For one, if you view Amazon's Look Inside, you'll be able to readily determine if the Look Inside has been updated yet (it may take several days for the Look Inside to match the revised files). Also, if you happen to see a customer's book, you'll be able to tell which version they purchased.

It's handy to keep records of your files in at least two different places so you know which files were the most recent. Also, backup your most recent files in at least two different places. Every once in a while, a computer pretends like a file isn't there when it is, and if you don't realize this, you could accidentally open a version that wasn't your most recent file and start revising that. Fortunately, Amazon KDP shows you the filenames of the cover and interior files that you uploaded last time, which can help with this.

A totally new edition can be made by adding a new title with a new ISBN, for example. This is common among textbooks, for which a new edition comes out every year or two (which publishers use not only to make improvements, but to help reduce the impact of used textbook sales). The previous edition can be unpublished by disabling sales channels (and it can even be retired by contacting support – but the listing may still remain on Amazon so that

---

[7] Originally (before CreateSpace merged with KDP), CreateSpace had advertised that this was supposed to cost $25 if you had the Expanded Distribution. However, this fee was never charged. Note that it can take several weeks for some changes to propagate through all of the Expanded Distribution channels.

[8] However, if you've already asked Amazon KDP to add a second browse category to your Amazon page, you should make this change by contacting support.

customers can resell used books). The two editions may be linked together on Amazon (probably, with the old edition less visible – a customer may have to click a link to see all of the editions). Any reviews on the old edition may automatically show up on the new edition.

5.1.11 Getting Help with Your Paperback

You may be able to get free help and advice from fellow authors. One place where this is possible is Amazon KDP's community forum. There are many authors and small publishers there who regularly share their expertise, and it's usually a friendly ambiance. You can also meet other authors like yourself.

Amazon KDP maintains a list of professional services on the KDP help pages, and you can find many other options online (even some members of the KDP community forum offer this).

5.2 Proofing Your eBook

5.2.1 Perfecting Your eBook

MUCH OF WHAT WE discussed about perfecting your paperback cover, interior, blurb, and biography in Sec.'s 5.1.3-5 also applies to your eBook. In this section, we will focus on details and formatting that are exclusive to eBooks, so as not to repeat what we have already discussed regarding paperbacks; but we will save picture formatting in the interior file for the following section. When you proofread your paperback book and revised it, hopefully you also took the time to update your eBook file. It's important to remember to revise both files any time that you make changes.

Virtually everything that applies to designing a print cover from Sec. 5.1.3 also applies to the eBook cover – even the part about the cover looking good in large size. The majority of Kindle buyers shop for eBooks on Amazon's website on their PC. The cover must look nice as a thumbnail to attract attention, but once they click on the listing, many customers will click to see the large cover image (they will also see this when they use the Look Inside). I've seen many covers that looked nice as thumbnails, but then some imperfections (jagged lines, blurry, pixelated, text not crisp, or stray marks) showed up in the large image. Since this can deter sales, you want to ensure that it looks nice both ways.

Since your cover will automatically be included inside of your eBook, don't include the cover in your eBook file (you should, however, have a title page; what you don't want is a duplicate cover in your book). Also, use the maximum resolution allowed for your cover (up to 2500 pixels for the longest side) because many customers will be viewing the large image on a

PC. The width of your eBook cover should be shorter than the height. Almost all of the other thumbnails look like this, so if your eBook cover is wider than it is tall, it will really stand out – but not in a good way. This will likely hurt sales.

The two-space issue described in Sec. 5.1.4 has a greater impact on eBook formatting than it does on paperback formatting. Don't use two consecutive spaces in your eBook – not even following a period – otherwise one of the extra spaces will either show up at the end of one line or the beginning of the next if the two spaces happen to come at the beginning or end of a line displayed on the screen of the eReader (and you can't plan for where this will occur, since the device user can vary font size, line spacing, etc. – plus, screen sizes vary).

Don't use blank lines to separate sections in your eBook. Instead, place asterisks (* * *) or other symbols on a single, centered line (with a single linespace above and below it) – or do the same thing, but use a glyph. However, there is an important formatting issue with glyphs that we will discuss in the next section. Note that drop caps won't format perfectly on every device. A better alternative is to write the first three words of each chapter in CAPS.

There are some places where you should use Shift + Enter instead of just Enter in your eBook. This yields a more predictable blank line, which you may have between elements of your table of contents, copyright page, before and after images, etc. Hold down Shift and press Enter twice to create a single blank line. When you do this, the last line of the previous paragraph will look funny on your screen. Don't worry about this because eReaders should display it correctly (well, it would be wise to check this among other things as described in Sec. 5.2.3). However, don't create blank linespaces this way in your paperback book file.

The best way to make dashes is to use Alt codes. Hold down Alt and type 0150 to make the en dash (–) and 0151 to make the em dash (—). The dashes that Word makes via AutoCorrect as you type often don't work on some of the older Kindle devices, but do work using the Alt method. If you have numerous dashes to update, copy/paste one of your old dashes into the Find field in Replace and use the Alt method in the Replace field. You don't need to make any changes to hyphens (-) typed directly from your keyboard.

It's also safest to use the Alt codes for other supported characters, such as standard curly quotes (" and "). Be sure to angle the quotation marks correctly. You can find a table of supported Kindle characters by going to the KDP help pages and looking on the left column for Preparing Your Book > Formatting Your Book > Character Encoding. After pulling up this page, click the second "here" link to see an image of supported characters and their Alt codes. Note that Alt codes for characters not on this list won't work on Kindle (and other eReader) devices. Here is the current link for the page of supported characters:

https://images-na.ssl-images-amazon.com/images/G/01/digital/otp/help/Latin1.gif

Actually, there are other characters that you can use. You can't use them in Word, but there is a simple way to use them. When your Word file is complete, click Save As in the File tab and set Save As Type to Web Page, Filtered (don't pick Single File Webpage and make sure it says Filtered). Click Yes and wait for the file to fully save. Then open the file in Notepad (not Word). Now you can type the ampersand symbol (&) followed by the name of a supported HTML symbol and a semicolon (;). For example, ⊥ makes the perpendicular symbol (⊥) and ♦ creates a diamond (♦). A list of supported HTML symbols can be found here:

http://en.wikipedia.org/wiki/List_of_XML_and_HTML_character_entity_references

One problem with eBook design is that text can wind up anywhere on a screen, since users read eBooks with different size screens, font sizes, line spacing, etc. One way to gain some control over this is to use Ctrl + Shift + Spacebar to create a space between two words (or a word and symbol) that you don't want to be split. For example, you can do this if you want to type "4 lbs." in such a way as to prevent the "4" from being on the end of one line and the "lbs." from being on the beginning of the next line. This is called a non-breaking space.

Remember, the eBook can be in color even if the paperback edition is black-and-white; there is no charge for adding color to the eBook. However, don't overuse color in the text; the most important function of text is that it be clear and easy to read. Color is most effective as a highlight or to catch attention when used sparingly. Another consideration is that some colors that ordinarily contrast well sometimes don't contrast well in grayscale (they may even blend together), yet many readers have black-and-white eReaders. For example, where red stands out on a color screen, it looks gray on a black-and-white device. These are all important considerations, which you can judge by viewing a preview on a black-and-white device (see Sec. 5.2.3). It would be ideal to make preliminary a sample when you first start making figures.

Consider avoiding long paragraphs in your eBook. Some readers – so this may depend in part on your audience – are easily overwhelmed by long paragraphs. Long paragraphs can easily occupy the entire screen on small devices, which makes them seem unending.

We will now explore some details that are quite important for perfecting the formatting of an eBook. There are many common formatting mistakes that arise from eBook files that are typed in Word that can be avoided, and which you want to avoid in order to make your eBook appear professional. The problem has to do with the fact that an eBook is designed to function more like a webpage, whereas a word processor is designed to perfect the look of printed pages on separate sheets of paper. The natural language of a webpage is HTML. Ultimately, your Word file will be converted to a mobi file for Kindle, and at some point in the process your Word document will be interpreted as a set of HTML instructions.

What does this mean to you? What you see on your monitor – and what you would see on a piece of paper if you were to print your document out – can be quite different from what you see on the screen of an eReader. Therefore, you want to learn how to make Word produce an eBook file that looks just as nice on any eReader as it appears on your screen; and you want to preview your eBook very carefully on every device before you publish it.

The problem is that documents typed in Word can result in HTML instructions that one or more eReaders may interpret differently than you expect. The solution is to learn techniques to format the Word document in such a way as to make the HTML cleaner and unambiguous.

One way to do this is to use the Styles on the top right half of the Home tab. Format every piece of your Word document with one of these Styles so that Word will add tags to the converted HTML – like Heading 1. You need to use at least 4 different styles: Normal, FirstNormal, Heading 1, and Title. Modify the default Normal, Heading 1, and Title styles to suit your needs, and add a new style for FirstNormal (a different style for the first paragraph of each chapter and other paragraphs or stand-alone lines that you don't want to have automatically indented by eReaders).

Right-click a Style to modify it. Set the font style to Times New Roman (and note that the user will be able to set the font on his/her eReader), the font size to 12 for the Normal and FirstNormal Styles (which the user will also be able to adjust; this is the best size for paragraph text), and the font color to Automatic. The Heading 1 and Title Styles should use a larger font size than Normal. To add a new style – such as FirstNormal – click the funny icon in the bottom right corner of the Styles group on the Home tab – which looks like ⬎ – and click the bottom left button (New Style).

In each Style, click the single spacing button. Click the justified full button for the Normal and FirstNormal Styles, and the center button for the Title and Heading 1 Styles. If you want any left-aligned text, use justified full in the Style, highlight the text, and click the left align icon in the Paragraph group of the Home tab (don't use the left align button in the Style) – after the Style has already been applied (and remember, like FirstNormal, you need to set First Line to 0.01" to prevent this paragraph from being automatically indented). Adjust the paragraph options for each style by clicking the Format button in the bottom left corner (where you modify the Style). Choose Paragraph from the list. Set the Spacing Before and After to 0 and the Line Spacing to Single (not Word's default of 1.15). Exception: For Heading 1, set Before to 18 pts and don't create a blank linespace before it. In the FirstNormal Style, set First Line to 0.01"; in Normal, adjust Special to First Line and By to 0.3" (or so – we'll improve upon this later in this section); and in Title and Heading 1, set Special to None.

To save your Styles, click the Change Styles button at the right edge of the Home tab, select Style Set, and click Save As Quick Style Set.

Don't adjust the font size in the Home tab; instead, defined Styles that have both the font size and formatting that you wish to apply to the text (with the exception of how to make left-aligned text that we described previously).

To help Word produce clean, unambiguous HTML, Select All and click the Normal Style. Now go through your eBook file and apply the other styles to any text that you don't want to have the Normal Style – such as headings. Use the Title Style (large font, centered alignment) for pictures centered on their own lines. Apply FirstNormal to the first paragraph of each chapter (to prevent it from being automatically indented) and any other non-centered paragraphs or stand-alone lines that you don't want to have automatically indented (like lines from your copyright page and table of contents).

Sometimes, the table of contents bookmark hyperlinks can take the reader to the chapter, but not show the chapter heading at the top of the page. The way around this is to insert a blank line above the chapter heading, press the spacebar a few times (this is the one exception to the rule to never have two or more consecutive spaces), highlight these spaces, apply the FirstNormal Style, place the cursor at the beginning of this row of spaces, and insert the bookmark there (instead of at the beginning of the chapter heading).

Aside from pictures (which we will discuss in the next section), this is satisfactory to achieve fairly good (a relative concept) eBook formatting in the eReaders (you still need to check the preview carefully, as described in Sec. 5.2.3 – however, not by using the convenient online previewer – and then you may need to tweak things a little to perfect the formatting). However, your eBook may suffer from a few problems in the Look Inside.

The Look Inside is the most important part of your eBook, and even when the equivalent of the Look Inside may look perfect on any eReader, there are still frequently formatting problems on the Look Inside seen on Amazon on a PC (where most people buy their eBooks). That's right: There can be formatting mistakes in the Look Inside on Amazon that aren't present when the eBook is read on a Kindle. The Look Inside is the most challenging part of your eBook to format properly because it uses the strictest interpretation of HTML. At the same time, the Look Inside formatting is the most critical toward earning sales. Perfecting the Look Inside formatting can give you a professional edge over the competition.

After perfecting your eBook file – including pictures, which are discussed in the next section – and prior to inserting supported HTML symbols – as described earlier – save it as a filtered webpage (we described this in the discussion of supported HTML symbols). If you have pictures, make a compressed zipped folder (as explained in the following section). This filtered webpage (which, if your file has images, is inside the compressed zipped folder) contains your HTML code.

There are programs available online (even for free) that can help you clean the HTML file that Word produced. A cleaner HTML file helps to achieve a more professional Look Inside.

You can view and edit the HTML file by opening it in Notepad. Most other HTML editors are likely to mess up the HTML code (as far as using it for an eBook is concerned), so Notepad or Notepad++ are your best options.

Note that you don't have to be an HTML expert in order to learn how to tweak your eBook file. Rather, you just need to learn what to look for and how to modify it, which is far easier than learning HTML.

For example, you can tweak the HTML to make more professional indents. To do this, look through your HTML to see what your paragraph styles look like. The paragraph styles start with a <p> and end with a </p>, but there are usually statements inside of the first <p>, such as <p style="text-indent:0.3in;">. There may be other statements inside the <p> besides the text indent, and some paragraph styles may not even include the text indent. You can also find the text indent statements at the top of the HTML file in the style definitions. They will look like text-indent:0.3in; (the same as when it's included in the paragraph style). It's the text indent that you want to modify.

If you formatted your eBook properly, you should have two types of text indents: One set to 0.3 inches or so (for Normal) and another set to 0.01 inches (for FirstNormal). Use the Replace tool in Notepad to change 0.01in to 0 and 0.3in with a percentage or a measure in ems. Be careful not to remove any semicolons (;) or quotes (") when you do this. Publishers tend to set indents in terms of the em (the width of the uppercase M in the font style and size); in this case, 1.5em or 2em are common values. A percentage is useful because a reader may view the book on a cell phone or an iPad. Setting the indent to about 8% or so bases the size of the indent on the length of the line on the screen. In the former case, replace "text-indent:0.3in;" with "text-indent:2em;" and in the latter case, replace with "text-indent:8%;" (don't use the quote; do use the actual indent size that you had previously set in Word).

You can find a list of supported HTML tags in the KDP help pages. Look under Preparing Your Book > Types of Formats in the left column, and then click Supported HTML Tags. Once there, you can also see a shorter table of Common HTML Tags. The current link to this page is:

https://kdp.amazon.com/self-publishing/help?topicId=A1JPUWCSD6F59O

KDP also has a guide for HTML publishing experts:

http://kindlegen.s3.amazonaws.com/AmazonKindlePublishingGuidelines.pdf

Some Kindle publishing experts use special programs to make epub and mobi formats from their HTML. These include Sigil, Calibre, Kindlegen, and others. There are many guides available that describe how to tweak the HTML or use such software to create epub and mobi files for an eBook. If you're new to styles and modifying HTML for eBooks, there is a handy guide called *Formatting of Kindle Books: A Brief Tutorial* by Charles Spender that provides a good visual introduction to both using just Word's styles and also modifying the HTML.

Another important aspect of the Look Inside is the front matter, which is often neglected. The details discussed in Sec. 5.1.5 regarding how to perfect the front matter and Look Inside also apply to eBooks, but the formatting is a little different with eBooks. For one, if there is a table of contents, the eBook edition should have hyperlinks. The title and copyright pages of a paperback may have design marks, which might not appear in an eBook. Making front matter that appears highly professional can make a great impression. Browse through bestselling eBooks by traditional publishers and see what they do to make the front matter look very professional. This will give you ideas that you can apply to your eBook. But remember, you want to get into the action quickly – in Chapter 1, which hopefully has a captivating start – so you don't want too much front matter. For short eBooks, it's not uncommon to move some front matter (like an Introduction) to the back in order to increase the amount of Look Inside available to prospective readers.

Remember, there are a few differences between Kindle and other eBook publishing services. For example, using Page Layout > Breaks > Next Page to create page breaks (instead of inserting ordinary page breaks) will create page breaks that are recognized by PubIt's preview tool for the Nook. (PubIt was replaced by Nook Press.) Also, remember to modify your copyright page to designate the Smashwords edition if you publish with Smashwords.

5.2.2 Perfecting eBook Images

Here's a funny Kindle fact: It's possible to have a picture that measures 600 pixels across look small on a Kindle screen that's only 600 pixels wide! One way this could happen is if you insert the picture into Word and Word downsizes the image so that it only fills the available margin width in the page. Also, make sure to use Insert > Picture and not copy/paste to add images to your eBook file.

One way to fix this is to right-click the image in Word, click Size and Position, choose the Size tab, and adjust the Scale to 100% for the width (and the height will automatically change to 100% if the aspect ratio is locked). Ensure that the box is checked for Relative to Original Picture Size. If you check a few of your pictures and suddenly realize that you have a large number of pictures with the scale set below 100%, there is a very quick way to rescale many images at once: Open the HTML file in Notepad (as described in the previous section) and use the Replace tool in order to change the percentage. Check that the width="100%" statement is inside of the image style, as in <img width="100%" src="filename.jpg">. **Note**: If you want an image to **automatically fill the width of any screen**, insert the width="100%" statement into the HTML (not Word); delete the old width/height statements (don't make height 100%).

The common size of 600 pixels by 800 pixels will fill the screens of most devices with the width scaled to 100% except for screens that are larger than 600 x 800 – such as the Kindle Fire HD, Apple iPad, and a PC monitor. See 4.2.2, which has a table of screen sizes for a variety of eReaders. Full-screen pictures on these devices require higher resolution images.

Pictures should be placed on a line all by themselves, with Wrap Text set to In Line With Text in the Format tab. Apply the Title Style to pictures. It may help to place blank lines before and after pictures using Shift + Enter to create the blank lines (but don't worry if this causes strange formatting with the last line of the previous paragraph in Word – as long as it looks good in the downloadable previewer). Center pictures that may be less than full screen. For full-page images, a blank page problem on the Kindle may be prevented by using a Style with First Line set to 0.01" and then clicking the left align button on the Paragraph group in the Home tab.

For the Nook, if you want to see a page break prior to the picture show up on the previewer at PubIt (replaced by Nook Press), use Page Layout > Breaks > Next Page to do this.

Note that if a picture file size exceeds 127 kb, the picture file size will be reduced when the book is published to Kindle, which may affect how the image appears on a device. If you compress your images (see Sec. 2.2.5; an alternative is a picture compression program that you may be able to find online), this will help you not only reduce the size of your pictures, but also the overall size of the content file, which can affect your list price and royalty as explained in Sec. 4.2.5. Also, you should save your file as a filtered webpage and send it to a compressed zipped folder, as explained in the last paragraph of this section.

Pictures saved in the jpeg format with a "clear" background actually will have backgrounds that look white even if the user sets the device background to sepia or black. This can cause some images to look funny when the user uses a sepia or black background. It poses a problem with using glyphs for section breaks, for example. This is also why the KDP publishing guide states that GIF format should be used for line art and text images (instead of jpeg). Line art and text should be saved in GIF format with a maximum size of 500 pixels by 600 pixels.

When your Word file is complete, go to the File tab, choose Save As, and select Web Page Filtered (not Single File Web Page, and make sure that it says Filtered). Click Yes, then wait for the file to fully save. Next, clean and tweak the HTML as needed and as described in the previous section (you may also want to modify the image statements in the HTML using Notepad). Once your HTML file is fully prepared, close the file and find it in your Computer or Documents folder. Right-click the file, choose Send To, and select Compressed (Zipped) Folder. Find the folder with your compressed images (it has the same name as the HTML file) that this creates, copy it, and paste it into the compressed zipped folder. Look inside the zipped folder to make sure that it has both the HTML file (the filtered webpage) and the matching folder of compressed pictures. Saving your file as a filtered webpage is necessary in order to prevent gray lines from showing up on one or more edges of the pictures on the eReader.

5.2.3 Proofing Your eBook

The best way to publish on Kindle is directly with KDP so that you can take advantage of the downloadable previewer to see exactly what your converted mobi file looks like. If you use an aggregator like Smashwords in addition to publishing with KDP, be sure to disable the Kindle sales channel from the aggregator (if available) as soon as the option appears. Nook Press has a previewer for Nook. For Smashwords, you actually have to publish your book first, and then preview the result; you can make changes afterward, but your book has a brief period of high visibility immediately after publishing, so it may help to avoid mistakes on the first go.

First upload your book cover to KDP; the thumbnail that you see for your cover is much lower resolution than the actual thumbnail will be. When you upload the content file, KDP will automatically add the cover to the first page (in the past, this was an option, but not any-more). There are two previewers available in Step 6 of the KDP publishing process. The common mistake is to use the convenient online previewer. This is a mistake because there are often formatting mistakes in the eBook that don't show on the convenient online pre-viewer that you can see right away with just the click of a button. Look closely and you will see that there is a downloadable previewer available in the same step. Use the downloadable previewer because it is more accurate.

Download the downloadable previewer by clicking the Windows or Mac link. Look carefully at which folder this is installed in on your computer and write down this path so that you can find it easily. You may also pin it to your Start Menu or add it as a shortcut. Then click the Download Book Preview File link. Also record the name and location of the downloaded book preview file. Once you have more than one Kindle tool for reading books on your PC (such as Kindle for PC and Kindle Previewer), the Kindle reader that you wish to use may not open by default; and if you open the tool you want (as opposed to clicking the book to read it), your book won't be on the history unless you've already read it with that tool. You may need to open the Kindle reader on your PC (either the Kindle for PC or Kindle Previewer), click File, select Open Book, and then find the downloaded book preview file on your computer.

First use the Kindle Previewer (not Kindle for PC). This is the Kindle reader that you in-stalled when you clicked the Windows or Mac link in Step 6 of the KDP publishing process. Open your downloaded book preview file in Kindle Previewer. In the Devices tab, there are three options: eInk, Fire, and IOS. When you choose eInk, you will see three buttons – Kindle Paperwhite, Kindle, and Kindle DX. There are two buttons when you select Fire – Kindle Fire and Kindle Fire HD. There are two more buttons for IOS: Kindle for iPad and Kindle for iPhone.

Be sure to preview your eBook carefully with all 7 options. The Fire, eInk, and IOS devices format a little differently, so an eBook that looks perfect on one device may have major for-matting flaws on another device. Customers who purchase your eBook may have any of these devices, and if there are formatting mistakes on any one of these devices, a customer is likely to point this out by leaving a 1-star review. You can prevent this by investing the time now to carefully preview your eBook on all 3 devices with all 7 options. Even on a single device, such as the eInk, the different eReaders can have significant formatting differences. For example, there may be serious problems with the Kindle Paperwhite even if the book looks fantastic on the Kindle. **The only way to be sure that you don't have any serious formatting mistakes is to view your eBook page by page with all 7 options.** This will take some time, but it is well worth it. You only need to read your eBook thoroughly once to proofread it, but you need to quickly browse through every page on all 7 devices to proof the formatting.

Don't browse too fast when you check the formatting: Maintain a slow enough pace that you see every page and are able to spot any formatting mistakes. Take breaks to rest your eyes and rejuvenate your brain frequently, and only check the formatting for one option at a sitting. Keep a pencil and paper handy to make a list of all of the formatting issues that you find and precisely describe where to find them in your eBook file. In addition to browsing for formatting mistakes 7 times, slowly and carefully proofread your eBook at least once.

There is yet an 8th option that you need to check: Kindle for PC. Find any eBook in the Kindle store on Amazon to find the option to download the free Kindle for PC to your computer. Make sure that you open Kindle for PC and not the Kindle Previewer (which you've already used to proof the first 7 options). Then go to File, click Open Book, and find your downloaded book preview file. Check the formatting of your eBook on Kindle for PC.

You're still not done! The most important way to check your eBook is on an actual device. If you have a Kindle, iPad, or iPhone, use it. If you know a friend or family member – or even an acquaintance – see if you can borrow their device. They might not want you to take their device to your home and use it, but they might be willing to upload your eBook on their device and allow you to quickly check the formatting in their presence – at the very least, they might be willing to let you put your eBook on their device and leave it there so that they can read it for free (that should get their attention).

Don't email the downloaded book preview file because this can apparently change the formatting of the eBook. Instead, use a USB cable to connect the device to a computer where you directly downloaded the book preview file to that computer from Step 6 of the publishing process (or download it again on a different computer, if needed). Now check the formatting of the eBook on that device. The greater variety of devices you can find, the better.

You need to check both the formatting and text. We already discussed how to proofread the text in Sec. 5.1.8. You should proofread your eBook (on one device of your choice) at least once even if you've already perfected the proofreading of your paperback. There are almost always some significant issues that are found this way. Also, reading the eBook instead of just quickly turning the pages will help you to see some subtler formatting mistakes that you might miss when checking the formatting.

When you check the formatting of your eBook with the 7 different options (plus Kindle for PC and actual devices), following are some issues that you should look for (in addition to the relevant formatting issues that were outlined in Sec. 5.1.8 regarding paperbacks):

- ✓ First inspect the cover on the first page. Check that the aspect ratio looks okay (no distortion) and that the image(s) and text look clean and sharp with good contrast.
- ✓ Most eBooks will look more professional with no space between paragraphs (or very little, like 0.1 pts), justified full (not left-aligned), and consistent indents. There are a few rare categories where non-indented block paragraphs with a linespace between are common, but most eBooks shouldn't use this format.
- ✓ Check for inconsistent indents. It's common to find occasional indents that are shorter or longer than the others. Very often, this is a sign of a tab that needs to be removed.
- ✓ A small space at the beginning or end of a line, which often results from having two or more consecutive spaces (especially, following a period when a sentence happens to end at the margin edge).

- ✓ Are there any unsupported characters? Look for boxes with question marks (?) inside them or streams of funny characters. Sometimes, characters that look fine on the Kindle Fire show up as ?'s on the Kindle and Kindle DX, for example. Look carefully for unsupported characters with all 7 (and more) options.
- ✓ Check that quotation marks are angled correctly. Also, check for consistency – don't mix the use of both straight and angled quotes.
- ✓ Test out the table of contents links, website hyperlinks, and links for email addresses (some of these may only function on the real devices and Kindle for PC, but not in the Kindle Previewer). Make sure that they work on the actual devices.
- ✓ If you used color, see if the colors look good on black-and-white devices.
- ✓ Are you satisfied with the size of the pictures on all devices? It's not too late to change.
- ✓ In Kindle for PC (and an actual device that has this option), go to View, click Show Display Options, and see how your eBook looks with White, Sepia, and Black backgrounds. Quickly browse through your entire eBook with each background to see how it looks. Check for images or colors that don't look nice on these backgrounds.

Also, use the convenient online previewer in Step 6. Don't trust the online previewer – trust the downloadable previewer, Kindle for PC, and especially the actual device. The convenient online previewer does mimic the device screen, which can help give you a feel for the aesthetics and check how large images look compared to screen sizes.

When proofing your eBook – with any of the options that we discussed – try changing the font size, switching between portrait and landscape, and other options. This will also help you gauge aesthetically the various ways that your eBook may appear to different customers.

Most formatting problems can be corrected by closely inspecting your original eBook file and making an adjustment. Other formatting issues can be resolved by tweaking the HTML (which we discussed briefly in Sec. 5.2.2). If you can't correct an issue that you see, try posting a question on the Formatting discussion in the KDP community help forum. There is a good chance that someone else has experienced a similar issue and found a solution.

After you upload your file to Kindle, you will see a list of possible spelling errors. Check this list, correct any mistakes, and ignore any that are actually correct until KDP tells you that there are now 0 spelling errors. (This does <u>not</u> mean that your book is free of mistakes.)

On page 2 of the KDP publishing process, look below the list prices in various countries to find the file size of your converted mobi file. If you wish to reduce this file size, the way to do it probably lies in picture compression, converting images to grayscale (small effect), or resizing or removing images.

It's very important to have your eBook perfected as much as possible prior to publishing. Mistakes in the Look Inside deter sales, and so do reviews that complain about formatting, spelling, or grammatical mistakes. If you take the time and effort to create buzz for your book, have a book launch party, send out advanced review copies, and succeed in having several sales when your eBook is first published, it will all backfire if it turns out that there are formatting or editing mistakes in the eBook.

The best time to submit corrections is prior to publishing. You can upload your cover and content files as often as you want. Once you publish, your original eBook will still be available for 12 to 24 hours (or more) after you submit revisions. So if you find any mistakes after publishing, they will be there for a day or so before the corrections take place.

After you publish your eBook, you should see what the published eBook looks like first-hand and check it very carefully.

Then there is one more thing that you have to preview: the Look Inside. First, view the Look Inside on your PC. If you have any mistakes in the Look Inside, you absolutely want to correct and update this. A common formatting problem on the Look Inside is an indented first paragraph of each chapter, even where you know you set First Line to 0.01".

Next, view the free sample on a Kindle device – or at least download the free sample file from Amazon and view the file on your PC (this is different from just clicking to Look Inside).

5.2.4 Making Revisions to Your eBook

You can revise your eBook after publishing. However, your original eBook will continue to be available until your submitted revisions go live – unless you first unpublish your eBook. Depending on where you publish your eBook, it may take quite some time to unpublish, also. If you have major issues, you should unpublish your eBook until you are able to resolve the issues so that no new customers experience those problems. (Obviously, the best course is to avoid the problems in the first place.) For minor issues, you just need to submit the revisions; don't worry about unpublishing. If you use an aggregator like Smashwords, once your eBook is distributed to various eBook stores, it may take much longer to submit revisions or unpublish. Therefore, you should check your eBook carefully as soon as it goes live with an aggregator and strive to correct any issues as soon as possible. When you submit revisions to just about any eBook publishing service, you will have to wait at least 12-24 hours for the revisions to go live before you can make any other changes to your eBook.

What if your files are fine, but you just want to revise your description, keywords, price, or other details? You still need to republish your eBook, unless you only want to change the description. For Amazon, the description can be changed using AuthorCentral (see Chapter 6).

Keep track of your files so that you always have a record of which version of the file is the most up-to-date. You'd hate to revise an older file by mistake, reintroducing old mistakes while correcting new ones. Save this list in at least two places in case you lose one (and when you update it, be sure to update both copies of the list).

Put some information on the copyright page to distinguish between the new and old versions of your eBook – such as "second edition," "updated on August 12, 2013," or "revised to include larger images." You can make this more subtle if you don't wish to advertise that minor corrections have been made. Either way, this information will help you determine if the Look Inside that you see on Amazon is the new version or the old one.

You may revise the interior file, cover file (for your thumbnail image), description, keywords, list price, DRM choice, and just about anything else (unless you have an ISBN, in which case you can't revise the title and shouldn't make drastic changes to the content) – in contrast to the paperback, where the title, subtitle, and contributors are locked after the ISBN option is selected. If you just want to modify your KDP Select enrollment, this can be done from your Bookshelf.

Note: KDP now overrides the AuthorCentral description when you republish. Save your AuthorCentral description (copy and paste the HTML into Word), then when your book goes live you can update it through AuthorCentral.

How do you notify customers of changes? For Kindle, go to the KDP help pages and click the yellow Contact Us button in the bottom left corner. Select Publishing Your Book > Making Corrections and enter the ASIN for your eBook (you can find this number on your eBook's Amazon detail page, and copy/paste it). Enter a subject and type a message explaining very clearly what corrections have been made and that you wish to notify the customers of this change. KDP will do one of three things (but note that their action may take 4 weeks):

1. If they decide that the changes are major, KDP will email customers to notify them that the book update exists (remember, this can take a month). Customers will be able to get the update at the Managing Your Kindle page on Amazon.

2. If they decide that the issues are minor, KDP will not email customers. However, customers can still obtain the update from Managing Your Kindle.

3. If your eBook has critical issues (this can happen if customers complain about your eBook, even if you didn't contact KDP), KDP will make your eBook unavailable for sale until you notify them that the eBook has been revised. KDP will then review the corrections and either ask you to make further revisions or notify customers by email that an update is available.

5.2.5 Getting Help with Your eBook

Try posting a question on the Kindle community forum. There are many authors and small publishers who frequent those forums and regularly share their expertise. You can also meet fellow authors. There is also professional eBook formatting help available. For example, go to the KDP help pages and click Preparing Your Book > Conversion Resources for a list of companies that offer such services.

Chapter 6

Creating Author Pages

Chapter Overview

This chapter answers questions about the following topics, and more:

- ☑ How to create an author page at Amazon.[9]
- ☑ Advantages of creating an author page at Amazon, like being able to track sales.
- ☑ Creating a biography, choosing and uploading photos, monitoring sales information, reviewing feedback, and adding feeds to blog posts on your Amazon author page.
- ☑ Formatting your book's description with boldface, italics, and basic HTML.
- ☑ Developing a blog that can attract members of your target audience.
- ☑ Writing blog posts and feeding them into your Amazon author page.
- ☑ Setting up an eStore.
- ☑ Creating a website for a personal author page or publishing company on the internet.
- ☑ Linking your Amazon listings from your website.
- ☑ Benefits of driving traffic to your book's Amazon page instead of your eStore or selling in person.
- ☑ Making effective use of social media, such as Facebook and Twitter.[9]
- ☑ Setting up an author page and Goodreads[9] and using free author tools there.
- ☑ Including your books on social websites, like Facebook pages.
- ☑ Driving traffic to your blog, author website, and social media websites.

---

[9] Amazon,™ CreateSpace,™ Facebook,™ Goodreads,™ and Twitter™ are trademarks and brands of their respective owners. Neither this book, *A Detailed Guide to Self-Publishing with Amazon and Other Online Booksellers*, nor its author, Chris McMullen, are in any way affiliated with any of these companies.

6.1 Creating an Author Page at Amazon

6.1.1 Setting Up Your AuthorCentral Account

YOU CAN AND SHOULD create an Author Page on Amazon. AuthorCentral is an Amazon program designed especially for authors. You don't have to be a famous author to have your own Author Page. Sign up at

https://authorcentral.amazon.com

There are several benefits of joining AuthorCentral:

➢ It's totally <u>free</u> (even though many authors would actually be willing to pay to join).

➢ Get access to graphs for sales rank history for print books sold in the U.S. There is even an option to see where your print books are selling geographically. (Although the sales rank is for print books, everything else at AuthorCentral applies to print and eBooks.)

➢ AuthorCentral provides email and daytime phone support for authors who sign up.

➢ Edit your description using boldface, italics, blank lines, and even basic HTML.

➢ Add your biography and author photos to your Author Page. Your biography and primary photo will show up on your book's detail page on Amazon, along with a link to your Author Page.

➢ Customers can learn more about you as an author by clicking on the link to your Author Page. In addition to your photos and biography, customers will be able to quickly find all of your books, and you can also add feeds from your blog and Twitter, videos, and information about author events (like book signings or tours).

➢ See your author rank to discover how you compare with other authors.

➢ Add editorial reviews, About the Author, From the Author, and From the Back Cover sections (all are optional) to your book's detail page on Amazon.

➢ Visit Shelfari to add Book Extras to your book's detail page.

You're a professional author now. Therefore, you should have your very own Author Page at Amazon. Make your book's detail page look more professional by having AuthorCentral include your photo, the beginning of your biography, and a link to your Author Page on your book's detail page on Amazon.

You can add an AuthorCentral account for a pen name. If you write in your own name and a pen name, for example, you can create separate accounts for each. This is very common when an author writes in two quite different genres, or when an author writes some books specifically geared toward adults and others that may also be suitable for a wider audience. You may have up to three AuthorCentral accounts linked to one email address.

When you login to AuthorCentral (after you sign up), you can claim books that you have written by going to the Books tab and clicking the yellow Add More Books button. Search for your books by typing in your name, the title of the book, or the ISBN or ASIN number for your book. Sort through the list of books carefully because there may be books on the list that you didn't write. If the paperback and Kindle editions of a book are linked together, you should only need to add one of these.

Note that a book can't be removed from AuthorCentral once you add it just because it's no longer in print. Suppose, for example, that you publish a paperback book, then later decide to unpublish it. If it was added to your AuthorCentral account, it will remain there forever. Amazon's reason for this is to help customers find all of the books that each author has written. Even though the book may be out of print, customers may still be able to buy it used. An eBook won't be available used if it's unpublished (unless Amazon starts permitting the customer resale of eBooks), so if your book is only available as an eBook and you unpublish it, you should ask AuthorCentral if they can remove it from your account in this case.

If you find any of my books on Amazon, you can explore my Author Page from there. Try finding Author Pages of other authors, including successful top selling authors – both traditionally and self-published. This way, you may see a variety of ways that different authors use AuthorCentral and get some ideas for what you can do with your own Author Page.

The big publishers have special privileges. As a result, you'll see a few things on their product pages – even things that their bestselling authors can do on those pages – that self-published authors can't do. Nonetheless, self-published authors do have a great variety of helpful tools available at AuthorCentral. In Sec. 6.1.4, we'll see that self-published authors can improve their product pages using formatting tools at AuthorCentral.

As an example of what a bestselling, traditionally-published author can do, check out *The Eighty-Dollar Champion* by Elizabeth Letts. Obviously, you can't say *New York Times* Bestseller like Ballantine Books put in her description (unless, of course, your book actually becomes a *New York Times* Bestseller). If you look further down the detail page for her book – in her editorial reviews – you will see that she has an Amazon.com review, which is actually a letter from the author herself. You won't be permitted to post an Amazon.com review this way (or review your own book). However, there is a From the Author section on AuthorCentral that you can use, and if you have legitimate reviews that qualify as editorial reviews, you can include them in the editorial reviews section. You can also achieve professional formatting in the blurb and other sections available from AuthorCentral, such as Elizabeth Letts has on her book's detail page (see Sec. 6.1.4). We'll return to the subject of editorial reviews in Sec. 6.1.7.

You can make a highly professional detail page for your book on Amazon using features available on AuthorCentral. The main thing that will probably be lacking on your page compared to traditionally published books and bestsellers is the number of editorial reviews and the distinguished sources of those reviews.

To find authors who use AuthorCentral extensively, try visiting Shelfari (there is a link to it from AuthorCentral), since this is where authors go to add book extras to their Author Pages at Amazon. Search for those authors on Amazon to see what their Author Pages look like.

Also, AuthorCentral has a few example pages. After logging into AuthorCentral, click the Help tab and you will find a few samples of Author Pages illustrating what you can do with them.

Note that you must be at least 18 years old in order to use AuthorCentral. See other eligibility requirements when you read the terms and conditions presented during sign-up.

6.1.2 AuthorCentral in Other Countries

In addition to creating an Author Page at Amazon US, you should also add an Author Page through AuthorCentral at Amazon UK. The link for UK's AuthorCentral is

https://authorcentral.amazon.co.uk

Unfortunately, you must separately login to AuthorCentral at each country's AuthorCentral site; your US Author Page does not automatically show up at Amazon's websites in other countries. However, once you login (using the same account as in the US), your AuthorCentral account in each country will be able to locate your list of books from your US AuthorCentral account. At least, you won't have to individually add all of your books for each country.

Not every country offers AuthorCentral. For example, presently AuthorCentral isn't available in Canada; but this may change in time. As of now, only the following countries provide Author Pages via AuthorCentral:

https://authorcentral.amazon.com (United States)
https://authorcentral.amazon.co.uk (United Kingdom)
https://authorcentral.amazon.fr (France)
https://authorcentral.amazon.de (Germany)
https://authorcentral.amazon.co.jp (Japan)

I just have Author Pages in the United States, United Kingdom, and France. Although I do sell a book in Germany or Japan occasionally, the vast majority of sales come from the United States and United Kingdom.

You will need to add your author photos and biography for AuthorCentral in each country. You may even choose to customize your biography for each country. If your books are in English, there really isn't any need to translate your biography into French, Spanish, or other languages – since anyone who can read your book will be able to read your biography in English. However, for non-English speaking countries, you may need some translation help in reading the website to understand what you're doing. Google's free translation service is better than nothing (for trying to understand the instructions – but using this service to translate your biography is not recommended). Also, by comparing controls in Amazon US with the other countries, you can often deduce the correspondence. Finally, try searching online for how to setup an AuthorCentral account in non-English speaking countries. By using an internet search engine such as Google, you may discover that other authors who have figured this out have posted instructions in English.

Note that your books won't show up under the main search results in non-English speaking countries (unless your books have been translated to the relevant language), but will show up as books in a foreign language. Social media that can be fed into your Author Page at Amazon US may not feed into your Author Pages for other countries. For example, presently only Twitter can be fed into your Author Page in the United Kingdom.

6.1.3 Adding Your Biography and Author Photos

Think about your image as an author as you search for a suitable photo (or take some new photos) and prepare your biography. Strive to come across as likeable, credible, competent, and professional. Look for an image that suggests these qualities, and prepare a biography that suggests this, too. Realize that the photo and biography – like just about everything else that you do – relate in a small way (but every way counts!) to marketing. Your photo helps to establish your brand as an author. Recognition is important. The more often readers see your photo – on Amazon, on your blog, on your website, etc. – the more likely they are to recognize you. Products often sell from recognition (kind of like laundry detergent – most customers go with a brand they remember having heard before).

Select a photo of yourself – readers want to see the person behind the words. They don't expect you to look like a model; they are interested in reading your ideas, not dating you for your looks. You should present yourself well so that you appear professional. It can be a head-and-shoulders shot, but doesn't need to be close-up; go with what you feel comfortable with, and explore what other authors have done. You can have your photo touched up, if done so that it appears professional. The photo should definitely be well-lit, any red-eye must be removed, the photo needs to be cropped nicely, you should look good against the background, the photo has to be clean (no stray marks, for example), and the background must look appropriate. Using a quality photo does make a difference.

If you're particularly self-conscious, there are a variety of ways to get a nice image of you – like getting a professional, low-cost sketch (along with written permission to use the sketch for this purpose). Whatever you choose to do, make sure that you come across as likeable, credible, competent, and professional – and also look like someone who may write a book in your genre. You can get a little personality into your photo, but it will only work out well if you meet the aforementioned criteria.

Try changing your photo after a month if you have any doubts about it, and see if it seems to have an impact on sales. I've tried changing my author photo a few times, and observed that the sales of some of my books can be significantly affected by the author photo.

Get input about your photo and biography from family, friends, acquaintances, and – perhaps this is more important – complete strangers who can provide honest feedback. The more credible you appear as the author of the type of book you wrote, the better.

You may load up to four different photos for your Author Page. Only the primary photo will display on the book's detail page; the other photos will be seen if shoppers click to see them on your Author Page. Remember that you must separately add photos for your Author Page in the United States, United Kingdom, and any other countries where you have an Author Page.

Go to the Profile tab after logging in at AuthorCentral to add photos. Click Add Photo to insert photos. If you have multiple photos, click Manage to reorder them or delete them; just drag to reorder or drag down to the indicated space to delete. The leftmost image will serve as your primary author photo.

Write your biography in the third person so that it sounds like someone else wrote it. You can also ask someone else to write it, but that's only a good idea if they write biographies well; if you do this, be sure to get written permission to use the biography for this purpose.

Your biography can help to establish your credibility as an author in your genre. Don't brag, though: Let your work speak for itself. You may list relevant, truthful qualifications and expertise, if you have any. Readers don't expect you to have a degree in English if you're writing fiction; while qualifications are particularly important for most nonfiction. Do you have relevant experience? For fiction, life experience can be implied from your biography. What qualifies you to write this book? For example, if you are detective or police officer, this may be relevant for a mystery. Have you spent a noteworthy (above average) amount of time researching your book, or working with editors, for example? Such things may fit in as minor points in your overall biography, but one minor point can make a difference.

The biography is not just about expertise and experience, though – especially, in fiction. If you have relevant expertise or experience (or even awards), you want to mention it, but the biography shouldn't just be devoted to this. Some readers are curious to learn more about the author – what the author does, hobbies, background, etc. These things give the reader an opportunity to relate to you in some way, or to want to share part of your unique experience. For example, if you happen to mention that you grew up in Brooklyn, this can attract interest two ways: "Hey, I lived in Brooklyn for a few years," or, "I wonder what it would be like to grow up in Brooklyn." When you meet a stranger, do you appreciate it when you discover that you have something in common? How about when you discover something unique?

You can also get your personality into your biography and have a little fun with it. However, you must appear likeable, credible, competent, professional, and ultimately like an author in your genre; don't let your personality and fun betray these qualities. Biographies do have a tendency to come across as boring for many readers, so if you're able to present yours in a way that interests readers – while still meeting the above criteria regarding your image as the author – that can be a plus (it bodes well for the actual book being interesting, too).

It's important to proofread your biography carefully, get proofreading help, and receive feedback on it. This, along with your blurb, will be highly visible, so these are important for marketing. Any mistakes in these relatively short writing samples (compared to the length of the book) may suggest major editing and formatting issues in the book itself. Give readers every reason to Look Inside, and strive not to give any reasons for them to walk away.

Note that only a fraction of your biography will be immediately visible, while the rest will only be read by customers who click the Read More link (unless you have a very short biography). By viewing other Author Pages, you can get a sense for approximately how much will show up front versus what will be hidden. There will be customers who read the visible portion, but who don't click to read more; and what is included in the visible portion may also influence how many customers decide to read the rest. Therefore, you might consider which parts of your biography should appear in this visible portion, while also ensuring that your biography is well-organized.

Go to the Profile tab in AuthorCentral to add or update your biography. After you add your biography, note that the Read More link doesn't quite coincide with the position of the Read More link that will appear on your book's detail page (although it is pretty close). Furthermore, the Read More link will be in a slightly different position on your book's detail page compared to your Author Page (but again, it will be close).

Unfortunately, you can't format your biography with boldface, italics, or even basic HTML; but you can apply this formatting to the About the Author, product description, and other features available in the Books tab (as described in the following section).

Note that AuthorCentral allows you to enter an About the Author section that is different from your biography. If you submit both of these sections, they will both appear on your book's detail page. It might not look professional to have two copies of the same biography. The one to remove, if any, is the About the Author section. It's okay to have both if they aren't completely redundant. The About the Author section might be much shorter, with the biography more elaborate, for example. If you publish a variety of books, you might cater the About the Author section to specific books. There is another possibility for books that have coauthors: Describe each author briefly in the About the Author Section, while each author has his/her own Author Page (multiple author pages *can* show on the same book's detail page). If so, separate the About the Author into paragraphs using AuthorCentral.

6.1.4 Formatting Your Blurb

Go to the Books tab in AuthorCentral to format or otherwise revise the description for one of your books. Click on the book. If it's available in multiple editions – e.g. paperback and eBook – you'll have to click each edition and edit the descriptions separately. Click the Edit button next to Product Description.

AuthorCentral allows you to format your description and other written sections (like About the Author or From the Back Cover) with *italics*, **boldface**, numbered lists, simple bullets, and even some basic HTML. Although you could use basic limited HTML in the description at KDP, you can't preview it there. Your AuthorCentral blurb can have up to 4000 characters.

Update: KDP now supports HTML blurbs (the same HTML as AuthorCentral, except that if you use the Enter key in the KDP description, it will add an additional linespace). However, KDP doesn't show a preview. Note that if you republish your book at KDP, the KDP description will override the AuthorCentral description (and your AuthorCentral description will be lost). Copy and paste the HTML from your AuthorCentral description into the KDP description before republishing. An advantage of using HTML in the description at Amazon KDP is that it will propagate to Amazon UK, BN.com, and other retailers. I recommend using AuthorCentral first, and then copying/pasting the HTML version of the description into KDP afterward.

Don't copy/paste text directly from Word or most other programs into AuthorCentral; copy/paste from Notepad instead to remove hidden formatting that will cause problems and delays (but see how it looks in Word at some stage to help catch spelling/grammar issues).

Keep your paragraphs short in the description and separate them by blank linespaces. In Compose mode, use the Enter key to create linebreaks; in HTML mode, use
 (put a space before it – AuthorCentral's HTML has a few idiosyncrasies) to do this (use it twice in a row following a paragraph for a blank line). Note that the Enter key won't start a new line if you're in HTML mode. Don't end a line in mid-sentence to force the sentence onto the next line.

Only very limited HTML works in AuthorCentral. It's generally best to avoid paragraph <p> tags in AuthorCentral's HTML. Some basic HTML that works in AuthorCentral includes:

❖ **Boldface**: type bold phrase here
❖ *Italics*: <i>type italicized phrase here</i>
❖ Linebreak: Type
 (with a space first) precisely where you want the line to break.
❖ Numbered or bulleted lists, <ol> and <ul>. It may be simpler to do this with Compose.

Following is an example of the effect that formatting can have on a description. This description is for a chemistry book, and is much longer than most effective descriptions in fiction and entertaining or less technical nonfiction. First, see it unformatted:

OVERVIEW: This eBook focuses on fundamental chemistry concepts, such as understanding the periodic table of the elements and how chemical bonds are formed. No prior knowledge of chemistry is assumed. The mathematical component involves only basic arithmetic. The content is much more conceptual than mathematical. AUDIENCE: This eBook is geared toward helping anyone – student or not – to understand the main ideas of chemistry. Both students and non-students may find it helpful to be able to focus on understanding the main concepts without the constant emphasis on computations that is generally found in chemistry lectures and textbooks. CONTENTS: (1) Understanding the organization of the periodic table, including trends and patterns. (2) Understanding ionic/covalent bonds and how they are formed, including the structure of valence electrons. (3) A set of rules to follow to speak the language of chemistry fluently: How to name compounds when different types of compounds follow different naming schemes. (4) Understanding chemical reactions, including how to balance them and a survey of important reactions. (5) Understanding the three phases of matter: properties of matter, amorphous and crystalline solids, ideal gases, liquids, solutions, and acids/bases. (6) Understanding atomic/nuclear structure and how it relates to chemistry. (7) VErBAl ReAcTiONS: A brief fun diversion from science for the verbal side of the brain, using symbols from chemistry's periodic table to make word puzzles. ANSWERS: Every chapter includes self-check exercises to offer practice and help the reader check his or her understanding. 100% of the exercises have answers at the back of the book. LENGTH: The paperback edition of this eBook has 176 pages. COPYRIGHT: All rights are reserved by the author. However, teachers who purchase one copy of this book or borrow one copy of this book from a library may reproduce selected pages for the purpose of teaching chemistry concepts to their own students. FORMATS: This book is available in paperback in 5.5" x 8.5" (portable size), 8.5" x 11" (large size), and as an eBook. The details of the figures – including the periodic tables – are most clear in the large size and large print edition. However, the eBook is in color, whereas the paperback editions are in black-and-white.

Here is the same description with formatting:

OVERVIEW: This eBook focuses on fundamental chemistry concepts, such as understanding the periodic table of the elements and how chemical bonds are formed. No prior knowledge of chemistry is assumed. The mathematical component involves only basic arithmetic. The content is much more conceptual than mathematical.

AUDIENCE: This eBook is geared toward helping anyone – student or not – to understand the main ideas of chemistry. Both students and non-students may find it helpful to be able to focus on understanding the main concepts without the constant emphasis on computations that is generally found in chemistry lectures and textbooks.

CONTENTS:
(1) Understanding the organization of the periodic table, including trends and patterns.
(2) Understanding ionic/covalent bonds and how they are formed, including the structure of valence electrons.
(3) A set of rules to follow to speak the language of chemistry fluently: How to name compounds when different types of compounds follow different naming schemes.
(4) Understanding chemical reactions, including how to balance them and a survey of important reactions.
(5) Understanding the three phases of matter: properties of matter, amorphous and crystalline solids, ideal gases, liquids, solutions, and acids/bases.
(6) Understanding atomic/nuclear structure and how it relates to chemistry.
(7) VErBAl ReAcTiONS: A brief fun diversion from science for the verbal side of the brain, using symbols from chemistry's periodic table to make word puzzles.

ANSWERS: Every chapter includes self-check exercises to offer practice and help the reader check his or her understanding. 100% of the exercises have answers at the back of the book.

LENGTH: The paperback edition of this eBook has 176 pages.

COPYRIGHT: All rights are reserved by the author. However, teachers who purchase one copy of this book or borrow one copy of this book from a library may reproduce selected pages for the purpose of teaching chemistry concepts to their own students.

FORMATS: This book is available in paperback in 5.5" x 8.5" (portable size), 8.5" x 11" (large size), and as an eBook. The details of the figures – including the periodic tables – are most clear in the large size and large print edition. However, the eBook is in color, whereas the paperback editions are in black-and-white.

You can apply boldface, italics, linebreaks, numbered lists, and bulleted lists to the About the Author, From the Back Cover, and other sections available in AuthorCentral, too – but note that you can't apply this formatting in the author's biography in the Profile tab. **Note**: KDP overrides AuthorCentral's description when republishing, so save it before republishing.

6.1.5 Monitoring Sales, Sales Rank, Author Rank, and Reviews

AuthorCentral is a convenient place to see the Amazon sales rank and reviews for all of your books – both print books and eBooks – at once. It also shows you your author rank and provides BookScan statistics for print books. The BookScan data even has an option to see how your books sell by geographic area in the United States.

One way to see the current sales rank for all of your books – including both print and eBook editions – is to select the Books tab. If you have paperback and Kindle editions linked together, you will have to click on the book and then select the other edition to see its sales rank. Another way to find sales rank is to choose the Sales Info tab and then click Rank Over Time below Sales Rank. Use the drop-down menu to view all of your books or to select one. There is even a third way to view your sales rank: In the Rank tab, click Sales Over Time under Sales Rank. These last two options also show how your sales rank is doing compared to the previous day: A number in green shows improvement, while a number in red shows a drop.

The lower the sales rank, the better. We will discuss Amazon sales rank in detail in Sec. 7.1.4, including the correlation between sales rank and sales frequency.

You can also find your BookScan data for print sales in the United States in the Sales Info tab. There are some sales that don't show in the BookScan data – like used books sales – as explained in the Help tab under Sales Information. KDP books sold through Amazon generally show up in these reports. If your books have the Expanded Distribution channel enabled, other sales may also show up here. However, the BookScan data isn't perfect, and there can be notable discrepancies between your actual sales and what BookScan suggests. The important thing is that BookScan data for sales does not reflect eBook sales (Kindle or otherwise).

You can click Weekly Sales or Sales by Geography under BookScan Data in the Sales Info tab, and you can also choose data from the last 4 weeks or up to all available data (from the inception of the program). Seeing your print sales by geography provides useful information about where your audience resides. Most of my sales are made in New York. I also have very strong sales support from California, which may be influenced a little by the fact that I was born and raised there. My Louisiana sales clearly reflect that I live and teach here, and this probably extends into my Dallas and Houston sales, too. In general, authors sell most of their books in major metropolitan areas like New York City, Los Angeles, and Chicago.

Of course, you can also see your sales reports for Amazon KDP books by logging into your account at Amazon KDP, and similarly you can login to KDP, Nook Press, Smashwords, and anywhere else that you may have published eBooks to see your eBook sales reports. One nice feature of the sales rank and sales info stats available at AuthorCentral is that you can corroborate sales (and sales spikes in the sales rank) with royalties that are reported.[10]

You can find your Author Rank in the Rank tab. Select as little as two weeks or up to all available data. As with sales rank, the lower the number, the better. See Sec. 7.1.4 regarding how to interpret you Author Rank.

If you have multiple books, you may appreciate that you can see all of the customer reviews at Amazon for all of your titles (at least, those registered to your AuthorCentral account) in the Customer Reviews tab. There is a noticeable delay between the time that the review first shows on Amazon and the time it appears on AuthorCentral, but the convenience for multi-book authors is easily worth the delay. We will discuss customer reviews in depth in Sec. 7.1.6.

6.1.6 Feeding Blog and Twitter Posts into Your Author Page

AuthorCentral allows authors to feed their blog and Twitter posts into their Author Pages. Do this from the Profile tab. All RSS and Atom blog feeds are supported.

If you have a blog that is relevant to your work as an author, feed it into your Author Page by clicking Add Blog beside Blogs. You should get a blog if you don't already have one (see Sec. 6.2.2). Two of the most popular blogs for writers are WordPress and Blogspot (or Blogger); I will discuss how to setup these feeds into your AuthorCentral account. For other blogs, you can learn how to do this by consulting their help pages or looking for the universal RSS feed icon (an orange square with white broadcast marks) where you run your blog.

For WordPress, simply add /feed/ to the end of your blog's url. For example, my WordPress site is http://chrismcmullen.wordpress.com, so the feed for my WordPress blog is http://chrismcmullen.wordpress.com/feed/. The feeds for Blogspot (or Blogger) have the form http://yourblogname.blogspot.com/feeds/posts/default?alt=rss (or the same without the ?alt=rss). For example, my blog's name at Blogger is McMullen4D, so my Blogger feed is http://mcmullen4d.blogspot.com/feeds/posts/default?alt=rss.

You can actually feed multiple blogs into your AuthorCentral page. I have one blog at WordPress and another at Blogger, and feed both into my Author Page.

Your three most recent blog posts will show up on your Author Page. There may be a delay of up to about 24 hours after you post before it shows up at Amazon.

---

[10] However, there may be occasional inconsistencies. For example, returns and used books affect sales rank, but don't show on your royalty report. Rarely, Amazon chooses to source a new sale made directly from Amazon through a third party. When this happens, Amazon KDP doesn't report the royalty until Expanded Distribution royalties are reported, which can be a delay of two months. At this time, Amazon KDP will correctly report the royalty as being an Amazon royalty instead of an Expanded Distribution channel royalty. Remember, this is rare.

After you add your blog feed(s) to AuthorCentral, any new posts will show up on your Author Page within 24 hours of the post, but any that you posted prior to adding the feed to AuthorCentral will not show up unless you repost them.

If you encounter problems with the blog feeds, select the Help tab and then click on Your Blog Feeds under Your Author Profile. The last three paragraphs that begin with "if" discuss common issues and how to solve them.

To add a Twitter feed, go to the Profile tab and click Add Account beside Twitter. Simply enter your username. Your most recent Tweet will show in addition to your three most recent blog posts (if you have both blog and Twitter feeds).

Note that there are differences in AuthorCentral functionality between countries. For example, you can add Twitter in the UK, but not blogs.

6.1.7 More AuthorCentral Goodies

Here are some more things that you can do with AuthorCentral:

> You can add Book Extras through Shelfari.com. Click the Books tab, select a book, choose the Book Extras tab, and click the Visit Shelfari.com link (or the Learn More link to find out more about Shelfari). The Book Extras might only show up if several of these fields are completed at Shelfari. A spoiler alert should show at the top of any Book Extra that spoils the plot – like the Ridiculously Simplified Synopsis (if not, mark it as a spoiler). You can easily go overboard with the biography, About the Author, From the Author, From the Back Cover, and all of the Book Extras. Some of these features may be more relevant for your book than others. Also check out what other authors have done.

> Editorial reviews from **reputable sources** can be added from the Books tab by clicking on a Book and then the Add button next to Reviews. Quote just 1-2 sentences – but adhere to the "fair use" copyright guidelines – in quotation marks, then use a dash to cite the source (as in the example at the top of the window where you add the review). There is a 600-character limit. Remember only to copy/paste from Notepad (not Word) in order to avoid formatting complications and delays.

> Add events like book signings, appearances, and presentations that relate to your work as an author in the Profile tab. If you do a book signing, for example, get a photo that you can use (with written permission, if someone else takes it). That could be one of the photos on your profile to help establish your credibility as a professional author. Your events help to convey this, too – in addition to spreading word of the events to your fans and new readers.

> In the Profile tab, you can also add a video – a book trailer, footage from a book signing, or an author interview, for example.

> ➤ The Help tab may also come in handy. For one, you will find a Contact Us button. There is also handy information on the Help page, such as Reporting Copyright Infringement.
> ➤ Click the Profile tab and update your Author Page URL. Share this link to your page.

6.2 Creating Your Own Websites

6.2.1 Different Types of Author Websites

THERE ARE DIFFERENT TYPES of websites that you can use to help market your book and establish your image and brand as an author. A very common type of website that most writers have is a blog. There are several free blog sites that allow authors (and others) to express themselves with images and text. Blogs can be helpful in a variety of ways, as we will learn in Sec. 6.2.2. Every writer should maintain a blog, and it's a simple way to get started online.

The next step beyond the blog is to have an author website. Some authors refer to their own website and really mean their blog site; a blog essentially is a website, and the url for it can even be www.yourname.com – just like a major website. However, in this book, when I refer to an author website, I will mean more than just a blog. The distinction that I have in mind is offering much more content on the author website than is available on a typical blog. We'll discuss maintaining a website for the author, book, and/or imprint in Sec. 6.2.3. I recommend having both a blog and a separate website with additional content; the blog can also be fed into the website (and AuthorCentral, and elsewhere). It's a good idea to first develop the blog site, and then develop a website (as we'll see, you can do this for free, and get hosting with free tools so that you don't have to do any technical "developing" by yourself) with additional content.

Your online presence may also extend into your own eStore (Sec. 6.2.4), Goodreads (Sec. 6.2.5) and similar websites, social media (Sec. 6.2.6), and elsewhere. We'll consider some of the "and elsewhere" in Chapter 8, such as making a video for YouTube and writing articles online (which can be highly effective).

6.2.2 Start Out By Blogging

A blog is a great way to begin developing your online presence as an author because it's easy to get started and maintain, and you can do it mostly by writing a little bit here and there – exactly the kind of work that writers enjoy doing. Starting out with easy things that lie in your comfort zone is a good way to get the ball rolling.

Two very popular blogging sites among writers are WordPress and Blogspot (or Blogger). There are several others, too, such as Posterous and Tumblr. There are many advantages of using the two main blog hosts – WordPress and Blogspot – when you start out. For example, they are free, highly regarded, include many helpful features, and because a large number of writers and readers already use them, this can help your beginning blog get noticed.

You don't have to choose just one blog. Presently, I have two: I blog about writing and math with two different WordPress blogs. My writing blog relates to my self-publishing books (there are many free self-publishing resources on my blog, including articles and Microsoft Word tutorials) while my math blog relates to my math workbooks – the *Improve Your Math Fluency Series* – and general science books – *Understand Basic Chemistry Concepts* and *An Introduction to Basic Astronomy Concepts*. I feed both of these blogs into my Author Page at Amazon. I update my writing blog more frequently than my math blog.

I recommend starting out with WordPress or Blogspot (aka Blogger), then once you get the hang of that, you should have both – widen your market this way. Differentiate between the two blogs, at least a little bit. Use the same author image and show the same book covers – recognition and repetition are important for establishing your brand. What you might do differently is develop your writing and pictures (other than your author picture and covers) around different concepts. You can widen your presence by adding more blogs, but then it becomes more challenging to juggle your blogs, writing, social media, and other marketing activities. Successful writers are very busy doing many other things besides just writing.

WordPress and Blogspot share some similarities, but do have some important differences. Personally, I like WordPress's system of Likes and Follows, which shows a little icon with the person's avatar. At WordPress, underneath each post, you see a table of photos of people who Liked that post; it's very easy to follow a blog, and when someone follows your blog, you see their avatar and can easily click to check out their blogs. Blogspot, being Google's blog, features Google's Plus button and also has a system of following blogs; I guess I just find WordPress's visual layout for Likes and Follows a little more appealing. On the other hand, Blogspot has a few other features that I like better; each has its benefits.

I will discuss WordPress first, Blogspot second, and offer a little more blogging advice toward the end of this section.

Note that there are two WordPress sites – www.wordpress.com and www.wordpress.org. The .com site is free and provides free web hosting, whereas the .org site requires web hosting (which means you either need experience as a web developer so that you can provide your own hosting, or you need to find a hosting service). Using the .com site is free and easy; the .org site allows for greater flexibility and a much wider variety of options, but is essentially just like developing your own website (see Sec. 6.2.3). I will describe the free, easy .com site.

The first step is to choose the name for your blog's web address. My blog's name is my name, so the url is www.chrismcmullen.wordpress.com. You can get a domain without the "wordpress" in it if you're willing to invest a little money; WordPress offers free blog hosting, but they also provide several add-ons that bloggers can invest in. The free services are actually pretty good. If you plan to have an author website in addition to your blog, as described in Sec. 6.2.3, then it might be preferable to leave the "wordpress" in your blog's url. In my case, my website is www.chrismcmullen.com, which is different from my blog site, which has the "wordpress" in it. Both domain names feature my name – reinforcing my brand as an author – while the "wordpress" distinguishes the author website from the blog site.

Once you have already signed up, when you login to www.wordpress.com, there are Reader, Stats, My Blogs, and Freshly Pressed tabs at the left, and New Post, a notifications icon, and your author picture (once you add one) at the right. Place your cursor over your author picture (or the placeholder for it at the far right) to find Settings. Be sure to update the information under Public Profile, including your Public Display Name, About You, and Current Gravatar (place your image here).

Three very useful places to go after you login to WordPress's .com site are the My Blogs, Stats, and Reader tab.

Compose and edit posts in the My Blogs tab. From there, you can quickly edit posts or view and approve comments. Click on the number of posts to see all of your posts and also find options for changing the appearance of your blog, for example. Clicking the Add New button from this page is the best place to add a new post – better than clicking the convenient New Post button at the top of just about every page. The workspace is larger and you can easily add tags and keywords this way. Just to be clear, go to My Blogs, select the icon that shows how many posts you have, and click Add New next to Posts at the top of the page; don't click the New Post button from any page.

There are many formatting options available, and you can add images and videos, too. Click the Preview button before you publish your post. Don't underestimate the importance of editing anything you post online. If you want to establish your credibility as a writer, it's important for all of your writing to look well-edited. Be sure to select a handful of relevant categories and tags for your post. On subsequent posts, you can check categories that you've used previously and click a link to choose from your most frequently used tags. Check the boxes to show likes and sharing buttons at the bottom of the page. At the bottom right, you can set a featured image, which could help with your image branding (see Sec. 8.1.6).

From the page that shows your posts (click the My Blogs tab and then the button that shows the number of posts), you can find other helpful options, such as Appearance. Select a theme that fits with your image as an author and the types of books and blogs that you write. You can find several valuable tools in Widgets. Following is a list of some handy widgets. Find them when you click on Widgets in Appearance. Drag the Widget to the Sidebar on the right side of the screen. Reorder the Widgets in the Sidebar by clicking and dragging. Place your cursor over your name/photo in the top right corner and select your domain on the bottom of the list to see what your site looks like. First, I recommend exploring a variety of other blogs to see what other bloggers do. This might give you some helpful ideas (but don't be a copycat).

- ➢ Follow Blog allows readers to follow your blog by email.
- ➢ My Community makes a table of avatars from your blog's community.
- ➢ Gravatar shows your author photo and About Me description.
- ➢ Recent Posts provides links to your latest blog articles, images, and videos.
- ➢ Top Posts & Pages highlights your most popular blog posts.
- ➢ Blog Stats displays a counter for the total number of views on your website.
- ➢ Search allows visitors to find specific information in your posts.
- ➢ Archives is a nice way to consolidate your older posts.
- ➢ Twitter feeds your Tweets into your blog.
- ➢ Facebook Like Box connects readers to your Facebook page.

The Stats tab provides a nice analysis of pageviews, both numerically and geographically. See how many followers your blog has at the bottom of this page.

In the Reader tab, you can choose just to view blogs from those you Follow or in your favorite categories, for example. Check this out each time you login to see what writers you Follow have recently posted. One way to get noticed is to click Like when you read a blog post that you enjoy and click to Follow blogs that interest you. A few writers expect everybody to reciprocate to every Follow, but this is unrealistic. There are a couple of good reasons to just Follow blogs that truly interest you. For one, people will know that you really like their posts, and aren't just hoping for reciprocity. Also, what you choose to Like and Follow is part of your brand. If you Like something controversial, for example, this can impact your image. It's okay to Follow several blogs, and a wide variety of blogs, including many far outside of your writing interests – like photography or investments. Just have your image in mind with all of your online behavior because the internet has a very long and far-reaching memory.

The notifications icon near your name at the top right will light up when someone Likes one of your posts, Follows your blog, or makes a Comment. Simply click on the notifications icon when it lights up. It will also show you when you reach new milestones, such as 50 Likes, 20 Follows, or 10 Likes in one day; this gives you something to look forward to even if things progress slowly at first.

When you click on the notifications icon, click on the notification, and then click on the user id to go to that person's blog. If you like their blog, you can easily Follow it by clicking the Follow link next to their user id that appears next to the notification.

Now let's turn our attention to Google's Blogspot, also referred to as Blogger.[11] You'll get the most benefits by signing up for Google Plus (it's free). After you sign up with Blogger and create your own free domain, when you login you will see your blog site and your reading list for blogs that you follow. Click on the domain name for your blog to see stats, change the

---

[11] Whether you search for Blogspot or Blogger, you wind up at the same website. The technical distinction is that Blogspot provides the domain service, which has to be used with the publishing platform Blogger, while it's possible to use a different domain service with Blogger.

layout (the option for this is on the left), and find other helpful tools and information – like the links under Blogger Guide (on the right). When you click Layout, you will find a list of handy Gadgets that you can add, such as:

> ➢ Profile (at the bottom of the list) displays your photo and About Me section.
> ➢ +1 Button is Google's version of the Like.
> ➢ Google+ Followers lets readers follow your blog and also highlights your Followers.
> ➢ Follow By Email provides a convenient way for people to keep up with your blog.
> ➢ Google+ Badge shows others that you're signed up with Google Plus.
> ➢ Translate is handy for potential readers who don't speak English.
> ➢ Popular Posts collects the links of your blog's best content.
> ➢ Blog's Stats displays the total number of times that your blog has been viewed.
> ➢ Search Box makes it easy for others to search your blog for specific information.
> ➢ AdSense allows you to earn a little money by displaying advertisements. This may be viable if and when you become fortunate enough to develop an extremely popular blog (e.g. if it goes viral). Otherwise, advertisements may deter readers and followers.

Don't be surprised if your blog develops very slowly; this is very typical of many very good bloggers. You may receive just a few Likes and Follows with each of your first several posts. It takes time for your blog to be discovered and for your following to grow. Similarly, don't expect the blog to drive instant sales or to drive many sales. Your blog isn't a tool that, used by itself, will reap many instant rewards. However, blogging does play a valuable role in your overall marketing campaign, offers some important indirect benefits, and helps to establish your brand and credibility as an author. It's also easy to do and a comfortable way to get started with your online marketing.

What you choose to do with your blog can be quite significant. Posts about your upcoming book, interviews, contests, and other direct marketing should be infrequent – no more than 10% of your posts. Blogging about yourself or what you're doing like a daily journal probably won't attract new readers and may not even interest your current fans (but you should do this occasionally to appear human) – unless you happen to be a celebrity. Using your blog as a fan page also probably won't work well until you become a famous author. Fans can learn more about you at Goodreads, follow you on Twitter, and Like your Facebook author or book page, for example, so you really don't need to use your blog that way.

Identify your target audience. Which people are most likely to read your book if they discover it? Answering this question and finding your target audience is the key to marketing. Your blog isn't the most effective way to reach them, but everything ties together and it's a start. You should be blogging with your target audience in mind. Prepare content that will interest your target audience; this same content should be of interest to your present fans.

Spend some time thinking about content that is relevant to the books that you write, which will attract your target audience. Avoid duplicating content from your books; a little crossover is okay. You want to develop useful content in your blog, with the hope that some readers who appreciate this will want more and check out your book. A typical post should be about 300 to 1000 words in length. Most readers aren't looking to read more than 1000 words in a blog. An occasional fun short post is okay. If you post poems, you may have shorter posts.

Nonfiction blogs have an advantage – these pull readers in who want to learn how to do something or are curious about a topic. If you write fiction, you might consider what nonfiction posts you can write that relate to your topic or genre and are relevant for your intended audience. Poets can post short poems, but don't give away too much for free if you also want to sell collections.

Look at what expertise or special knowledge you have, which others in your target audience may want to know and relates to the books that you write. If you write fiction, at the very least you have knowledge and experience that relates to the genre that you write in and the topics involved in your books.

Fiction writers can occasionally post some fiction. This can be a very short story, a very short piece to work on character development and solicit feedback, or a chance for you to explore a different type of writing. If you're hoping for feedback, respectfully ask for readers to please post some comments, explaining that you would appreciate some feedback. At the same time, if you receive brutally honest criticism, absolutely do not sacrifice your image as an author by retaliating, making any negative comments, or showing any poor behavior. If you react this way – which can be natural, because your work is personal and we tend to take pride in our work – take a couple of days off from the computer before responding, and then only respond with a brief thank you note. An author who exhibits any form of bad behavior online can find a quick end to his or her writing career; see Sec. 7.1.6. Keep in mind that it's difficult to develop an audience by writing exclusively fiction on your blog.

Your blog should have a main theme, which is relevant to your writing. It's okay to have some fun, show some personality, and offer some variety, so long as you keep a main theme that relates to your writing and maintains your author image. You want to appear knowledgeable in your genre, credible as a writer, and professional. Since your blog is your territory, you can and should be personal – interact with people who post comments, but be courteous and professional.[12] See how other authors do this on their blogs.

Keep in mind that your last three posts will feed into Amazon (provided that you activate this feature at AuthorCentral – see Sec. 6.1.6). Ideally, you should always have one post with valuable content for your target audience in these last three links. Your blog doesn't just help a little to drive sales; customers from Amazon may also discover your blog. Include the url for your blog in the About the Author sections of your books. Post a link to your blog at Facebook, Twitter, and your author website. Feed your blog into your Author Page at AuthorCentral, Goodreads, and elsewhere. Everything ties in together, and traffic can go both ways.

---

[12] Commenting on customer reviews at Amazon or Goodreads is a different story, and can cause many problems, as we will explore in Chapter 7 and Sec. 6.2.5.

Choose a name for your blog that's easy to spell and remember, and use the same author photo that you use elsewhere to help establish a recognized image – your brand of author and book. Develop a theme that fits in with your writing.

It's the content that may attract a readership and maintain a following. Remember, not everyone who reads your blog will purchase your book. When you start out, you will have a very small following, which may grow rather slowly, and only a small fraction of your readership may actually buy your book. But everything is multipurpose, and indirect benefits often outweigh the direct ones. Your blog serves many functions:

- ✓ Attracting a small number of new readers from your target audience.
- ✓ Providing additional content for customers who have already read your book.
- ✓ Helping to establish your credibility as an author and develop/reinforce your image.
- ✓ Feeding your posts to other websites, including Amazon and Goodreads.
- ✓ Pulling a few customers from Amazon and Goodreads to your blog.
- ✓ Adding information to your Author Page at AuthorCentral through the RSS feed.
- ✓ Giving you a chance to explore new writing and request feedback on it.
- ✓ Letting you express yourself creatively with words, images, and videos.

Ideally, you should begin blogging before you publish your first book. This helps you develop a small following and stir up a little more buzz before its release. If you missed this opportunity with your first book – as most new authors do – then there is always the next.

A successful blog may lead to other possibilities. Publishers, for example, may be more interested in your work after you establish a large following. Also, advertisers tend to favor popular websites. However, if you want to maintain a large following once you build it, keep any advertising to a bare minimum so that it doesn't seem intrusive.

Let's look at a few examples. One of my favorites is www.kelihasablog.wordpress.com. What I love about this blog is the combination of imagery and content. Her poetry is, in my humble opinion, quite a treat, and it is always accompanied by the perfect artwork.[13]

Here is a short blog dedicated toward self-publishers who need help formatting their eBooks: http://notjohnkdp.blogspot.com. This blogger is very active in the KDP community help forums, and had this blog up long before his book was released. The content is effective as the resources are of interest to a wide audience, and his credibility and following had been established well in advance of the book release. Observe that the simple theme matches the content of the blog site.

As I already mentioned, my WordPress site is http://chrismcmullen.wordpress.com. This may be of interest to you as there are many free self-publishing articles on my blog. For

---

[13] If you use images, get permission to use them; or use your own photos or drawings; or use pictures that are in the public domain (e.g. over 90 years old or created by the federal government). Consult an attorney with your legal questions – including the use of photos, plagiarism, and even possible copyright infringement when quoting or citing the source (search "fair use" online – and speak with an attorney – to learn more about this).

example, the first link is for an article on cost-benefit analysis as it applies to book marketing. The second article below describes the art of branding and its importance in marketing. Not all of my posts are strictly about self-publishing, though. For example, the third link below is a fun post that may be of interest to anyone who appreciates books, as it is about both reading and writing with passion.

http://chrismcmullen.wordpress.com/2013/04/16/cost-benefit-analysis-for-marketing-books/
http://chrismcmullen.wordpress.com/2013/03/15/marketing-the-4-rs-of-branding/
http://chrismcmullen.wordpress.com/2013/01/05/reading-writing-with-passion/

6.2.3 Creating an Author Website

As explained previously, in this section I mean something separate from and in addition to your blog site. There are many places online that allow you to create an author website for free, such as Wix, Weebly, and Webs.com. Free is great when you're on a low budget or have no idea how much you might make in royalties.

The main problem with the free domain services is that your url will contain an extension. This extension makes it more difficult for people to remember the name of your website, and also shows that the website is part of a free domain provider.

It's possible to buy a domain name for a long period at a very affordable price – like $10 per year or less. If you purchase your own domain name – from a site like Go Daddy – and find a free web hosting service, this will be a great way to keep your costs very low while also eliminating the problems of an automatic url extension.

Most of the websites that sell domain names also offer paid web hosting and other services. If you draw hundreds of dollars per month in royalties, then investing $10 per month or so for web hosting and other services might make sense; but if you publish a single book and sell less than one copy per day, any monthly fee will gobble up just about all of your royalties. A compromise might be to start out with a paid domain name and find free web hosting, then when you achieve modest success, switch to a paid web hosting service.

Go Daddy and other sites that sell domain names and provide web hosting and other services are very clever with their marketing strategies. They tempt you with add-ons. Also, the costs always seem cheaper until you go to checkout – when all of the little things add up, plus they hit you for the total cost up front (it sounds like X dollars per month, except that many of these websites don't bill you monthly – they bill you up front for a year or more). Many of the services are also discounted when you book them for a longer period of time.

Don't get me wrong. I use Go Daddy myself and am quite pleased with the services. I'm just warning you that if you're on a low budget, you have to exercise self-control and buy just the services that you actually need and can modestly afford.

The first step is to get your own domain name. As I already mentioned, it's worth investing about $10 per year for this in order to avoid having an extension added to your url. You can search for a domain name on Go Daddy or similar websites to see what's available. Get a .com website; they'll try to sell you .net, .info, .co, and so on, but most authors really just need .com. Although one year is usually quite affordable, they usually provide a large discount to entice you into buying several years. If you can afford a few extra dollars, this is a good deal. However, it's only a good deal if you'll still be using your website so many years from now. Are you ready to make this commitment?

Next, you need web hosting. Paid web hosting can come cheap – as little as a few dollars per month for the most economical service, even with a big name like Go Daddy. There are also free web hosting providers that you can find online. I suggest going free or economical at first. I highly recommend WordPress.com. When your monthly royalties start to show at least modest success, then you can think about upgrading to better services.

Unless you have HTML or web design expertise, what you need is web hosting. Go Daddy and similar websites provide both website building or design and website hosting; the former is for HTML experts or web designers, while the latter is for the rest of us. Unfortunately, some of these websites don't make it clear that you don't actually need both. For most writers, I recommend a domain name and web hosting, which means you don't need website building or design (you'll be able to "build" and "design" your website with the tools included in the web hosting package). Hosting may come with free stock images that you can use on your website without copyright infringement (see the web hosting site for details about this, and contact an attorney regarding your legal questions).

You should have an author website, preferably with a domain like www.authorname.com, if available. Using the author name in the url helps with branding. The url should be both easy to spell and easy to remember. In addition to an author website, there might be a separate website just for the book, perhaps www.booktitle.com. For authors who write numerous books, this can become a challenge to keep up with. If you publish using an imprint, you can also help establish the imprint's credibility and brand with a publisher website, of the form www.imprintname.com. Using a single imprint for all of your books, you don't need to have a separate website for each book. In this case, you only need to register two domain names – one for the author and another for the imprint (it would be wise to see what is available before locking in your imprint name – in addition to what imprints are already in use).

A photo and information about the author should appear on the author's website, and this should match other branding efforts across the web (e.g. using the same photo). The author's website also needs to include pictures of the front covers. You can sell your book directly from your website, include a link to your own eStore, or link to your book on Amazon. As we will discuss in Chapter 8, although you can earn a greater royalty in the first two cases, there are many incentives for promoting sales directly through Amazon. In this case, you can also use Amazon Associates (see Sec. 7.1.8) to earn a commission for this.

You can also provide a forum for customer discussions or comments, a form for people to provide feedback, or an email address. If so, you'll want a web hosting service that can help filter out potential spam, and you might want to create an email address (there are many places to sign up for free email accounts, such as Yahoo and Gmail) specifically for this purpose (but if you do, you must then remember to check it periodically). A page on your website can even be dedicated to a fan club, although this may fit better on the book's website (or the book's page on an imprint's website), if you have one. Feed your blog into your author website. Link to your social media pages, your author pages at Amazon and Goodreads, and other related websites where you have an author presence.

Amazon does <u>not</u> allow content to be copied onto your website. However, you can link to books using thumbnail images. You can't copy reviews – in whole or in part – but you may be able to link to an excerpt that pulls up the full product page (including the reviews) when clicked. Again, consult an attorney for all of your legal questions. Sign up for Amazon Associates (as explained in Sec. 7.1.8) and use this program to create links to Amazon pages.

As with your book, blog, and everything else, be sure that you only use images that you own, are in the public domain (e.g. over 90 years old), that the web host provided for your use on the website, or otherwise do not infringe on copyrights. Also, be sure that any para-phrasing or quotes adhere to "fair use" (it's worth searching for this on the internet to learn more about it). I'm not an attorney; contact an attorney to ask about copyright infringement and what does or doesn't constitute fair use.

Even if the author website is www.authorname.com, it shouldn't be just about you. The website will be much more effective if it includes valuable content that may attract members of your target audience. People probably aren't going to discover the website because they happened to search for your name and wanted to learn more about you (although this might happen rarely), unless of course you are or you become famous.

Identify your target audience. Strive to think of what content you can provide on your website that would be of interest to them, which relates to your writing. Make significant content the main theme of your author website. Your presence should be visible, but let the parts about you be on their own pages or off to the side, with the homepage featuring the valuable content. Other valuable content that you may add is supplemental content for readers who have finished reading your books. Include your web url on the About the Author pages of your books, and let them know what they can find of value – e.g. supplemental content for readers who want more, or a fan page. People are more likely to go to a website when they know that something interesting or helpful is waiting for them there.

Be sure to announce promotions – giveaways, contests, freebies, discounts, etc. – on all of your different websites, including your blog, social media sites, and so on. Include a way for potential booksellers to contact you about the prospects for buying books wholesale. You could just mention that your book is listed with Ingram (if you have the Expanded Distribution) or you could provide a link to your own eStore, but most booksellers will probably want a greater discount than those options offer along with the option to return them. Therefore, they may be more likely to buy and resell books if they can buy them directly from you (and you can afford to provide this discount because author copies are quite inexpensive). We'll discuss this further in Sec. 8.1.16.

If and when you can afford to upgrade and may be considering this, here are a few of the add-ons that web hosting services may try to sell you: A malware scanner to help protect customers who may download your content, programs that help with search engine optimization, a seal to certify your domain name, tools to sell books and accept payments directly from your website, or an SSL certificate for secure transactions.

Search for author, book, and publisher websites to see what options may be available and to generate ideas, but note that some of the cool things out there may not be possible with all web hosting services. If you visit the author websites of popular authors, such as Stephen King (www.stephenking.com), you'll see that their websites are usually not just blogs. On the other hand, because they are very popular, their websites are all about their books and related merchandise. (Sure, even you can sell t-shirts and bookmarks on your website, if you want.) These professional websites often have striking imagery and interactive features. They will also show you a lot of ideas that you probably hadn't thought of, which may be useful to you. But remember, the main thing you need to do differently compared to the popular authors is provide valuable content – since you don't have the same name recognition, you need another way to drive traffic to your site (as described in Sec. 6.2.7).

Most indie author websites are essentially the same as blogs or mostly feature the authors and their books. The latter kind is a mistake. It can start that way, but the important thing is to add regular content to transform your website or blog into an effective content-rich website. It can start out very slow, but keep your eye on the goal – to attract your target audience through search engines. This stat is much more important than likes or follows.

I began with one author website, www.chrismcmullen.com, and one self-publishing blog, www.chrismcmullen.wordpress.com. The self-publishing blog has grown into a full-blown website; it's a content-rich website that attracts hundreds of visitors daily through search engines. I've since added additional blogs (which are also growing into content-rich websites). My author website is now organized into various topics (self-publishing, math, etc.).

A website for a book should feature the book. Use striking imagery from the front cover for the background. Feature the front cover on the website. Include a free sample (but not more than the Look Inside available on Amazon). Ideally, the website should be developed before the book's release and help you to build "buzz." In this case, you can add a countdown counter for the coming release date. If it's available for preorder (see Sec. 7.1.8), make this clear and include an Amazon Associates link.

The book's website should also include supplemental material for readers who want more. Give people reasons to visit the website. Include links to the author's website, blog, publisher website, social media sites, Goodreads, the Amazon page, etc. Of course, you can offer bookmarks, t-shirts, etc. here. Anyone coming to the book's website expects the website to focus on the book and must have already heard about it (or read it) to be there. If you're already adding content to your author website to draw readers from your target audience, you don't need to do this for the book's or publisher's website, too.

Check out a variety of publisher's websites, both big and small, to see how they look – they are significantly different from author or book websites. For big publishers, look at Random House and Simon & Schuster, for example. A couple of smaller publishers include www.booknook.biz and www.barefootbooks.com.

While having a publisher website might help give a little credibility to the imprint (ask yourself this: if you see a publisher you don't recognize when buying a book, do you search for that publisher's website?), the other side of the coin is that it might look odd if the imprint only features one book or only features books by one author. One way to have books by a few different authors is to also publish with a couple of pen names, but then you may lose many sales from customers who enjoy your book and would have bought some of your other titles. If you know a few other upcoming authors in similar genres, you could get together and use a common imprint. Some experienced indie authors advance to become small indie publishers.

6.2.4 Setting Up Your eStore

Before CreateSpace and KDP merged together, CreateSpace provided an eStore free to authors. The eStore also paid a higher royalty (by 20% of the list price) compared to the Amazon royalty. Authors were also able to offer a discount code for purchases made through the CreateSpace eStore. This all sounds great, right? Except for one thing: Very few authors succeeded in driving significant traffic to the CreateSpace eStore. Why not? Here are the main reasons:

➢ Customers had to pay shipping charges to purchase books from the CreateSpace eStore. Even if you offered a discount code, very often customers could purchase the book at a lower price simply by going to Amazon instead and qualifying for free shipping. Amazon's price with free shipping was generally less than the discounted CreateSpace eStore price due to CreateSpace's shipping charge. How did customers qualify for free shipping at Amazon? Some customers have Amazon Prime. Others simply needed to add a minimum amount to their cart (like $35) to qualify for free shipping.

➢ The CreateSpace checkout process wasn't customer friendly like Amazon is. First of all, customers had to setup a new account with CreateSpace; they couldn't use their Amazon account to make purchases at CreateSpace (even though Amazon owned CreateSpace). CreateSpace was designed to help authors self-publish books; it wasn't designed as a customer friendly storefront.

➢ Another issue was trust. Most customers hadn't heard of CreateSpace. Most customers trust Amazon enough to make a purchase there. It's much easier to drive customers to a trusted storefront like Amazon.com or BN.com than it was to get customers to visit a site like CreateSpace, which they hadn't heard of before.

➢ You couldn't even search[14] for books within the CreateSpace eStore very well. There was a counterintuitive search feature. If you simply typed in a search and pressed Enter, it didn't search in the eStore: It searched in the community forum instead (unless you had an eagle eye and realized that you needed to toggle between community and store). If the eStore had better searchability, customers may have purchased multiple books at a time, which would have helped to offset the shipping charge. But it wasn't.

Now that CreateSpace and KDP have merged together, Amazon no longer offers an eStore like the CreateSpace eStore. Well, if you think about it, Amazon has the world's bestselling eStore: The Books department at Amazon is the best eStore you can find. If you want to send customers online to buy your book, directing traffic to Amazon is a compelling option. Customers trust Amazon, the store is customer friendly, the checkout process is excellent, and the site is easily searchable (especially compared to CreateSpace).

However, a few authors were successful at using their eStores, and they must now either direct traffic to Amazon or setup their own eStores elsewhere.[15] If you can drive your own traffic to an eStore, you can potentially earn a higher royalty from your eStore than you can from Amazon. Most authors struggle to drive traffic to online storefronts other than Amazon, for the reasons that I mentioned previously regarding the disadvantages of the CreateSpace eStore. But if you can drive traffic to an eStore, setting up your own eStore gives you an additional sales channel, and depending on how you go about it, there is potential to earn higher royalties for any traffic that you do drive to your own eStore.

Even if you can get customers to purchase books through your eStore, there may still be benefits to sending the customers to Amazon instead. Here are some benefits to sending your customers to Amazon:

➢ Every purchase at Amazon helps you maintain a better sales rank. Better sales rank helps with visibility at Amazon. If your book lands on a top 100 bestseller list or a hot new release list, the exposure can be tremendous, but even a modest improvement in sales rank sometimes yields better visibility.

➢ Every purchase at Amazon improves your book's chances of showing up on customers-also-bought lists for other books. When this happens, it gives your book much added visibility on Amazon.

---

[14] This used to be a great way to discover books by self-published authors. If you were looking for a book, you could consider searching on CreateSpace to see if any of your indie colleagues had written one similar to what you were looking for. Although the CreateSpace eStore is now gone, you can actually still do this at Amazon. Try adding CreateSpace (for older books) or "Independently Published" (without the quotes) to your search at Amazon, as this may help to pull up some self-published books in the results.

[15] I actually sold some books through the CreateSpace eStore. But I'm not outraged by the loss of the Create-Space eStore. I understand the reasons for the change, and see the value of sending customers to Amazon instead.

> ➢ If a customer purchases your book at Amazon (and if Amazon doesn't determine that the customer is likely to be a friend or family member), and if the customer reviews your book at Amazon, the Verified Purchase review will show up on your Amazon product page.
> ➢ The customer is far more likely to follow through with the purchase at Amazon than any eStore that you might direct them to, for the reasons mentioned previously.

So you must decide whether, for your book and your situation, it is better to try to direct most customers to Amazon or to your own eStore. There are rare authors who are successful with their eStores; I'm not saying that it can't be done, just that for most authors Amazon is the better way to go.

There are three main ways to go about setting up your own eStore:

> ➢ Try to find a print-on-demand service with an eStore option that will let you use the eStore sales channel (but which won't force you to use their own Amazon sales channel, meaning that they will allow you to use KDP for Amazon sales and their company for eStore sales). For example, you might see whether Lulu will meet your needs.
> ➢ Find a place that makes it easy to setup your own website and add payment options. If your eStore will be part of a major trusted site, this would help with customer trust issues. If instead the website URL for your eStore seems unfamiliar to customers, it will be harder to get them to visit the eStore and make a purchase. There are some major businesses that make it fairly easy to setup a website with customer friendly payment options, but will you also use your own customer-unfamiliar domain name or will your site be an extension in an already familiar storefront? That's a question you should get answered. Another issue is whether it will be free or relatively low-cost, or if it would take many regular sales just to break even.
> ➢ A few authors have excellent HTML skills and can setup their own websites rather easily. The challenge here though is the trust issue, if customers are being directed to your own customer-unfamiliar domain name. The better you are at creating customer trust in your own interactions with customers, the more their trust in your author name will translate to trust in your domain name. But first you must build that trust in your own name.

There is actually one more option: Buy author copies – which are very inexpensive – and sell them directly. This is a great option for people you know or meet in person – friends, relatives, acquaintances, and resellers that you visit. Instead of driving them to your own eStore or sending them to Amazon, you could sell the book in person and potentially earn more. You can also make this mutually beneficial by offering a discount. Since author copies are very cheap, you can easily offer a substantial discount for in-person sales and still make a much greater royalty than when customers buy the book from Amazon.

Another reason for creating an eStore option isn't for selling directly to customers, but for selling to local bookstores or other stores. When you initially approach a bookstore with a PR kit, your bets prospects for selling some books to them are to sell them author copies in person. If they resell your author copies and want more, you don't want to have to drive out there every time. Once they see that your books are selling (if that happens), they might be willing to have copies sent to them.

You could direct booksellers to your own eStore. Another option is to refer them to Ingram. By selling directly or using your own eStore, you can negotiate a discount off your list price. If you're using the Expanded Distribution channel to get your book in the Ingram catalog, your book will have a minimal discount (40%). If you wish to use Ingram and offer a better discount, you could use Ingram Spark instead of Amazon KDP. (But if you wish to use Amazon KDP for Amazon sales and also use Ingram Spark for the Expanded Distribution channel – rather than use Ingram Spark for all of your sales channels – be sure to research this online to find out exactly how to go about doing so, and to learn about the pros and cons of this strategy.) Note that Ingram Spark charges a setup fee, there may be other significant differences between Ingram Spark and Amazon KDP, such as the cost of author copies, shipping costs, and royalties.

Before you setup your own eStore, I recommend that you do some research to find some eStores that successful indie authors are using. This will help you figure out how to create and setup your own eStore.

Once you setup an eStore, you need to learn how to drive traffic to your eStore; otherwise you're unlikely to sell any books through this sales channel. If you have a blog, social media account, or business card, for example, you can include the URL for your eStore. Try to interact with potential readers in person (both offline and online), and direct them to your eStore (or even better, sell copies in person). Authors who frequently interact with potential readers in person tend to be more successful with eStore (and in-person) sales. This is common with authors who give seminars and workshops, who give readings or book signings, who go on tours, or who visit schools, for example. When you interact with people in person and build a sense of trust, they are more likely to visit your eStore and make a purchase. They are more likely to trust your own domain name. They are also more likely to write customer reviews, and are more likely to tell friends and family members about your book (provided that they enjoyed reading your book or found the information helpful). Personal interactions can also be helpful authors who are just starting out.

6.2.5 Author Pages at Goodreads

There are reading-oriented websites like www.goodreads.com that allow you to create an author page, and which provide many helpful tools. First sign up as a reader. While you are signed in, search for yourself on Goodreads. Click on your published author name in the search results. Toward the bottom of the page, look for the link that asks, "Is This You?" Within a few days, you should receive an email notifying you of your upgrade to an author account. You can also manually add a book before it is published. Click the Author Program link at the bottom of their website to find the instructions for this. Goodreads can help you create "buzz" for your book and generate early reviews by having your book manually added prior to its release.

If your name gets associated with someone else's book(s), or if not all of your books are added to your author account, you will need to consult the help pages and read the instructions carefully to resolve this. Also, note the Email Us link on the page that describes the Author Program.

When you sign in, note whether you are looking at your reader or author account page. Your author page shows you recent activity from friends (if you've added any). Visit your author dashboard to see your book ratings and customer reviews on Goodreads, and to find a variety of helpful tools. Add friends you know who use Goodreads. As a reader, add books, rate books you've read, review books you've read, mark books as to-read, identify yourself as a fan of your favorite authors, and follow authors who interest you.

Here are some helpful tools available from your author dashboard:

➢ Add an Author Widget to your website to let fans quickly add your book at Goodreads.

➢ Read the author newsletter for news, tips, and advice.

➢ Feed your blog posts into your Goodreads author page. You can also write blog posts at Goodreads, but it might seem more professional to feed your blog into Goodreads.

➢ Make your eBooks available on Goodreads.

➢ Display Goodreads ratings and reviews on your Facebook Fan Page.

➢ List your book for a Giveaway to help create buzz for an upcoming or recently published book; this may also help stimulate a few early reviews. It's recommended that you give about 10 free copies with this promotion – if you strongly believe in your book's success and have good marketing motivation and plans; if you're a little more tentative, try a smaller number. Order your books from Amazon KDP at your author price and mail them out professionally with careful packaging. Note that shipping can be quite expensive if you allow international participation. This advance review copy option only applies to print editions of your book (not eBooks).

➢ Create a Q&A group to interact with fans and answer questions for a brief period. This is intended to help you create buzz for an upcoming or recently published book. If you use this, be sure to behave very professionally.

➢ There are some advertising options available. Advertising isn't magical – if you think you can just throw money to advertisers and reap instant success, it just doesn't work so easily. See Chapter 8 regarding free and low-cost marketing options. Even if you advertise, you still have to market actively; advertising doesn't relieve you of this need.

There are many horror stories floating around from authors who have made the mistake of responding to reviews on Goodreads (as well as Amazon) – especially, replying defensively to negative reviews, getting into discussions with reviewers, and displaying unprofessional behavior. I strongly recommend <u>not</u> commenting on any review at Goodreads for any reason whatsoever. If a customer wants to interact with you, there are many ways for the customer to initiate this – email, commenting on your blog, using a fan page, etc. Don't thank customers for positive reviews, don't ask Goodreads reviewers to also review your book on Amazon, and definitely don't respond to negative reviews at Goodreads. If they point out mistakes, don't ask which mistakes (I realize this would be helpful, but think about it – when you read a book, you notice mistakes, but you don't get out paper and make a list of them, so the reader doesn't have such a handy list to give you; therefore, don't ask for it). We'll discuss customer reviews in much more detail in Sec. 7.1.6 (but know that Goodreads "police" are more strict).

Don't engage people who add your book to their to-read list, rate your book, or review your book. Authors have been flagged as spammers for doing this, and can actually get their accounts suspended. At Goodreads, the best policy is to completely not interact with readers. The sole exception is the limited interaction with fans in a Q&A group specifically designed for fans to interact with authors for a brief period – and just in that author's group setting.

Note that almost all of your activity on Goodreads – including comments, adding books as to-read, or even just liking a review – is publicly displayed on your author page. So, for example, suppose a group on Goodreads says something bad about you or your book. That group itself is fairly invisible, but if you make the mistake of commenting in that group, now your behavior has turned an insignificant problem into a very public ordeal – which does not look good for you. The best thing you can do is nothing at all. Try to exercise restraint.

Read all of Goodreads' policies and recommendations carefully, as they provide good advice. For example, read the Author Program FAQ. A related point to note is that after you send out books to the giveaway winners, you're not permitted to contact those readers ever again. Some readers will report you if you send them material again, which will get you banned from doing giveaways and can get your account suspended or terminated.

If you want to see samples of author pages at Goodreads, try searching for your favorite authors. If you wish to find my humble Goodreads author page, search for Chris McMullen.

6.2.6 Author Pages at Social Media Websites

The two main social media networks are presently FaceBook and Twitter. Authors also get some use out of Pinterest, Google Plus, and LinkedIn. These are the main places to start, but there are other sites like these if you're looking for more. I will focus on FaceBook and Twitter.

Some authors swear by social media, and others claim that it's not really effective. Part of the difference may be your target audience. The first rule of marketing is to identify your target audience, then gear your marketing toward increasing your book's visibility among them. Who is most likely to read your book? What age group is this? What interests do they have? How many of them are likely to be using Facebook and Twitter actively? Are they mostly using these to interact with friends and family, or to follow celebrities? What are your prospects for connecting with them through Facebook and Twitter?

You don't necessarily need to connect with them directly. Especially, if you're an adult, while your target audience is minors, you want to find ways to spread the word without direct contact. Certainly, don't add minors as friends to your personal Facebook account. There is a distinction between fans following the posted activity of celebrities, and celebrities who interact directly via personal accounts, emails, or text messages.

Teen fiction, for example, can have a huge market on Facebook and Twitter. Just imagine the buzz among teens on social media that was generated before, during, and after the release of the books in the *Harry Potter* and *Twilight* series. There is potential to tap here. The question is how to tap into it.

If you simply create an account, who will look for it and start following? Unless you're a celebrity, you need to market your following; people aren't likely to just show up on your page. Of course, you can provide links to your social media pages in your books, but those readers already have one of your books. You can link to Facebook and Twitter from your blog and website, but again, it's like you're going in circles. What you really want to do is increase your visibility among people who don't already know about you. Think about this.

Let's start with the easy way to use social media. Some people already have a large following on Facebook and Twitter. If you already have hundreds or thousands of followers on a personal account, make use of this popularity. These are your relatives, friends, and mostly acquaintances. Seek input on your title, cover, and blurb before publishing, post an occasional note about how the writing is going, and let everyone know when your book becomes available. **But only mention your book very occasionally!** Most of your posts must be the usual things that Facebook friends tend to do; only a very small fraction can relate to your book, otherwise you'll get tuned out. Don't be a commercial or a salesman. If you do it just once in a while, you can use your following to help build buzz, and if you just send out one message projecting the release date and a few weeks later post another short, "Ta-da! I did it," kind of message – that lets everyone know your book is live, rather than asking for sales – then you're much more likely to generate early sales.

The next easy way to use social media is to develop a following among your readers. For this, create fan pages – or author pages, book pages, and/or publisher pages. People who read your book and enjoy it, and who also check out your About the Author section and decide to visit your social media sites may Like or Follow your social media author presence. You need separate personal and author accounts, so that your fans and readers are joining your author (or fan, book, or publisher) pages. You need to have one personal account for friends, family, and acquaintances, and a separate account for you as an author.

This fan following may be interested in your subsequent books. You can similarly create some buzz with your established fan base by allowing fans to vote on a choice of covers, for example, or announcing contests. Provide content or other material that will attract readers or fans to these pages; it's unlikely that people will follow pages that simply advertise or showcase the author's books, for example. What would draw your interest if you were a fan? Explore how other non-famous authors successfully utilize their fan pages.

These are the two easy ways to effectively use social media – the established connections in your personal account help you spread the word about your new book, while readers and fans added to your fan pages help with the marketing of follow-up books.

It's not as easy to use social media as a marketing tool to reach a large number of people in your target audience who don't know about you or your book, but there is some potential here. The first step is identifying your target audience (see Sec. 8.1.9). Then think about how these people use social media and, ultimately, how to make them aware of your book. You don't want to be a salesman advertising your book. Marketing isn't about salesmanship, but about discoverability. Advertisements and requests to purchase a book tend to turn people away. It's different when they briefly discover a book that interests them, or when they happen to discover that someone whom they've interacted with personally is an author.

If you're socializing online with members of your target audience and have a profile that they can check out if you attract their interest, this is one way to get discovered. Everybody has hobbies, interests, passions, etc. Most people spend a little time once in a while – not necessarily everyday, but perhaps once a week or so – pursuing these interests online. They could be reading blogs or articles, or they may be engaging in discussions with others. Spend some time writing down interests that people in your target audience are likely to have that relate to your book. Search online to see where people can pursue these interests online – the big sites have forums where people can interact with others with similar interests, plus there are many niches online for this. People like to buy books by authors who have personally interacted with them, and people are more likely to buy books that they "discover." Keep this in mind, but don't expect instant success. Sometimes you discover a product you like, but don't get around to buying it for many months. It can take a year for all of your marketing efforts to really start paying off. Twitter hashtags, which will be discussed shortly, provide a more direct way to reach your target audience (yet you still need to operate indirectly through discovery).

Another way that social media can be highly effective is when word-of-mouth about your book spreads from John to Jennifer to Jerry to Jenny to Jim and so on. Word-of-mouth sales can be invaluable, but aren't easy to generate. First, you must have a book that is not only very good, but which also elicits powerful emotions, has memorable characters, or features an impressionable plot, for example. Next, you need people in your target audience who tend to socialize – both online and in person – to find, read, and enjoy your book. The part you have the most control over is writing such a book and perfecting it. If you have such a book, all of your marketing efforts will help to stimulate word-of-mouth sales.

Gifting books to social people in your genre might help to create such a spark, but you must have the right book to increase your chances. This requires meeting people socially – online and in person – in your target audience. The Goodreads giveaways are geared toward this, and holding your own online contests – on your blog, website, or fan pages – may help. If your main audience is highly social – especially, with Facebook and Twitter – that's a plus.

To make author and related pages on Facebook, first login. At your Facebook Home, find and click the Like Pages link in the left column. Click the + Create Page button. In Artist, Band or Public Figure, select Author or Writer to create a Facebook author page. In Entertainment, select Book for a Facebook book page. In Company, Organization or Institution, select Media/News/Publishing for a Facebook publisher page. Read the terms and conditions carefully as there is plenty of material there about what is or isn't allowed regarding advertisements, contests (under promotions), etc. You don't want to violate any policies and lose your privileges (or worse, violate any laws). Remember to use images that help with your branding.

At Twitter, add a banner (wide, but short) that fits with your author brand. Explore hashtags and find those that are most relevant to your genre and the probable interests of your target audience, which relate to your book. Relevant hashtags can help you reach people in your target audience. Research hashtags at www.hashtags.org before you use them.

One key to Twitter is to first follow people that appear successful in areas that interest you and also follow top selling authors in your genre. For the first couple of months, just follow the posts and check out Twitter pages. Don't post content yourself during the first month. Develop and refine your Twitter page and learn what successful Twitter users do. There is an art to using the limited character count effectively. You want to master this and learn the secrets. Try to build a humble following and master the craft before you begin Tweeting yourself.

What you really want to learn is how to use the limited character count to provide useful content for people in your target audience. Very often, the useful content is a link that is likely to be of interest to people in the author's following or the assigned hashtags. People are much more likely to pay attention to your Tweets when the content that you Tweet – or reTweet – has proven to generally be helpful. Also, don't over-Tweet.

Authors who frequently advertise their own books and sites tend to get ignored. At least 90% of the time you should be providing valuable content that doesn't involve your own books or websites. Direct advertising and salesmanship often doesn't work; marketing in such a way as to provide valuable content and potentially have your work discovered is usually much more effective. Remember that you can feed your Tweets into your AuthorCentral account at Amazon in addition to your blog – and both will show separately.

Don't provide links to your Facebook author, book, or publisher pages or to your Twitter page until your sites are up-and-running with regularly updated content that will attract interest from your target audience. Fans will be disappointed if they discover a link that you provided to a social media site and take the time to visit it, only to find that the page isn't finished or hasn't been updated in a long time; the same holds for your blog, author website, and other online marketing efforts.

On the other hand, if these pages aren't listed in the About the Author section at the time of publication, when you finally get them together, you've missed some potential traffic. Still, this is better than driving traffic into dead-end streets. When your sites become ready, you can update your books to include them.

Ideally, you would have all of your online pages running when your book is released, and you would actively maintain all of these pages. However, there is a great deal of work involved in this and each page that you add carries a large long-term commitment. Unless you are really motivated and diligent regarding your blog, social media, website maintenance, etc., you probably need to be somewhat selective and choose wisely. Authors tend to choose what's easiest and most natural for them to do, and not necessarily what will be most effective with their target audience in mind. But it's the latter point that's far more important. To be successful, you must be willing to market outside of your comfort zone. You don't have to market every way imaginable; but you do need to use tools that may be effective at reaching your target audience. Very often, the most effective tools are the ones that lie outside of our comfort zones. So try to choose based on potential effectiveness, not based on what you feel most comfortable doing.

I have two blogs which I update regularly. I put together an author website, planning for that to be my main site; however my blogs have grown into full-blown, content-rich websites that net much more traffic than my main site. Regular content can do wonders for search engine traffic. I feed my blog posts into Twitter and Facebook, rather than posting separately to each. If you do this, don't also feed Twitter into Facebook and vice-versa (even though you will be prompted to do so; be sure not to select this option), otherwise you'll wind up getting double-posts on Twitter and Facebook. This allows people who prefer Twitter and Facebook to follow me without using my blog, and saves me from having to post separately to three different sites. I try to visit Facebook periodically to keep up with comments. Because you can only do so much (and you definitely want to save time for writing), you must choose wisely what you can do and which commitments you can make.

Commitments are important. If you drive traffic to a website that you haven't maintained for quite some time, this dead-end leaves a negative impression and affects the author brand that you're striving to establish through marketing.

6.2.7 Driving Traffic to Your Websites

There is a great deal of cross-linking among your various online sites – i.e. one site includes links to all of your other sites. Once someone discovers one of your sites, this helps to drive traffic to your other sites – some of which, like your Amazon detail page, offer your book for sale. Of course, you don't just want to create a circle where every site drives traffic to every other site – ultimately, you want new members of your target audience to discover your sites. All of these sites are like a giant net: The larger the net, the greater the chance that they will catch new traffic. First establish and expand your net, then work on finding new traffic.

One way to receive new visitors is through your choice of keywords and tags. For example, you choose keywords and tags when you post a blog, Twitter has hashtags, and some website tools allow you to associate words and phrases with each of your webpages. There is a high volume of web traffic, and you hope to direct a tiny fraction of this traffic to any and all of your websites.

You can type words and phrases into a search engine like Google to try to gauge what is popular and see what the results look like. There are also many tools out there to help with keyword selection; Go Daddy, for example, offers search engine optimization (SEO) tools. You might search online to see if there are free tools of this sort available. There are three issues to consider: (1) Which keywords are most relevant to your content? (2) Which relevant keywords are used most often? (3) How visible will your page be in search results? You must decide on the first point, while SEO or keyword selection programs can help with the second. Then you have to balance the second and third points: Would you rather have your page higher up on a less popular search, or further down on a more popular search? Relevance is very important – nobody will stay on a page that fools them into clicking on a link that doesn't actually relate to what they are looking for.

You also need to have valuable, regularly updated content on each of your sites. It's the content that can attract new visitors to your sites. Without the content, you just get the same small group of visitors circulating among your sites. Since the ultimate goal of marketing is to find new customers for your book, you need valuable content that relates to your genre and book to attract them.

If you just blog about yourself and your book, have a website that just shows your books, have a Facebook fan page for your book, Tweet about your book, get a few bloggers to interview you, and have a Goodreads author page... then let me ask you this: What is attracting new people to any of these websites? **Nothing!** That's a great deal of work to do for very little gain. Sure, a few new readers may discover your book or blog and add to the traffic, but these are small apples.

Compare that to this: Write an article that may interest your target audience and get it published somewhere online that has modest traffic, post content on your blog that is relevant for your readers, include free resources on your website to attract potential customers, and provide relevant and useful links with your Tweets. Do you see the difference? This has so much more potential to bring traffic to your "net" of websites.

Here are a few tips to help improve the visibility of your websites in search results:
➤ Older websites with a history of visitors are favored as they are more established.
➤ Unique content with relevant links and references looks good to search engines.

➢ Relevance of the content to the keywords is critical for good visibility.
➢ Specific keywords that are used frequently tend to better than general keywords.
➢ When other sites link to your content, this helps.
➢ Search engines favor pages that are easy to navigate and visually appealing.

There are other highly effective ways to market, too, such as through personal inter-actions (which tend to make a more lasting impression than online interactions via social media). We'll explore marketing in much more detail in Chapter 8. Those techniques not only help you market your book, but also to market all of the websites in your online "net." The more traffic in your net, the more customers will discover your book.

The primary key to driving more traffic to your marketing "net" is to post free content that will help attract your specific target audience. The free content is generally nonfiction, even for fiction authors, that relates to the content of the book and will interest most of the readers. One of the latest trends in marketing is less use of social media with much emphasis on creating a content-rich website. It's valuable content that can attract new readers; you don't simply want to direct current readers to new sites, so creating valuable content that will attract your target audience and posting it on your websites is an effective marketing tool at your disposal.

It's also important to go beyond your "net" to reach new customers. So don't just post content on your own websites. Write articles and make videos that will interest your target audience and submit them to high-traffic websites, newspapers, and magazines. Too many authors don't realize the value of posting an article where there is much traffic from the target audience, for which the target audience will be interested in the article. Just imagine hundreds of potential readers seeing Your Name, Author of Book Title at the bottom of the article. You can't do it if you don't try. Find ways to go beyond your "net" to effectively reach your target audience and you can get yourself a significant marketing advantage.

Chapter 7

Useful Tips about Amazon and Other Booksellers

Chapter Overview

7.1 Understanding Amazon's Website
7.2 Exploring Other Online Booksellers

This chapter answers questions about the following topics, and more:

☑ Information about sales rank in Amazon books and Amazon Kindle.[16]
☑ Interpreting sales rank and author rank at Amazon.
☑ What determines the order in which books appear in Amazon's search results.
☑ Various ways that customers will be able to find your book on Amazon's website.
☑ How add-ons help your sales, and when similar books can actually improve your sales, rather than compete for them.
☑ Information about used and new paperback books sold on the internet.
☑ Information about Amazon's browse categories, keywords, and tags.
☑ Using Amazon Advantage[16] to arrange for preorders of your book.
☑ Customer book reviews on Amazon and other online booksellers.
☑ The best and worst ways to deal with bad reviews of your book.
☑ Earning money through affiliate links with Amazon Associates.[16]
☑ Finding your paperback and eBook on other booksellers' websites.
☑ How to find the online booksellers that have picked up your paperback book through Amazon KDP's expanded distribution.[16]

---

[16] Amazon,™ CreateSpace,™ Amazon Advantage,™ and Amazon Associates™ are trademarks and brands of their respective owners. Neither this book, *A Detailed Guide to Self-Publishing with Amazon and Other Online Booksellers*, nor its author, Chris McMullen, are in any way affiliated with any of these companies.

7.1 Understanding Amazon's Website

7.1.1 Your Book's Amazon Detail Page

AFTER YOU CLICK Approve Proof, your book will go live to all of your sales channels. It won't show up on Amazon instantly, but usually appears within 2-5 days (although there are occasional exceptions). When your Amazon product page first shows up, it may look relatively empty; it will continue to grow as features are added to it over a period of time:

❖ You might not see anything but the title and it may not even appear to be for sale when you first find your book on Amazon. Don't worry; this will change.

❖ Check the title, subtitle, author, and all other information on our book's detail page carefully. You can make revisions to the blurb or Author Page from AuthorCentral, and you can change the cover, interior, keywords, and categories at Amazon KDP. If there are other mistakes that aren't your own fault (e.g. if you type your title incorrectly, that's your own fault) then contact Amazon KDP, explain the problem clearly, and politely ask if they can please resolve it for you. Amazon has over twenty million books listed, so there may be a rare issue. Don't contact them if a feature simply isn't showing yet; exercise patience, as some features take time.

❖ The first items that will appear on your book's page are the cover and description.

❖ It can take weeks for the Look Inside to be activated.

❖ If you update the description through AuthorCentral, it may take several hours for the revision to show up.

❖ The tagging system appears to have been phased out. There were both authors and customers abusing this system, which is probably the reason for this. However, you can still add keywords to your book (see Sec.'s 4.1.3 and 4.2.6). If the tagging system happens to be available for your book, it allows customers to associate tags with it.

❖ You may not see Likes. It appears that the Like feature is being phased out, perhaps from authors who have abused it. If the Like feature happens to be available for your book, it allows customers to show that they like it.

❖ Check your list price. If Amazon discounts the price, you should be happy ☺ about it. Why? Because they pay you the same royalty whether it's discounted or not. If anything, the discount may stimulate sales. On the other hand, if it is discounted now, it may just be temporary, so enjoy it while it lasts; you can't count on it. It's also possible that your price will never be discounted. You have no control over this.

❖ After the price, above the words "In Stock," it will probably say, "…& FREE Shipping on orders over $35." Above the Add to Cart button on the right, it will probably indicate that Amazon Prime is an option. These are incentives for customers to buy your book.

❖ CreateSpace books with a list price of $9.99 or less used to qualify for the 4-for-3 program. This program appears to have been discontinued in February, 2013. On the other hand, Amazon had rarely been discounting CreateSpace books in the 4-for-3 program, but recently Amazon KDP books in this price range are sometimes put "on sale." Amazon changes its practices and programs periodically, in their effort to maximize their profits. You can't count on any discounts or programs – you can just be aware of what there is and enjoy them while they last.

❖ If you have paperback and Kindle editions of your book with the exact same title and author(s) – spelled exactly the same way (if you have a subtitle for the paperback, this means that you have to include the exact same subtitle for the eBook, too) – they should automatically link together within a couple of days. If the title or author(s) do not match and you would like to have the two editions linked – or if they don't automatically link within a few days – sign into KDP, click the yellow Contact Us button in the bottom left, click Product Page, select Linking Print and Kindle Editions, fill out the form (you can copy/paste the ISBN and ASIN from the books' detail pages), and submit it online.

❖ When there are two or more paperback editions of the same book – such as regular and large print – linked together, one edition may be "hidden" by a + sign where it shows available editions. For example, if you have a large print edition linked with your regular edition, only the regular edition will appear in search results unless large print is specifically searched for, but customers will be able to discover it by clicking on the + sign. If the large print (or other) edition is newer than the regular edition, you can request Amazon to add a link at the top of the regular edition book's detail page indicating that a newer edition is now available.

❖ You won't have Frequently Bought Together or Customers Also Bought lists until you have several sales – and then it takes time for this to be added and updated.

❖ Customer reviews may not appear until you have hundreds or thousands of sales, but once in a while one of the first customers may review the book quickly.

❖ There may be third-party sellers offering your book for sale new or used. We'll discuss this in the following section.

❖ For paperbacks, the publisher will be listed as Independently Published unless you used an ISBN option that allowed you to use your own imprint.

❖ Your cover will automatically show up in a few days; there is no need to upload customer images. The Look Inside will also appear in a few weeks or so.

❖ There probably won't be a discussion forum about your book. I do not recommend starting one because this will look unprofessional. We'll talk about Amazon discussion forums in Sec. 7.1.7.

❖ You will probably see a few sponsored links beneath the customer review area. This is normal and you have no control over this.

Next, look for your book's detail page in the United Kingdom and any other of Amazon's international websites that may interest you. In the non-English speaking countries, your book may show up under foreign authors (and you may need a translator to help understand these websites). Following are Amazon's current websites (you can also find a link to each at the bottom of Amazon's homepage):

www.amazon.com (United States)

www.amazon.co.uk (United Kingdom)

www.amazon.ca (Canada)

www.amazon.es (Spain)

www.amazon.fr (France)

www.amazon.de (Germany)

www.amazon.it (Italy)

www.amazon.cn (China)

www.amazon.co.jp (Japan)

You should know the short link to your book's detail page. This will be very handy when you want to provide someone a link to check out your book. The first step is to find your book's 10-digit ISBN (for paperbacks) or ASIN (for Kindle) as it appears on your book's detail page. The short link has the form http://www.amazon.com/dp/ASIN, where you must replace ASIN with the numbers of the ASIN or ISBN. For example, if the 10-digit ISBN for a book is 1479134635, the short link to it on Amazon is http://www.amazon.com/dp/1479134635.

The wrong way to make the link is to search for your book on Amazon, then copy/paste the link from the top of your browser. The problem with that is that the link is then much longer than it needs to be. It looks much more professional when you use the short link instead of a longer one.

You can shorten it down to http://amzn.com/ASIN if you want, but this isn't a whole lot shorter, and some people might wonder if "amzn" is some third-party site imitating Amazon. Therefore, I recommend using http://www.amazon.com/dp/ASIN.

In other countries, change the .com to the extension for Amazon's homepage in the other country. For example, in the United Kingdom, Amazon's site is www.amazon.co.uk, so the .com gets changed to .co.uk. Thus, the short link to your book in the United Kingdom has the form http://www.amazon.co.uk/dp/ASIN.

7.1.2 Third-Party Sellers on Amazon

For your paperback book, you may notice third-party sellers listing copies of your book new and used in addition to new books sold directly by Amazon. This may happen immediately if you opt for the Expanded Distribution, and will probably occur at a later time otherwise.

If you have the Expanded Distribution, you will probably see several sellers offering your book for sale both new and used almost as soon as your book goes live. You might be wondering how on earth they already have copies of your book. The answer is very simple: They don't! If they don't have your book, how can they sell it? If your book sells, they will place an order for it at that time. After all, your paperback book is print-on-demand.

In Sec. 4.1.7, I provided a few compelling reasons why customers may prefer to purchase your book new directly from Amazon instead of one of the third-party sellers. You may sell an occasional book that way, but unless they offer a significant discount (which is unlikely if they are getting their book through the Expanded Distribution – except in the case of a very high list price), most of your sales are likely to go through Amazon. Also in Sec. 4.1.7, I explained that in many cases, these third-party sellers may help more than they hurt.

When your book sells through a third-party seller who orders your book through the Expanded Distribution, you earn the lower Expanded Distribution royalty instead of the higher Amazon royalty. Also, the royalty appears in two months (or more) when your Expanded Distribution royalties are reported, whereas royalties for new purchases from Amazon are reported when the book is printed – very often, within one or two days.

Every once in a while, for whatever reason, Amazon chooses to fill an order for a new purchase directly through Amazon from one of their third-party affiliates. When Amazon does this, they report it when Expanded Distribution royalties are reported. However, at this time KDP will correct the mistake and report it as an Amazon royalty. The problem is that, in this rare event, the royalty is not reported within one or two days as usual, but a couple of months later like the Expanded Distribution sales. Those of us who have been using CreateSpace or KDP for a few years and who have sold several books through the Expanded Distribution know this because CreateSpace used to send out an email about this to us every month about these adjustments. They used to report it as an Expanded Distribution royalty and then make an adjustment, but now it just shows up as an Amazon royalty when the Expanded Distribution royalties are reported. If you monitor your sales spikes carefully, but don't see a royalty report within a few days, this is one possible explanation.

A peculiar thing about these third-party sellers is that a few will list their books for outrageous prices – way above your list price. It's absurd to worry that these booksellers are making tremendous profits and that you're missing out on the deal: What customer will pay much more than Amazon's price to get their book from some unknown seller? Those overpriced sellers don't actually expect to sell any copies (but if anyone is foolish enough to buy their books, they won't complain). It may be some scheme for them to try to improve their SEO rankings, for example; if they are way overpriced, they have some other agenda besides selling books. Don't worry about them – they're not affecting your royalties.

Eventually, a few customers may resell their books used on Amazon. You don't earn any royalty when this happens. Only a small percentage of customers will probably try to resell their books used this way. If there are several customers doing this, it's a good sign that your sales have been mildly successful. Customers can qualify for free shipping by purchasing directly from Amazon, but have to pay shipping when buying used or from third-party sellers (except for the rare Fulfillment by Amazon, which costs them more money to do), so customers have incentives to buy your book new from Amazon. In most cases, these things are not worth worrying about.

Third-party sellers usually list the book by ISBN so that their book shows up on your book's detail page as one of the used or new options. Rarely, a seller will create a separate listing for your book, using their own cover image and a title as they enter it, which will only show their own book for sale. It's to their own disadvantage to do this, which is why it's rare. Theoretically, they should only do this for editions of books that aren't in Amazon's system. There is a slight chance that you will notice such a page. If so, it should appear further down in the search results than your book's main detail page. If you find such a page, don't click on it (or you might inadvertently make that page more visible).

7.1.3 Finding Your Book on Amazon

With twenty million paperbacks and two million Kindle eBooks showing in search results on Amazon, you may be wondering how in the world anyone will ever discover your book. If you expect your book to show up on the front page of its category or broad searches (like "mystery"), that's quite unreasonable. Amazon wants the most relevant, top-selling, likely-to-be-purchased books to show up on the front pages. When your book is released, there are already tens of thousands in their search results that already have an established history of (at least) mildly successful sales frequency. Your book won't leapfrog past all of these titles without good cause.

But don't despair: There are ways that your book can be discovered in search results. This doesn't mean that it will be discovered and purchased; just that there is potential. Most books don't sell by simply being discovered in search results. Most books sell because of good marketing, great covers, great blurbs, great Look Insides, great beginnings, and good content. The better you do at these things, the more your book will also be discovered in search results and purchased that way. The let's-just-throw-it-out-there-and-see-what-happens approach (i.e. zero marketing) usually doesn't pan out – what it generally does is establish a history of low sales frequency, which makes it more challenging for marketing to help later. This is, unfortunately, a common approach from new indie authors.

My point is this: Although I will show you a few ways that your book may be discovered initially, most books won't sell much this way unless you also market your book effectively and have done a good job with the cover, blurb, etc. Don't rely on your book selling through discovery in search results; rather, foster sales through marketing and improve the potential for your book to sell this way, too.

Obviously, if you enter the ISBN or ASIN into Amazon's search, your book should be the first and only search result. However, the only people searching for your book with these numbers are those who already know about your book.

Similarly, if your book has a long title or unique words in the title, your book may show up at the top of search results where customers enter the title. Again, only someone who knows about your book is likely to enter most or all of the title into a search. On the other hand, if your book's title is short, this may pull up hundreds or thousands of search results, and your book may not even be on the first page of the list (and there may even be books on the first page with titles that aren't even direct matches with your search). This is kind of like searching for keywords, so hold this thought for a moment.

Your book will also be searchable by the names of the authors (and other contributors) as they were listed when the book was published. If you happen to have a name like Robert Jones, this can pull up a large number of search results, but if your name is much less common, your own book may be the only search result. Some people who know you will search for your book by your name, so you should go to Amazon and see how far down the search results your book is when you try this.

But you're not interested in searches by ISBN, ASIN, title, or author. What you really want to know is how potential customers might discover your book through category or keyword searches. So we'll focus on this now.

Suppose, for example, that you have just published a romance. If you go to Amazon and search for "romance novel," for example, your book might be a hundred pages down the search results. If instead you browse by categories and select, for example, the Contemporary Romance category, your book will still be very far down the search results.

So how will anyone ever discover your book? Surely, nobody will browse through a large number of search results to find your book.

The answer lies in filtering. Many customers don't want to sort page by page through thousands of search results, so they usually filter the results in one or more ways.

One way to filter books is to check out the new releases. After searching for a keyword or browsing in a category (or both), once the customer has selected Books or Kindle eBooks (as opposed to All Products), in the top left corner they will find links for New Releases – Last 30 Days, Last 90 Days, and Coming Soon (this last is for preorders – see Sec. 7.1.8).

The New Releases links provide you a window of visibility. Take advantage of it by marketing your book actively before and during your book's release. If you wait a few months and then decide to start marketing because sales aren't what you'd hoped for, you will have missed this golden opportunity.

For the first 30 days after your book's publication date,[17] if a customer clicks on the Last 30 Days or Last 90 Days link, your book will suddenly be part of a much shorter list of search

---

[17] If you back-date your book's publication date – instead of using the date when you click Approve Proof – then you may miss out on this opportunity.

results.[18] These links greatly enhance your book's prospects for being discovered. The more customers you drive through marketing to search for your book on Amazon and purchase it shortly after its release, the more visible your book is likely to be – both within the Last 30/90 Days search results and other search results. If you just let your book "go-it-alone," you're squandering this wonderful opportunity.

Another way that a customer may filter the search results is by using the Sort By drop-down menu on the right side of the page. One option that may help your early sales potential is Publication Date. There is also New and Popular; your book is new when you publish it, but it will have to earn the popularity part.

Some other filters (these are on the left side of the page of search results) that may help your book include FREE Super Saver Shipping, Amazon Prime, New (as opposed to Used – not as in recent), unchecking Out of Stock, and Paperback or Kindle Edition.

Success can help bring your book more success. A history of a high sales frequency can help your book attain greater visibility; especially, the more customers search for your book by keywords or in browse categories and then purchase it. More sales get your book added to the Customers Also Bought lists. If your book has amazing success it can get featured on the top 100 bestseller lists in a category or subcategory.

The 30-day and 90-day periods are short. After that, your book needs to have developed different legs to stand on. Creating "buzz" for your book prior to, during, and shortly after its release can help. Sending out advance review copies can help. Launching a successful marketing campaign when your book is released can help your book not only thrive during the first three months of sales, but also gain long-lasting visibility in other ways.

When the 90-day period ends, your book needs to have developed strong relevance for a variety of searches so that it shows up on the first pages for some keywords, and it needs to have maintained a strong sales rank in order to be highly visible within its subcategory. A large number of sales may lead to a modest number of reviews, which is another way to help your book's visibility. Customers can order search results by the total number of reviews (this is a new feature) or by the average review (strictly highest to lowest, regardless of number).

Your keywords should be relevant to your book – not just kind of related. Customers use keywords because they are looking for specific types of books. If your book shows up high in the search, but isn't the type of book that the customer is seeking, it will almost certainly be passed over.

Broader keywords tend to be more popular searches. For example, "sci-fi" is a very broad and extremely popular search, whereas "sci-fi alien romance" is much more narrow and not

---

[18] Obviously, the customer must first do a search or browse in a category where your book is somewhere on the list to begin with (even if dead last) in order for it to be in these filtered search results. If the Last 30 Days and Last 90 Days links are not active for your book, contact support (KDP or AuthorCentral) for help. Explain clearly what you would like and make your request polite. Amazon doesn't have a responsibility to put our books here (and hasn't always done so); we hope that they do this and should be grateful when they do.

searched for nearly as often. While it would be great to have your book show up on the first page of a very broad and popular keyword, it's also highly unlikely because there is so much competition for it. If you have a sci-fi alien romance, for example, the narrower keyword will probably net more sales even though the search is far less popular – because your book (if that's what you wrote) would be a better fit for the results (i.e. it is more relevant). On the other hand, if the narrow keyword is really unpopular – only used by customers a few times per month, then such a keyword isn't too helpful. Remember, you get 7 keywords at KDP – you could have both "sci-fi" and "sci-fi alien romance," along with three others. The "sci-fi" would help with some filtering, such as Last 30 Days (i.e. when a customer chooses two or more filters). So you should have a broad, popular keyword and a narrow, highly relevant, and not too infrequently used keyword as two of your choices.

Including your keywords in your blurb may affect your book's positioning in search results. It's not reasonable to expect this to make the difference between page 1 and page 100, but there may be a noticeable effect. The trick is including your keywords as less than 15% of your description while still writing it effectively (and without just ending the description with a list of keywords, which is rather tacky); it's more challenging for fiction.

Remember, you can have your book added to two browse categories at KDP. First, visit Amazon and browse the categories to find one relevant for your book.

What determines the order in which books appear in Amazon's search results? That's the million dollar question. Amazon isn't publishing their algorithm – in order to try to prevent people from taking advantage of it. Nonetheless, we can observe the visibility of different books and see which factors appear to affect this. The following may affect search results. Keep in mind that Amazon does change its algorithm periodically. Obviously, they want to fine-tune their algorithm to maximize their profits, and they will revise it as they see fit.

❖ The search term must match your keywords, or a combination of words from your title, subtitle, author, and imprint.

❖ A history of customers clicking on your book after using the same or similar search may improve your book's visibility – especially, if they purchase the book after performing the search (on the other hand, if several customers click on your book in the search results and don't purchase it, this might establish lack of relevance).

❖ Sales rank plays some role in determining relevance. The lower the sales rank number, the better.

❖ Reviews also affect relevance to some extent. Having more reviews and a higher review rating both help.

❖ Some traditionally published books appear to have special privileges. You can hardly blame Amazon if they give some traditionally published books a little boost. Even so, there are many cases of self-published books showing up very high in search results.

❖ Tags and Likes appear to have been phased out. These may have affected search results, but also were abused by authors (and even customers, to some extent).

❖ A book that suddenly finds itself with very high placement (or winds up on a bestseller list, or gets featured on the Customers Also Bought list of a hot seller) has a limited window of opportunity – to run away with it or fall back off the map. If a book gets promoted to a special position and doesn't seize the moment, this may quickly affect its placement (and the chance of this recurring). If your successful marketing gets your book onto such lists, step up your marketing even more.

❖ Returns may have some effect. Obviously, it's in Amazon's best interest to offer better placement to books that have a lower return rate – all other things being equal. Customer satisfaction is very important to Amazon's future.

❖ Sales history in the last 24 hours, week, and month is also important. A book that is usually ranked in the millions, but presently has a sales rank of 200,000, may not be as visible as a book that's usually ranked near 40,000, but is presently at 200,000 – again, all other factors being the same. Also, the latter book's ranking will climb much more slowly than the former book.

It's easy to see the importance of creating buzz for your book, sending out advance review copies, and marketing to try to get early sales and, hopefully, a few reviews to go with those sales – these things impact your book's visibility and discoverability at Amazon.

Another thing that's significant is where and how you attempt to drive sales through your marketing efforts. You can make a greater royalty when you sell books at your eStore or in person, but those sales don't affect your Amazon sales rank. If you expect to sell most of your books at Amazon, then any book that you might have been able to sell in person or at your eStore which you instead sell at Amazon helps to improve your sales rank.

Furthermore, if you provide a link to your book, or if customers search for your book by ISBN, title, or author name and then buy your book, that doesn't help your book's visibility in keyword searches. Ideally, you would like your customers to search for your book with some popular keywords and then purchase your book. On the other hand, it's most convenient for customers when they can simply click on a link to your book; they might not buy your book at all if finding your book proves to be inconvenient. So it's tough to promote the ideal situation.

Meeting people in person and word-of-mouth sales can help improve your chances that customers will click on your book in keyword search results and then buy your book. They might remember what your book is about – but forget the title or author name – and try searching for it that way.

However, the most probable way that your book will get sales through keyword searches is when your marketing efforts yield good results – frequent sales and some reviews, especially in the first three months – can help to improve your book's discoverability among new customers who are just performing searches on Amazon.

A very significant percentage of customers actually buy books by browsing the 100 bestseller lists in their favorite genres. It's not easy to get on these lists – and can take dozens of sales per day (or many more, depending on the list), on average, to get on these lists – but if you can get your book there, sales can really skyrocket.

Remember, Amazon.com isn't Amazon's only website. There are also many English-speaking customers at Amazon.ca and Amazon.co.uk, for example.

7.1.4 Sales Rank and Author Rank at Amazon

At Amazon, sales rank is a number with 1 to 6 digits that provides a measure of how frequently a book is selling. A lower number represents more frequent sales.

The sales rank for your book is a number that is constantly changing. You can't look at a book's sales rank just once and pinpoint precisely how well it is selling. Rather, you must monitor sales for a longer period, such as a week, and see what its average sales rank is.

You can monitor your sales rank by checking your book's detail page at Amazon or by logging into AuthorCentral (see Sec. 6.1.5). A handy feature at AuthorCentral is a chart that shows how well each of your books has sold over a period of time.

When a book sells, the sales rank drops down to a significantly lower value. Sales rank then starts to climb until the book sells again. The following numbers are for **print** books.

Sales rank is a combination of how frequently a book has sold in the past 24 hours, week, and month. A book that has no sales rank hasn't sold yet.[19] When a book first sells, its sales rank will start out at around 200,000 and quickly rise upward, reaching 1,000,000 if it doesn't sell again in the next couple of days. A book with a sales rank of 1,000,000 or more hasn't sold for a few days or more; if the sales rank is well over 1,000,000, it may not have sold for weeks.

A book's sales rank climbs more slowly when it has a history of frequent sales in the past 24 hours, week, and month; a book's sales rank climbs very rapidly when it has sold only rarely (or not at all) in the past month.

The following table provides an approximate correspondence between average sales rank and frequency of sales. These numbers change with time. Every year, a million new books are added and there are changes in the economy, so you can't interpret this table literally and expect to know *exactly* how many books you've sold just by looking at your sales rank. However, these numbers should hold approximately true for a long period of time.

Average Sales Rank (Print Books)	Approximate Sales Frequency
around 100	100 per day
1,000 to 5,000	10 per day
around 200,000	1 per day
around 500,000	1 per week
1,000,000 to 2,000,000	1 per month

---

[19] It could have sold recently; sales rank isn't always quite up-to-date.

First note that this table is for physical books sold on Amazon. Kindle eBooks form a similar pattern, but with slightly different numbers, and have different ranks for paid and free.

There is some room for error in this table – don't take it too literally. For one, it depends on Amazon's overall sales figures, which can fluctuate greatly and have seasonal effects. Also, there can be a marked difference between a sales rank of 1,000 and 5,000, so the 10 per day figure can't apply to both ends of this range. These rough figures do help to give you some indication, and others have observed similar numbers. Remember also that this table involves average sales rank, whereas the sales rank itself can change considerably in just a few days.

My own books have been ranked anywhere from around 5,000 to the millions; I usually have multiple books in the 30,000 to 200,000 range at any given time. The sales frequency for a sales rank of around 100 is a figure that I've heard from multiple sources; the other sales frequencies I can corroborate with my own experience. The sales frequency in the top 100 is sensitive – it could easily be 500 per day instead of 100 per day depending on various factors.

Sales rank is based on the sale of one book relative to other books. The bestselling book at any given time has a sales rank of 1. A sales rank of 100 means that only 99 other books have a better sales frequency (the actual formula used weighs sales from the past 24 hours, week, and month together to make the sales rank; there are 99 other books selling better according to Amazon's sales rank formula).

Since sales rank is relative to other books, this means that sales rank can actually drop a little without a sale. Suppose that several books with a sales rank in the millions suddenly sell. Their sales ranks climb very quickly. Other books that generally sell once a day but haven't sold recently will have a sales rank that climbs more slowly. As such, the quickly climbing sales ranks can actually cause the slowly climbing sales ranks to drop a little even though they haven't sold. I've been talking about overall ranks; there are also ranks within categories.

Sales rank includes both new and used books, including direct sales from Amazon as well as those by third-party sellers. Note that different editions receive separate sales ranks. Unfortunately, this is one disadvantage of making regular and large print editions, or color and black-and-white editions – if you just have one edition, all of the sales improve the sales rank of the only edition available. (On the other hand, a few customers may not buy the book at all if the edition they prefer isn't offered.)

It's nice to know that if someone buys an Expanded Distribution book on Amazon that it still improves sales rank – so although the royalty is less than Amazon's royalty, we still receive this benefit. Also, if you ever have so many sales that many customers are selling your book used for cheap, all of these used sales will be helping your sales rank, which might help to get more new sales. There are often ways to find a silver lining. Almost all sales have a positive effect, even if we don't receive a direct royalty payment. (In addition, every sale widens the awareness of your book and improves your prospects for word-of-mouth sales.)

Occasional returns do not appear to affect sales rank (i.e. the sale seems to still improve the ranking – but might impact visibility in search results); cancelled purchases do not affect sales rank (i.e. it doesn't have the effect of a sale). Customer reviews do not improve sales rank. If a single customer places a large order for your book on Amazon, it has the exact same effect as a customer who purchases a single copy. However, if the same customer places multiple orders for your book, each separate order does improve your sales rank.

Beware that at any time Amazon may revise their algorithm for computing sales rank. Therefore, these practices are subject to change with time.

The sales ranks for Kindle eBooks are similar to print sales ranks, but the correspondence between sales frequency and sales rank is a little different. In addition, there is a separate sales rank for free and paid sales. If you have a book enrolled in KDP Select, when you run a free promo, it doesn't have a paid rank during that time (in contrast, a Countdown Deal has a paid rank). When the free promo ends, it reverts back to a sales rank for paid sales – except that at first the sales rank is worse because no paid sales occurred during the free promo period (so the sales rank has steadily climbed). However, if the free promo is successful, there may be a flurry of sales two or three days after the free promo period ends. Such a sales flurry is what authors hope for when they run a free promo, but not all books are successful at this.

In addition to overall sales rank in books – and separately in Kindle eBooks – there are category and subcategory ranks. Your book will receive a splendid dose of additional exposure if it reaches the top 100 in a subcategory. It's very difficult to reach the top 100 in overall sales rank or the top 100 in a category, but the top 100 in a subcategory is much more viable. Since the top 100 sellers in a subcategory get nice exposure, this is one more incentive to try to create buzz for your book and market your book actively before, during, and after its launch. It also provides a compelling incentive to try to drive traffic to Amazon, rather than sell in person or on your own website.[20]

Amazon has recently introduced a new type of rank called author rank, which you can view at AuthorCentral (see Sec. 6.1.5). Like sales rank, the lower the number the better for author rank. The overall bestselling author will have an author rank of 1. If you have an author rank of 20,000, this means that 19,999 authors have a better author rank than you.

All of your books affect your author rank. Authors who write multiple books in the same name have a distinct advantage when it comes to author rank. For example, a writer who has 3 books that each sell an average of 40 copies per day will have a better author rank than another writer who just has 1 book that sells an average of 100 copies per day. The second writer in this example has the more successful book, yet the first writer has a better author rank by having more books. A book that sells poorly doesn't hurt your author rank. Both print books and eBooks help your author rank; even audio books help. Also, note that author rank just depends on the number of books sold, and not on list price or royalty.

---

[20] It does depend on your circumstances. Some authors sell the majority of their books in person or through their own websites, in which case the Amazon sales rank isn't as important. If you're in this position, then you should strive to earn the higher royalty by selling in person or on your own website – or your eStore. For those authors who will sell most of their books on Amazon, there is good reason to prefer Amazon sales.

An author selling an average of 10 books per day may have an author rank of about 20,000. Selling 30 to 40 books per day results in an author rank of about 5,000 to 10,000. Just a couple of sales per day will lead to an author rank of about 50,000 to 100,000.[21]

As with sales rank, these numbers can fluctuate. Since most authors write multiple books, every time an author writes a new book, this helps improve his or her author rank. With the large number of new books being released each month, these new books may affect the correlation between author rank and sales frequency in the future. Other factors, like the current state of the economy, can also affect these numbers.

At AuthorCentral, you can view your author rank in specific categories, just in books, just in Kindle eBooks, and your overall author rank.

Customers will only be able to see your author rank if you sell enough books to make the top 100 overall or the top 100 in a browse category. If your goal is to be a top seller, you should be marketing with the goal of getting on as many top 100 lists as possible. Books and authors that get on these lists get amazing exposure.

It would be useful before you publish – even before you choose your book idea – to be familiar with the top 100 bestsellers and bestselling authors overall and in genres that interest you. If you're wondering which genres sell best, the answer is readily available. These authors and books are successful. Studying them can help you understand what works – and whatever they are lacking (i.e. features that you don't find in their books, covers, blurbs, etc.) might be things that don't work. You can experiment with your own writing by just putting your book together and publishing it, or you can look at the results of experiments that other writers have done. One might even search to see what these authors have done in the way of marketing. Some hints for how we might succeed are right before our very own eyes.

It's not just about what's hot. You also have to weigh what you're a good fit to write (in terms of knowledge, experience, and writing style), as well as what has a need and how much competition there is in that genre. If there happens to be a genre with very hot sellers, not much competition, and tailor-made for your writing, then you should be in Heaven. That's unlikely, but it gives you some goal to strive toward.

Not all book ideas will sell well, and not all writing makes for good reading. There are limits to what research and marketing can do for you, but these can be very helpful tools. Join a writing club to help gauge how well you write and learn what you might improve.

Your sales rank in the United Kingdom and at other Amazon websites works the same way as in the United States, but the correlation between sales frequency and sales rank is somewhat different. You can monitor your sales rank at the UK AuthorCentral, but presently they don't show a UK author rank.

---

[21] I've published books in my own name and a pen name, and have also published books for fellow authors, so I have a few different author ranks ranging from 5,000 to 120,000 to judge by. You can also find screenshots that other authors have posted on the internet. Your research may come up with somewhat different numbers, as these figures do vary with time.

7.1.5 Complementary Versus Competitive Titles

Two books are competitive if customers will probably buy one book, but not the other. Two books are instead complementary when many customers who purchase one book will also purchase the other book.

Most authors think of other books similar to theirs as being the "competition," but this instinct is false. Almost all similar titles are more complementary than they are competitive. Think about this: Similar titles will most likely help stimulate sales for your book rather than take them away.

Every book on Amazon that has any sort of regular sales frequency has an extensive Customers Also Bought list. The first books on this list are almost always similar books. That's because customers often buy several similar books together when they make a purchase, and over the course of several purchases, many of the books belong to the same genre. It's extremely common for customers to purchase similar titles – either all at once, or over the course of time.

Other titles similar to yours will actually help market your book. (It won't be a substitution for the many things you should be doing to market your book, but it can be a big help.) Once enough customers buy your book together with similar titles, your book will show up on their Customers Also Bought lists. It works both ways – their books will also appear on your book's Also Bought list. At first, your book might not be on the most popular books' Also Bought lists, and when it is, it might be buried far down the list; but it's a start. The better your sales, the more exposure your book will receive. This way, your marketing efforts may be doubly rewarded. It takes time for the Also Bought list to show up and grow. Be patient.

Your book also receives this kind of exposure when a customer adds a title that is similar to yours to the shopping cart. After a customer views or buys a similar title, your book may appear on their Amazon homepages – with the Customers Also Viewed or Bought lists.

Occasionally, a cutthroat author conspires to "eliminate" the competition by giving bad reviews to similar books. What he/she doesn't realize is how adversely this will affect his/her own sales. If the author actually succeeds in hurting the sales of similar books, this will in turn hurt the sales of his/her own books – those Customers Also Bought lists only help when the similar titles are selling frequently. Also, if the image of all of the similar titles deteriorates, many customers may search for a different kind of book all together.

When you wish your colleagues good luck with their books, you should *really* mean it – because it may very well have a positive impact on your own sales. To carry this idea a little further, there are a few authors who have achieved success who disparage other self-publishers for their writing and formatting mistakes. Think about the contradiction that occurs when they're trying to market their own positive image while at the same time they are marketing a lousy image for indies in general. If eBook sales drop as a result, this hurts their own sales. Sell a positive image for yourself, other writers, Kindle, Amazon, etc. It all helps.

You should have been **outraged** when I suggested that an author would consider blasting the competition. Unfortunately, on occasion this has been done. It shouldn't happen for the simple reason that the author is shooting him- or herself in the foot by doing so. But obviously they don't realize this. You could also argue that it shouldn't happen for the simple reasons of integrity and scruples – but, alas, we know that everyone doesn't behave this way.

However, there is an even better reason that it shouldn't happen – **it's against Amazon's customer review policy**. Authors are not allowed to review other books in the same genre (good or bad – so giving 5-star reviews to similar titles isn't permitted either). Authors who violate Amazon's policies are looking for serious trouble – they shouldn't bite the hand that feeds them. These unscrupulous authors risk suspension, loss of privileges, and termination.

7.1.6 Amazon Customer Reviews of Your Book

Customer reviews are important, hard to get, often not what you expect, agonizing once in a while, and even occasionally entertaining. Anyone can review your book – and it shows in a wide variety of reviews – yet only a small percentage of customers actually review books.

The major problem that indie authors face is that books with only a few reviews are quite vulnerable. One lousy review right off the bat can be a huge hurdle. Everybody who reads 100 customer reviews knows that he or she will personally disagree with many of them. However, if a book has a single one-star review, hardly anybody will check out the book in search results. This is sort of contradictory, but that's the way it is.

Check out your favorite bestselling author and you'll discover that everybody gets bad reviews. Not everyone will like any book – no matter how good it is. If people give bad reviews to the most highly respected books – and they do – you can bet that some people will do the same with your book – and once you have enough reviews, it will, unfortunately, happen.

If you have dozens of reviews, one bad review isn't going to hurt – rather, it will help provide balance if most of your other reviews are good.

But if you only have a few reviews, a bad review can really hurt. Not all bad reviews hurt; much depends on what is said and how. However, when there are only one or two reviews, a low-star review may prevent several potential customers from even clicking on the book to read the reviews. There is a way around this problem. Try to stimulate early sales and reviews by sending out advance review copies – such as through the Goodreads program described in Sec. 6.2.5 – when your book is released (but note that those won't be Amazon Verified Purchases). Also, try to stimulate many early sales by creating buzz for your book and actively marketing: The more books you sell, the more reviews you're likely to get.

Once you have a handful of good reviews, one bad review probably won't hurt. Your book becomes far less vulnerable to the effect of a single low-star review once it receives a handful of good reviews.

Too many good reviews is also a problem! **Customers are suspicious of a book that has just four- and five-star reviews.** A number of authors who abused the system in the past have aroused this suspicion in customers. No writer *wants* to receive a bad review, but an occasional low-star review is needed to achieve a sense of balance.

It's not just the number of stars that matters – what is written can actually carry more weight. Reviews that simply say, "This was the best book ever," or, "It was awful," will be ignored by most customers unless they also describe what they did or didn't like about the book. Similarly, reviews that describe the author instead of the book aren't helpful. There are many such reviews out there – they just aren't helpful to customers.

Good reviews that explain specific features that made the book worth reading tend to carry more weight, and bad reviews that describe spelling, grammatical, formatting, writing, plot, and storyline mistakes tend to get more credibility. Unfortunately, unscrupulous individuals who may be out to shoot a book down can easily lie about such mistakes to create a false impression (and Amazon will do absolutely nothing about them – unless it can be proven that the reviewer is an author in the same genre, which is unlikely to happen unless they actually used their own name). However, the vast majority of such reviews do have merit.

The problem is that there are many self-published books that do have several spelling, grammatical, and formatting mistakes, so most of the reviews that point this out are correct. Customers are aware of this, so they tend to believe such a review and usually don't even bother to check the Look Inside to see if the review is correct (especially, since the mistakes might come after the Look Inside). If you happen to have a book that is virtually free of mistakes and you receive such a review that really is false, then I feel your pain. As I said, a book with very few reviews is quite vulnerable. Advance review copies and early sales give you good prospects for getting some early reviews that can help offset any such nonsense.

Although there are a few books that have been attacked with malicious reviews, **most books are not.** I didn't mean to scare you with this. Chances are that it won't happen to you unless you do something to provoke it. It does happen to a few books: Some authors have sworn enemies or jealous rivals, plus there are a few anti-self-publishing people out there.

You also want to try to keep clear of the self-proclaimed "behavior police." There are such "policemen" and "policewomen" on Goodreads and several discussion forums – like KDP – where indie authors frequently participate. They like to give "citations" – i.e. bad reviews on Amazon or Goodreads – when they see self-published authors comment defensively on a review, post bad things about reviewers on the KDP discussion forum, etc. Strive to maintain a professional image as an author and you can greatly reduce your chances of being targeted by the Goodreads and KDP forum "police."

At some point, every author who sells enough books will get some bad reviews. **Most of these bad reviews are <u>not</u> malicious like the few that I've already described.** No book can please every reader, people like to disagree with others, readers have many different interests, and so on. Eventually, you will receive a "legitimate" bad review. Brace yourself.

Authors need to develop a thick skin. Successful writers don't let reviews get to them. A bad review may hurt – even those authors who don't show it. Successful authors analyze the bad reviews for possible areas of improvement as a writer. If a review complains of poor writing, assess to what extent this review may have merit. Should you invest in an editor, read a book on writing style, and strive to develop further as a writer? The author who becomes a better writer because of a bad review grows and has the promise of a more successful future.

You can't do everything that every review tells you that you should do. Customers will come up with all kinds of ways that they believe a book could be "better." You can't please everyone. Therefore, some reviews you just have to shrug off and ignore. Don't try to make a change in your writing based on *every* comment you read.

The important thing is not to let your emotions provoke unprofessional behavior on your part. Replying to reviews emotionally has cost some authors their writing careers. If you tend to react emotionally, maybe it's best not to read your reviews at all – or to shut your computer off after reading the review and not turn it back on for a few days. Give yourself a chance to cool off first.

Our books are our babies, so it's easy to take any criticism personally. We put so much time, thought, and effort into our books; we're very attached to them. We worked hard to do our best. Thus, hearing that a customer didn't like the result of our hard work can really hurt.

But customers are reviewing the book; they're not reviewing you as a person. Remember that. The purpose of customer reviews *isn't* to provide feedback to the author. Nope. The purpose is to help other customers decide if this book is for them. A reviewer isn't writing a note to the author, but to other customers. The review isn't directed at you, so don't take it personally. Even if a review does attack you personally, still you just have to shrug it off.

A bad review isn't necessarily an instant sales killer, unless perhaps all of the reviews are bad – if the book has an average rating of one to two stars, then customers may not even click on the link. A bad review mixed with good reviews doesn't tend to kill sales. First of all, every review increases the total number of reviews, and more reviews make the book seem more popular – books that sell more tend to have more reviews. A few bad reviews provide some balance and differing opinions for potential customers to consider. I've seen some books' sales improve significantly after receiving a low-star review, so bad reviews are not all bad.

The most important thing about a bad review is how you handle it. Don't let it get to you. Try to see if there is anything useful that you can extract from it. Try not to take it personally. Don't dwell on it. Strive to grow a thicker skin so that it doesn't bother you. Everyone is entitled to his/her own opinion. You're not going to like everybody's opinion. You want people to review your book, you want to receive a diversity of opinions, and you want your reviews to be balanced. Nobody wants a bad review, but having just five-star reviews arouses suspicion.

The self-published author's initial reactions to a bad review are often (1) to try to get it removed, (2) to downvote it with No votes, and (3) to post a comment on the review. Amazon almost never removes a bad review (there must be a very clear violation to their review policy from Amazon's perspective – not the author's point of view – for this to happen), so any effort to get the review removed probably won't pay off. We'll discuss Amazon's review guidelines later in this section.

Resist the temptation to downvote the review by pressing the No button to vote that the review wasn't helpful. Why? Before you react emotionally, think about how it will look. Especially, if there is a No vote shortly after the review was left, customers will assume that the author did this. It doesn't look professional. It's possible that other customers will vote No, indicating that the review didn't help them; if so, there's nothing you can do about it. But what you shouldn't do is vote No thinking, "How do you know it wasn't a customer?" Even if it was a customer, they may still believe it was the author. It's how it looks in the eyes of the potential buyer that matters, now what actually happened.

Suppose that you make the mistake of voting No. What might happen? The customer might see that – or the "review police" might take notice – and they can send their friends (or army) over to your product page and vote Yes to the bad review and No to any of your good reviews. It would have been far better if the author didn't vote at all.

Sometimes, when this happens, the author recruits his/her own posse of friends to vote the good reviews up and the bad review down. Now how will this look to potential customers to see reviews with 16 Yes votes and 9 No votes, for example? **Unprofessional!** The reviewer and his/her friends have nothing to lose by looking unprofessional; the author has a reputation and image at stake. The way to avoid this problem is to not vote at all.

If a random customers votes No, the same chain reaction probably won't occur because – unlike the author – that customer will only vote No once and be done with it.

Commenting on a bad review out of frustration is another common mistake. Very often, the author's emotions show through, the author appears defensive, or – worse yet – the author attacks the reviewer. This looks highly unprofessional and creates a poor image for the author. It's far better to have a bad review with no comments or No votes, as this looks much more professional. Every book will have bad reviews once enough customers have reviewed it, and ideally the reviews should be balanced. Accept that everybody won't like your book.

Some authors jeopardize their writing careers by commenting on a review in a negative way and then letting it get out of hand. Once you comment on a review, the reviewer is likely to reply to your comment – very often, in such a way as to entice you into posting another comment. This quickly turns into a long discussion in the comments section, which discourages sales and may catch the attention of the "review police."

If the "review police" feel that an author has misbehaved, they may recruit their friends to post a series of negative reviews. That's far worse than having one bad review with no comments or No votes.

Don't be tempted to get your own posse of friends together to downvote reviews or comment on reviews. It will just look unprofessional. An occasional customer will comment on a review, and there's nothing you can to prevent it; but it will just be occasional.

I've been describing possible problems because you need to be ready for it and prepared to deal with it professionally. Don't do anything rash. Don't do anything to jeopardize the potential success of your book. I hope I haven't misled you to believe that there will be several bad reviews. If your book is good, there should be a good balance with several good reviews, a few neutral reviews, and a few critical reviews. I didn't mean to make you worry that there might be loads of bad reviews or that many customers are out to get you.

The vast majority of customers who leave reviews provide honest feedback, which is helpful to both other customers and to authors. Many customers try to find good things to say about the books they read. Many customers make wise purchase decisions and tend to be happy with the books that they buy. We wouldn't sell any books if not for customers, and we wouldn't have any reviews if not for the customers who take a few moments to post them. Take a moment to be thankful for customers and reviewers. We absolutely need them.

On the other side of this, a good review isn't an instant sales booster. When an author's first review – or even first handful of reviews – is glowing with five stars, very often sales don't pick up; sometimes they even slip a little. Many authors find this surprising and frustrating. In the customer's mind, it's suspicious when every review just has great praise for the book – they wonder if maybe all of the reviews were written by friends and family. Some authors have abused the system in the past, and many customers have heard about it, which makes them wary. **Fake five-star reviews are a much greater problem than fake one-star reviews.**

If you read the reviews of any book that has a hundred of them, you'll surely see some crazy remarks. A few have nothing whatsoever to do with the book. Some reviews will outright contradict others. A review with three spelling errors may complain about mistakes. There may be a couple of reviews that don't seem like they're describing the right book. Customers will even admit to not having read the book. If you can dream of it, someone has probably written such a review.

With this in mind, you can't take any single review too seriously. Most customers know this, too. The total number of reviews you have and the kinds of remarks therein outweigh the number of stars received. What you hope for is that some of the good reviews will outline specific things that made your book good (like a memorable character, a great plot, or suspenseful writing) and that the bad reviews won't be too bad. Customers won't be swayed by a review that attacks you or says the book is awful without giving a credible explanation – so just disregard those. In fact, when the bad reviews don't look bad or credible, they actually make your book look good. Another thing you hope is that the low-star reviews will come in moderation; nobody wants to receive these in high frequency.

Just as reviews show a wide variety of comments, customers analyze the reviews in many different ways. Some look just at the bad reviews. Others ignore the first handful of reviews, assuming that they come from friends and family. A few only trust neutral three-star reviews. There are customers who just look to see if anyone has complained about formatting and editing. Many ignore the stars all together and just look for statements that explain what they did or didn't like about the book (this might be one of the wiser practices). Fortunately, there are also customers who mainly look at the cover, blurb, and Look Inside, virtually disregarding the reviews (this may be the wisest practice of all). Although I've identified two practices that I believe are wisest, most customers apply a different method. Everybody has a different method of making decisions that they feel comfortable with; we just have to accept this.

Note that customers don't have to buy a book in order to review it. According to Amazon's policies, a customer doesn't even have to read the book in order to review it. Don't shoot the messenger; that's Amazon's decision. (We'll get to their review guidelines later in this section.)

If a customer does buy your book, when they review your book they can check a box to mark the review as an Amazon Verified Purchase (if bought at Amazon). They may also choose to review using their Real Name. Remember, customers can review your book even if it's not an Amazon Verified Purchase. For print books, customers may actually have the book even if the review doesn't show that the purchase is verified: They could have borrowed it from a library, received it as a gift, bought it from a different bookseller, etc. Even if they bought it from Amazon, they may have unchecked the box so that it doesn't show as an Amazon Verified Purchase. For a Kindle eBook, they might have bought the eBook elsewhere (if available that way). Amazon doesn't care if it's an Amazon Verified Purchase. Amazon doesn't care if they even have the book. They're still allowed to review it.

On the other hand, reviews declared to be Amazon Verified Purchases tend to have more credibility among potential customers than those that aren't. Another way that customers can check on credibility is to check out the reviewer's profile and other reviews. When the reviewer only has one review or a small number of reviews, or if most of the reviews are not for books, customers tend to be suspicious – if it's a good review, it could be a friend of the author, and if it's a bad review, there may be malicious intent. Many reviews are actually legitimate even though the customer has reviewed just one book and it's not identified as an Amazon Verified Purchase; the problem is that many similar reviews in the past have abused the system, so this creates suspicion – legitimate or not. You're going to have some legitimate reviews that look suspicious – that's just the way it is (so authors who abuse the system have an inordinate number of these). You should also have many that don't seem suspicious.

Don't worry about what you have no control over. You don't have any control over what reviews customers might post, how customers may vote on other reviews, what comments they might make, how many other products the customer has reviewed, or whether the review will show as an Amazon Verified Purchase. So don't sweat these things.

You do have control over some things. You can try to create buzz for your book, you can send out advanced review copies (such as through Goodreads), and you can most definitely refrain from downvoting or commenting on reviews in order to maintain a professional image as an author. You have control in writing, editing, and formatting your book as well as possible. You control how much time and effort you are willing to put into marketing, and whether or not you will utilize effective marketing techniques. Focus on perfecting your book, creating buzz, attempting to stimulate early reviews of your book, and marketing your book – since more sales tend to lead to more reviews. Do your best and the reviews will take care of themselves. Statistically, reviews should average out once you get enough of them.

Since many customers understand that the reviews are inherently limited in their potential helpfulness, it's very important to have a great cover, blurb, and Look Inside. Some buyers will judge how professional these elements are in lieu of reading the reviews; others will check these things out to try to corroborate what is written in the reviews. Perfecting the cover, blurb, and Look Inside, as well as marketing effectively to achieve and maintain a good sales rank and earn steady reviews are more important than the reviews themselves. Professional appearance, sales rank, and the total number of reviews tend to influence buying decisions far more than any specific review – good or bad.

Customers are more likely to review a book if they feel strongly about it – really loved it (great characterization or plot) or hated it (not their style or found something to complain about) – or if it moves them emotionally (made them cry or giggle). Most customers don't review books. For some books, it can take hundreds of sales to get a review; for others, every few dozen or so sales spark a review. Some genres receive more reviews than others.

A free promotion through Kindle Select can sometimes have interesting effects. Authors intuitively expect to receive some great reviews by customers who receive the book for free, but it often doesn't work this way. First of all, most of the customers who download the book for free never even read it; they tend to download many more free books than can be read in several lifetimes. Some who read it won't start it for months – it will sit on their Kindles until they eventually get around to it. Others will start it right away, but spend months reading it. Only a few will start reading it immediately and finish it soon. So if you give away a thousand books, there might only be a few customers who finish reading it within a month. It's not reasonable to expect a large number of reviews shortly after giving away your book for free.

Back to the point where authors might think customers are grateful to get a very good book for free and will therefore leave a great review: The other side of the coin is that many customers believe that you get what you pay for. That is, some customers have a prejudice that free books must not be worth paying for. Sometimes a free promo results in bad reviews, not good ones. It happens.

Another thing to consider is that the free promo attracts readers from outside of your genre who may not understand what is typical of the genre. As a result, they may have unreasonable expectations. Sometimes this shows up in low-star reviews.

Finally, there are a few authors and publishers who loathe the free giveaways and believe that these free books are hurting everybody's paid sales. A few of these people are mean enough to go around blasting freebies with one-star reviews, unleashing their frustrations at fellow authors. Unfortunately, this practice hurts the image of eBooks in general, and may have a negative impact on their very own sales. However, this is rare. Most of the reviews are by actual customers. **The vast majority of one- and two-star reviews come from customers who just weren't happy with the book**, and are not malicious reviews from people who have an agenda. There are such people in the world, but fortunately most people aren't like that.

Amazon doesn't police reviews to prevent spiteful or malicious reviews. This makes it all the more important to behave professionally and establish a positive image as an author. Refrain from making any comments that may spark an attack from the "bad behavior police." Amazon won't remove their reviews, votes, or comments (except in very extreme cases). All you can do is try not to attract the attention of people who may leave malicious reviews.

On the other hand, Amazon does police suspicious four- and five-star reviews. Since many authors and publishers have abused the review system, Amazon does strive to prevent this. Amazon is far more likely to block or remove a suspicious five-star review than it is to remove a one-star review. Amazon isn't publishing exactly what data they look at to determine whether or not a good review is legitimate because they don't want people who know too much to try to game the system. If an author asks why a review has been removed, Amazon won't disclose the specifics. From all of the authors who have complained about the removal of good reviews, we have some ideas for what Amazon may look at in order to judge which good reviews to block or remove. This may include the following:

➢ The author has reviewed his or her own book. This is not allowed.

➢ The author's spouse or immediate family member has reviewed his or her book. If Amazon determines that the reviewer may have a financial interest in the book, the review will be removed.

➢ An IP address that a reviewer has used at least once matches an IP address that the author has used at least once. If a reviewer and the author have ever used the same computer or IP address, the review will be removed.

➢ Multiple reviewers have a correlation with at least one IP address. To Amazon, this looks like one person has created multiple accounts to give the same book multiple reviews. These reviews may be removed.

➢ A reviewer has the same last name as the author. Amazon may suspect that this is a family member. If Amazon removes reviews based on this, that's bad news for authors whose last names happen to be Smith or Jones. Maybe they also look at location. Again, there is no guarantee that Amazon uses this criteria; it's speculation based on what Amazon might do combined with stories that authors have told.

➢ A reviewer and the author appear to be friends. Amazon may be able to judge this based on Facebook or Goodreads' friends lists, for example. Or someone who believes that a reviewer is a friend of the author may contact Amazon to report this. There are some authors who believe Amazon may do this, but only Amazon knows for sure.

➢ Two authors exchange reviews – i.e. they agree to mutually review each other's books. In Amazon's eyes, this may look like two authors are trying to game the system.

➢ Anything else that Amazon deems to be suspicious.

Thousands (perhaps millions) of four- and five-star reviews have been either removed or blocked by Amazon. Most of these are reviews where Amazon suspects that the author or someone who may have a financial interest in the book's success may have written the review. If you have a good review that disappears, one of the reasons listed previously could be the cause. Another possibility is that the customer removed his/her own review; nothing prevents a customer from doing this.

Unfortunately, Amazon may occasionally remove a legitimate review in their effort to prevent and remove reviews that truly violate their policies. Amazon would rather remove a few legitimate reviews by mistake than allow a few authors to abuse the system.

At the same time, Amazon almost never removes a bad review. A one- or two-star review has to be a very clear violation of Amazon's review policy in order to trigger its removal. Following are some types of reviews that are not allowed:

> Authors can't review their own books.

> People who may have a financial interest in the book's success – including household family members or the publisher – are not allowed to review the author's book.

> Authors are not allowed to pay or compensate (except for mailing out free, legitimate advanced review copies) people for their reviews.

> Reviews may not include advertisements, personal information (like contact info), external links, or requests for helpful votes. However, it's okay if the review includes a link to another book on Amazon (provided that the reviewer doesn't have a financial interest in the sale of the linked book).

> A review shouldn't mention the price, availability, or shipping. Nonetheless, there are thousands of reviews that describe the shipping time or condition of the package.

> Authors are not allowed to review books in a subject or genre that is similar to their own books, or to review books with content that is similar to their own. Authors are not permitted to review complementary or competitive titles.

> Obscenity, profanity, and spitefulness are not allowed. However, Amazon does not remove *all* reviews that have some measure of spitefulness. Some authors have mildly (or even moderately) spiteful reviews that Amazon has elected not to remove.

> Reviews are not supposed to comment on other reviews on the product page.

If you see a review that you believe may be a violation of Amazon's review policies, you may report it to Amazon. Make a polite request. Reviews are removed at Amazon's discretion. They will look into it, and may choose to let the review stand. Amazon will not offer any explanation for their decision. You just have to accept it.

Although the customer review system isn't perfect, all in all it serves a valuable purpose: It offers potential customers some opinions from previous readers. The number of reviews is often far more important than any single review. It's only a rare occasion that a low-star review has an agenda. It's unreasonable to suspect every low-star review of having malicious intent. Very many customers leave positive reviews and provide helpful suggestions. When customers do offer criticism, they usually have a valid point.

Compared to independent movies, indie authors should be very happy with Amazon's customer review system. Many independent films – and even some major productions – get streams of one- and two-star reviews at websites like Redbox. Fortunately, there don't appear to be nearly as many harsh book critics as there are harsh movie critics. That's good for indie authors; the image of indie authors in general is nearly as important as each author's individual reputation. Like I mentioned before, the authors who sell a bad image regarding self-publishing with negative comments contradict their own efforts to market their own books. In addition to marketing your own books, help to rebuild a positive image of indies.

Don't focus on the shortcomings of the review system or the occasional abuse of the system. Focus on the fact that customer reviews – both the good and the bad – can serve as a helpful tool for potential customers.

Let's return to the controversial issue of whether or not it's okay to comment on reviews. The vast majority of authors and customers feel that authors should generally not comment on customer reviews. That alone should tell you that if you do it, it's going to upset a large number of customers and potential customers – not to mention the "review police."

Not commenting on a review is never a mistake. Not commenting on a review will never be interpreted as bad behavior. Not commenting on a review won't lead to retaliation from a customer or the "review police." Not commenting on a review will look professional.

Commenting on a review carries a great risk. It risks looking unprofessional. It risks possible retaliation by the customer and their friends (but only your image is at stake). It risks your image as an author. It risks future sales. It risks your writing career.

However, there are some authors – who are in the minority with their opinions – who believe that there may be occasions in which it is okay to comment on a review. This may include when the reviewer asks the author a question, to provide notice of updates, or to post that a new edition is available. In the former case, including some means of contacting you in the About the Author page may be the better option. In the latter cases, it's really not necessary: You can place this notice in the blurb, where it will be far more visible.

Other authors feel that replying to reviews offers customers that personal touch. Their feeling is, "What traditional author will take the time to reach out to his/her readers this way?" There are, however, many other ways to interact with readers who want the author to be personable – such as a fan club, the author's blog, or a temporary author/fan forum on Goodreads. Many reviewers don't want the author commenting on their reviews.

The majority of reviewers claim that customer reviews are their space, not the author's space, and don't want authors to invade this space. Whereas the author may feel that a simple, "Thank you for reading my book and taking time to share your thoughts," provides a personal touch, many reviewers feel that this is tacky – and something only a self-published author would do. When you thank a reviewer, other customers suspect that you are friends.

I recommend not commenting on reviews. Before you do some research and accuse me of being hypocritical, let me point out that I have commented on a couple of my reviews. I have done this, rarely, with my own books thinking that this experience may be useful prior to advising other authors – in this book – about commenting on reviews. By doing so, for example, I discovered that you can remove your comment afterward, but if anyone else has commented, too, when you remove your comment, it will say, "Deleted by the author on…" Here, the word "author" really means the customer who commented, but potential customers will interpret this literally as the author (so if a stranger posts and removes a comment – and there are other comments showing – that might create a little confusion; however, customers rarely comment, except when the author's comments provoke their participation).

If you do comment on a review, you must absolutely do so tastefully, politely, tactfully, and respectfully. Your image is at stake, and a negative author image can have a brutal impact on sales. No comment at all is more professional than a tasteful comment. Don't attack the reviewer; don't accuse the reviewer of anything; and don't be defensive. This behavior can lead to catastrophic results. Even tasteful comments place your image at stake and can get the attention of the "review police." Better to not comment and better not to thank customers for their reviews than to risk this.

Responding to bad reviews is even riskier, and takes a great deal of tact. First read the review carefully. If the writing suggests the possibility that the person could react quite negatively to your response, then your comment will likely attract negative attention. If the person has only reviewed your book, this person probably has an agenda. Commenting on reviews where the reviewer may have an agenda or may react emotionally is like playing with fire – and only you can get hurt. Part of the problem is that you can't always tell from a short writing sample that the person has an agenda or might react negatively, and it might be an onlooker who reacts this way – not the reviewer him- or herself. No wonder the vast majority of authors will advise you not to comment on your reviews.

You don't want to look needy, whiny, or defensive. You don't want to look like you sell so few books that you need to respond to your reviews. The cons of commenting far outweigh any pros.

Another thing you must avoid is blogging or posting on a forum (or anywhere online, like Facebook or Twitter) anything negative about any reviewer. It's tempting to want to blow off steam and/or seek some comfort and support by describing a bad review on your blog or a forum. However, this is unprofessional and very likely to attract the "bad behavior police." Your image as an author takes much time to establish, but can very quickly be ruined in just a heartbeat. Don't risk it by saying anything bad about reviewers or customers.

There are many mistakes that indie authors frequently make regarding reviews. A common one is to post a question online – such as at a discussion forum – asking for reviews. This looks tacky and unprofessional, and again tends to attract the "review police." Even worse is asking other authors to exchange reviews – i.e. review each other's book (providing feedback privately to each other is useful, but mutually exchanging public reviews is frowned upon). A few authors have even gone so far as to ask how they might buy reviews (and, believe it or not, some have actually done this). Paying for reviews is a violation of Amazon's policy. Amazon will remove a review if they believe that compensation has been provided for it (other than a free review copy). Furthermore, such behavior risks account suspension or termination.[22] Begging for reviews isn't good either – that also hurts your image as an author.

The proper way to get reviews is to send out advance review copies to people who are allowed to review your book (Goodreads, for example, has a program that can help with this), offer a relevant blogger (start small, as major bloggers are likely to get numerous requests) a free copy to read if they may have an interest in reviewing your book (as with advance review copies, there is no guarantee that your book will get reviewed or that the review will be good – it's a chance that you take), and market as best you can because the more books you sell, the greater the chances that your book will get reviewed.

If you explore Amazon UK and other international websites, you may find reviews on your books there that don't (presently) show up on Amazon US. If you have good reviews there, you will be wishing that the reviews showed up on all of Amazon's websites; but if you have bad reviews internationally that complain about differences between American and British English or customers who didn't understand what they were buying because of language differences, you may be glad that those reviews don't show up in the United States. This may change in the future. It's possible that all of Amazon's websites' reviews will be consolidated. If so, it is generally the case that having more reviews is better.

I've been fortunate to receive multiple reviews on several different books, including many good reviews. No amount of good reviews can make me appreciate them any less; every good review that I receive brings a smile to my face. I have a few critical reviews, too. I realize that these help to provide a balanced picture. I have even revised a few of my books, making improvements based on these suggestions. Some critical reviews help us write better books.

As a reader, my review policy is different than that of many other reviewers: I only review books that I believe merit five stars. For one, as an author myself, I understand how much time and effort goes into all of the stages of writing and publishing a book, and I know what it's like for an author to be very passionate about his or her work. I don't feel comfortable writing a review for which I would give less than five stars. So rather than review every book that I read – which would be very time-consuming – I only take the time to review those books that impress me the most. Some will argue that it may look biased that I don't give any bad reviews. On the other hand, this balances those reviewers who only give bad ones.

Also, I don't review books by request; I find my own books and review only those.

---

[22] Some of the people "selling" good reviews on Amazon actually leave nasty one-star reviews! Those are people who are appalled by the thought of authors paying for reviews and who are taking matters into their own hands, trying to "teach" such authors a lesson. If you see an advertisement offering to leave a good review for payment, don't think, "So that's how some authors are doing it." This unscrupulous tactic probably isn't working.

Do you review books that you've read? If you're hoping to have your book read and reviewed, it's kind of hypocritical if you're not taking the time to review books yourself. One way to help foster a better image for indies is to occasionally read indie books and review indie books that you like. Giving great reviews for bad books won't help our image, but giving good reviews for well-written indie books will help in a small way; if a great number of indies do this, the effect will be more significant.

In conversations and blogs, speak positively about indie authors; refrain from complaining or making disparaging remarks publicly. When you hear a negative comment about indies, take a moment to briefly and tactfully respond with a statement of the form, "Actually…" Keep it brief, sound positive, don't be defensive, and don't get in an argument. The small things we might do to help our image impact every one of us. If you have a friend or acquaintance who is self-publishing, provide some honest feedback. If you can tactfully persuade them to improve some aspect of their books, this also helps to improve our image.

Also, if you review books by other indies, remember that you're not permitted to review books that are similar to yours in content, subject, or genre.

7.1.7 Customer and Author Discussion Forums

If you participate in Amazon's customer discussion forums or the KDP community's forums, you have a choice of doing so anonymously or you may choose to reveal your identity in your profile. If you reveal your identity in your profile (or if your profile is anonymous, but you reveal your identity explicitly or implicitly in any of your posts), do so with your image as an author in mind. Be professional. Appear knowledgeable, trustworthy, and likeable. Write well. Proofread your posts because they are samples of your writing. Don't post anything that may attract negative attention, create controversy, or otherwise adversely affect your image as an author. You especially don't want to attract the self-appointed "bad behavior police."

Self-promotion is not allowed in Amazon's customer discussion forums. You're not permitted to say, "I wrote a book called __," for example, or to include the title of your book at the end of your posts. Customers will become very irate if you self-promote in forums where this is not allowed, and a moderator may edit or remove your post. It paints a bad image, too.

You can be a helpful, thoughtful participant in the discussions. If someone likes your writing or ideas, they may click on your user profile. If your profile reveals your name and indicates that you're an author, they may indirectly learn about your book this way. Most customers are not clicking on many profiles and buying books from authors this way. It's probably not the best place to promote – especially, since you're not allowed to include a signature line, and few people will indirectly discover your book by clicking on your profile. Also, most other indie authors are promoting only on Amazon, and most customers are weary of the self-promotion that occurs from thousands of authors who didn't know better.

When you visit your book's detail page at Amazon, you'll see a place where a customer could begin a discussion about your book. This is highly unlikely except for very popular traditionally published authors. Don't start your own discussion here, as customers may perceive it as tacky and unprofessional.

The KDP community forum is a good place to meet other authors, exchange ideas, get help with your Kindle eBook, and help others. You can benefit from these things anonymously. If you reveal your identity – even through a hint in a single post – remember that your author image is at stake. Always behave professionally. If you simply support others who are complaining – say, about a bad review – there is a possibility that you will be targeted by the "bad behavior police" indirectly just through your association (this has happened).

Some authors request feedback on their blurbs, covers, etc. on the KDP community help forum. Ideally, one would do this prior to publishing – you only get one chance to make a great first impression. You can get some honest feedback there, but beware that sometimes it's brutally honest. That's the most useful kind of feedback, but you have to be prepared for it and put on a thick skin. At the same time, not everyone who participates there is necessarily an expert on the subject, so you have to sort out the good advice from the bad; on the other hand, customers will have a variety of opinions, so hearing a variety of opinions from fellow authors might be helpful. Obviously, sharing your blurb or cover will reveal your identity, so remember the importance of appearing professional.

There are better places to promote your book than the KDP community forum. Almost everyone there is an author like you, busy writing and marketing their own books. A few authors there do occasionally buy books from other authors – especially, when they like the writing style and character displayed in the posts – but many other authors simply aren't looking for books to read while they are in author help forums. The more effective way to market online is to figure out where your target audience is likely to engage in conversations, and try to get discovered through your helpful participation at those sites.

7.1.8 Preorders and Affiliate Links

Go to Amazon's homepage, scroll down to the bottom, and find the Make Money with Us list. As a self-published author, you will probably be interested in Amazon Advantage and/or Amazon Associates. The links under Make Money with Us include – some of these won't be relevant for you – Sell on Amazon (you can make products or buy them wholesale, then sell them in a store on Amazon; you can sell your used books online as a third-party seller; or you could sell the books you've published as a third-party seller, but I don't recommend this last option), Become an Affiliate (earn a commission for any sales you generate by referring customers to Amazon via product links), Advertise Your Products (if you have any goods or services to advertise), and Independently Publish with Us (via KDP).

Find both Amazon Advantage and Amazon Associates by clicking the See All link under Make Money with Us. Amazon Advantage allows you to ship books (or other products) to Amazon to stock them in their warehouse and let Amazon sell them on their website. If you want to make your book available for preorders, use Amazon Advantage to do it. This allows you to create a listing for your book before it is published, and allows customers to buy your book in advance of the release date. A couple of days before your book will be released (i.e. when you will click Approve Proof, which enables the Amazon sales channel at from KDP), go to the Amazon Advantage control panel and submit a request that Amazon Advantage switch control of your Amazon orders over to KDP.

You have to be very clear and precise about what you want in your request to Amazon Advantage, and you may need to exchange a couple of messages with them. You don't want them to close your book; you want it to remain open until the release date. This shouldn't be a problem because it's only available for preorder – you listed the date that it will be available, and it's not available yet. If they tell you that they've closed the book, you want to respond and explain that you want it to remain open, and remind them why this should be okay (because it's not yet available – you set a release date which hasn't come to pass). You want a smooth transition so that KDP can simply fulfill the orders that have already been placed and for Amazon to fulfill future orders through KDP, too.

If Amazon Advantage tells you that you can't source orders through both Amazon Advantage and KDP, explain that this shouldn't be a problem because it's a preorder. Again, you need to tell them that you would like it to remain open until the release date so that customers may preorder it, and then have KDP take over when it's published.

Once you have suspended (not closed – at least, not prior to the release date) your book at Amazon Advantage, you can ignore Amazon's email alerts about stocking your title – since you have requested Amazon Advantage to have KDP fulfill your orders.

The important thing is to check your book's Amazon detail page. You want the preorder option available prior to the release date with the Add to Cart button live, and you want this to change to being available and In Stock once your book is published. Your title should remain open at Amazon Advantage until the release date, and change to Closed when KDP takes over fulfillment.

At some point in the process, you may need to go to your Amazon Advantage control panel, click on Purchase Orders, and mark them as Cancelled: Not Yet Available. If done correctly, this shouldn't cancel the order completely, but should hold the orders until the book is available. You want the orders to be transferred to and fulfilled by KDP.

If you have questions, contact Amazon Advantage to explain what you are trying to do (and if they misinterpret your intentions, try to clarify). You might also search the Amazon KDP community forum for discussions about preorders or post a question there.

Note that preordering is presently only available for books, but not for eBooks. (However, you may notice that the big publishers have special privileges.)

Join Amazon Associates in order to earn commissions from sales that you refer to Amazon's website through an affiliate link. You can get an affiliate link for specific Amazon pages from Amazon Associates and then use it at your own website. You can also link to a book or product using a thumbnail image. The commission applies to any products that customers may purchase at Amazon after clicking on the affiliate link. This only works from websites – it doesn't work when the link is included in an email or an eBook (you're not permitted to include affiliate links in an eBook; you can include relevant links in an eBook, but you can't use affiliate links to earn commissions on referrals from an eBook).

Beware that a new limit on affiliate links to free promo books has been imposed by Amazon. If you use your affiliate links primarily to link to free promo books or if customers download 20,000 or more free promo books in a month after clicking on your affiliate links (of which 80% or more of the free downloads are attributed to your affiliate links), then you will not earn any commissions for that month. Some websites were avidly promoting free books through affiliate links, hoping that the customers would also buy others products while at Amazon. These program changes are evidently directed toward this practice.

If you use your real name or a pen name as your Associates name, the address bar will reveal this name when the affiliate link is clicked. This is something to keep in mind if you want to use affiliate links from a website without revealing your identity.

7.1.9 Changes in Amazon's Website

Amazon's website, programs, policies, and practices change periodically. These changes can seem scary at first, especially once you've achieved some level of success. Amazon strives to improve. Like all business, their goal is to maximize their profits, and like all consumer-driven businesses, this means optimizing the quality of the products and customer satisfaction. When you think about it, improvements that Amazon may make regarding the quality of their products or customer satisfaction benefit all of us – not only as customers, but as authors, too. Customers are more likely to buy books when they are generally pleased with the products and services. So we shouldn't fear possible changes at Amazon.

A couple of years ago Amazon began removing and blocking reviews – mostly with four and five stars – that they suspected of violating their policies. A small number of these reviews may have been legitimate, but overall this has improved the customer experience by helping to prevent review abuse that had been previously occurring. Customers and authors should generally view this change as for the better.

Recently, the 4-for-3 program was discontinued. I was concerned about this at first be-cause most of my books had been in the 4-for-3 program, and frequently sold by the fours. However, Amazon now periodically discounts some of my books that had previously not been discounted. If anything, this change seems to have improved my sales.

There will surely be other changes, too. It doesn't help to worry about them. The changes usually provide improvement, which help both customers and authors. We should welcome this type of change.

Sometimes, there are temporary changes or glitches in the system. Once a year or so the sales rank feature seems to disappear for a day or two. Sales often plummet in such cases, and can take a while to rebuild afterward. However, this is very rare and doesn't last long. If this happens and you notice it, remember that it probably won't last long and it probably won't occur again for another year or so. Occasionally, there is a glitch in the detail page for a book at Amazon. These glitches often resolve on their own, but if you notice a glitch, you should report the problem to Amazon.

7.1.10 Contacting Amazon

If you have an author-related issue, you can contact Amazon from AuthorCentral. After logging into AuthorCentral, select the Help tab and look for the yellow Contact Us button. For issues that relate to a book that you've published with Amazon KDP, you can contact support from your Member Dashboard. You can also receive much help from the Amazon KDP community forum. For issues that relate specifically to your Kindle eBook, you can contact KDP from the KDP community help pages: Click the yellow Contact Us button in the bottom left corner. One way for customers to contact Amazon is to look for the small Help link at the bottom of their homepage and then find the yellow Contact Us button on the right side.

7.2 Exploring Other Online Booksellers

7.2.1 Online Paperback Booksellers

MOST SELF-PUBLISHED AUTHORS are primarily interested in the nuances and subtleties of Amazon, many of which we have discussed in detail. Most other booksellers have much simpler websites, and most self-published authors sell only a fraction of their books there. For these reasons, I will focus on listing a variety of online booksellers and only mention a few pertinent details about them (and for another reason – that this book would be extremely long if I described each of these booksellers in as much detail as I have described Amazon's website).

If you've enabled the Expanded Distribution channel with Amazon KDP, you may want to check where your paperback book is available. Visit http://www.gettextbooks.com and enter the ISBN for your book to see where it's for sale online. Of course, it takes time for online booksellers to learn about your book, decide whether or not to add it to their catalog, and, if so, make a product page for your book. Some sellers will do this very quickly, others very slowly. If you search for your book on this site shortly after you publish, there might not be any matches. Give it time, and you should see a variety of online booksellers listed. With even more time, you may notice many more sellers. Some books have a very large number of online sellers listed. If you want to verify this information, simply visit any of the websites (you don't have to click on the links – you can visit each directly) and search for your book there.

Even if your book is available at dozens of websites, most customers tend to buy Amazon KDP paperbacks through Amazon. Some of the sellers listed may never sell a single copy of your book (especially, because a few list outrageous prices). A few of these sellers, such as The Book Depository, do sell some Amazon KDP paperbacks. The Book Depository advertises free shipping worldwide and is very popular in many countries.

A couple of major bookstore chains in the United States that may sell your book online through the Expanded Distribution channel include Barnes & Noble and Books-a-Million. Powell's Books, Alibris, and Abe Books are large online booksellers that may also choose to include your book. The Book Depository is a major online retailer that I've already mentioned. Some small businesses and even individuals might list your book for sale on Half.com and eBay (and customers can resell their copies there, too – but in the case of resale, you don't earn any royalty). You will probably also discover other booksellers carrying your book "virtually in stock." Most (if not all) of these booksellers will not carry your book in their warehouses – it's print-on-demand, so they will only order it if and when it happens to sell. Since it can take 2-3 months for an Expanded Distribution sale to show on your royalty reports, it may take several months before your Expanded Distribution sales take off (and, like sales in general, there are no guarantees that it will). If you cancel the Expanded Distribution channel, you run the risk of stopping such sales right when they're starting to pick up, without even realizing it (because the royalties may not show for a couple of months).

None of these booksellers have any obligation to carry your book. Amazon KDP lists your book with Ingram's catalog. That's the end of Amazon KDP's obligation. Then it's up to bookstores to discover your book and decide whether or not to carry it. There are no guarantees. However, there are many booksellers that want to have the widest selection possible; these are very likely to pick up your book, too – at least, online (probably not on-hand).

Similarly, every bookseller will individually decide what information to display for your book, and what price to charge. Many will only display the thumbnail image and title. Some won't include your description, categories, or keywords. You can try asking Amazon KDP politely to have select bookstores (such as Barnes & Noble – although the relations between Amazon and Barnes & Noble may inhibit this possibility) add your description, if possible (it may not be). You might also consider trying to contact the booksellers directly; some may be more receptive than others. If you publish an eBook through Nook Press, your description, keywords, and/or categories may get linked with your paperback edition on Barnes & Noble.

You should visit Barnes & Noble and other online booksellers' websites to search for your book and learn more about their websites and how they work. Find out firsthand what your list price is, whether or not there are periodic discounts, if your description shows up, which categories (if any) your book is listed in, whether or not your book is searchable by any keywords other than words from the title, what the sales rank is (if it's sold), and if there are any reviews. Monitor your sales rank by visiting the sites periodically as this will help you estimate how often your book may be selling there. Note that customer book reviews are most common on Amazon and Goodreads, and are very rare at most other online booksellers.

As we discussed in Sec. 6.2.4, customers won't discover your eStore unless you provide a link to it, and many customers will prefer to buy your book on Amazon instead of through your eStore. As noted in Sec. 6.2.4, although CreateSpace used to offer authors an eStore, the eStore option disappeared when CreateSpace merged with KDP. CreateSpace also used to have an affiliates program. Amazon still has affiliate programs: For example, check out the Amazon Associates program, which allows you to earn a commission (depending upon where you live) on sales (of most products, not just your book) that result from traffic that you send.

Search for your book and also search for your name on popular internet search engines such as Google. Note that some places may appear to be giving your book away for free (some will go so far as to quote the number of alleged downloads), but most of these are false appearances. They often don't have your book at all, but have some ulterior motives. I recommend avoiding websites that pretend to be giving your book away for free – if they are dishonest about that, who knows what else may be going on there (and if they are honest about your book being free – when it's not free anywhere else – then they are dishonest in their practice of giving it away, which again is a good reason to avoid that website).

7.2.2 Online eBook Retailers

Your eBook should only be available specifically where you publish it – and if you use an aggregator like Smashwords, at any outlets where sales distribution is enabled (check carefully, as you may have to disable your eBook's distribution anywhere you don't want to publish – or where you've already published, like KDP or Nook Press – rather than enabling its dis-tribution where you do want to publish). Therefore, you won't have to hunt all over the internet to find your eBook: You should already know exactly where to find it.

Go to Kindle (on Amazon), Nook (at Barnes & Noble), Smashwords, Sony's Reader Store (www.ebookstore.sony.com), the Apple iBooks website (www.apple.com/apps/ibooks), the Kobo bookstore (www.kobobooks.com), and wherever else your eBook is available. Search for your book to see what the listing looks like and which searches pull it up successfully. Check your list price, description, categories, keywords, and free sample carefully. Monitor your sales rank to estimate your sales frequency and see if there are any customer reviews.

Try searching for your eBook with a variety of devices (e.g. Kindle, Nook, Sony Reader, Kobo, iPhone, iPad, etc.) and see what the sample looks like on the device. It would be wise to see what one full-length copy of your eBook looks like on each device (from each eBook store where it is available for that device), since your eBook can easily look great on one device, but have serious formatting issues on another. Ideally, you should test the formatting carefully before publishing, whenever possible. You want to see how your book looks on each device firsthand before your customers do (who will probably complain about any serious formatting issues in a review, if there are any). If you don't have the specific device, you may have a friend or acquaintance that has one that you can borrow (or, more likely, they can do this for you and you can watch).

If you publish an eBook on Nook and have the same title available on Barnes & Noble through Amazon KDP's Expanded Distribution, the two editions may get linked together and the description, categories, keywords, and/or author biography may show up for your paperback edition through this linkage.

Remember that if you enroll in KDP Select, you're not permitted to sell your eBook online through any other retailer until your enrollment period ends. **Enrollment in KDP Select automatically renews every 90 days unless you go to your KDP Bookshelf, check the box next to the book, click the Actions button, choose See KDP Select Details, and uncheck the box for automatic renewal.** If you uncheck this box or even if you unpublish your book from KDP, you're still obligated to publish exclusively through KDP until the enrollment period expires – there is no way to opt out early (except for a very brief grace period of a few days when you first sign up).

You may publish a paperback with Amazon KDP or publish other print editions while your eBook is enrolled in the KDP Select program – only the eBook edition of your book is exclusive to KDP. Note that you are <u>not</u> even allowed to give away more than Amazon's free sample on your own website when your book is enrolled in KDP Select.

Some eBooks sell best on Kindle. Some sell very well for the iPhone and iPad – yet, strangely, sometimes more iPad and iPhone users buy the eBook through Kindle than from Apple iBooks. A few eBooks sell very well on Nook. Success with different eReaders can vary widely depending on the genre and even the book. The only sure way to know what works better is to try it. Note that some eBook publishing services have a very long delay in sales reporting, and that some aggregators have a significant delay in distributing the eBook to various eReaders. For this reason, your eBook could be selling well through a variety of outlets and you might not even know it for a couple of months. Just because you don't see sales initially doesn't mean that your eBook isn't (or won't be) selling.

Many authors who aren't satisfied with their eBook sales try switching their options. Some who try KDP Select for its benefits opt out after 90 or 180 days to try Nook, Kobo, Smashwords, and others. On the other hand, authors who first publish with Smashwords, but notice that most of their sales come from Kindle, often decide to try out KDP Select. However, note that there can sometimes be lengthy delays in getting eBooks successfully unpublished from some distribution channels. Amazon sometimes sends emails to authors stating that they are in violation of the KDP Select terms and conditions because their eBooks are still showing as available through one or more other retailers, whereas the authors had unpublished their eBooks from those channels. If this happens to you, first try politely responding to the email (or contact as directed in the email) to explain the situation. Also contact the service where you published the eBook about getting it unpublished.

Yet other authors start with KDP Select, then try to publish elsewhere, and finally return to KDP Select. Some authors claim that they sell mostly through Kindle, while others say that they sell many through Nook, Kobo, and Smashwords. Some claim that KDP Select's free promo days tend to bring them successful results within a few days, others state that it doesn't help them at all. Some authors receive many borrows through KDP Select, but many eBooks very rarely get borrowed (if ever). Again, the only way to know for sure is to try it out for yourself and see firsthand. This is why so many authors switch back-and-forth between these different eBook publishing services.

If you can find authors of eBooks that are very similar to yours – genre, price, length, style, etc. – who have tried both with and without KDP Select, then you may be fortunate enough to save yourself from the trials and tribulations of switching – you can then have some measure of confidence with your initial decision and choose to stick with it, whether it is for better or for worse.

7.2.3 Customer Book Reviews Other than Amazon

The vast majority of customers post their book reviews on Amazon. Very few customers post reviews at Barnes & Noble and other online booksellers' websites. Customers who buy most of their books from Barnes & Noble are far more likely to post reviews there. Barnes & Noble can sell your paperback if you have the Expanded Distribution and if they elect to include your book on their website, and they can sell a Nook edition of your eBook if you publish through Nook Press or an aggregator like Smashwords. Unless you have a strong sales rank at Barnes & Noble for a long period of time, it's unlikely that you'll get more than an occasional review there; you may not receive any. If you're not selling frequently at Barnes & Noble and other online booksellers, don't sweat the reviews – or any lack thereof – on their websites.

Next to Amazon, Goodreads tends to garner a large number of customer reviews. A few customers will post the same review on both Amazon and Goodreads, but many will just take the time to do one or the other. Don't ask a reviewer who posts a good review at Goodreads to also post it at Amazon; it looks tacky and unprofessional – you don't want to appear needy. As mentioned in Sec. 6.2.5, don't comment on any reviews at Goodreads. Don't invade any customer space there – like customer forums discussing books and authors.

Goodreads has a reputation for very strict "review police" and "author behavior police." Many customers at Goodreads absolutely do not like to have their space invaded and feel strongly that authors should not comment on reviews. Defensive comments, appearing needy, taking reviews personally, making requests of reviewers, and especially accusing reviewers of anything – these things can bring responses from the "review police" in swarms, and they may post on Amazon in addition to Goodreads. Many of the Goodreads customers also frequent the Amazon customer forums, KDP community forums, review books on Amazon, and visit several other places online. It's very important to always behave professionally with your author image in mind, remembering that it's at stake anytime you post any information online (even on your own blog). Don't say bad things about reviews or reviewers. Don't get involved in discussions with reviewers. Only *your* reputation is at stake.

Occasional reviews will be bad: It's a fact of life as an author that we must deal with. Customers are entitled to their opinions. Some bad reviews help us grow as writers. Don't react emotionally (you will feel some strong emotions, just don't let those emotions cause action or written words). Don't take it personally – they reviewed the book, not you. Try to wear a thick skin and hope that there are many good reviews to balance occasional bad ones.

There are small customer groups on Goodreads that identify authors and their books who they believe have "misbehaved." Sometimes, you can get on this list just by association – maybe you said something to another author who got on this list, whom you don't even know. Don't try to discover these groups. How you might discover them is when someone sends you a message to let you know that you and/or your book have been mentioned in one of these groups. This message tempts you into making a grave mistake. Don't go there! No customers are going to discover your name or book in that small group. But if you post there, your posts will show up on your author page at Goodreads along with all of the group's responses, which can destroy your credibility and image as an author.

Anything that you post anywhere on Goodreads – and anything that you simply vote on – shows up on your author page at Goodreads. Don't do or vote on anything or rate any books or write any reviews or vote on any reviews that in any way can be construed as being negative by any potential customers.

An interesting feature at Goodreads is that customers can rate books without reviewing books. When customers rate a book, they give it 1 to 5 stars. When customers review a book, they write comments about what they did or didn't like. On Amazon, customers must do both; on Goodreads, customers may rate a book without writing a review. This is kind of neat because some customers don't know what to say or don't want to take the time to write a review, but are willing to rate the book.

Customers can also mark books as to-read on Goodreads, which shows you if there is some future interest in your books. Don't thank customers for marking your book as to-read – again, this looks tacky, unprofessional, and needy.

Another place where you might see reviews of your book is on blogs (see Sec. 8.1.15).

Chapter 8

Marketing Strategies

Chapter Overview

8.1 Low-Cost Marketing Ideas
8.2 Other Marketing Options

This chapter answers questions about the following topics, and more:

☑ The importance of marketing, and why every author has to do it.
☑ Marketing that every author should be doing prior to publishing.
☑ Simple things everyone can easily do to market their books.
☑ Free ways to market your book and eBook.
☑ The importance of positive feedback.
☑ Effectively marketing through discovery instead of self-promotion.
☑ Techniques to brand your book's image and your author image.
☑ Identifying and reaching your target audience.
☑ Friends, family, acquaintances, and word-of-mouth publicity.
☑ Preparing a professional press release package.
☑ Taking advantage of free media coverage.
☑ Book signing, seminars, and other social marketing strategies.
☑ Contacting local bookstores that feature local authors.
☑ Selling your paperback book directly.
☑ A few Amazon[23] programs that relate to marketing.

---

[23] Amazon™ and CreateSpace are trademarks and brands of their respective owners. Neither this book, *A Detailed Guide to Self-Publishing with Amazon and Other Online Booksellers*, nor its author, Chris McMullen, are in any way affiliated with any of these companies.

8.1 Low-Cost Marketing Ideas

8.1.1 Why Marketing Is Necessary for All Authors

I T'S SIMPLY A MATTER of numbers. With millions of books to choose from and thousands of new books released every day, your book is just another faint star in the sky. Just a small percentage of customers buy their books after searching for keywords online. Most books are bought from customers browsing bestseller lists or specifically for the title or author – as should be expected, since the popular authors and bestsellers account for a huge fraction of book sales. Many customers buy books because of promotional discounts or giveaways. Amazon's Customers Also Bought marketing tool attracts a significant number of customers. Only a few books per hundred are purchased through online searches.

These online searches are very significant though because of the very large number of books purchased. But there are also millions of books available, which is why the vast majority of books sell only a few copies per month (or less). Out of millions of books, only the top hundred thousand or so average about a sale per day.

Unfortunately, books just don't sell themselves. Let's consider the life of an unmarketed book. When it's first published, it's at the bottom of the pack both in its category and in keyword searches. Sure, the Last 30 Days filter helps a little, but there are thousands of other books in this category, many of which have developed great sales ranks and have received some good reviews because of effective marketing. Those books are far more likely to be discovered than an unmarketed book. The unmarketed book sells very little, so it's sales rank – once it acquires one – quickly rises up to the millions, which adversely affects its visibility. It hasn't sold enough for the Customers Also Bought lists to help it out.

The successfully marketed book, on the other hand, sells many times when it's released, giving it a healthy sales rank, which aids its visibility and helps create an early Customers Also Bought list. It may have a few early reviews earned through advanced review copies. Not all of these reviews may be good reviews, but it's better than no reviews. The effectively marketed book is selling frequently and generating new reviews through those sales. Buzz has been growing since before the book's launch and word-of-mouth sales are helping its sales along. If it's very successful, it may reach one of the top 100 bestseller lists and receive great exposure.

It's a tale of two stories. If you want your book sales to be successful, you must help promote sales through effective marketing, and the sooner you begin this, the better. Amazon helps authors who help themselves: The more you perfect your book prior to publishing and the greater you stimulate sales through effective marketing, the more Amazon's Customer Also Bought and top 100 bestseller lists may reward your efforts. Amazon gives every book a chance, but the odds are highly uneven: Unmarketed books have very slim chances, while effectively marketed books are the clear favorites.

Even traditionally published authors must market their own books. Publishers mainly help with editing, typesetting, formatting, sending out advance review copies, and including the books in their catalogs, but still expect authors to do much marketing on their own. In fact, publishers expect this – and may contract for it – because they know that they won't sell enough books unless the author is willing to follow through with effective marketing. Many writers are becoming self-publishers not just to avoid the countless rejection letters that are typically involved in the hunt for a traditional publisher, but because they are still going to have to do the marketing themselves anyway. Authors who have highly successful marketing skills are desired by publishers, but these authors can just as well market their own self-published books – and that's what many of them are now doing.

8.1.2 Effective Marketing Isn't an Afterthought

Hopeful authors who just throw their books out there to see what happens are almost always very disappointed: not much happens. After seeing firsthand that books don't sell themselves, they begin to realize that everybody may have been right – indeed, marketing skills might be required to sell books. **By then, it's too late!** They have missed the golden opportunity. Once the sales rank has risen very high, it counts against the book's favor – it becomes more and more challenging to rebound from this history of poor sales.

Starting off with a strong sales rank gives your book its best chance of success. This gives your book greater visibility, improves your prospects for getting early reviews, and helps to quickly generate Customer Also Bought lists. Also, a great start can lead to increased exposure on the top 100 bestseller lists.

Marketing is something that should begin before the book is published – when the book is still being written. There is a great deal that you can do for <u>free</u>:

➢ Utilize the ideas described in Sec. 8.1.7 to generate "buzz" for your upcoming book both in person and through social media.

➢ People like to buy books from authors whom they've personally interacted with – in person or online. Let them discover that you're a writer, rather than advertising this openly. Many people should be aware of your writing before you ever publish.

➢ Let others see your passion for your writing. This increases their interest in your book.

➢ Get feedback on your cover, title, and blurb before you publish. This not only lets you see how people react firsthand, but also helps to create interest in your book.

➢ Think about what is special about your book – such as extra time spent doing research or multiple revisions from a professional editor – and let this slip naturally in conversations once in a while (don't overdo it).

➢ Don't talk about your book every time that you interact with friends and acquaintances or you'll be tuned out. Rather, let them inquire about your book.

➢ Use Amazon Advantage to enable preorders of your paperback (see Sec. 7.1.8). This can give your book a headstart in sales rank and Customer Also Bought associations.

➢ Send out advance review copies via Goodreads or relevant blogs, for example, to help improve your chances of earning a few early reviews.

➢ Perfect your cover before your book is published because it's a valuable marketing tool. It can attract attention and signify the genre with a relevant, striking image. A memorable cover makes it easier to recognize and describe to others.

➢ Write a killer blurb and perfect the Look Inside before you publish because these can have a profound influence on sales.

➢ Perfect your editing, formatting, and storyline before you publish. If people love your book and the writing, they are far more likely to leave good reviews and recommend your book to others by word-of-mouth.

➢ Develop your websites and post relevant content there before you publish your book.

➢ Start your blog and gain a small following before you publish. Post content relevant to your book and genre that will help attract customers and also interest fans. You don't want readers who enjoy your book to visit your blog only to find it mostly empty.

➢ Setup your social medial (Facebook, Twitter, etc.) with relevant content prior to publishing. Your friends, family, and acquaintances can help you generate early sales.

➢ Setup fan, book, author, and/or imprint pages at Facebook. Fans who go to your author pages should find fresh material. Your preexisting fan base may give you some early sales and a few early reviews.

➢ Don't tackle more than you can handle. Definitely, create online webpages or sites that require very little maintenance. However, for things that require you to make regular content (blog, Twitter, Facebook, etc.), you need to budget your time wisely because these are commitments that you are making to your readers.

➢ Use the same author image and logo everywhere to help with brand recognition.

➢ Choose an imprint before you publish and develop a website (free, perhaps) to help lend it some credibility.

➢ Setup your AuthorCentral and Goodreads author pages.

➢ Develop a marketing plan in three stages – before, during, and after publication.

8.1.3 Marketing Is Different from Advertising and Salesmanship

Many self-published authors often fear marketing because they believe they lack the skills of a salesman and the motivation to sell and advertise. But marketing is different from advertising and salesmanship. In fact, direct advertising – especially, outright self-promotion – and direct persuasion don't tend to generate book sales. Advertising and persuasion may sell cars, but they don't tend to sell books. Marketing is more subtle and can be far more effective.

Effective book marketing has more to do with discovery and branding. If a stranger walks into a room and says, "Hey, I just published a book. You should go check it out," most people will think, "Great. Another salesman telling me what I need to buy." The same is true even in an online forum. If a writer posts, "I just published a book. Here's the link for it," in an online forum, such self-promotion does <u>not</u> tend to sell books. That's because most people don't like self-promotion, and it's not permitted in many online forums where people interact. Marketing isn't about self-promotion.

Discovery tends to be more effective. Consider the following two scenarios. (A) One person walks up to you and says, "I just wrote a book and now I need to find people to read it." (B) Another person comes to sit near you, a conversation begins, and because you enjoy the interaction, you each inquire about what the other does for a living. You discover that you've just met a writer. In which case are you more likely to check out the book? With the vast majority of people, the correct answer is (B).

People like to read books by authors whom they have personally interacted with. People who have read hundreds of books sometimes don't know any of the authors, which makes the occasion special when you can read a book by an author you've actually met. People are more likely to know a few authors in this age of self-publishing, but out of every hundred books read, knowing a few of the authors is still a treat. Don't think self-promotion. Think discovery.

Just as marketing is often confused to mean self-promotion rather than discovery, advertising is often misinterpreted. Many people believe that commercials work like this: A company says, "This is our product and you should buy it because it's the best," and that this works because millions of people are foolish enough to listen to it, march right out to the store, and buy the product. Advertisements actually make very few (if any) sales this way.

The reason that advertising is successful has to do with branding, and not because people are foolish enough to listen to instructions about which product is better or that you should buy a particular product the next time you're at the store. (Okay, maybe they do make a few sales this way, but that's not how *most* of the sales occur.) The main goal of commercials and other advertisements is to get as many people from the target audience as possible to remember and recognize the brand. Companies strive to build brand recognition, not to generate direct sales. Advertisers know that brand recognition results in indirect sales. Such indirect sales are plentiful and long-lasting when the advertising is successful.

I'm not suggesting that you spend money on advertising. You can create a similar effect for <u>free</u>. I want you to understand the true nature of advertising, and to see how this fits in with the marketing suggestions of this chapter. You want to brand your image as an author, using a variety of free techniques, so that readers in your target audience remember and recognize you and your book(s). Paying for advertisements may not be effective for book sales, but there is no reason to pay for it when you can do this for free. Some writers wish that they could "buy" their way out of marketing by just paying for advertisements, but doing the work and marketing with free methods tends to be more effective.

Here is an example of how advertising works, which you may be able to relate to (it doesn't involve books). Imagine that you're in the grocery store buying detergent, and you're looking at two similar products. You've heard of detergent A, but not detergent B. Which one will you buy? Very many people will go with detergent A, simply because they recognize the brand. Most aren't buying it because a commercial said that it was better; most aren't buying it because a commercial told them to run down to the store and buy it; most are simply buying a product that they recognize. A brand name is a brand that customers recognize.

Sure, some people will buy the cheaper product to save money. Others will buy the expensive product hoping to get what they pay for. A rare customer will actually do research to see what others have to say about it. But if they're buying online, many customers will check out customer product reviews. Not everybody makes purchase decisions the same way. Nevertheless, successful branding does influence a very large number of consumers.

The same holds true for books. If you can get members of your target audience to see your cover, read your title, hear your name, and/or view your author picture multiple times, this helps to brand your book and image as an author.

Let's consider a second non-book example of marketing, which involves more than just advertising. Suppose that you decide to buy or sell a home. Which realtor will you choose? Most people will choose a realty company that they've heard of, which relates to company branding, or an agent whom they know, which relates to discovery and/or person branding. If you've ever met a real estate agent socially who made a nice impression during your brief encounter, this may greatly influence your decision. This is the discovery method that we discussed earlier in this section; you discovered that this person sold homes during a conversation. This gives the small hometown realtor a chance against the major brands. Similarly, discovery, branding, and marketing give self-published authors a chance to sell books alongside popular authors and major publishing houses. These are your most valuable tools, and they're free; you just have to learn to use them effectively.

Some people may choose a specific agent whom they haven't even met. Maybe they recognize the name and photo of the realtor from signs, posters, business cards, ads, etc. Authors can similarly brand without personal contact. Readers may recognize your photo, title, or book cover from your website, blog, and other online activities (e.g. maybe clicking on your profile somewhere). The more visible you are – in a positive way – among your target audience (not just anybody with eyes), the greater such discovery may impact your sales.

Another way that you might select a specific realty company or a particular agent is by word-of-mouth recommendations. If any friends or family members, for example, personally recommend a realty company or agent they've done business with before, this may have a very significant influence on your decision. The better job they do, the greater the prospects for receiving word-of-mouth recommendations. This can have a very significant impact on book sales, too. The way to achieve this is to have a great story that's perfected as much from the front cover to the back, and then to get a large number of customers to read it.

Discovery, branding, and word-of-mouth are three major methods of marketing books that relate to marketing and advertising techniques that big businesses use. These are the main ideas, but there are several specifics – which we will explore in this chapter. We can also relate many of the specifics to big business marketing.

For example, authors should devise a hook for their books, which works sort of like a catchy slogan. The hook is a very short sentence that's easy to remember, which helps stir interest in your book. It should tell something about your book so that your target audience will recognize the genre. If mystery readers hear a hook for a mystery book, but can't tell that it's a mystery, for example, then the hook won't be as effective. A highly effective hook will also create interest in reading the book.

Another similarity is the use of a product name that's very easy to spell and remember. What brands come to mind? Coke, Sony, Levi's. Similarly, a book title should be short (two to three words), easy to spell and remember, and relate to the genre and content.

8.1.4 Ways that Marketing Can Be Ineffective or Even Backfire

There are several different ways that marketing can be ineffective. This is very important, and not all of it is obvious – otherwise, there wouldn't be nearly as many books suffering from such ineffective marketing. In addition to discussing how marketing can be ineffective – even when the marketing techniques employed are often highly effective – we'll learn how to avoid mistakes that can make normally sound marketing decisions produce poor results.

The last thing you want is to successfully market hundreds of people to your book, but have most of the potential customers decide not to buy your book – or purchase the book only to return it shortly afterward. If you get people interested in checking your book out, you want to close the deal, and then you want them to keep the book once they have it.

What determines whether people will buy your book once they find it?

➢ A lousy cover says, "This author didn't put much effort into the book, and didn't seek feedback from others to learn what suits his/her target audience."

➢ Suppose that the cover looks like a great sci-fi book, but it's really a fantasy. The readers who are attracted to the cover think, "That's not what I was looking for."

➢ If the blurb contains mistakes, this doesn't bode well for the content. The same goes for the Look Inside. Proofreading or formatting mistakes can blow the deal.

➢ Does your blurb create interest in your book without giving too much away? Does the blurb seem like a good fit for your target audience? A great blurb helps to stimulate sales; a lousy blurb may inhibit your marketing efforts.

➢ The Look Inside should look professional and the beginning of the book should create interest in the book. Wise customers try the Look Inside before buying the book. If the sample impresses them, they buy it; if it's just so-so, they're more likely to pass on it.

What determines whether people will keep your book after they purchase it?

> ➢ They enjoy the first part of the book (more than just the Look Inside). For fiction, the story must engage their interest. For nonfiction, they must appreciate the information and the way that it is presented.

> ➢ The content is what the reader was expecting. Prospective customers have some idea of what they expect the book to be about based on the title, cover, and blurb. If they begin reading the book and it doesn't seem to agree with these expectations, they are likely to abandon their efforts.

> ➢ The book is well-edited and well-formatted. When people invest money in a product, they expect to receive something that appears professional. For a book, this means that it should be well-written and visually appealing.

After customers read the entire book, you want them to recommend it. They might recommend it in a customer review, by word-of-mouth to friends, family, or acquaintances, or even online (e.g. at a blog or website). The customer has to feel strongly to recommend a book. Most readers don't recommend a book; only a fraction do. Customers who dislike a book, however, are more likely to post a bad review. Marketing is most successful when most customers enjoy the book and when a significant percentage of the customers recommend it to others, while marketing is ineffective when few customers enjoy the book and a significant percentage dislike it strongly. Following are some factors involved in customer reactions:

> ➢ Customers who love it or hate it are most likely to leave a review. If they enjoy it or dislike it mildly, or if they feel indifferently about it, they are less likely to review it.

> ➢ Only customers who love some aspect of the book are likely to recommend it to others. Even then, it must be well-formatted, well-edited, and suitable for the people they recommend it to; they're unlikely to recommend books that seem unprofessional.

> ➢ For fiction, memorable characters, scenes that evoke strong emotions, and great plots tend to generate more reviews and recommendations. For nonfiction, useful content and clear explanations achieve this. For either, a wonderful way with words can leave a good impression.

> ➢ There are also genre-specific issues. Readers in each genre have certain expectations and if you violate these unspoken rules, it could have a very negative impact on sales. For example, an action thriller should have a fast pace and a romance should have a happy ending. Protagonists shouldn't have character traits that upset the readers.

> ➢ Controversial books are more likely to be reviewed. In this case, the reviews are likely to be mixed with both very good and very bad reviews.

Self-publishers tend to make titles that sound good to them, covers that have images that mean something to the author, and other styles that they appreciate. But you're not selling the book to yourself! Take the time to find out how others – especially, strangers in your target audience – will react to your book. Don't just go with a minority of reactions that happen to agree with what you wanted to hear. Listen to things that you hear repeated, even if you disagree with them. The difference between selling just a few books or selling very many books can often be something simple in the title or cover that makes the book less or more appealing to your target audience.

I've seen many authors solicit feedback on their title, cover, and blurb after a few months of slow sales, only to discover that something – an image on the cover that didn't seem to fit, colors that didn't work well together, etc. – was putting people off. It's especially common for the author to be partial to an image that really doesn't belong on the cover – and to be quite stubborn about it. For example, the story might involve a ring, which at some point becomes important in the story, but only the author knows this. Unless the title mentions a ring, this ring just confuses prospective readers. Consistency and unity among the title, cover, and blurb – and signifying the right genre and content – are far more significant than most indie authors tend to realize. Inconsistency there can be a sales deterrent.

There are also some other important ways that marketing can be ineffective. One major problem that can arise is a target audience mismatch. If your marketing efforts are attracting mostly adult romance readers, for example, but your book is actually a teen romance, many of the customers who check out your book may pass on it. The first step in effective marketing is to identify, as precisely as possible, your main target audience. Then you gear your marketing efforts toward that specific audience. The title, cover, blurb, and Look Inside need to send a unified message about the genre and content so that the same audience who comes to check out the book feels that the book is a good fit for them. This is another reason why it's so important to invest the time to get representative people from your target audience to offer you opinions on your title, cover, blurb, first chapter, and even the entire book. Companies use a focus group in their marketing efforts for this very reason.

One of the worst things that can happen is that hundreds of people buy the book, but then find a glaring mistake that you missed. Almost all books have a few minor mistakes. What I'm talking about is a major mistake that would ruin the book (and your image). A misspelled word in the title, grammatical mistake in the title, misspelled author name, major formatting mistake inside the book, or a major problem in the appearance of a key picture, for example, can produce a very negative reaction from customers who order your book. It's critical to catch all major problems before you publish your book. Scrutinize your printed proofs and eBook previews very carefully. There are a few horror stories circulating the internet from authors who delivered hundreds of books with major mistakes that they missed prior to publication. Don't let that happen to you.

If you succeed in generating much buzz for your book, resulting in a large number of preorders or early sales, it becomes even more crucial that the book be free of major issues.

Perhaps the most common marketing mistake – aside from not marketing at all – is to only do what the author feels most comfortable doing or to only do what seems easiest. For example, many authors mainly market through Facebook and Twitter. Social media is great for generating early sales among your friends, family, and acquaintances, and for early sales and reviews among your established fan base for your subsequent books. You can also reach some new readers using hashtags, for example. But social media is very limited in its ability to attract new members of your target audience, so if this is the only thing that you do, your marketing efforts are not likely to yield long-lasting success.

Just browsing through this chapter, you will find a wide variety of ideas that you can use to market your book. If you decide not to utilize all of these ideas, don't simply discard those that fall outside of your comfort zone and don't simply look for those few that seem like they might involve the least amount of work. Instead, try to determine which of these ideas are likely to be most effective in driving your specific target audience to your specific book. Some strategies work better for some kinds of books than for others. You definitely want to apply the techniques that are likely to be most effective for your book. The only reason that you should discard an idea is if you have good reason to believe that it won't be effective for your particular book. Unfortunately, most authors choose based on what's easiest and most comfortable for them. Or maybe I should say "fortunately," since having fewer people do what's most effective leaves the door wide open for those who choose to do it. Get out of your shell and market in ways that you don't prefer – it could make a big difference in sales.

Another common mistake is giving up with marketing efforts prematurely. Marketing involves work. Writing is the kind of work that authors like to do; marketing isn't. So when we begin marketing, we want to see results. It's easy to use the lack of quick results as an excuse to stop doing this work – marketing – that we didn't want to do in the first place.

Unfortunately, marketing doesn't always pay immediate rewards. Branding, for example, can be a long-term process. Branding takes repetition – so first people in your target audience need to see your cover and photo, hear your name, and read your title a few times over a period of months. Then they're not likely to be in the market for their next book in your genre immediately. Branding pays off when they finally get around to looking for a book like yours, which can be several months down the road. It's the same way with advertising on television: We get branded over a period of months, then several months after that when we're making a purchase decision in the store, the branding may finally make a difference.

One of the best marketing tools is often hidden and very slow to develop: this is word-of-mouth sales. First, customers have to find your book. They might not buy it when they first find it. When they finally do buy it, they need to read it. The might not read it as soon as they buy it. When they finally start reading it, they need to finish it. This might take many months. Most readers aren't going to recommend your book to others until they finish reading it themselves. It can take several months before a significant number of people have read your book, at which point – if your book is very good – they may recommend it to others. Don't get discouraged if you don't see early results. Keep marketing actively and your patience may pay off down the road. Continued marketing is essential to long-term success. Don't give up!

Marketing doesn't supply instant satisfaction. You must be very patient. It can take a year before consistent marketing efforts really begin to pay off. If you give up prematurely, you may never fully realize the fruits of your early efforts. Don't give up; keep at it. Focus on your next book and the prospects for the first book helping the second book. Visualizing positive success in the future can help you be patient with your marketing efforts.

The way that you market can also impact its effectiveness. As discussed in Sec. 8.1.3, self-promotion tends to be highly ineffective, whereas branding and discovery tend to be more effective. Similarly, with social media and blogs, posting about yourself and your book tends to be less effective, whereas posting useful content tends to be more effective. No more than 10% of your posts should be geared toward yourself, your own book, or your own websites; in fact, you needn't do this at all since anyone who is interested in learning more about you, your book, or other websites can find such information on your profile or end-of-posts.

A marketing tactic that can backfire is making a book sound far better than it really is. Making a book sound like the best book ever loses customers two ways. First, potential customers often avoid books where the blurb or author brag about how great it is. They're skeptical: If the book is great, this should be easy to see on its own merit, so there shouldn't be any need to boast. Let readers discover how good it is and judge this for themselves. Secondly, customers who do read the book are very likely to be disappointed that the book isn't the <u>best</u> book ever written. Don't create expectations that are impossible to fulfill.

On the other extreme, you can't sell many books if you lack confidence in yourself. If you make statements like, "My book probably isn't very good," you might draw a little sympathy, but most people are going to think, "Well, if you don't believe in your own work, it must not be worth reading." Somewhere there is a fine line: You need to show confidence, but don't sound boastful. Your confidence and passion for your work help to create interest in your work, but any bragging tends to detract from it.

Let me conclude this section with the bad news: Not all book ideas can be good sellers, and not all writing styles make for good reading. Marketing has its inherent limitations. For marketing to be successful, the first step is to develop a book idea that has good potential, perfect the book cover to cover, and have a writing style that will appeal to many readers. If any of this is a significant problem, no amount of marketing can offer you long-term success.

With that said, you must show confidence in your book. Don't worry that it might not pay off. Worry and doubt don't help at all. Instead, worry and doubt affect your attitude and mood, hampering your ability to successfully market your book. You must believe in your book wholeheartedly. If you can't sell your book to yourself, you definitely can't sell it to others. Remember, show confidence, but don't boast.

Let prospective readers see your passion for your book and your passion for writing, and your confidence but not your ego. Your image as an author is very important toward your success. Be knowledgeable, trustworthy, and professional. Behave like someone who may write such a book as yours to establish credibility as a writer.

8.1.5 How to Motivate Yourself to Market Diligently

Most authors easily motivate themselves to write because they either enjoy the topic that they're writing about or the art of writing itself (or both). However, most writers feel that it is quite challenging to motivate themselves to market. I will try to convince you that this is not logical – that authors who are motivated to write should be equally motivated to market their books when they finish writing.

Writers tend to look at marketing as persuasion and salesmanship. They see writing as an art, but book sales as a business. Most authors love the artistic elements that they see in writing, but not the business side of writing – well, selling books and earning royalties they appreciate, but striving to earn this through marketing they don't.

Let's look at the business perspective for a moment. Don't worry, you don't have to become a business person to sell books. I'm not trying to convince you to think like a business person. I'm not suggesting that you gear your writing toward money. It is, however, useful to see how the business-minded person approaches writing because business-minded people are often successful at marketing. Have a little patience and I will try to show you how you may become successful at marketing without thinking like a business person. But – like it or not – we're going to look at the business model first. Then we'll modify it significantly for writing.

Editors and publishers often see the business side of writing more than the artistic side. Those who favor the view that writing is a business tend to be successful marketers. The business-minded writer doesn't want to waste his/her time writing. The first thing he/she does is research: Which books are already on the market, which are selling well, what kinds of book does he/she have the expertise to write, of these is there a need that he/she can fill, what large potential target audience can he/she reach, what kind of writing will appeal to this audience, and what is most likely to sell well?[24] This person is writing to sell and everything revolves around how to sell books beginning with the writing. Since this person is motivated to sell, marketing comes very naturally. The business person uses his/her passion to sell in order to motivate himself/herself to write.

If you're not a business-minded individual, what you have to do is invert this: Use your passion for your writing to motivate yourself to market your books.

It's simple, really. You infused your passion into your book, and now you wish to share it with others. If you're passionate about your writing, then you must develop a passion for sharing it, which means that you must be passionate about marketing it – for that's how it will be successfully shared. If you can't get passionate enough about your very own writing to feel that it's worth sharing with others, why on earth should others want to read your writing? Use this to motivate yourself to market your book. Let your passion for your work show.

---

[24] When an editor looks at a query letter and book proposal, they're thinking about the business side of writing. Editors want to find books that were written to sell because publishers are businesses that sell books. One great thing about self-publishing is that the non-business-minded author can succeed without giving in to this mindset.

Passion is the secret ingredient that can bring writers and readers together. Readers want to read books (in genres that they enjoy reading) which are written with passion by authors who are passionate about their work. Which writers have so much passion for their work? Those authors who actively market their books, whose sense of passion shows – not those who advertise their passion overtly, but those whose passion is implicitly, yet clearly, present.

From the reader's point of view, authors who don't market their books must feel that their books are lacking in some way or must not have passion for their work. Why else would they be so reluctant to share their books with the world, if not for some inherent problem? Therefore, you must first perfect your book in order to convince yourself that it is ready to be shared with the world, and then when you believe in your own book, you must market diligently in order to share your book. You must also be passionate about your work within. First convince yourself that your book is worth sharing. If you cannot do this, then why should anyone else want you to share it with them?

But don't go overboard expressing your passion. Boasting, bragging, and overconfidence tend to turn readers off. They want to discover your passion – not have it thrust upon them. You want your passion for your writing to show without overdoing it. Let others inquire about your work, then show your passion as you discuss it. This way, they are discovering it. Don't tell others what to think – e.g., "This book is the best," "It will make you cry," etc. Bragging like this doesn't allow others to discover it for themselves. Statements of the form, "Oh yeah, when an idea hits, I just can't stop writing," don't tell others what to think, while conveying your sense of passion and dedication.

Also, don't let your passion for your writing let you take criticism or negative reviews personally. When it comes to criticism, you must wear a thick skin and keep your passion in check. They are reviewing your work – which you are very passionate about – but not you personally. While you love your writing, not everybody will. You just have to accept this. Although you have passion for your book, you can't afford to react emotionally or this will quickly ruin your reputation and credibility as a writer. The trick is to use passion to motivate yourself to market and create interest among potential readers, without letting your passion show in boasts, overconfidence, or difficulty receiving criticism.

Why must you market your book? You published your book, so it's available. Isn't this sharing, since others can now read it? Why can't people discover your book this way? If my book is good, won't people realize it and spread the word? Why should you have to sell a great book? Shouldn't great books sell simply because they're great? These are thoughts that most new self-publishers wonder. If you have similar questions, perhaps you can use one or more of the following answers to continually remind yourself why you need to market:

➢ There are millions of books out there, and thousands of new books released every day. How will people find your book if you don't market it?
➢ For the author who wonders why he/she must market his/her book, the reader is wondering why the author doesn't care enough about his/her book to market it.

- ➢ No sales rank or poor sales rank suggests to the reader that the book isn't very good. While you wait for your book to be discovered amongst millions, the low frequency of sales will have a long-lasting effect on your sales rank.
- ➢ Nobody will know if you're book is great until it's discovered. Without marketing, it will be buried in the search results. This means that it may take months or years for the book to get any attention, and by then it will be too late to overcome its slow start.

Some self-published authors may be able to let traditional publishers fuel part of their motivation. Until recently, big publishing houses have been deciding what people can read. Self-publishing provides freedom and opportunity for both authors and readers. Some writers have a stack of rejection letters from publishers that they use for motivation. Others draw motivation from the hope of succeeding without publishing traditionally. Another option is to let the freedom that self-publishing provides fuel part of your motivation.

Self-publishing doesn't tend to reward laziness. Writing successfully is hard work. Success takes a great idea, months of writing, months of editing and formatting, honest feedback, and effective marketing. Even if you publish traditionally, you still need a great idea, months of writing, and effective marketing – and you may have a contract for marketing expectations. Publishers require authors to market their own books, knowing that this hard work is what it takes to be a successful writer. If traditional publishers need their authors to market their work in order for sales to be a success, it's even more important for self-publishers. The more that you realize how important marketing is (without having to learn this the hard way, hopefully), the more diligent you are likely to be in your marketing efforts.

Once you start marketing, you must be patient and constantly remind yourself that continued marketing is essential if you're to sustain long-term success. Resist the urge to give up. Keep marketing. Don't let early results fool you: If sales start with a bang, that doesn't mean that you can slack off; and if sales start out slow, you must keep marketing in order to give your book a chance. Remember, it can take a year for your marketing efforts to fully pay off. Branding takes months. Word-of-mouth referrals can be especially slow in coming. Keep marketing to give your book its best possible chance.

Visualize a positive future for your book sales. Keep up your marketing in an effort to achieve this positive outcome. You must work toward it; sales won't just come to you. Focus on writing your next book. Working diligently on your marketing and writing your next book help to keep your mind off sales and reviews. Sales tend to fluctuate, so anytime they seem to be slipping, it can be agonizing; and reviews are sometimes critical. Instead of focusing on sales and reviews – or worse, responding to reviews – devote your mind to your marketing campaign and to writing your next book.

Think about the prospects for your next book improving sales of your first book. This will give you something to hope for and to work toward. It may help you exercise patience, keep your mind off of numbers and reviews, and help you stay positive. ☺

Another thing you can do to try and stay positive is to keep track of milestones. This can be fun and give you something to look forward to, whether you just notice it and enjoy it for a moment or keep a scrapbook. Here is a sample of some milestones that you can look for:

- ✓ Your first sale. Heck, you could even buy it yourself and frame it.
- ✓ When you sell your 10th, 100th, 1000th, etc. book (paperback and eBook, separately).
- ✓ When you first make $100, $1000, etc. overall (i.e. not just in one month).
- ✓ The first time that you make $100, $200, $300, etc. in royalties in one month. Fourth quarter sales may help you show improvement; so can releasing your next book.
- ✓ The first time that you sell 100, 200, 300, etc. books in one month.
- ✓ Also keep track of annual totals for both royalties and sales; try to improve each year.
- ✓ When your sales rank first cracks 200,000, 100,000, 50,000, 20,000, 10,000, etc. I have screenshots from a few of my books the first time that they cracked 5,000, and several other authors have done the same (because it doesn't always last long).
- ✓ Your first good review and your first five-star review.
- ✓ The first time a fan contacts you to say something nice about your book.
- ✓ When you sign your first autograph.

The best thing about these milestones is that no matter how good or poor your sales are, there is always something to look forward to – i.e. there is always a way to improve. On the other hand, your happiness can't depend upon reaching the next milestone, otherwise you will never be happy. Use the next milestone to help you revamp your marketing efforts.

8.1.6 Branding Your Author Image

As described in Sec. 8.1.3, branding is largely about recognition. The more you see and hear a brand name – like Heinz, Skechers, and Dell – the more you are likely to recognize it. Branding isn't about getting people to go out and purchase a product immediately. Rather, the idea is that if people recognize the brand from having seen and heard it enough, this may influence their purchase decision when they eventually shop for such a product. It can take months for branding to take effect, and many more months before customers are searching for such a product. This is the case with books. Branding doesn't bring immediate results, yet it can be a very powerful tool: When most customers are buying a product in the store, they very often choose a brand that they've heard before.

Branding a book or author isn't quite the same as branding laundry detergent or soda, but – as we will see – there are many close parallels. One of the main differences is that paid advertising probably won't be as effective for branding books. For one, everybody buys laundry detergent, but not everybody reads books similar to yours (yes, almost everyone does read books – but they read many different kinds of books – whereas any single laundry detergent is suitable for nearly anyone; also, there are millions of books for readers to choose from, but only a dozen or so laundry detergents – a huge difference in buyer-to-product ratio).

The similarities between branding a book or laundry detergent can help us apply common advertising methods to our books. For one, most brand names are very short and easy to spell and remember, like Nike, Timex, and Ford. Why? Because that makes it easy to remember, type in a search engine online, or refer to a friend. Would you like for your book to be easy to remember, type in a search on Amazon, or refer to friends and family? Then you should strive for a short title with three words or less, which is easy to spell and remember. It will be easier to remember if the title fits the genre and relates to the content. This is very common in traditionally published fiction.[25] Another advantage of short titles is that at the bottom of your email, blog posts, and online profiles, you can concisely say, Your Name, Author of X, Y, and Z. With a long title, you can just mention one book this way, instead of two or three.

Your cover plays a similar role in branding – the more people see the same cover, the more likely they are to recognize it. It might seem intuitive that if you had a wacky picture on your cover that would make it easier to recognize, but research suggests otherwise. Also, you don't just want your cover to get noticed by making it look zany – it needs to signify the genre and content, and it must look professional. The covers that work best for branding feature one striking, memorable image, where the title and cover send a consistent, unified message that relates to the genre and content. When the title, picture, genre, and content all easily relate to one another – without having to know anything about the book! – this makes the cover easier to remember. Unity is very important and too often ignored: Authors tend to favor cover images that mean something only to people who have read some of the book, but you're trying to sell the book to people who haven't yet read it. Keep this in mind.

Use the same book and author photos everywhere. Many authors make a temporary cover, feeling that it's better than nothing and that they can upgrade it later. When they change their covers, this hurts their branding efforts. It would be far better to perfect the cover prior to publishing. Similarly, post your same author image on all of your websites to help with branding your author image. There is a time issue – every few years you may need to update your author photo – but it should still be the same at all of your websites.

There is more to branding than just creating recognition. Companies want their brands to symbolize a particular trait – such as quality (like Sony), luxury (like Mercedes), or affordable (like K-Mart). One way that companies try to achieve this is with a catchy slogan. This helps people remember something about the brand. There is a similar tool that authors use with books: the hook. This is a short sentence that helps create interest in the book, and will give potential readers a glimpse of what to expect – something they will associate with the book.

---

[25] Perhaps I should have simply called this book *Self-Publishing with Amazon*. Titles are sometimes longer in nonfiction than in fiction, as a couple of additional words can help to match the content to a specific audience. In fiction, extra words usually hinder rather than help. For this book, the combined title and subtitle are too long. Even if you publish nonfiction, I recommend keeping this combination much shorter than mine.

Use your hook whenever you talk about your book in person. You can also use your hook at the end of a book reading. It's useful online, too – at the bottom of an email, blog post, or other online activity where you write your name and title (under that you can write the hook).

Companies also use a logo to help with branding. If you use your own imprint, you should develop some logo to put on your cover and copyright page, and anything else – such as a website – that is associated with the imprint. All of the books using the same imprint will feature the same logo.

Brand names establish status. You want your book to have status, too. Part of status is actually established with price. An underpriced book loses status – the price makes it seem cheap. Being way overpriced won't work, but a modest price may. The quality has to match. If people thumb through the book and it appears highly professional and if the book is very well-written, this signifies quality. However, a book with poor formatting or spelling and grammar mistakes won't command the higher price of a higher-quality book.

Some status comes by word of mouth. For example, if you list an editor by your name and readers are talking about how well-written your book is, while other authors are asking you if your editor may be interested in helping them – this greatly helps your status. Sir Arthur Conan Doyle had a different type of status with his protagonist, Sherlock Holmes. In fact, his sidekick, Dr. Watson, immensely helped build up Holmes's status as a super sleuth. In this case, the status is two-fold: a very memorable character and clever mysteries.

Another important part of branding is visibility. You need to get your target audience to see your book's title and cover along with your name and author photo in order for branding to take effect. Both discovery and branding require first identifying and then reaching your target audience. We'll discuss this in Sec.'s 8.1.9-10.

Branding the author's image is just as important as branding the book's image. Anything that you post online – including your biography and photo (see Sec. 6.1.3) – must help to reinforce your image as an author. You want to sound confident and knowledgeable, with a personality that relates to your book. All of your behavior must be professional.

Credibility takes much time to establish, but can be lost online in a heartbeat through forum clashes, arguments, rash behavior, controversial remarks, political comments, replies to reviews, etc. Don't risk your credibility by looking unprofessional. As explained in Sec. 7.1.6, perceived bad behavior by authors can lead to No votes and negative reviews, and sometimes a mob mentality develops when an author responds to reviews – especially, when done so emotionally, defensively, or repeatedly.

Maintaining good public relations is an important part of becoming a successful author. A single post anywhere online can destroy your author image. You must always be thinking about how each post may affect your brand as an author.

It's not always easy. Once you have several reviews, you are likely to have at least one critical review. If you attain success, some people will make accusations and try to show that you've done something wrong. You must wear a thick skin, avoid commenting on reviews, avoid complaining about bad reviews anywhere online, never get into an argument online, not behave defensively or react emotionally, and always behave professionally.

Branding occurs in person, online, and also through social media. Consider how you appear in your Facebook and Twitter activities. Posting bad things about negative reviews through social media, for example, hurts your reputation.

In addition to your own image, there is also the image of self-publishing in general to consider; both are important. On the one hand, the self-publishing industry has already been branded with some criticism (which indies have largely brought upon themselves), including:

- ☹ Authors who have abused the system with numerous fake five-star reviews for books that turned out to be not so good, giving malicious reviews to other books, getting into forum arguments, etc. Bad behavior doesn't just hurt your own image: it affects indies at large.
- ☹ Some websites that criticize indie covers.
- ☹ References to self-published books that were poorly written, edited, formatted, or thought out. Even if nobody reads them, the Look Inside of the worst books still affects the image of self-publishing.
- ☹ There is some criticism of free promo and 99-cent books cheapening the market – especially, those books that didn't turn out to be good.
- ☹ Very short books seem to be the new fashion – sometimes, just a chapter that's not even self-contained. Some authors are hoping to create interest by giving a short sample away for free; others are even just looking for feedback before completing their books.[26] Customers like to get their money's worth.

Unfortunately, there are even self-published authors who are contributing toward the negative image of self-publishing by frequently talking about the "slush pile" of poorly written and formatted indie books. The better the image of self-publishing, the more customers will be willing to buy self-published books. Similarly, the better the image of eBooks, Kindle, Amazon, or Smashwords – the more customers will be willing to buy these products.

Consider this: If you invest time and effort marketing your own books, while at the same time you're often disparaging other indie authors, eBooks, or eBook sellers, this is neutralizing your own marketing campaign. The better the image of self-publishing, the better for your own sales. If indie sales or eBook sales decline because this image declines, that hurts sales for all authors – not just those at the bottom. Fewer eReaders = fewer eBooks for everyone.

Everyone can help to improve the image of self-publishing:

- Don't disparage other indie authors or indie works.
- Don't complain about the slush pile, free promo books, or review abuse. Reminding people about these problems is negative advertising.

---

[26] You want your first impression to be a great impression. Don't publish material that's not ready for publishing, especially not just to get feedback. Go to a writer's forum and exchange feedback there.

- Strive to paint a positive picture for indies in your blog, conversations, etc.
- When you hear someone disparage indies, refer to the slush pile, etc., make a quick, positive, tactful, "Actually…" comment. Don't get in a debate, don't sound defensive. Just make one short, swift, positive statement and let it go.
- When someone asks you, "Don't you hate the effect that all of those lousy self-published books have on your image," politely and quickly refute this.
- Do your best to perfect the covers, editing, formatting, and stories of your own books.
- Once you have achieved mild success, occasionally lend a hand to help a newbie start out on the right foot and avoid some common mistakes.
- When your friends and acquaintances self-publish, give them honest feedback and help them improve their covers, blurbs, Look Insides, storylines, and writing.
- Bring attention to great indie covers, great indie books, and indie success stories.
- Recommend quality indie books to others.
- Don't give good reviews to lousy indie books. Do give good reviews to good indie books. Be careful what you say in any bad reviews of lousy indie books.

One thing we have going for us is strength in numbers. There are over a million self-published authors. Add to this number their friends, family, and acquaintances. Almost every-body knows somebody who is a self-published author. Together, we can help overcome this stigma and build a positive image for self-publishing. Discuss advantages of self-publishing, like not having an editor decide what we can read and artistic freedom for the author.

8.1.7 Creating Buzz for Your Book

The importance of marketing before your book is published – or even written – was stressed in Sec. 8.1.2, which listed several marketing techniques that you should be applying prior to publishing your book. Many of these help to generate "buzz" for your upcoming book – i.e. to get people talking (in person and online) about your book. This process should begin a couple of months prior to the release date, and you want to create buzz before, during, and after its release. This helps greatly in stimulating early sales and reviews, and gives your book the best possible start.

It should all begin when you first start writing your book. "What have you been up to?" Questions like this provide you an opportunity for friends, family, and acquaintances to discover that you're working on a book. Weeks later, they may ask, "So how's your book coming along?" This way, they can follow your progress.

The trick is to create interest in your book, but not to give too much away. The more you reveal about your book, the less they need to read to learn about it. Arouse curiosity. Don't answer every question – let them read it and find out. Also, let people ask you questions so that they can discover that you're writing a book, or look for opportunities to bring this up naturally – e.g. if it happens to relate to the conversation. Refrain from advertising out of the blue that you're written a book, as this doesn't tend to generate nearly as much interest as when people discover it.

Feedback is invaluable for two reasons: It provides you with a variety of opinions about things that people do and don't like (so if there is any feature that is widely disliked, you may improve your book's chances of success by correcting this prior to publishing) and helps create some buzz in the process.

As described in Sec.'s 5.1.1-2, you should separately solicit feedback on your title, cover, blurb, Look Inside, and even the book itself. Strangers in your target audience (who aren't yet fans) will most likely give you the most honest, relevant opinions. Friends and family are far more likely to be supportive, even if you feel that they are usually very critical. Don't rely on just friends and family to provide feedback. Besides, the more people who provide feedback, the more buzz you can generate.

Begin with family, friends, and acquaintances. If you happen to have a conversation with someone, you can pull out your title or cover, for example, and request a little feedback. Any busy (yet safe; bring a friend) place where soliciting isn't prohibited can help you solicit feedback from strangers in person. You can also post questions – including a link to your prospective cover – online at discussion forums (best if it includes your target audience), your blog, social media, and your website. (Remember, the fewer posts about you – like 10% or less – the better. Providing valuable content for your target audience helps to attract followers.)

You generally don't want the same person to offer feedback on everything at the same time. Start out with the title. First, show people your title and ask them what they think the book is about – if they can't guess, a better title is desirable. Also ask their opinion of your title, and any suggestions that they may have. Then show your cover. The better your cover is the first time you show it, the greater will be the effect – especially, if there is a striking image. The blurb requires some reading and thought, so opinions won't come in as quick and casual a setting as the title and blurb.

You need a few people who can provide good critiques to carefully comb through your Look Inside. Your goal is to make this immaculate – beautifully formatted, perfectly edited. You need to approximate the Look Inside and get this feedback before publishing. The first couple of paragraphs can be shared more widely. You want to know if the first couple of paragraphs hook the readers into the story.

A bigger challenge is getting some people to read your book – and not all at once, so you can make one set of revisions before seeking further help. Ideally, the first person to help with this would be an experienced editor, whose previous work (one way to verify this is if they are listed as the editor and you – or someone with great grammar skills – checks a sample of it) looks excellent. Most very well-written books have gone through a few separate edits. Don't rely on a single person to do all of the editing. A few close friends can help, too.

The more positive publicity your book gets prior to publishing, the more you may get people talking about your book before, during, and after its release. Do you know people who love to socialize? You want them to know about your book, so that if there is something about your book that they like (just the cover, perhaps; they don't necessarily need to read it), they might be more inclined to say something like, "Did you know that so-'n'-so is writing a book?"

Think about what makes your book special. You would like to find ways that people can discover this – i.e. without your prompting. Multiple edits might make it seem well-written, use of a professional formatting service might make people want to check out what it looks like, a couple of years doing research helps make you seem knowledgeable about the subject, sharing excerpts about a memorable character can get people discussing the characterization, a few people who've read the whole book can advertise if the storyline is excellent, etc. There are many things out of your control, but one thing in your control is what you say when you answer questions about your writing and what parts of your book you reveal to others. For the purpose of branding, if most people are describing just one or two main things that really make your book stand out, this helps with recognition. People have their own opinions and express ideas differently, so it won't just sound like the same thing is being repeated over and over – but, for example, if a prospective reader happens to hear from a few different sources that your book is very well edited, this could make a favorable impression (but then if the facts contradict the gossip, it will backfire).

Any professional services that you use might give you a little publicity. For example, if you hire a professional illustrator or editor, find out if he/she has a website and, if so, if he/she will feature your thumbnail image on his/her website. This person might also mention your book to his/her friends, family, and acquaintances in order to help create some buzz for your book.

Sending out advance review copies can help you create word-of-mouth buzz and earn some early reviews. Goodreads can help with this (Sec. 6.2.5), and so can bloggers who have a following among your target audience (Sec. 8.1.15).

The more early sales that you can stimulate through effective marketing, the more people may be talking about your book shortly after its release. Word-of-mouth publicity is among the best marketing that your book can get. The first step toward this is getting many people to read your book. The next step is for your book to be as good as possible. Some books tend to garner word-of-mouth referrals more than others. Nonfiction that is very clear and helpful or fiction that evokes powerful emotions are more likely to benefit from this. Memorable characters and great storylines can help, too. Poor editing or formatting detract from this – or worse, provide some negative publicity.

Amazon Preorders allow you to generate a sales rank before your book is even published, and can get your book listed in the Coming Soon category. We discussed this in Sec. 7.1.8.

Many of the other marketing ideas described in this chapter – such as writing articles, book signings, and book readings – can help generate buzz before, during, and after the release of your book.

8.1.8 Launching Your Book

The launch of your book should involve more than merely pressing the button to publish your book. The large number of authors who do just that are missing out on many possible benefits. First, you should create buzz for your book, as described in the previous section. For your paperback, arrange for preorders on Amazon (this was discussed in Sec. 7.1.8). Of course, you should be marketing from the get-go (in fact, starting a couple of months in advance). In this section, we'll mention a few specific marketing strategies that you should be using when you release your book, but you should also be applying many of the other techniques from this chapter, too – like how to make a press release kit (described in Sec. 8.1.14).

Arrange a book launch party among friends and family on the release date. I recommend not investing in decorations or a fancy dinner; this is an occasion to start earning royalties, not to be spending money. Maybe someone will be nice and treat you to dinner in celebration of your accomplishment. If not, a low-cost barbeque or pizza party might be in order. If you frequently go out to dinner, you might be able to use a "normal" dinner occasion to celebrate your book launch without incurring any additional monthly expenses.

You might want to have some paperbacks available to sell during your party. Friends and family might wish to get them free, but you need sales. If they buy your book on Amazon, this affects your sales rank. They might appreciate buying copies in person as a compromise, as you can earn more royalties while they can also receive a discount due to the low price of the author cost. Remember, anyone with a financial interest in your book – a family member who lives with you, for example – isn't allowed to review your book.

Two other events you should be arranging around the publication date are book signings and book readings. A signing is when you sit down at a table and autograph paperback copies of your book, such as at a bookstore. At a reading, you read part of your book for 10 to 30 minutes and answer questions. Such events help stir interest in your book, establish your credibility as an author (it looks professional), and can earn early sales. We'll explore this much further in Sec. 8.1.11.

Many authors fail to take advantage of <u>free</u> media (newspaper, radio, and television) opportunities. Local press especially likes to feature local authors, and local papers often have column inches that need to be filled somehow (your story might just be that "somehow"). You should get some local press when your book is released, and may earn better publicity later if your book really takes off. We'll describe how media can help you market your book in Sec. 8.1.14 and the use of videos and writing articles in Sec. 8.1.13.

Decide whether to release your paperback book and eBook at the same time. Traditional publishers often release different editions in stages, often by price. Usually they begin with a more expensive hardcover edition, then come out with less expensive paperback and eBook editions. If the paperback is more expensive, but you draw a greater royalty from your eBook, then this strategy doesn't really make sense for you.

8.1.9 Identifying Your Target Audience

All of your marketing efforts will be wasted if they are not directed at and geared toward your target audience. You must first take the time to identify and truly understand the target audience for your book. Then spend time thinking about and researching precisely where you can find your target audience. If you have visibility with an audience that's not a good match for your book, you won't be attracting much interest in your book.

Your audience is <u>not</u> anyone with a pair of eyes. Sure, anyone who can read could read your book, but almost all readers buy books in just their favorite genres. Very, very few book sales come from readers who don't ordinarily buy in your book's genre – except for those people who buy your book primarily because they already knew you or met you and became interested enough to buy your work. Marketing toward a very specific audience that's a great match for your book is far more effective than marketing across the board.

If you want a wider market, write books in very popular genres like romance or suspense. There is a trade-off, though – there is a great deal of competition in the most popular genres. Meeting a need in a niche market may have a smaller audience, but you're more likely for a good book to attract a high percentage of a niche audience.

Note that combining genres that are too different may hurt more than it helps. Intuitively, some authors expect a mystery/romance to attract more readers than either a mystery or romance novel because it could be of interest to every mystery and romance reader. But it may not work out that way. Most mystery readers are looking for a good mystery; if it has some romantic elements, that's fine, but if the blurb says it's a romantic mystery, it may sound like too much of a romance. Similarly, romance readers are looking for a good romance novel; some mystery in it is okay, but if it seems more like a mystery that has some romance, they may prefer another book. You really need to choose one or the other and gear your book that way. The problem is that the romantic mystery isn't attracting – as intended – all of the readers from both genres; instead, it's only attracting the few readers who read both mystery and romance frequently. The difficulty lies in writing a blurb that is attractive in both genres.

Similarly, authors want to list their books in as many categories as possible, thinking that this widens the book's visibility. However, some readers will actually check out the categories to see what kind of book they are getting. If they see two significantly different categories listed, like mystery and romance, they might think, "Oh, that's not what I was looking for."

To make matters worse, if you run the idea of combining genres by friends, they will often support your intuition. They will probably even give you an example, such as, "I buy both sci-fi and fantasy, so I think a crossover is a great idea." Gearing your book toward a specific genre is best for marketing your book.

In the other extreme, the toughest books to market are books that blend three or more categories and books that don't quite fit into any category. A few books have a blurb that states that they are part romance, mystery, horror, and fantasy, for example. Such books are very difficult to sell. Your best chance of having stellar sales is to write a book geared for a popular genre, which adheres to the unspoken rules of that genre (i.e. read the bestsellers in that genre to learn what is allowed, not allowed, and generally expected).

On the other hand, if you write a mystery book where the majority of the book involves bowling, for example, then it is a good idea to target both mystery readers and bowlers. Here, we're not combining two separate genres. In this case, we're instead identifying both a genre and a common interest among the target audience.

You want to identify your target audience not only by genre, but also be age group, gender, occupation, hobbies, interests, and any other category that may be relevant. It's to your advantage to pinpoint this precisely. The more precisely your marketing efforts match the perfect audience for your book, the greater will be the yield. It's a common mistake to try to find every possible audience member. For example, if you think, "Oh yeah, fantasy readers might be into computer programming, too," and start reaching out to computer programmers to brand your fantasy book, you're wasting your time unless your book features this skill, too.

Identifying the specific audience for the book is what publishers do, and it's what the editor expects to find in your book proposal when you try to get traditionally published. If there is a mismatch between the book you propose and your target audience, the editor will likely think that your marketing efforts won't be successful and reject your proposal. For self-publishers, it's equally important: If you don't market your book to the right audience, it really hurts your prospects for good sales.

Note that romance, for example, isn't a precise genre: You must distinguish between teen romance, adult romance, and erotica. Even within adult romance, there is contemporary, historical, gothic, and more. First, pinpoint the target genre.

Next, do some research to try to learn more about your target audience. You can try searching online for help or conducting surveys, for example. When you meet and interact with fans, you can get some idea directly (without making them feel that you're collecting and analyzing statistics). Are they mostly male or female? What age group is predominant? What main interests and hobbies are they most likely to have? How about their careers? Will they have anything in common among their educational backgrounds?

The more you know about your target audience, the easier it will be to find them. In the next section, we will discuss how to reach your target audience, assuming that you have already correctly identified who they are.

8.1.10 Reaching Your Target Audience

Now that you've identified your target audience, the next step is to find them. For example, if you write a book to help troubled teens, you need to start thinking about where to find troubled teens and their parents. In this case, doing volunteer work in your community to help troubled teenagers or to help their parents deal with them will let you personally interact with members of your target audience – and there may be indirect benefits, such as authority figures getting to know and trust you, who may recommend your book once they discover it, if they believe that it would be helpful. There are discussion forums online for parents to share experience and advice with one another. If you're an active and helpful member there, you improve your presence – and if the website allows you to fill out an online profile, you may be discovered or branded. You could post articles on a blog to help troubled teens and their parents, try to publish articles in magazines (in print and online), and ask bloggers on this topic if they would consider reading an advanced review copy and, if they like your book, consider posting a review on their blog.

As another example, suppose that you wrote a book that closely relates to golf – it could be a nonfiction book about golf, or a fictional work that is set on the golf course. In this case, you should be visiting golf courses and golf shops with several books in your trunk. Sell them at a healthy discount that's a good compromise for both you and the seller. Have a press release package, business cards, and a sample book handy. Start locally where people know you and work your way up. Keep some copies handy when you visit the driving range or play a round of golf. Contact golf magazines, starting with smaller publications, to see if they have an interest in showcasing your book or writing an article about you. Look for online golf websites, too. If you write a golf article, you may be able to get it published in print or online, indicating that you're the author of Your Book at the bottom. Figure out where golfers hang out online: You may be able to write an online golf article or interact with golfers at a discussion forum.

Unfortunately, I can't work out every possible example. Let me do one more, and hope that these examples will help to inspire ideas for your unique book. Suppose that you wrote a science fiction book. If so, then you should already be a member of one or more sci-fi clubs and organizations. Many of these allow you to meet and interact with others online, where they may be able to learn more about you from your user profile. They also have parties and get-togethers (you could throw one yourself, but if you have a good social presence, you will receive invitations), where everybody gets to dress up. You can meet several people at sci-fi conventions. Try to find a science fiction book club (being a member would help). A blog is a little trickier because it's difficult to attract many new readers with short fiction pieces – it's a big commitment to read blog fiction when you're not already familiar with the author, and it's hard to know what to expect until you start reading. Instead, it may be more effective to post nonfiction articles that are relevant for a sci-fi audience.

Once you've established who your target audience is, it's just a matter of resourcefulness, willpower, and motivation to find them. You can do it! You're not under pressure to find every avenue today; other ideas may pop into your mind from time to time. Keep pondering this and good ideas will come.

The most effective way to market your book to your target audience is to meet and interact with them in person. This is more personable than online interactions, and benefits from the fact that the reader can say that he/she actually met the author of a book that he/she has read. The next time they see you, they can even get your autograph. A significant number of self-published books are actually sold to customers who have personally interacted with the author. It's important to let them discover that you've written a book, rather than advertising this information – i.e. let them ask, or at most work this into the conversation at a relevant moment.

Of course, there is a limit to how many people from your target audience you can meet in person, so you must also use social media and/or online tools. These may not provide as large a percent yield, but this is compensated by the much greater number of people whom can potentially be reached this way. You can use branding and discovery effectively with social media, online forums, your blog, your websites, writing and posting articles online, and other online resources – provided that you're interacting with or presenting information to your target audience (not just to people in general).

Most places (including Amazon's customer discussion forums) don't allow self-promotion, which means that you're not allowed to say, "I'm the author of This Book." That's okay because self-promotion isn't effective anyway. Instead, many forums do allow you to include your name, occupation, and sometimes a link in your profile. When you interact with members of your target audience, people whom you interest may click on your user profile to learn more about you. It's not reasonable to expect to generate many sales in the near-future this way. This is just one step in your overall discovery and branding scheme, which helps people recognize you when they finally (which may be months from now) go to buy their next book.

One of the more effective marketing resources available to you online is the opportunity to write and post an article with content geared toward your target audience in a modestly high-traffic area on the internet. There are very many online magazines and other websites that feature articles – so many that you can find several where useful content is in demand. This will be described in more detail in Sec. 8.1.13.

You can also make a video and post it online, or publish a poem or short story in a magazine, journal, or high-traffic website. We'll also discuss this in Sec. 8.1.13.

Social media can be useful at a few different stages. When you publish your first book, Facebook and Twitter help you reach out to family, friends, and acquaintances for useful feedback, to help generate buzz, and to stimulate early sales. As you gain new readers, they help you establish a fan base. When you publish subsequent books, social media can help you utilize your fan base to get early sales and reviews. Attracting new readers from your target audience requires posting valuable content that will be useful to your target audience. At least 90% of your posts must include valuable content for this to be effective; only 10% can be links to your own websites or posts about you and your book (except, perhaps, for a separate Facebook fan page, which will consist almost exclusively of already established fans). At Twitter, research relevant hashtags at www.hashtags.org to understand them prior to using them with your posts. We discussed the use of Facebook and Twitter in Sec. 6.2.6.

Socializing in person is generally better than the distant, impersonal interactions with social media. Interacting face-to-face provides the personal touch. When people meet the author in person, they feel like they have really met the person; interacting with the author online doesn't produce the same feeling, and definitely not nearly to the same degree. Face-to-face socializing with the right audience is more likely to impact sales. Get out of the house and interact with your audience in person. It's only because there is a limit to how many people you can interact with in person that social media is effective – although it is less likely to stimulate a sale with a single person, social media can easily reach much larger numbers.

Ordinary media is often more effective than social media. Too many authors aren't taking advantage of newspapers, radio, and television opportunities. Local papers usually like to cover local authors and normally have free column inches to fill. Free media coverage is the subject of Sec. 8.1.14.

Ideally, you should have your blog up-and-running prior to publishing. This helps you establish a small following prior to your book's release, and ensures that there is some content available when your first fans check out your blog. As with everything you do online, post valuable content to get people interested in checking out your profile. This is true whether you blog, use social media, or just post online in a forum. Posting about yourself or your book won't attract people unless you're a celebrity, but content will slowly develop a small following. A highly successful blog may also lead to other possibilities, such as advertisers that pay you. We discussed blogging in Sec. 6.2.2. Remember to feed your blog and Twitter posts into your Author Page at Amazon (see Sec. 6.1.6).

An author website – i.e. more than just a blog – can also include valuable content to attract prospective readers from your target audience. If you add a mailing list for fans to sign up at your author website, be sure to send valuable content – don't just plug your books. Sec. 6.2.3 described how to go about creating a website for you as an author.

Whenever you post a link to any of your books at Amazon, be sure to use the short link, as explained in Sec. 7.1.1, or an affiliate link, as described in Sec. 7.1.8.

Think of where to meet people from your target audience in person. Find a book club for your genre. Knowing what interests are common among your target audience will help you immensely, which is why it's so important to first identify and try to learn more about the people who are the best fit for your book. This is a little easier with nonfiction, and with fiction that features a main topic or hobby. For example, a book may be geared toward raising kids with disabilities, involve a great deal of basketball, or have much to do with aviation. You just need to find where you can meet people with similar interests. Since you wrote about this topic, hopefully you will naturally fit in there; you don't want to seem out of place, like you're only there as an author hoping to sell books.

Get involved in community service that relates to interests that are common among your target audience. You can arrange workshops, guest lectures, and other presentations. You may be able to setup book readings at libraries, schools, bookstores, churches, theaters, big brother or sister organizations, civic centers, etc. Don't sign up for readings everywhere – focus your energy on your target audience. You can also do book signings at libraries and bookstores. We'll discuss readings, signings, presentations, and workshops in Sec. 8.1.11. Organize other types of events (or get involved in events organized by others) that let you meet potential readers.

The more you socialize, the more your work may be discovered in person, which can significantly impact sales. Anyone you interact with could buy your book – maybe not right away, but sometime down the line. They might also recommend your book to someone else even if they don't buy it themselves. For example, if you interact with someone who doesn't read mystery, they probably know a friend who does. Socializing with people in your target audience is most effective, but all interactions are useful. I can't emphasize enough the importance of letting them discover your work, rather than you advertising your book.

When you meet people, charm them. Make a good impression. Think of your image as an author. Brand yourself as professional, knowledgeable as a writer in your genre, passionate about your work, engaging in conversation (people may expect your book to be as exciting or boring as your conversations – true or not, this impression is likely), and credible as the author of the type of book that you've written.

People who enjoy interacting with you and happen to discover that you're an author are not only more likely to buy and read your book, they're also more likely to spread the word about your book among friends and family (provided that they like your book). Many authors tend to be highly introverted, and so would rather sit comfortably at their computers and type than socialize. As I mentioned earlier, some of the most effective marketing strategies involve doing things that lie outside of your comfort zone. Get out of the house and meet new people – it will be a healthy change for authors who tend to prefer being unsocial.

It's not just people from your target audience whom you want to interact with. You also need to attend events where you can meet other authors, editors, literary agents, publishers, bloggers, advertisers, and publicists. Build useful contacts. In life, who you know is sometimes more valuable than what you know. Like it or not, you can benefit from this principle if you simply accept it. It's the underlying principle of marketing – people need to learn about you and your book before they will buy it. It's "who you know" first (i.e. your marketing campaign is designed to get more people to know you as an author through branding and discovery) and then "what you know" later (once they read your book, they get this from the content). Similarly, if you want to find a good editor who is willing to work with you, get good press from a high-traffic blogger, or get traditionally published, you must first market yourself in these circles so that they can learn "who you are" before you can sell them "what you know." Even careers tend to follow this principle.

People often wear many hats or change hats. Most authors are also bloggers, and many authors who have a humble blog now will have a high-traffic blog in the future. Some authors who write very well and gain some experience helping others revise their work will become freelance editors someday. A few people who enjoy major success marketing their own books may transform into publicists to help aspiring authors succeed. As you begin to wear more hats or as you change hats in your own career path, the various contacts that you build in the world of writing may come in handy in ways that you would never have imagined.

What is unique about you – the author? Do you have any marketing advantages? For example, if you happen to be a triplet, this improves your prospects for getting great press coverage. If you have expertise – such as an advanced degree – it should help you publish a nonfiction article in a magazine with high circulation. If you have marketing contacts – e.g. in the media, or a publicist – they may be able to help you promote your book. Everybody has something special going in his/her favor. Think about what it is and how to use it to your advantage. You have interests and experience that relate to your book: This not only helps you connect with readers who have similar interests and experience, but can also help you get exposure in these areas, too. People you already know in this area may be able to help you promote your book. If you feel that nothing is special about you and that you don't know anybody that can help, then you need to spend more time pondering this or ask others for ideas. For example, if you write a suspense novel that features chess, you must know some chess players or instructors, be in a chess club, or play online. Start with these contacts.

Your successes and accomplishments can sometimes help you work your way up the ladder. For example, climbing up the bestseller list, improving your sales rank, and earning reviews may show that your work is serious enough for higher-traffic websites to consider working with you. Publishing articles on smaller venues and achieving mild success with it may open doors with larger venues. You can't leap from local to national exposure in a single bound, but you can slowly work your way up the ladder.

There are sometimes opportunities to plug your book or eBook. Discovery and branding tend to be most effective, while self-promotion tends to be ineffective. In between, someone may plug your book for you or prompt you with a question. During a radio, television, or blog interview, for example, the host is likely to plug your book or directly ask you about your book. A plug can greatly increase your exposure in a high-traffic zone. There are sometimes creative ways to plug your book. For example, I was watching a baseball game once when one of the announcers mentioned the name of a book that a fan had sent him in the mail. The fan had written a baseball book that consisted of pictures of memorabilia. The television station even took a moment to show excerpts from the book. That was a great plug, as there were over a million viewers in the author's target audience.

Plugs, YouTube videos, and publicity stunts can help you get a little exposure among a very wide audience. However, you must strive for positive publicity. Remember, your author image is at stake. Negative publicity of any kind – including publicity stunts – can ruin a writing career. Don't do anything that may give you a bad name.

Use your hook – a short sentence that helps to create interest in your book. This comes in handy during conversations, interviews, and all of your personal interactions.

Are there any popular books that are very similar to yours? If so, drawing a comparison can help you describe what your book is about. For example, when someone asks you what to expect from your book, you might say something like, "It's a cross between *The Lord of the Rings* and *Harry Potter*" (and for a case like this, it arouses curiosity – they will want to know how that's possible). You can also write statements of the sort, "If you enjoyed *Twilight*, you may also like *My Book Title*."

But you must be careful. Saying, "If you like Book A, you'll love Book B," is dangerous. First, it sounds boastful. If Book A is a bestseller and Book B is self-published, saying that Book B is better creates unrealistic expectations. People are more likely to check out your book if you say that they may like Book B, and less likely to do so if you say that they will like or will love Book B. Those who do buy Book B expecting it to be better than Book A are likely to leave a negative review if Book B doesn't live up to these lofty expectations. Even worse is saying, "*My Book* is better than *This Book*." Be confident and passionate about your writing, but don't be overconfident or boastful. Bragging deters sales, while passion encourages them.

Always carry business cards in your wallet or purse; you can't have too many, but you can have too few. Your cards should include your cover photo, book's title, author name, and mention your website(s). If you wish to sell some books through your eStore (see Sec. 6.2.4), consider including a discount code on your business card. There are other press release materials that may come in handy, too, in addition to business cards (see Sec. 8.1.14). You should always have books on hand – i.e. in the trunk of your car (nicely stacked in a box where the covers won't get wrinkled or start to curl).

If you can get inexpensive bookmarks printed that look nice and feature your book, these will probably be more effective than business cards. What do you do with a business card that you find in your pocket when you get home? Many people toss it in the garbage or a pile of other business cards. What would you do with a nice bookmark that includes information about a book, but doesn't look like an advertisement? Many readers will actually use these, especially if they enjoyed personally interacting with the author. Guess what? They will be reminded of your book every time they read.

We'll discuss promotional contests and giveaways in much more detail in Sec. 8.1.17, including discounts and freebies.

8.1.11 Book Signings, Readings, and Presentations

A book signing is an event – often hosted by a library or bookstore – where the author sits down at a table and fans wait in a line to get their copies of the book signed. A reading is an event – which could be at a theatre, school, or church, for example – where the author stands before a podium and reads a portion of the book for 10 to 30 minutes, followed by a question and answer session. Very often, an author will sign books at the conclusion of a reading.

Bookstores have an incentive to work with authors in arranging book signings: Customers may purchase the author's book while in the store – and may even buy other books and products (like bookmarks or coffee). Local bookstores – especially, smaller specialty shops and antique stores that sell books – are most likely to be receptive. With this and many other marketing strategies, starting small and working your way up is a good idea. For one, this gives you some experience and confidence – plus, you can honestly say that you've done this before – prior to approaching the bigger bookstores.

Why won't all bookstores be receptive? Unfortunately, whenever a bookstore may have a bad experience with a book signing, this ruins the chances for other authors to do this. Make your book signing professional and successful, leaving a good impression with the bookstore managers and owners, and you're more likely to get additional opportunities in the future (not just with the same bookstore – news tends to spread).

But don't be discouraged – some bookstores, libraries, and other places will be receptive to book signings. It's a valuable opportunity to meet people from your target audience who you know in advance have some interest in your book. Many authors don't think to try this or don't realize how effective it can be when done right. Book signings and readings lend you credibility as a professional author.

With bookstores, you'll need to make arrangements in advance regarding the sale of your book. They might expect you to sell copies to them at a discount, which they can then sell to customers, with the option of returning unsold copies to you for a refund; or they might allow you to sell them on consignment while you're there – i.e. they will take a commission for each sale. We'll discuss all of the ways that you might sell books to bookstores in Sec. 8.1.16, but the best option usually is for you to buy the books directly from Amazon KDP at your author cost and then sell them to bookstores in person at a significant discount.

For libraries and other places that won't sell your book, you will probably bring your own stack of books to set on the table where you do the signing and sell them yourself (since author copies are quite cheap, you can offer a discount from the list price and still make more than your Amazon royalty).

Always clarify the arrangements in advance – especially, the exact arrangements for how to sell your book at the signing. Bring a few nice pens. Even though you're the one who should be using the pen, nice pens have a tendency to disappear, so you want backups. Also, use a pen that looks very nice, yet which you can afford to replace if you must. Dress appropriately – you should look credible as the author of the type of book that you wrote.

Be polite, personal, and charming, while also appearing professional and confident (but not boastful or overconfident). Get their name and remember it, but clarify the spelling. Write with care and absolutely avoid any need to cross anything out (that's very tacky). Mistakes happen though. How do you cover up non-erasable ink? With a sticker or adhesive label that will look very nice inside the book. A sheet of these may come in handy. Come prepared to answer questions about you or your book. Don't give away too much information about the story. Make eye contact with each reader and strive not to blush (this makes you appear amateurish). Engage in a brief conversation individualized to each reader – this makes every-one feel special and worthy of your attention. If someone is dragging things on too long and holding up the line, make eye contact with the next person briefly and gently wave him/her forward. Develop an autograph that differs from your bank signature.

Help populate your book signings, readings, and other events. It's totally embarrassing for both you and the host if you sit at a table for half an hour and scarcely anybody shows up. You have to promote your event. At least get friends, family, and acquaintances to populate some of your events (maybe try to spread them around so that they don't all show up to the same event, leaving others empty – while still getting enough to attend each event that in the worst-case scenario, it's not too vacant).

Have a friend take pictures of you signing books. You can post one of these on your Author Page at Amazon, your blog, or your author website. It will help to establish your credibility as a professional author. If the photo features you and just one other individual, ask for that person's permission to post it on your author pages. If it features you signing a book with many others in the background, since they came to a public event, as long as they aren't doing something embarrassing in the background, posting the picture shouldn't be a problem. Of course, if you want legal advice, you should consult an attorney; beyond legalities, you also don't want to offend or embarrass any of your fans.

Let your fans know about your signings and readings through your fan page, author website, blog, social media, Goodreads, and your Author Page at Amazon (you can post infor-mation about events and tours there). Remember, you need a regular dose of relevant content on your blog and social media sites so that when you have an event to announce, the posts about you and your other websites don't amount to more than 10% of the overall posts.

There are many places where you can give readings of your book, such as theaters, schools, churches, civic centers, big brother and sister organizations, etc. Theaters and other businesses that often market events may help you promote your reading – they might even have contacts in the press to place a note in the local paper.

When you call or visit in person (don't email or text – it's far too impersonal) to make arrangements, sound (and appear, if in person) professional. Avoid saying, "I don't know." Prepare for questions and think of details that you should ask about. If they've done readings before, inquire about prospective attendance counts and expectations for what percentage of the audience may purchase books. Make arrangements for selling your books – e.g. all on your own, will they take a commission, or do they want to sell them? Some theaters have a gift shop and may even want to keep some extras for a few days because people who couldn't attend sometimes call afterward to inquire about the event. Ask if they will help promote your book and how – e.g. with press coverage or sending emails to their fan base.

Be sure to place an order for author copies well in advance. In fact, just having several extra copies lying around the house and in the trunk of your car can come in handy. It's quite embarrassing to not have a book when you need it. If you can get a good estimate for the prospective attendance count, this will help you bring the right number of books. Some authors sell copies to 70% of the audience at a book reading. A few authors like to bring enough books for 100% just in case. If you bring too many copies, you will be able to use the unsold copies in other ways. Business cards and press release material can come in handy for the unlikely case that you run out of books (well, it should be unlikely if you're well-prepared).

You might not sell 70%. Prepare for the possibility of only selling books to a small fraction of your audience, but don't be discouraged if that happens. Everyone who shows up is interested in your book – otherwise, they wouldn't be there. Some might not buy your book for months. Having attended your reading, they now know about your book, which is one step in branding your book and image. So even if sales are dismal at your reading, you should be encouraged by the prospects for future sales. You've planted the seed.

However, if sales at a reading aren't too good, you should also request some feedback a couple of days later from a few individuals. They might have suggestions for something that you could have done better. Don't ask for criticism at the reading, but politely accept any suggestions that may be offered at this time. Don't ruin your image by getting into a debate at a signing or reading, and don't make any disparaging remarks about anybody or anything.

Many readings last 10 to 30 minutes and allow for about 15 minutes of questions and answers. Contact your host regarding expectations for the duration of your reading. Keep in mind that we tend to speak twice as fast when we're on stage as we do when rehearsing at home. Err on the side of your reading being a little short rather than too long.

Choose suitable material. Rehearse to see if you have too much or too little material for your allotted time. Reading the first couple of chapters is typical, but if it contains material that may not be suitable for the audience, you can read something else. Select material that is likely to be engaging and get people interested in reading your book, without giving too much of your story away. The end of your reading should leave them hanging in suspense so that they feel like they have to read more. At the end of your reading, use your hook – that short sentence that you use to generate interest in your book.

Show up early and test the microphone out before your reading begins. Introduce yourself to the people in charge and shake hands with them when you show up. Also, shake hands with and introduce yourself to people as they enter instead of waiting alone by yourself.

If you may be using technology – such as a PowerPoint presentation – inquire in advance about exactly which hardware and software they have and visit the venue a few days in advance to check that everything will work. Test it out again a half hour or more prior to the reading – occasionally, there are room or equipment changes and the same equipment does not always work the second time. If there is a helper on-hand on your first visit, the same helper may not be there on the day of the reading. You must have a back-up plan in case there are any technological problems. Things don't always go as planned, and the last thing you want to do is cancel your reading for lack of preparation on your part.

Use the restroom shortly before the reading begins. Have a bottle of water with you near the podium or desk where you will read.

Don't read your work in a monotone. Show your passion and make it sound interesting. Vary your tempo and pitch to match the story, and stress select words for emphasis. Pause between paragraphs. Slow yourself down if you have a tendency to speak too quickly on stage. Pronounce your words clearly. Your audience will forgive occasional stutters and other speech issues if your passion shows through and the material engages their interest.

When audience members ask questions, repeat them for everybody to hear. Don't show any frustration or anger regardless of the nature of any questions. Be polite, courteous, and professional at all times – your reputation and future success is at stake. Prepare in advance for obvious questions:

- ❖ What is the significance of your book's title?
- ❖ Where did you get the inspiration for your characters?
- ❖ What challenges did you encounter in writing and publishing your book?
- ❖ Where did you learn how to write?
- ❖ Have friends and family members who have read your book ask you their own questions a few days before the reading so that you can practice answering them.

It would be wise to attend book signings and readings of other authors to learn more about them before arranging your own. You may find video footage posted online (e.g. try YouTube). Study them and decide what you believe they did well and poorly. Did the reading bore you or entertain you? Would you have bought the book when it was over?

Arranging and preparing for workshops, lectures, and presentations are very similar to handling book readings. You may be able to give workshops or lectures to provide valuable training or knowledge that relates to a nonfiction book, for example. Once you become a successful self-publisher, you can even get involved in workshops to help share your skills and experience with new authors.

8.1.12 Word-of-mouth Publicity

Word-of-mouth referrals can be the best publicity for your book, and it's also the hardest to come by because you can't get it directly. To some extent, friends, family, and acquaintances who like your book may be able to help spread the word locally. But for word-of-mouth sales to be highly successful, you need complete strangers who have never met you simply to enjoy your book so much that they mention it to their friends.

The best thing you can do toward this end is to have your book be the best it can be. People are less likely to refer a book that has editing mistakes, formatting problems, or a lousy cover – even if they loved the story – because it reflects poorly on them if they recommend a book that looks unprofessional. In fiction, a great storyline, memorable characters, or a book that evokes strong emotions tends to gain more referrals. In nonfiction, a very informative book with clear explanations achieves this. There are also some genres and specific kinds of books that tend to garner more word-of-mouth sales than others. The more initial sales you get through effective pre-marketing, the more people there will be who have read your book; and the more readers you have, the more potential there is for referrals. If you write a series, many readers may wait until it's complete before recommending it to others.

Branding (see Sec. 8.1.6) plays an important role in word-of-mouth sales. An easy-to-remember title that relates to the content and genre helps – if a customer can't remember the name of your book several months after reading it, they won't be able to recommend it.

Gifting your book to others may or may not pay off. It depends on your audience and the likelihood of your book being recommended. For example, if you write a book geared toward teenage girls in a genre that is very popular among them and if they love your book (that's a big IF), just imagine the incredible publicity that your book could receive if many of them get their hands on your book and start texting about it and posting comments about it with Facebook and Twitter. In this case, giving copies of your book to teenagers you know could very well pay off. Gifting books is an investment, and like all investments, it carries a risk. There are no guarantees that people will like or recommend your book. The more social your target audience is, the more likely they are to spread the word if they enjoy your book.

8.1.13 The Power of Articles and Videos

There are numerous online websites with thousands to millions of daily visitors that need content that will continue to attract their readership. The most popular sites have a high demand from authors who are trying to publish their articles with them, but the very large number of websites out there means that there are also many sites with modest traffic that have a need for valuable content. Some magazines and newspapers also have significant circulation numbers. While it's a challenge to get articles accepted in the most popular magazines, it's easier to get an article accepted by a more modest magazine – and, again, there are so many magazines out there that this increases your chances of a quality article being accepted somewhere. Just imagine having an article published someplace where a thousand or more viewers will read it every day for a month or so, with your name followed by *The Title of Your Book* appearing at the bottom.

You really have nothing to lose. In the absolute worst-case scenario where nobody wants your article, you can always post it on your blog. So no matter what, it will get used.

Start out by writing some articles for your blog. This is something you should be doing once per week anyway. You gain some experience when you post articles on your blog and see firsthand which types of articles tend to generate more interest. This experience can be useful when you prepare a query letter to send with your request for publication. Start out with a modest website. Success that you achieve there may help you breakthrough with higher-traffic sites. Focus only on websites that are great matches for the interests of your target audience. Check out each website and read several articles before submitting your query letter (which describes your proposal) to see how relevant it is for your work and to get an idea of what kinds of articles they publish. Read the submission guidelines.

Try small print magazines and newspapers, too. If you have an advanced degree that's relevant for your book, this can help you to break in with scholarly magazines in your field. Journals are more appropriate technical publications; if your work is more popular and less technical, then you should be looking for magazines that will be of popular interest with your target audience. Either way, well-researched and thought-out articles have an advantage.

Poetry and short fiction can also be published in relevant magazines – in print and online. A short story in a high-traffic area among your audience can gain you some nice exposure.

Maintain a professional image in your interactions with prospective publishers. See the following section regarding how to prepare a press release kit.

Another way to gain exposure is to make a video with content that relates to your book and will likely interest your target audience, and post this video online in a place that will be highly visible and attract your target audience. The most obvious place to upload a video is YouTube. Be sure to link to this video from your author websites and social media.

Relevance is key. It doesn't do you much good to make a cute video about cats purely for the sake of attracting attention and then mention that you're an author of a book that doesn't relate to cats in any way whatsoever. You want to attract your target audience, so you should make content relevant for them. Also, don't try to make a video that will go viral with negative attention. You want positive publicity in order to build credibility as an author.

Nonfiction writers can make a video lecture or demonstration that provides useful skills, knowledge, or training that is relevant to your book and target audience. The video may attract new readers, and you can also provide a link to it in your book – this way, it also serves as supplemental content for your current readership.

Some authors make a video introduction – or trailer, like a movie preview – for their books. These can be posted on YouTube or your AuthorCentral page, for example. A video to go along with a free short story is another way to garner interest in your writing. You can find a few sample video trailers that authors have made for their books by searching YouTube or the Amazon KDP community forums.

8.1.14 Free Media Coverage

Local newspapers, magazines, radio stations, and television networks have many readers in your area, without much competition. In contrast, the online sites with the highest traffic have much more competition – both in terms of competing sites and with the number of other writers trying to get their work published there, too. Local also seems more personal.

Another advantage of local press coverage of your book and/or you as an author is that it helps you build credibility. You can post a link to it from your author websites, for example, and include information about it on your Author Pages at Amazon and Goodreads. Most other authors aren't doing this (but they should be!), which makes it look more professional for you when you get featured in a newspaper, in a magazine, or on a radio or television show.

In the previous section, we discussed how to publish an article that you write. In this section, we're talking about an article that a journalist writes about you and/or your book(s). This is great exposure for you, and can be far more effective than a blog (but you should mention it and post a link to it on your blog and social media sites – remembering to post at least nine times with useful content for every post about you, your book, and your websites).

If you already have contacts in the media, use them. If not, you should be establishing these as you gain media attention for your work. Contact local newspapers and local radio and television stations. For radio and television, make sure that your target audience fits in with their image. It would be kind of funny for you to be interviewed by a radio station, for example, where neither you nor your book relate to the listeners in some way. Local and regional public broadcast stations that often feature talk shows and interviews are a good place to start for radio and television appearances. You have a better chance to gain national exposure if you're a celebrity, if your book becomes a bestseller, or if the topic of your book is a perfect fit for the radio station or television network. For example, if your book relates to tennis, see if you can get any press with a tennis or sports channel. Some smaller cable or satellite stations may be more receptive. If they can just briefly post a note about you and your book somewhere on their website, that in itself will be a great step in the right direction.

Newspapers often have column inches that they need to fill. Radio stations and television networks occasionally have minutes to fill; some shows are looking for ways to use all of their airtime. Contact local newspapers, radio stations, and television networks (and specific shows, separately) regarding your book. Tell them that you're looking for local press to write an article or do an interview about you as a local author and your book. Many small-time authors have gotten featured this way. The first step is to ask (while appearing professional).

Even newscasts online can give you unique publicity as a writer. Some high-profile bloggers interview authors periodically. Your interview will be most effective when their audience coincides with your target audience. See Sec. 8.1.13 regarding videos.

What is unique about you that might help you gain more press coverage? You can gain some press coverage even if nothing seems to stand out. But if there is something about you that's newsworthy – like overcoming long odds – use it to your advantage. Many people have a marketing advantage and don't even realize it. For example, universities have internal marketing departments that not only recruit new students, but assist faculty with press coverage. Even if an instructor writes a nontechnical book (instead of a journal article or a textbook), it still benefits the university to help the instructor receive press coverage for the book – as the increased popularity of what the instructors are accomplishing helps attract new students. Even students and alumni who publish books can receive help from the university in getting local media coverage. Former students can get featured in an alumni magazine.

A press release package can help you appear more professional in your interactions with the press, making arrangements with book signings and readings, bookstore dealings, etc. Your press release package may include one or more of the following (the combination that you use should depends on the circumstances):

❖ A well-written announcement for the launch of your book, featuring your cover photo. (You can make similar announcements for awards and other achievements.)

❖ An informational sheet about your book, including the description, cover, price, and any quotes that you have permission to use.

❖ Your author biography with your photo. Customize your biography for the occasion and the market of whomever you're submitting your press release package to.

❖ A professional-looking book review request form (for an editorial review).

❖ Your business card for your work as a writer, or relevant expertise for nonfiction.

❖ A bookmark. What reader wouldn't mind enjoying the benefit of a visually appealing bookmark that doesn't look like an advertisement? If it features your cover, title, and name, this is a product that's likely to get used while helping you with branding.

❖ A copy of your book. If you may use this on a wide scale, you could consider making a separate edition (with no sales channels enabled) that says Advance Review Copy on it in large letters, noting that it's not available for resale in smaller print. (Instructors can make a similar evaluation copy when they publish textbooks.)

❖ If you want bookstores and other retailers to stock your book, they may want to see sheets that outline your marketing plan and provide sales figures, copies of reviews, and other data that can convince them that your book may be worth stocking.

❖ Post a digital copy of your press release material on your author website (but don't post personal info) and link to it (or email it as an attachment) in your online dealings. On your website, this material may help lend you credibility as an author.

Just like sending cover letters and resumes to a company when you apply for a job, your press release package should look highly professional in appearance. You want it to look impressive at first glance. It should also be completely free of mistakes if you wish to make a good impression of your ability to write well. All of your material should look uniform, with similar imagery. Your front cover may appear on most of it, and so might your logo. Use the same page border for each full-sheet document.

Following is the link to a local paper that included an article about myself and my books: http://www.natchitochestimes.com/view/full_story_2/19369910/article-Northwestern-State-faculty-member-writes-book-on-basic-astronomy?instance=nsu_news.

8.1.15 How to Get Book Reviews

Let's begin by discussing some <u>wrong</u> ways to go about getting reviews. Some of these violate Amazon's review policy and may cause the review to be blocked or removed (and can also lead to account suspensions or worse). Most are unscrupulous, and provide a negative image for the author as well as self-publishing. All make the author look unprofessional and needy.

➢ Don't review your own book. Don't create fake accounts or use other accounts to review your own book. This is against Amazon's customer review policy. It is also frowned upon as highly unscrupulous and will permanently tarnish your reputation as an author. Amazon has found and removed thousands of such reviews, outsmarting the authors who thought that they were outsmarting Amazon's system.

➢ Don't allow anyone who may have a financial interest in your book – spouse, parents, children, household family members, editor, illustrator, coauthor, publisher, etc. – to review your book. This is against Amazon's customer review policy.

➢ Don't allow genuine customers that you've sold books to in person to post reviews from any computer or IP address that you've ever used. It will be blocked or removed. If multiple customers post reviews from the same IP address – even if you've never used it – the same result is likely.

➢ Don't buy reviews or offer to pay for reviews. This is against Amazon's customer review policy. Believe it or not, there are ways to track this and Amazon and others are trying to prevent such abuse – which means that people may be investigating this and setting "traps" for authors. There are stories circulating of authors who have responded to advertisements from customers willing to sell good reviews, claiming that the customer actually left a negative one-star review instead.

➢ Don't offer anything other than an advance review copy (i.e. one free book to read) in exchange for a review. Don't approach just *anyone* with this offer; see the list for the right way to seek reviews to find ways to use advance review copies appropriately.

➢ Don't beg for reviews. Don't go to online forums and ask for people to review your book. Don't go to online forums and ask people how to get reviews. All of this makes you look needy, branding you as unprofessional.

➢ Don't exchange reviews with fellow authors. Don't offer to review other authors' books if they will review yours. Amazon is likely to remove one or both reviews if they see (and they have a computer program that searches for review abuse, so this is likely at some point) that two authors have reviewed each other's books. (Critiquing each other's books and exchanging these critiques personally is fine. Posting them on Amazon is a problem.) Now if you review a book and that author discovers your book and decides to review yours, you did nothing wrong; but it won't look good if others see that there is a mutual review, and Amazon may remove the reviews at some point. Amazon won't know that it was an accident, and may treat it like it was intentional.

> ➤ Anyone who has written a book that is similar to yours is not permitted to review your book on Amazon.
> ➤ Similarly, don't use any of these strategies to get Amazon or Facebook Likes, Google Plus One's, etc.

Following are some legitimate methods of getting customers to review your book on Amazon, Goodreads, blogs, media, etc.:

> ➤ Effectively market your books to stimulate sales. Nothing is better than the reviews that customers who discover your book leave at Amazon and Goodreads. They look more genuine than any reviews that you request, and it's most useful for prospective customers to see what other customers have to say. Unfortunately, only a small percentage of customers post reviews, which is why it takes active marketing to get more sales to improve your chances of getting customer reviews.
> ➤ Traditional publishers encourage early reviews by sending out advance review copies. Goodreads has an author tool to help with this (see Sec. 6.2.5); some recipients will rate and/or review your book on Goodreads, and a few on Amazon, also – but some won't review your book. Keep in mind that any customers who don't buy your book from Amazon won't have Amazon Verified Purchase showing on their reviews; it may look suspicious if you have many reviews with unverified purchases, even though the customers have read (and sometimes purchased, just not from Amazon) your book.
> ➤ Find bloggers on your topic (e.g. health food) who review books in your genre. First, Like their blog posts and Follow their blogs to learn more about them. Then, when you feel that they are a good fit and you've been a follower for a while, politely ask if they would mind reading an advance review copy. If they enjoy your book, they may post a review on their blog. They may or may not post a review on Amazon, and Amazon, at their discretion, may decide not to post bloggers' reviews that aren't Amazon Verified Purchases (just speculating). If your eBook happens to be free – through KDP Select, for example – during that time (if not, you can gift it), they can "buy" it that way. Bloggers with a large following are likely to receive numerous requests, so they are less likely to review your book – and if they do, there may be a lengthy delay (plus the time it takes to read a book). Bloggers with a smaller following may be more receptive. Amanda Hocking, for example, credits bloggers for helping her get noticed.
> ➤ Try to get newspapers, magazines, and online websites that do book reviews to review your book. This will show in print or online – not as a customer review on Amazon – but you can get legitimate editorial reviews to appear on your book's Amazon detail page through AuthorCentral. Your press release kit (described in the previous section), including the book review request form, can come in handy for this. It's best to call – as it's more personal – but prepare a professional, well-written (proofread carefully) letter for a book review request when you can't make the request by phone.

➤ Some professional review services, like Kirkus reviews, provide a neutral editorial review for a fee. This isn't considered buying a review when it's a well-known company that provides a neutral review – i.e. there is no guarantee that it will be good. Amazon will definitely support Kirkus reviews because this used to be a marketing service that you could purchase from CreateSpace. This will show as a Kirkus review on your book's Amazon detail page. You must have a lot of faith in your book to do this because the review won't necessarily be glowing or even good. It's also a significant investment. On the other hand, it helps to provide customers with a neutral review.

➤ You may be able to get permission to use some legitimate review quotes (not from Amazon customer reviews) in the editorial reviews section on your book's Amazon detail page, in the Look Inside, and on the back cover – depending on the restrictions of where the review appears. You're not allowed to quote Amazon customer reviews anywhere, but you can provide a link to them from your websites.

➤ If a fan contacts you and tells you that he/she read the book, you could try to tactfully and carefully encourage him/her to leave you a customer review on Amazon. Many authors refrain from doing this because they don't want to appear tacky or needy. Rather, they will simply strive to provide a personal yet professional-looking response, and hope that their professionalism and personal interaction (which was invited, if the customer contacts you by email, for example) helps to implicitly encourage a review.

See Sec. 7.1.6 for more information about customer reviews on Amazon. Note that it's possible to send .mobi and .epub files of your eBook or PDF's, which is cheaper than sending paperback copies. However, some reviewers may only accept print editions for review. If your eBook happens to be free through KDP Select, the review will show as an Amazon Verified Purchase (but the reviewer has the option not to reveal this).

8.1.16 Bookstores, Libraries, and Direct Sales

Recall that we discussed what more you might do – i.e. in addition to selecting Amazon KDP's Expanded Distribution option – in order to improve your chances of getting your book in libraries and bookstores in Sec. 4.1.7. I will try to avoid repeating too many details from that section and focus primarily on the pertinent marketing aspects.

It's extremely unlikely for brick and mortar bookstores to pick up your title to stock in their stores simply by finding it in Ingram's database. You must approach bookstores to make this happen. Small, locally-owned bookstores, antique stores that sell new and used books, and other kinds of retailers that sell books are more likely to be receptive. Major bookstore chains like Barnes & Noble will be much more reluctant. A few companies actually have title request forms that specifically prohibit CreateSpace books. Remember to start small.

Look for local bookstores that feature local authors on their shelves. That's a great place to start. If they won't carry your book, they might give you helpful suggestions about who might and how to go about this. Since you write books, you probably read books, so they should realize that you're a potential customer, too. Providing you with good service is in their best interest (but, of course, we don't always get good service everywhere we go, do we?).

Bring your press release kit (see Sec. 8.1.14). Some bookstores will be quite interested in your marketing plan (written professionally and included with your press release kit), copies of reviews, and your sales figures. They want evidence that you're actively and effectively promoting your book. Dress up like a business person; bring a briefcase and wear dress shoes. Make sure you speak to someone who has the authority to decide on this before you begin your spiel. You may need an appointment. However, if you call to schedule an appointment, you could get turned down on the phone; if you show up, at least you made it in the door (though you can still be refused, just prolonging it). Have a business card in your pocket – you might leave it for the manager, for example, if nobody present can help you.

If you have multiple listings, you may want to create a professional-looking catalog of your books and include that with your press release kit. Include contact info and your website in your catalog. You might include your eStore URL and discount code, too.

There are a couple of more professional things that you could potentially do if stocking your book in a retail bookstore chain is a major goal. Check out Sec. 8.2.3 for more details.

Bookstores can purchase your book a few different ways. If your book has the Expanded Distribution option, just knowing that your book is listed with Ingram is enough for them to stock it. However, this probably won't appeal to them because the discount is very low and the books are nonreturnable (unless you use Ingram Spark, as mentioned in Sec. 4.1.7). The option to order through Ingram has appeal because it comes across as professional, but sometimes the cons outweigh the pros. When you sell author copies in person, offer consignment, or refer stores to your eStore (Sec. 4.1.7), you have the opportunity to negotiate the price, and with in-person sales the stores don't have to pay shipping charges. (Bookstores used to be able to order books through CreateSpace Direct, but CreateSpace has since merged with KDP.)

The best option is generally to buy author copies yourself, which are relatively cheap for you, and sell them directly. This way, you can offer a significant discount from your list price while still earning a healthy royalty. You can accept cash in person, money order by mail and ship the books, or sell them from your website or by email using PayPal, for example. Keep in mind that you can order books from Amazon KDP at your author price and ship them directly to businesses or customers (the packing slip doesn't reveal the price).

If you succeed in getting your books stocked in any bookstores, reward them by helping to drive traffic their way. You want to sell books there or you won't have the same success with getting your book stocked the next time you publish a book.

Another option is to search for wholesale distributors and contact them about the prospects for including your title. Major wholesalers may want exclusivity agreements that restrict where you can sell your book. You may be able to find small wholesalers online willing to work with you. Some authors have been known to contact new and used bookstores who sell on Half.com and eBay, for example, to see if they have any interest in selling their books. If so, they will probably need a hefty discount to offset all of their costs and fees.

Include information on your website regarding how potential booksellers can contact you. If nothing else, this makes your website look more credible when customers and fans check it out, and when prospective bookstores verify your information.

Always have books in the trunk of your car when approaching businesses about stocking your book. It would be awfully embarrassing for someone to say, "Sure, we'll take 10," pull out some cash, and watch your jaw drop as you wonder how you're going to get the books. Be prepared (and be prepared for the same line to be a joke, too – assume it's not a joke unless and until proven otherwise, and behave professionally).

There are other places where you can sell books, too, besides bookstores. For example, teachers can post books and other teaching materials for sale at Teachers Pay Teachers, while golf books may be able to get stocked at golf stores and pro shops.

When you approach libraries, much of the same applies, except they will want to know that your book is available through Baker & Taylor. That's the most professional way for them to order your book, although a small, local library might be willing to purchase through other means. You should have a few copies in your briefcase just in case, at least to let them look it over. Some libraries want to see neutral reviews – especially, editorial reviews. It doesn't have to be at the level of the *New York Times*; a book review printed in a local paper or from a legitimate online book review website would be better than nothing.

There are a variety of ways for you to sell your books directly to customers. Pricewise, the best deal for everyone is for you to buy the book at your author price. This way, you can provide a significant discount while still making a substantial royalty. You don't have to accept cash, checks, or take payments directly through PayPal (although this is a good option for selling books directly from your website): You can order books from Amazon KDP and ship them directly to customers (the packing slip shows Amazon as the billing address, and there is no receipt with pricing – send a copy to someone you know to check it out).

You can also provide a link to your eStore and optionally provide a discount code (see Sec. 6.2.4). However, with this option, customers must pay shipping and handling charges, which may offset the benefit of any discount.

There are many advantages for both you and your customers to encourage sales directly from Amazon. For customers, they tend to trust Amazon and their guarantee, may qualify for Free Super Saver Shipping (and two-day shipping if they have Amazon Prime), might find your book on sale, and can check out customer reviews. It's beneficial for you because when customers buy from Amazon, this improves your sales rank and if they leave a review, it will show as an Amazon Verified Purchase. You can also earn a commission on sales that you refer to Amazon from your website using your affiliate link (see Sec. 7.1.8).

For a few rare books that tend to sell much better in person than they do through Amazon, it may be better to try to sell books directly. This is sometimes the case, for example, for businessmen who tour the country giving presentations and sell many books in person when it's over.

If you have expertise, going on tours to give lectures, presentations, and workshops in major metropolitan areas is a good way to sell your books – and possibly get paid for your presentation, too. Stack up books on a table at such events so that people can thumb through them and offer to sell them in person.

The main challenge of marketing books to the United Kingdom and other countries is overcoming the shipping charges. If you enable the Amazon UK and Europe channels, customers can buy your books with low-cost (or free, if their purchase qualifies) shipping from European Amazon websites, in which case Amazon has them printed in the United Kingdom or Europe. Sometimes there are other worldwide online booksellers offering low-cost or even free shipping to various countries; for example, check out the Book Depository (which may also be a good option if you need to send a book internationally). For direct sales or eStore orders, you could have author copies shipped directly to the customer from Amazon KDP (and for some destinations, like Europe, the book can be printed and shipped from a printer in that region to save on shipping costs), you could look for a worldwide online bookseller like the Book Depository, or you could pack and ship the book yourself (but you should first visit your local post office with some of your books and try to get precise shipping estimates).

8.1.17 Free Book Promotions, Discounts, Price-matching, Giveaways, and Other Promotions

Many authors try to generate interest in their books using free book promotions, creating discounts through price-matching, and promoting giveaways and other contests. Note that freebies and discounts are sometimes unsuccessful. Like all investments, giving your book away for free is a risk that may or may not pay off. When it doesn't, there are dozens or hundreds of customers who now have your book for free, who might have purchased it sometime in the future if not for the free giveaway.

The most common way that authors make their books free for a limited period of time is through enrollment in KDP Select. Bear in mind that you can only make your eBook free for 5 out of every 90 days with the KDP Select program. Enrollment in KDP Select has a few other benefits – like paying royalties on borrows – but doesn't permit you to publish an eBook edition with Nook, Kobo, Apple, Smashwords, or anywhere else during the enrollment period (paperback is not restricted). Some authors take advantage of the benefits of KDP Select for the first 90 days, and then if they aren't happy with it, try publishing with other eBook sellers. Other authors sell a significant number of eBooks through Apple, Sony, and Kobo, for example, and don't want to lose those sales by agreeing to KDP Select's terms and conditions.

A significantly growing number of authors feel that the free promo days are becoming less effective than they had been when the program was first introduced. Many are preferring the new Kindle Countdown Deal (see Sec. 4.2.7). Here are some things to consider carefully:

- ❖ The free promo days tend to be most effective when the first eBook in a series is made free, or when an author has multiple eBooks that are very similar. See Sec. 8.1.18.
- ❖ Many customers hoard the free eBooks, but never get around to reading them. If you succeed in giving away 1,000 books, only a fraction of those will get read.
- ❖ Of those customers who will read the eBooks, some won't begin reading them for a few months, and then it may take them a month or more to read it.
- ❖ Authors do receive increased exposure from those customers who do read the eBook. The more people who read the eBook, the greater the chances for word-of-mouth sales and customer reviews.
- ❖ On the other hand, you may be losing sales by not having your eBook available on Sony, Apple, Kobo, Smashwords, etc. If so, the customers you are losing this way may be in your genre, whereas many of the free promo readers may be outside your genre.
- ❖ Customers who believe that they get what they pay for often undervalue free eBooks.
- ❖ Indeed, an increasing number of customers are avoiding free eBooks because of one or more poorly written or poorly formatted free eBooks that they have downloaded.
- ❖ Free eBooks attract readers from outside of the genre, who often don't have realistic expectations. This is occasionally revealed through low-star reviews.
- ❖ Customers who buy the eBook are more likely to read the description and Look Inside to see what they are getting. Those who get free eBooks usually don't take the time to do this, yet may be unhappy with what they get and might state this in a review.
- ❖ Unfortunately, there are a few readers (and worse, authors and publishers) who loathe the free promo days and maliciously leave bad reviews to eBooks that were free. Note that these show as Amazon Verified Purchases. This is quite rare, but does happen.
- ❖ With recent changes in Amazon Advantage (Sec. 7.1.8), many websites have stopped advertising free eBooks through affiliate links, which appears to have significantly diminished the number of eBooks that are given away for free during the promo.
- ❖ However, there are some dedicated blogs and websites that still promote free Kindle eBooks (they just don't use the affiliate links). Research the blogs and websites that do this (use Google, for example) and contact them to let them know when your eBook will be free. Politely ask if they could include your eBook, too.

I still have most of my eBooks enrolled in KDP Select. I used the free promo days more frequently until 2013, at which point I have started using them only occasionally and for just a few of my eBooks. I have some sets of arithmetic flashcards, for which the free promo days have a similar effect as series (see my first point above). There are other benefits besides free promo days and the Countdown Deal (such as the new **Kindle Unlimited** program).

Some eBooks sell a significant number of copies through Apple, Sony, or Kobo. If you have such an eBook, you may benefit greatly from selling it through as many sales channels as possible. The problem is that you don't know until you try. Another problem is that once you try, you may experience some delays and hassles trying to return to KDP Select: When you publish with an aggregator like Smashwords, it may take a month or so to completely remove your eBooks from all of the catalogs where your eBook was published. KDP will email you if your eBook is available in another catalog while enrolled in KDP Select. If this happens to you, send them a polite explanation that your eBook has been unpublished. I did this once, and they replied to confirm that it wasn't actually available for purchase where they had found it. I had to go through this again a few weeks later for the same eBook, but that was the end of it.

Another way to offer your book for free or at a discounted price is by price-matching. Of course, you can create your own "discount" at any time by simply adjusting the list price (but at Kindle, you can't set the list price lower than 99 cents – and if your converted .mobi file is larger than 3 MB or 10 MB, the limits are $1.99 and $2.99, respectively). However, this doesn't look like a discount – it just lowers the list price. If you have a paperback and Kindle edition linked together, the eBook will appear as a discount off of your paperback price.

Amazon may choose to price-match an eBook if they discover a lower price elsewhere. There is no guarantee that Amazon will do this, and it may take months before they do. It's solely at Amazon's discretion. However, customers may report a lower price, which may or may not influence whether Amazon will match the price.

Some authors have succeeded in getting their eBooks price-matched by setting a lower price elsewhere. Note that if you publish with Nook, you're not permitted to set the list price lower than the Nook list price. Authors who want to make their eBooks permanently free (as opposed to the five free promo days that come with KDP Select) price their eBooks free at Kobo or someplace that allows free eBook pricing, and hope that Amazon price-matches it. Amazon may be more likely to price-match a retailer like Kobo than Smashwords, but again it's solely at their discretion. You don't earn royalties for eBooks that are given away for free.

If you succeed in getting a free price-match from Amazon, it may take several weeks to undo this if you later change your mind. Simply raising your list price at the original eBook publisher (e.g. Kobo) by itself won't work: Amazon will still be giving your eBook away for free (or whatever the discounted price was). You must contact KDP and specifically request the ability to regain control of your price; you will need to agree to stop discounting the price of your eBook elsewhere. Note that it may take 4-6 weeks for all of the prices to raise if you used an aggregator like Smashwords, and that Amazon may continue to price-match until the price is successfully raised in all published catalogs that they can find online.

There are other kinds of promotions and giveaways that you can use besides freebies and discounts that may attract interest in your books. Some of these may even be more effective than making your book free. For one, if you want to put your book on "sale" temporarily, you can do this. Price-matching may result in delays of weeks or more, as noted previously. The alternative is to simply change your list price for a day or so and announce this change on your blog, through social media, by email, etc. Just like any other retailer that has a sale, you simply announce that your eBook is on sale for today only, this week only, or whatever the period may be. Remember, no more than 10% of your posts should be about your books.

Note that eBook price changes made through KDP may show up in 12 hours or so (in the United States), while paperback price changes made through Amazon KDP may take longer – especially, through the Expanded Distribution channels. (A Countdown Deal doesn't require republishing.) Short-term price changes are best made on your eBook and not your paper-back. Remember, Nook doesn't allow you to price your eBook lower anywhere else.

It's very important to realize that price doesn't sell books. Marketing is what it takes to sell books. A discount can bring success when you use it as a marketing tool – i.e. you promote the discount. Just playing with the price by itself probably won't help. Even "free" is just a price unless you actively promote your eBook.

You can also announce free giveaways and contests. Facebook, for example, has a special page just for this (see Sec. 6.2.6). Announce and promote your giveaways and contests on your blog, through social media, at your website, etc. This helps you create market buzz for your book. The prizes can include bookmarks, signed paperbacks, t-shirts, etc.

Bookmarks make for great gifts. You can print a large number for a low cost. They should look professional (people are very picky even about free merchandise – but mainly you want the bookmark to be used, so the nicer it looks, the better), feature imagery from your front cover, and include the title and author. Don't make it look like an advertisement.

There may be legal restrictions on how often your book can be on sale in a given time period. There may also be rules and regulations concerning prizes and giveaways (e.g. to ensure fairness). If you have legal questions, consult an attorney.

Authors of textbooks have an issue with students reselling their used textbooks at a deep discount. If you publish a textbook where this may be a problem, you can deal with this the way that the big publishers do: They make revisions every year or two to create a new edition. Some old exercises that instructors didn't like disappear, being replaced by new exercises, with the order of the exercises changing. For courses where exercises are assigned from the textbook, this compels students to buy new editions. On the other hand, this upsets many people who feel that it's unscrupulous. If you simply make changes for the sake of forcing students to buy a new edition, the complaints may be justified. However, if the revisions are what you would honestly do anyway to improve your textbook, that's a different story.

8.1.18 Marketing Series and Similar Books

Some highly successful indie authors have derived much of their success by publishing series of books and strategically pricing them. If you have a series – or, to a much lesser degree, a set of similar books – then you have a significant advantage at your disposal. Provided that the first book in the series is very good and hooks the reader, then your focus should be on how to get as many people as possible to read the first book. The other books in the series will virtually sell themselves if, in fact, readers enjoy the first book enough to want to finish the series. Authors who have a series for which they believe that the first book will hook the reader often strive use price-matching to make the first eBook free or price it at 99 cents.

However, price doesn't sell books, and free and even 99-cent eBooks suffer from some of the problems listed in the previous section regarding free promo days. For this strategy to be successful, you must do more than just make the first book cheap:

- ❖ Have a great cover on the first book to attract attention. All of the covers in the series should match to help with branding.
- ❖ Write a super blurb for the first book that encourages potential readers to Look Inside. Have a great start to the first book that compels readers to try it out.
- ❖ Perfect the first book. It has to be very compelling to get readers to buy the next volume or purchase the omnibus, leave reviews, and refer the series to friends.
- ❖ Perfect the series so that subsequent books also get good reviews.
- ❖ Actively promote any free or discounted books or editions on your blog, through social media, on your website, etc. (but no more than 10% of your posts can do this – at least 90% must provide useful content that attracts your target audience).
- ❖ Give away as many copies of your first eBook as you can to your target audience. Offer to gift the first volume to anyone you know in your target audience. Buy paperback copies of your first volume and give those away, too; even sign them.
- ❖ Place a sample of the next volume at the end of the previous volume (but not longer than Amazon's Look Inside). But beware of having too much front and back matter to the point that customers feel that they haven't received much content for the money.
- ❖ Price an omnibus edition (i.e. a special edition that includes the entire set) such that readers have an incentive to buy it. For example, if you have 4 books in your series, the first is 99 cents, and the other three are $2.99, pricing your omnibus at $6.99 is like getting the fourth volume for free. Some buyers will try the first volume for 99 cents and then buy the omnibus (which includes book one) if they are hooked. Referred customers may go straight to the omnibus.
- ❖ Occasionally discount the omnibus – e.g. regular $5.99, now just $1.99 or 99 cents. Promote the daylights out of this sale. Do this just rarely and it will be more effective, and you will also sell many books at the regular price. When the sale comes too frequently, word spreads. Then customers will wait for the next sale (as your sales rank plummets), and the expected sale price will cheapen your book in some minds.

If you just have a single eBook by itself, a 99-cent list price may not be the best price (unless it's very short) because it suggests that the eBook is cheap and it only provides a 30-

cent royalty. However, when you have a series of eBooks, pricing them all at 99 cents makes them impulse buys, and when the omnibus is cheaper yet, that's a good deal, too. But don't forget the fundamental rule that price doesn't sell books for you. You must promote your books in order for them to sell. Discounts and sales can help with your promotion and make the promotion of a series more effective, but they don't promote the books for you.

If you write multiple books that are similar, this strategy may also help you sell these books, although it probably won't be as effective – unlike a series, customers don't have to purchase the other books to discover how the story ends. Also, there is no "first" book in this case. If you give one eBook away for free one day, and give another for free another day, then eventually customers can collect all of your eBooks without spending a dime. Instead, if you always give the same eBook away for free, it helps to sell your other, similar eBooks.

Recently, many authors have been trying to take advantage of the business strategy for marketing series using a free short story. It doesn't have the same effect. For one, a series usually has roughly equal-length volumes, so the first volume is representative of what to expect; a short story is simply different, not representative. If the "short story" is really the first chapter, this tends to frustrate customers – who are then unlikely to buy your other books, but are more likely to leave bad reviews. Even if it's free, many customers expect to get more than a short story when they download an eBook (even if the word count is clearly stated in the description). I'm not saying that a short story can't be used effectively – just that there are some possible pitfalls. It's definitely not an easy way out for writers who are hoping to avoid the need for marketing their own books. The short story idea is most likely to work well if you market your short story and other books effectively and if you are able to succeed in generating many early sales and reviews for the short story.

8.1.19 Book Contests and Awards for Authors

Note that there are two distinct kinds of contests: There are contests where customers can win a prize (mentioned in Sec. 8.1.17) and contests that authors can enter (which we will discuss in this section).

I highly recommend entering your book in several different contests (but first read each contest description to make sure that your book is eligible and is also a good fit). There are hundreds of contests for authors to enter their books into, such as the annual Amazon Breakthrough Novel Award, which you can enter through Amazon KDP.

Entering these contests helps give you some free exposure and may also improve your writing skills – including the art of writing an effective blurb, since some contests make their first cuts solely based on the blurb. You don't have to win the contest to gain exposure: Just getting your name on the list of quarterfinalists would give you nice visibility, for example (which you could link to from your websites).

Thousands of authors enter any given contest, so you can't be disappointed if you don't win. There are thousands of excellent writers, so winning the grand prize is sort of like winning a lottery. However, if you enter several contests, there are reasonable prospects for great writers to make it to the later rounds in an at least one contest. Many contests reveal the winning titles and blurbs, which may help you generate good ideas for how to improve next year if you don't have any success your first time. You can also check out the winners; reading their books and comparing with your own may help you grow as a writer.

If you make it to the later rounds, some contests have authors critique one another's work. It's very beneficial all around for top writers to get together and exchange criticism this way. There are many benefits to entering contests and striving to do your best, then entering again the next year with an improved book – even if you never win. If you do win, several contests have amazing rewards – such as publishing contracts with an attractive advance.

There are many contests and awards out there, such as awards for the best indie cover. Use your favorite search engine to find websites and blogs with contests and awards for authors. Check out the contest to make sure it's legitimate before submitting your manuscript to them (because, unfortunately, there are some people who try to take advantage).

8.1.20 Follow-up Work: Thank You's and Fan Mail

Take time to respond to your fan mail. When readers contact you via email, on your fan page at Facebook, through Twitter, by posting on your website, via a private message at Goodreads, or on your blog, for example, take a moment to respond. Don't reply immediately – as that makes you look needy – but do respond in a timely manner. Think about what your fan wrote and also consider your response carefully before you reply. If you respond right away, you're much more apt to let your emotions get into the message or make a blunder.

Remember that your author image is at stake. Anything you write may be copied and pasted elsewhere and used against you (even out of context) – even if you wrote it in a private email (whether or not this is legal is a separate matter – even if it's illegal, it may not be worth the hassle to take action, and it's certainly negative publicity to take any action against a reader for just about any reason). Be courteous. Don't be disparaging or defensive.

Write a professional, yet personal response. Keep it concise. The less you write, the less the chance of making a mistake. Be careful to address him/her by name and to spell his/her name right (copy/paste of the name may help). Just accept any criticism (don't be defensive).

But don't respond to reviews – not even to thank customers. If you write a thank you note to good reviews, it makes it look like the reviewers are your friends (i.e. as if the author had fake reviews planted, which discourages sales). If you respond to negative reviews, it looks like you're needy and can't handle criticism. If customers want to interact with you, they will contact you by email or some other way. We discussed reviews in Sec. 7.1.6.

Check your email periodically (including any special email accounts for fan mail), and also your fan page at Facebook, customer discussions or feedback at your website, posts at your fan club, and anywhere else readers may go to contact you. They're not likely to leave a good review or refer your book to friends if you leave them hanging for several days.

8.1.21 The Team Marketing Concept

Companies often use the concept of teamwork in their marketing efforts. A few authors also apply this to self-publishing. If you know fellow self-published authors, you might consider collaborating together in some way. But don't apply any unethical or unscrupulous team marketing ideas (like reviewing each other's books), as this can ruin your reputation as an author (or cause account suspensions or worse).

The general business notion is that team marketing trumps an individual's marketing efforts. There are a couple of ways that authors can use the team marketing spirit (ethically). One way is combine skill sets. For example, one author may be highly regarded for editing, another for cover design, another for website development, another who has achieved much marketing success, etc. This way, one author has the primary editing responsibilities, another designs the covers, another gets the website up-and-running and maintains it, another does much of the marketing work, and so on. It's not easy to meet and recruit a good combination of authors willing to do this, and it can be a challenge to iron out the details and establish enough trust in teammates (and that the distribution of work is fair) to pull this off – and then there is the problem of an author who wants to opt out. However, a successful publishing team such as this has much more potential than one self-publisher trying to do all of these tasks by him- or herself.

It almost sounds like a small publishing company, which it sort of is. They can put the same imprint on all of the books and develop a website specifically for the publisher. If one person has the finances to invest in a company and hire others on contracts, then there is even greater resemblance to a small publisher.

8.1.22 So Much to Do, So Little Time: Choose Wisely

If you're feeling overwhelmed with the many different things that you could be doing to market your book, just focus on doing one thing at a time and eventually you'll have many things working for you. You can do it all the same way that you run a marathon – one step at a time will get you to the finish line. Try to get several marketing ideas up-and-running prior to publishing your book. Don't start out with the things that are easiest to do or which you feel most comfortable doing. Instead, base your marketing priorities on what's most likely to be effective and relevant for your unique book (what's most effective for others may not be for you). When you're unable to do everything, you must choose wisely. Specifically, consider which ideas are most likely to reach the most new members from your target audience.

I myself haven't applied *every* idea from this book, but I have utilized the vast majority of it. There are many things that I've been doing for years, while others I've only implemented recently. Next on my to-market list is more use of social media. You'll have to make similar decisions about which tools you believe suit your specific needs the most and use those first.

Another thing I don't do is send out advance review copies. Most of my books are math workbooks. Many similar titles earn reviews at a very slow rate, including a few relatively popular series. I thought that it may seem strange if I sent out several advance review copies and earned a modest number of reviews this way right off the bat. Customers may wonder how this relatively unknown, new author (not anymore, but when I started) might suddenly have more reviews than other series with somewhat more well-known names. I also have the benefit of having a Ph.D. in physics and being a university professor; I sell many books just from my expertise, and so the reviews aren't as critical for my math and science books.

To be clear, I absolutely treasure every single review that I receive; I'll never reach the point where a good review fails to make me smile and lift my spirits for the next few days. But I don't use advance review copies or other methods to attempt to garner more reviews.

Most books need the benefits of advance review copies. Most fiction, for example, needs several early reviews to help customers decide whether or not the book is for them, and are critical toward success for new authors. The same is true for many areas of nonfiction. You shouldn't avoid sending out advance review copies simply because I mentioned that I don't use them. In fact, I have a couple of fictional works that I may be publishing in the future, such as *Romancing the Novel* (an extended analogy about dating a book), for which I may be using the Goodreads author tool to send out advanced review copies.

8.1.23 Providing Related Services

Many authors who self-publish excel at one or more of the tasks, such as proofreading, cover design, illustrations, formatting, cleaning HTML, marketing, etc. Especially, once you have several years of experience and have perfected an art, others may be interested in your services. There aren't enough very good proofreaders to go around, so if you happen to excel at this, people may be interested in your service even if you don't yet have much experience. Formatting, on the other hand, is a precise art with many technical issues that the majority of indie authors never even realize they are doing wrong. The formatting of print books, in particular, really requires extensive experience working with graphics and printing before you can compete with the many small publishers out there who do exceptional jobs. A different art is involved in the formatting of eBooks, which also entails much experience to perfect.

If you excel at one or more of these skills in order to provide valuable help to others, you may be able to offer these services freelance. You can mention them on your websites, but you really must market these services much the same way that you would market your books. A benefit of this – aside from supplementing your royalty income – is that your efforts to market your publishing services help a little to market your books, too. You get more traffic coming to your websites this way. When you satisfy customers with a publishing service, it helps your branding – i.e. creating a positive image for yourself and a reputation to associate with your name. They might check out your books, and may refer your services and/or books to their friends.

Realize that it works both ways. Your reputation is adversely affected every time you have a dissatisfied customer. There are also many other experts out there competing with you to offer these services. They might feel that you're stepping on their "turf" when you first come on the scene. You want to uphold your image as a credible author by behaving professionally at all times. As with book promotion, discovery and branding are much more effective than self-promotion. At some discussion forums (where permitted), editors or illustrators, for example, indicate at the bottom of their posts that they provide such services (and may provide a short link to their websites) – or they will make this clear on their online profiles.

If you decide to offer any publishing services now or in the future, you'll need to draw up a contract. It's common to request a partial payment (such as half) upfront and the remainder once the customer is happy and accepts the service. Allow yourself a reasonable time period to complete the work, and expect numerous requests and suggestions for changes. Customers like to see signs of progress, and want to be involved in the ideas. Remember that it's their work, not yours. The quality of the final product does reflect well or poorly on you, but their books are their babies and not yours. Request to mention your name on the copyright page and the service you provided (for example, "Cover design by Your Name") – you can include this in the terms of the contract. Don't let the author write your name on the front cover – it's very tacky, and there is a trend that the larger the name, the worse the quality of the service – unless you are the editor (then there is a special field to declare you as the editor) or illustrator (not a cover designer). Professional cover designers have their declarations on the back cover in fine print by the price or UPC bar code; amateurs have their declarations in a large font on the front cover. The contract should specify, among other things, when the project will be completed, how much will be paid when, who owns the copyright for the work, and that you have the right to mention the work on your website (if you're a cover designer, you also want the right to display the artwork and front cover on your website and any promotional materials that you use to market your services).

Simple proofreading is something that you can get involved in with little experience, provided that you're good at it. Offer to edit a sample chapter (limit the word count) free or at a low cost. After designing a few awesome covers, you can get into cover design easily by making your samples available and doing some effective marketing.

8.1.24 Other Marketing Resources

One of the best ways to learn about marketing is to read about the success stories from self-published authors. They obviously did something right, and many describe their rise to the top in articles or blogs on the internet. Their results show that self-publishers can succeed. When you read their stories, it may help provide you some needed inspiration, motivation, and/or confidence that you can do it, too. Study the sales tactics that they reveal to try to learn their secrets. Follow their blogs and social media posts to learn what they do. But beware, now that they're celebrities, they can afford to blog much more about themselves and their own books and websites – and even advertise – whereas you must restrict such activity to 10%.

There are a few things in common with many of the indie success stories:

➢ They usually have a pile of rejection letters from traditional publishers that helped to fuel their motivation.

➢ These authors often researched and studied business plans. The most popular authors often approach both the writing and publishing from a business perspective.

➢ They wrote books in very popular categories and wrote them in a way that would likely appeal to a very large target audience. They didn't break the "rules" of the genre.

➢ Their books generally have great covers and short, easy-to-remember titles.

Amazon KDP has some free marketing resources on the KDP help pages. You can also find several free marketing articles on my blog (www.chrismcmullen.com); look for the tab labeled Marketing. Another great way to get free marketing advice is to find successful self-published authors, then watch and learn. Not everything you see will work for you, but you can learn a lot by seeing some of the things that bestselling indie authors do. When you're an upcoming author, it can help to find other positive upcoming authors: When a group of positive authors get together, their enthusiasm can feed off one another and they can help offer support.

CreateSpace used to offer paid marketing services, but those disappeared in the merger with KDP. For paid marketing services, see Sec. 8.2.

8.2 Other Marketing Options

8.2.1 Paid Marketing Services

PAID ADVERTISING FOR books might not pay off; you might not even recover the money that you invest in it. Unfortunately, paying for advertisements does not provide an easy way out of the necessity of marketing. One problem with advertisements is that books are genre-specific and so have a much narrower audience than other inexpensive products, like bath soap. For an advertisement to be effective, it must be geared specifically toward your target audience. Since few authors advertise their books – compared to cereal and many other products – it may seem out of place if you do this. Also, as noted before, books tend to sell better through discovery and branding, not through self-promotion. Any branding that you might achieve through advertising may be little better than what you can achieve for free with an effective and diligent marketing campaign. Since branding can take months of dedicated marketing, advertising to help brand your book is likely not to pay off for a very long time. Finally, advertising can be expensive, so you must sell a large volume of books just to recover your investment. Therefore, I don't recommend paying for advertisements. There are many free marketing tools that you can use, which can be highly effective for a very good book and don't involve risk.

You can find many individuals and companies willing to offer you paid marketing services. Marketing yourself is much more personal, and personally interacting with people sells books better than any service that you might buy to market for you. A marketing service that you use in conjunction with all of the free tools that you should be using is likely to be more effective than any service that you try to use in order to get out of doing the work yourself.

CreateSpace used to offer paid marketing services, but you can find other individuals and businesses that provide similar services. One thing to consider carefully is whether the service might boost your sales enough to make the investment worthwhile. You can easily calculate how many books you must sell in order for the royalties to add up to the cost of the service (just divide the service fee by your royalty). If you have money to invest in your book, buying a great cover and very good editing or formatting may provide the best yield.

CreateSpace's paid marketing services used to include writing services (for the blurb or a press release), bookmarks, business cards, and Kirkus reviews. You can find such services on your own, and you can find options that CreateSpace didn't offer (like creating a bookmark that doesn't look like a sales pitch). There are many printing services online (or at local stores) that offer business cards or bookmarks. A bookmark can be handy, especially if it looks nice enough for readers to want to use. Imagine if every time a reader opened a book, they saw a picture of your book cover and were reminded of your book. With this in mind, many authors prefer bookmarks to business cards. A business card will likely end up in a junk drawer, pile, or garbage can, but a really nice bookmark is likely to get used.

8.2.2 Audio Books and Other Formats

Consider making an audio book edition of your book, or other media, such as a video DVD. The KDP newsletter advertises the Audiobook Creation Exchange (ACX), which is an Amazon platform. From the KDP help pages, click Announcements near the top of the list at the left, then click on a recent newsletter from the KDP Newsletter Archive to find a link to ACX. (Once you are signed up with KDP, you should also receive these newsletters monthly by email.)

There are many truckers, for example, who listen to audio books during their long drives. If audio books may be a good match for your target audience, it may be worth doing. Search for books in your genre and see if there are any audio books available with a good sales rank.

If you or someone you know has any potential for being an indie filmmaker, CreateSpace offers DVD on Demand and Amazon Instant Video options for publishing movies.

8.2.3 Other Publishing Options

Once you've published a couple of paperbacks with an imprint, you might be eligible to publish with Lightning Source (LSI) – a major print-on-demand company that many small publishers use. This may be appropriate if your self-publishing efforts are growing toward becoming a small publisher. CreateSpace provides an unbeatable value. Lightning Source offers hardcover print-on-demand books and more options than CreateSpace does, and is highly regarded for their full-color books (if you choose the better of the available formats). It's possible that publishing with Lightning Source might look more professional in the eyes of bookstores that you might want to work with, but it's still a print-on-demand service – so it won't open all of the doors for you. At least, one or more major retail chains that specifically state that they don't work with CreateSpace published books don't (yet) also list Lightning Source as a deal-breaker (to be fair, most don't specifically state anything about CreateSpace, and some CreateSpace authors have gotten their books stocked in various bookstores).

Note: Since the original publication of this book, Lightning Source (LSI) has offered Ingram Spark for self-published authors and small publishers. It's very easy to work with Ingram Spark (there is no application process). You should look into Ingram Spark, not Lightning Source.

Another option very similar to, but not as affordable as, CreateSpace is Lulu, which does have more printing options.

8.2.4 Publicists, Agents, and Traditional Publishing

A good old-fashioned publicist for authors who feels that the author's work is highly marketable can really help with branding, marketing, and especially helpful connections. Such publicists may charge a very hefty fee. Someone advertising him- or herself as a publicist charging a much more affordable fee probably isn't providing nearly the same degree or quality of services and probably doesn't have the same experience and contacts.

Authors who are able to gain the interest of a reputable publicist have a significant advantage in the publishing world. At the early stages, such a publicist can provide direction in the writing itself from a business and marketing perspective, recommend excellent editors, and connect authors with relevant literary agents. When these authors submit their query letters and book proposals and prospective publishers see that these authors have been working with publicists for several months, this looks very favorable as a book that is likely to be written following a good business model and very successfully marketed. This is what traditional publishers want – authors whose books are easy to market and who are likely to be successful marketers. They don't want authors who lack marketing experience or authors who make empty promises. Previously published authors who have successfully marketed their books have an edge. New authors are more likely to get a foot in the door by having a publicist.

The same business models and publicity plans that traditional publishers seek can also work for self-publishers. Whether you want to self-publish or get traditionally published, studying business models, marketing strategies, and the techniques that publicists use can help you achieve high levels of success.

Did you know that Amazon has some publishing companies? Check out Amazon Encore and Kindle Singles, for example. Like traditional publishing, Amazon's publishing companies are highly selective. There are very many submissions, and most are rejected. You can find Amazon's imprints at http://www.amazon.com/gp/feature.html?docId=1000664761. To learn more about Kindle Singles, visit Amazon's homepage, click Kindle and then Kindle Books, and choose Kindle Singles from the list at the left.

HOW TO
SELF-PUBLISH
a Book on
AMAZON.COM

Chris McMullen

How to Self-Publish a Book on Amazon.com:
Writing, Editing, Designing, Publishing, and Marketing

Revised and updated in February, 2019
Significantly expanded in March, 2014

Copyright © 2009, 2013, 2014, 2019 Chris McMullen

Cover Design by Melissa Stevens
www.theillustratedauthor.net
Write. Create. Illustrate.

All rights reserved. This includes the right to
reproduce any portion of this book in any form.

Fourth Edition (February, 2019)
Third Edition (March, 2014)
Second Edition (May, 2013)
First Edition (May, 2009)

ISBN: 1442183012
EAN-13: 9781442183018

Nonfiction > Reference > Publishing
Nonfiction > Reference > Authorship

Contents

THIS BOOK WAS first published in 2009. Much has changed between then and now. For example, KDP and CreateSpace have merged together into a single company that offers both paperback and Kindle editions. Microsoft Word continues to release new editions with significant improvements. More and more books are being self-published as eBooks in addition to paperbacks, whereas this book was originally geared primarily toward paperback self-publishing – and the formatting of eBooks is considerably different from the formatting of paperbacks. Also, the world of marketing has changed considerably since 2009 – especially, with ways to achieve this effectively without seeming like a salesperson and without investing big money on advertising. The author has experienced each of these changes firsthand.

Hence the need for this edition: **to significantly update the content**.

This book should answer the vast majority of your publishing questions, but in case it doesn't answer *all* of them, try asking your questions on the KDP community forum. There are many knowledgeable self-publishers (including the author of this book) and small publishers who frequently share their expertise there.

Introduction

I HAVE SELF-PUBLISHED over a dozen books on Amazon.com using Amazon's print-on-demand self-publishing services (KDP and CreateSpace, which since merged into a single company, KDP). I have considered reasons for self-publishing versus searching for a publisher or literary agent. I have edited and formatted several manuscripts to turn them into published books. I have designed most of my own covers, but also have experience working with a cover designer. I have learned tips for making books more marketable, and I have explored a variety of marketing strategies.

But it wasn't all easy: I have run across numerous issues, especially formatting my books into PDF files and having the final product match my vision. Having solved several formatting and editing problems and delivered numerous books to market myself, it occurred to me that it might be useful for other aspiring authors to have a self-publishing guide available to them.

My publishing experience started when I was halfway through writing a book on extra dimensions – a subject I really enjoy contemplating. I read various books on how to get published. I wrote a query letter and invested many hours in writing a lengthy book proposal – which was very much like a book itself. And then I embarked on the daunting task of convincing an editor or literary agent to publish my work.

After I had begun my search in 2008, a new link on Amazon's website caught my interest: in regards to self-publishing a book on Amazon.com. I clicked the link and learned about Amazon's self-publishing service (at the time, it was CreateSpace, but CreateSpace has since merged with Kindle Direct Publishing). I read this information over a few times and considered the prospects of self-publishing versus working with a publisher.

There were several advantages of self-publishing a book that would be available on-demand which appealed to me immediately:

- I wouldn't need to invest any money.
- My book would be on the market in a month, not a year or longer.
- I could publish my work the way I like it; I wouldn't need to revise it until I found an angle that appealed to an editor, nor would an editor ask me to change it.
- I would save myself from the hassles of finding a literary agent or editor willing to work with me.

Prior to this, when I had considered self-publishing, I had ruled it out because I thought it would require a large investment and much entrepreneurship. However, Amazon's self-publishing service would save me from a financial investment and the problem of how to get my book to market: If someone buys my book on Amazon, then Amazon prints the book and ships it out. One beautiful aspect of print-on-demand is that you don't need to have a garage full of books to self-publish.

I still had some concerns about self-publishing. If I could get published, I expected the publisher to print thousands of books and pay a royalty up-front based on this. Through self-publishing, I would instead get paid as the books sell and there would be no guarantee that a certain number would sell. So I saw both pros and cons.

Obviously, I finally decided to self-publish my books. Two more ideas weighed in on this. First, I noticed that if I self-published my book on Amazon, it would be available for several years to come; whereas the book may soon go out of print with a regular publisher. I wanted to share my work for many years, not just a couple of years. Next, I had a backlist of material that I had been writing for 20 years: I decided to edit and self-publish some of these books to better acquaint myself with the publishing process and test the print-on-demand concept out. It worked out well for me and I have since self-published several books; I have also collaborated on professional projects with other authors and designers.

Self-publishing on Amazon.com may or may not be the best option for you. Several ideas in the first chapter can help you decide this for yourself. The remaining chapters aim to help you with your entire project, from developing the concept for your book to editing your manuscript to making your work available on the market to promoting your book.

I hope that you find this book helpful. I wish you success in your writing and publishing endeavors.

Sincerely,

Chris McMullen

Disclaimer

T HE INFORMATION IN this book is presented as accurately as possible based on policies and practices that were put in place at the time of publication (most recently, in 2018). The policies and practices of various companies, such as self-publishing companies, are subject to change. The author makes no guarantees regarding the information contained in this book. However, the author has worked hard to ensure that the information is as accurate as possible as of the time of publication. You should check directly with the companies themselves in order to receive the most up-to-date, accurate information about their policies, practices, pricing, etc.

Kindle Direct Publishing, CreateSpace, and Amazon are trademarks of Amazon.com, Inc. These and other trademarks and brands referred to in this book are property of their respective owners; these companies did not endorse this book and the opinions expressed in this book are not necessarily shared by these companies.

1 Reasons for Self-Publishing

CHOOSING WHETHER TO self-publish, search for a literary agent, or directly contact a publisher that doesn't require an agent is an important decision for an author to make – one that an aspiring author does not wish to regret later. Let us consider the advantages and disadvantages of print-on-demand self-publishing versus searching for a publisher that will distribute your book to the market.

Print-on-Demand

This new concept is becoming increasingly popular, especially on Amazon.com. Instead of printing a large number of your books and storing them in a warehouse, a print-on-demand self-publishing company prints and binds your book as soon as it sells online. In this way, you are able to avoid the large investment that would otherwise be required to publish a book yourself.

Advantages of Self-Publishing on Amazon

(1) No investment is required if you publish a book with Kindle Direct Publishing (Amazon's self-publishing company for both paperback books and eBooks).

You'll probably spend more money (and time and effort) on books that teach you how to write a book proposal and list addresses of publishers (unless you borrow these from a library) and the postage to cover the dozens of query letters, self-addressed stamped envelopes, book proposals, and manuscripts that you will need to send to various publishing houses and/or literary agents.

(2) Your book can be on the market in as little as a week.

Once your book is written, you need only make it into two PDF files – one for the book interior and one for the cover – as described in Chapter 7. A couple of days after you submit your PDF files, you can order a proof of your book (for as little as about two dollars plus shipping). Your proof will arrive in about a week. If you are happy with your proof, you go online to approve your proof, and then you will be able to find it in searches on Amazon.com in a few days, where it will be available for sale around the world.

If instead you publish with a publisher that prints thousands of copies of your book and distributes physical copies to bookstores across the nation, it often takes six months to a year before your book hits the market.

This is especially important if you are publishing a nonfiction book with time-sensitive information. For example, if you are writing a book about how to survive in the real estate market in a tough economy, you want your book on the market before the economy rebounds.

(3) Save yourself from the hassles of contacting publishers and agents, and from the prospect of numerous rejection letters.

When you self-publish, you don't have to sell your work to a publisher or agent. You don't have to perfect the art of writing an effective, eye-catching query letter. You don't have to learn how to write a book proposal that identifies your target audience and convinces an editor that your book will sell very well. And you don't have to deal with rejection letters.

Instead, you can focus on writing your book. You can put the emphasis of being an author on the writing itself, not on being a salesman. (However, applying some marketing techniques, as described in Chapter 10, will help you increase sales; but this is something you are expected to do whether or not you self-publish.)

(4) Self-publish with a company you trust: Amazon.

You don't have to self-publish your book by investing a large amount of money in a publishing company you've never heard of. Now you can self-publish with a company that is part of the Amazon group of companies, and without the investment.

(5) Publish your book just the way you like it.

You don't need to modify the concept of your book in order to appeal to an editor's preferences. To you, your book is a work of art. It's your baby. Through self-publishing, you don't have to sacrifice features of your book in order to reduce the cost of printing your book or make your book more marketable in the editor's eyes. You can be your own boss.

On the other hand, your book may sell better if an editor suggests or requires you to modify your book. Even if you self-publish, you should first test-market your book to receive valuable feedback from others (Chapter 8). You should consider the suggestions that

1 Reasons for Self-Publishing

they make – and prepare yourself to handle constructive criticism well – as they represent a sample of how others will view your work.

(6) You can leave your book on the market indefinitely.

When you publish a book with Amazon, it remains available indefinitely (though you may choose to make it unavailable at any given time). So readers may purchase new copies of your book at Amazon.com for many years to come.

Most publishing companies print a limited number of copies and only print new copies or new editions for a limited period of time – only for as long as the publisher feels that there is sufficient demand. Many books go out of print after about a year, since demand is often greatest shortly after the book is released onto the market. However, those rare books that are popular over a long period may remain on the market for several years.

(7) Revisions are easy to make, and you can make them immediately.

If you spot a typo, printing error, or other mistake after you make your book available, you can make it immediately unavailable until the problem is corrected. To correct the problem, you submit a revised PDF file in the same way that you submitted the original, order a new proof, and once you are happy with the proof, you approve it and the book becomes available once again. Of course, you should examine your first proof carefully to avoid the need for corrections, but if you find the need to make revisions, it is quick and easy to do.

You can also update your book as needed without creating a new edition. However, if you do this, you should consider the possible ramifications of different readers discussing your book and realizing that their copies are not quite the same. You might include a printing number (e.g. third printing) on the copyright page to help distinguish slightly different copies.

A publisher that prints numerous copies of your book and then distributes them will expect your first proof to be final. You are stuck with what you get unless your book is successful enough to warrant new editions.

(8) It's okay if you change your mind after making your book available.

You're not committed to self-publishing once you begin it. Even after receiving an ISBN and making your book available on Amazon.com, if you publish with Amazon you can retire your book – just choose to make it no longer available for sale at Amazon.com. You are free to change your mind and try the traditional publishing route. This affords you some flexibility, in case you have reservations about print-on-demand self-publishing. You

- 424 -

can try it out with virtually zero investment. (Amazon may choose to leave your book's photo and description available on their website, and may allow readers who have a copy of your book to sell their used books on their webpage.)

(9) You can choose to promote your book as little or as much as you like.

There is no pressure to promote your book. If you write a book proposal, editors generally expect to see a description of promotional strategies that you will engage in that will help to market your book. The publishers are already investing a large sum of money to print and distribute copies of their books, and so are not willing to make additional large investments to promote all of their books. They are more likely to do this for authors who have proven success or celebrity status. Publishers expect other authors to invest time and money in their own books, including self-promotion. This can include radio or television appearances, presentations with back-of-the-room sales, writing promotional articles or soliciting book reviews, using part of your advance to purchase copies and sell them directly, maintaining a website, and so on.

If you want to focus more on the writing and spend less time with the business side of authorship – i.e. feel less like a salesman – then self-publishing can help you relieve this sense of external pressure to promote your book. However, any promotional activities you are willing to perform will help you increase sales (Chapter 10). But you don't have to make promises for how much promotion you will undertake, there are ways to help promote your book with zero or minimal investment, and there is no rush to promote your book heavily when it first comes on the market (although marketing can sometimes be more effective when a book is released). Because print-on-demand self-publishing with Amazon allows you to keep your book on the market indefinitely, you can start out with little or no promotion and gradually promote your book more and more, if you wish. This way, you can see firsthand to what degree, if any, your promotional activities are affecting sales. If you see it helping significantly, you are apt to be more motivated to promote your book.

(10) You can still distribute physical copies to bookstores if you want.

While you can make your print-on-demand self-publishing book available on Amazon.com, you can still buy and distribute copies to bookstores. Authors can purchase copies directly from the publisher at a cheap price: At Amazon KDP, books with a black-and-white interior start at about two dollars for up to one hundred pages, and then cost about a penny a page after that, while color interior books run about three-fifty for up to forty pages and about seven cents a page beyond that. You can order as little or as much as you want (there is no discount for ordering large quantities – or look at it this way: there is no extra charge for ordering small quantities), and distribute them to bookstores.

Print-on-demand self-published books have virtually no chance of being stocked nationally in chain bookstores. However, there are favorable prospects of local bookstores stocking a few copies of your book. The best way to achieve this isn't through Amazon KDP's Expanded Distribution channel (that helps to expand your online presence through online booksellers), but by approaching local bookstores in person with copies of your book on-hand and a press release kit. If your book appears professional and marketable, that's a big plus. You can also approach libraries and other stores that specialize in other products, but also sell books (sometimes those stores are more receptive).

(11) If you have your own webpage, you can include a link to your book's product page at Amazon.com (or you can sell author copies directly).

If you have a webpage for your book, or are willing to get and maintain one, you can include a link to your book at Amazon.com. If you publish with Kindle Direct Publishing (KDP), you can choose to sell author copies directly from your own website. Customers may be more willing to buy your book at Amazon.com since this name is much more recognizable. Selling books directly from Amazon's website is also far more convenient. You can start a free website at WordPress.com, for example (and turn it into a professional-looking domain name for an additional fee).

(12) You can skip the struggle of breaking through the publishing industry as a first-time author.

The publishing industry is very competitive. Millions of people are willing to write a book that will appear in bookstores (physical or online) and sell. Publishers are swarmed with more query letters and book proposals than they can read. The largest publishers do not accept unsolicited manuscripts, book proposals, or even query letters; you need a good agent just to get your foot in. It is difficult, and can be time-consuming, to get a publisher interested in your work, and similarly challenging to find a good agent to represent you. It is especially hard to break through as a first-time author. Many publishers and agents are not willing to take a chance on a first-time author, and so do not consider their requests at all. They have enough query letters and book proposals to consider already, so they can afford to be quite selective.

But you can put your first book on the market through print-on-demand self-publishing. If your book becomes moderately successful, you may be able to use the success of your first book to get a publisher interested in a second book; they might even be willing to publish your first book if you sell enough copies over a six-month period (it can be a selling point). Though if your book is successful, you might feel even more compelled to self-publish subsequent books.

Disadvantages of Self-Publishing on Amazon

(1) You won't receive an advance on your royalties.

When you elect to publish your book with a print-on-demand self-publisher, you receive your royalties as you sell your books. (Actually, you typically get paid for a month's royalties at the end of the following month.) You don't receive any money until after a book sells.

Publishers sometimes offer authors advances on their royalties. The amount of the advance depends upon the author and the book; the publisher is not apt to risk losing money by paying too large of an advance. If you are a celebrity or if you are already a successful author, you have good prospects for receiving a rather large advance.

But if you had celebrity status or have already published several books, chances are that you wouldn't be reading this book. For the rest of us, it's a challenge just to get published, and then the advance may not be too large. Part of the advance would probably be invested toward promoting the book, and part may cover probable book expenses anticipated by the publisher – e.g. travel expenses to take photographs for the book.

However, a traditional publisher would likely pay you some amount upon receipt of your completed manuscript based on probable sales from the number of books they intend to initially print and distribute. Unless they have reason to print a large number of copies, though – i.e. some reason to expect your book to be very successful – this might not translate to a large advance.

If you're not anticipating a large advance, the lack of an advance on your royalties may not be too important.

(2) Being self-published isn't quite the same as being published.

Having a publisher accept your manuscript for publication, offer you a contract, distribute physical copies of your book to bookstores, and pay you royalties in the traditional manner carries some status – a respectable accomplishment in the eyes of some.

Self-publishing your work bypasses the editorial review process. You can publish anything, whether or not it is good or useful. Having an editor accept your book for publication signifies that your work is worthy of being published.

But it would be naïve to assume that a book is not good simply because it was self-published. On the contrary, when a book is sold through Amazon.com, all buyers have the opportunity to post reviews of the book. So if a book does not meet readers' expectations, it will receive poor reviews. This customer review process is one means of establishing the quality of a book. A reviewer can also submit a book review to a newspaper, magazine, or website.

In this way, many books are self-published and highly regarded. The worth of the book is measured by what's actually between the covers, which can be measured regardless of whether or not it went through the editorial publishing process.

In fact, some traditionally published books turn out to be flops; so having a publisher accept a manuscript for publication does not necessarily provide a measure of the book's quality.

Still, there is some perceived status with the traditional publication process. It's more important if this status means something to *you* than if it is important to other people you know.

(3) If your first book is published through the traditional route and becomes successful, it will be easier to publish subsequent books and you will probably command higher advances on the royalties.

Looking ahead to future books, if you have high expectations for a very successful first book – considering many other books that will be written by already popular authors in this competitive market – then if you are able to publish your first book with a traditional publisher, you may have better opportunities available when you are ready to publish subsequent books. Of course, this means that first you must have your first book accepted for publication and that it also needs to be as successful as you envision.

If you have a highly successful first book that is self-published, you may still be able to advertise this as a selling point when trying to get a second book published. If you self-publish and build a good name for yourself, the audience that you have already created may be looking for subsequent works; so self-publishing subsequent works may still be a good option.

(4) There might be some book features that you could get from a publisher that you can't get by self-publishing on Amazon.com.

Self-publishing with Amazon KDP presently offers a full-color or black-and-white interior with a full-color cover. You can choose between white and off-white pages, and glossy or matte covers. There are a variety of sizes to choose from, from as small as 5" x 8" to as large as 8.5" x 11".

However, if you want a smaller or larger book, a trim size that's not available, a hard-cover book, a spiral bound book, embossed lettering on the cover, any other feature that is not offered, then you either have to sacrifice the feature or find an alternative publisher. Some traditional publishers may offer more options.

It is possible to find another print-on-demand self-publishing service for a hardcover or spiralbound cover. Another option is to place a special order with a local printer and sell your copies through Amazon Advantage.

(5) Print-on-demand self-publishing might not be the best option for producing super low-priced books.

You can purchase books directly for a pretty good price (starting at about two dollars for a hundred black-and-white pages or about three-fifty for forty color pages), and you receive pretty good royalties (sixty percent minus the cost of the book). However, there is a minimum price that you can charge for your book (which is higher for color than for black-and-white, and which depends on your page count). You can still make a book reasonably cheap if you want – say, around five dollars for a black-and-white interior that is not too long. But if you want to make a very inexpensive book – say, under four dollars – this will be difficult to do. Or if you want to publish in color and keep the cost down, if you have a large number of pages, this may also turn out not to be manageable. Going with a publisher that is willing to print and distribute a large number of books (e.g. mass market) may help you keep the price down. So if you're writing a book for which there is already a lot of low-priced competition, print-on-demand self-publishing may not be the best option.

For most books, though, print-on-demand self-publishing is a relatively inexpensive process, and you can set a very fair price and still keep a larger than normal royalty. If you sell fewer copies than you would through traditional publishing, a larger royalty helps to compensate for part of this difference. We'll consider how to set the prices in Chapter 9. The point here is how print-on-demand self-publishing might not be the best option for producing very low-priced books (but most books do not fall into this category).

A better way to compete in the low-price market may be with eBooks. You can publish an eBook with Amazon KDP, for example, in addition to a paperback. In fact, this is something you should consider regardless of your price-point, in order to maximize your book's exposure (unless you're writing a workbook or other book where eBooks aren't practical).

(6) If you are writing a nonfiction book or textbook for which you have expertise and a strong resume or image, you may be able to draw on your expertise in order to get published more easily and draw a higher advance on your royalties.

Some nonfiction and textbook publishers are looking for authors with expertise, experience, and strong qualifications to publish books. If you fall into this category, you can also advertise your expertise in your book description and back cover as a self-published author, but you might find better opportunities in traditional publishing and have an easier time getting published. However, even this field is growing competitive, so if your degree is new, you are inexperienced, or your resume and image are not yet strong, you might still find it challenging to get your work published regardless of your expertise.

(7) You need to create PDF files for your cover and interior in order to use Amazon KDP.

If you publish with a traditional publisher, you just have to focus on writing the book. Many publishers will accept a physical manuscript printed on paper; some may prefer a file, but often with some freedom in the format of the manuscript.

However, Amazon KDP only accepts PDF files. It is pretty easy to convert a document to PDF (as described in Chapter 7), and it is quite manageable to make a cover and convert it to PDF, too. Even if you have trouble with this, chances are that you can find someone knowledgeable enough with computers to help you out (though you should find what you need to know in Chapter 7). For technical reasons, PDF files do not always print exactly as they look on the screen, as sometimes happens with certain color images (yet this problem is also addressed in Chapter 7).

So you shouldn't be worried about making PDF files – but if you are, you can find free helpful information on KDP's community forum. There are also many free PDF converters available online.

You can focus on writing your book (versus formatting), and completely avoid the issue of making PDF files, by getting published – but then you still won't be concentrating solely on writing your book because you then have to divert some of your energy to query letters and book proposals.

Suppose you do publish your book, or maybe you have already published a book, and it goes out of print. At this point you may be able to self-publish your book on Amazon.com. You should check on the legal details yourself, though. If you are publishing a book now, you might inquire about the prospects for self-publishing the same book once it goes out of print.

2 Developing the Concept

BEFORE YOU WRITE a book, you should decide whether you want to write fiction or nonfiction. For fiction, you should decide whether you want to write prose or poetry. For prose, you can choose from romance, science fiction, fantasy, horror, etc. Similarly, with nonfiction, you can choose from subjects such as science, how-to, games, computers, photography, cooking, and so on. But whatever your format and subject, you should consider the concept before you write. Even if you have already written your book, you may want to consider the concept, and potential revisions, before you publish your work.

There is an exception: An author who envisions himself or herself as an artist may write in the spirit of Edgar Allen Poe, and create a written work of beauty from a blank canvas – i.e. writing without preconceptions. There is much aesthetic merit to be found in this process. However, from a business perspective – i.e. if the number of books you sell has some importance to you – it may be worthwhile to consider the concept of your book first.

Will it Be Worthwhile to Publish Your Book?

How you determine whether or not it will be worthwhile to you to publish your book depends on how you measure your book's worth. If you care mostly about the artistic merit of your book, you should judge the aesthetic value of your work. If you care mostly about making something useful or entertaining available so that you can share it with others, you should measure how useful or entertaining your work is. But if you are more concerned with the royalties your book will draw, you should consider how well your book will sell.

The aesthetic worth of your book should mean more to you than anyone else. If you are pleased with your final product and you are almost entirely concerned with its artistic merit, you should be happy with your book regardless of the sales. If you wish to judge how it is artistically perceived by others, you can receive their feedback. Reviews can help convey this, too, though some reviews will focus on other aspects of your book, such as whether or not it is useful or entertaining.

If you are primarily aiming to write a book that is very useful, you should research the market first to see what other books are already available in the area you have in mind. Then you have to ask yourself if there is a need, which you can fill. If you don't have an area in mind, you can browse different types of books and try to find a need – thinking like an inventor: Look for a need, then try to fill that need. You also have to consider how well-suited you are to fill that need. If there are many experts in that area, and you are not an expert, that area might better be left to the experts. But sometimes amateurs can fill a need in ways that experts can't. Writing from the perspective of utility, you want your book to be useful, stand out from the competition, and be easy to find by your anticipated market. You can judge your book's usefulness from feedback and reviews.

Perhaps your primary goal is to entertain. There are many other books, in a variety of subjects, which aim to entertain in some way – not just comedy, but many works of fiction, and even nonfiction. You should consider what may make your book sell when there are so many forms of entertainment available, many of which are already popular and well-known. If you don't envision your book selling very well, ask yourself if entertaining a smaller audience may be sufficient for your needs. Again, entertainment is something you can judge from feedback and reviews.

But most of us have to pay the rent. If you want to write full-time, you definitely need to earn good royalties. If you're considering self-publishing, though, hopefully you already have a day job. Don't quit it unless and until at some point you become fortunate enough to have a steady income from your royalties that is good enough to do so. You probably already have your royalties spent even if you already have a full-time job – no matter what you make, you probably have several things in mind that you'd like to do with the revenue you make from sales of your book. (Don't forget that you'll have to pay taxes, and that the royalties will be reported to the IRS. Many people expect, incorrectly, that a 1099 will only be issued if the amount exceeds $600, but while $600 is the limit for many kinds of 1099's, the limit is just $10 for the reporting of royalties. If you receive $10 or more in royalties, you should get a 1099.)

So from the business perspective, you should consider the concept of your book and what its financial worth may be. If you haven't started writing yet, when you choose your concept, you will be better motivated if you have confidence that your concept will pay off to some degree financially. If you've already written your book, you may still want to consider whether any revisions may be worthwhile.

A good place to start is to research the competition. How to go about this is described in the next chapter. If you have a concept in mind, look for competing books with similar concepts. You can measure their success to some extent. You can also see how much competition there is. If you don't have a concept in mind, you can still browse available books in various subjects to help you develop your own concept. Researching what is already available on the market is a very useful tool available to writers.

Decide what aspects of the book are most meaningful to you: How will you measure the success of your book? To what extent are you interested in the aesthetic value, the usefulness, the entertainment value, or the royalties of your book? Then choose, or revise, the concept of your book with these criteria in mind.

Your goal of researching the competition that most closely matches your concept is to establish whether or not there may be enough demand for your book, in terms of what you want to get from your book – financially and otherwise. We'll return to the research issue in the next chapter, where you can get a better feel for how to estimate the potential success of your book.

Considering the Market for Your Concept

There are millions of ideas for books, and millions of books have been written. But not all book ideas are successful, including many that have been published. There are a lot of factors that may affect the success of a book idea, such as:

- writing about a popular subject (but see the next bullet, as these two are related).
- if there are already more books related to your idea than the market demands.
- how easy it is for your potential audience to find your book.
- how useful or entertaining your book is.
- if the book is well-organized and well-written.
- if the content is free of conceptual mistakes.
- what marketing strategies are employed.
- whether the cover attracts the target audience.
- if the content of the book fulfills what the cover, book description, and book reviews advertise.
- if readers appreciated the book enough to encourage family and friends to read it.

If you want your book to be successful, you need to consider the market for your book when you choose the concept and develop it more fully, and consider it again when you write and then revise your book.

Ask yourself who the target audience is – i.e. what groups of people are most likely to be interested in your book. How large is your audience? How will your audience learn about your book? (Not everyone searches for books on Amazon.com, of course. Amazon does have a very large audience, but many customers go to Amazon knowing specifically what they will buy, which means they've learned about the book they want before they visit the site.) How many other books are on the market for this audience? What distinguishes your book from the competition? Is it enough to drive sufficient sales? How willing are you to promote your own work?

It's important to consider the market for your book because you can't expect to sell copies to others if you don't first sell your concept to yourself. Also, identifying your intended audience is a necessary prelude to writing a book with that particular audience in mind.

You need to sell your book to yourself before you can expect to sell it to others.

Once you have the main concept for your book and have ways in mind that will help to distinguish it from the competition, explore your concept more fully. Write a chapter outline if your book is nonfiction, or write a story outline if you are writing fiction. This will help you organize your thoughts and make sure that your idea is complete. It will probably force you to think about a few things that are missing or that you haven't yet thought through.

As your concept develops more fully, reassess the market for your book and its potential worth. Show your outline to family or friends for valuable feedback. Prepare yourself to accept constructive criticism, and realize that you are still free to decide whether or not to accept any advice. The feedback will provide some measure of how others may view your book. Your outline is a sketch of your vision for the book. Bear in mind that other people may look at your outline and see a different vision. Receiving feedback from your target audience, e.g. in a focus group, can be especially helpful. It may also be useful to join a writer's forum.

Once you are happy with the vision for your book and understand who you are writing the book for, you are ready to begin writing. Having thought the concept through and satisfied yourself that your book is worth writing, be ready to use this to motivate yourself to start and then continue writing. There will periods where your motivation dips or you question yourself or you get frustrated with the writing. When this happens, remind yourself that you thought this through already, and that you are confident that writing your book is worthwhile.

3 Researching the Competition

I**T'S IMPORTANT TO** identify books that are competitive titles, complementary titles, and otherwise related to the concept for your book. As you develop your book, this will help you see what is already on the market. Knowing what is presently available will help you to develop a book that is distinguished from the competition and fills one or more needs.

Complementary Books
Complementary titles serve as useful companions to one another, like a dictionary and thesaurus, which complement one another nicely.

Competitive Books
Competitive titles represent a choice that a reader has; once the reader selects one title, the reader will not have need of the others.

Part Competitive, Part Complementary
The definitions above are extreme; many related titles are not quite either. Most books are more complementary than they are competitive, since readers tend to buy many similar books and the "frequently also bought" lists tend to help the sales of both complementary and competitive titles.

Complementary titles are books that go well together – once a buyer has one, it will be useful to have the others. Once a few buyers buy your book and another book together, these other titles will show up on your book's product page, and your book may show up on the other books' product pages. Amazon encourages multiple sales (e.g. with free shipping on orders over $35), so when customers buy one book, they often browse related books. Complementary books often show up at the top of the page as "frequently bought together." So complementary, as well as competitive, titles affect the sales of your book.

If you are writing nonfiction, you will need to compile a list of references and cite related works. This provides one more reason for searching for competitive, complementary, and other related works.

Finding Related Works

Start out by visiting a couple of bookstores. Here, you can walk right up to shelves of books on your topic and find current books that the bookseller deemed popular enough to stock on their shelves. These books you can pick up and browse through. This will get you acquainted with a few related books. You don't need to spend an arm and a leg buying every related book you find; just get a feel for the market for now. You might carry a pocket notebook on which to write down the titles and authors, though, and perhaps jot down a few notes.

A major library will have some older books that bookstores likely will not have. Library books you can check out without putting a dent in your budget.

It's good to browse through physical copies of books, as you can learn quite a bit about them that way, but you won't find many of the books on the market at bookstores or libraries – so this won't complete your search. Remember to check the references at the back of these books, as many of these works may be related to your work.

Next, search online. Amazon has a large database of current and old, used and new books. First try browsing subjects, where you can find all of the books related to a single subcategory. Next try searching by a variety of keywords in books (not in specific categories, as some books will not appear in the categories you expect). Useful books will not always appear at the top of your search, so you'll want to spend some time browsing through search results. You can get ideas for other keywords to use by reading descriptions, covers, reviews, and contents of related books. Friends, family, and colleagues may suggest a few more keywords that you hadn't thought of.

Some online books will let you search inside – front and back cover, front matter, back matter, and contents. You can also see sample pages, but you won't be able to browse as much of the book as you can in a bookstore. When browsing through a physical book, you can see how many figures it has and how good they are, learn how technical the writing is, find out how well-written the book is, and several other aspects that may be of interest. Other online books will not have the Search Inside feature.

It will be useful to learn more about the online books, including those with no Search Inside. You might be able to find book reviews to offer some input, or you may be able to find physical copies of these books somewhere. If the cost is cheap and you're willing to invest, you might purchase a few of the books you find online that seem most useful. Remember, on Amazon you can recover some of your investment later by reselling these books used.

Compiling Your Research

For each book, you want to learn enough about it to decide if it's mostly competitive, mostly complementary, otherwise related, or not useful. Also note which seem most useful and relevant for your purposes.

These related works have much information that can be useful to you. For one, you want your own book to be distinguished from the competition, so you need to acquaint yourself with the market to achieve this. You really would like to learn what the market needs and supply this need. Browsing through related works may help you organize your ideas for your own work. You will also see a variety of styles and formatting – decisions you will need to make when you begin writing your own book. These titles will help you establish a fair price for your book.

Record notes now, which may prove to be useful later. List the books, indicate how they relate to your work (e.g. competitive or complementary), record the price and whether it is softcover, hardbound (since softcover generally sells for less), or an eBook, and make useful notes about each book – with more description for related works that you deem to be more useful to you. Separately, you may want to jot down ideas you get about your own book as you sort through the market.

You also want to measure the success of these books. Some may be bestsellers – this could be noted on the cover, on the book rack in a bookstore, on a description of the book, or on a bestseller list. If so, note this and consider why the book sold well. Was the author already well-known? Was the book promoted well? Was it distributed by a major publisher? Is it well-written? Does it fill a useful market need? Etc.

You can also gauge how well a book sells by searching for it on Amazon. Note that many books will have different editions available on Amazon, and some editions may sell better than others. If the book has sold on Amazon.com, it will have a sales rank on its webpage. (So if a book doesn't have a sales rank, it has yet to sell its first copy.)

Amazon.com Sales Rank

A book with a very low sales rank (like 5,000) sells with higher frequency, and a book with a very high sales rank (like 1,500,000) sells with very low frequency.

> The smaller the number of the Amazon.com sales rank, the better the book has been selling recently.

After a book has not sold for two or more days, the sales rank grows into the 200,000's and begins to climb. A book with a sales rank in the 1,000,000's has not sold for several days; some of the books with sales ranks in the millions may have not sold for a month or more.

For a book that has not sold for two or more days, if it suddenly sells on Amazon.com, shortly afterward the sales rank drops to about 100,000 and begins to climb back up. A book with a sales rank between 100,000 and 300,000 has probably sold within the last day or two. (The same concept applies to Kindle eBooks, but the numbers are somewhat different.)

In this way, the sales rank is more a measure of how long it has been since the book last sold. Since it can fluctuate considerably – being a very high number because it hasn't sold for several days, and then suddenly dropping down to a much lower number after a sale – it is not what you might intuitively expect. Sales rank combines sales data for the past day, week, and month.

Fortunately, the sales rank is not tied to the total number of copies that have sold on Amazon. This way, relatively new books can compete with popular books that have been on the market for a long period of time. If you do a search on Amazon that sorts results by bestselling, new books that have sold well recently can come up early in the search, and old books that have sold numerous copies but have been inactive recently will show up later in the search. This has a positive impact on your sales when you self-publish on Amazon, especially since your sales largely depend upon customers finding your book in a search. We'll discuss other ways that customers might find your book in a search in Chapter 10.

Books with sales ranks under 50,000 have probably sold two or more copies within the last day. A book with a sales rank under 10,000 has been selling well recently.

The sales rank can be deceiving, especially if you view the sales rank at a relative low or high for a particular book. However, if you monitor the sales rank over a period of time – like a couple of times a week for a few weeks – you can get a better measure.

If a book maintains a sales rank under 10,000 for a few weeks, it's a pretty hot seller. It is selling multiple copies every day.

If a book averages with a sales rank from 100,000 to 300,000 over a period of a few weeks, it is probably selling about a copy a day. A book that never drops below 1,000,000 probably has not sold at all while you've been monitoring its sales rank.

In addition to the sales rank, a book that is one of the top 100 sellers in a subcategory will give its rank, from 1 to 100, in that category. For example, a book that is #37 in sales in geometry is one of the top fifty sellers in the subcategory geometry. If instead it were #37 in mathematics, it would be an even better seller (since mathematics is a much broader category with numerous subcategories).

The sales ranks of related works can give you some idea of how well, or poorly, books like yours may sell on Amazon.com. This is important if you are trying to predict whether or not it may be financially worthwhile to write your book and self-publish it.

Bear in mind that many of the books that you find on Amazon also sell as physical copies in bookstores. Those books are selling more copies than Amazon's sales rank indicates.

If you intend to sell your books mostly on Amazon.com, then the sales rank is quite important to you as it will determine how often you receive royalties. If your book is only available on Amazon.com, then every copy you sell affects your book's sales rank. Note that there might be other books that sell reasonably well, but don't have a strong sales rank because only a fraction are sold through Amazon.

Ask yourself how many copies you expect to sell each month, and then try to determine if this is plausible. Browse the top sellers in the category that would be the best fit for your book. How often do these books sell on Amazon? This serves as an idea of the absolute best that you might expect.

You should also ask yourself what a reasonable expectation for your book is. Do you really have reason to expect your book to be a top seller? What is the competition in this category? Are the bestsellers written by popular authors or highly qualified authors? Are the bestsellers promoted well?

Try searching for books in your potential category that seem comparable to your book in some sense. Try searching for books published by Amazon to see how well these print-on-demand self-published books do in your category. This might serve as a better indication. Enter "CreateSpace Independent Publishing Platform" or "Independently Published" into the search field at Amazon.

Browse through the bestselling self-published books at Amazon to see what types of books are selling well at the moment. Keep in mind that these stats can change considerably over the course of a month – a book that is selling very well today might not be selling well in a few weeks. Check out some of their sales ranks. Look for books that seem like they could be comparable to your book in some ways. Note that there are hundreds of thousands of books that are self-published on Amazon, but not all of these sell well. Also, there are thousands of books self-published that use an imprint; many of these sell well, but won't show up in your search for self-published books because they have an imprint name rather than CreateSpace Independent Publishing Platform or Independently Published listed under the publisher field at Amazon.

There are ways to help your sales grow once you make your book available. So whatever your sales rank is when your book starts out, it can improve over time. We'll look at marketing strategies, including some specific to Amazon.com, in Chapter 10. If you're concerned about how well your book will sell, you might browse through Chapter 10 now. If you're willing to implement some of these marketing strategies, you might develop some confidence that your book can be successful.

4 Preparing the Manuscript

I F YOU INTEND TO use Amazon KDP to publish your book on Amazon.com, you will eventually need to create a PDF file, as described in Chapter 7. This is very common among self-publishing services. If you prepare your manuscript with Microsoft Word, you will be able to convert it to PDF later. Microsoft Word is convenient for most self-published authors because the most writers are familiar with this software and it is more economic than many specialized publishing programs, like Adobe InDesign, although Serif Page Plus is much more affordable. If you don't have access to Microsoft Word, consider Open Office.

In this book, I will provide formatting instructions for Microsoft Word 2003 and 2010 for Windows, as these are the most popular word processing programs used by self-published authors. Note that Microsoft Word 2007 and 2013 are very similar to 2010.

Before You Begin Writing

Collect and organize your thoughts into an outline. If you are writing nonfiction, prepare a chapter outline. First decide which topics to cover and in which order to present them. Next, give each chapter more detail: Either divide the chapters into sections or write a paragraph to describe what you will cover in each chapter. This will help you prepare a well-organized, structured, and complete manuscript. It will force you to think the concept for your book through, and the result will be a more detailed vision for your work.

For fiction, prepare a story outline, such as a summary of events. You might also develop some of your characters in advance by writing descriptions of them. This will help you stay organized as you write your story; you can refer to these notes to ensure that your book is self-consistent (posting your notes, character development, outlines, and related preparatory materials on your blog – see Chapter 10 – can help to build buzz for your coming book and can help develop a professional image). A few artistic writers of fiction like to write with a fresh canvas, so to speak – i.e. without any preconceptions. If this describes you, that's fine (some fiction authors strongly prefer it), but most of us benefit from organizing our ideas before we write.

Focus on writing your manuscript first, and save most of the formatting details for when your writing is finished. We'll discuss formatting in the next chapter, where the emphasis is on editing your manuscript. Much of the formatting requires more and more memory, so your computer is less likely to encounter problems if your document consists mostly of plain text as you write your manuscript.

Concentrate just on writing text. Don't worry about figures, tables, headings, footnotes, the title page, or any pages that require special formatting until the text is complete. Headings, footnotes, figures, and tables, for example, require more active memory just to open your document. Even if your computer has a lot of memory, you will be doing yourself a favor to save the formatting for later. If you want to draw pictures or create tables while they are fresh on your mind, make them in separate files – just one picture or table per file – to avoid memory-related problems.

> Save figures, tables, headings, footnotes, and all other formatting until after you complete writing the text in order to maximize the active memory of your computer while you type your manuscript. If you want to draw figures or create tables sooner, put them in separate individual files.

Save your file frequently. After you type a page of work, if you don't want to risk losing it, save it before writing more. Don't always save your manuscript with the same filename. I suggest including a version number with the filename, and updating the version regularly. For example, as you write the first chapter, you might save the file as Mystery 1.doc. Once you begin the second chapter, save it as Mystery 2.doc. You can have both chapters together in the same document. The idea is that if the most recent version of the file becomes corrupt, for example, you will have older versions to fall back on. Save your file in at least two different places, so that if you lose your file you still have another copy somewhere else. Unfortunately, computer problems are somewhat too common, but you can take measures to avoid losing your work. Save the file on a jump drive and also email it to yourself, for example.

> Save your manuscript regularly, and save it to two different places, like a jump drive and email. Change the version number frequently so that if you have problems with the most recent version, you can fall back on an older version.

Get a notebook or journal to carry around with you everywhere you go – such as a pocket notebook or journal that fits in a purse. You never know when you will think of a good idea for your book, so you want to be prepared to write it down whenever it comes. It's frustrating to remember that you had a good idea, but forgot exactly what it was. You might wake up at 2:00 a.m. with book ideas, so keep your notebook or journal near your bed, too.

> Be prepared to jot down book ideas whenever they may come. Keep a notebook or journal with you at all times.

Writing the Manuscript

To begin with, give some thought to writing a good title and subtitle. You want your title to be catchy, yet you want it to attract attention while still being informative – i.e. it should fit the genre or category well and convey something about your book. An optional subtitle can help you to elaborate on what your book is about.

Shorter titles tend to be more effective, especially in fiction. Shorter titles also have an advantage when it comes to marketing, as they are easier to remember and take up less room in online posts.

Nonfiction authors can include a few relevant keywords in the title and subtitle. However, it's more important for the title to read well and effectively convey the content; any keywords are secondary. If the title and subtitle are loaded with keywords, this strategy will probably backfire.

If you plan on selling largely through Amazon.com, including a couple of keywords that potential buyers may be searching for, which are related to your book, may help improve the visibility of your book in search results. Nonfiction authors can usually do this and still create effective titles; it's not as easy to squeeze keywords into fiction titles without making the title less effective (note that most bestselling fiction titles have just three words or less).

Keep in mind that you will have the opportunity to enter five keywords that aren't in the title or subtitle when you publish your book, so if there are relevant keywords that don't fit well in your title, you'll still have a chance to use them.

Give some thought to these keywords, and consider what keywords were useful when researching the competition for your book. You want your book to show up with searches of competitive and complementary titles, so you need to know what keywords are linked to those titles. You can't get every keyword into your title and subtitle, and it won't read well at all if your title is nothing but a jumble of keywords, so you will have to selectively identify just the most useful keywords. Once you submit your book for publishing, your title is fixed in stone, so choose it wisely. Consider feedback that you may receive from friends and family regarding your title. Focus on writing an effective title and subtitle. Keywords are secondary, and you get to add five keywords that aren't in your title or subtitle when you publish, so don't let keywords dictate your title for you. Remember, fiction titles usually don't have keywords; nonfiction titles usually use a few.

As you write your manuscript, bear in mind the importance of your book being well-written, well-organized, thorough, and self-consistent. You will receive reviews of your book once customers have bought your book and read it, and you want readers to recommend your book to their friends and family. So these details are important.

Invest in a book (or borrow one from a library) that describes rules of grammar and style. There are several such books, so you can easily find one that suits you. You will also want a dictionary and thesaurus handy. You want readers to focus on the content of your book, but any time they come across a grammatical or spelling mistake, it will distract their attention. Many mistakes can be caught with a word processor such as Microsoft Word, but this process is not foolproof. For example, if you misspell a word that turns out to be a different word, this mistake will not be caught. For example, if you mean to write the word *spite*, but instead write the word *spire* – which is easy to do since these two letters are adjacent to one another on the keyboard – this mistake will not be caught by the computer.

A style manual will help your book read better. For example, it will remind you to think about the sentence structure, so that it is not too repetitive. You will also remember to avoid fragments and run-on sentences and a host of other details that can help you write better.

Many guides will also have word lists to help you mix things up. When you read your draft, look for repetitiveness. Your work will read better if the writing exhibits some variety. Word lists will include a variety of action verbs and descriptive adjectives, for example.

Decide whether to write in the first person, second person, or third person, and whether to use the singular or plural – i.e. using *I*, *me*, and *my*; or *we* and *our*; or *you* and *your*; or *he*, *she*, and *they*. There may be reasons to use more than one person – e.g. mostly *you* and *your*, but other times *I*, *me*, and *my*. This could be the case if you are writing a book to give advice to your audience, in which case *I* refers to the author and *you* the reader.

Also, choose a tense – past tense or present. For fiction, you will need to have a setting in mind, which may change in different scenes of your book.

Check out similar titles to see which person and tense they use. Use a search engine to find out which of these tend to appeal better to readers, which are easier to write, and which tend to be accepted in which genres.

Note that there are three popular conventions for dialog tags:

- Use a simple "he said" or "she said" to indicate who the speaker is. For example, John said, "My book is almost finished."
- Use a precise verb, with an adjective if helpful, when this helps to convey meaning or tone. For example, Martha whispered slowly, "The monster is right behind that door."
- Don't use any dialog tags when the speaker, tone, and meaning are clear from the context. For example: Roger bumped his head on the wall after slipping on Fred's roller skate. "Ouch! Fred, you're in big trouble, son."

Sometimes you will need to refer to page numbers, chapters, figures, or tables, or you will need to cite references. The page numbers you refer to can change frequently as you write and revise your book, and so can the numbers to chapters, figures, tables, and references. The best thing is to write ### or something else that will be easy to find later and save this for when your book is totally complete. When there is no longer a chance that these numbers may change, do a search on your word processor to find all instances of ### and then replace the ###'s with the appropriate numbers. Readers will be frustrated if you refer to incorrect chapters, pages, figures, tables, or references. Alternatively, you can use Word's built-in cross-reference tool.

> Save referrals to page numbers, chapters, figures, tables, and references until your book is 100% complete in order to avoid referring to incorrect numbers.

There are a few different popular styles for how to cite references. Choose one that is appropriate for the type of book you are writing; look at some related works to develop a feel for this.

Plagiarism

Copying the work of another and passing it off as your own – even as little as a single phrase – is called plagiarism. Plagiarism is a very serious problem with serious legal consequences. Quote any sentences that you copy and properly cite the source(s) of your quotes or paraphrases, and stay within limits to how much you are permitted to cite, in order to avoid engaging in an instance of plagiarism.

Be sure to avoid plagiarism. If you copy one or more sentences, or even just a phrase, from another source, you must enclose this in quotation marks (") and cite the source as a reference – following the style guidelines for citing references. Even if you paraphrase the sentence, you need to cite your source. You also need to cite any research you may use to write your book. Failure to properly cite your reference for sentences that you copy or paraphrase can carry very serious legal consequences, so you definitely want to avoid this. There are limits to how much you can quote and paraphrase; an attorney can help you determine what constitutes "fair use."

Copying just one line from song lyrics can lead to legal action. Research "fair use" before quoting or paraphrasing anything for your book.

Note that citing your source does not relieve you of possible legal liabilities. Use a search engine to research "fair use." If you use just a single line from song lyrics, for example, the company that holds the rights to the lyrics can sue you for copyright infringement and even prevent the sale of your book until the issue is resolved.

Write with your intended audience in mind. Who is likely to read your book, and what will they be looking for? The answers to these questions affect how you should write your manuscript. For example, you need to consider at what level you should write, how much detail is appropriate, and what the reader will already know before picking up your book.

You want to make sure that you get your ideas across clearly and effectively. Consider the fact that different people think in different ways. If you ask a large group of people to describe how to eat an orange, you might be surprised by the results. Try it! Someone who thinks scientifically might describe this like a laboratory manual – starting with a technique for peeling the orange and finishing with putting the first bite in your mouth. Someone who thinks more passionately may instead describe how to enjoy the taste of the orange and savor the juices that shoot out when you bite down on it. It's important to consider how different people might interpret what you write. Being familiar with how your target audience thinks can help you out with this.

Some sections you will enjoy writing more than others. At some point, almost every writer gets frustrated. When this happens, you might take a little time off. Clear your mind and approach it when you feel fresh. The notion of completing a book can also feel overwhelming at times. The best way to deal with this is to force yourself to write one page at a time. Make a little progress here and there and this will add up – eventually, you will see that you are getting somewhere and this will lift your spirits. Look forward to the next part of the book that you will really enjoy, as this can help you with your motivation.

While you do want your writing to be very good, you're being too much of a perfectionist if you find yourself frequently deleting a large portion of your work and starting over. If this happens, you need to force yourself to write *something* and complete your work. Finish a draft of your work and you will gain a sense of completion. You can always go back and improve upon it afterward. It's important to feel that you are accomplishing something; it's better to finish a draft and then revise it than to spend too much time writing your first version.

5 Editing and Formatting the Manuscript

O NCE YOUR BOOK IS complete, it is time to proofread your book for necessary revisions, add figures and tables, add front and back matter, and format your book interior, thereby transforming the design of your manuscript into a professionally formatted book interior.

Amazon KDP has a variety of template Word documents (both blank and with sample formatted content) that you can use to prepare your manuscript with. Some authors find these helpful; some authors get frustrated trying to adjust the formatting.

The formatting prepared in the templates is minimal – it divides your document into sections for you. You gain much freedom starting with a blank Word document and formatting it yourself, and you can achieve everything the templates would do for you and much more without using them. Doing it yourself also spares you from having to figure out how to revise the formatting of the templates, add new sections, and adjust settings that might not appeal to you.

If you elect to use the templates, one thing you should do is change Amazon KDP's pagination settings. In Word 2003, these are in Format > Paragraph > Line and Page Breaks; in Word 2010, go to the Home tab and click the funny icon in the bottom right corner of the Paragraph group, then choose the Line and Page Breaks tab. Uncheck Widow/Orphan Control, Keep With Next, Keep Lines Together, and Page Break Before (it's better to deal with these issues manually, as explained later in this chapter). You want to select all and apply these changes to the entire document (remove the blue dots from these checkboxes).

You have a choice between working with a .doc or .docx extension. If your book is mostly text, like a novel, the .doc extension will probably be simpler. Some rich formatting, such as the new equation tool (as opposed to the equation editor from 2003) is only supported in .docx format. If you use newer formatting features only available with .docx, you'll want to check how these features convert to PDF in Chapter 7. (You can make a test PDF now of the work that you've done so far.)

Revising Your Manuscript

When you finish writing the text, examine the content and organization. You will probably see some conceptual or organizational changes that you would like to make. These are the first types of revisions that you should attend to.

Next, you should proofread the text. Make sure that it reads well. Look for misspelled words, instances where you may have inadvertently used the wrong word, and grammatical mistakes. Also look for sentences or paragraphs that need more than just minor revisions. Rethink the content through as you read your manuscript. Check for content mistakes and self-consistency. Reconsider how the content is presented. Imagine yourself as a sample of your target audience reading the book for the first time, and highlight parts of the book that may be worth revising. Ask yourself if each part of the book reads well.

It is well worth having friends or family read your manuscript. Prepare yourself for some constructive criticism, then ask for honest constructive comments – what they like and what they don't. Consider their ideas, comments, and suggestions, as this is a sample of what readers may notice and think when they read your book. Ultimately, you have to judge whether or not to make revisions based on one or more of these suggested revisions; not all of them will be for the best. Everyone will have a different vision for what your book could be. It is your writing, so you are responsible for making these decisions, but many people (hopefully!) will be reading it, so your decisions will impact them (and perhaps how many people read your book).

Focus your attention on the basic text first. Once that is done, then move onto other aspects of your book.

Figures, Tables, and Equations

Note: You might want to add headers, footnotes, and page numbers prior to adding figures, tables, and equations. Otherwise, the placement of figures, tables, and equations may shift after adding these formatting features. See the last section in this chapter for information about headers and page numbers.

Before you add figures, tables, and equations to your manuscript, save your plain text document. Then resave it with a different filename – like MystFig1.doc instead of MystPlain4.doc. This way, if you experience any problems with your file after adding figures, tables, and equations, you will still have your plain text file to fall back on. Remember to save your files with different version numbers, so if after adding the tenth figure you have a file problem, you may still be able to open a version that has some of the figures. Also save your files in more than one place – like on a jump drive and email it to yourself, just in case (too safe is better than sorry).

Let me remind you that I will focus on how to use Microsoft Word 2003 and 2010 for Window in this book, since most self-published authors use one of these programs (2007 and 2013 are very similar to 2010). Some of these techniques can also be applied to other programs, but it's not feasible for me to try to explain how to use every software package on the market.

Photographs and other pictures that you have already saved in individual files can be inserted into your manuscript. In Microsoft Word, go to the Insert tab and choose Picture. Once you insert your picture, you can right-click on it and choose from an assortment of options. If you simply left-click on the picture once, you will be able to access a toolbar for formatting the picture. Some of the basic options include cropping and resizing (lock the aspect ratio first). However, it's better to crop and resize the picture in the native picture program and not adjust it after inserting the image into your Word file, otherwise the picture may print with less than its maximum resolution (see Chapter 6).

I strongly recommend choosing a wrapping style that is in line with the text, which you can find under Layout after you right-click on the picture (and choose Format Picture). Other types of layouts require much more of your computer's active memory, which slows your system down and makes it much more susceptible to serious problems – like the file closing while you are working on it or becoming corrupt. With the picture wrapped in line with the text, you can simply click the centering icon in order to center the picture.

> When you can format a picture to be in line with the text, this helps minimize memory and other problems.

If you want a picture to appear centered horizontally and placed on its own line (or its own page), adjust the layout to be in line with text. If you want the paragraph to wrap around the image, use square or tight wrapping instead (but note that the positioning can change as you edit the document). Depending on your needs, placing the picture in front of or behind text may be the best option: This takes more memory, which may be an issue if you have numerous pictures (in which case it might help to separate your file into smaller documents).

You can draw black-and-white as well as color pictures that appear very professional in Microsoft Word. Once you acquaint yourself with the basic drawing tools, as described in the next chapter, you should see that you have much more flexibility in drawing than you might expect. Every diagram in my books on extra dimensions was drawn using Microsoft Word and/or Microsoft Excel. All of the covers for my books, including those that feature drawings of golf holes, were drawn in Microsoft Word (except for the cover of this book and *Spooky Word Scrambles*, which were designed by artist Melissa Stevens at www.theillustratedauthor.net). Every picture was drawn from scratch using basic drawing tools – there was no clipart or copying and pasting of other pictures (except for pictures that I had already drawn myself, and where I needed another picture like it). If you browse through the covers of my books (you can find them easily on Amazon), you will see a sample of the drawing possibilities offered by Microsoft Word. (The two exceptions include the covers for this book and *Spooky Word Scrambles*.)

I have used specialty drawing programs in the past, like Corel Draw, yet Microsoft Word is fairly good. It's also very convenient if you type your text in Microsoft Word and plan to have your completed manuscript in Microsoft Word, too. Some people like Paint, but I find that pictures drawn in Paint often come out looking very unprofessional on the screen as well as in print (e.g. edges often appear jagged and if you look closely, you may see stray marks). If you explore the drawing tools that I describe below for Microsoft Word, you will be able to make illustrations that look more professional.

However, if you have access to PhotoShop and have some expertise with it, you can create some highly professional pictures with that. More than just having the software, you want to have some experience with PhotoShop and a good understanding of the graphic arts techniques that it entails (in order to avoid common design mistakes made with filters and layers, for example).

Regardless of how you make your diagrams, you should save your figures in separate files. So even if you use Microsoft Word to draw your figures, start with a blank document and save them in individual files. That way, if the interior file with both text and figures becomes corrupt, you may still be able to retrieve the figures individually. Save your figures separately, save your text file by itself, and once all are complete, save yet a new file with both text and figures together.

If you draw diagrams in Microsoft Word, once a diagram is complete, select all of the objects in your drawing and group the objects together to create a single drawing. Where viable, right-click the image to change the layout to be in line with the text. Again, this will help to conserve memory and avoid problems.

Consult the next chapter for instructions on how to use Microsoft Word's drawing tools.

If you use another program to draw a picture, make a graph, or make a photo, after inserting this picture into Microsoft Word, you can still use Microsoft Word's drawing tools to add to the picture. You can also add textboxes to create labels. Use basic textboxes. Right-click textboxes, then choose no outline and no fill for the outline and fill colors – since diagrams look more professional when the labels aren't surrounded by rectangles, and if the fill is instead white the label will block out part of the picture.

> Change the outline color from black to no outline to make textboxes look like professional labels. Similarly, change the fill color to no fill so that the labels do not block any parts of the pictures.

Note that if you crop, resize, or otherwise edit imported pictures in the Word document, the images may get compressed. Ideally, you want your images to be 300 DPI. Some images look fine at 200 or 150 DPI, while others look noticeably better at 300 DPI. Word has a tendency to compress images such that they print at 200 DPI or less. You must take steps to avoid this compression, as described in Chapter 6.

In older versions of Microsoft Word (2003 and prior), you may be able to group imported pictures, textboxes, and drawing elements that you create in Microsoft Word together into a single object (but see the note in the previous paragraph). Then you can right-click this single object to change the layout to be in line with the text. Some of the newer versions of Word may restrict what can or can't be grouped together. If possible, avoid having many images floating around your document that are not in line with the text as this leads to memory and file problems.

If you have a large number of tables, figures, and/or equations, I recommend separating your book into several files – one file per chapter. This makes the file size more manageable and frees up active memory so that your programs work faster and are less susceptible to problems. When each chapter is complete, you can copy and paste them all into one large document (or, better yet, if you have a PDF converter that allows you to join separate PDF files together, you can simply leave your Word files separate).

You can draw tables in Microsoft Word by going to Insert and choosing Table (or in older versions going directly to the Table tab). When your cursor is in the table, you will be able to access design and formatting features as well as table tools. Table properties let you change the width and height of cells, rows, columns, or the whole table, modify text position, and more. You can easily add or remove rows or columns, split cells, merge cells, and so on. The tools are very intuitive. It just takes a little exploration to get used to where to find the features you are looking for. Remember that Microsoft Word has a Help feature to help you figure out what you need. In the worst case, you can probably find someone to ask for a little help.

You may want to type a numbered caption beneath each figure and table. If so, prepare these meticulously: Make sure that you follow the exact same format each time, otherwise the alert reader may be distracted by non-uniformity. If you plan to describe the tables and figures in the text, numbering them can help the reader find the tables and figures that you refer to. This is particularly useful if the tables and figures that you describe are not near the text that refers to them – for example, if you refer to a figure in Chapter 3 when you are writing Chapter 7. Some books do not have table and figure captions, though. It's partly a matter of function and partly a matter of style.

If you use any math in your book you will need to include equations. Microsoft Word has a built-in tool for creating equations, which is pretty intuitive. If you are writing a mathematical or scientific book that will involve regular use of equations, you might prefer Microsoft Word 2007 or later, as the newer equation tool has many improved formatting possibilities compared to the 2003 equation editor. You must save the file as .docx, not .doc, in order to use the new equation tool. (Find the new equation editor in Insert > Equation; find the old editor in Insert > Object > Microsoft Equation 3.0. In Word 2007 and up, you must use the old editor in .doc mode, but can use the new editor in .docx mode.)

If you have extensive use of equations, an alternative is obtaining, learning, and using LaTeX – which lets you write equation commands in a basic text editor, which transform into formatted equations when a compiler converts your text file to PDF.

If you type equations, following are some conventions that you should be aware of. Symbols that represent constants (e.g. the speed of light c) and variables (e.g. position x) should appear italicized (the default setting in Microsoft Word's equation editor), but units (like m/s) should not be italicized (you will need to change these to normal). Vectors should appear in boldface and/or have an arrow over them (like $\vec{\mathbf{A}}$). Browse through various mathematics textbooks and papers for more style choices.

If you need to add an equation to a diagram – perhaps creating a mathematical label – in Microsoft Word 2003 you can right-click the equation and change the layout to be in front of text. In Microsoft Word 2007 and up, you can first insert a plain textbox (removing its outline and fill) and then insert an equation into the textbox (or, if the equation is already typed, cut and paste the equation into the textbox). Afterward, remember to group objects together and to make the group in line with the text, whenever this is viable.

Front and Back Matter

Front and back matter are sections that appear at the beginning or end of the book. Front matter commonly includes the title page, copyright page, table of contents, and one or more of the following: introduction, prelude, dedications, and acknowledgements. Acknowledgments may also appear at the end of the introduction instead of in a separate section. Back matter commonly includes one or more of the following sections: appendices, references (or bibliography), glossary, index, about the author, and advertisements for other books. Trying to include all of these sections is overkill. Choose those that are most relevant for your work.

Almost all books begin with a title page, which has a copyright page on its back side. The title page should include the title, subtitle, and author, and may have other information and even figures; it could simply be a black-and-white copy of the front cover (unless you are writing a book with a color interior). The title page should be centered both horizontally and vertically. To center it vertically, highlight the text and go to Page Layout, where you can choose to vertically center only the highlighted text (not the section or entire document). After, check the page(s) that follow to see that they didn't get vertically centered, too. It might help to temporarily add an extra blank line to the end of the title page and highlight only the text preceding this line before centering vertically. Sometimes a new blank page will appear after, which you will have to delete – with trial and error you can delete any blank pages without undoing the vertical centering.

Including a copyright page will make your book appear more professional. The copyright page should include the title and subtitle, but in a smaller size font – whereas the title page should use a larger font for the title – and the author's name. Indicate the year after a copyright symbol, like © 2009. You may want to include a note about the rights being reserved and that no portion of the book may be copied in any form without the author's permission. You should write this in your own words to avoid plagiarism. (However, you have permission to copy and use the copyright note that I used on the copyright page of my book – or modify it as you see fit.) Most fictional works also include a statement to the effect that all persons and places are purely fictional and that any resemblance to real people or places is purely coincidental. Of course, an attorney can advise you best.

Examine traditionally published books similar to yours and study their copyright pages, title pages, front matter, back matter, headers, footers, layout, design, font styles, indentation sizes, justification or centering, vertical justification or centering, and so on. These models can help you perfect the design of your book.

Find books similar to yours in libraries and bookstores (also explore Look Insides at Amazon) and study their front matter, back matter, headers, footers, and other formatting, layout, and design features. Use these as guides for the formatting of your book (but don't plagiarize their designs).

A copyright page may also indicate the category for your book. You should include the ISBN number on the copyright page. You don't know this yet (unless you happen to already have one), so save this until you are ready to submit your files for publishing. Once you set up your account to load your files, you will receive an ISBN-10 and EAN-13, which you can simply copy and paste into your copyright page before making your final PDF files. Publishers also indicate the edition number and a series of numbers for the print number. You can include an edition number, optionally, but those printing numbers don't make sense for print-on-demand. Study traditionally published copyright pages to find other ideas, like including the category.

I suggest inserting a table in Microsoft Word with two columns and several rows for your table of contents. Move the column divider far to the right – just enough to type a three-digit number like 256 (try this to check that it's wide enough). You can change the formatting of the table so that it doesn't show the cell borders (actually, it will turn these gray in color so that you can see them on the screen, but the borders won't print – well, you should check this to be sure). Alternative to the table, you can make two uneven columns of text (by changing the format to two columns). There is also a Table of Contents tool under References.

The other front matter and back matter sections are straightforward to make – they mostly consist of text. Basically, you just need to look at some samples from traditionally published books to develop an idea for how these should read and appear.

Formatting Your Manuscript

It's good to save the formatting for last. Doing all the formatting in a short period of time helps to have a uniformly formatted book – otherwise you might forget what choices you have made and format parts of the book differently. The placement of figures, tables, and equations is sensitive to the structure of your document. That is, if you insert a figure prematurely and later add or remove text before the figure, the figure will appear in a different place – perhaps partway between two pages. So it's best to wait until the text is completed, then insert figures, tables, and equations exactly where you want them to appear. Subtle formatting like manual hyphenation, widows, orphans, and kerning can't be implemented until the pages are otherwise finalized – you have to redo these features every time you make any revisions to the text or page layout.

Examples of Justified Text

This paragraph is aligned left. This paragraph is aligned left. This paragraph is aligned left. This paragraph is aligned left. This paragraph is aligned left. This paragraph is aligned left. This paragraph is aligned left. This paragraph is aligned left.

This paragraph is aligned right. This paragraph is aligned right. This paragraph is aligned right. This paragraph is aligned right. This paragraph is aligned right. This paragraph is aligned right. This paragraph is aligned right. This paragraph is aligned right.

This paragraph is centered.
This paragraph is centered.
This paragraph is centered.
This paragraph is centered.
This paragraph is centered.

This paragraph is justified full. This paragraph is justified full. This paragraph is justified full. This paragraph is justified full. This paragraph is justified full. This paragraph is justified full. This paragraph is justified full. This paragraph is justified full.

For most books, the body text should generally be justified full – that is, both the right and left edges of the text should appear to line up very nicely. Contrast this with left alignment (also called ragged right), right alignment (ragged left), or centered. Chapter headings, figures, tables, equations, and notes that you want to stand out might be centered on their own lines. The copyright page and a few other pages might be aligned left (or centered) instead of justified full.

Microsoft Word lets you justify, align, or center text easily by clicking an icon that mimics the structure of the text. First highlight the text you wish to justify, align, or center, then click the icon.

Many new authors don't like the gaps they see with fully justified text, but if you think about it, the gaps at the right edges of left-aligned text are even bigger. This is why left alignment is often termed ragged right. Since almost all traditionally published books are justified full, if your book is aligned left, it may have a self-published look to it.

Here is a tip: Use hyphenation with your fully justified text. This will reduce the gaps in many cases. You can do this manually (but consult a dictionary first), or you can turn on Word's hyphenation tool to do this automatically. Don't do any manual hyphenation until your text and page layout are perfected, otherwise you'll get stray hyphens mid-line.

> Use full justification and hyphenation for a more professional appearance.

In Word 2003, look for Tools > Language > Hyphenation. In Word 2010, look for Page Layout > Hyphenation; also, go to File > Options (below Help) > Advanced > Layout Options (at the bottom) and check the box to hyphenate like WordPerfect for improved hyphenation. Increase the hyphenation zone to about 0.4, otherwise you get an excessive number of hyphens. You might also wish to limit the number of consecutive hyphens. To undo an automatic hyphen, place the cursor at the beginning of the word and press Shift + Enter. With automatic hyphenation turned on, you can still insert hyphens manually, if desired (but once you insert manual hyphens, any revisions you make to your document may cause those hyphens to appear mid-line instead of at the end of the line where you inserted them, so you must watch out for this possibility).

Another way to reduce the gaps in fully justified text is to use a single space after the period, instead of two. Many well-educated people believe that you're supposed to use two spaces after a period, but this rule actually applies to using a typewriter, not publishing books. If you study the typeset of traditionally published books carefully, you can actually see that it's "correct" to only use one space after the period. This practice also spreads the spaces out better for fully justified text. If you already have two spaces after your periods, you just need to use the Replace tool to fix this quickly. If you doubt that one space is correct, I encourage you to Google a fascinating article called "Space Invaders" in *Slate Magazine* by Farhad Manjoo.

> When publishing a book, it's correct to use one space after a period, not two.

You'll want to note the distinction between hyphens (-) and dashes (– or —); dashes are longer. Use hyphens in hyphenated words (like good-hearted), to create hyphenated adjectives (like red-haired, blue-eyed girl), or to hyphenate a word that would otherwise go onto the next line, leaving large gaps in the previous line of justified text (like the word "justified" in this sentence). In contrast, dashes are used as separators – like this—or like this; they help to separate phrases that interrupt the main flow of the text.

The hyphen (-) appears on your keyboard. In Microsoft Word, you can create a dash automatically by typing a space, hyphen, then space or two consecutive hyphens (--) if the AutoCorrect feature is enabled. A better way (if you might make an eBook, this method is better at preserving these symbols) is to hold down the Alt key and type 0150 or 0151 to create the short (–) and long (—) dashes, respectively called en and em dashes. Include spaces around the short dash – like this – but not around the long dash—like this. Choose either the short or long dash and be consistent throughout your book; don't use both as I've done in this paragraph.

The long dash can also be used to set off a quotation (in this case, with a space), as in the example below.

> Better to write for yourself and have no public, than to write for the public and have no self. — Cyril Connolly in *The New Statesman*

Choose the style and size of your font. Times New Roman 12-point font is particularly common for the body of the text, but some people view Times New Roman as amateurish because it's used in many self-published books. This book utilizes Georgia, which is a little bolder than Times New Roman (the fact that Georgia looks similar to Times New Roman may be a drawback); another common choice for fiction is Garamond (it's somewhat lighter, though some readers feel it may be too light). It's worth researching fonts and choosing wisely for your unique book. For most common fonts, 10 to 12 points is a good place to start: The best test is to print out a sample page and compare it with traditionally published books serving as your models (don't make an exact replica, though – just use these models to guide your own ideas). The title, subtitle, chapter, and section headings often use a larger font size or appear in boldface (or both).

When you convert your book to PDF format for publishing, you'll need to embed the fonts. If you're not using one of Word's preinstalled fonts, you'll want to check that it allows commercial use and that it can be embedded in the PDF file. When you download a font or buy a font package, check the font license and see if commercial use is permitted. If so, once you download the font, find the font file (it may be in the fonts folder in the Control Panel or a location that you specified when you saved it; if not, try searching for it by name on your computer), right-click the font file, click Properties and Details, and look under Embeddability. If it says "No embedding permissions," you won't be able to embed the font in the PDF file. If it can be embedded, this doesn't guarantee that the font can be used for commercial use, so you must also check the font license. Check Font Squirrel and Font Space online for a selection of fonts to choose from. However, sticking to a common font like Georgia or Garamond may make your book more readable. At the very least, search online to find opinions on a font before adopting it.

You want your readers to be able to read your book without too much eye strain, but the larger the font size, the more pages your book will have and therefore the more your book will cost. In Times New Roman, Calibri, Georgia, Garamond, and many common fonts, the 12-point size is quite readable for most people. If your book is very long, you can save pages with a 10-point font, which is sometimes used. Publishers sometimes offer large print books with larger font sizes, for books popular enough to print a special edition for readers who require a larger font size. Some font styles often appear larger or smaller than other fonts of the same point measure; you can type a sentence in a variety of font styles and print the page as a means of comparison.

The default indent size in Microsoft Word is 0.5", but many traditionally published books use a smaller size, especially for books with smaller page sizes. You can measure the indents of traditionally published books similar to yours to see what's common. Don't use the spacebar to create tabs. If you'll be making an eBook version, too, don't use the tab key (or you'll wind up with crazy formatting for your eBook). Instead, use the First Line option in the Paragraph dialog box (in Word 2010, click the funny icon in the bottom right corner of the Paragraph group on the Home tab; in Word 2003 look on the Format menu): Change Special to First Line and manually set the numerical measure to properly indent a paragraph. You don't have to do this manually to every paragraph though: You can use the Styles feature built into Word. Right-click on the Normal style (at the top of the Home tab in Word 2010, or on the Formatting toolbar of Word 2003), choose Modify Style, click Format, select Paragraph, and set First Line. (You may also need to adjust other properties of the style, such as font style and size: The easy way to do this is to highlight a paragraph with the style set the way you like it, right-click on Normal style, and click Update. Then adjust the First Line in Normal style.) Once the Style is modified, it's easy to "paint" formatting.

Another issue is the leading. Basically, this determines the space between lines. Professional designers are familiar with measures specified in terms of font points (or relative to the em). If you don't want to get technical, the practical method is to play with the linespacing, print out sample pages, and compare with traditionally published books to get this right.

There are two common ways to create section breaks: Use three asterisks between two blank lines (like the one below) or use consecutive blank lines. Some traditionally published books indent the beginning paragraph of the subsequent section, others don't. Explore books that are similar to yours to see what's common (that's what readers will be accustomed to).

* * *

Go to Page Layout to choose the size of your pages. First go to the publisher's website (e.g. Amazon KDP) to see what trim sizes are available for your book. Note that there are restrictions on the number of pages permitted for your book based on the trim size and whether the interior is black-and-white or color – so make sure that the page count doesn't exceed the limits for the trim size that you select. In Page Layout, choose to apply this to the entire document (otherwise, you might only change the page size for one section) and set the page size to match the desired trim size.

Determine the sizes of some related books to help you choose a suitable trim size. The 5.5" x 8" trim size is close to mass market size. Trade paperback is somewhat larger. Note that it will be challenging to compete with mass market pricing, so marketing your book as a trade paperback may have an advantage. At Amazon KDP, a larger trim size costs the same as a smaller trim size – but the larger trim size means fewer pages, which will reduce the cost of your book (unless it has fewer than about a hundred pages for black-and-white or forty pages for color, in which case page count doesn't affect price). So you don't actually save money with a smaller size book; rather, this might cost you more money.

Set the page margins in Page Layout. I recommend .5" for the left, right, top, and bottom margins, plus a 0.5" gutter (what Word calls a gutter is really a half-gutter). Alternatively, if you adjust the setting of Multiple Pages, the options will include inside and outside margins instead of left and right: In this case, choosing 1" for the inside margin, 0.5" for the outside margin, 0.5" for the top and bottom, and 0" for the gutter will be equivalent. But before implementing my suggestion, first check to see what's common in your genre. Also, if you need to reduce your page count, one thing to consider is adopting narrower margins. Be sure to meet the minimum inside and outside margins that Amazon KDP specifies: 0.25" outside margins, and an inside margin of 0.375" for up to 150 pages, 0.75" for up to 400 pages, 0.875" for up to 600 pages, and 1" for more pages.

In Page Layout, choose different odd and even pages, and different first page, too. The gutter is an extra 0.5" width (it's only 0.5" in my example – it may be different for your book) added to the right or left margins: If you check the box to have different formatting on odd and even pages, then the gutter will automatically place the 0.5" on alternate sides of odd and even pages to leave an extra 0.5" on the edge of the page that fits into the binding of the book. I highly recommend this. (Again, if you work with inside and outside margins instead of left and right, then just make the inside margin larger – it would be 1" in my example – and set the gutter to zero.)

Insert page numbers and browse through the options for style and numbering. I like to choose a basic style that has the page number positioned where I would like it, and then format the page numbering after inserting it. Note that you can type symbols before and after the page number, like ~ 4 ~ instead of just 4. You can choose the page numbers to show on the outside or inside – meaning that it will alternate position on the left and right sides of the pages to always show up at the outside or inside edge of the page. Alternatively, page numbers can be centered. Also, page numbers can appear at the top or bottom of the pages.

Most books also have page headers (not to be confused with headings – a header appears at the top of nearly every page, whereas a heading precedes a chapter or section). You probably want different headers for odd and even pages. You might put the title on odd-page headers and your name on even-page headers, for example. I like to enter a linespace after the title or name, select the header text and linespace, go to format paragraph, switch from text to paragraph, and insert a horizontal line in the middle of the paragraph (all this while in the page header) – that's how I created the header that appears at the top of the pages of the paperback edition of this book. But browse other books and play around with this to see what suits you best.

Another common option is to put chapter names on the even pages and the title of the book on odd pages. There is a trick to doing this with Microsoft Word. The same trick is used to omit the page numbers from the first few pages, use Roman numerals for front matter, use Arabic numbers for most pages, and omit page numbers from the first page of each chapter. The trick has to do with creating sections. Backup your file and save it with two different filenames before you play with the headers and footers: Sometimes the file becomes corrupt, and if it does you'll be happy if you have another copy of your file saved somewhere (save it in a couple of places, like jump drive and email, just in case).

To use different kinds of page numbers (e.g. Roman numerals, Arabic numbers, and no numbers on selected pages) or different kinds of headers in different parts of your book, you must use section breaks. You want to divide your file up into sections where each "section" is a part of your book that will use a different style of page number or header. Remember to look at traditionally published books similar to yours as a guide for page numbering and header options.

Most books have no page numbers until the introduction, in which case the second "section" would start at the introduction. Then page numbering typically switches from Roman numerals to Arabic numbers in Chapter 1, which would begin a new section. If you want each chapter to have its name on the even-page headers, you must begin a new section with each chapter. You'll also need to decide how to separate your back matter into sections.

When a new "section" (as I've just defined it) needs to begin, remove the page break beginning the section and insert a Next Page break under Breaks in Page Layout instead. Don't use an ordinary page break because that won't define where a new section needs to start; the Next Page feature tells Microsoft Word where the page numbering or header style needs to change.

Next, start at the beginning of the document and systematically go through – section by section – and insert and adjust the page header and numbering options. When you place your cursor in the header of footer area, uncheck the box that says to link to the previous section until the Same as Previous flag disappears; then you can modify the current section's header or footer without messing up the previous section. After you change a section, go back to the previous section and make sure it's still okay. Occasionally, Word gets fussy and you need to use the Undo button, remove the current page break, insert a new Next Page section break, and try again.

The first page of a chapter often doesn't start at the top of a page. You can use the Enter key to drop it down a few lines, or you may find it more reliable to go into the Paragraph dialog box and enter a numerical measure for how far it should drop down. The chapter heading usually has a larger font style. The first letter often has a drop cap (Word has a built-in tool for this), and the first few words may also APPEAR IN CAPS.

Headers and footers can serve a function by providing valuable information (like page numbers and chapter names). They can also include a design that fits the theme of the book well. One other thing that they may do, which can be a problem, is distract the reader from the main text.

Most traditionally published books avoid widows. A widow is a single line of a paragraph that winds up on a page separated from the rest of the paragraph. You could revise the text to deal with widows, but ideally you would first perfect the text and design the page layout around the content, not revise the wording to fit the layout. There are a variety of methods to deal with widows, such as adding or removing hyphenation in end-of-line words, adjusting the kerning (look for the Advanced features in the Font dialog box), adding a tiny indent to either side of a paragraph, or making a slight adjustment to font size in one paragraph. The goal is to create an effect that the reader won't notice (like an indentation so small you can't see it with your eye unless you know to look for it) that eliminates the widow. Don't worry about widows until your content is otherwise perfected, otherwise you'll have to undo and redo these changes every time you revise the text or layout. Perfect and proofread your book carefully before worrying about widows.

In addition to eliminating widows, every page of the book lines up at the top and bottom (set the Vertical Alignment to Top in Page Layout) in most traditionally published books. This is especially important for novels and books that consist mostly of text. Some pages, like those with chapter or section headings, might not align at the bottom with the rest unless you play with the space before or after paragraphs for the heading text or make some other tiny adjustment to the paragraphs.

When you finish adding in all the figures and complete the formatting, scan through your document to see how all this formatting may have affected your book. You'll probably find extra or missing linespaces, strange page breaks, and other odd formatting features. You definitely don't want to publish your book without finding and correcting all of the formatting problems.

Proofread your book thoroughly. Receive feedback from friends and family. Make all of the final changes. Then put in the references to chapter numbers, page numbers, figures, tables, equations, and sources cited. If you wrote these as ### earlier, search for ### (using the Find option) and change all of these ###'s to the appropriate numerical values.

Now you should check that these changes didn't affect the formatting, and double-check these cross-references. Then your book interior will be complete – except for adding the ISBN and EAN to the copyright page, which you can do before making your PDF file and after setting up your account with Amazon KDP (who can supply you with an ISBN before you upload your files).

If you have to make more changes for some reason, you'll want to check the formatting and cross-references carefully to make sure that these changes didn't cause more problems than they were worth. You can make changes even after your book is published and you start selling copies, but you want the quality of your book to be excellent when the first copy sells because the first customer could leave you a review that affects your sales for the life of your book. It affects not only the book, but your reputation as an author. We all make mistakes (if we're human), so if you find one, don't sweat it. Just do your best to keep the mistakes to a minimum.

Making an eBook

Don't upload your PDF file directly to KDP. Even if your PDF looks wonderful on your computer, when a PDF is uploaded to KDP, it will probably suffer many formatting problems. Even a Word file that looks great on your computer may suffer from a variety of formatting problems unless you reformat your Word file specifically for Kindle formatting. Don't worry: This guide shows you how to do this. (Note: For an illustrated kids book or a textbook, Amazon offers free conversion tools.)

Make a new version of your Word document for Kindle. You should have two files for your book – one for your paperback and a separate file for your eBook.

Remove the following features from your paperback book file because they don't apply to eBooks:

- Remove headers, footers, page numbers, borders, bullets (the new Kindle supports bullets, but not perfectly – you should test them out across all devices before adopting them), and references to pages (like "see p. 42," which you can change to "see Sec. 5.2," for example).
- Remove the page numbers from your table of contents. Format your table of contents as a single-column list for now. (Later, you will add bookmark hyperlinks to it.)
- Remove the index if you have one, since there are no page numbers (and it's not really necessary, since eReaders have a search function).
- Remove any instances of two or more consecutive line breaks (made by pressing Enter).
- Remove any tabs. (If you used the spacebar to create indents, you need to remove those spaces.) You will need to make indents with the First Line method (to be described later) instead in order to avoid inconsistent and automatic indenting.
- Change multi-column text to a single column.
- Remove any text from textboxes and paste it into the main document.
- Remove any drop caps. A better alternative is to just type the first few words of the chapter in CAPS. Kindle supports drop caps, but they won't look perfect across all devices; you can also just change the first letter to a large font size, but that has problems, too.
- Remove any instances of two or more consecutive spaces (i.e. made using the spacebar). Even after a period, you want only one space, not two (otherwise, when a period happens to come at the end of a line, an extra space will appear at the end of the line and it won't look like the book was justified correctly).

- Remove tables. The new Kindle version is supposed to support simple tables, but you should first test this out in a preview on all devices to see how they look. You can make a table into a picture, but details may not show on a small screen.

- Some eReaders may not support footnotes or endnotes. Kindle supports basic endnotes that function as bookmark hyperlinks (not displaying on the "page," of course). As with your entire book, you should preview it on every device to see how it looks and works before publishing.

- Remove any fancy text effects (i.e. fancier than underlining, boldface, and strikethrough) – like glow or WordArt (you can format these as pictures instead, if they are legible on small screens and if it's done in moderation).

- Page breaks that are removed and replaced with Page Layout > Breaks > Next Page section breaks may format better on a couple of devices.

Even though indents may look perfect on your screen when you're using Microsoft Word, they might appear much different on a Kindle device. That's because eReaders treat indents much differently. If you use the tab key or spacebar to create indents, your eBook will probably suffer big problems with indents.

To create indents properly for eBook formatting, you must go into the paragraph dialog box (in Word 2010, click the funny icon in the bottom right corner of the Paragraph group on the Home tab; in Word 2003, look on the Format menu), go to Special, choose First Line, and set the value. It's common to use 0.2" to 0.3" for eBooks (because 0.5" would be large on an iPhone).

Don't do this paragraph by paragraph. Use the Style feature built into Word. You need to use the Styles to achieve proper eBook formatting in Word for more reasons than just indents. Ultimately, eBooks work like HTML files and the Styles feature helps translate your Word file to an eBook file properly.

You need to make at least four different Styles: one for body text with indents, one for non-indented paragraphs or lines, one for headings, and one for titles. You might name these styles Normal, FirstNormal, Heading 1, and Title (that's what I will call them in what follows):

- Apply the Normal Style to most of your document. This Style will create an indent using First Line (click Format when modifying the Style to get into the paragraph settings).

- For any non-centered paragraphs or lines (like the first paragraph of a chapter, subheadings, or lines from your copyright page) that you don't want automatically indented, apply the FirstNormal Style. For this Style, you must set the indent to 0.01". **Unfortunately, if you select "none" for no indent, Kindle may automatically indent the paragraph!**

- Apply the Heading 1 Style to headings. This Style should have a larger size font.
- Apply the Title Style to the title on the title "page" and to figures. The Title Style will have a larger font and will be centered.

To modify a Style (find it on the Home tab in Word 2010 or the Formatting toolbar of Word 2003), right-click it and choose Modify. Adjust the font style, size, alignment, and paragraph settings for each Style. The user can adjust the font to his or her liking on the eReader, so just use a basic, common font like Times New Roman. The user also has the option of adjusting the font size, which works best if you set Normal and FirstNormal to size 12 and make the Header 1 and Title Styles somewhat larger. Set the font color to automatic. In the paragraph options, set the linespacing to single and set First Line to 0.2" to 0.3" for Normal and 0.01" for FirstNormal (but set First Line to "none" for the Heading 1 and Title Styles). Set the justification to center for the Heading 1 and Title Styles, and to full for the Normal and FirstNormal Styles. In the paragraph options, there should be no space before or after paragraphs, except for Heading 1, which should have about 18 points set for the spacing before (because the first page of a chapter typically begins a couple of lines down from the top of the "page" – or in this case the "screen"); you might also include after space for Heading 1 to give more separation between the chapter heading and text.

You can select all and apply the Normal Style to save time from having to format paragraphs properly one at a time. However, this may remove formatting like boldface, underlining, italics, and other text features, which means you must then go through the document and restore these attributes. If you have a richly formatted document, it may be better to update the paragraphs one by one, updating each paragraph's style without disturbing formatting.

Next go through the document and apply the FirstNormal Style to any non-centered paragraph that you don't want to get automatically indented (including the first paragraph of each chapter and stand-alone lines or paragraphs, such as subheadings or lines from your copyright page). Apply the Heading 1 Style to chapter headings. Apply the Title Style to the title on the title "page" and to figures.

Kindle accepts only the most basic bulleted lists, and the justification may not be perfect. Test these out carefully on all devices in the previewer before publishing. If you publish your eBook elsewhere, check their guidelines to see if they support bullets.

Pictures need to be formatted differently for eBooks than for paperbacks. For paperbacks, you want 300 DPI; this doesn't matter for eBooks. What matters for eBooks is the pixel count. 600 pixels by 800 pixels looks good on many screens, except for devices with large screens like the Kindle Fire HD, iPad, PC, or laptop. Higher pixel counts mean more memory, and memory can affect both the minimum possible price and your royalty for the Kindle eBook (and there is a maximum file size that varies by eReader; it's 50 Mb for the converted file size after uploading to Kindle, and much smaller elsewhere).

Microsoft Word may make your pictures come out smaller than the pixel count would suggest: The way to prevent this is to right-click on the picture, click Size and Position, go to the Size tab, and set the Width to 100% (the Height will adjust automatically if the Aspect Ratio is locked).

For your paperback file, you want to prevent Word from compressing images, but for your eBook file, you want to compress images to minimize the file size (they will display just fine, provided that your pixel count is sufficient and Width is set to 100%). In Word 2003, right-click on a picture, go to Format Picture > Picture, uncheck the box that says, "Apply to selected pictures only," and choose Email Resolution (96 DPI). In Word 2007 and 2010, select the image and click Compress Pictures on the Format tab at the top of the screen; also go to the File tab, select Options > Advanced, find Image Size and Quality, and uncheck the box that says, "Do not compress images in file" (you want that box checked in your paperback file, however).

All images should be inserted as JPEG files except for text and line art. Pictures that consist only of text and line art should be saved as GIF images with a maximum size of 500 pixels by 600 pixels; all other pictures should be saved as JPEG images, usually 600 pixels by 800 pixels unless you want them to appear larger on devices with large screens (then you can research the screen sizes of devices that you have in mind) and don't mind that large pixel counts add to the file size (this affects your minimum price and royalty).

If you have equations, if you can retype them as text with simple subscripts and super-scripts, this is the best way to format them. However, if you have equations that require more advanced formatting (like subscripts and exponents for the same symbol or special characters, like integration symbols, that Kindle doesn't support) you can turn them into GIF images and insert them as pictures (each picture should appear on its own line with the text wrap set to in line with text). Note that it may be difficult to read detailed equations, especially on small screens like an iPhone. Test out equations with the previewer on all devices to see if they are acceptable before publishing.

Many of the special symbols that you can create in Microsoft Word don't show up in eReaders – instead, they will display as question marks (?) or a jumble of strange characters. Therefore, you want to make sure that you don't use any unsupported symbols. The following Kindle page lists supported characters for the Kindle devices:

https://images-na.ssl-images-amazon.com
/images/G/01/digital/otp/help/Latin1.gif

There may be a few common characters that Kindle supports, which don't appear on the graphic given in the previous link. For example, hold down Alt and type:

- 0150 for an en dash (–)
- 0151 for an em dash (—)
- 0147 for an open curly quote (")
- 0148 for a closed curly quote (")
- 0145 for an open single quote (')
- 0146 for a closed single quote or curly apostrophe (')

You should check each device carefully in the preview to be sure that the characters come out okay. Supported characters may not format correctly on all devices when you make them with Word's AutoCorrect feature (e.g. typing space hyphen space to generate an en dash through AutoCorrect) instead of using the Alt codes.

One problem with eBook formatting is that you can't predict where a line will break (since the eBook can be read on anything from the size of an iPhone to a PC, and the user can adjust the font size and style). Kindle gives you a little control with the non-breaking space. Hold down Ctrl then Shift and press the spacebar to create a non-breaking space (press the Show/Hide button on the paragraph group of the Home tab if you want to see the difference visually). Use a non-breaking space when you have two symbols that naturally go together, like 3 hrs or 8 kg. In the case of 3 hrs, if the "hrs" extends onto the next line, this forces the 3 to go with it. Avoid using non-breaking spaces with long words or where it's non-essential, otherwise it can create large gaps in justified text (especially on devices with small screens).

Similarly, you can't predict where blank line spaces may appear: A blank linespace can appear at the top or bottom of the screen, for example, where it may not be noticed. For this reason, it's not a good idea to use two consecutive blank linespaces to create a section break in an eBook. It's better to use three asterisks (* * *) between blank linespaces. That way, the section break will be visible regardless of where it appears vertically on the device's screen. An alternative to the asterisks is a glyph or design that matches the theme of the book without distracting the reader.

Using Shift + Enter can yield a more predictable blank linespace in an eBook. Don't use Shift + Enter at the end of a paragraph in your paperback, as it will make the line fill the margin. If you do this in your eBook file, the last line of the paragraph won't look good on your monitor, but when you view it on the preview, it will probably look fine (as always, test out how it looks on each device in the preview). If you want to create a blank linespace in your eBook, use Shift + Enter twice (once at the end of the previous paragraph, then again for the blank line). For example, if you want to insert blank lines between elements of your table of contents (or anywhere else), use the Shift + Enter method for more predictable results. Use this to create blank lines before and after images, too. Don't worry that the last line of the previous paragraph will look funny on your monitor in Word (as long as it looks fine in the preview).

A table of contents must be formatted much differently for an eBook than for a print book. Instead of including page numbers, use bookmark hyperlinks. This lets the reader click on the bookmark and go directly to that chapter or section of the eBook.

First, you must create the bookmarks before you can insert bookmark hyperlinks into the table of contents. Find the first item that will appear in your table of contents (e.g. the Introduction or Chapter 1). Go to the actual heading in the book (not the heading from your table of contents). Don't bookmark the heading itself. Instead, insert a blank line above the heading, press the spacebar a few times at the beginning of the blank line, highlight these spaces, and apply the FirstNormal Style to the spaces (which appear above the heading).

Highlight the spaces on the blank line above the heading then Insert > Bookmark. Type the name of the section without spaces (like Chapter1, not Chapter 1) and click Add. Repeat all of these steps for every component of the table of contents (but bookmark the actual headings in the book; don't bookmark headings from the table of contents).

Once you've made the bookmarks, you're ready to add bookmark hyperlinks to your table of contents. Now highlight the first item on your table of contents list (e.g. the Introduction or Chapter 1 – you should have a space in the text in your list and in your headings, just don't name the bookmarks with spaces), go to Insert > Hyperlink, select Place in This Document, choose the corresponding bookmark, and press OK. Repeat these steps for each item of your table of contents (but don't link the table of contents heading to itself). Don't use any bookmarks that Word may have generated automatically; make sure that any bookmark you add is one that you made yourself.

Bookmarks have other uses besides just making a table of contents. For example, suppose you refer to Appendix A. If you turn this text into a bookmark, the reader can jump directly to the appendix by activating the hyperlink. These are called internal hyperlinks. You make these bookmarks the same way that you make the active table of contents.

You can also add external hyperlinks. For example, if you provide a link to a website in your book (you should have your own author website or blog, which you can make for free, and include it with an about the author page in the back of your book; you can also link to your social media pages this way), this is an external hyperlink. To create an external hyperlink, if Word automatically converted your url to an active hyperlink, deactivate it (right-click it to get this option), then highlight the url (once deactivated), go to Insert > Hyperlink, type the full web address (including the http:// part, otherwise it won't work in the eReader).

Check all of your hyperlinks to ensure that they work properly. Click on the table of contents hyperlinks and internal bookmarks to see if they take you to the proper destination. Press Ctrl and left-click the external hyperlinks to open a browser and check that each url works correctly.

Editing/Formatting Resources

- You can find free editing and formatting articles on my blog: www.chrismcmullen.wordpress.com. Once there, click the Editing/Formatting tab.
- The KDP help pages include articles on formatting: After visiting KDP, click Help and look for Prepare Your Book.
- Although KDP doesn't offer paid services, KDP does maintain a list of professional editors, designers, translators, and conversion services. Visit KDP, click Help, under Prepare Your Book click See All Formatting Resources, and find a link under Professional Services. Ask if you'll get to keep the edited file (and in what format), and what happens if you need to make changes after the process is complete.
- You can find freelance professionals who offer editing and formatting services. As with shopping for any service, try to learn about the person's character and qualifications, and seek objective opinions from someone who has used the service. Ask to have a sample chapter edited or formatted as a token of what to expect. Read your contract carefully. Find out exactly what you're getting for your investment.
- Amazon has a free guide for basic Kindle formatting called *Building Your Book for Kindle*. You can read it on a PC or Mac.
- If you need help with formatting issues (for paperback or eBook), try searching the KDP community help forum and posting your question if you don't find the answer there. Chances are that someone else has had the exact same problem and will be happy to share the solution.

- The Kindle help pages (see the link below) have many useful tips.

  https://kdp.amazon.com
  /help?topicId=A3R2IZDC42DJW6

- It is possible to pay someone to format your Kindle eBook for you. KDP lists a variety of companies who specialize in Kindle conversion services (see the link below):

  https://kdp.amazon.com
  /help?topicId=A3RRQXI478DDG7

6 Designing the Book Cover

DESIGNING A GOOD book cover is important because it's the first thing the reader sees. We would like readers to judge our books by the content, but a shopper has to first decide whether or not to even read the content. Potential buyers can read reviews, the description of your book, see the cover, and look inside your book on its webpage at Amazon.com. Since the cover is one of the first things a shopper might look at, you want the front cover to make a good impression, the back cover to include information that describes your book well and helps to sell your book, and the cover to appear professional.

A cover functions as an important marketing tool:

- When customers see your book, based on the cover they will decide in average of three seconds whether or not to click on it and learn more.
- Many customers browse for books by viewing several thumbnails on a page of search results. More appealing covers attract more customers.
- Customers are much more likely to click on your book to learn more about it if your book's cover attracts your specific target audience.
- A book cover helps an author brand the image of a book. If a customer recognizes your cover from having seen it in the past, this improves your chances of catching the customer's interest.
- A poor cover suggests little effort was put into the content; an appealing cover seems professional.

You have five options for getting a book cover:

- Hire a cover designer. It's reasonable to spend $100 to $300 for a custom design.
- Shop for premade covers. Many sell for $10 to $100. It's hard to get a perfect match for your book, and there may be other covers like yours.
- Design your own cover for free. You can draw your own images on the computer, take photographs, scan images (hand-drawn usually doesn't work well on a cover), or shop for free stock images (make sure they are 300 DPI).
- Make your own cover, but invest a small amount of money in stock images (be sure

they are 300 DPI) that fit your cover well.
- Use Cover Creator, Amazon's free tool. Your design will be limited in some ways and your book may look like many other covers, but it's convenient and easy.

I've designed almost all of my covers myself. In 2013, I invested in some covers, paying $300 each, and am very pleased with the results. Investing $100 to $300 in a book cover is a lot of money to spend: If your royalty is a few dollars, you may have to sell a hundred books just to break even. If you wind up selling just a couple of books per week, it may take several months to recover your expense.

However, if you have a highly marketable book, a professional-looking cover that attracts your specific target audience can make the difference between selling several copies per day versus just one or two per day. The challenge is predicting how marketable your book is and what effect the cover will have.

Did you do the research prescribed in Chapter 3? This data can help you see how well similar books are doing. Your book may or may not do as well, but at least this gives you something to judge by. Other things to consider include: How confident are you in your book? Have you published previous books to help you judge your potential? How motivated are you to market your book? Are you prepared for the possibility of the investment not paying off?

If you choose to hire a cover designer, do some research first. At a minimum, you want reasons to expect a much better cover than you could make yourself (a portfolio of previous covers may help you judge this – also see if there are any in your genre). You want a cover that will look professional and attract your specific target audience (so browsing similar covers will help you see what those readers are accustomed to).

You could make a cover yourself or pay for a low-cost cover to start with, reserving the option to upgrade to a better cover later. Some authors do this hoping to learn if the book is worth it first, or to acquire the funds to pay for a cover from the initial royalties. The main disadvantage of this is that the first three months are your best opportunity to attract sales, since your book will be visible in the Last 30 Days and Last 90 Days new release categories when it's first published.

In this chapter, I will show you how you can make your cover – in whole or in part – by yourself using Microsoft Word. If you have access to PhotoShop and some experience with PhotoShop, you have the potential to create a better cover there (but there are also some pitfalls of using PhotoShop, such as filters that sometimes do more harm than good). If you do make your own cover, it will help to keep your initial investment to a minimum. This way, you won't put yourself in a position where you need to sell a hundred or more copies of your book just to break even. If you can write your own book, you can surely design and make your own cover – and a good one – following the prescription described in this chapter. At the very least, try it yourself and see how it turns out; that way, if you do hire help, you will see firsthand how much that improves on your own effort.

You can make a professional cover using Microsoft Word. If you have Microsoft Word 2007, you might obtain better results saving your file as a .doc file (the 2003 format), unless you use features specific to Word 2007, in which case you must use .docx to retain those features. I encountered a few bugs designing covers with 2007; I haven't had these problems with 2003 or 2010. The .docx format works better for me with Word 2010.

After discussing the cover design in the next section, I will describe specifically how to make your cover in Microsoft Word. If you create your cover using different software, the design of your cover may follow a similar prescription and many of the design tips may still apply – so you may wish to read the following section even if not using Word. In the last section of this chapter, I explain how to use Microsoft Word's drawing tools.

Designing a Professional Cover

Study the covers that you see on a variety of books, including books that are or are not similar to yours. This will give you ideas for what features to include on your cover and help inspire your own cover style.

Obviously, you need to include the title, which should stand out well in large letters, the subtitle, and the author's name. The title and subtitle should attract the reader's attention and, especially if your work is nonfiction, give the reader an idea of what your book is about. If any words are emphasized (e.g. with a larger font size), they should be key words.

Some nicely drawn (usually, not by hand) artwork or a photograph on the front cover can help catch attention and lend your book a professional appearance. You would like readers to imagine your book sitting in their hands. The cover should be attractive. What is attractive to one may not be attractive to another, but you want the cover to be appealing to most of your audience.

Most back covers include text that will help to sell the book to a potential customer. On Amazon, the back cover will be visible where the Look Inside feature is accessed, but the back cover is more valuable for people who see your book in person (such as on a customer's coffee table). Most online buyers see just the thumbnail image of your front cover until they buy your book and it arrives in the mail, so it's very important for your front cover to form a good impression.

Amazon KDP will make the ISBN and UPC bar code for you. They will identify the exact location and size (within their printing tolerance) of this label so you can design your cover around it. With the instructions that follow, you will be able to predict the UPC's location.

Your book will be more professional if you include the title and author's name on the spine. However, Amazon only permits text to be included on the spine if the book has at least 102 pages. The spine text must also be narrow enough to leave 0.0625" between the text and the spine edges. For narrow spines, writing the spine text in CAPS will allow you to use the largest possible font size (since some lowercase letters, like g and q, have tails that limit the usable space).

It's important that the spine label be centered very well on your cover file so that it prints as professionally as possible – it will stand out like a sore thumb if it is off-center. You do have to allow for a small printing tolerance, though (an estimate may be available on the publisher's webpage). Eventually, you will receive a proof of your book, but it is just one sample; if afterward you order multiple copies of your book, you will obtain a better measure of how reliable the printing is. (Overall, in my experience viewing over a thousand copies in person, it is very good, but nothing is perfect so you want to understand any limitations.)

If you plan to try to market your book to any bookstores, you will need a label on the spine to help customers identify your book when it is sitting on a bookshelf. Some bookstores will simply not purchase books that do not have a spine label.

Including a cover price is optional. Some retailers in the Expanded Distribution channel may wish to mark up the price of your book, so having a cover price might frustrate customers who pay more than that. If you succeed in getting local bookstores to stock your book, chances are that they will place a label on your book anyway, so including a cover price won't matter to them (but if they wish to charge more for your book, again any cover price might pose a problem). You can see that I tend to include prices on my covers. I did this because many readers are accustomed to seeing this; the more your book looks like what your audience is used to, the better it will fit the buyer's eye. However, many indie authors prefer to leave the price off the cover, especially if they intend to sell copies to local bookstores.

> Your cover should include – at a minimum – a title, subtitle, author's name, ISBN with UPC barcode (automatic), spine label (if the width permits), back cover text (optional, but can be helpful), and front cover art.

Even if your book interior is black-and-white, your cover will print in color. So take advantage of this and use color when you create your cover.

However, color images often do not print exactly the same way as they appear on the screen. This is not the fault of the publisher, but a problem that plagues the publishing industry in general. The publisher's printing process is excellent, but for technical reasons relating to the color scheme used to print an image on the screen versus the color scheme used to print an image on paper, your book cover (and interior if it is color, too) may have slight variations in color compared to what you expect from viewing your cover on the screen.

Computer monitors use a RGB (red, green, blue) color addition scheme. Any color can be created by combining the right amounts of red, green, and blue at any point on the screen. Printers, on the other hand, use a CMYK (cyan, magenta, yellow, black) color subtraction scheme. The technical reasons for the differences have to do with the physical processes involved – i.e. the difference between producing an image on a screen that emits light of a given color versus combining pigments on paper that reflect light of given color. (This is actually an engineering issue – it's not like selling hot dogs in packages of six and hot dog buns in packages of eight.)

Here's what this means to you: Using the RGB color scheme, monitors can make virtually any color, but printers are much more limited with their use of the CMYK subtraction scheme. Thus, the printer may not be able to reproduce every color you can view on your monitor exactly the way it appears on your screen. The printer the publisher uses is not the same as your own home printer, so a color could print one way in your house but slightly differently in your book.

One common problem is that images tend to look much brighter when displayed on a monitor and much darker in print. Most authors strive to perfect the image as seen on the monitor, only to be frustrated to see it appear much darker on the printed cover. Here is a tip: Print out a sample with a deskjet printer to give you a rough idea of how much darker it might appear in print; order a proof of your book with the tentative cover for a better indication. You really want your cover to look great both in print and on the monitor, since many customers will first see it when shopping online and later hold your book in their hands.

When you draw your own artwork and make your text, you may minimize problems if you stick to standard RGB colors. When selecting the color of an object in Format, choose More Colors > Custom and enter the RGB values. You can find the RGB values for many standard colors in the table below. Note that in Word 2007 and later, many of the preset colors (like green) are not standard colors.

Color	Red	Green	Blue	Color	Red	Green	Blue
aqua	0	255	255	navy	0	0	128
black	0	0	0	olive	128	128	0
blue	0	0	255	purple	128	0	128
fuchsia	255	0	255	red	255	0	0
gray	128	128	128	silver	192	192	192
green	0	128	0	teal	0	128	128
lime	0	255	0	white	255	255	255
maroon	128	0	0	yellow	255	255	0

Fortunately, when your PDF files are ready, you first purchase an inexpensive proof copy, so you will see exactly how the colors print. If you are not happy with your proof, you have as much time as you like to make revisions. Once you do approve a proof, you should know approximately what your customers are receiving: Their copies will look just like your proof, within reasonable printing tolerances.

If you publish with Amazon KDP, you can use the Cover Creator feature. However, it is pretty straight-forward to follow the prescription outlined in the next section to make your own professional cover. Doing it yourself gives you the flexibility to design a cover exactly the way you want it. With Cover Creator, your cover may look like many other books.

Drawing Your Cover in Microsoft Word

Microsoft Word has a tendency to make images at a lower resolution, since it's generally intended for showing images on a screen (where 96 DPI is just fine) or printing on a household printer. This helps to reduce the active memory. These tendencies are a problem when publishing a book, however. Images print best when they are 300 DPI or greater.

Before inserting or drawing any images, you want to disable Word's automatic tendencies. You can find instructions for how to do this in the next section (following the pages of sample covers).

Disable Word's automatic compression feature before inserting or drawing any images. Skip to the next section to learn how to do this.

You need to have your book cover saved in one file and your book interior saved in a separate file. So open a blank document in which to begin designing your book cover. Go to Page Setup in the File tab of Word 2003 or Page Layout in Word 2007 and up to set the page size. Set the page size exactly to the size of the full-spread cover including bleeds. If you submit a PDF cover larger than this, it increases the chances of encountering readjustments during file review.

Determine your cover's full-spread (i.e. with front, spine, and back together) size:

- width = trim width x 2 + spine width + 0.25"
- height = trim height + 0.25"
- spine width = 0.002252" x page count for black-and-white interior on white pages
- spine width = 0.0025" x page count for black-and-white interior on cream pages
- spine width = 0.002347" x page count for color interior on white pages

Here, trim width and trim height form the trim size of your book. For example, if you choose a trim size of 6" x 9", the trim width is 6" and the trim height is 9". If your book has 130 pages with a black-and-white interior on white paper, then your cover width will be 6" x 2" + 0.002252" x 130 + 0.25" = 12.54" and your cover height will be 9" + 0.25" = 9.25". In this example, you would set the page width to 12.54" and the page height to 9.25" in Microsoft Word.

It will be handy to zoom in and out periodically in the View tab. Sometimes you'll want to see how the cover looks as a whole page, other times you'll want to zoom to see just the front or back cover, and when perfecting the details you'll want to zoom in further for a closer look. Note that the alignment may be a little off when viewing the entire cover as a whole page, whereas 100% is usually more reliable (also, zooming in far in Word 2003 has some alignment issues). Print out a test copy and you won't have to wonder.

If you are not already familiar with drawing objects in Microsoft Word, you might want to read the tutorial in the following section to become better acquainted with the drawing tools and then return to this section.

Insert a rectangle. Right-click on the rectangle and change the size to the trim size of your book (e.g. 6" x 9"). Change the fill color to no fill. After removing the fill color, you will need to click on the border of the rectangle in order to grab it. Copy and paste this rectangle so that you have two identical large rectangles. Make a third rectangle (with no fill) with a width equal to your spine width (this is defined in the previous bullet list, you can find a calculator for this on KDP's website, and will also find this value after you submit your interior file) and the height equal to the height of your trim size (e.g. 0.29" x 9").

Position them roughly so that the spine width rectangle is in the center and the other two large rectangles are just to its left and right. Grab all three of these rectangles and align their tops with the Align tool from the Format tab. Then grab the left rectangle and use the left/right arrow keys to move it horizontally until its right edge matches up with the spine width rectangle's left edge. Also join the right rectangle's left edge to the spine width rectangle's right edge.

Group the three rectangles together into a single image. Then unclick the object, right-click on it, and go to Format Object > Layout > Advanced, where you can choose to center it horizontally and vertically on the page. Now your cover will be centered on your file. At some point in your work you may want to ungroup these rectangles (at least temporarily) – e.g. if you want to center a picture or WordArt with just one of the three rectangles by using the align command.

Make a new rectangle (it's okay to leave a white fill for this one) and change its size to 0.25" x 0.25". Copy and paste it until you have 8 of these squares. Put these 8 squares in the corners of the front and back cover rectangles (the large rectangle on the right corresponds to the front cover, while the large rectangle on the left corresponds to the back cover). The purpose of these 8 squares is to define the active area of the front and back covers. Don't put any text within 0.25" of the border defined by these squares.

Make a new rectangle (white fill is okay) that is 2" wide and 1.2" high. Put it in the bottom right of your back cover rectangle such that its lower-right corner matches the upper-left corner of the 0.25" x 0.25" square that you just put there. This is where your ISBN and UPC bar code will print. Anything you put in this space, such as artwork, will be covered up by the bar code. So don't put any text (or anything else you don't want to get covered up) in this area.

Select all of these objects – the original three rectangles for the front and back cover and spine, the 8 squares, and the bar code rectangle – and group them together. These are your guides. You will want to delete the guides when you are completely finished so that the guides don't print on your actual cover. If you ungroup these rectangles at some point during your work (useful, for example, for aligning objects with just one of these rectangles), you can regroup them afterward.

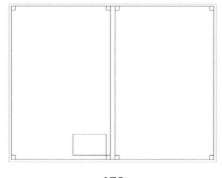

Thus far, your document should look like the previous image (where the back cover is on the left, the front cover is on the right, and the ISBN/bar code rectangle appears near the bottom right of the back cover).

The background color or pattern for your cover needs to extend beyond the cover size (i.e. all the way to the outer rectangle). Your cover prints on a larger size sheet from which your cover is cut out. So you need your background to extend beyond the size of your cover to allow for tolerance in the printing and cutting processes. This is why the actual page size extends 0.125" beyond the front and back cover edges. Your background image should completely fill the outer rectangle.

The background image could simply be a rectangle the same size as the page and properly centered with a simple fill color or gradient, or it could be a picture (ideally at least 300 DPI). Click on your background image and change its Order to the back (or place it behind text in Page Layout) so that all other images and text appear in front of your background. I recommend inserting this background rectangle after the remainder of your cover is complete – it will be easier to select, move, and alter other objects in your cover if the background image is not there. However, you might want to have the background color in mind to make sure that your color scheme works well.

Any art or images must either extend all the way to the edge of the outer rectangle (i.e. beyond the 3 cover rectangles), or must not get closer to the cover edges than 0.25" (the 8 squares help to mark this area). Text must also not get closer to the cover edges than 0.25".

Add separate textboxes (or WordArt) for your title, subtitle, author name, and other text that you might include. Change the outline to no color to remove the rectangle from the textbox. Change the fill color to no color also in order to prevent its fill color from blocking out other images. If you insert WordArt, remove any shadow that may appear in the default. Choose a large font size for your title. You might want to divide your title up into two or more textboxes if you want a couple of the words to appear much different than the others. Make sure that your title stands out well and is very readable in terms of size and color. Center the title, subtitle, and author's name relative to one another and to the front cover rectangle.

Insert WordArt to make the spine label. Choose a horizontal line for the WordArt shape. You will probably want a fill color, but may not want an outline color, for this text (but neither for the shape – i.e. compare the similar tools Shape Fill and Text Fill). Type the title, then several spaces, then the author's name. Some trial and error will help you get the spacing right. You can adjust both the size of the WordArt as well as the font style and size in order to change the appearance of the spine label (but be careful to preserve the aspect ratio).

Right-click the spine label to change the Layout to in front of text. Now you can click on the spine label to rotate it 90° to the right (not left). Center it in the spine rectangle. Leave a little room around the spine text for printing tolerance, making the spine text smaller if necessary. Check that the orientation of your spine matches that of books that you have. (If you have a book with a few hundred pages or more, your spine might be wide enough to include a spine label that is not rotated. However, most books have a rotated spine label.)

Spine text must be at least 0.0625" from the spine edges (otherwise, Amazon KDP will reject your cover or resize your spine text). If your spine is narrow (not much longer than 102 pages), write your spine text in CAPS to maximize the available space (since some lowercase letters like g and q have tails). If your page count is 100 pages or less, you can't include spine text.

Add some textboxes for your back cover (with no shape fill or shape outline). Draw interest to your book. What is your book about? How is it distinguished from the competition (but don't put your competition down)? Do you have qualifications worth mentioning? If you have any book reviews yet, you can use quotes from these (citing your source if it is a magazine or website, and ensuring that you have permission to use the review quote). Read several book covers to get ideas for what kind of information you might want to include on your back cover.

Textboxes and WordArt have changed somewhat from 2003 thru 2010. In Word 2010, it's easy to change the font size (working in .docx mode). In some of the older versions of Word, it may seem intuitive to resize WordArt, for example, but in such a way so as to change the aspect ratio of the text. If possible, change the font size to resize your cover text. If you must resize the box itself, first lock the aspect ratio (right-click and choose Size and Position).

For artwork, you can draw your own artwork (using the Microsoft Word drawing tools described in the next section or a different drawing program) or you can insert photographs – or both. If you are working with photos, you might prefer to open them in a program designed for viewing and editing photos, then crop them and format them, if needed, before inserting them into your document (cropping and editing images in the native program – rather than adjusting them in Word – and inserting them as you want them to appear may help to maximize their resolution in the Word file, along with other precautions described in the next section).

Don't forget to remove the cover guide before you upload your book cover for publishing.

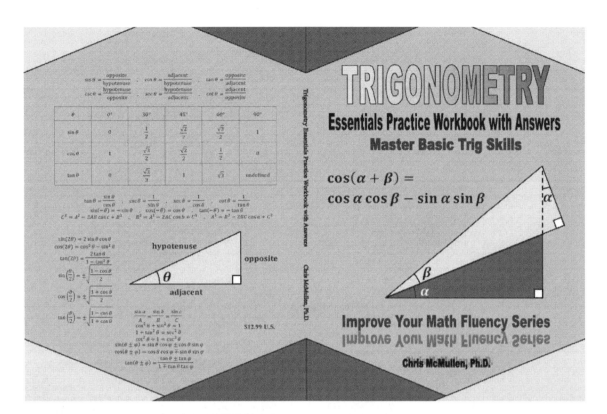

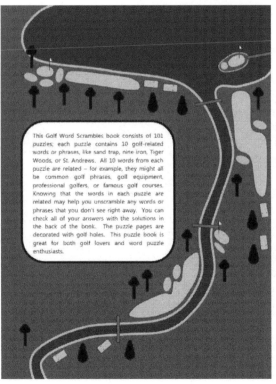

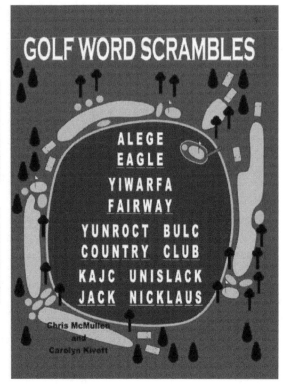

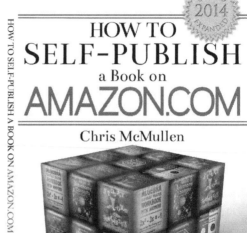

This book will show you how to prepare and submit files to a print-on-demand self-publishing service that is part of the Amazon group of companies – a self-publishing service that you can trust, which requires virtually no investment (just a few dollars for the cost of your book plus shipping). Following the steps outlined in this guide, your book can be selling in as little as a week once your manuscript is completed.

The author, Chris McMullen, has self-published over a dozen different types of books on Amazon.com. He is experienced with the techniques and details, and is sharing his knowledge with you through this guide. This handy reference takes you through all of the steps of the self-publishing process, from writing your manuscript to editing and formatting to preparing PDF files to publishing your book to low-cost promotional strategies for improving sales.

$11.99 USA

Below are some sample eBook covers:

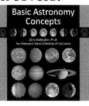

Using the Microsoft Word Drawing Tools

Before drawing or inserting any pictures into the Word file for either your interior or cover, you must first disable Word's tendency to automatically compress your images. Even that won't prevent Word from reducing the resolution of your pictures: There are a couple of other things you need to know, too.

Here is how you can turn off automatic picture compression in Word (you must do this again for every Word file that you create, and do it before inserting or drawing any images):

- In Word 2003, right-click on a picture (ideally, do this the first time you insert a picture; if you don't have any images in your file yet, you can insert one temporarily), select the Show Picture Toolbar, click Compress Pictures, select All Pictures in Document, and uncheck the box next to Compress Pictures.
- In Word 2007, right-click on a picture, go to the Format tab, click Compress Images, uncheck the box marked "Apply to selected pictures only," select Options, and uncheck the box marked "Automatically perform basic compression on save."
- In Word 2010, click the File tab, scroll down to the bottom of the list (it might be hidden at first, in which case you just need to scroll below Help to find it), select Advanced, scroll down to find Image Size and Quality, and check the box marked "Do not compress images in file."

Ideally, you want images to have 300 DPI for your print book, but Word likes to reduce them to as little as 96 DPI. For your eBook file, you want 96 DPI instead, as that will save memory. Create separate files for your paperback and eBook, but remember to make any revisions to the text to both files. For your eBook, you want to do the opposite of the instructions above, compressing images automatically instead of turning picture compression off (for your eBook, you want 96 DPI).

You must take additional steps to avoid picture compression for your paperback. In addition to turning off picture compression, don't crop or resize any pictures after inserting them into Word (otherwise, Word may reduce the resolution). If you've already cropped or resized pictures that you inserted into Word from files, delete those and reinsert them (you *can* crop or resize them in the native program). Also, don't copy/paste images into Word: You must go to the Insert tab to add pictures if you want to avoid having the resolution reduced. In the next chapter, we'll learn that you must also print to PDF via a Word-to-PDF converter instead of using the convenient Save As feature (since Save As PDF results in lower DPI for your images).

> For your print book, deactivate Word's automatic picture compression before drawing or inserting any pictures. Don't crop or resize images after inserting them from files. Use Insert > Picture instead of copy/paste. To create the PDF file, don't use Word's convenient Save As PDF feature if you have images in your file. These actions will reduce the DPI of your images.
>
> For your eBook, you instead want to activate automatic picture compression. You want 96 DPI for your eBook, but 300 DPI for your print book.

If you use Microsoft Word 2003, I highly recommend that you click the Tools tab, choose Options, select the General tab, and uncheck the box that says, "Automatically create drawing canvas when inserting AutoShapes." I find it much more convenient and flexible to put shapes anywhere I want on the page rather than the confines of the drawing canvas. (In Word 2007 and beyond, there is no default canvas to worry about.)

In Microsoft Word 2007, the various drawing tools can be found in tabs at the top of the page. You begin with the Insert tab, selecting one of the options in Illustrations, such as Shapes. Once you have a diagram going, you may need to go to the Home tab and choose to select (or deselect) objects by checking (or unchecking) this box – you can find this at the far right of the Home tab, with the Editing options. If you have a drawing object selected, a new tab will appear – Format. Yet other drawing tools are located at the far right of the Page Layout tab, with the Arrange options.

Here is where to find the Microsoft Word 2007 and 2010 drawing tools:

- Insert tab: This where you can insert shapes, textboxes, and WordArt. Start your diagram here.
- Format tab: This has most of the drawing tools and options. This tab is only accessible when you have selected an object that has already been drawn. From here, you can change the fill and outline colors and styles, picture layout, and much more.
- Page Layout tab: This tab has Arrange options. It is useful for grouping objects to-

gether, aligning objects, rotating objects, and positioning objects in front of text, behind text, or in line with text. You can find these same options in the Format tab, too.

• Home tab: If you want to select multiple objects, you can go to Select and check a box to do this (then to select text you have to go back and uncheck this box). In Word 2007, you can then draw an outline rectangle by dragging the mouse and any drawing objects inside this rectangle will all be selected. There is also a handy Selection Pane on the Format toolbar in Word 2010.

In Microsoft Word 2003, all of the drawing tools are conveniently located in the same place – a drawing toolbar. Simply click the View tab, click Toolbars, and check the Drawing toolbar.

In any version of Microsoft Word, you can access many of the drawing options by right-clicking on an object – e.g. under Format Autoshape or Format Object.

> Many of the drawing features can be found by right-clicking on an image.

You need to understand the grid to help align objects well (the align tools on the Format tab can help, too). Alignment tends to be more reliable when the View is set to 100% (or to the page width, except for large page widths, like 12").

Explore and understand the grid before you begin drawing. Students (and others) tell me that they have tried drawing in Microsoft Word 2003 and found it to be very limited. In every case, this turned out to be because they didn't understand the grid options. Once you understand the grid options well, you will be able to use it to your benefit – instead of it preventing you from what you would like to accomplish (Microsoft Word 2007 is slightly more restrictive than Microsoft Word 2003, but I expect that this came about to reduce file problems associated with active memory required to work with your document).

Experiment with turning the grid on or off. In Microsoft Word 2003, you can separately choose whether or not to snap objects to the grid. In Word 2007 and 2010, find Grid Settings by clicking Align from the Format tab or the Page Layout tab.

You must be flexible with the grid options (i.e. don't insist on always having the grid turned on or off). There will be times when you need the grid on and others when you need it off, and in Microsoft Word 2003 there will be times when you do want to snap objects to the grid and times when you don't. Keep the grid options on your mind: If you're having trouble aligning things the way you would like, you probably need to change the grid options.

You will want the grid on (and to snap objects to the grid) if you are trying to join two objects at a specific point, when these points on each object both lie at grid corners. The grid is also useful for making horizontal or vertical lines, or for making one object a given multiple of times wider or taller than another object (you can also set the width and height precisely in Format > Size).

You will want to turn the grid off (and not snap objects to the grid) if you are trying to attach an object to a precise point that lies between gridlines. This is also sometimes visually useful.

Sometimes you need the grid off, sometimes on. It pays to be flexible with the grid (and snapping) options.

Suppose you want to join two objects together and have them connect at a precise point. For simplicity, imagine that you have one vertical and one horizontal line segment, which you would like to join at the endpoints. If your grid is off and you are not snapping objects to the grid, if you try to line these up with your eyeball, they will not match up perfectly – this will look less professional when you print the diagram. (Zooming in considerably does not prevent this problem.) If instead you turn the grid on and snap objects to the grid (remember, you have to choose these separately in Microsoft Word 2003), it is much easier to line these up precisely. The Align tool in the Format tab can also help to align images precisely (but look closely; in Word 2010, for example, you can sometimes get funny results if any of the images have been rotated, for example; sometimes, you get better results manually).

In the illustration that follows, the diagram on the left was made without snapping the objects to the grid whereas the diagram on the right was made by snapping the objects to the grid. Look closely at the corner and you will see the distinction. If you want to create professional diagrams, this is an important distinction. (This particular image can alternatively be drawn with the freeform tool.)

On the other hand, sometimes you want to position something precisely, but if the grid is on and you are snapping objects to the grid, you will be prevented from putting the object exactly where you want it. In this case, you need to choose not snap objects to the grid (turn the grid off in Microsoft Word 2007 or 2010).

If you are snapping objects to the grid, it will be easier to draw very horizontal and vertical lines. If you are not, you can still draw very horizontal and vertical lines if you draw them with care: Look closely and you will see that the line appears smoother on the screen when it is horizontal or vertical, and a little less smooth when it is slightly off.

If you need to grab two or more drawing objects, you can drag your mouse to draw a rectangle around the objects, in which case any object inside the rectangle will be selected. Note that I don't mean to insert a rectangle shape. In Microsoft Word 2007, go to Select on the far right of the Home tab and check the box for selecting drawing objects (in Microsoft Word 2003, just click the arrow on the drawing toolbar), then you can select objects by making this rectangle. In Word 2010, you can't select with such a rectangle, but you can turn on the Selection Pane.

Alternatively, you can grab one object, press Ctrl, and continue holding Ctrl as you grab the other objects.

It just takes a little exploratory practice to master the drawing tools. Once you get used to them they turn out to be pretty intuitive.

So let's get started. Open a blank document in Microsoft Word and prepare yourself to get acquainted with some of the drawing tools and features. We'll discuss how to insert various shapes and make diagrams from them and you will develop Microsoft Word drawing skills by trying this on your computer as you read this book. Don't be shy: You will learn much better by trying; simply reading will probably not be very helpful.

Grab the line tool from the Insert tab (or drawing toolbar in Microsoft Word 2003). Position the cursor at a point where you would like to start drawing the line segment, then press and hold the mouse button down to drag the line out as far as you like and in the direction you want, and release the mouse button when your line segment is ready.

Try to make a horizontal or vertical line both with and without snapping objects to the grid. Notice how the line is smoothest when it is horizontal or vertical, but a little less so when it is slightly off.

Make two different line segments and explore your manual alignment options both with and without snapping objects to the grid, as we discussed in a previous example. Also, explore the Align tools available on the Format tab.

Now try to insert an arrow instead of a line. Try reversing the arrow's direction or making a double arrow. Change the size and style of the arrow.

Insert other AutoShapes, such as circles and rectangles. Choose different fill and line colors. Change the line thickness and style. Explore some of the fill effects, like the gradient.

See if you can rotate and flip an AutoShape. You can rotate an object 90 degrees with standard buttons. In Microsoft Word 2003, you can also choose Free Rotate. In any version, you can right-click the object and choose any degree value from 0 to 360 degrees for its orientation: Format AutoShape (or Object), go to the Size tab, and enter the rotation angle. Try entering a few different rotation angles to explore this option.

Select a rectangle and adjust its size using the mouse. Stretch it out horizontally, then vertically, then diagonally. Now right-click to format the object, and in the Size tab check the box to lock the aspect ratio. This does not guarantee that the aspect ratio will not change. You can still stretch it horizontally or vertically. If you want to preserve the aspect ratio, check this box and then stretch it only along a diagonal. Go back to the Size tab and note that you can manually enter the dimensions of the object instead of stretching it out visually.

With multiple drawing objects on your screen, try selecting two or more of them and aligning them in various ways – center, middle, or top, for example. Group them together. Select the group and then click on one of the objects: Notice how this results in an extra set of markers to indicate the boundaries of the selected AutoShape in addition to the entire object. Try this again if necessary to see the difference between selecting the grouped object and selecting an object within the group. It's important to understand the distinction so that you can manipulate grouped objects correctly. If you have the group selected, instead of one object in the group, you can format the group as a whole. Try rotating the group.

Change the layout of the group by right-clicking the group, choosing Format Object, and going to the Layout tab. See what happens when you choose in line with text. Write some text. Grab the object and move it to a different position in the text to understand this formatting option. Try to center it on its own line (use the Enter key to create a blank line, center the blank line from the Home tab, and move the object to this line).

With multiple solid two-dimensional AutoShapes on your screen – like circles and rectangles – filled with different colors, arrange them so that they overlap and notice how one blocks out the other. Try changing the order so that a different one appears in the front. The objects are generally layered in the order in which you make them, but you can override this by with the Order tool. In Word 2010, the Selection Pane helps you select objects that are behind other images.

You can also make an image partially transparent so that images behind it show through. You can do this by right-clicking the object and adjusting the transparency level in the Color tab of Format AutoShape (or Object). If you use transparency, you'll want to note the following: The publisher has to manually implement transparency that appears in your PDF file, which may result in color shifts or other problems with formatting your images. If you use transparency, see my tip in the next chapter to avoid this problem.

Insert a textbox. Remove the rectangular outline by changing the line color to no color. Observe how the textbox's fill (the fill is the region inside the textbox) blocks out other drawing objects where they overlap. Remove the fill by changing the fill color to no fill. Notice that the background of the textbox no longer blocks out other drawing objects. The textbox has to be sufficiently wider and taller than the text or some of its text will get clipped. Always check to see that the bottoms of letters like 'g,' which extends further downward, are not cut off (they will be if the textbox is too short).

Compare WordArt to a textbox. A textbox allows you to include text in an arbitrary position in a diagram that easily matches the style of text in the document; you have many of the standard text formatting options in a textbox. WordArt allows for some more artistic formatting. In Word 2003 and 2007 especially, you have to be careful when resizing text so as not to distort the aspect ratio; in Word 2010, change the font size to resize the text without distorting the aspect ratio of WordArt.

Insert WordArt. Enter some text. Try changing the WordArt shape. Explore the effects of adding, removing, and otherwise changing the fill and line colors. Try rotating the WordArt, which is useful for making a spine label for a book cover.

Personally, I prefer to avoid using 3-D style or shadow style, but you may wish to explore these options. I find that I can make a greater variety of 3-D styles or shadows manually than are available here, but I have seen some nice images created with these, too.

The variety of callouts provide comic strip type bubbles. When selected, you can drag the yellow diamond-shape marker, and you can separately move or resize the cloud. Try typing text in the cloud.

If you insert an oval shape, it first looks like a circle. When you resize the oval, you can stretch it into an ellipse. If instead you want it to remain a circle, lock the aspect ratio and stretch it diagonally.

The arc is one of my favorite AutoShapes. You can make a lot of useful curves with this simple tool. It is also useful for labeling angles. Try playing with the arc AutoShape. The yellow markers let you choose the initial and final positions. You can stretch it out so it looks more like a hyperbolic arc, or you can wind it around so it makes a complete circle or ellipse. Try adding a fill color to see what happens.

As an example of the arc tool, try to draw a cylinder. You could draw a circle and use the 3-D option, but if you want to draw modified cylinders, like a coaxial cable, the 3-D option turns out to be less flexible. So another way to draw a cylinder is to make an ellipse, then use the arc to make a semi-ellipse. If you snap objects to the grid and lock their aspect ratios, you can get the ellipse and semi-ellipse to match almost perfectly. Then spread them apart and align them vertically. Add a rectangle, and place it behind the ellipse. Fill all three objects. Remove the outline of the rectangle, and add two horizontal lines at the top and bottom of the rectangle. You may need to adjust the horizontal position of each object a little (without snapping to the grid). There are other ways to draw a cylinder, also. I find this to be pretty flexible: For example, I sometimes need to draw coaxial cylinders, where this works out pretty well. See if you can reproduce the following example.

There are two variations of the line tool that are very useful: freeform and curve. The freeform tool allows you to drag the mouse around like you are drawing with a pencil, but I don't recommend this. Instead, if you use freeform, I suggest you click once at a time to make a polygon-type shape. You can use this, for example, to draw three sides of a cube with different colors (as shown below).

The curve tool can be used to create just about any curved object, which can be open or closed. You can also fill curved paths that you make. I suggest not snapping objects to the grid when you are using the curve tool to give yourself more flexibility. When you first practice using the curve tool, it will probably seem pretty limited. Try using the curve tool to see what I mean, then read the following paragraph.

Make a closed curved path with several points using the curve tool (closed means that the endpoint is coincident with the starting position). If you right-click the image, you will be able to edit the points, add a point, delete a point, or open the path. This allows you to perfect a curve considerably. Explore these options and practice for a while if you want to learn how to create curved drawings that look very professional. Below is a golf hole that was drawn using the curve tool. The other images were drawn using the circle and rectangle tools.

Here is an example that illustrates alignment and rotation. Start with an ellipse. Copy and paste it five times so that you have six ellipses in all. Give them rotation angles of 0°,

60°, 120°, 180°, 240°, and 300°. Align these ellipses two at a time to arrange these ellipses into a rose petal formation. Group these together, then add a circle and center the circle with the group in order to complete the following diagram.

You can also find a host of clipart images, including some available directly from Microsoft. This clipart may not be available for commercial use – you should contact Microsoft or the clipart owner to find out. Some clipart collections do permit commercial use, but some paid collections do not. Always check the documentation to find out; also, you should consult with an attorney for legal advice.

Personally, I find that I can make any image I need, and prefer to do this because it gives me greater flexibility. If I draw a car myself, I find it easy to open a door or add a moonroof because I know exactly what I did to create it. You can edit some clipart images, especially if they are designed for use in Microsoft Word, but you might not find it as easy to make exactly what you want as if you had made the original object yourself. As you draw more and more images, you can develop a personalized clipart collection. All of the images in my self-published books I have drawn from scratch using Microsoft Word (and occasionally Microsoft Excel), except for some of the decorative images used for this book and *Spooky Word Scrambles*, which were designed by artist Melissa Stevens at www.theillustratedauthor.net (I purchased these interior images along with the cover design). The shapes and pictures that you see interspersed throughout this chapter I drew myself in Word.

You can also insert pictures into your Microsoft Word document that were created with other programs. You can add photographs, too. If you are trying to make a specific curve, like a sine wave, you can graph it in Microsoft Excel, remove the outline of the plot as well as the axes and paste just the curve into Microsoft Word.

The possibilities offered by the basic drawing tools in Microsoft Word are virtually limitless (although there are programs, like PhotoShop which can produce professional images efficiently for experienced users, and which also have many possible pitfalls, such as with layers and filters). I wish you success in your endeavors to create professional diagrams.

For your eBook file, all images must be JPEG files with the text wrap set to In Line with Text (not in front of text, behind text, or square). However, images that only consist of line art and text should be GIF images. If you draw a diagram in Word, you can copy and paste it into Paint, for example, to convert it to JPEG or GIF format, although you can get a cleaner image using a more professional graphics program (there are some free graphics programs available, like Gimp).

> Each image must be in JPEG or GIF format for your eBook, placed on a line by itself, with the text wrap set to In Line with Text.

Cover Design and Illustration Resources

- You can find free cover design articles on my blog: www.chrismcmullen.wordpress.com. Once there, click the Cover Design tab.

- Although KDP doesn't offer design services, KDP does maintain a list of professional editors, designers, translators, and conversion services. Visit KDP, click Help, under Prepare Your Book click See All Formatting Resources, and find a link under Professional Services. Ask what happens if you need to make changes after the process is complete.

- Amazon KDP offers a free Cover Creator tool. This can help you design a basic cover for free. However, the designs are limited, and your cover may look very similar to many other covers.

- It's possible to hire a cover designer. You can find premade covers from $10 to $100, which aren't likely to fit your content perfectly and help attract your target audience as well as a custom cover. You can find custom cover design help from $100 to $300 (and up). I've hired Melissa Stevens (www.theillustratedauthor.net) to design covers, and have been very pleased with the results. Many small publishers who actively participate in the KDP community forum offer their cover design and illustration services. As with shopping for any service, try to learn about the person's character and qualifications, and seek objective opinions from someone who has used the service. View a portfolio of previous work to help judge what to expect. Read your contract carefully. Find out exactly what you're getting for your investment.

7 Preparing the PDF Files

THERE ARE SEVERAL software programs used to produce documents that have text, figures, or both, and these programs can save the documents in different file formats, which have different file extensions (.doc, .txt, .jpg, etc.). Even those files that are written with one program (such as Microsoft Word), yet are saved in a common extension like .txt, may lose features and quality when saved in the more common format. Rather than restricting all authors to use a particular software program, which inherently can not be the best program to produce all types of books that can be written, most print-on-demand self-publishing services ask authors to submit files in a Portable Document Format (PDF). Authors can thus prepare their manuscripts in whichever program they prefer, in principle, and then convert the document to PDF. The conversion of a file to PDF is a means of making it universal – i.e. anyone can open a PDF file on any computer if they have a program that can view a PDF file, even if they don't have the program that was used to write the original document. Acrobat Reader is freely available so that everyone can read PDF files.

PDF File

A PDF file is a portable document format that any computer can read (with a PDF reader like Acrobat), which has instructions for how to display the text and figures of a document on a screen, even without knowledge of the software program that was used to prepare the original document.

Here is the essential idea behind PDF files. Regardless of what program you use to make a document, you are able to print the document by sending the printer a set of instructions for what the document looks like. The printer is not familiar with all of the programs that a computer might use to make documents, which would not be practical. Rather, all programs send a similar set of instructions to the printer to tell the printer what the document looks like. If you can tell a printer what a document looks like, then you can just as well tell a file what a document looks like. So creating a PDF file is sort of like printing to a file, but not quite. If you simply open a document and try to print it to a file, this by itself will not make a PDF file. However, this is the main underlying idea: A PDF file is a universal way of converting a program's document to a file that any computer can view on the screen, even if the computer doesn't have the software program that was used to make the original file.

PDF Conversion Basics

If you have access to a computer that has Microsoft Word 2007 or later and you have prepared a Word document or other text document that was saved in a format with a .docx, .doc, .rtf, or .txt extension, the simplest way to convert the text document to PDF is as follows. However, if your file contains any pictures, this convenient method will decrease the resolution of your images; in that case, it's better to use a different method (such as described later in this section).

- If it is not there already, bring your file to this computer (via CD, floppy disk, or jump drive, for example). It is not necessary to save the file to this computer.
- Open Microsoft Word 2007 or later. Open your file in Microsoft Word.
- Go to Save As and look at the options. If the PDF conversion add-on feature has already been installed, choose to Save As PDF.
- Otherwise, where this option would be there will be a link to download and install this option. Do this. It's free and easy: Just follow the instructions, which you will see when you reach Microsoft's website.
- Save your file in PDF format. It may take a couple of minutes, depending upon your file size and the speed of your computer. (If you had to install the PDF conversion add-on, you may need to repeat these steps before you reach the Save As PDF point.)
- If the computer has Acrobat Reader, the PDF file should open automatically. If not, go to where you saved the PDF file and open it manually.
- If the computer does not have Acrobat Reader, you should get this – it's available freely. Search for it with your favorite internet search engine. Look for a website that is clearly part of Adobe's extensive website (it's best to download it from a reliable source).

This is not the only way to prepare a PDF file. There are a myriad of programs available on the web, some free and others not, for converting files of a variety of formats to

PDF. I recommend going with a website that you can trust. You should have a reliable antivirus program working before downloading software. Adobe, for example, is one of the major PDF experts, and offers PDF conversion processes (they give you a handful of trials for free).

Some of Adobe's PDF software is relatively expensive (except for Acrobat Reader, which is free) to purchase, but Adobe also offers a conversion service. While there are many free Word-to-PDF converters online, if you prefer to purchase a copy, Nuance PDF Professional is fairly affordable and includes several features. Among the free PDF converters recommended on the KDP community forum is DoPDF (I haven't used DoPDF myself, though; I have used the Adobe and Nuance software programs that I've recommended).

If your book includes images, you want to install a Word-to-PDF converter and print the file to PDF. Don't use Word's convenient Save As PDF option. When printing to PDF, explore the options (e.g. you'll probably need to manually change the page size, since the default setting probably won't match the size that you set in Page Layout). Two convenient features to look for in PDF converters are the option to embed fonts and to flatten transparency in pictures.

Don't use Word's convenient Save As PDF feature if your file has images; otherwise, your images may print with a lower than recommended DPI. Instead, install a Word-to-PDF converter and print to PDF.

Although Amazon KDP allows you to submit a .doc, .docx, or .rtf file, this is not recommended because the formatting of your document is very likely to change. It's better to convert your file to PDF, check the PDF carefully, and submit that.

Beyond the Basics

If you didn't use any features specific to Word 2007 or 2010, you may find the conversion to PDF more reliable by first saving your file with the Word 2003 format (i.e. with a .doc instead of .docx extension). If you used the new equation editor, drawing tools, or other features from Word 2007 and beyond and try to save the file in the 2003 format, those features may not format as well that way; in that case, it's worth trying to maintain the

.docx extension. This was a bigger problem in 2007 when the new .docx extension first came out; with Word 2010 and various updates to PDF converters as well as Amazon, the conversion to PDF from .docx seems to be smoother (as long as you convert to PDF yourself and upload a PDF file; don't upload a .doc, .docx, or .rtf file to Amazon KDP). If you happen to have Word 2007 specifically, the Save As PDF feature might cause some strange formatting issues when trying to do this from a .docx extension (so try installing a PDF converter and printing to PDF instead – something you should do anyway if your file contains images).

Chances are that a basic PDF conversion, such as the one available with Microsoft Word 2007 or 2010, will work just fine for you if your book consists of just text (like a novel). Otherwise, you should look for a PDF converter (there are many available for free online). If you have rather complex images, it's possible that the conversion of your files will involve some technical issues. If so, you might need to seek some expertise with PDF formatting (see the list of resources at the end of this chapter, and first try seeking free help).

Amazon KDP will review the PDF files for your cover and book interior and send you an email with their comments. They will tell you if the files are just fine, if they notice minor problems, or if there are major problems that must be corrected. They are very good at identifying problems like insufficient margins, text too close to the page edge, and low-resolution images; but they do not check for formatting, writing, spelling, or grammar issues (those are entirely up to you). If you observe a problem with your proof and ask them about a technical printing issue, they are also very good at understanding your problem and identifying the technical issue(s) that caused the problem. However, Amazon KDP is a self-service publisher – i.e. they will only identify the problem for you, but not help you resolve the problem. So if you are unfortunate to have a technical problem, you will have to solve it yourself or look elsewhere for the expertise you need to solve it (unless you invest in paid formatting or design services). Try posting your question on the KDP community forum; if your question doesn't get answered (most questions posted there, even when highly technical, do get answered) or if you'd like an experienced formatter to help you, many of the small publishers active on the community forum offer paid formatting help.

If you need more than just a basic PDF conversion, you can try one of the many programs or services available on the web. Adobe offers a PDF conversion with many options that are not available when you convert with Microsoft Word 2007 or 2010. They also offer some rather expensive PDF software, which has a ton of detailed features, but again I recommend spending as little as possible when you are starting out. If you use Adobe's web-based conversion, for which you can use for five free conversions, if you explore the options you will see that there are numerous advanced options for formatting your PDF file. You might look into these if you require a specific formatting feature. Alternatively, you might see if a free PDF converter, like DoPDF, can meet your needs.

Following are a couple of problems that I have encountered with my PDF conversions. I am sharing them in case they also apply to you.

If you prepare figures with transparency – i.e. you make the color of an object partially transparent so that objects behind it show through – this may cause a bit of trouble. If you use Amazon KDP, they will notify you that your file includes objects with transparency. They manually flatten (that's the jargon) the transparency in your figures, which may cause slight color shifting. If you have rather complex images, the process of manually flattening the transparency might cause the images to come out considerably different than how they appear on the screen.

They recommend flattening the transparency yourself. If you happen to use a PDF conversion program that has a box to check to flatten transparency, this will be convenient; some free PDF converters have this feature. An alternative is to convert your images to JPEG files and insert the JPEG files into your Word document before converting to PDF (depending on the method you use to do this, you might notice stray marks on your images; e.g. using Paint is convenient, but not the best method available).

There are some other issues that are rather common, which are either minor problems or easy to solve. One is that the images in your PDF file might have less resolution than the images in your original document. If the resolution is low, the publisher will let you know that you have figures with low resolution. You can either choose to accept this or try to make them higher resolution. A PDF conversion process that lets you select the desired resolution will help you make higher-resolution images; Microsoft Word's built-in conversion process is very basic, and presently doesn't offer any options (you get options by printing to PDF from Word with a different PDF converter installed, instead of using the Save As feature). Also, be sure to follow the prescription outlined in the previous chapter (following the images of book covers) regarding how to avoid Word's tendency to decrease the resolution of your images.

It may also help if your PDF file has the fonts embedded in the file. If you use common fonts like Times New Roman, Garamond, Georgia, and Calibri, this should not be a problem. If you use rare fonts, you might have to learn how to embed them in the PDF file through the conversion process (provided that the font provider enabled embeddability and that commercial use is permitted by the font license). A PDF conversion program that has embedding options can help you with this. If you're using Word's built-in converter, when you Save As, click Tools, select Save Options, and check the box marked "Embed fonts in the file."

Look your proof over carefully. It might not look exactly the same as your document, or even how your PDF files appear on your screen. The formatting differences could be slight, or they could be substantial, but it's definitely worth looking this over carefully before you make your book available for purchase.

PDF Conversion Resources

- Visit www.adobe.com to get Acrobat Reader to view PDF files. Adobe also offers some paid conversion services. Nuance at www.nuance.com offers a fairly affordable software package, although Adobe is highly regarded by publishers.
- There are several free Word-to-PDF converters available online, such as DoPDF. If you download a file from the internet, be sure to have an updated antivirus program installed on your computer and check that the site is trustworthy.
- If you need help converting to PDF format, try searching the KDP community help forum and posting your question if you don't find the answer there. Chances are that someone else has had the exact same problem and will be happy to share the solution.
- It is possible to pay a reasonable fee to an experienced formatter if you run into a technical problem and free help and advice don't work out. For example, you might contact one of the experienced small publishers who regularly participate on the KDP community forum. Most of the time, authors can convert their books to PDF format just by taking time to find a suitable converter and asking a question on the forum.

8 Receiving Feedback

FEEDBACK THAT YOU receive from others can be quite valuable. Once your book is available for sale, anybody who reads your book is liable to leave you permanent feedback in a review, so it is worthwhile to receive some feedback prior to this moment and consider any merit that it may have. You know how you view your book. Different people have different views, though, so you want to assess what your target audience might think about your book.

Using Constructive Criticism

Feedback can be useful throughout the production of your book, from when you first conceive of the idea to when you publish your book, and even after your book is on the market. In order to allow yourself to benefit from this feedback, and to handle it well, you must prepare yourself for some constructive criticism. When you request feedback, ask for the reader to give you an honest assessment, and to try to provide comments objectively and tactfully, if possible. Ask them to make comments that are good, not good, and neutral.

People have different views, beliefs, and opinions. What works well for one person may not work well for another. There is not one method of teaching that works best for everyone because different people learn better in different ways: Some learn very well visually, others learn better by speaking and listening; some learn best individually, others learn better in groups; some learn better by participating, others through observation. Similarly, a book style that appeals to one person may not appeal as well to another person.

So some criticism that you might receive may not mean that a certain aspect of the book is necessarily bad – it could just be a matter of a difference of opinion or style, which could appeal to some people better than others. But that doesn't mean you should just dismiss the comment. You really want to know for what percentage of your target audience this works for, and what percentage it does not.

Some who read your book to offer feedback will catch spelling and grammatical mistakes, formatting problems, inconsistencies, organizational problems, conceptual problems, etc. Notes like these will lead to helpful corrections.

You will also receive a variety of other comments and suggestions. Ultimately, you have to decide whether to make revisions based on these comments and suggestions, and to what extent. If you can gauge what percentage of your target audience feels the same way, or otherwise, or is neutral on this point, this may help you in your decision. It's your book, and your vision, so you're in charge and it's your responsibility, but the more your book appeals to your audience, and the wider the audience for your book, the better your sales.

You can receive helpful feedback from close friends and family when you are first developing the concept for your book. You can discuss the concept with them or show them an outline for your book. As you try to share your vision for your work with them, they may provide useful feedback in the early development of your work.

When you finish writing the text for your book, feedback that you may receive at this point is very useful for revisions because the more revisions you make prior to formatting your book for publication, the less hassle you will experience with editing and formatting.

Additional mistakes can be caught, especially those that may have appeared as a result of editing and formatting, when the book interior is complete. Once again, after creating the PDF file, feedback is useful.

When you proofread your own book – which you need to do, since you should have a greater interest in your book than anyone else, and therefore should be more motivated to find mistakes – you sometimes read what you intended to type instead of what you actually typed. Feedback that you receive from others can help you correct mistakes of this sort.

But you want more than just a list of corrections. You also want organizational, stylistic, and conceptual comments and suggestions. You want to know what people think about your book, whether or not it is useful or entertaining, whether or not the book is worth buying, which type of audience may be interested in your work, ideas for improving your book, the quantitative worth of your book, etc.

Feedback is the best way to sample how people will react to reading your book.

One helpful way to receive feedback is to join a writing group. If the group includes other authors like yourself, you may be able to exchange feedback. Another way to receive feedback is to find people or fans who would be willing to serve as beta readers. Once your book is published, they might also help to spread the word.

Test-Marketing Your Book

When your book is complete and you are ready to publish your work, it may be worthwhile to test-market your book. Distribute copies and solicit some input. This time, you might try to reach a wider audience than close friends and family. If you have a nonfiction book, you could give a presentation and offer some copies to interested readers in exchange for their input (you might even sell pre-publication copies, possibly at a discounted price). If your work is fiction, you could instead hold a storytelling session and similarly distribute copies.

Someone who receives a free or discounted copy and likes your book might help spread the word about your book, which could serve as good promotion for your book. They may appreciate that you asked for their input – people often like to give advice.

You might ask people to make comments in the book itself and return it to you, or just to read it and discuss it with you (and keep the book). You can order inexpensive copies of your book directly from the publisher (if doing this for the purpose of test-marketing, you may not want your book to be available on Amazon.com until later). You might even provide a form with specific questions you would like to have addressed. Whatever method you choose, you would like to receive feedback.

If you're considering investing money in your book at the outset, the results of test-marketing your book can help you decide if the investment may be worthwhile.

If you are able to solicit any good reviews of your book prior to publication, you can include quotes from these reviews on the cover of your book. Include the source of your quote if it is from a magazine or website. Note that you can post editorial reviews on your book's product page through Author Central (see Chapter 10).

Your test-marketing results might be good, and they might not. If they are good, you will have some confidence in your book, and you are ready to publish your book. If the results are not good, it's better to learn this now than later. You have the opportunity to make improvements before publishing your book. The comments, suggestions, and corrections you receive give you the opportunity to revise your book for the better. The next go-around may yield more encouraging results. Believe in your book and go back to the drawing board, if necessary. You might also try presenting your work to a different audience. Maybe others will appreciate your book better than your first sample audience.

Once you develop a fan base (you can create a Facebook page for your book or an email newsletter and provide information about how to sign up at the end of your book), some of your fans may be willing to form a focus group to help provide feedback on your next project (this may also help to build some buzz).

9 Publishing on Amazon.com

ONCE YOU HAVE a completed manuscript, publishing on Amazon.com is easy. One way is to use Amazon's Kindle Direct Publishing (KDP). If you self-publish with them, you can make your title available for sale directly on Amazon.com as well as through Expanded Distribution channels (which are now free – the cost used to be $25). When your book sells, Amazon KDP prints your book and ships it out.

In addition, you can publish an eBook through Amazon KDP, which will be available for sale on Amazon for Kindle devices (and can also be read with Kindle for PC, iPad, and iPhone). You can also publish your eBook with Nook, Kobo, and other retailers.

If you visit Amazon.com, at the bottom of their home page, you will see a link that says, "Self-Publish with Us." Click this link to learn about how you can publish with Amazon. Amazon KDP allows you to publish a paperback to be available on-demand at Amazon (plus Expanded Distribution channels) and also allows you to publish a Kindle eBook. (Note: CreateSpace has now merged with Kindle Direct Publishing.)

---

kdp.amazon.com

If you already have an Amazon account, the same login information will work at KDP. Otherwise, you can sign up for a new account.

Amazon KDP is not your only self-publishing option. Ingram Spark is the main alternative to Amazon KDP, though a downside is that Ingram Spark charges a setup fee. A few self-published authors also use Lulu. Amazon KDP is a popular option because it is Amazon's self-publishing company: Many authors trust Amazon through experience or reputation, and using Amazon KDP is a natural way to sell your books on Amazon.com. I have published dozens of books with Amazon KDP and recommend it highly (though I still encourage you to do your homework – i.e. compare your options to see what suits your needs best).

You can publish your eBook with Nook, Kobo, and other companies in addition to KDP (unless you enroll in KDP Select, in which case you are choosing to publish your eBook exclusively with Kindle – we'll discuss this option later in the chapter). There are also aggregators like Smashwords and Lulu that help you publish with several eBook retailers at once. I recommend publishing your eBook directly with each retailer when this option is possible – that way, you can view a preview of your eBook directly with the source.

Publishing a Paperback

Amazon KDP offers softcover book printing. The covers are printed on coverstock and are laminated. You can choose from glossy or matte. They can assign you a free ISBN-10 and EAN-13 and print the ISBN with a UPC bar code on the back of your cover (also free of charge). Alternatively, you can purchase an ISBN through Bowker to publish with your own publishing imprint.

First, visit Amazon KDP's website and setup an account. In order to publish your book and receive royalty payments for sales, you will need to provide information for them to report taxes and bank account information so that they can deposit your royalty checks. They will send you a 1099 after the year ends, reporting your total royalty payments for the year. (Amazon's 1099's are mailed out on January 31, which means you should expect it in the mail one to two weeks into February. You don't want forget and file your taxes before your 1099's arrive. They used to mail out multiple 1099's for different countries, but now they are consolidated.)

Once your account is setup, log in. When you log in, you will come to your Bookshelf. This is where you can see any books that you are working on or already have published. Once you have published a book, you can keep track of your sales by clicking the Reports link at the top of the page. If a book sells on Amazon, you typically see the sale register within 1-2 days on your Sales Dashboard (but note that there are occasional delays of up to two months). Click the Help link at the top of the page to find the KDP help pages. There will then be a Contact Us option down at the left.

You should visit the KDP community forum, where you can interact with other members of the community, such as other authors like yourself by asking or answering questions about self-publishing on Amazon. The KDP help pages and KDP community forum are packed with helpful information about every stage of the self-publishing process. Some knowledgeable formatters and small publishers frequent the KDP community forum. You may even find helpful marketing ideas.

If you are ready to publish your book, first go to your KDP Bookshelf, and then click to add a new title. You will see that this is a multi-step process. The process is organized into three pages: book details, book content, and pricing. You may save your progress and continue later (you will probably not be able to do it all at one sitting).

The first step is to enter Title Information. Choose your title and subtitle carefully. These and other fields that are indicated with an asterisk (*) will become permanent when you receive your ISBN.

Here is a tip: Don't enter a publication date. If you enter a publication date, by the time you upload your files, order a proof, revise your proof, and are ready to publish, the date you entered will be weeks in the past. By not entering a publication date, when you press Approve Proof, that date will automatically become your publication date. Why is this important? Because Amazon has new release filters (Last 30 Days and Last 90 Days) that give your book added visibility when it's first published. You get the maximum benefit of the new release filters by not entering a publication date.

> Don't enter a publication date. This will give you maximum exposure with the new release filters.

Enter your author information. You can also add coauthors, illustrators, editors, and so on. Anyone who contributed toward your book should be credited for their effort: Some may wish to have their names entered in these fields (if so, their names and roles will also show up next to your author name at the top of the book's Amazon page); others may just wish to be mentioned on the copyright page. If you study traditionally published books, you may note that most only mention cover designers in small print on the back cover and in one note on the copyright page, but not in the contributor fields (fantastic covers often don't mention the cover designer on the front cover).

When your Title Information is complete, save it and move onto the second step. The second step is pretty short: Select an ISBN option carefully. You can either take KDP's free ISBN option or purchase your own ISBN directly from Bowker. If you select the free ISBN, Amazon will write "Independently Published" in the publisher field for your book. If you buy an ISBN from Bowker, you can use your own imprint. If you consider the number of self-published authors and their friends and family, you will see that there is a very large support group for self-publishing. In this way, it's possible for the free option to be more of an advantage than a disadvantage. It depends in part on your genre or content, your target audience, the appearance of your book, etc.

Once you save page two, you will receive your ISBN-10 and EAN-13. I suggest that you add these numbers to the copyright page of your book, if you have such a page. If you had already made your PDF, you will have to make a new PDF file for your book interior after adding the ISBN info to it.

Choose whether to have a black-and-white or color interior. A color interior costs much more. You pay the same price for a color interior whether you have just one page in color or every page in color. Note that your cover can be in color regardless of whether or not the interior is black-and-white. If your interior is black-and-white, you can choose between white or cream pages. Note that different trim sizes have different restrictions on how many pages your book can have, and that this also depends on whether your interior is color or black-and-white; there are also more distribution options if you select one of the "standard" trim sizes. Ensure that your trim size, interior color, and page count match.

The next steps, submitting your interior and cover files, just involve browsing your computer for the PDF files for your book interior and book cover, and selecting and submitting them. (Although you may submit a .doc, .docx, or .rtf file for your book's interior, PDF is highly recommended in order to reduce the chances of significant formatting changes.) Using Interior Reviewer allows you to inspect the live zone and potential problems (but note that some issues that get flagged may not be critical, and Interior Reviewer is not always 100% accurate; if in doubt, proceed to submit your files for review and get a report within 12-24 hours).

You may choose the Cover Creator option if you don't wish to design your own cover. Note the links to learn more about creating a cover.

In the next step, you get to review all the information that you have entered thus far. Check this over carefully. When you are happy with everything, submit your book for publishing. Once you do, you won't be able to make any more changes to the steps that you just completed until after someone has reviewed your submission (so if you suddenly realize you need to correct something, you just need to wait about 12-24 hours).

After submitting your files for review, you can proceed to select sales channels, enter pricing information, your book description, and more (you don't need to wait for file review to finish to make *these* changes).

Select your sales channels. The Expanded Distribution channels used to cost $25, but are now free. The Expanded Distribution channel helps to make your book much more visible online (e.g. BN.com, The Book Depository, and many other online retailers are likely to sell your book online). While it makes your book available through some physical channels (like schools and libraries), it's highly unlikely that a bookstore will stock your book by simply adding Expanded Distribution (your best bet is to order author copies to sell to local bookstores directly and approach them with a professional press release kit). Depending on the list price that you have in mind, Expanded Distribution might affect your options to some extent – e.g. it affects the minimum price you can set, so if you were planning on a relatively low list price, you might want to explore this (you can play with the royalty calculator to find out).

Before CreateSpace merged with KDP, there used to be an eStore option. The eStore offered authors a storefront that paid higher royalties than Amazon, but few authors succeeded in landing significant eStore sales. Most authors sell more books by driving traffic to Amazon than some other storefront because customers trust Amazon, they might be able to qualify for free shipping, and Amazon's website is functional and convenient. If you are among the rare authors who could drive traffic to a site other than Amazon, you can setup your own website and sell copies directly (or sell them on your own website and have the books shipped from KDP).

Set the list price for your book in dollars, pounds, and euro. Choosing a good price is not easy. You should check the list prices of competitive titles, complementary titles, related titles, and even self-published titles that seem somehow comparable to your book. If the price is too high, this may discourage shoppers from buying your book. If the price is too low, you make a much smaller royalty.

A lower price will not necessarily result in more sales (in fact, it can even deter sales, as many people believe that you get what you pay for). I explored this with a few of my first books: After reducing the price by a dollar or two, sales were virtually unaffected. But this doesn't mean that you can get away with a high price. There is a limited price range that will seem like an appropriate value. If the price is higher than this, it will discourage sales. If the price is lower than this, it might not improve sales (and might even deter sales).

Another thing to consider is this: What's a fair royalty? The price and royalty go together, so you need to consider both. Publishers often pay a royalty of about 15%. However, publishers also print a large number of books, and expect to sell a large number if they agree to publish your book. If you self-publish, you probably expect to sell fewer books. If you sell fewer books, a somewhat larger royalty may be fair to make it worthwhile to you, financially, to write and publish your book. You're not just an author – you may also be the editor, formatter, cover designer, etc. If you're filling many roles, a higher royalty than a traditional publisher pays just to an author is certainly fair. If you also invest your money for promotional activities, you need to use a portion of your royalties to pay for this.

So it may be fair to earn a royalty that is somewhat greater than 15% of the list price. But you don't want to be greedy, either. If you want a really large royalty, you'll have to make the list price very high, which probably means you'll sell many fewer books and make less revenue from your book.

Keep in mind that you can change the list price once you set it. Shoppers probably won't appreciate it if you raise the list price,[1] but won't mind if you lower the list price. Amazon often discounts the book (but don't worry: if they do this, they pay you the royalty based on the list price, not on the sale price, so it's a good thing). The higher your list price, the more room Amazon has to play with to create a sale price.

Finally, think about what kind of book you are offering. Is it like a mass market paperback, for which there are already numerous popular works available for about five to seven dollars? If so, you will find it difficult to compete at the top of the price range. Is it more like a trade paperback, which can sell for more? (Physically, Amazon KDP paperbacks tend to resemble trade paperbacks much more than mass market paperbacks; marketing-wise, self-published authors are also more apt to reach a niche audience than a mass market audience.) Does your book involve expertise that may drive the price up? What is the value of your book? What would you be willing to pay for it? Test-marketing can help you establish a fair value.

Royalties depend on the author cost. Books with a black-and-white interior cost $2.15 for up to 108 pages and $0.85 plus $0.012 per page for longer books. Books with a color interior cost $3.65 for up to 40 pages and $0.85 plus $0.07 per page for longer books.

You receive a 60% royalty, based on your list price, for books sold through Amazon.com, minus the cost of your book. If you sell a book directly through Amazon KDP, your royalty is 80% minus the author cost. The Expanded Distribution pays 40% minus the author cost.

You receive a direct deposit (if you sign up for it) into your bank account of your royalty payments for a given month near the end of the following month.

Now we'll move onto the book description. Type a description that has up to 4,000 characters (with spaces). Note that shorter descriptions tend to be more effective for fictional works; nonfiction can be somewhat longer if divided into block paragraphs with spaces between or by including bullet points (either you need to learn basic HTML to do this or sign up for Amazon's Author Central – see the resources at the end of the chapter – after you publish; using HTML is better as it will transfer to BN.com, too, but first preview your description on Amazon to ensure that it came out well). I highly recommend that you

---

[1] I have actually done this, but I had a good reason. I was selling the first volume of a two-volume set for $11.99. When I published the second volume, I realized how silly this was. Customers buying both would have to pay $23.98 plus shipping. So I raised the price to $12.50 so that buyers would qualify for free Super Saver shipping (back then, Super Saver shipping applied to $25 purchases and self-published paperbacks were rarely discounted; now, there is a good chance that Amazon will discount the list price by 5 to 10% – but pay you the *full* royalty, so it's a good thing – and the minimum purchase for Super Saver shipping has jumped up to $35).

first type your description in Microsoft Word and then paste it into the description field later (but if pasting into Author Central, you must first paste into Notepad and then copy/paste from Notepad to Author Central, then reformat in Author Central). For one, Microsoft Word will help you catch spelling or grammatical mistakes. For another, Microsoft Word will let you keep track of how many characters you've used and how many are left.

You want your description to read well, to draw interest to your book, and to help sell your book. Browse other book descriptions on Amazon to get some ideas. Shoppers who come across your book's webpage will probably want to know what your book is about, what it will be like to read your book, and how your book differs from similar titles (without saying negative things about other books or authors). Your description is a sample of your writing, so if it doesn't read well, this might adversely affect your sales. Shoppers might not know that *you* wrote the description, but even so, the quality of the writing of your description can have a positive or negative influence on the customer's first impression.

The next step is to indicate the reading level and enter categories. Browse through all of the category options. More than one category will probably apply to your book, so you'll have to choose the best categories from the list. However, there are special keywords that can get your book listed in additional categories: Search the KDP help pages regarding keywords and categories. There are also special requirements for teen categories. You might search for competitive and complementary titles to see what categories they appear in (but the browse categories on Amazon and the BISAC categories listed here are not the same).

> Once your book has been published, if your book doesn't end up in the categories that you expected based on your selections, contact KDP support to request up to two categories. Make a separate request for Amazon UK.

You can enter up to five keywords that shoppers might search for on Amazon.com, which relate to your book. A keyword can be a single word or a short group of words (there is a limit for the number of characters, though). I recommend that you not use keywords that already appear in your title or subtitle – words that appear in your title and subtitle may be searchable even if you don't list them as keywords. You will be able to test this out once your book becomes available on Amazon.com (it can take a week after you publish it before you can find it on Amazon), and you can modify these keywords later. Give some thought to what keywords will be useful and appropriate. Bear in mind that shoppers won't be happy if your book shows up in a seemingly unrelated search, so be sure to choose keywords that relate to your book. **See the note in the following section regarding how to use keywords to get your book listed in special categories.**

You can also enter an About the Author section. It's better to sign up for Author Central after you publish and add a biography. If you do both, the biography will show in addition to the About the Author section (and if both are the same, this will seem like a glaring mistake on your product page). Author Central also allows you to easily keep track of sales ranks and reviews, shows you geographic sales data for most of your paperback sales, and has other nice features. Beware that once a paperback book is added to Author Central, it's there permanently (whereas an eBook can be removed by request, once it's unlinked from the paperback edition).

You may receive automatic emails (depending on your account settings) when you create your account, submit your files, revise files, make purchases, and submit your book for publishing. After submitting your book for publishing, within 12-24 hours (usually) you will receive an email from someone who has reviewed your files. This email will let you know if your files are acceptable, and will tell you if there are concerns about the format of your book (like the resolution of your images, or whether the title you entered matches the title of the cover and the book interior); but they won't check for spelling, grammar, writing, or formatting mistakes (those are all up to you).

If your files are unacceptable, you will have to correct the specified problems and re-submit them. If they are acceptable, but they identified concerns, you can either choose to accept your book as it is and continue with the publishing process (it might be best to order a printed proof to see exactly how it looks), or make changes and submit your files again.

Once your files are acceptable and you are content with them, you can order a proof of your book. There are two options for proofing your book – a digital proof and printed proof. I recommend using the Digital Proofer first, and once you're satisfied with that, ordering a printed proof. You really need to have a copy of your printed proof to know exactly what your customers will be getting. Also, you're sure to catch typos in your printed proof that you would miss when viewing the screen.

You will have to place an order for the printed proof, including shipping charges. My proofs *usually* arrive in about a week – faster than the dates that they indicate.

When your proof arrives, review it carefully. Chances are that, no matter how careful you have been and how much feedback you have received, you will spot one or more mistakes. Think of it as Murphy's law if you want. It's important to read through your proof carefully, though, since if you choose to approve your proof, this is exactly what you can expect buyers to receive. If there are any mistakes, you want to catch and correct them now. If you do find mistakes, correct them and submit new files, and order a new proof.

Once you have a proof that you are happy with, login to your KDP account to approve your proof and publish your book. You should be able to find your book on Amazon.com within about a week. Check this Amazon page carefully to make sure that there are no mistakes (there shouldn't be, but nobody's perfect).

If you encounter problems or have questions, visit the KDP community forum or contact KDP support.

If you need to revise your book after making it available, you can make your book unavailable and go through the process once again to make corrections.

You will probably want to monitor your sales and royalty payments on your Member Dashboard. Once your book sells, you might also want to keep track of your Amazon.com sales rank. Realize that sales fluctuate. They will be better sometimes and slower other times. Don't get discouraged if sales start out pretty slow. First, people have to find your book before they can decide to buy your book. Promotional strategies (Chapter 10) can help with this. If sales are slow when your book first hits the market, there is still the hope for sales to increase as awareness of your book grows, and there is the hope that any promotional activities that you might choose to engage in will help increase sales of your book. On the other hand, if sales take off early, there is a chance that they will taper off later.

> Be patient. Give your book a chance and see how things evolve before you judge the success of your book.

Now you should consider promotional strategies. Even if you don't plan to market your book at all (which I don't recommend), I bet you will find a few useful tips in the next chapter and be glad that you read it. ☺

Publishing an eBook

Don't use the PDF file for your paperback edition to make your Kindle edition because PDF files tend to suffer formatting problems when converted to Kindle. Instead, convert your Word document to eBook format as described in Chapter 5. (However, you might check out Amazon's free Kindle conversion tools: Kindle Create, the Kindle Kids' Book Creator, the Kindle Textbook Creator, and the Kindle Comic Creator. These tools help to simplify the Kindle conversion process.)

After you login to KDP, visit your Bookshelf. Click to add a new title.

The box at the top asks if you wish to enroll in KDP Select. If you're not sure, you can leave this box unchecked for now – it's something you can elect to do at any time. However, you can't get out of the program so easily – if you sign up, you must wait for your 90-day enrollment period to end before opting out. Also, enrollment automatically renews, so you must uncheck the box to disable automatic renewal and also wait until the 90-day enrollment period ends in order to opt out of KDP Select.

Since it's not easy to get out of the program, it's important to consider this decision carefully. KDP Select has some enticing benefits. Let me mention the one disadvantage first: If you sign up for KDP Select, your eBook may only be available in Kindle format while it's enrolled in KDP Select. Your eBook can't be available for sale with Nook, Kobo, Sony, Smashwords, your website, or anywhere else in electronic format unless and until your 90-day enrollment period ends (and you have to disable automatic renewal to avoid entering into a subsequent 90-day enrollment). However, you may publish a paperback with KDP and have your eBook enrolled in KDP Select, and you may select the Expanded Distribution channel at KDP (the exclusivity agreement only applies to the electronic edition).

So why would you give up the opportunity to publish your eBook with Nook, Kobo, Sony, and other retailers? Some authors choose to do this because KDP Select does offer some enticing benefits (while other authors prefer not to give up this opportunity):

- You can schedule one Countdown Deal during each 90-day enrollment period. If your eBook price is at least $2.99 in the US (the minimum is £1.93 in the UK), a Countdown Deal lets you create a temporary sale (up to 7 days). Customers will see the list price, sale price, and when the sale ends.

- Instead of a Countdown Deal, you can make your eBook free for up to 5 days per 90-day enrollment period. You don't earn royalties for free eBooks, but this can help you get some early readers. (Personally, I prefer the Countdown Deal, as you're more likely to attract readers from your target audience – plus, you earn a royalty.)

- Kindle Unlimited subscribers can borrow your eBook. You receive a royalty (around $0.005 per page, but it varies) for each page read.

Should you sign up for KDP Select? It's a tough decision to make. Authors who join KDP Select and receive many sales from Countdown Deals and get many borrows usually stay in the program. Those who don't get much out of the Countdown Deals or borrows often opt out of the program. On the other hand, authors who at first avoid KDP Select who don't sell many eBooks with other retailers often join KDP Select to try it out. The only way to know for sure is try it both ways.

Enter the title exactly the same as you entered it for the paperback (use copy/paste). If you entered a subtitle for the paperback, include the title and subtitle together in the title field at KDP (separate them with a colon and a single space after the colon). When you add contributors, be sure to spell and punctuate the names exactly the same way (copy/paste them). This way, the paperback and Kindle editions should link together automatically. If they don't link in a few days, use the Contact Us feature at KDP to place a request.

> If your Kindle and paperback editions don't link together on Amazon within a few days, log into KDP, click the Contact Us button, select Product Page, click Linking Print and Kindle Editions, and copy/paste your ISBN and ASIN directly from your product pages.

Enter a description of your eBook. Just like for the paperback version, you can use limited HTML for the eBook description. In fact, you can simply copy/paste the description from your paperback into your eBook. Alternatively, you can use Author Central.

As I explained for the paperback edition, I recommend leaving the publication date blank.

Don't use the same ISBN as your paperback when publishing your eBook. Paperback and eBook editions can't use the same ISBN. However, you don't need an ISBN for Kindle: Just leave this field empty and you will receive an ASIN instead.

Similarly, don't enter Kindle, Amazon, or KDP as the publisher. You can either leave this field blank or enter the name of your own publishing imprint, if you have one.

You can select up to 7 keywords at KDP (two more than CreateSpace allowed) and two categories. There are some special categories that you can only get in through the use of special keywords. See the link below to a KDP help page that lists the special keywords needed to get your book listed in special categories.

> Visit the following KDP help page to learn how to get your book listed in special categories through keywords: https://kdp.amazon.com/help?topicId=A200PDGPEIQX41. Once there, click on one of the categories at the bottom to pull up a table of special keywords.

Select the option to declare your publishing rights. Click the "What's This?" link to learn more.

Upload the image for your cover or use the free Cover Creator option. You can upload a JPEG or TIFF file for your cover. Neither the width nor height may exceed 2500 pixels. Amazon recommends a 5:8 aspect ratio (i.e. the image should be 1.6 times taller than it is wide), in which case the cover would be 1563 x 2500. The thumbnail that you see on Amazon is usually sharper than the sample that you see after you upload your cover. However, it's important to upload a cover that looks sharp and clean full-size because that's how most shoppers will see it when they first look inside your eBook.

Select your preference for Digital Rights Management (DRM). Click the "What's This?" link to learn more about DRM.

Upload the content file for your eBook. If you have images, you should upload a compressed zipped folder (otherwise, you're likely to see subtle formatting problems): Save as a Web Page Filtered, close the file, find the file on your computer (e.g. in My Documents or wherever you saved it), right-click, choose Send To, select Compressed (Zipped) Folder, find the folder with the compressed images (the folder has the same name as the HTML file had), and copy/paste this image folder into the compressed zipped folder.

If you don't have images, you can upload a .doc or .docx file. In the early days of .docx, it seemed that .doc worked better in many ways; recently, I've had better luck with .docx (while many people who recall the early days of .docx continue to advise against it); which is better also depends in part on the nature of your content. If you're not happy with your preview, this is one thing you can try changing to see if it has an impact. (The "pros" will upload an EPUB or HTML file, and will clean and tweak the HTML to perfect subtle features.)

The maximum content file size for Kindle is 50 Mb. If you opt for the 70% royalty option, it's in your financial interest to minimize the file size. If you have pictures, these usually take most of the memory. Compress your images for your eBook file, as explained in Chapter 5, to keep the file size down.

Check your eBook carefully in the preview. Note that there are two previewers. There is a convenient online previewer and there is also a downloadable previewer. The downloadable previewer is more reliable than the convenient online previewer. Check your eBook on all 7 devices: eInk > Paperwhite, eInk > Kindle, eInk > Kindle DX, Fire > Kindle Fire, Fire > Kindle HD, IOS > Kindle for iPad, and IOS > Kindle for iPhone.

It's possible for your eBook to look fine on some devices, but format poorly on one device. The only way to know for sure is to check your eBook carefully on each device. You don't want your customers to be the first to discover any problems.

Use the downloadable previewer, which is more reliable than the convenient online previewer. Check your eBook carefully on all 7 devices. Even if it looks perfect on a few devices, there may still be major formatting issues on other devices. Resolve any issues before publishing.

On the second page of the publishing process, first select the locations where you have the rights to publish your eBook and set your list prices. Note: If you're enrolled in KDP Select and set the list price at $2.99 in the US, make sure the list price in the UK is at least £1.93, otherwise your book won't be eligible for Countdown Deals in the UK.

The 70% royalty option isn't quite 70%. First subtract the delivery fee from your list price, then multiply by 0.7 to figure your royalty. You don't have to do the math, though: There is a royalty calculator built into page 2 of the publishing process (where you set your list price) that will do the math for you. Under the table that lists the countries, you will find the converted MOBI file size for your Kindle eBook (look below the long table). This determines the delivery fee (multiply by 15 cents in the US). If you have a large file size, it's worth comparing the 35% and 70% royalty options to see which gives you a higher royalty.

The file size affects the minimum list price. If the converted MOBI file size exceeds 10 MB, the minimum list price is $2.99, and if it exceeds 3 MB, the minimum list price is $1.99. You can only set the list price between 99 cents and $1.99 if the file size is under 3 MB.

If you have a paperback edition of this eBook, you may choose to enroll your eBook in MatchBook. This allows you to offer customers an incentive to purchase both your paperback and Kindle editions – the incentive is a discount off your Kindle edition.

The Kindle Book Lending box (not to be confused with KDP Select borrows) will automatically be checked. You can only uncheck this box if you select the 35% royalty rate.

Read the terms and conditions carefully, check this box, and you're ready to publish (maybe you should check everything carefully once more first). Your Kindle eBook should be available in the Amazon US store in about 12 hours (you should receive an email, depending on your account settings).

Check your Kindle product page and explore the Look Inside once your eBook goes live. If you don't have a Kindle, find someone who does who can let you check out exactly how it looks on a Kindle device.

You can revise your eBook at any time (once it goes live). You might want to put a note in the front matter (e.g. the copyright page) so that when you view the Look Inside on

Amazon, you'll know which edition you're looking at.

If you don't enroll your eBook in KDP Select, you should also publish your eBook at other sites. The following list will help you get started:

www.nookpress.com
www.kobobooks.com/kobowritinglife
www.smashwords.com

Smashwords can distribute your eBook to Nook, Kobo, Apple, and other retailers. However, an advantage of publishing directly with Nook and Kobo is to see exactly what your preview will look like (if you do publish directly with them, you'll want to disable distribution to these retailers from Smashwords). When you publish at Smashwords, be sure to read the *Smashwords Style Guide* carefully (it's a free guide). Smashwords has other free guides that are also worth reading, such as one on marketing. Smashwords has a few special requirements, like writing "Smashwords Edition" on your copyright page.

Publishing Resources

- You can find free publishing articles on my blog: www.chrismcmullen.wordpress. com. Once there, click one of the following tabs: Cover Design, Blurb, Editing/Formatting, Writing, Marketing, or Publishing.
- Sign up for Amazon's Author Central at https://authorcentral.amazon.com (for the UK, change .com to .co.uk). You can monitor sales rank and reviews conveniently there, add formatting to your description, and find other helpful features.
- For full-page picture books, you may want to visit the KDP help pages to learn about fixed-layout Kindle eBooks.
- When publishing at Smashwords, read the *Smashwords Style Guide* by Matt Coker carefully before you publish. You can find many helpful free resources on Smashwords' website.
- Although KDP doesn't offer paid services, KDP does maintain a list of professional editors, designers, translators, and conversion services. Visit KDP, click Help, under Prepare Your Book click See All Formatting Resources, and find a link under Professional Services. Ask if you'll get to keep the edited file (and in what format), and what happens if you need to make changes after the process is complete.

- You can find freelance professionals who offer editing and formatting services. As with shopping for any service, try to learn about the person's character and qualifications, and seek objective opinions from someone who has used the service. Ask to have a sample chapter edited or formatted as a token of what to expect. Read your contract carefully. Find out exactly what you're getting for your investment.
- Amazon has a free guide for basic Kindle formatting called *Building Your Book for Kindle*. You can read it on a PC or Mac.
- If you need help with formatting issues (for paperback or eBook), try searching the KDP community help forum and posting your question if you don't find the answer there. Chances are that someone else has had the exact same problem and will be happy to share the solution.
- The Kindle help pages (see the link below) have many useful tips.

https://kdp.amazon.com
/help?topicId=A3R2IZDC42DJW6

- It is possible to pay someone to format your Kindle eBook for you. KDP lists a variety of companies who specialize in Kindle conversion services (see the link below):

https://kdp.amazon.com
/help?topicId=A3RRQXI478DDG7

10 Marketing Strategies

MARKETING HAS TWO sides. On the one hand, promotional strategies help authors spread awareness of their work, reaching more customers and, hopefully, increasing sales of their books. This is also beneficial to your target audience: Someone who might not otherwise have known about your book who buys and reads your book, and who enjoys your book or draws usefulness from your book, similarly benefits from your effort to market your book.

As I have said all along, I recommend not investing much in your book until your book starts to sell and you establish some measure of how well your book is selling. By using part of your royalties to invest in promotional activities, you can stay in the positive as you undertake such tasks. Also, by being patient this way, when you finally do some work to promote your book, you will be able to see firsthand what effect, if any, it may have had on your sales. This way you can see what is or isn't worth trying again so that you put investments where they are most effective.

Two places where it might be worth investing initially are cover design and editing. If you have friends and acquaintances with some measure of editing skills, they might be able to help you catch mistakes and offer valuable feedback. You definitely need a second pair of eyes to read your book because the author very often sees what he or she meant to write instead of what is actually written (you can gain a pair of ears using text-to-speech – this can help you catch phrases that sound funny to your ear).

Cover design is an important part of your marketing: The cover should quickly show the target audience that this book is for them. Your cover is also part of your branding process. If you have a highly marketable book (that's a big 'IF'), paying for a cover that attracts your target audience may pay off. (This requires the content to appeal to the audience, the cover to succeed at its job, and the description and Look Inside to be effective.)

Your book's description and Look Inside are also important aspects of your marketing. Only a fraction of the potential customers who view your book on Amazon will actually make a purchase. The effectiveness of your description and the quality of your Look Inside are huge factors. The description needs to concisely convey what to expect without giving too much away, and it needs to create interest in your book. The Look Inside needs to look professional, read well, and engage interest. It's worth studying top-selling books similar to yours to learn how to write effective blurbs and what a professional Look Inside looks like (especially, find blurbs of top-selling books that aren't selling because of the author's or publisher's big name).

The content is another huge factor in your marketing. Once customers read your book, the quality of the content will determine whether or not they recommend your book to others. This can come in the form of reviews and word-of-mouth sales. When customers spread news about your book through conversations, this is among the best marketing you can get. It's also the hardest marketing to get because the quality of your book must earn it. People read many average and good books without recommending them. It takes something special, like a book that moves them emotionally or a character they fall in love with to do this. Editing and formatting factor into this, too, because it's harder to recommend a book that has many mistakes in it.

The most effective marketing you can do tends to be free. Most authors struggle with marketing because they don't really know what to do or don't want to take the time to learn and try out ideas (and most of the ideas don't yield immediate results, but take months of patience). The result is that many authors are hoping to throw some money at marketing to get it to work, but it doesn't work that way.

Why does free book marketing tend to be better than paid marketing? Because personal interactions are a huge part of book marketing. You meet people at readings or signings, social media, and most of your online and offline marketing endeavors. Other people (e.g. publicists) can help arrange events for you, but *you* are the person who will have to make the appearance and do the bulk of the "work" involved in marketing anyway.

When people see your passion firsthand, have a chance to judge your character, realize that they share commonalities with you, and experience your charm, for example, such things can significantly improve your chances of creating interest in your book. When you look at the reasons that people by books (such as browsing bestsellers, recommendations, also bought lists, and keyword searches), one reason that may be most effective for independent authors is personal interactions with the author. Nobody else can do this for you. You're selling (and branding) yourself in addition your book.

Many of the free and low-cost things that you can do to market your books are easy to set up and just require putting a little time into them here and there over a long period of time. You don't build a professional author platform overnight, but you don't need to try. Develop it slowly over a long period of time and your platform and following will both grow and have substance.

Time is on your side. A little here, a little there is all it takes... if you keep it up. Focus on what you can have several months down the line. Don't dwell on what you don't have today. Don't expect instant results. A following and fan base can start out very tiny and grow very slowly, but if you have continued growth, a time can come – often many months down the line – where it begins to accelerate. It often pays to be very patient.

Another thing that can help significantly in the long run is having several similar books. When you market a handful of similar books, some customers will buy multiple books. Some customers will buy one book today, and if they like it, will check out your other books in the future. Amazon may show your new books to previous customers, and some will check them out. Every new book that you release gives you additional exposure in the new release categories. Just having multiple titles published over a period of time shows readers that you're a serious author: If they like your book, there is plenty more where that came from.

So don't let your marketing efforts detract from writing more books. Put most of your time into writing, but put some regular time into marketing. Don't worry about perfecting your marketing in the beginning. Focus on gradually building a professional author platform step-by-step. Work on one step here, one step there, thinking how each step can be part of something much bigger several months down the line. You're not marketing for instant sales (though any of those are a sweet bonus) – set your sites on a successful future.

Marketing with Little or no Cost

It's a common mistake for authors to "hope" that they won't need to market their books. Then after they release their books, when sales are very slow, they realize that marketing is an important factor. But then it's too late. Why is it too late? Because of how sales rank works.

Amazon's sales rank is a combination of daily, weekly, and monthly sales. If your book has scarcely sold in the past month and suddenly sells today, its sales rank drops to about 100,000 and then starts climbing rapidly. If another book has sold steadily this month, but suddenly stopped selling today, its sales rank climbs much more slowly. A history of slow sales works against you, while a history of frequent sales helps you.

Sales rank factors into some customers' buying decisions (not everyone knows about sales rank and not everyone wants to buy what's "trending now," but it is important to a significant number of customers). Sales rank also affects your book's visibility on Amazon in various ways. The more sales you get, the more you benefit from Customers Also Bought lists and other forms of Amazon marketing.

What does this mean? It means that authors who hope to avoid marketing, but learn the hard way that they must learn how to market their books are sort of shooting themselves in their feet, so to speak. It's easier to try to maintain a history of frequent sales than it is to overcome a history of slow sales.

The solution is simple: It's called premarketing. If your book is ready to publish today, don't. Wait a few months. Unless you have time-sensitive nonfiction information, you *can* wait a few months. This will give you time to do some premarketing; you can use this time for extra editing; and also use this time to start working on your next project.

You can do effective premarketing by just spending a little time each day on the following activities. You don't need to build Rome in one day. Spread it out. The main thing is to start early and accomplish a little of the work each week. A nice thing about premarketing is that it will make an easy transition to marketing. Remember, you want writing your next book and perfecting your current book to be your main priorities, but you also want to squeeze a little time for marketing into your weekly activities. Here are some premarketing ideas:

- Strive to build buzz about your book. Keep friends, family, acquaintances, and coworkers informed about the progress of your book so they look forward to it. Every time you solicit feedback (even a simple cover reveal), it's an opportunity to create more interest.

- Start a blog months before you publish for two reasons: (1) It helps you build a small following that might lead to a couple of sales and (2) when you direct readers to your blog, there will be some content there instead of an empty blog.

- Create an author page and/or book page at Facebook. You can feed a WordPress blog into a Facebook author page, so you don't need to make separate posts for the two sites. You can also feed your blog into Twitter (but don't feed between Twitter and Facebook or you'll get double posts).

- Prepare for a fan club. The main site for this could be your Facebook author page or it could be a page from your blog. Find an email subscription service that will let you begin an email newsletter for your fan club.

- Create an about the author page for the back matter of your book. Include the url to your blog, Facebook author/book page, and Twitter page. Include the email to subscribe to your fan club.

- Order business cards or bookmarks. When you interact with people personally and mention your book, pass out a business card or bookmark.

- Find bloggers who share a similar target audience who may be interested in reading and reviewing your book. You can also give review copies to people you know. (If you give out a free copy in exchange for a review, the reviewer is required to state this in the review.)
- Try to generate early sales from people you know both in person and online (e.g. Facebook).

Your hope is that premarketing will stimulate some initial sales and that regular sales will follow. If your premarketing and packaging (cover, description, and Look Inside) are effective and your content is excellent, that's what *should* happen. But even if sales turn out to be fairly slow at first, don't panic. For one, your premarketing has given you a headstart toward building a professional author platform. You might solicit feedback on your packaging and content. However, the bigger factor may be that it takes time to get discovered.

On Amazon, your book is just one of millions. It's hard for new books to get discovered there. Your book will show up at the bottom of search results and won't appear on any Customers Also Bought lists until customers find and purchase your book. With effective marketing, you can improve your book's discoverability, but it still takes time. It won't change overnight.

Marketing tends to start out very slowly. When you first setup your blog, you get a few followers and a little traffic, and may not even get any direct sales from it. Social media followings develop slowly and many of the followers may be outside your target audience. Don't focus on how slow things start. Set your sights on what they might become over the course of several months.

One of your online goals should be to develop a content-rich website that will attract your target audience. Start out with a simple blog and work your way toward transforming it into a content-rich website. A blog is something easy to do and appeals to writers because it involves writing, but a content-rich website that attracts people who aren't already fans or followers can be a highly effective marketing tool.

You can't start out with a content-rich website because it takes time to develop the content. What you can do is create a little content here and there over the course of several months for your blog.

I recommend WordPress: www.wordpress.com. The .com site is a free and easy way to create a blog website. You don't need to know HTML or anything about web development. (Those with expertise in these areas might want to look into the .org site.) I've used Blog-Spot, too, but had much better success with WordPress.

If you mostly blog about yourself, this won't attract new readers. If you blog short stories, you'll probably discover that it's no easier to give them away than it is to sell them on Amazon. What you want to do is create nonfiction content that will attract your target audience – i.e. it needs to relate to the content of your book, even if it's a novel. It's very important that your website and book share the same target audience. You can occasionally post something personal, which helps to show that you're human and reveal your character, but if you mostly post about yourself, your blog won't serve as an effective marketing tool (unless you're a celebrity).

When you post your first few nonfiction articles, hoping to attract your target audience to your blog, you'll probably be very disappointed. It's not easy to get discovered, especially in the beginning. You have to think long-term. Initially, you have very little content to attract anybody and your blog has had very little time to get noticed. Things generally start out very slowly.

If you just post one article every week or so, you can still put most of your writing toward your next book, and eventually you will have a content-rich website and your blog will start to get noticed more. Mention your book at the bottom of each of your posts, with a link to your book's product page at Amazon (it may not lead to any sales in the short-term – think long-term). Include a relevant image that will attract interest in your article. Test out relevant keywords on Google: Ideally, these will be specific to your article, searched for frequently, but not so popular that your article won't be found.

In the beginning, each post may get a dozen views, a handful of likes, and a couple of followers. This will help to slowly grow a following. What's more important is getting a few articles discovered through search engines. This takes planning and much patience. Learning about search engine optimization (SEO) can help to some extent, but ultimately it's the quality and value of the content that you write that makes the difference. Even if you write novels, you want to think about nonfiction content that you can create that will help to attract your target audience through search engines.

After a few months, you might have a humble following of 50 or 100 followers, you might get a couple dozen views of your posts, and you might have a dozen or more likes of each post. You'd like these numbers to grow over time as it's a show of support, but these aren't the stats you should worry about. For one, only a fraction of your followers will actually read your posts and only a fraction of those are in your target audience. Focus on reaching people beyond your blog. The external traffic that checks out your old posts are the more important numbers. Many months from now, once you have several content articles, you can add a page to your blog that serves as a table of contents or index.

If you view your WordPress stats and see posts from weeks ago getting a few views per day, you're headed in the right direction. After several months, you might have a dozen or more older posts that get an average of 1-10 visitors per day. If one year from now, you have 50 or so people discovering your blog each day through search engines, that's a lot of traffic (multiply this by 365 – that's 18,000 visitors per year).

The goal of your blog should be to gain discovery through search engines from your target audience. It can take several months to reach this point. If you see activity on older posts and if you see that your blog is being discovered through search engines, this is a positive sign. If these numbers (not the likes and follows) grow a little each month, things are going well. If not, you need to reevaluate your content.

You can also try to publish an article with a high-traffic website, online magazine, print magazine, newspaper, etc., in addition to your blog. Really, you have nothing to lose: In the worst-case that nobody accepts it, you can still publish your article on your blog. However, there are so many websites out there, you have good prospects for getting an article posted where there is moderate traffic. The main thing is to submit to places that share the same target audience. If you get your article accepted and list Your Name, author of Your Book at the end of your article, this can lend you some helpful exposure and help to build credibility.

Your blog isn't just about developing a content-rich website. Interactions and connections are valuable parts of your blogging. Visit other blogs, meet other authors, find editors and designers, and interact with people in the comments sections. When you visit other blogs, you'll get ideas for things you could be doing. When you interact with other authors, you'll share tips and develop a support network. You'll make connections that may prove valuable in the future. You can mix in occasional fun posts, try out a new writing style, show a little of your personal side, or spread some goodness, and you'll enjoy the writing variety that a blog offers (but you want most posts to provide valuable content).

You also want to take advantage of the benefits of social media. This was huge when self-publishing started, but the tide is turning toward content-rich websites. Still, you want to have both. There are many people who love Facebook and Twitter, so you'll get some followers if you simply have a presence there.

This doesn't necessarily mean more work. The simple thing to do is feed your Word-Press posts into your Twitter and Facebook pages. Create a Facebook author page (you can do it from your personal profile – it's not a separate account) and feed your blog posts into that instead of your personal profile. But don't feed posts between Twitter and Facebook (they will both invite you to do this) or you'll wind up making double or triple posts, which will deter followers.

You might want to do something different for your fans. People who have read your book might want to learn more about the characters, read about your work in progress, find supplemental content from the book, learn about promotional pricing for your new release, and learn a little more about you as a person. People who haven't read your book want to find valuable content and might want to know about a promotional price for the first book in a series. These are two separate audiences. You might want to have a fan page or book page (at Facebook, for example) dedicated just to fans, and a content-rich website to attract new readers. This requires a little extra work, but may be worth it. Your fan base will pay off when you notify them about your upcoming book.

An email newsletter offers something that your blog and social media don't do: It provides an effective filter. Most of your followers don't read your posts or aren't in your target audience. Most people who subscribe to an email newsletter have some interest in the content. This means you have to send out an occasional email with content that will interest your target audience. You can give away a free PDF booklet, for example, as an incentive to subscribe to the newsletter. If your newsletter provides valuable, engaging content, you can grow a following that will actually read what you have to say. You don't have to spend too much time on this: A biweekly or monthly newsletter is easy for you to keep up with, and won't feel like spam to your readers. You must provide an unsubscribe option with your email (many email subscription services will do this for you).

Another thing you should work on is a press release (PR) kit. This will be useful for approaching bookstores, libraries, local newspapers, local radio stations, and potential reviewers, for example. A press release kit includes a press release announcement, a cover letter (which needs to fit each occasion), a business card, a tip sheet, a copy of your book, and a sales sheet with relevant sales data and review excerpts (sales and editorial reviews being pertinent to bookstores and libraries – you won't include this sheet where it's not pertinent).

You can post your PR kit on a page on your website, too. When your PR kit is relevant for online interactions (like trying to get news coverage online or seeking online reviews), you can include a link to your online PR kit. (You won't include a copy of your book on your website, but if you have an eBook, you can gift it or attach it to an email – but don't send files via email without prior consent from the recipient.)

There is a prescription for how to write a press release announcement. Anyone in the media or bookstore relations is familiar with this. So if you don't follow the convention, it will stand out like a sore thumb. I recommend reading *Get Your Book in the News: How to Write a Press Release that Announces Your Book* by Sandra Beckwith, a former publicist. It guides you step-by-step through the process and includes examples (also check out

Sandra's press release on her website – some formatting comes out better there than it does in eBook format – www.buildbookbuzz.com; this also serves as a good example of a content-rich website and an effective email newsletter).

Your PR kit is a tool that can help you get your book stocked in local bookstores or libraries, help you get your book in the news (in print, on the air, and online), and help to solicit book reviews through review copies. Start small and local and work your way outward.

Your best chance to get your book stocked in bookstores is to approach small, local bookstores (and other stores that sell books in addition to other merchandise) in person with your press release kit, including a copy of your book (have more nicely packed in your car). Bookstores could order your book through Ingram (via the Expanded Distribution channel), but your book won't be returnable or include any discount. Selling in person tends to be more effective than referring to Ingram since you can discount the sale of author copies. Chain bookstores probably won't stock your book nationally, but local stores may work with you.

You can offer 40 to 55% off the list price by selling author copies. It would be ideal for you to sell copies to the bookstore, but the bookstore is more likely to want consignment. It's a negotiation. Try to sell your book at 40% off, but be willing to go up to 55% and be willing to settle for consignment. Some authors specify something like 45% off for consignment, 55% off for purchase, giving an incentive to avoid consignment; but be willing to settle for what you can get.

Personal interactions are one of a self-published author's best marketing assets. Even in this age where there are hundreds of thousands of authors, it's still cool to be able to say you've actually met the author of a book. When you meet people, let them discover that you're an author, rather than advertising this. People usually don't like advertisements, like, "Hey, I just published a book," but they like to make discoveries, like when they ask you, "What do you do?"

You can interact with people at readings, signings, following presentations, at conventions, in community service, and many other ways that you can involve yourself with activities where you're likely to meet and interact with your target audience. Show professionalism, reveal your passion for writing and your topic, and charm your potential readers. A significant percentage of books are purchased by readers who had previously interacted with the author and enjoyed the meeting. You can interact with more people online, but personal interactions are much more meaningful and can make a more lasting impression. Readings, presentations, workshops, and seminars allow you to sell copies in person when the event ends.

Branding is an important marketing concept. It's the idea behind commercials and billboards. If you see an advertisement, you don't run to the store immediately and buy the product. Rather, the advertisement brands a name, image, or idea. Months later when you're shopping, you see a few brands to choose from, and you think things like, "I've never heard of this," and, "I recognize this brand."

Advertising doesn't tend to be effective for books, except in special circumstances like promoting a special sale price (and even then it may not pay off). Unlike advertising a brand of coffee where there aren't many to choose from, there are millions of different books on the market. But you don't need paid advertising.

You can achieve the effect of branding for free. Every time someone in your target audience sees your cover, sees your author photo, or hears or reads your name, for example, you are branding the image of you or your book. The more exposure you get, the more readers will recognize your brand when shopping for a book.

Marketing very often doesn't result in an immediate sale, but works through branding. For example, when people read your online posts and see your name at the bottom as the author of a book, they probably won't go straight there and buy it, but they might recognize your book sometime in the future.

Branding requires patience. A potential customer might see your book, photo, or name once today, again in a month, and once more a few months from now, then recognize your book a few months after that while shopping. Hence, it can take months of active marketing for branding to show its effects. Don't dwell on short-term sales; build for long-term potential (but do analyze your marketing strategies, seek feedback, and try to improve your marketing effectiveness).

Strive to brand a professional image as an author; positive branding is far more likely to result in sales than negative branding. Also, you want exposure, but not to seem like an advertisement – i.e. you don't want to get tuned out (like repeatedly announcing your book through social media).

Finally, let's consider your book's product page on Amazon. I recommend that you buy a copy of your own book on Amazon.com. You can buy a copy cheaper through KDP, but you should still buy one from Amazon. After you buy your book, you can see how long it takes for your royalty to show up at KDP.[2] You will see how this affects your sales rank. By the way, with a better sales rank, your book shows up sooner on a search sorted by Bestselling. Plus, you can double-check that books bought through Amazon.com are, in

---

[2] Well, occasionally a royalty can be delayed by a couple of months. Once you get your book, if the royalty doesn't show up for several days, contact KDP with the printing numbers from the last page and ask if they can track the royalty for you.

fact, identical to your proof copy (except, of course, that your proof copy has the word "PROOF" written on the last page).[3] Finally, it's nice to have a memento of your self-published book.

Beware

It is against Amazon's policies for anyone who has a financial interest in the book to review it. This includes the author, household family members (e.g. spouse, children, or parents), as well as editors, agents, and publishers. These people are not allowed to review your book on Amazon.

If a review is posted that violates Amazon's policy, it will be removed (if not immediately, eventually). Abuse of the customer review policy can lead to account suspensions, removal of the book, and even revoking the right to sell on Amazon. Some reviews are also removed that may not seem to violate the policies. For example, if a friend reviews your book, it's possible that the review won't show up or that it will be removed later. Amazon compares IP addresses, shipping addresses, and other data in their customer and author databases, and any matches will likely block reviews from showing up. Never let a customer review a book from your computer; if you and a customer have ever logged into Amazon from the same computer, or if you've ever shipped a gift from Amazon to the customer, the review is likely to be blocked. When authors do review swaps, the reviews may be removed. I'm not asking if you agree with this (Amazon isn't asking us, either), I'm just letting you know it might happen so you're not surprised. ☺

When you are next in the market for a book, you might see if there is a suitable self-published book for your needs. Support your fellow self-published authors when possible. Don't do this blindly: Make sure that the book does suit your needs, and check that it looks well-written and has good reviews. Reward self-published authors who produce quality books. The more good self-published books there are, the better image self-publishing will have. If you enjoy a self-published book, or find it useful, please write them a favorable review and explain what you liked about the book – the authors will greatly appreciate your effort.

---

[3] I did this once (years before CreateSpace merged with KDP) and the book bought through Amazon actually had some formatting errors that my proof did not have. I contacted CreateSpace: They corrected the problem and apologized. Fortunately, I was the first customer, and no other copies had been sold yet. I was glad that I had bought a copy. They said that it was a very rare occurrence. It hasn't happened again with any of my other books.

Amazon reviews can be hard to get. For some books, it takes an average of 500 books or so to get one review. It depends on the genre and content. There are books that tend to get more reviews, such as the one you're reading now. Most of the readers of this book are self-published authors, and nobody understands the importance of reviews better than us. As of February, 2014, this book has received 41 reviews (and I'm thankful for each and every one). I didn't ask anyone for a review, and none are from friends or family: The best reviews are the ones that come naturally from customers.

It may be tempting to recruit reviews, but what you really want is honest feedback. Friends and family are more likely to post five-star reviews that really don't say anything useful ("This book was awesome," isn't helpful to shoppers), and they're also likely to be blocked or removed by Amazon. If you write a five-star review for a fellow author and ask for one in return, it will be hard for that author to be honest (if he or she doesn't like your book, do you think he or she will really leave a two-star review after you just left a five-star review?), and again Amazon may remove the reviews. You're not allowed to pay for reviews – that's against Amazon's policy (however, you may give a free book – but nothing more – in exchange for a review).

Publishers typically send out several advance review copies, hoping to generate some early reviews. You can do this, too, but if you wind up with a dozen reviews and a sales rank indicative of virtually no sales, customers who notice this may be suspicious.

The best thing you can do to generate reviews is to generate sales through quality content, effective packaging (cover, description, and Look Inside), and effective marketing. The natural reviews that you get from actual readers who don't know you and who take the time to leave an assortment of honest feedback is best. They come about slowly, but that's okay – this way, the number of reviews is more likely to match your sales rank.

Every book has strengths and weaknesses. Even if you just look at the writing style, no writing style pleases everybody. Find the most highly rated books of all time and you can find hundreds of people who feel that they were horribly written. That's because no writing style appeals to everyone. For example, many readers like writing to be easily understood, but some want the ideas to be expressed with complexity – there is no way to please both audiences with the same book.

This means that your book has strengths and weaknesses, too. A balance of honest opinions will reflect both your book's strengths and its weaknesses. If grammar is one of your weaknesses and a review exposes this, don't fret about it. The review is helping customers who value grammar highly, but won't deter customers for whom it's not as important as a great storyline or wonderful characterization. On the other hand, you can get your book edited and note this in the description, and then customers who value grammar won't be deterred (ideally, you would have your book edited before getting a review that complains about this).

Any review that doesn't provide an explanation is essentially worthless – it's affecting your average star-rating, but won't matter to customers who read the reviews. If a review says, "The story is wonderful," or says, "This book stinks," but doesn't explain why, customers will simply ignore those reviews – they aren't helpful. You'll get some reviews that don't have explanations; just realize that they won't factor into purchase decisions. What reviewers say is more important than the number of stars. Interested shoppers will also inspect the Look Inside to see if it agrees with reviews. For example, if the review says that the book is well-written or horribly written, checking out the first few paragraphs can easily show if the review has merit.

Having all four- and five-star reviews might make you feel good inside, but might seem suspicious to customers. It's possible that you'll have mostly good reviews. In fact, if most of your reviews come from customers who personally interacted with you during your marketing endeavors, this is quite likely. Customers don't know how the reviews came about, but they do know that authors have abused the system in the past (they also don't realize that Amazon has cracked down on this and made it much more difficult to abuse the system in recent years). Many customers assume that the first reviews are written by friends and family.

On the other hand, getting a one- or two-star may not deter sales. In some circumstances, it can actually help sales (though you'd be a fool to *try* to get a negative review – unfortunately, these come enough without any help at all). A negative review is more likely to affect sales if you don't have other good reviews to balance it or if it exposes a problem that's important to your target audience (in which case, you might address that problem with a revision and note it in the description).

It's really tempting to comment on reviews, but very wise to avoid this temptation. Some customers feel very strongly that reviews are for customers and authors should stay out of this space (*these* customers don't buy books when they see comments from the author).

The last thing you want to do is comment on a review and show your frustration or otherwise react emotionally and ruin your reputation as an author. If you do comment on a review, you must do so tactfully, but even then it's better not to comment at all. If the review was left by a spiteful individual, your comment is just inviting more spite. Guess what the reviewer will do: He or she will ask you a question in his or her response to your comment. Now you have to answer the question, right? Pretty soon, what you intended to be a single comment turns in to a discussion with several comments. It just doesn't look good to customers. Instead, by not commenting, you show that you're a professional author.[4]

Another Amazon feature that may interest you is how search results work. Customers search for books by keywords and by category. Choose the most relevant categories and keywords for your book to benefit from these searches. When customers search for your book, click on your book, and purchase your book, this helps to improve your book's visibility; and sales rank factors into search results to some extent.

Sign up for an account at Amazon's Author Central (https://authorcentral.amazon.com and change .com to .co.uk for the UK) and you can add your biography and photo to your book's product page. Author Central lets you add basic formatting to your description, add other sections to your product page, quickly see sales rank and recent reviews, and has other cool features. For example, you can feed your blog posts into Author Central.

Other Promotional Opportunities

I'm a light promoter myself. I appreciate the aesthetic value of having completed the task of preparing a professional-looking book, and I'm happy just to have my work available to those who might be interested in it. I'm content with regular sales, but don't feel a need to be a bestseller. I do give copies of books to my students, occasionally – e.g. when they earn high scores on exams. I have also donated some copies of my books to the school where I teach, for my students to use as part of their course (I make problem sets and laboratory manuals in physics, for example, in addition to my other books). I write because I enjoy it, not for a living.

I do market my books with a content-rich website, but I do this to provide free resources to other authors and to share my passion to be part of the indie-publishing revolution, not to boost sales (that's just a sweet bonus). I interact with people in my target audience, but again it's about helping others, not generating sales (though I'm happy with any sales, of course). I don't do much in the way of promotion, like advertising or contests.

You may be able to motivate yourself to market your books with a similar approach. If you write with passion, but don't write with royalties as your main goal, motivate yourself to market your books as a way to share your passion.

---

[4] I have commented on a few reviews, and I've seen many other authors attempt this (sometimes unsuccessfully). The best that can happen may not offset the risk of the worst that can happen.

I do have a little experience with advertising and click-through rates from promoting a special event that I created called Read Tuesday. This is a special sales event in December, similar to Black Friday but just for books (you can check it out at www.readtuesday.com). I started this to help promote reading and literacy, and to create a promotional opportunity for indie authors (you're welcome to participate – at no cost to you).

One thing you might do to help promote your book is create a temporary sale price. Kindle has a tool that can help you do this for your eBook: If you participate in KDP Select, you can do a Countdown Deal (if your list price is at least $2.99). If you're not in Select, you can simply lower your price temporarily (unless your price is already at its minimum).

Prices don't sell books. You need to promote a sale for it to be effective. This means you need to spread the news about your sale price to your target audience. Just posting this on your blog may not help much, especially if most of the traffic comes from people who already know about your book. You might be able to find bloggers who share the same target audience who are willing to announce your sale. There are also some popular reader websites that may be willing to advertise your book's sale (see the resources at the end of the chapter).

Another way to generate a little interest in your book is through a giveaway or contest. For example, Goodreads has a giveaway program, or you might look into Rafflecopter. You must promote the contest effectively to get the most out of it.

One kind of contest is to give away a bookmark, book, or related item. Another kind of contest is to enter a writing competition like the Amazon Breakthrough Novel Award. There are many contests open to self-published books. If you get into the later stages of a contest, this may give you some nice exposure.

Authors who write series have additional tools at their disposal. Some price the first book cheap (or even free, through price-matching – i.e. they make the price free at another retailer like Kobo or Smashwords, get customers to notify Amazon about the cheaper price, and succeed in making their eBooks permanently free), while others create an omnibus at an enticing price to encourage the sale of multiple volumes at once.

Fiction books may get significant sales in audio book format. This entails a large upfront cost, but there is less competition among audio books (and there is an audience, e.g. truck drivers). The Audiobook Creation Exchange (ACX) is an Amazon platform mentioned in the KDP newsletter.

What's best? That's the million-dollar question, and varies from author to author and book to book. A few things that have much potential for most authors are content-rich websites, personal interactions, and writing more similar books with highly marketable content. The best thing is to do a little here and there, explore different options, and strive to build a successful future.

* * *

I hope that this book has been useful to you, and wish you the best regards in your writing and publishing endeavors. Thank you, kindly, for reading my book.

Marketing Resources

- You can find free marketing articles on my blog: www.chrismcmullen.wordpress.com. Once there, click on the marketing tab.
- A great way to learn about marketing is to follow other self-published authors via social media, including those with established success and those who are just now becoming successful.
- Visit www.buildbookbuzz.com to see a website maintained by a former publicist. It's a good model for a content-rich website, an effective subscription newsletter, and how to write a press release announcement. There are some free marketing resources on this website (in addition to some paid services).
- Here is a sample of eBook promotion websites:

www.bookbub.com
http://ereadernewstoday.com
www.fkbooksandtips.com
www.bookgorilla.com
www.bookblast.co
www.pixelofink.com

FORMATTING PAGES FOR
PUBLISHING
on
AMAZON
WITH CREATESPACE

Chris McMullen

Formatting Pages for Publishing on Amazon with CreateSpace

Chris McMullen

Copyright © 2013, 2014, 2019 by Chris McMullen

Note: This book was revised in 2019 to reflect the merger between CreateSpace and Kindle Direct Publishing.

All rights are reserved by the author, including the right to reproduce any portion of this book in any form.

Amazon and CreateSpace are trademarks of Amazon.com, Inc. These trademarks and brands are the property of their respective owners. Neither company has authorized, endorsed, or sponsored this book in any way (explicitly or implicitly).

UPDATED 2019 EDITION (February, 2019)
FIRST EDITION (revised May, 2014)
ISBN-13: 978-1482545715

Books › Education & Reference ›
  Writing, Research & Publishing Guides ›
  Publishing & Books › Authorship

Books › Education & Reference ›
  Writing, Research & Publishing Guides ›
  Writing › Technical

Contents

Introduction

This book shows you how to format your pages for publishing a paperback book with Kindle Direct Publishing (Amazon KDP). Although Amazon KDP does have templates, many writers who use them encounter a variety of formatting issues, and there are many formatting options that aren't included in those templates. This guide will show you how to apply a variety of formatting options yourself using Microsoft Word 2010 for Windows. If you're already using one of the Amazon KDP templates, you might also learn how to resolve problems by reading this guide.

Since authors want to spend more time writing and less time learning how to publish their work, this guide is concise and focused on the main challenge that most authors face — how to properly format their book in terms of layout, structure, headings, page borders, page numbering, etc. As such, it is not a comprehensive guide to self-publishing, but a quick and handy resource to perfecting your pages. It has the technical details to help you master the formatting, clear explanations to help you understand what to do and how to do it, and it's short and to the point so that you can quickly get back to writing.

If you haven't already done so, visit Amazon KDP at kdp.amazon.com and sign up for an account. There are no setup fees, so you can publish for free while also making your book available at Amazon. While this guide will answer your formatting questions, you can find many of your other questions about publishing with Amazon KDP on their website. Once you get there, click Books near the top of the page and then click Publish a Trade Paperback. After checking out the Amazon KDP website and reading this guide, if you still have questions, try asking your questions on the Amazon KDP community forum. There are many knowledgeable members who frequently participate in the Amazon KDP community forum. If you would like to ask the author a question, consult the About the Author section toward the end of this book.

This guide is geared specifically toward formatting the interior file of your book because these are the most frequently asked questions about how to publish a book with Amazon KDP, and tend to be the most troublesome for self-published authors. Other general questions, like royalties and distribution, are easier to learn about on your own. Therefore, it made sense to prepare a book that focuses on a technical subject that self-published authors frequently need help with, without cluttering the book with a lot of general information that many writers might already know.

The author, Chris McMullen, has published dozens of paperback books with Amazon KDP since 2008 using Microsoft Word. His other books on self-publishing include *How to Self-Publish a Book on Amazon.com* (a basic guide for novices written in 2009 and featuring Word 2003) and *A Detailed Guide to Self-Publishing with Amazon and Other Online Booksellers* (which is very detailed and comprehensive, and features Word 2010).

Chris McMullen is a physics instructor at Northwestern State University of Louisiana, who has experience explaining difficult concepts in a way that is easy to understand. He enjoys writing and publishing books in his spare time. He is an expert at using Microsoft Word 2010 to format manuscripts professionally. He shares his formatting knowledge and experience in this guide.

1 Why You Shouldn't Use the Templates

CreateSpace offers templates for the interior file in every trim size. Most self-publishing experts advise against using these templates. Although it seems like this should be convenient, many authors who use the templates wind up wishing that they hadn't. In the Amazon KDP community help forum, questions are frequently asked about how to correct formatting issues in the templates.

One problem is that the templates have some default settings that need to be adjusted. If you decide to use the templates (or if you've already used them and now need help correcting problems), click the funny icon – which looks like ⌐ – in the bottom right corner of the Paragraph group (at the top of the screen in the Home tab) if you're using Word 2010. This will open the paragraph dialog box. In this popup window, go to the Line and Page Breaks tab and uncheck all of the boxes. (One of the boxes is Widow/Orphan Control, which we will discuss in Chapter 16.)

Another common issue is customization. Many writers encounter formatting problems when trying to make changes to the template, like trying to add or remove sections or chapters. Go to the Page Setup group (in the Page Layout tab), click Breaks, and choose one of the Section Breaks (instead of inserting a page break), such as Next Page, in order to insert a new section or chapter. If you need to remove sections, it may be helpful to press the Show/Hide button – which looks like ¶ – in the Paragraph group (in the Home tab). Press the ¶ button again to hide these codes.

Another reason to avoid the templates is that you retain much greater flexibility by doing your own formatting. Since you're reading this guide, you will be able to do all of the formatting for your paperback book by yourself. The templates are also very basic. You will find options in this guide that aren't in the templates.

2 How to Do a Better Job than the Templates Using Word 2010 for Windows

In this guide, you will learn how to create the same effects that you can find in the templates, as well as other effects that you won't find in the templates, using Microsoft Word 2010 for Windows. Other versions of Microsoft Word are similar, such as the 2007 version. This guide will show you a variety of options at your disposal and teach you how to implement each formatting feature. This will give you the flexibility and knowledge to customize your book exactly the way that you want. Also, by not using the template, your book won't look very similar in layout to thousands of other self-published books that used the templates. Devote some time to the formatting of your pages in order to make your book appear professional, and this will help your book stand out in a good way.

The left image below shows a page designed from the Amazon KDP templates, while the image on the right shows a page created without using the templates.

3 Choosing the Trim Size and Setting the Page Size

If you haven't already done so, first you must select the trim size for your book. The following tables show you what options you have. If your book is full of text, a smaller size book will have more pages, which may affect your royalty. You should search for similar books to see what size is common for paperbacks in your genre.

The following trim sizes are industry-standard for black-and-white books that allow 24-828 pages (white) or 24-740 pages (cream). Note that industry-standard trim sizes are eligible for the bookstore and online retailer distribution channels (provided that you enroll your book in the expanded distribution).

5" x 8"	6.14" x 9.21"
5.06" x 7.81"	6.69" x 9.61"
5.25" x 8"	7" x 10"
5.5" x 8.5"	7.44" x 9.69"
6" x 9"	7.5" x 9.25"

The following trim sizes are also industry-standard for black-and-white books, but do not permit as many pages as those from the previous table. The 8" x 10" size allows up to 440 pages (white) and 400 pages (cream), while the 8.5" x 11" size allows up to 630 pages (white) and 570 pages (cream).

8" x 10"	8.5" x 11"

There are also a few non-standard trim sizes for black-and-white books. The first two sizes allow up to 220 pages (white) and 200 pages (cream), while the 8.5" x 8.5" size allows up to 630 pages (white) and 570 pages (cream).

8.25" x 6"	8.25" x 8.25"
8.5" x 8.5"	

The previous tables are for black-and-white books. The following tables are for color books The following trim sizes are industry-standard for color books with 24-480 pages.

5.5" x 8.5"	7" x 10"
6" x 9"	8" x 10"
6.14" x 9.21"	8.5" x 8.5"
8.5" x 11"	

The following trim sizes are non-standard for color books. The sizes in the first three rows allow up to 480 pages, while the sizes in the last row allow up to 212 pages.

5" x 8"	6.69" x 9.61"
5.06" x 7.81"	7.44" x 9.69"
5.25" x 8"	7.25" x 9.25"
8.25" x 6"	8.25" x 8.25"

The page size will be the same as the trim size unless you have images that need to bleed. If you don't have pictures, then you won't have bleed. If your book has any pictures that need to extend to the page edges, then your interior file will have bleed. We will discuss bleeds in more detail in Chapter 12. For now, we will just discuss how bleed relates to the page size.

If any of your interior file images need to bleed, add 0.125" to the width and add 0.25" to the height of your pages. For example, for a 6" x 9" trim size where images bleed, the page sizes must be 6.125" x 9.25".

Actually, Word may round down and this can cause a problem. So you should round up to the second decimal place to be safe. With this in mind, the page size for the previous example would be 6.13" x 9.25".

Click the funny icon — it looks like ⬕ — in the bottom right corner of the Page Setup group (in the Page Layout tab) to open the Page Setup dialog box. For now, just go to the

Paper tab and enter the width and height of your book. Be sure to select Whole Document in the Apply To drop-down menu (otherwise, some pages will have different sizes than the others). Remember, if you don't have images that need to bleed, enter the actual trim size, but if you do have images that need to bleed, you must add 0.125″ to the width and 0.25″ to the height of your trim size (and then round up to the nearest 0.01″).

4 How to Set the Inside and Outside Margins

The inside margin refers to the margin on the side of the page that glues to the spine. For odd-numbered pages, the inside margin is on the left side of the page, while for even-numbered pages, the inside margin is on the right side of the page. The other three margins are called outside margins.

Odd pages	Left = inside
Even pages	Right = inside

The outside margins must be at least 0.25″. The minimum inside margin depends on the page count of your book, according to the following table:

Page Count	Minimum Inside Margin
24-150	0.375″
151-400	0.75″
401-600	0.875″
601+	1″

Although the outside margin can be as small as 0.25″ and the inside margin can be 0.375″ for a book of 150 pages or less, it is recommended that all margins be at least 0.5″. Also, if you're planning to use any of the minimum margins, consider adding 0.1″ in order to avoid possible problems with text being just slightly out of bounds.

Word 2010 uses left, right, top, and bottom margins along with a gutter margin. The inside margin equals the left margin plus gutter for odd-numbered pages and the right margin plus gutter for even-numbered pages. (Word's definition of gutter is what most publishing manuals would refer to as a half-gutter.) The gutter refers to extra space in the inside margin (compared to the outside margin) to account for unusable space near where the pages join to the spine.

Make sure that the left margin plus gutter exceeds the inside margin minimum for your book, and the same for the right margin plus gutter. Ordinarily, your left and right margin values should be equal.

Using 0.5″ for left, right, top, bottom, and gutter works out pretty well, in general, and will meet the inside margin specifications regardless of your page count. I recommend filling a page with text (if you don't already have a full page of text, write a line of text and copy/paste it to fill the page), printing it out, and cutting the paper down to your trim size to see exactly what the printed page will look like.

If your book has bleeds — as described toward the end of Chapter 3 (and discussed in more detail in Chapter 12) — then the margins must be a little different in order to accommodate the bleeds.

If your book mostly consists of text, but also has images that need to bleed, add 0.125″ to the top and bottom margins, add 0.125″ to the left and right margins, and subtract 0.125″ from the gutter (it's really a half-gutter) margin. This accounts for the fact that the page is oversized (we added 0.25″ to the height and 0.125″ to the width in Chapter 3 for a book that has bleeds), and that a book with bleeds needs an extra 0.125″ on the outside margins.

For example, suppose that the trim size is 8″ x 10″ (this means that your page size is 8.125″ x 10.25″, which we rounded to 8.13″ x 10.25″ in Chapter 3 for Microsoft Word) and that you would like an inside margin of 1″ and outside margins of 0.5″ in your paperback book. In this case, set the left, right, top, and bottom margins to 0.625″ and the gutter to 0.375″. Rounding to the nearest 0.01″, these become 0.63″ and 0.38″, respectively. See Chapter 12 for more details and to learn how to insert pictures that properly fill the page.

If your book consists mostly of full-page pictures — as many children's books do — then you should set all of the margins — left, right, top, bottom, and gutter — to 0″ in Word. Any text must still adhere to the margins that we discussed, but you need 0″ margins all the way around in order to have a picture in-line with the text and bleed to the page edges. See Chapter 12 for more information about working with bleeds.

Click the funny icon — it looks like ⬛ — in the bottom right corner of the Page Setup group (in the Page Layout tab) to open the Page Setup dialog box. Enter the margins for Top, Bottom, Left, Right, and Gutter. Select Left from the Gutter Position drop-down menu. In the Layout tab (still in the same pop-up window), check the box for Different Odd and Even pages (this way, the half-gutter will alternate between the left and right sides of the page).

The following picture illustrates margins, the half-gutter, and bleeds. Word's gutter (which is really a half-gutter) is labeled ①, the inside margin is labeled ②, the outside margin is labeled ③, and the trim size is labeled ④. Note that the actual page size in Word exceeds the trim size. (This picture shows two pages as they appear in the opened book. In Word's, two-page view, the even page would incorrectly appear on the right-hand side.)

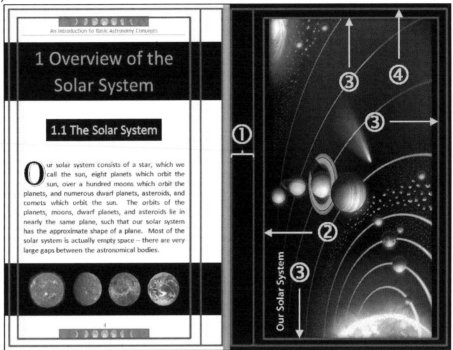

5 The Problems with Word's Default Paragraph Options
and What You Should Change

Microsoft Word 2010's default paragraph options are not the best choice for publishing a book. Everyone has some experience reading traditionally published books, and therefore everyone has an expectation for what a book should look like. If you use Word's defaults, your book will appear substantially different from this expectation. When used to prepare a book, Word's defaults often give the impression that the book is amateurish. You must format your book as professionally as possible in order to help it compete among the millions of other books on the market.

Text is aligned left instead of justified full in Word's default setting. This causes the body text to have a jagged right edge instead of being even on both sides. Traditionally published books are justified full — not left aligned. We will discuss this point further in the next chapter, including how to change the default alignment.

The default line and paragraph spacing is also significantly wider than what readers are accustomed to seeing in traditionally published books. Microsoft Word 2010's default linespacing is 1.15 (instead of single) and the Spacing After is set to 10 pts (instead of 0 pts). Adjust these by right-clicking the funny icon — it looks like ⬛ — in the bottom right corner of the Paragraph group (in the Home tab) to open the Paragraph dialog box.

You may also wish to explore other font styles and sizes. There are some fonts, like Comic Sans, which many readers particularly dislike. It's worthwhile to search online to learn which fonts are recommended for your genre and also to learn which fonts may be disliked. Wikipedia even gives a statistic related to how font styles affect readers. A 12-pt font size is fairly standard for most fonts.

Tip: Don't judge the font size as it appears on the screen. Instead, print out a page and judge how it looks in print. A variety of font styles appear below.

This sentence was typed with Calibri.
This sentence was typed with Times New Roman.
This sentence was typed with Garamond.
This sentence was typed with Palatino Linotype.
`This sentence was typed with Courier New.`
This sentence was typed with Arial.
This sentence was typed with Baskerville Old Face.
This sentence was typed with Bookman Old Style.
This sentence was typed with Book Antiqua.

The best fonts may not come preinstalled with Word. For example, Minion and Dante are popular with traditionally published fiction. Of the preinstalled fonts, Garamond and Palatino Linotype are popular choices for fiction. Times New Roman and Calibri are popular for self-published books mainly because they are defaults on various versions of Word. Using these fonts may be an advertisement that your book was self-published.

Word's defaults are also lacking page headers, page numbers, and other features that are common in traditionally published books. Add these features (as described in this guide) in order to make your book appear more professional. Compare the previous pages: The left page was written with Word's defaults, while the right page was not.

6 How to Justify Text and How to Deal with Gaps in the Lines

I f you open several different books that were published through the big publishing houses — and even most small publishers, too — you will notice that the text is justified full, like the paragraph that you are reading presently. Observe how the left and right edges of the paragraph both line up at the edge. The default paragraph alignment is left instead of full. You can switch from left to full by clicking the ☰ icon in the Paragraph group in the Home tab.

When the text is justified full, the computer automatically adjusts the spacing between words so that each line has the same length. When a long word is just a hair too long to fit on a line, the spaces between words can be fairly large. Some authors don't like these large spaces, and choose to align their text left instead of justifying it full. However, left-aligned text puts even larger spaces at the end of each line, making the right side look ragged. Almost all professional publishers justify full instead of aligning left. Therefore, when a self-published author aligns left, the result is often perceived as amateurish. Compare left alignment and full justification in the figures that follow.

There is a way to reduce the gaps between the words when text is justified full: hyphenation. You can hyphenate words manually (consult a dictionary to find the accepted break positions). Word actually has a built-in hyphenation tool that can do this for you. Go to the Page Layout tab and click Hyphenation. Select Automatic. Note that this may hyphenate words in your title, headings, and other lines that you might not want to be hyphenated. Under Hyphenation options, increase the hyphenation zone from 0.25" to about 0.4" (otherwise, many short words will be hyphenated). You can also force a break by holding down Shift and pressing Enter at the beginning of a word to eliminate an unwanted hyphen. If instead you choose to manually hyphenate, don't bother doing this until your book is 100% complete – otherwise, you will make revisions and suddenly find hyphens where you don't want them. The pictures at the end of this chapter show how hyphenation can reduce the gaps in fully justified text.

Here is a tip: WordPerfect's justification is a little better than Word's, and Word actually has a built-in option to use WordPerfect's spacing. Go to the File tab, scroll down below Help and click Options, select Advanced, and click on Layout Options way down at the bottom of the list. It doesn't look like Layout Options is something that you can click, but you can. When you click on Layout Options, a long list will appear. Check the box to use WordPerfect's justification (it's about the twelfth box down the list; you can find many other interesting options here, too).

While the body text should be justified full, there is some text that should be centered or aligned left. The title page should be centered. Headers (described in Chapter 8) are often centered. Portions of the copyright page might be aligned left (like a title that exceeds the text width). Main headings (not to be confused with headers) – like chapter titles – are often centered, whereas subheadings are often aligned left. Pictures are often positioned In Line With Text (click on the picture, go to the Format tab, and choose Wrap Text to set this) and centered.

It's worth browsing through a variety of traditionally published books to see how they are formatted. In particular, see which types of text seem to be justified full, aligned left, or centered.

Use the ≡ and ≡ buttons in the Paragraph group in the Home tab to center and align left, respectively. Alternatively, you may use the Styles at the top of the Home tab to apply quick formatting. Before you use the Styles, you must modify the font style, font size, justification, etc. in the styles that you want to use in your document. Right-click on a style to Rename it or to Modify it. After you click Modify, you can select the font style, font size, set the alignment, choose italics or boldface, and even find more options by clicking Format.

A nice feature of the Styles is that once Word associates various Styles with different blocks of your text (like body text and headings), you can easily re-format those blocks of your text by modifying the style. This is very convenient if you wish to publish your book as an e-book and paperback both, for example. This guide will focus on how to format the paperback, so if you want to make an e-book, you should learn about e-book formatting. However, here is one format-ting tip: Go into the Paragraph dialog box (click the funny icon – which looks like ⌐– in the bottom right corner of the Paragraph group in the Home tab) and set First Line Indent to a value like 0.2" and use this to create indentations (instead of using the Tab key, which will cause inconsistent indentations in an e-book).

This will help to reduce the effort needed to convert your paperback book to an e-book.Similarly, for any non-centered paragraph (which could be a single line, like a subheading) that you don't want indented, set First Line Indent to None for the paperback book (but change it to 0.01" to avoid automatic indentation in the e-book).

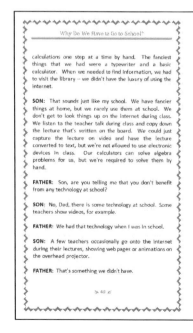 

7 Which Text Needs to Be Adjusted Vertically and How to Adjust It

Most pages in a book are aligned at the top, vertically. That is, when you type the text, the first line appears at the top and each successive line that you type appears below the previous one. All such pages begin at the same position at the top of the page – so they are aligned at the top. There may be space at the bottom of the page at the end of a chapter (where a page break was inserted – however, you should insert a section break instead of a page break to go onto the next page, as described in Chapter 8).

A few pages tend to be vertically centered instead. The title page and copyright page are usually centered vertically in traditionally published books. I suggest browsing through a few traditionally published books that are similar to your book (at a bookstore or library, for example) to see which other pages they may center vertically.

Traditional publishers often begin a new chapter (or introduction, contents, and so on) a few lines down from the top of a page. These pages are still top-aligned, but have space at the top before the chapter number. (When an introduction or one-page section does this, if the section is short enough that there is also space at the bottom, that page might look centered when it's actually aligned at the top.) See the difference between the two pages illustrated at the end of this chapter.

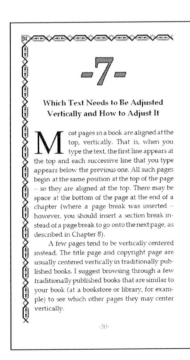 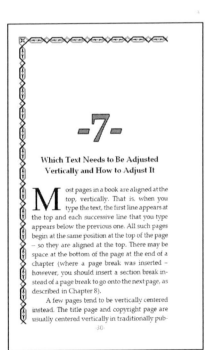

You could use the Enter key to start a new chapter a few lines down from the top, but the professional method is to adjust the spacing in the Paragraph dialog box. Definitely, don't use the Enter key to center a page vertically. To set the vertical alignment of your page, go to the Page Layout tab and click the funny icon — it looks like ⌐ — in the bottom right corner of the Page Setup group to open the Page Setup dialog box. In the Layout tab of the Page Setup dialog box, you can change the Vertical Alignment to Top or Center — after choosing This Section next to Apply To. Then use section breaks instead of page breaks, as described in the next chapter.

In the pair of pictures that follow, the picture on the left is aligned at the top, while the picture on the right is centered vertically.

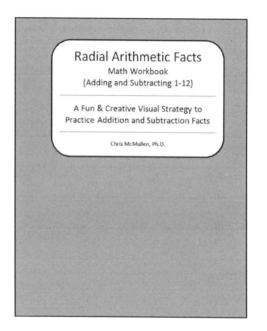
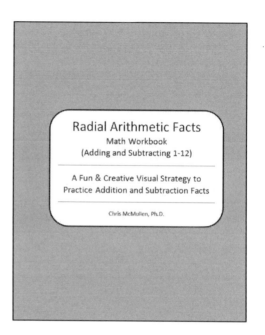

8 Whether to Insert Section, Page, Column, or Other Types of Breaks

Don't use the Enter key to start a new page. Instead, insert a page break. However, don't go to the Insert tab and click Page Break, and don't go to the Page Layout tab, choose Breaks, and select Page. Rather, go to the Page Layout tab, choose Breaks, and select Next Page.

Why? Using the Next Page option creates a section break instead of merely going onto the next page. This distinction is critical for (1) using Roman numerals for the first few pages and Arabic numbers for the remaining pages and (2) creating different headers in different sections of your book. We will discuss page numbering in Chapter 9 and headers in Chapter 10. Both involve using section breaks discussed here.

If you have text arranged in columns, if you wish to start a new column (instead of a new page), go to the Page Layout tab, click Breaks, and select Column.

Another common break is a section break between two bodies of text in the same chapter. Such a division may arise with a change of scene, for example. There are a few common methods for creating such a section break. One convention is to simply use 2 to 3 blank linespaces between the paragraphs (with the Enter key). Another popular convention is to place three asterisks (* * *) on their own centered line between blank linespaces. Sometimes, both techniques are combined: A blank linespace may be used except when the blank line would appear at the top or bottom of the page, in which case the asterisks are then used to make the section break clear.

Check books in your genre to see what is common, and whether or not they indent the line following the section break. Occasionally, an artistic section break is used. Rather than using asterisks, you could use a short picture (this is called a glyph). If you use glyphs for your section breaks, they should relate to the theme of your book.

The following pictures show various types of section breaks.

9 What You Need to Do in Order to Use Both Roman numerals and Arabic Page Numbers

Roman numerals (I, II, III, IV, etc.) are usually used to number pages of front matter, whereas the remaining page numbers tend to be Arabic (1, 2, 3, 4, etc.). Browse through some traditionally published books to see the variety of page numbering styles that are common.

The title page, copyright page, contents, dedications, acknowledgments, and preface often have no page numbers. Front matter that does have page numbers – such as an introduction or foreword – usually has Roman numerals. When page numbering does start, it usually isn't with a 1, but corresponds to the actual page in the book. For example, if the fifth page in the book is the first page to include a page number, and if this page is front matter, this page will be numbered with a Roman numeral v. The Roman numerals often appear in lowercase (i.e. i, ii, iii, iv, etc. instead of I, II, III, IV, etc.).

Each sheet of paper in a book is called a leaf. There are two pages per leaf – one page on the front side and one page on the back side of the leaf. When you open a book, you see the odd page numbers on the right and the even page numbers on the left. (Note that if you change the View to Two Pages in Word, what you see is different than an actual book – as Word puts the odd pages on the left instead of the right. You can temporarily correct this by inserting an extra blank page at the beginning, but you'll need to remove the extra blank page before you publish. If you add this blank page, note that its presence may affect page numbering and references to page numbers.)

The first chapter almost always begins on an odd-numbered page (so that it appears on the right-hand side of the open book). Publishers may insert a blank page in order to achieve this, but often you can tweak your choice of front matter in order to do avoid the blank page while still starting the first chapter on an odd-numbered page. Arabic numerals (1, 2, 3, 4, etc.) are used to number the pages from Chapter 1 thru the end of the book.

However, Chapter 1 almost never begins on page 1. Rather, the pages are generally numbered by their actual position in the book. For example, if the introduction is on pages v to vi and Chapter 1 begins on the next page, Chapter 1 will begin on page 7.

As described in the previous chapter, go to the Page Layout tab, click Breaks, and choose Next Page (rather than Page) in order to start a new page with a section break (instead of beginning a new page with a page break). This is necessary in order to gain the flexibility of removing page numbers from some sections and using both Roman and Arabic numerals in the same book.

Go to the Insert tab, click Page Numbers, choose a position, and select one of the page numbering styles. Return to Page Numbers and choose Format Page Numbers to choose the number format (e.g. Roman or Arabic) and to choose the starting page for each section (or to simply continue from the previous section).

Modify the page numbering style by clicking in the page number area. Highlight the page number to change the font size and style. You may type characters before or after the page number to make page numbers that look like -24- instead of 24, for example.

If you would like to add a border above or below the page number, click the arrow on the right edge of the Borders and Shading icon (it's the bottom right icon) in the Paragraph group in the Home tab and select Borders and Shading from the bottom of the list. Find Preview on the right side of the dialog box and look for the top line and bottom line buttons. Click one of these buttons. (Check that Apply To is set to Paragraph instead of Text in order to insert a long line.) Now you can choose a Style, Color, and Width to your liking.

You must separately insert and format page numbers for odd pages, even pages, and first pages (if this box is checked in the Page Setup dialog box) in each section that was created by using Next Page. In the Page Layout tab, click the funny icon – which looks like ⌐ – in the bottom right corner of the Page Setup group in order to open the Page Setup dialog box. In the Layout tab of the Page Setup dialog box, check the box for Different Odd and Even pages and you may also want to check the box for Different First Page. These boxes allow you to create dif-ferent headers and footers (including page numbers) on odd and even pages for each section of your book.

You can also remove page numbers by selecting this option from Page Numbers on the Insert tab.

After you insert page numbers in one section, you may see page numbers appearing in other sections. If you want to change the style in a subsequent section, go into the footer in the next section. When your cursor is in the footer, you will see a Design tab for headers and footers at the top of the screen. Click the Link to Previous button and the Same as Previous flag will disappear, allowing you to use a new footer style in the new section. This way, you can start using Arabic numerals in Chapter 1 after using Roman numerals in the front matter, for example. (If you click the Link to Previous button again, this will return the page numbering to the style of the previous section.)

You can find many useful header/footer options in the Design tab. Click in a header or footer to open the Design tab. You can quickly adjust the vertical position of the header and footer in the Position group, for example.

Start with the first page of your book and count the pages to ensure that the page numbering worked out correctly. It's especially important to check that odd-numbered pages actually came out on the odd pages.

Word can get a little fussy sometimes with page numbering, headers, and footers. If you have a PDF program that allows you to combine multiple PDF's together, the simpler option is to make separate files for each portion of your book. When your book is complete, you can then convert each portion to a PDF file and then merge the files together into a single PDF file for the whole book.

As you add features like page numbers, headers, and page borders to your document, the Word file becomes increasingly complex. This significantly increases the chances of the file becoming corrupt or encountering other problems with your Word file. There are a few ways to combat this.

For one, you might save these features until your book is completely typed. Save your file frequently using different numbers at the end of the name – e.g. Book1.docx, Book2.docx, etc. Save your file in multiple places – on your hard drive, on a jump drive, email it to yourself, etc. This way, if your computer crashes or you lose your jump drive, you may still have a recent copy of your hard work.

Another way to help fight large file size issues is to first write your chapters in separate files. If you do this, you must be careful to use the same styles throughout each chapter. This includes using the same page size (and make sure it's the same size on every page in the document), same header and page number styles, same page borders, and the same font styles and sizes for the body, headings, etc.

You can link your documents together using master and subdocuments, or you can merge them into a single file yourself later. The best option for a highly complex book is to create separate PDF files for each chapter and merge the PDF files together. Since the master and subdocument method also has frequent file corruption issues, I'm not going to outline how to do that here (but it's easy to find online if you search for "master and sub-documents Word 2010"). If you copy/paste your files together, there may be some formatting changes – so you'll have to look for these and correct them. Also, when you merge separate Word files, you must use Next Page to create section breaks and go section by section to adjust headers and page numbers.

For a book that mostly consists of plain text, such as a novel, it may be simplest to work with one large file. Working with a single file may also be convenient if you use cross-references (see Chapter 13). As the file grows larger and larger, be sure to save new version numbers frequently and to back it up on other devices.

The picture on the following page provides a sample of page numbering.

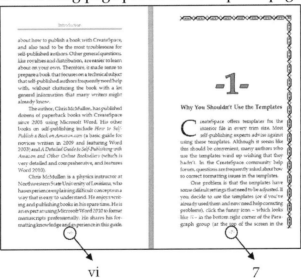

10 How to Insert, Format, and Position Headers and Footers

Page headers appear at the top of every page in a book. Note the distinction between a header and a heading. A heading refers to text at the beginning of a chapter or section, whereas a header refers to text that is repeated at the top of each page.

Traditionally published books almost always include page headers. The title may appear at the top of the odd pages, while the author or publisher may appear at the top of the even pages. The author's name is appropriate for bestselling authors and celebrities. As alternatives, the subtitle or chapter could be used at the top of the even pages.

You can make a different header for odd pages, even pages, and the first page (including having no header at all) by checking the appropriate boxes in the Page Setup dialog box (as described in the previous chapter). It's also possible to use different headers between sections (like indicating the chapter number and name on the headers of even pages) by using section breaks (created by clicking Next Page in Breaks in the Insert tab) instead of page breaks (this technique was described in Chapter 8).

Add a header or footer by clicking on the Header or Footer buttons on the Insert tab. If you choose the basic header at the top of the list, you'll be able to customize it.

Modify the header by clicking in the header area (or choosing Edit Header from the Header button on the Insert tab). Highlight the text in the header to change the font size and style. If you need a little clearance between the header and text, insert a blank line (using the Enter key) following the text of your header.

If you would like to add a border below the header, click the arrow on the right edge of the Borders and Shading icon (it's the bottom right icon) in the Paragraph group in the Home tab and select Borders and Shading from the bottom of the list. Find Preview on the right side of the dialog box and click on the bottom line button. (First check that Apply To is set to Paragraph in order to insert a long line.) Next choose a Style, Color, and Width for the border. (Note that a border that you add to the header in this way is different from – and will be in addition to – a page border that you can add.)

You must separately insert and format page headers for odd pages, even pages, and first pages (if this box is checked in the Page Setup dialog box) in each section that was created by using Next Page. To remove a header, click the Header button on the Insert tab and select Remove Header. The title page, copyright page, contents, and first page of each chapter usually do not have a header.

If you want an odd-page or even-page header to be different from the previous section (e.g. if you want to use the chapter names on even pages), click on the odd-page or even-page header in the new section to open the Design tab and choose Link to Previous in order to remove the Same as Previous flag. This will allow you to create a new header style in the new section.

You can also add a footer the same way that you add headers and page numbers. However, the technique for inserting footnotes is different. See chapter 13 regarding footnotes.

This book has no header on the title page, copyright page, table of contents, or beginning of most chapters. It also has the title on all the odd pages and the chapter number and name on all the even pages (except for front and back matter). The images below show pages with headers.

A header can be a decorative feature that helps your book look more professional, and it can provide helpful information (like the chapter title). However, if the header is not providing useful information (e.g. if it only repeats information that can be found on the cover), re-moving the header may help the pages appear less cluttered. For this reason, there are books that intentionally do not have headers.

11 How to Insert and Adjust a Page Border that Will Pass File Review

Word 2010 has many built-in page borders that you can use to decorate your pages. A page border can add an artistic touch to your book. On the other hand, it could provide a distraction from reading and it might make the page seem cluttered. You might try adding a page border just to see how it looks. Try to gauge whether your pages look better with or without the page border. Which seems more professional?

It may also help to check out traditionally published books in your genre. In many cases, you will find that traditionally published books don't use page borders; and when they do, it's often just a line beneath the header or above the footer (which we described how to add in the previous two chapters). The page border might be a nice touch when the imagery matches the theme of the book or if the content of the book relates to art in some way.

The page border doesn't need to appear on all four sides of the page. You can add the page border on one to four sides.

Go to the Page Layout tab, click on Page Borders, and select the Page Border tab in the popup window. Select any border in Art and then use the up (↑) and down (↓) arrows on your keyboard to quickly scroll through all of the options. You will see a preview of each in the upper right corner of the window as you scroll. If you scroll far enough down, you will find the black-and-white page borders.

Click the Options button in the Page Borders dialog box and change Measure From to Text (instead of Edge of Page) if you have a Gutter setting in your page margins (Chapter 4). Otherwise, there will be a noticeable gap between the page border and the inside text margin.

You may need to modify the distance between the page border and text in Options in order to center the text (including any header, page number, and footer) inside of the page border. You may also need to adjust the From Edge values of the Header and Footer in the Page Setup dialog box (in this dialog box, choose the Layout tab) in order to center the header and footer vertically between the page border and text. You can perfect these values with a little trial and error.

The original edition of this book used the following distances in Options in the Page Borders dialog box: 1 pt top and 10 pts left (or right, depending on whether it's an odd or even page). Also, the From Edge measurements for Header and Footer are 0.5" and 0.25", respectively. The values that work well for your book may be somewhat different depending on the thicknesses of your page border, header, and footer.

If your page borders extend to the edge of the page – or just beyond the minimum margins (see Chapter 4) – this may cause your file to be rejected by Amazon KDP during file review. First of all, images in the out-of-live zone must bleed 0.125" beyond the page edges (as described in the following chapter). Secondly, many of the designs have glyphs or decorative marks that Amazon KDP will treat as text, meaning that it's not permitted to be in the out-of-live zone.

Therefore, you should go to the View tab, click One Page, check the box next to Ruler, and inspect the distance from the page edge to the page border to ensure that it isn't in the out-of-live zone. This means that the distance between the outside edges and border must be at least 0.25", and the distance between the inside page edge and border must be at least the minimum inside margin for your page count (see Chapter 4). (Add an extra 0.125" to each distance if your book will have bleeds.) The closer your page border is to the page edges, the more noticeable will be any printing variations in your book's trim size.

In addition to page borders, Word also has options to change the page color or insert a watermark. You can find gradients and patterns by choosing Fill Effects. These options may be better-suited for a full-color picture book.

You may want to test out your selection of page border or Fill Effects with your PDF converter to see how well the graphics will display in the converted PDF (a few of the more intricate designs may appear significantly different in PDF, depending on your PDF converter and its settings).

The images that follow show a couple of sample page borders.

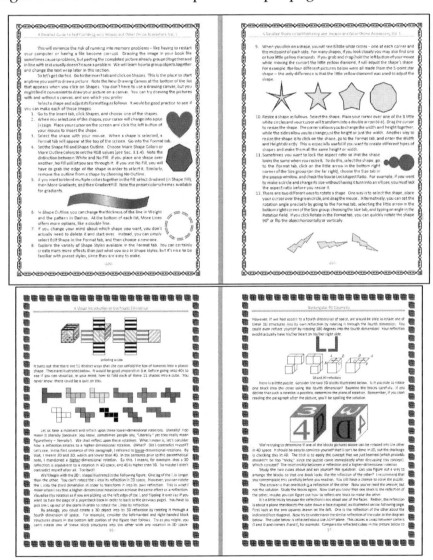

12 How to Deal with Bleeds

Books that include at least one picture in the interior file (separate from the cover file) that will extend to the page edges must be designed to bleed. This means that the picture must actually extend 0.125" beyond the trim size of the book. This requires making the page size larger than the trim size and also adjusting the margins accordingly.

If your book has figures, but none of the figures extend to the page edges, then your book won't have bleeds. In this case, make sure that none of your figures extend into the out-of-live zone (described later in this section).

Recall that in Chapter 3 we discussed modifying the page size in Word by adding 0.25" to the height and 0.125" to the width of the trim size in order to make room for pictures to bleed 0.125" beyond the edges. Also, we discussed rounding up to the nearest 0.01" to avoid possible problems with Word rounding down. In Chapter 4, we explained that 0.125" must be added to the outside margins (again, rounding up in the adjusted margins) in order to increase the out-of-live zone in your interior book file. (That's if your book will consist of a combination of pictures and text. We will discuss the different case of a pure picture book later in this chapter.)

For example, for a 6" x 9" book with bleeds that has 0.25" outside margins and a 0.75" inside margin, set the page size to 6.13" x 9.25" and the margins as follows: Set the left, right, top, and bottom margins to 0.38" and the gutter to 0.37". (The value of 0.375" was rounded to 0.38".) This assumes that the book will consist of separate text and pictures. We will discuss the case of a pure picture book later in this chapter.

There are two types of images to deal with – images that will bleed to the edge and images that won't extend into the out-of-live zone. Images that will be closer than 0.25" from the actual page edges (which means closer than 0.38" from the page edges that you see in Word, since the pages in Word are oversized to allow for bleed) must extend 0.125" beyond the page edges (which means to the very edge of the page that you see in Word). Unless you have a full-page picture book, you will need to select such images individually, change Wrap Text to In Front of Text in the Format tab (which only appears when the image is selected), and place the image at the very edge of the page that you see in Word. You can move the picture either by dragging it or by right-clicking it, selecting Size and Position, going into the Position tab, and setting the appropriate Alignment field and changing the Relative setting to Page (but only after you change the wrapping to In Front of Text).

Images that don't bleed must remain inside the out-of-live zone. The out-of-live zone is 0.25" from the actual page edges (which means 0.38" from the page edges that you see in Word). You can't have an image that extends partway into the out-of-live zone. Either push the image all of the way across the margin to the very edge of the page that you see in Word (which is 0.13" beyond the actual trim size) or keep it at least 0.38" from the edge of the page that you see in Word. If you check the box for Ruler in View, it will help you see the text margins (you want non-bleeding images within your text margins).

Text, glyphs, symbols, and some designs must also remain inside of the out-of-live zone. This means that if a picture contains text (or text-like marks), you must make sure that this part of the picture isn't in the out-of-live zone.

You don't have to wrap non-bleeding pictures In Front of Text. Setting the text wrap to In Line With Text (centered on its own line) will help with the active memory of your file in Word. Other text wrap options, like Square, allow you to place images next to paragraphs.

For a full-page picture book, you can make all of the margins zero, including the gutter. Since each page will be a picture, just insert a picture on each page, separated by page breaks (no need to use section breaks if the picture will be the entire page), and wrapped In Line With Text. (Centering should be irrelevant if the picture completely fills the page and is set to In Line With Text.)

Whether you have just a single full-page picture or a whole book of pictures, there are a couple of details that you need to check. First, you must size the picture to the exact same size as the page width and height that you are using in Word (i.e. the oversized page that allows for bleeds) – not the trim size of your book. As explained in Chapter 18, it's better to do this in the native picture program than in Word (but if you still prefer to do it in Word, you can find the options in the Format tab when the picture is selected). Since you rounded the margins up to the nearest 0.01" in Word, you must do the same in the native picture program. It would be wise to have the foresight to size the picture properly when making the picture in the first place – otherwise, resizing a full-page picture may change the aspect ratio (in which case, the picture will appear distorted). (If you want to change the aspect ratio in Word – remember, it's better to do this in the native picture program – right-click on the picture, click Size and Position, choose the Size tab, and uncheck the box for Lock Aspect Ratio.)

Next, ensure that your full-page pictures do not have text, glyphs, symbols, or other text-like marks in the out-of-live zone (otherwise, you must modify your pictures). Finally, check for any tiny gaps at the edge of your pages, which may arise from slight differences between your picture's size and the size of the (oversized) page in Word.

Word likes to compress images, whereas for optimal printing you want to prevent the images from being compressed. There are ways to prevent Word's automatic picture compression (and it takes more than just checking or unchecking a single box). I highly recommend that you read about this in Chapter 18 before inserting any pictures.

Consider the following pictures. The 'N' of Neptune is in the out-of-live zone in the top left, nothing is in the out-of-live zone in the top right, a full-page picture appears at the bottom left, and the image and text are both out of position in the bottom right.

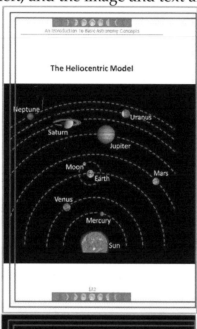 

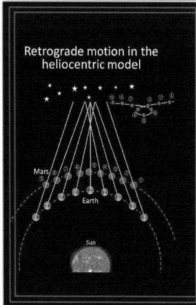 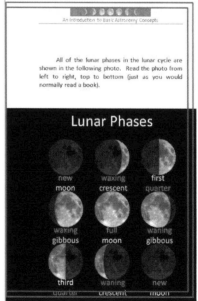

13 Footnotes, Endnotes, Cross-references, and How to Insert Them

Footnotes and endnotes allow you to insert notes without interrupting the flow of the text or to cite references. You can insert a footnote or an endnote by clicking a button on the References tab. Footnotes[*] appear at the bottom of the page, whereas endnotes[1] appear at the end of the section or at the end of the book.

You can find the Note Options by placing your cursor in the footnote or endnote and right-clicking. In Location, you can choose to place an endnote at the end of a section (determined by using section breaks – see Chapter 8) instead of at the end of the document. Choose whether to number the notes with letters, numbers, Roman numerals, or symbols in Number Format.

Highlight the text in the footnote or endnote in order to change the font size and style or to change the alignment from left to justified full.

If you have multiple sources of information to cite, you should create a bibliography or references section. Word has a built-in bibliography tool in the References tab. Choose a style that is relevant for your genre (the default is APA, which is fairly common in the humanities). In the body of your text where you cite a source of information or where you quote or paraphrase a reference, position your cursor immediately after this text and click Insert Citation on the References tab. Enter the information for your bibliographic entries in Add New Source and add citations with Add New Placeholder. Toward the end of your book, place your cursor where you would like to insert your bibliography and choose one of the options in Bibliography on the References tab. You can rename the heading References or anything else.

Be sure to place any direct quotes inside of quotation marks (in addition to citing the reference). For example, in *The New Statesman*, Cyril Connolly wrote, "Better to write for yourself and have no public, than to write for the public and have no self." Here, I stated the reference with the quote, but I could also have done so with a citation and bibliography.

Be careful not to plagiarize. Copying the work of another (even if it is just a single phrase) and passing it off as your own is called plagiarism. Failure to cite your source – even if you paraphrase instead of quote – is an instance of plagiarism. Plagiarism may result in serious legal consequences. Limit your paraphrasing and quotations to reasonable "fair use."

---

[*] This footnote appears at the bottom of the page.

You can't use song or poem lyrics or even quote one line from a song or poem in your book without written permission from the songwriter or poet (who will likely charge a royalty for its use) unless the song or poem was written over 80 years ago (that's in the US – copyright law varies from country to country). You can refer to the title – but not lines from the lyrics – provided that it's clear that the songwriter, band, poet, record label, etc. has not endorsed your work. I'm not an attorney; you should consult an attorney for all of your legal questions, including copyright law.

Word also has a cross-reference tool that can be handy. If you want to write "see Chapter 6," "as shown in Figure 4," or "on page 24," you can type this directly or you can use the cross-reference tool. The problem with typing this directly occurs, for example, when you write "see page 96" and the information that was on page 96 moves to page 97 after you make revisions. It can be tedious to track down all of these references and update them. The cross-reference tool allows you to refer to a specific page, figure, or chapter, for example, and it automatically updates the number if it changes.

Before you can use the cross-reference tool, there must be material that the tool can find. One way to do this is to use the Bookmark button on the Insert tab. Highlight the heading or text that you want to bookmark, click Bookmark, and type a name for the bookmark without spaces. Click the Cross-reference button in the References tab to insert a cross-reference. Choose Bookmark, for example, in Reference Type, and select the bookmark that you want to reference. You may want to uncheck the box that says to create a hyperlink if you will only be publishing in paperback (or at least reformat the text to remove the underline and color from your paperback edition – you may have to press the underline button twice to do this).

You can also create an index or table of contents using tools from the References tab. The more built-in tools that you use, the more complex your file may become, which makes your file more susceptible to problems.

The images that follow show footnotes and endnotes, and illustrate citations and references.

---

[1] This endnote appears at the end of the chapter.

Formatting Pages for Publishing on Amazon with CreateSpace

FBD for the basic swinging problem: There are two forces acting on the object in the basic swinging problem illustrated above – tension, $\vec{T}$, along the cable (or rope, cord, etc.) and weight, $m\vec{g}$, pulling downward. To setup our coordinate system, we first identify the center (C) of the circle. The inward (in) axis is then directed from the instantaneous position of the object to the center of the circle. In the side view of the diagram below, corresponding to the instantaneous position in the diagram above, the inward direction is instantaneously horizontal and to the right. The tangential (T) direction (not to be confused with the magnitude of the tension force) is tangent to the circle – it is instantaneously coming out of the page in the side view below. The third independent direction, z, is perpendicular to the plane of rotation, and is therefore vertical.

side view   top view

Newton's second law applied to the basic swinging problem: Set the sum of the inward components of the forces equal to ma_c and the sums of the other two independent components equal to zero for UCM:

$$\sum_{i=1}^{2} F_{i,in} = ma_c \quad , \quad \sum_{i=1}^{2} F_{i,T} = 0 \quad , \quad \sum_{i=1}^{2} F_{i,z} = 0 \quad (\text{UCM})$$

$$T\sin\theta = ma_c \quad , \quad 0 = 0 \quad , \quad T\cos\theta - mg = 0 \quad (\text{basic swinging problem})$$

$$T\sin\theta = ma_c \quad , \quad T\cos\theta = mg \quad (\text{basic swinging problem})$$

Eliminating the tension: The most efficient way to eliminate the tension in the above equations is to divide the two equations.[205]

$$\tan\theta = \frac{a_c}{g} \quad (\text{basic swinging problem})$$

---

[205] If $a = b$ and $c = d$, it follows that $\frac{a}{c} = \frac{b}{d}$, since the numerators and denominators are both equal.

Chapter 2 – Answers to Conceptual Questions

7. 3.0 N, 13.0 N.   8. –5.0 m j̄.

9. (A) 1.0 mi. ĵ (north), 3.0 mi. (B) The set of points near the South Pole that are one mile north of the latitude that has a circumference of one mile, half a mile, a third of a mile, a quarter mile, etc.

10. 15 km/s, 0.   11. Zero.

12. Product rule: $\vec{a} = \frac{d\vec{v}}{dt} = \frac{d}{dt}(v_r\,\hat{r}) = v_r \frac{d\hat{r}}{dt} + r_p \frac{d t}{dt} = a_r\hat{r} + a_c\hat{n}_c$. The object has a normal component when the direction of the velocity changes – i.e. the direction of the unit tangent, $\hat{t}$, is time-dependent.

The external push, $\vec{P}$, acts directly on the gray box, and so is only included in the FBD and sum of the x-components for the gray box. Its effect on the black box is indirectly communicated through the horizontal normal forces.

Notice that $\vec{N}_{1,2} = -\vec{N}_{2,1}$, but $N_{1,2} = N_{2,1}$. Magnitudes of vectors can't be negative, but vectors and components can; signs are directional.

If you can remember that fluids 'flow,' this may help you recall the meaning of the word 'fluid.'

It's the weight of the amount of fluid that is displaced by the object's submersion, and not, in general, the weight of the object (however, the object's weight equals the weight of the displaced fluid if the object is floating due to its buoyancy, like a boat – but in that case, the object is only partly submerged). If you place an object in a fluid, such as a beaker of water, the fluid level rises by an amount equal to the volume of the object. If you weigh this displaced fluid, it will equal $\rho_f V g$, where ρ_f is the density of the fluid.

Observe that helium – and any other gas that is less dense than air (it would be a conceptual mistake to say 'lighter' than air) – has a negative apparent weight when submerged in air.

The speed is only zero because the banana was thrown straight upward. If instead the banana were thrown upward at an angle, its speed would not be zero at the top of its trajectory – only the vertical component of its velocity would be zero.

---

on their phenomenological ramifications that have been published in leading physics journals in the past decade.

Don't worry if some of these ideas seem Greek at this point. We will develop them more fully as we encounter them in later chapters.

Further Reading:

The original research papers that motivated large extra dimensions include work by Antoniadis [T1] and Arkani-Hamed, Dimopoulos, and Dvali [T2]. These papers are highly technical; for a much more accessible article on this topic, see [A4].

References and Further Reading

These references are divided into two categories: References beginning with an A, such as [A3], are reasonably accessible to a general interest audience; those beginning with a T, as in [T2], are highly technical papers. The technical references have been kept to a minimum and are included primarily to pay tribute to a few researchers who have motivated modern-day experimental searches for large extra dimensions.

Accessible References

A1. *Flatland: A Romance of Many Dimensions*, Edwin A. Abbott, Book Jungle, 2007.

A2. *Flatterland: Like Flatland, Only More So*, Ian Stewart, Perseus, 2001.

A3. *The Fourth Dimension: A Guided Tour of the Higher Universe*, Rudy Rucker, Houghton Mifflin, 1984.

A4. "Large extra dimensions: A new arena for particle physics," N. Arkani-Hamed, S. Dimopoulos, and G.R. Dvali, *Phys. Today* 55N2, 35, 2002.

A5. *Projective Geometry*, H.S.M. Coxeter, Springer, second edition, 2003.

A6. *Regular Polytopes*, H.S.M. Coxeter, Dover, 1973.

A7. *Spaceland: A Novel of the Fourth Dimension*, Rudy Rucker, Tor, 2003.

Technical Papers

T1. "A possible new dimension at a few TeV," I. Antoniadis, *Phys. Lett.* B246, 377, 1990; "New dimensions at a millimeter to a Fermi and superstrings at a TeV," I. Antoniadis, N. Arkani-Hamed, S. Dimopoulos, and G. Dvali, *Phys. Lett.* B436, 257, 1998.

T2. "The hierarchy problem and new dimensions at a millimeter," N. Arkani-Hamed, S. Dimopoulos, and G.R. Dvali, *Phys. Lett.* B429, 263, 1998; "Phenomenology, astrophysics and cosmology of theories with submillimeter dimensions and TeV scale quantum gravity," N. Arkani-Hamed, S. Dimopoulos, and G. Dvali, *Phys. Rev.* D59, 086004, 1999.

14 How to Insert and Format a Drop Cap

M any traditionally published books use a drop cap for the first letter of each chapter. For example, the letter 'M' of the word 'Many' at the beginning of this sentence appears in a drop cap. Some books also write the first few words in CAPS, too. If the book you are reading had done that, this chapter would have begun, "MANY TRADITIONALLY PUBLISHED…"

Highlight the first letter of the chapter and click Drop Cap on the Insert tab. Select Dropped from the list. You can adjust the distance to text and number of lines dropped in Drop Cap Options. Select the drop cap to modify the font style or size. A fancy font is often used for the drop cap, but it's important for the letter to be legible. If the drop cap isn't flush against the left margin, try placing your cursor to the left of the letter and pressing the backspace key.

The images that follow show a few samples of drop caps.

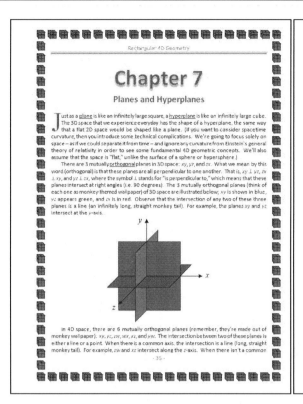
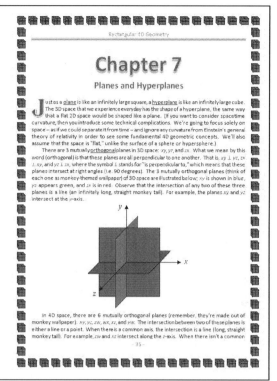

15 Formatting Columns and Bulleted Lists

Books are generally written in single-column format. Newspapers and some magazines use double columns. However, there may be some sections of books where two or more columns are desirable. For example, an answer key at the back of a book may have multiple columns.

Click Columns in the Page Layout tab. You can find more options in More Columns. For example, you can increase the space between columns or add a line between them.

To insert a column break, select Column in Breaks on the Page Layout tab.

If you type a list, inserting bullets will allow you to insert symbols, automatically number, or create an outline, for example. There are three bullet icons to choose from in the Paragraph group of the Home tab – one for symbols, one for numbers, and one for outline. Click the arrow at the right of the icon to find more options. In the bullet icon for symbols, for example, it is possible to use a picture for a symbol by clicking Define New Bullet and then selecting Picture (or choose a standard symbol by selecting Symbol).

Make sublevels by using the Tab key (or undo sublevels and levels with the Backspace key). Advance to the next bullet in the list with the Enter key. Check the box next to Ruler in the View tab and look for the markers on the ruler. Adjust these markers to reset the automatic tabs in the bulleted list. Place the cursor in the list and right-click to find more options, like Increase Indent or Adjust List Indents.

The following images show samples of columns and bulleted lists.

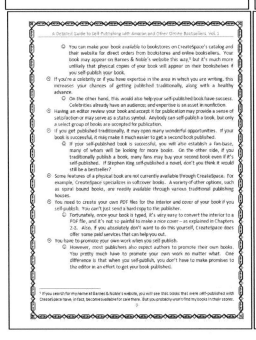

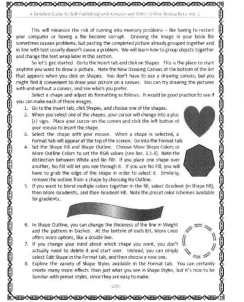

16 Other Text and Paragraph Formatting

Recall that we have already discussed some text and paragraph features in Chapters 5 and 6. For example, we have already covered the proper way to create indents (instead of using the Tab key), the problem with Word's defaults and how to adjust them, setting alignment, and how to use Word's Styles.

I'll try not to repeat what has already been described, but let me begin by adding a couple of notes to what we learned in Chapters 5 and 6. Word's default indentation of 0.5" is larger than most traditionally published books use. You should print out samples with different indentation sizes and compare them to traditionally published books. This book features a 0.35" indent. Note that 0.35" is not the standard, and most traditionally published books use a smaller indent – such as 0.15" to 0.20" – especially for fiction (and publishers express this measure in terms of the "em" instead of the inch).

When you browse for fonts, highlight a sentence, choose a font from the Font group in the Home tab, and use the up (↑) and down (↓) arrows on your keyboard to quickly scroll through fonts and see how they look. Readability is very important. It's also important to check the font license to see if commercial use is permitted and the font can be embedded (see Chapter 18).

Headings and subheadings should stand out – through larger font size, boldface, and/or other formatting. Chapter headings are usually centered, whereas subheadings (when the book has these) are often aligned left. Any subheadings should be smaller than headings.

Basic formatting includes **boldface**, *italics*, underline, ~~strikethrough~~, color, and highlighting. There is a button for each of these in the Font group of the Home tab. Click on the arrow at the right of the underline icon to find the underlining options (and there are yet more options under More Underlines). Many people believe that underlining doesn't look right in print, but some feel that it can be effective when used sparingly; extensive use is hard on the eyes.

For a black-and-white book, the only color that makes sense is gray. There are many different shades of gray, but two shades close together might look the same in print. You can use color, but it will print in grayscale. The big problem with using color is that a customer who sees color in Amazon's Look Inside feature may be disappointed to receive a printed book that's really black-and-white.

Click on the A button in the Font group of the Home tab to find the fancy formatting features, including outline, shadow, reflection, and glow. Select Options from the bottom of the list for Shadow, Reflection, or Glow to explore more options. This opens a dialog box. Choose an item from the list on the left and then adjust the settings on the right to customize the text effect. These fancy formatting options may come in handy for a title, subtitle, or chapter heading, for example. Make sure that the text is clear (that's more important), and try not to overdo it.

Another way to make fancy formatting is to insert WordArt. You can place the WordArt on its own line by selecting it and changing Wrap Text to In Line With Text. Insert WordArt by clicking WordArt on the Insert tab. There are several default styles to choose from. Select the WordArt and go to the Format tab to customize it. Look for Text Fill, Text Outline, and Text Effects (not to be confused with Shape Fill, Shape Outline, and Shape Effects). If you want to insert a paragraph in a box on a page, choose Text Box on the Insert tab.

WordArt

Special symbols can be found by clicking Symbol and then More Symbols on the Insert tab. You can find many standard symbols in "(normal text)," but many more by changing to one of the other fonts. MS Gothic has a vast collection of symbols, for example. Webdings and Wingdings have a variety of icons. If you're looking for mathematical symbols, try clicking Equation on the Insert tab, selecting the bottom arrow to the right of the symbol collection, and then clicking Basic Math to find more symbols.

$$\P \ © \ ® \ ¢ \ § \ ä \ é \ æ$$
$$⅝ \ \Omega \ ☺ \ ✋ \ ✝ \ 📷 \ ❶$$
$$↘ \ ✂ \ 📖 \ ✈ \ ☠ \ ❋ \ ♫$$
$$\pm \ \infty \ \geq \ \ell \ \perp \ \Leftrightarrow \ \equiv$$

How many spaces do you use after a period? Many people believe that the correct answer is two (largely because that's what they were taught in school). However, all traditional publishers actually use one space after a period. Check out some traditionally published books and convince yourself that this is true. If you want your book to look professional, use one space after a period instead of two (a simple search and replace can fix this).

I'm a two-spacer myself, and was quite shocked to discover that traditional publishers use one space. The reason for two spaces actually relates to typewriters, but has been carried forward because our teachers often teach what they were taught. Search online to find an interesting article in *Slate Magazine* called "Space Invaders" by Farhad Manjoo. Furthermore, in an e-book, having the second space after the period may occasionally cause subtle alignment issues (when a period happens to come at the end of a line).

A standard keyboard has a hyphen (-), but not a dash. The hyphen (-) is used to hyphenate words. There are two types of dashes – the shorter en dash (–) and the longer em dash (—). The dash is used as a separator. Use space around the en dash (–), but not around the em dash (—). For example, the en dash (–) following "two types of dashes" above is surrounded by spaces. If using the em dash (—) instead, it would look like this: "There are two types of dashes—the shorter en dash (–) and the longer em dash (—)." It is generally best to use one dash or the other, but not both. Be consistent in your style. Not everyone agrees which is better – it's partly aesthetic. However, you will probably find em dashes (—) more common in traditionally published books. Hold down the Alt key and type 0150 to get the en dash (–) and 0151 to get the em dash (—). If you also publish an e-book, you may find that some e-readers don't recognize one or both dashes (especially, older e-readers, which are still in use).

You can apply borders or shading to text or paragraphs using the icon in the bottom right corner of the Paragraph group on the Home tab. Click the arrow at the right of this icon, then select Borders and Shading at the bottom of the list. You can toggle Apply To between Paragraph and Text.

A few subtle formatting issues that can help your book look more professional involve features that are called widows, orphans, and rivers. When a short word appears by itself on the last line of a paragraph, the stranded word is called an orphan. Some designers tolerate orphans, as a little editing is required to improve them. When the first or last line of a paragraph appears all by itself at the end or beginning of a page, the stranded line is called a widow. Professional publishers correct widows in order to improve the appearance of the book. Another no-no is having just a couple of lines on a page at the end of a chapter.

Although Word has an option for automatic Widow/Orphan Control (see Chapter 1), you can achieve best results by dealing with all widows and orphans manually (e.g. by editing the text, changing the kerning – highlight the text, right-click, choose font, and select Advanced – or adjusting spacing between paragraphs).

A book that mostly consists of text – like a novel – will look most professional if every single page has the exact same number of lines (except for the first and last pages of each chapter) and all pages are aligned exactly the same vertically (see if the bottoms match up, except for the last page of each chapter).

Rivers appear when several consecutive sentences happen to have spaces that line up vertically. These can be removed if you're willing to edit your paragraphs. If so, save these until your book is virtually complete.

This short paragraph illustrates widows and page orphans (not to be confused with paragraph orphans, or runts). Having just one line of a paragraph on a page is a problem.

If you want to force a linebreak in the middle of a paragraph (e.g. to manually deal with widows and orphans), hold down the Shift key and press Enter. This will separate the paragraph into two parts while preserving full justification.

If you have data that you would like to organize in a table, click the Table button on the Insert tab. After you insert a table, place your cursor in the table (or highlight part of it) to find the Design and Layout tabs, where you can find all of the formatting options.

The images that follow show examples of a shaded paragraph, a widow, a paragraph orphan (different from a page orphan), and a river. The last image shows a table.

17 Front and Back Matter

Every book begins with a title page. The title page should include the title, the author(s), and other contributors. If your book has a subtitle, you may include that, too. You might list any relevant qualifications that you have, such as an advanced degree in the subject in which you are writing. Traditionally published books

Chris McMullen

You will see that this is a five-step process. You may save your progress and continue later (you will probably not be able to do it all at one sitting).

The first step is to enter Title Information. Choose your title and subtitle carefully. These and other fields that are indicated with an asterisk (*) will become permanent when you receive your ISBN (this happens after you complete the second step).

Type a description that has up to 1,000 characters. I find that my draft of my description is invariably longer and so I always have to labor over how to shorten it enough. I highly recommend that you first type your description in Microsoft Word and then paste it into the description field later. For one, Microsoft Word will help you catch spelling or grammatical mistakes. For another, Microsoft Word will let you keep track of how many characters you've used and how many are left.

You want your description to read well, to draw interest to your book, and to help sell your book. Browse other book descriptions on Amazon to get some ideas. Shoppers who come across your book's webpage will probably want to know what your book is about, what it will be like to read your book, and how your book differs from the competition. Your description is a sample of your writing, so if it doesn't read well, this might adversely affect your sales. Shoppers might not know that you wrote the description, but even so, the quality of the writing of your description can have a positive or negative influence on whether or not the shopper will be attracted to your book.

You also need to indicate the reading level and enter a category. Note that you have to submit your category, not simply select it. Browse through all of the category options. More than one category will probably apply to your book, so you'll have to choose the best category from the list. You might search for competitive and

- 100 -

How to Self-Publish a Book on Amazon.com

7 Preparing the PDF Files

There are a plethora of software programs used to produce documents that have text, figures, or both, and these programs can save the documents in different file formats, which have different file extensions (.doc, .txt, .jpg, etc.). Even those files that are written with one program (such as Microsoft Word), yet are saved in a common extension like .txt, may lose features and quality when saved in the more common format. Rather than restricting all authors to use a particular software program, which inherently can not be the best program to produce all types of books that can be written, most books-on-demand self-publishing services ask authors to submit files in a Portable Document Format (PDF). This way, each author can prepare their manuscript in any program they prefer, in principle, and then convert the document to PDF. The conversion of a file to PDF is a means of making it universal – i.e. anyone can open a PDF file on any computer if they have a program that can read PDF, even if they don't have the program that was used to write the original document. Acrobat Reader is freely available so that everyone can read PDF files.

Here is the essential idea behind PDF files. Regardless of what program you use to make a document, you are able to print the document by sending the printer a set of instructions for what the document looks like. The printer is not familiar with all of the programs that a computer might use to make documents, which would not be practical. Rather, all programs send a similar set of instructions to the printer to tell the printer what the document looks like. If you can tell a printer what a document looks like, then you can just as well tell a file what a document looks like. So creating a PDF file is sort

- 85 -

A Detailed Guide to Self-Publishing with Amazon and Other Online Booksellers, Vol. 1

you view reflected light from the page. Here, the colors mix according to the rules for pigmentation, which is different than for mixing light.

The CMYK process used by printers is, from a conceptual standpoint, more limited than the RGB process. As a result, it is difficult to achieve the exact same color with a printer as that color appears on a screen. There may also be a difference in brightness, contrast, and other qualities between the image that you see on the screen and the actual cover.

The printing process used by CreateSpace is excellent, but – as with printing in general – does not perfectly reproduce the colors that you see on the screen. You may notice slight variations in color. For example, a blue may appear a little darker on the printed page and a little brighter and lighter on the screen. You can print your cover if you have a color printer (scaled down to a smaller size, unless your printer accepts large sheet sizes – like 11" x 17"). Although it won't be the same printer that is used by the publisher, it might be better than only looking at the screen.

On a related note, you can draw with hundreds of colors on your computer monitor, but the publisher's printer won't print in this many different hues and shades. So if your cover has three different shades of green, for example, you might only see two different shades of green on your actual cover. If you use a few different shades or hues of the same color, try to ensure that no two of the colors look too similar.

Color	Red	Green	Blue
Aqua	0	255	255
Black	0	0	0
Blue	0	0	255
Fuchsia	255	0	255
Gray	128	128	128
Green	0	128	0
Lime	0	255	0
Maroon	128	0	0
Navy	0	0	128
Olive	128	128	0
Purple	128	0	128
Red	255	0	0
Silver	192	192	192
Teal	0	128	128
White	255	255	255
Yellow	255	255	0

- 16 -

---

include the publisher's name. If you select an ISBN option (starting at $10) that allows you to choose your own imprint, you can include this on your title page, too (you can even create a logo). You may want to add some decorative art to your title page.

I recommend checking out the title page, copyright page, table of contents, and other front and back matter sections of a variety of traditionally published books to get ideas for what you might do to make your book appear more professionally published and less self-published.

The copyright page should list your book's title, subtitle, authors and other contributors, imprint name (unless you use the free ISBN option), ISBN-13 (which you will get just before you need to upload your files, if you don't already have one), the copyright date, and a copyright notice.

The copyright date should be in the following form: Copyright © date by Your Name. Publishers list the author's name after the copyright date when the author holds the copyright and the publisher's name after the copyright date when the publisher holds the copyright.

Traditionally published books state the edition number and printing number. A CreateSpace book is printed on demand, so a printing number is not relevant on the copyright page (the printer, however, will add an extra page at the end of your book when your book is printed, which has a barcode and printer number), but you can give an edition number.

You can get some ideas for your copyright notice and other material to include in order to help make your copyright page look professional by checking out traditionally published books. For example, fictional works usually include a statement that the book is a work of fiction and that any resemblance to actual persons, living or dead, is purely coincidental.

Front matter should have the title page, copyright page, table of contents, and any other sections like dedications, acknowledgments, foreword, introduction, or prologue. See how these sections are ordered in traditionally published books. Back matter may include an afterword, epilogue, about the author, references or bibliography, glossary, index, or catalog.

There is a little room for marketing in your front and back matter. For example, an about the author page can include links to the author's social networking sites (like Facebook and Twitter), the author's blog, the author's website, and the author's email address. An email account could get spammed if made public, but does provide readers a chance to connect with you. You might make a special email account for your book, but then you have to check it. Your blog, website, or social media sites may also provide a means for readers to contact you, if they wish.

Publishers sometimes have quotes in the front matter from people who have read and enjoyed the book, and occasionally have previews of a sequel or a new release in the back matter. Beware that most people don't like overt advertising. If you do any marketing of this sort, keep it light and try to avoid having it come across like a sales pitch.

The following pictures show samples of front and back matter.

EXCERPT

SON: Dad, why do we have to go to school?

FATHER: Son, you need to learn valuable skills, like the three R's.

SON: What's the third R? I can think of A-R-E, as in, "Are you going to let me stay home?" and O-U-R, as in, "Our time is being wasted in school."

FATHER: No, Son, you misunderstood. The three R's are reading, writing, and arithmetic.

SON: Why do they call them the three R's? Two of those words don't even begin with an R.

FATHER: Well, they do have an R in common. What would you call them?

SON: War!

FATHER: Now, Son, there's no reason to become so violent about it.

SON: But, Dad, hear me out. W.A.R. stands for Writing, Arithmetic, and Reading.

Why Do We Have to Go to School?

AFTERWORD

I didn't set out to write a book about educational policy and practice, or even about the use of technology in school. Actually, I sat down at the computer one Saturday morning, as I often do, expecting to work on one of my other projects. I always have a few books in progress – I have to put them on hold until the inspiration comes. This time, I couldn't work on any of my books in progress, so I stared at a blank screen, wondering what to write about. That's when it hit me – the countless students who have asked me, "Why do we have to learn this?" I revised this to, "Why do we have to go to school?" The rest of this book evolved from there.

This is not my first fictional work, but it is the first time that I have been able to muster the courage to publish my fiction. So here it is. I'm laying my heart on the line. I wouldn't call this full-fledged fiction, but more of a crossover between the nonfiction world where I have the most experience and comfort and the fictional world that I'm stepping into.

This dialogue does mark the first time that I have ever sat down and let the art of writing evolve from scratch without any preconceived ideas. I almost always work some of the ideas for my books out in advance and then shape them on my computer screen. When I do that, I always feel as if Edgar Allen Poe is looking over my shoulder with a pained expression, shaking his head in dismay. On this occasion, if he is shaking his head, it must be for a different reason since I have finally succeeded in

---

INTRODUCTION

I have written and self-published over a dozen books with CreateSpace, which is an Amazon company. I write non-fiction books in areas that interest me. Most of my books are math workbooks, as I am very passionate about helping people improve their fluency in fundamental math skills, like arithmetic and algebra. It all started after I had written a pair of volumes on the fourth dimension – another of my passions, and also the topic of several papers that I have written in the field of collider physics – when I discovered, in my search for a publisher, that Amazon had a self-publishing company.

Writing, formatting, and publishing books – the technique of trying to turn ideas into a printed work of art – has evolved into a hobby for me. I wrote this book with the aim of helping many other writers who, like myself, were not entirely satisfied with the traditional publishing industry and were considering the prospects of print-on-demand self-publishing. I have also published some puzzle books, golf books, chess books, and science books. I have learned much about the self-publishing process – many ideas that I wish I had known when I started out. While I can't pass this book in such a way that it reads well if you read it straight share it with other writers, such as you. This is the spirit with which I have written this book. I sincerely hope that you find much of the information to be helpful, and I wish you the best of luck with your own work! ☺

One of my main goals in writing this book was to provide a wealth of practical information, and also to state the information concisely. I expect that you want to spend more time writing your own book, and less time listening to some other author drone on along some tangent. Thus, I have tried to stick to the point, and I have deleted several paragraphs which didn't actually provide any valuable information. I hope that you appreciate this. Also, I have tried to adopt a friendly, conversational tone, so that, hopefully, you will feel that someone (but not me – that would be creepy) is right there speaking with you, helping you publish your book with confidence.

I have tried to write this book in such a way that it reads well if you read it straight through, yet is also organized so that you can easily find the information that you're looking for if you consult the book as you need it: For example, you will probably want to have this book handy while you are applying any of the step-by-step techniques – like how to submit your book to the publisher or how to modify the content of your manuscript in order to format it as an eBook. With this in mind, the subsection headings and many instances of "See Sec. such and such" in the body of the text should help you find the relevant content quickly.

THE AUTHOR

Chris McMullen has written and self-published over a dozen paperback books with CreateSpace and over a dozen eBooks. He enjoys writing books, drawing illustrations on the computer, editing manuscripts, and especially the feeling of having produced a professional-looking self-published book from cover-to-cover.

Chris McMullen holds a Ph.D. in physics from Oklahoma State University, and presently teaches physics at Northwestern State University of Louisiana. Having published a half-dozen papers on the collider phenomenology of large, extra, superstring-inspired extra dimensions, he first wrote a two-volume book on the geometry and physics of the fourth dimension geared toward a general audience, entitled *The Visual Guide to Extra Dimensions*. When he learned about self-publishing on Amazon through CreateSpace, he wrote a variety of golf and chess log books, and published these to gain some experience as a self-publisher before self-publishing his work on the fourth dimension.

Since then, Chris McMullen has self-published numerous math workbooks, a couple of books on self-publishing, and several word scramble puzzle books. The math workbooks were written in response to his observation, as a teacher, that many students need to develop greater fluency in fundamental techniques in mathematics. He began writing word scramble books along with his coauthor, Carolyn Kivett, when he realized that it was possible to make over a thousand words using only the elements on the periodic table. Chris McMullen and Carolyn Kivett first published a variety of chemical word scrambles using elements from the periodic table, and have since published several 'ordinary' word scrambles using the English alphabet instead of chemical symbols.

18 Picture Compression and PDF Conversion

Pictures look best in print-on-demand books when their resolution has a minimum of 300 DPI. Word has several tendencies to automatically compress pictures. There are a few things that you must do in order to avoid this.

First, go to the File tab, scroll down below Help to find Options, select Options, choose Advanced, scroll down to Image Size and Quality, and check the box that says, "Do not compress images in file." But that's not enough.

In order to avoid picture compression, add pictures to your file by clicking Picture on the Insert tab and finding the file. Don't copy/paste pictures into Word. Also, do any picture editing (like cropping, resizing, etc.) in the native picture program (or other software program that allows you to edit pictures without compressing them). If you edit pictures in Word, they might get compressed.

The other side of the coin is to use images that already have 300 DPI to begin with. Many free images on the internet have 96 DPI and so may look blurry or pixelated in print. Some cameras take photos at higher resolution than others. It's the dots per inch (DPI) on the paper that matters for a print book, not the pixel count or pixels per inch (PPI) on the screen.

It's best to work with images that have at least 300 DPI. If the image has less than 300 DPI, you can increase the pixel count to make it 300 DPI using picture-editing software (Paint can do this, if you don't have anything better). These "invented" pixels aren't as good as having 300 DPI to start with, but it may be better than nothing. See what your image looks like after increasing the resolution. (Look at how many pixels you get per inch of the picture's actual size in print.)

Most images that you find on the internet or in clipart collections have copyright restrictions, and so you can't legally use them without express written permission (which may come with a fee). Again, I'm not an attorney. If you have questions about copyright or other legal issues, you should contact an attorney.

There are some clipart and photo collections that do allow commercial use. Make sure that it clearly states that commercial use is allowed. There are some collections that cost money, but do not allow commercial use. When commercial use is not permitted, it's not always easy to find such notice. However, when commercial use is permitted, the notice should be easy to find.

Also, if you take a photograph of something that is trademarked, like the Eiffel Tower at night, you can't use that in a book either (without express written permission).

If you include color pictures in a black-and-white book, beware that they will show up in color in Amazon's Look Inside. Customers who see color on Amazon, but black-and-white in person, might not be happy about it. Therefore, you may want to convert your images to grayscale if your book will be black-and-white.

Pictures tend to look different on a computer monitor than they do in print. Physically, the computer monitor is emitting light, whereas you view reflected light when reading print. The colors displayed on a monitor are made using a color addition scheme based on red, green, and blue (RGB), while printers use a color subtraction scheme based on cyan, magenta, yellow, and black (CMYK). Printers also have slight variations and some limitations, and print often appears darker than the bright images produced on a monitor. Therefore, what you see on the screen may not be exactly the same as what you see in print. You will see what your images look like in print when you order your printed proof; there is no better substitute than seeing this for yourself.

Amazon KDP allows you to upload a .doc or .docx file, but you should upload a PDF file instead. If you upload a .doc or .docx file, inspect it very carefully in Interior Reviewer and the Digital Proofer because the formatting sometimes changes. Prevent unwanted formatting changes by uploading a PDF file instead.

If you have pictures, don't use Word's built-in Save As PDF feature because it will compress your pictures. Use some other PDF converter in this case. (If you have designs like page borders, they may be treated like pictures, too.)

If possible, if you have pictures, try to find a PDF converter that can flatten transparency and embed fonts. There are many free PDF converters on the web, but you have to be careful of possible malware, spyware, and viruses when downloading programs from the internet. One of the best (paid) converters is Acrobat XI Pro.

In Word, go to the File tab, choose Options (scroll down below Help), click Save, and check the box to embed fonts. But what you really want is to have the fonts embedded in the PDF. Some fonts have a restricted license and won't embed in a PDF. There are very many fonts that are embeddable and do allow commercial use, but, again, if you have legal questions, you should contact an attorney.

When you convert your file to PDF, examine the PDF carefully. Occasionally, something appears a little different in the PDF than it does in the Word file, and this is the best time to notice it. It's helpful to first view the pages two at a time and then zoom out and view many pages at once (your eye may catch funny formatting by viewing several pages together this way).

Leave the box checked to use Amazon KDP's Interior Reviewer when you upload your interior book file (available in Guided Setup). Interior Reviewer superimposes the minimum margins on your pages so that you can see if anything is in the out-of-live zone. It will also flag images that have less than 200 DPI. Not every comment that the Interior Reviewer makes is accurate, and not every error message has to be fixed (sometimes, it's just providing information, and you can decide whether or not to improve it, while in other cases, the change is required). If you think that Interior Reviewer may be wrong or that the issue doesn't really need to be corrected, submit your files for review and a Amazon KDP representative will inspect your files. Amazon KDP will either approve or reject your files, and they may provide comments even if your files are approved. If your files are rejected, they will specify exactly what needs to be fixed.

After your file is approved, view your book using the Digital Proofer. You can view your cover in 3D with the click of a button and even rotate it. View your cover and interior carefully. Sometimes there are slight changes to your files.

Order at least one printed proof to see how your book looks in print. This is very important because what you see on paper may differ somewhat from what you see on the screen (and you don't want your customers to be the first to notice this).

If you have trouble with functionality when using Amazon KDP's website, try using a different browser (like FireFox or Chrome instead of Internet Explorer). This sometimes resolves the issue.

ADDED CONTENT

Microsoft Word's Styles

There are five simple rules to follow to achieve very good Kindle formatting from Microsoft Word:

1. Don't use the tab key for anything.
2. Don't use two or more consecutive spaces (not even after a period).
3. Don't press the Enter key three or more times in a row.
4. Use Word's styles for any and all formatting that can be done through the styles (including indents—yes, it is possible).
5. Avoid special characters and formatting that may not be supported on all devices.

The first three rules are really easy to follow. If you didn't, you can use Word's search and replace feature to easily remove tabs, extra spaces, or extra Enters. (Tab removal: Make a tab, cut it and paste it into the find field and leave the replace field blank. Double-space removal: Type two spaces and replace with one space, then repeat this find until no matches are found. Triple Enter removal: Click More > Special > Paragraph Mark three times to create three Enters in the find field and replace with two enters; repeat as needed.)

Rule 4 is critical toward achieving consistent Kindle formatting from Word. How to do this is the focus of this article.

The last rule just requires a little research. Beware that some fancy features, like dropcaps, are supported on many devices, but don't format properly on all devices. When in doubt, simple works better.

Using Word's Styles

The secret to good Kindle formatting is to apply any and all formatting through Microsoft Word's styles. Don't apply formatting directly to highlighted text or paragraphs—not even for first line indents. Instead, set the formatting in a style and apply the style to the paragraphs (or text).

You can find Microsoft Word's styles on the right-half of the Home ribbon at the top of the screen. (These instructions are specifically for Microsoft Word 2010, which is similar to 2007 and 2013, for Windows.)

Note: Some styles (e.g. Normal) apply to entire paragraphs, other styles (like Emphasis) apply to text, and yet others can apply to either. The distinction is important because if you highlight just some text and apply a paragraph style, it will modify the entire paragraph rather than just the selected text. You can tell what a style applies to by clicking the little arrow-like icon below where it says Change Styles. Then look next to the style name to see if it has a paragraph symbol, an 'a,' or both.

Modify Word's Styles

Right-click a style on the Home ribbon in order to modify it.

For Kindle e-book formatting, leave the color set to Automatic in the Normal style (because a customer might choose to read in night or sepia mode, for example). You needn't set a font, as the customer will choose the font from his/her device, though if you do pick a font, using a very common font like Georgia is apt to work best (but, again, the customer gets to control the font from his/her device).

Apply the font style, font size, linespacing, indents, and all other formatting through Word's styles. Don't highlight text or paragraphs and apply formatting directly to the text. Instead, modify a style to suit your needs and apply that style to selected paragraphs (or, when applicable, highlighted text).

All styles other than Normal allow you to check a box to Automatically Update after right-clicking and choosing Modify. This is convenient to apply changes to that style throughout your document.

How to Indent Paragraphs for Kindle

Not with the tab key! Not using the spacebar! Not by going into the paragraph menu and using first line indent. Close, but no cigar! Instead, right-click the Normal style, then:

1. Choose Modify > Format > Paragraph.
2. Change Special to First Line.
3. Set the value to 0.2" or so (definitely, not 0.5" as that's huge on a small screen).
4. Apply the style to paragraphs you want formatted this way.

How to not Indent

Not indenting is even trickier. Kindle automatically indents non-indented paragraphs. So the trick is to copy the Normal style and give it a different name, like NoSpacing (don't put a space in the name). This new style will be modified and used for non-indented paragraphs.

To copy a style, click the little arrow-like icon below Change Styles at the right of the Home ribbon to pull up the styles menu. Find the three buttons at the bottom of this menu (this menu pops up at the right side of your screen). Click the left button (of these three buttons) to add a new style. Choose the style you want this based on (pick Normal). Name the style (e.g. NoSpacing). Modify the style as needed.

Modify this new style as follows: Click Format > Paragraph, change Special to First Line and set the indent to 0.01" (not smaller).

Note: Setting this to zero will backfire!

As always, modify the style and apply the style to the paragraphs. Don't apply First Line Indent directly to paragraphs.

The first paragraph of the chapter is typically not indented. This is typical of most traditionally published books.

Stand-alone, non-centered lines like subheadings or lines from your table of contents also need to be non-indented. There are typically many such lines throughout the book. Remember, if they appear non-indented in Word, they'll be automatically indented on Kindle.

Unless you apply the NoSpacing style to those paragraphs. Indenting isn't an issue with centered text, e.g. using styles like Heading 1 that center text.

Page Breaks

You can even use Word's styles to create page breaks. You should be using Heading 1 to create your chapter headings.

If you want each chapter to automatically start on a new page, and if you only apply Heading 1 where you want to begin a new page, you can remove all of your current page breaks and instead implement them through Word's styles.

Right-click on Heading 1 to modify it. Choose Format > Paragraph > Line and Page Breaks and check the box for Page Break Before.

Why Do You Need to Use Styles?

When you upload your file to KDP, it gets converted to a .mobi file. In this conversion, KDP reads your Word file as an HTML file (yes, even if you upload a Word document). The top of your Word's HTML (even if you don't upload an HTML file, this still applies) defines all of Word's styles.

If you highlight selected text or paragraphs and apply formatting directly to them, you introduce formatting contradictions: The styles say one thing, while the specific paragraphs or text says another. This confusion can lead to inconsistent formatting in the all-important Look Inside or on specific devices.

If you only apply formatting through the styles, then you won't have contradictions, which leads to more consistent formatting.

Page Numbering in Word 2010

Introduction

There are several problems that one must solve when numbering pages in Word, and this can be the source of much frustration:

- You change the page number on one page, and it changes the style or numbering on one or more other pages.
- You insert a page number on a page, but the formatting doesn't match that of the other pages.
- You try to make the front matter have **Roman numerals**, but all the page numbers switch from **Arabic** to Roman.
- You discover that the same page number appears twice in a row.
- You add page numbers and the file freezes on you. Worse, it won't open back up.

WHY doesn't it work? **WHY** can't it just be easy? Calm down. Take a deep breath.

It is possible to number the pages exactly how you want them. The problem is that the way to do it isn't intuitive. You have to use section breaks, and you have to implement the page numbering a certain way.

If you follow the procedure that Word is looking for, you can master pagination in Microsoft Word.

Before We Begin

Microsoft Word is somewhat more prone to file **freezing** or **corruption** when making changes to page numbering.

What does this mean to you?

It means you should **back up your file** before you edit Word's pagination.

Save your file with a **new filename** (like Book v2.docx) and **save it in two different places** (like jump drive and email). If you've already spent months typing hundreds of thousands of words for a book, the worst that can happen is that you have to start over... unless you wisely back up your file in multiple places.

Procedures

Follow these steps in Microsoft Word. This outline is specifically for the **2010** version, but 2007 and 2013 are nearly identical and 2003 follows the same ideas (but the toolbars are different).

A picture is worth a thousand words, right? At the end of the procedures you can find some screenshots of the key steps.

1. Insert a section break anywhere you want the style of page numbering to change. For example, if you want to number your first page on the fifth page of your manuscript, you need a **Next Page section break** at the end of the fourth page. If you'd like to switch from **Roman numerals** (v, vi, vii, viii, ix, x) to **Arabic numbers** (11, 12, 13) on the eleventh page, insert a Next Page section break at the end of the tenth page. Remove the ordinary page break (if that's what you have presently) and instead go to **Page Layout > Breaks > Next Page** to insert a section break instead of an ordinary page break. This section break tells Microsoft Word that you wish to change the header or footer style (your page numbers are either part of the header or footer, depending on where you place them).

2. Press the **Show/Hide** button (it looks like ¶) on the Home toolbar. This will help you identify page breaks, section breaks, and blank lines, for example. (If your page numbers aren't lining up between different sections, this will help you see if you accidentally pressed the Enter key while formatting the page numbers in one of the sections, for example.)

3. Start at the very **beginning** of your Word document and **work your way forward one section at a time**. Very often, sections link to previous sections (though you can choose to unlink them), so if you make changes to one section, it often affects every section that follows (sometimes it also affects previous sections). Problems are best minimized by starting at the beginning and working forward one section at a time. After you make any change, **immediately review all the previous sections to double-check that none of the previous page numbers have changed**. You can save a great deal of frustration by nipping problems in the bud. It's worth checking. It might seem like it's a lot of extra work, but in the long run it might be much less work.

4. If you don't already have page numbers, go to the page where you'd like to add them and find Page Numbers on the Insert toolbar. Choose one of the options (it's possible to customize it after inserting them); the simpler options are less likely to result in freezing or file corruption, but nothing is foolproof. Return to the same place and click **Format Page Numbers**. This gives you the option to change the starting number, continue from the previous section, or change the style from Roman numerals to Arabic numbers, for example. You can highlight the page number and

change the font size or style. You can also place your cursor just before or after the page number and type characters (such as ~ to make your page numbers look like ~17~).

5. You can remove page numbers the same way as you add them. Just go to Insert > Page Numbers > **Remove Page Numbers**.

6. Remember to **check the previous sections** each time you add, remove, otherwise make changes to page numbers. You don't want previous sections to change. It's okay if following sections get changed; you'll be able to correct that once you get to those later sections. If previous sections do change, hit the **Undo button** at the top of the screen (what a handy button!). Then you need to unlink the current section from the previous section before trying to make these changes. See the next step.

7. The magic button is called **Link to Previous**. It's actually a checkbox. Simply place your cursor in the page number area to open the Design toolbar for page numbers. Uncheck the box to remove the **Same As Previous** flag and that will allow you to modify the current page numbers without affecting previous page numbers. (Changes you make might affect page numbers in following sections, but that's okay—you'll be able to fix those when you get there. It's the previous sections that you need to check on repeatedly. You don't want previous sections to change.) Sometimes you do want the current section to follow the same style and numbering as the previous section. In these cases, you want the Link to Previous checkbox to be checked.

8. When you want a new section to have different page number formatting from the previous section, remember to uncheck the Link to Previous box and verify that the Same As Previous flag disappears before making the changes. Otherwise, previous sections will change, too. It's easy to forget. Remember also to go back and check all the previous sections anytime you make changes. Once in a while, a previous section (sometimes, it's *way* back) changes even though the Link to Previous box is unchecked. So it pays to check. Also, remember to insert a Next Page section break (see Step 1) instead of an ordinary page break anywhere you'd like to make changes to the page numbering style. Not sure if you have a section break where you need it? See Step 2.

9. Place your cursor in the page number area on a given page to open the **Design toolbar**. Two of these options can be quite useful. One is the option to have **different page number styles on odd and even pages**. For example, this helps you place page numbers near the outside edges, which would be the right side for odd-numbered pages and the left side for even-numbered pages. Another option is to have a different style on the **first page of each chapter**. Many books don't number the first page of the chapter, so this option allows you to remove the page number from the first page of each section without disturbing the other pages. Well, if you suddenly remove the page number from the first page of the chapter, you may need to go in and reinsert the page numbering on subsequent pages of the same chapter (in addition to just checking the box for a different first page).

10. Note that the **two-page view** in Word does **NOT** show you an actual book view. In a real book, such as one you self-publish at Amazon using CreateSpace (www.createspace.com), odd-numbered pages appear on the right-hand side and even-numbered pages show up on the left-

hand side. Word shows it backwards. Just ignore the way that Word shows it; don't try to adjust your page numbering based on Word's incorrect two-page view. If you would like to see how your book will really look, save your file as a PDF file and open it with Adobe Acrobat Reader (you can get the Reader for **free** from Adobe's website, www.adobe.com/products/reader.html). Then go to View > Page Display > Show Cover Page in Two Page View, then View > Page Display > Two Page View.

11.   If you're having trouble getting two different sections to display page numbers the same way, try clicking the **Show/Hide Codes** button (see Step 2) and comparing the formatting marks in both sections. Also check the settings in the **Page Setup Dialog Box** (click the funny-looking, arrow-like icon in the bottom right of the Page Setup group on the Page Layout toolbar to open this dialog box); check all three tabs there—Margins, Paper, and Layout. Especially, check the From Edge values in the Layout tab (which should be the same for every section if it's applied to the Whole Document).

12.   You can change the **position** of page numbers relative to the body text using the From Edge values (see Step 11). The right combination of margins and From Edge values should allow you to get the body text and page numbers to look exactly how you want them to appear.

13.   Note that headers and footers are set differently. For example, **if you unlink one section's header from the previous section, the footer may still be linked to the previous section**. So, for example, if you have both page headers at the top and page numbers in the footer below, unlinking the page numbers won't unlink the page headers. This is important to keep in mind when you're trying to format both headers and footers in the same document.

14.   If at first you don't succeed, vent some of your frustration, get some rest and relaxation, and try again. See the suggestion in Step 15.

15.   Unfortunately, once in a while Word seems to go haywire. That is, you're sure did everything right, but it doesn't seem to be working. **Sometimes, it helps to undo the last change, remove the section break, reinsert the section break, and then try again.** It's also possible for a Word file to become corrupt, in which case it's best to start over with your **back-up file**. Didn't back it up like I recommended? Ouch!

16.   If you just can't hammer the square peg through the round hole, there is an alternate solution, which can really come in handy for self-published authors formatting books for print-on-demand services like Amazon's CreateSpace. You can break your file up into smaller files. Before you do this, see if you can find a **Word to PDF converter** that allows you to join multiple PDF files together (e.g. Adobe Acrobat XI Pro offers a free trial period, and also offers a monthly subscription; Nuance PDF Converter Professional offers this feature; and there are also many **free** converters available on the internet). When you publish with CreateSpace or Ingram Spark, it's best to submit a PDF anyway. If you're able to join PDF files together, then you can break all the separate sections of your Word document into separate files. The trick is to ensure that all the page sizes, layout, and formatting is consistent across all of your files. Then you just need to get

the page numbering right in each individual file, which is easier than getting it right in several different sections of a large file.

17. If you're also self-publishing an **e-book**, remember to remove page numbers (and all headers and footers) from the e-book version of your file.

Page Headers, too

Headers and footers in general work the same way as pagination.

For example, if you would like to have even-page headers show chapter names and odd-page headers show the book title, you can do this by formatting the page headers the same way as page numbers are formatted. It's also common to exclude the page header from some pages, such as some of the front matter and the first page of each chapter. It would be wise to see what header and page numbering styles are common for the type of book you're publishing before you decide on the formatting.

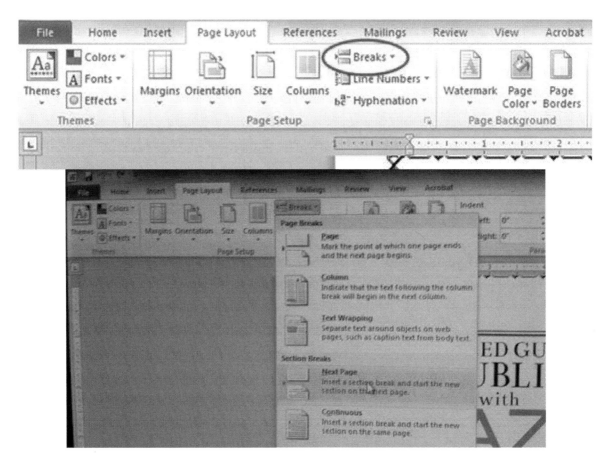

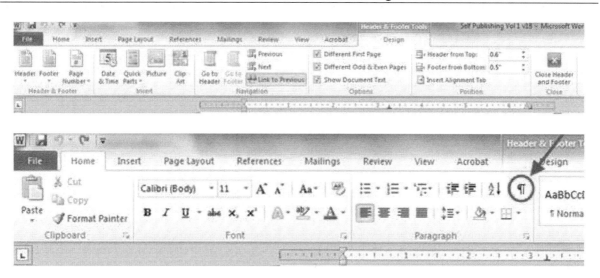

More recommended articles:

Visit http://chrismcmullen.wordpress.com and type any of these article titles into the search field (about midway down the sidebar on the right-hand side).

- Marketing: Why Isn't It Working?
- How Do People Buy Books?
- Which Fonts Can You Use?
- Kindle Promotions
- Advertising on Amazon
- Sideload to Kindle
- Kerning in Microsoft Word
- Kindle Kids' Book Creator
- Kindle Textbook Creator
- Marketing Children's Books
- Kindle Preorders
- How to Find and Hire a Cover Artist
- Book Blurb
- Where Are Your Amazon Sales?
- Should You Publish with an Imprint?
- Once Upon a Time
- Which Part of a Book Is Best?
- When Amazon Buys Heaven

THE AUTHOR

CHRIS MCMULLEN HAS written and self-published over a dozen paperback books with KDP and over a dozen eBooks. He enjoys writing books, drawing illustrations on the computer, editing manuscripts, and especially the feeling of having produced a professional-looking self-published book from cover-to-cover.

Chris McMullen holds a Ph.D. in physics from Oklahoma State University, and presently teaches physics at Northwestern State University of Louisiana. Having published a half-dozen papers on the collider phenomenology of large, extra, superstring-inspired extra dimensions, he first wrote a two-volume book on the geometry and physics of the fourth dimension geared toward a general audience, entitled *The Visual Guide to Extra Dimensions*. When he learned about self-publishing on Amazon through CreateSpace, he wrote a variety of golf and chess log books, and published these to gain some experience as a self-publisher before self-publishing his work on the fourth dimension.

Since then, Chris McMullen has self-published numerous math workbooks, a couple of books on self-publishing, and several word scramble puzzle books. The math workbooks were written in response to his observation, as a teacher, that many students need to develop greater fluency in fundamental techniques in mathematics. He began writing word scramble books along with his coauthor, Carolyn Kivett, when he realized that it was possible to make over a thousand words using only the elements on the periodic table. Chris McMullen and Carolyn Kivett first published a variety of chemical word scrambles using elements from the periodic table, and have since published several 'ordinary' word scrambles using the English alphabet instead of chemical symbols.

Check out the blog with free self-publishing resources:
   http://chrismcmullen.wordpress.com
The author website: https://chrismcmullen.com
Email: chrism@chrismcmullen.com
Facebook author page:
   https://www.facebook.com/pages/Chris-Mcmullen/390266614410127
Twitter: @ChrisDMcMullen

Free marketing opportunity created by Chris McMullen:
   http://readtuesday.com

CATALOG

Self-Publishing

Kindle Formatting Magic
How to Self-Publish a Book on Amazon.com
A Detailed Guide to Self-Publishing with Amazon and Other Online Booksellers, Vol. 1
A Detailed Guide to Self-Publishing with Amazon and Other Online Booksellers, Vol. 2

The Fourth Dimension

The Visual Guide to Extra Dimensions, Vol. 1
The Visual Guide to Extra Dimensions, Vol. 2
Full Color Illustrations of the Fourth Dimension, Vol. 1
Full Color Illustrations of the Fourth Dimension, Vol. 2

Science Books

Understand Basic Chemistry Concepts
An Introduction to Basic Astronomy Concepts (with Space Photos)
An Advanced Introduction to Calculus-Based Physics (Mechanics)
A Guide to Thermal Physics
Creative Physics Problems

Improve Your Math Fluency Series

Addition Facts Practice Book
Subtraction Facts Practice Book
Multiplication Facts Practice Book
Division Facts Practice Book
10,000 Addition Problems Practice Workbook
10,000 Subtraction Problems Practice Workbook
7,000 Multiplication Problems Practice Workbook
4,500 Multiplication Problems with Answers Practice Workbook
Master Long Division Practice Workbook
Addition and Subtraction Applied to Clocks
Practice Adding, Subtracting, Multiplying, and Dividing Fractions Workbook
Practice Adding, Subtracting, Multiplying, and Dividing Mixed Fractions Workbook

Practice Arithmetic with Decimals Workbook
Practice Addition, Subtraction, Multiplication, and Division with Negative Numbers Workbook
Fractions, Decimals, & Percents Math Workbook (Includes Repeating Decimals)
Algebra Essentials Practice Workbook with Answers
Trigonometry Essentials Practice Workbook with Answers
Calculus Essentials Practice Workbook with Full Solutions

Word Scramble Puzzle Books (Coauthored)

Christmas Word Scrambles
Fun Word Scrambles for Kids
Football Word Scrambles
Golf Word Scrambles
Teen Word Scrambles for Girls
Song & Artist Music Word Scrambles
Negative/Positive Antonym Word Scrambles Book
Positive Word Scrambles (A Fun Way to Think Happy Words)
Positive Word Scrambles (Fun Positive Visualization)
English-French Word Scrambles (Level 1 Basic)
English-Spanish Word Scrambles (Level 1 Basic)
Igpay Atinlay Ordway Amblesscray
Word Scrambles that Make You Think
VErBAl ReAcTiONS – Word Scrambles with a Chemical Flavor (Easy)
VErBAl ReAcTiONS – Word Scrambles with a Chemical Flavor (Medium)
VErBAl ReAcTiONS – Word Scrambles with a Chemical Flavor (Hard)
Chemical Word Scrambles Anyone Can Do (Easy)
Chemical Word Scrambles Anyone Can Do (Medium)
Chemical Word Scrambles Anyone Can Do (Hard)
Travel-Size Chemical Word Scrambles (Easy to Medium)

54100555R00328

Made in the USA
San Bernardino, CA
18 September 2019